PSYCHOPHYSICS
BEYOND
SENSATION

LAWS AND INVARIANTS OF HUMAN COGNITION

SCIENTIFIC PSYCHOLOGY SERIES

Stephen W. Link and James T. Townsend, Series Editors

MONOGRAPHS

Louis Narens • *Theories of Meaningfulness*

R. Duncan Luce • *Utility of Gains and Losses: Measurement–Theoretical and Experimental Approaches*

William R. Uttal • *The War Between Mentalism and Behaviorism: On the Accessibility of Mental Processes*

William R. Uttal • *Toward a New Behaviorism: The Case Against Perceptual Reductionism*

Gordon M. Redding and Benjamin Wallace • *Adaptive Spatial Alignment*

John C. Baird • *Sensation and Judgment: Complementarity Theory of Psychophysics*

John A. Swets • *Signal Detection Theory and ROC Analysis in Psychology and Diagnostics: Collected Papers*

William R. Uttal • *The Swimmer: An Integrated Computational Model of a Perceptual–Motor System*

Stephen W. Link • *The Wave Theory of Difference and Similarity*

EDITED VOLUMES

Christian Kaernbach, Erich Schröger, and Hermann Müller • *Psychophysics Beyond Sensation: Laws and Invariants of Human Cognition*

Michael Wenger and James Townsend • *Computational, Geometric, and Process Perspectives on Facial Cognition: Contexts and Challenges*

Jonathan Grainger and Arthur M. Jacobs • *Localist Connectionist Approaches to Human Cognition*

Cornilia E. Dowling, Fred S. Roberts, and Peter Theuns • *Recent Progress in Mathematical Psychology*

F. Gregory Ashby • *Multidimensional Models of Perception and Cognition*

Hans-Georg Geissler, Stephen W. Link, and James T. Townsend • *Cognition, Information Processing, and Psychophysics: Basic Issues*

TEXTBOOKS

Norman H. Anderson • *Empirical Direction in Design and Analysis*

For more information on LEA titles, please contact Lawrence Erlbaum Associates, Publishers, at www.erlbaum.com.

PSYCHOPHYSICS BEYOND SENSATION

LAWS AND INVARIANTS OF HUMAN COGNITION

Edited by

Christian Kaernbach
University of Leipzig, Germany

Erich Schröger
University of Leipzig, Germany

Hermann Müller
Ludwig-Maximilians-Universität München, Germany
and
University of London, UK

2004

LAWRENCE ERLBAUM ASSOCIATES, PUBLISHERS

Mahwah, New Jersey   London

Editor: Bill Webber
Editorial Assistant: Kristin Duch
Cover Design: Kathryn Houghtaling Lacey
Textbook Production Manager: Paul Smolenski
Full-Service Compositor: TechBooks
Text and Cover Printer: Sheridan Books, Inc.

This book was typeset in 10/12 pt. Times Roman, Bold, and Italic.
The heads were typeset in Americana, Americana Bold, and Americana Bold Italic.

Lawrence Erlbaum Associates, Inc., Publishers
10 Industrial Avenue
Mahwah, New Jersey 07430
www.erlbaum.com

Library of Congress Cataloging-in-Publication Data

Psychophysics beyond sensation : laws and invariants of human cognition / editors,
    Christian Kaernbach, Erich Schröger, Hermann Müller.
        p.   cm.
    Includes index.
    ISBN 0-8058-4250-0 (casebound : alk. paper)
    1. Cognition.   2. Psychophysics.   I. Kaernbach, Christian.   II. Schröger, Erich.
III. Müller, Hermann.

    QP360.5.P795   2003
    153.4—dc21

                                                            2003044891

Books published by Lawrence Erlbaum Associates are printed on
acid-free paper, and their bindings are chosen for strength and
durability.

Printed in the United States of America
10 9 8 7 6 5 4 3 2 1

This volume is dedicated to Hans-Georg Geissler for his extraordinary knowledge and contributions

Contents

Abstracts to all Chapters and Supplementary material:
http://www.erlbaum.com/Kaernbach.

Preface

Since its origins, psychophysics has studied the relation of physical stimulus (outer psychophysics), its neurophysiological correlate (inner psychophysics), or both to sensation. In the 1950s (cognitive term, "new look"), sensation was linked to memory and other higher-order cognitive processes. Subsequently, psychophysical methods were used not only to study sensation as such but also to explore the complex interrelations among physical stimulus, sensation, and internal representations.

This volume presents a series of studies that expand laws, invariants, and principles of psychophysics beyond its classical domain of sensation. In spite of the equivalence of methods, such contributions are often not regarded as "psychophysics." For example, can studies on memory be considered as psychophysical in the same way as studies on sensation? A strong cue to an answer derives from neuroanatomy: It is a fascinating fact that the cortex of the human brain is composed of the same types of neurons, organized in the same assemblage of layers, with the same variety of intralayer and interlayer connections, for primary sensory cortices, secondary and higher-order sensory cortices, up to complex areas with cells sensitive to objects such as hands and faces, for association areas, and for motor cortices. Thus, it is the similarity not only of methods but also of the substrate that suggests an extension of psychophysics beyond sensation.

It is our goal to demonstrate the extent of the *domain* of psychophysics, ranging from sensory processes (but linked to internal representations), through sensory memory and short-term memory issues, to the interaction between sensation and action. The dynamics and timing of human performance are a further important issue within this extended framework of psychophysics: Given the similarity of the various cortical areas in terms of their neuroanatomical structure, it is an important question whether this similarity is paralleled by a similarity of processes. These issues are addressed here by state-of-the-art research methods in behavioral research, psychophysiology, and mathematical modeling.

The idea of putting this volume together originated at a symposium organized to mark Hans-Georg Geissler's 65th birthday. In this symposium, which was attended by many renowned scientists, issues and perspectives of psychophysical research were examined. On the basis of presentations and discussions, we concluded that it was timely to demonstrate the reach of psychophysical methods and theorizing in a special volume. It was Hans who suggested the title for it: "Psychophysics Beyond Sensation." Of course, this volume is not the first of its kind: efforts to portray the state of psychophysical art have a long tradition. In his guest editorial (following this preface), Hans-Georg Geissler gives a lively and intimate insider description of this tradition and his personal view on today's research perspectives in psychophysics.

The volume is divided into four sections. Section 1 presents contributions concerning the classical domain of psychophysical judgment. Sections 2 and 3 describe elementary (perception and action) and higher-order (memory) processes, respectively, and Section 4 presents psychophysical models. Although this structure provides a useful framework for grouping related chapters together, most contributions fit well under more than one section heading. The grouping into four sections follows the central focus of the individual contributions. However, the cohesion across authors imposed by the psychophysical approach precludes consideration of the various sections as entirely separate. The sections are introduced by guest editorials contributed by independent authors. These editorials present the authors' personal views on the respective section, providing an integrated account of the various contributions or highlighting their focus of interest among them, while also voicing their own and sometimes different points of view, thereby contributing to the process of discussion that makes science so exciting.

In summary, this book explores psychophysical approaches to issues concerning internal representations, memory, and action, which consider general questions of the timing of brain dynamics and provide frameworks for context-dependent and multidimensional generalizations of psychophysical theory, in order to advance psychophysics as a seminal approach to psychological science and the understanding of the human mind. The book should be of great interest to advanced (postgraduate) students in neuroscience, cognitive science, psychology, neuropsychology, and related areas who seek to evaluate the range and power of psychophysical work today, and to established scientists in those fields who will appreciate the variety of issues addressed within the same methodological framework and their multiple interconnections and stimulating cross-talk.

This volume required the help of numerous people. First, we thank the contributors who accepted our invitation to write a chapter or a guest editorial for this volume—and who complied readily with our numerous change requests resulting from the review process as well as from our attempt to produce a coherent volume. Peer reviewing was performed not only mutually among contributors (and approximately every second contributor, including the guest editors, had to serve as reviewer for one or several chapters) but also with help from external scientists. We are grateful in this respect to Wolfram Boucsein, Boris Burle, Greg Davis, Laurent Demany, Mieke Donk, Randall Engle, Patrick Haggard, Hans Irtel, Dylan Jones, Helena Kadlec, Werner Klotz, Jan J. Koenderink, Sigrid Lipka, Adrian von Mühlenen, Jochen Müsseler, Wolfgang Prinz, Bertram Scharf, Friederike Schlaghecken, Werner X. Schneider, Joel B. Talcott,

Robin D. Thomas, and Hirooki Yabe. This book is part of the Scientific Psychology series. We thank Series Editors, James T. Townsend and Stephen W. Link, for their patient and continuous support. Especially without Jim's enlivening and encouraging running commentary, the process of putting this volume together would have been less fascinating. From Lawrence Erlbaum Associates, we were obligingly supported by Editor Bill Webber and his assistants Erica Kica and Kristin Duch. Special thanks go to Karsten Jost in Leipzig, who cross-checked every manuscript, solicited any missing piece of information, did a final touch-up on several figures, put together the total manuscript, and compiled the subject and author indexes. His thorough and careful effort contributed considerably to the coherence and consistency of the book. Maria Etzkorn helped us to marshal the considerable amount of communications among contributors, referees, editors, and publisher. We already mentioned that the title of the volume came from Hans-Georg Geissler; what is more, Hans was a stimulating person and inspiring scientist to all of us during our common time in Leipzig, and he is still enthusing us with active research projects and is always ready to discuss our own projects now that he is retired. Editor C. K. is deeply grateful to Hans for being his long-time mentor. Finally, and in the name of all contributors, we thank all those unnamed scientists that helped us to give birth to and clarify our ideas, by putting forward their own and discussing ours. We hope that by bringing out this volume we return some of this debt.

—*Christian Kaernbach, Erich Schröger, Hermann Müller*
Leipzig, Germany

Guest Editorial

Hans-Georg Geissler
Universität Leipzig, Germany

As in any scientific publication, the chapters collected here aim to represent the state of art (see the preface). From a historical perspective, the same contributions may be viewed as representing links in a chain, reflecting the interactive development of the ideas of groups of researchers under the influence of other disciplines and constrained by the conceptual and technical tools available at the time as well as by facilitating or restraining conditions in the respective societies at large. Rarely do these determinants become clearly discernible to those directly involved. This volume, to a certain degree, provides an exception that deserves comment.

It may be taken as a sign of coherence that most chapters were written by (co-)authors who, since 1976, had contributed to a sequence of five volumes that formed what can be considered a "virtual" book series and that ended, in 1992, with the first volume of a "real" series, *Scientific Psychology*, to which this volume provides a continuation. It was in the midst of the cold war, in the winter of 1974, on a taxi ride with Russian colleagues to the Moscow Belo-Russian Train Station, when the plan for the first of these books was conceived, with the idea of exploiting the preparation of a session of the 20th International Congress of Psychology in Paris to organize a joint endeavor with Western colleagues. The intention of the book—to accommodate a rich variety of perceptual–cognitive phenomena within a broadened concept of psychophysics—exactly caught a worldwide trend that had emerged in response to the narrow, power-function focus of "new psychophysics." To denote this turn toward a generalized psychophysics, later, following a small meeting in Frankfurt (am Main) in 1983, I coined the term "psychophysics beyond sensation"—hitherto never used as a title for a book. By this time, a multitude of sessions during the 22nd International Congress in Leipzig in 1980 had already demonstrated that the trend toward this type of approach, encompassing complex representational issues and modeling of decision processes, was fairly robust. On the occasion of the centenary of Fechner's death in 1987, it was again Leipzig, in her role as a place of exchange between East and West, that hosted sympathizers of this approach from all over the world.

The past decade saw an immense progress in physicotechnical and conceptual instrumentation, to mention only the rise of brain imaging, neoconnectionism, and novel epistemological approaches to consciousness. Thus, one might ask whether extrapolation from psychophysical concepts is outdated and can no longer provide a suitable frame of reference for a book. I do not think so. First, given perception-related world cognition as the common theme, the specific features shared by the contributions to this book can be neither delimited by a particular set of paradigms or contrasting methodologies nor tied down to a specific programmatic vision. In fact, the volume embraces brilliant examples of the most advanced data acquisition and neural modeling, and a multitude of theoretical and methodological approaches abound in free competition with each other. Indeed, it would seem easier to define the common ground by negative imperatives, such as the endeavor *not* to adhere to any reductionism or *not* to radically exclude opposing standpoints. However, this is exactly what the "exact science of mind–body relations," as Fechner had referred to psychophysics, actually implies. It binds the authors together with what I call the implicit rigor of a scientific ethics—not that of an established discipline but rather of an ultimate shared goal "respected" as a whole in all its known and yet-to-be-discovered facets.

This position sharpens sensitivity to large-scale interrelationships, thus promoting working stratagems based on them. In this respect, what strikes me is that the guiding role in the search for psychophysical correspondences is attributed here to behavioral analysis. Not accidentally, this stratagem is part of Fechner's—more than once rediscovered—functional principle for establishing "inner psychophysics." From a phylogenetic point of view, this stratagem seems essential, because, in shaping perceptual–cognitive architectures, natural selection acts directly on behavioral outcomes and only indirectly on the neural substrate. An often-overlooked corollary of this is that, in the identification of psychophysical correspondences, no unconditionally unique reversal of the direction behavioral construct → neural substrate is possible. Resulting loopholes are known from Wasserman's and Wang-Bennett's (1989) insightful analysis. In the present volume, Grossberg's bold ideas on complementarity and uncertainty provide an example of a constructive solution. Another variant of the problem surfaces in Elliott and Müller's and Kompass' chapters, which show that the precision of mental timing may many times exceed that known from physiological indices. In agreement with the winner-takes-all principle, this may be taken as indicating that merely a small fraction of interrelated brain activities participate directly in a ultimately behavior-determining chain of processes—a conclusion that would be fatal for any purely physiological approach.

Another important stratagem, referred to in the subtitle of the book, is reduction to (processing) invariants. In contrast to their universal counterparts in physics, these invariants are conditional by nature, defined only relative to architectural structures of cognition. Thus, the corresponding constructs, depending on the context, may mean widely different things. For example, invariances concern sensory characteristics under varying conditions of conscious access (Vorberg et al.), item independence of storage time (Kaernbach), constancy of operation time under varying task constraints (Geissler), or common metrical structures of color spaces constructed from judgment data versus electroencephalographic potentials (Izmailov and Sokolov). At the same time, as a cross-validation criterion, invariance is part of a system-oriented analysis that goes far beyond plain single-case modeling.

Apart from novel scientific and technological developments, the years separating the former editing efforts from the present volume have witnessed a most dramatic and unexpected change in the political scene, which is still difficult to realize in its full scale and potential consequences. The project of the first international book in 1974 was, and had to be, a secret shared among three people. Editing at that time in East Germany was a strange task, as one was confronted with all sorts of technical and political obstacles. Let me mention, just as an aside, that after invitations for a contribution had illegally crossed the "iron" border, submissions were received with great delay, and surprisingly—as became clear after a while—in reverse order of their mailing. It took the naive editor a while to discover, with feelings oscillating between horror and amusement, that someone had obviously filed the incoming manuscripts in a stack and, after a signal of permission from wherever, passed them on to the editor, piece by piece in a top-down fashion from the stack.

What a happy contrast now. From remote parts of the world, contributors to the volume could meet freely in Leipzig, laying the basis for this truly international collaboration. Again, there has been a considerable delay between submission and publication. This delay time, however, was spent on careful reviewing and editing, in a process in which manuscript versions, mostly several times, changed "sides" by means of the Internet. I can only congratulate the Editors on the outcome of their efforts.

Finally, this Guest Editorial offers a unique opportunity for me to gratefully acknowledge the resourceful efforts of a few of my many colleagues in those difficult times: Friedhart Klix, who kept scientific psychology going in East Germany; and Viktor Sarris, Emanuel Leeuwenberg, Hans Buffart, Stephen Link, Wolfgang Prinz, and Allen Parducci, who opened a window and then a door for me to the West before barriers were pulled down.

Obviously, the intentions that once, under difficult circumstances, brought together a group of researchers have stood the test of time and survived even political-system transformation. It looks as if the virtual project of "psychophysics beyond sensation" has also succeeded in terms of recruiting researchers from a younger generation. However, true progress lies in the unexpected, and what has been said here is not to imply that the way into the future will be a direct extension of a track from the past.

—*Hans-Georg Geissler*
Berlin, Germany

REFERENCE

Wasserman, G. S., & Wang-Bennett, L. T. (1989). Unity and diversity of neurelectric and psychophysical functions: The invariance question. *Behavioral and Brain Sciences, 12*, 297–299.

I

Theories of
Psychophysical Judgment

Guest Editorial

R. Duncan Luce
University of California, Irvine

The five chapters of this section provide a sample of current approaches to psy-chophysical theories based entirely on observed behavior. (Izmailov and Sokolov, chap. 2, provide a partial exception in that they treat aspects of evoked potentials in much the same way as behavioral data.) In each case the stimuli are simple phys-ical signals such as pure tones or monochromatic lights. Two chapters (chap. 3 by Petzold and Haubensak and chap. 4 by Sarris) focus on context effects such as sequential and range effects arising in absolute identification, category, rating, and magnitude estimation methods (as they are usually carried out). Little doubt remains that psychophysical judgments are relative, and the focus of these studies is to make guesses as to what the respondents elect (consciously or unconsciously) to use as references for judgments of these types. The other three (i.e., chap. 1 by Dzhafarov, chap. 2, and chap. 5 by Townsend and Spencer-Smith) focus to vary-ing degrees on the issues of representing stimuli geometrically and on the related question of their perceptual separability. Both of these issues, context effects and perceptual separability, are well within the domain of sensation. That accords with the role of this first section to treat classical sensation from a modern perspective. The cognitive aspects that go beyond sensation arise in the later sections.

The present studies are representative of part of the field in the sense that, first, a variety of types of judgments are collected and modeled: discriminations in the

Fechnerian tradition (chap. 1), judgments of dissimilarity (chap. 2), or some form of more or less specified category or other numerical judgment (chaps. 3 and 4), with chapter 5 not being specific about the source of data but focusing mainly on the nature of representations. Second, some, but by no means full, agreement exists about the specifics of the representation. Three chapters (chaps. 1, 2, and 5) focus on geometric representations, and the other two focus on numerical ones.

One unrepresented approach, although chapter 5 mentions it briefly, is the class of information processing models. Presumably they were excluded because a good deal more than observed behavior underlies them. One example of such modeling is that grounded in neural mechanisms, which is treated in the fourth part of this volume.

My favorite approach, representational measurement theory, is also largely missing, although to a degree some of Dzhafarov's approach is quite similar. Let me outline what I see as the advantages and some of the present weaknesses of this approach.

First, one seeks sets of behavioral properties (axioms), each having no free parameters and each suitable for empirical study in isolation from the others. An early example of this axiomatic approach, one that attempted to deal with context effects of a certain type in vision, is that given by Krantz (1968); it has been largely and unjustifiably ignored. In chapter 1, one finds two defining properties of separability of stimuli that are behavioral. As axioms, these are spatially local in character and are then pieced together to get a global representation. In my work, the axioms themselves are global and require no sort of additional Fechnerian hypothesis. Unfortunately, mine do not admit any sort of imperfect discrimination as seems to be inherent in the data. Meshing local probabilistic behavior with global algebraic structure has proven to be quite elusive.

The testing of behavioral properties is rather different from asking how well a representation fits numerical responses that are generally subject to context effects. Usually such representations have free parameters, whereas behavioral axioms almost never do. The axioms are focused, and when one is rejected empirically it is clear what aspect of the theory requires modification. Three of my recent papers (Luce, 2002, 2003a, 2003b) reflect just such an interplay of behavioral data followed by selectively modified theory.

Second, these axioms, together with a rich domain of stimuli, lead (purely mathematically) to some sort of representation. In chapter 1 it is a Minkowski power metric of dimension $r \geq 1$. In my work it is the one-dimensional, nonnegative real line with some arithmetic operations reflecting behavioral structures. The behavioral axioms dictate the representation; the responses are not in themselves in any way treated as direct measures of sensation, of loudness or brightness. Indeed, in my work the responses are all choices of signals in the domain being studied, not numerals selected by the respondents (see the paragraphs that follow). Numerical measures of intensity arise only in the representation; they are a creature of the scientist's compact description of behavior and not a part of the behavior itself. A price of this approach is that often the mathematics establishing the nature of the representation is not simple.

From the perspective of three of the papers in this section, my current work is too limited because it is not geometric in character and so cannot possibly capture such features as perceptual separability—however, that concept may be defined. Consensus on that definition has yet to be reached, as chapters 1, 2, and 5 vividly demonstrate. This limitation only means that a next stage is to incorporate more complex aspects of, for example, audition rather than just loudness. This would include pitch and possibly other attributes of stimuli varying in more than just intensity. The theoretical task, which is formidable, is to arrive at testable properties that give rise mathematically to a representation in a suitable geometric space whose nature is dictated by the behavior. To a considerable extent this was done for color by Krantz (1975) although, as chapter 2 and other work suggest, that modeling has to be extended in some fashion to four dimensions to be fully comprehensive. In principle, this kind of work should be cumulative, with each new complication encompassing the earlier more limited results. This process will not be easy and so shortcuts are tempting, but I venture to guess that ultimately the principled effort will be worthwhile.

Third, both Dzhafarov's work and mine attempt to use empirical methods that may reduce or eliminate the roles of anything but known, temporally local contexts. So, for example, in my work the respondents are assumed to make two kinds of judgments. To talk about these, we need notation for two concepts of order— spatial and temporal. Let (x, u) denote the presentation of intensity (measured in intensity units above the relevant threshold intensity) x to the left and u to the right ear. (Other interpretations of the primitives are possible.) For stimuli A and B, let $\langle A, B \rangle$ denote the presentation of, first, A, quickly followed by B. Let $\sim$ denote loudness matches of successive presentations. The respondent is asked to select stimuli z_l, z_r, z such that

$$(x, u) \sim (z_l, 0), \quad (x, u) \sim (0, z_r), \quad (x, u) \sim (z, z),$$

where the successive presentations, for example, $\langle (x, u), (z_l, 0) \rangle$, are close in time. The other judgment involves successive presentations of two pairs of temporally ordered stimuli: for $x, x' > y$, $\langle (y, 0), (x, 0) \rangle$ followed by $\langle (y, 0), (x', 0) \rangle$, where this temporal separation is, usually, somewhat greater than within the pairs. The experimenter chooses x, y and a positive number p, and the task of the respondent is to select x' so that the subjective "interval" $\langle (y, 0), (x', 0) \rangle$ stands in the ratio p to the "interval" $\langle (y, 0), (x, 0) \rangle$. Such data are reported in Steingrimsson and Luce (2003).

If the term $(y, 0)$ is omitted in each case, then this is a version of magnitude production in which the referent is implicitly held fixed at $(0, 0)$. Data suggest that this special case is dealt with differently than when $(y, 0)$ is presented, and so, perhaps, should be avoided or modeled separately (Luce, 2003b). In our method the referent $(y, 0)$ is explicit on each trial and can, if one wishes, be varied from trial to trial. One potential advantage of this unusual method is that it makes clear on each trial what the reference signals should be, and we hope that the respondent will refrain from using his or her own reference levels from previous trials that seem to generate unwanted context effects. Whether or not these two types of judgments actually do avoid context effects remains to be established, but the attempt to search for such procedures raises the following important philosophical point.

Is it reasonable for the field to continue to use a method, such as category scaling, after it has been shown to have messy context effects, and then challenge theorists to account for them? To answer Yes would argue that 16th- to 17th-century physicists erred and should have accepted the challenge of developing theories of mass measurement able to describe what happens when pan balances are highly imperfect, such as when they are made of nonrigid materials with unequal arms and sticky pivots. These are context effects in that situation. Rather, merchants as well as scientists perfected balances to the point where the observations were highly reliable and a simple measure of mass resulted. Much later, with the elaboration of physical theory, it became possible, in principle, to explain in detail what would happen with imperfect balances, but that is hardly basic physics. The alternative for psychophysicists is similar—to devise data collection procedures with the goal of bringing the context effects under experimental control, although we can never hope to eliminate the reality of imperfect, unaided human discriminations.

We should never forget that absolute identifications, rating or category scales, or magnitude estimations are not in any way holy—especially if, as has been shown, they invite respondents to make unknown comparisons and possibly lead them to use the several categories approximately equally often no matter what the actual distribution of stimuli. Let us focus on better ways to collect data as well as on modeling that does not pretend respondent's judgments are themselves the measures we seek.

ACKNOWLEDGMENT

My thanks to A. A. J. Marley and Ragnar Steingrimsson for comments and suggestions on earlier drafts.

REFERENCES

Krantz, D. H. (1968). A theory of context effects based on cross-context matching. *Journal of Mathematical Psychology, 5*, 1–48.

Krantz, D. H. (1975). Color measurement and color theory. I. Representation theorem for Grassman structures. II. Opponent-colors theory. *Journal of Mathematical Psychology, 12*, 283–303, 304–327.

Luce, R. D. (2002). A psychophysical theory of intensity proportions, joint presentations, and matches. *Psychological Review, 109*, 520–532.

Luce, R. D. (2003a). Symmetric and asymmetric matching of joint presentations. Revised manuscript submitted for publication.

Luce, R. D. (2003b). Increasing increment generalizations of rank-dependent theories. Manuscript submitted for publication.

Steingrimsson, R., & Luce, R. D. (2003). Empirical evaluation of a model of global psychophysical judgments. Manuscript under revision.

1

Perceptual Separability of Stimulus Dimensions: A Fechnerian Analysis

Ehtibar N. Dzhafarov
Purdue University, Indiana

Consider a situation in which, say, elliptically shaped visual stimuli continuously vary in the lengths of their radii, a and b, all other parameters being held fixed. This is a simple example of a two-dimensional continuous stimulus space: Each stimulus can be described by two coordinates, (x^1, x^2), taking their values within a region of Re $\times$ Re.[1] The dimensions $\langle x^1, x^2 \rangle$ can be chosen in an infinity of ways. One can put $x^1 = a$, $x^2 = b$, or $x^1 = a{:}b$, $x^2 = ab$ (aspect ratio and size), or one can even choose dimensions for which one has no conventional geometric terms, say, $x^1 = \exp(2a + 3b)$, $x^2 = \log(3a + 2b)$. The number of dimensions, in this case two, is a topological invariant (i.e., it is constant under all-continuous one-to-one transformations of the space), but the choice of the dimensions is arbitrary: With any given choice of $\langle x^1, x^2 \rangle$, one obtains other representations by arbitrarily transforming these dimensions into $\bar{x}^1 = \bar{x}^1(x^1, x^2)$, $\bar{x}^2 = \bar{x}^2(x^1, x^2)$, provided the transformations are one-to-one and smooth. If one imposes a certain "subjective"

---

[1]Following the traditional differential-geometric notation adopted in Dzhafarov and Colonius (1999, 2001), I use superscripts rather than subscripts to refer to point coordinates and (later) coordinates of direction vectors. The notation $\langle x^1, x^2 \rangle$, $\langle x^1 \rangle$, $\langle x^2 \rangle$ refers to frames of reference, or axes, whereas (x^1, x^2), (y^1, y^2), (x^1), (y^2), etc., denote coordinates of different stimuli with respect to specified frames of reference, or axes.

(computed from perceptual judgments) metric on the stimulus space, this metric must be invariant with respect to the choice of stimulus dimensions. In multi-dimensional Fechnerian scaling (MDFS), on which this work is based, this invariance is achieved automatically by the procedure of computing Fechnerian distances.

The choice of the dimensions describing elliptically shaped visual stimuli, however, may interest one from another point of view, pertaining to the focal issue of this work. One might hypothesize that with some choice of $\langle x^1, x^2 \rangle$, say, $x^1 = a{:}b$ (aspect ratio) and $x^2 = ab$ (size), the two dimensions are processed separately, so that perceptual distinctions between two ellipses can be, in some sense, computed from the perceptual distinctions between their aspect ratios (irrespective of size) and their sizes (irrespective of aspect ratio), whereas, one might hypothesize, such a reduction to individual dimensions cannot be achieved with other choices, say, $x^1 = a$ and $x^2 = b$, in which case the dimensions have to be viewed as processed integrally.

Ashby and Townsend (1986) analyze several theoretical concepts (separability, orthogonality, independence, performance parity) proposed in the literature in an attempt to capture this intuitive distinction. They propose to interpret these concepts within the framework of the General Recognition Theory (Ashby & Perrin, 1988), as different aspects of the mapping of stimuli into hypothetical random variables that take their values in some perceptual space. If one can define in this space two coordinate axes, $\langle p^1, p^2 \rangle$ (or two subspaces spanning two distinct sets of axes), such that the p^1 component and p^2 component of the random variable representing a stimulus (x^1, x^2) depend on only x^1 and x^2, respectively, then one can say that the dimensions $\langle x^1 \rangle$ and $\langle x^2 \rangle$ are perceptually separable. (The separability, perhaps by an abuse of language, is sometimes attributed to the perceptual dimensions $\langle p^1 \rangle$ and $\langle p^2 \rangle$ rather than the stimulus dimensions.) With this definition, the stochastic relationship between the p^1 and the p^2 components of the random variable representing (x^1, x^2) may depend on the (x^1, x^2) in an arbitrary fashion, provided the selective correspondence $(x^1 \leftrightarrow p^1, x^2 \leftrightarrow p^2)$ is satisfied on the level of marginal distributions. Thomas (1996) adapts this approach to the situation in which pairs of stimuli are judged on the same–different scale, which is especially relevant to the Fechnerian analysis presented in this chapter.

A different attempt to rigorously define perceptual separability is made by Shepard (1987) within the framework of multidimensional scaling. Shepard posits that stimuli are represented in a perceptual space by points separated by distances negative-exponentially related to some "stimulus generalization" measure, that, for our purposes, can be thought of as a probability of confusing one stimulus with another. It is traditionally postulated in multidimensional scaling, or derived from equivalent premises (Beals, Krantz, & Tversky, 1968; Tversky & Krantz,

1970), that one can define in this perceptual-space coordinate axes $\langle p^1, \ldots, p^k \rangle$ with respect to which the interstimulus distances D in the space form a Minkowski power metric:

$$D\left[(p^1, \ldots, p^k), (q^1, \ldots, q^k)\right]^r = \left|p^1 - q^1\right|^r + \cdots + \left|p^k - q^k\right|^r.$$

From the multidimensional scaling of several stimulus spaces, Shepard (1987) suggested that the exponent r of this power metric equals 1 (city-block metric) if the stimuli are analyzable into separately processed dimensions, and it equals 2 (Euclidean metric) if they are not. Although the relationship between subjective distances and stimulus confusion probabilities is central to Shepard's theory, he did not define the perceptual separability in terms of these confusion probabilities, relying instead on operational criteria external to his theory (such as those described in Garner, 1974). He also did not seem to consider the possibility that, just as stimuli with perceptually separable dimensions (by some criteria) can always be presented in a frame of reference whose axes are not perceptually separable (by the same criteria), so the "perceptual integrality" of stimuli corresponding to $r = 2$ could generally be a function of a specific choice of stimulus dimensions, rather than a property of the stimuli per se.

In this chapter I present a new approach to the issue of perceptual separability of stimulus dimensions, based on the theory of MDFS (Dzhafarov, 2001, 2002a, 2002b, 2002c, 2002d; Dzhafarov & Colonius, 1999, 2001). This chapter closely follows Dzhafarov (2002c).

Historical precursors of MDFS can be traced back to Helmholtz's (1891) and Schrödinger's (1920) reconstructions of color metrics from color-discrimination data. In MDFS, subjective (Fechnerian) distances among stimuli are computed from the probabilities with which stimuli are discriminated from their close neighbors in a continuous stimulus space. Accordingly, the concepts explicating the intuitive idea of perceptual separability are formulated in this chapter solely in terms of discrimination probabilities. Specifically, I propose to treat dimensions $\langle x^1 \rangle$ and $\langle x^2 \rangle$ as perceptually separable if the following two conditions are met:

1. The probability with which a stimulus $\mathbf{x} = (x^1, x^2)$ is discriminated from nearby stimuli $\mathbf{y} = (y^1, y^2)$ can be computed from the probabilities with which $\mathbf{x}$ is discriminated from $\mathbf{y}_1 = (y^1, x^2)$ (differing from $\mathbf{x}$ along the first dimension only) and from $\mathbf{y}_2 = (x^1, y^2)$ (differing from $\mathbf{x}$ along the second dimension only);

2. The difference between the probabilities with which $\mathbf{x} = (x^1, x^2)$ is discriminated from nearby $\mathbf{y}_1 = (y^1, x^2)$ and with which $\mathbf{x}$ is discriminated from itself does not depend on x^2; and analogously for $\mathbf{x} = (x^1, x^2)$ and nearby $\mathbf{y}_2 = (x^1, y^2)$.

If the probabilities with which each stimulus is discriminated from nearby stimuli are known, then MDFS allows one to uniquely compute the Fechnerian distances among all stimuli comprising the stimulus space. The following question therefore is a natural one to ask in relation to the definition of perceptual separability just outlined: Given that $\langle x^1 \rangle$ and $\langle x^2 \rangle$ are separable, how is the Fechnerian distance between stimuli $\mathbf{a} = (a^1, a^2)$ and $\mathbf{b} = (b^1, b^2)$, not necessarily close, related to the corresponding coordinatewise Fechnerian distances, between $\mathbf{a}$ and $\mathbf{b}_1 = (b^1, a^2)$ and between $\mathbf{a}$ and $\mathbf{b}_2 = (a^1, b^2)$? The answer to this question is the main result of this work. It turns out, with the Fechnerian distances denoted by G, that

$$G(\mathbf{a}, \mathbf{b})^r = G(\mathbf{a}, \mathbf{b}_1)^r + G(\mathbf{a}, \mathbf{b}_2)^r, r \geq 1.$$

This means that the Fechnerian metric in a stimulus space with perceptually separable dimensions is a Minkowski power metric with respect to these dimensions.

This result may appear similar to Shepard's (1987) suggestion. The resemblance, however, is rather superficial. First, in MDFS the metric is imposed directly on the stimulus space rather than on a hypothetical perceptual space (which may even have a different dimensionality). Second, it is the power function form per se of the Fechnerian metric that is indicative of perceptual separability, rather than a specific value of the exponent r. I show below that the value of r is determined by the value of the fundamental characteristic of MDFS, μ, the *psychometric order of stimulus space*. Specifically, $r = \mu$ if $\mu \geq 1$, and $r = 1$ otherwise. Roughly, the psychometric order μ determines the degree of flatness/cuspidality of discrimination probability functions at their minima, and this characteristic has nothing to do with perceptual separability.[2]

The theory to be presented is formulated for two-dimensional stimulus spaces, but it can be readily generalized to arbitrary dimensionality, or even to an arbitrary number of subspaces spanning several dimensions each. This generalizability is the main reason why I keep in this chapter the notation adopted in Dzhafarov and Colonius (1999, 2001) for n-dimensional stimulus spaces.

PERCEPTUAL SEPARABILITY: DEFINITION AND PROPERTIES

Consider a two-dimensional stimulus space $\mathfrak{M}$, an open connected region of Re^2, and let $\langle x^1, x^2 \rangle$ be a coordinate system imposed on this space. The stimulus space is assumed to be endowed with *psychometric* (discrimination probability) functions

$$\psi_{\mathbf{x}}(\mathbf{y}) = \mathrm{Prob}\,(\mathbf{y} \text{ is discriminated from } \mathbf{x}),$$

---

[2]A new theoretical development described in Dzhafarov (2002d), based on two fundamental properties of perceptual discrimination (called regular minimality and nonconstant self-similarity), shows that μ generally cannot exceed unity. This means that in the case of perceptual separability $r = 1$, precisely as Shepard suggested but with a very different justification. This and other relevant results from Dzhafarov (2002d) are not reflected in the present chapter, as they were obtained long after the chapter had been accepted for publication.

where $\mathbf{x} = (x^1, x^2) \in \mathfrak{M}$, $\mathbf{y} = (y^1, y^2) \in \mathfrak{M}$. I refer to the stimulus space together with the psychometric functions defined on it as the *discrimination system* $\langle \mathfrak{M}, \psi \rangle$.

Given a stimulus $\mathbf{x} = (x^1, x^2)$, the stimulus that lies $s \geq 0$ units away from $\mathbf{x}$ in the direction $\mathbf{u} = (u^1, u^2)$ can be denoted by $\mathbf{x} + \mathbf{u}s = (x^1 + u^1s, x^2 + u^2s)$; u^1 and u^2 may be any real numbers, except that they cannot vanish simultaneously. The difference

$$\Psi_\mathbf{x}(\mathbf{x} + \mathbf{u}s) = \psi_\mathbf{x}(\mathbf{x} + \mathbf{u}s) - \psi_\mathbf{x}(\mathbf{x}), \quad s \geq 0$$

is referred to as the *psychometric differential* (at $\mathbf{x}$, $\mathbf{u}$), and it plays a central role in Fechnerian computations. The underlying assumptions of MDFS ensure that following, if necessary, a certain "elimination of constant error" procedure whose description can be found in, e.g., Dzhafarov & Colonius, 1999, 2001, the psychometric differentials are positive (for $s > 0$) and continuously decrease to zero as $s \to 0+$. The definition of perceptual separability is formulated below in terms of the psychometric differentials Ψ rather than the discrimination probabilities ψ per se.

In the subsequent presentation I also use the following convention. Given a direction vector $\mathbf{u} = (u^1, u^2)$, I denote its coordinate projections $(u^1, 0)$ and $(0, u^2)$ by $\mathbf{u}_1$ and $\mathbf{u}_2$, respectively.

Definition A (Refer to Fig. 1.1). The coordinate system $\langle x^1, x^2 \rangle$ forms a *dimensional basis* for the discrimination system $\langle \mathfrak{M}, \psi \rangle$ if for any stimulus $\mathbf{x}$ one can find an open neighborhood $\mathfrak{N}_\mathbf{x} \subseteq \mathfrak{M}$ of $\mathbf{x}$ such that, whenever $\mathbf{x} + \mathbf{u}s \in \mathfrak{N}_\mathbf{x}$,

$$\Psi_\mathbf{x}(\mathbf{x} + \mathbf{u}s) = H_\mathbf{x}\left[\Psi_\mathbf{x}(\mathbf{x} + \mathbf{u}_1s), \Psi_\mathbf{x}(\mathbf{x} + \mathbf{u}_2s)\right], \tag{1}$$

where H_x is some function differentiable on $\mathfrak{N}_\mathbf{x}$.

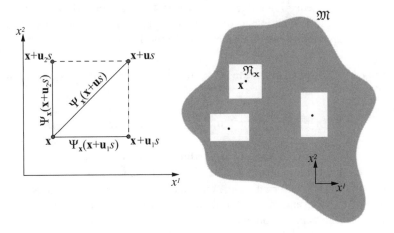

FIG. 1.1.   A diagram for Definition A (dimensional basis).

Observe that the functions H_x are allowed to be different for different x. One should note the following two important properties of H_x. First,

$$H_x\left[\Psi_x(x + u_1 s), 0\right] = \Psi_x(x + u_1 s),\ H_x\left[0,\ \Psi_x(x + u_2 s)\right] = \Psi_x(x + u_2 s),$$

$$H_x(0, 0) = 0 \tag{2}$$

The second property is

$$\left.\frac{\partial H_x(a, b)}{\partial a}\right|_{a=b=0} = \left.\frac{\partial H_x(a, b)}{\partial b}\right|_{a=b=0} = 1. \tag{3}$$

See Dzhafarov (2002c) for the proof.

As a simple example of H_x, consider the discrimination system in which

$$\Psi_x(x + us) = 1 - \left[1 - \Psi_x(x + u_1 s)\right]\left[1 - \Psi_x(x + u_2 s)\right]. \tag{4}$$

H_x here does not depends on x. If, in addition, $\psi_x(x) \equiv 0$, this equation can be rewritten by substituting ψ for Ψ, and it can be interpreted as saying that the discriminations along $\langle x^1 \rangle$ and $\langle x^2 \rangle$ are stochastically independent and that two stimuli are discriminated whenever they are discriminated along either of these dimensions.

One can obtain a wealth of special cases for H_x by choosing an arbitrary strictly monotone (differentiable) function $T_x(a)$, $0 \leq a \leq 1$, vanishing at $a = 0$, and putting

$$\Psi_x(x + us) = T_x^{-1}\{T_x[\Psi_x(x + u_1 s)] + T_x[\Psi_x(x + u_2 s)]\}. \tag{5}$$

In particular, this equation reduces to Equation 4 if $T_x(a) = T(a) = \log(1 - a)$.

The following lemma is part of the foundation of the Fechnerian analysis of perceptual separability (see Dzhafarov, 2002c for the proof).

Lemma A (Additivity in the small). If $\langle x^1, x^2 \rangle$ forms a dimensional basis for $\langle \mathfrak{M}, \psi \rangle$, then

$$\Psi_x(x + us) \sim \Psi_x(x + u_1 s) + \Psi_x(x + u_2 s)\ (\text{as } s \to 0+). \tag{6}$$

(The symbol $\sim$ indicates that the two expressions it connects are asymptotically equal, i.e., their ratio tends to 1. The term in the small means "at the limit" or "asymptotically".) As $u = u_1 + u_2$, one recognizes in Equation 6 an asymptotic version of the conventional factorial additivity (of the main effects of changes along the two dimensions on Ψ).

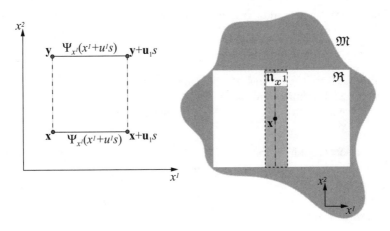

FIG. 1.2. A diagram for Definition B (detachability, shown for the horizontal axis only).

The next definition requires that we confine the consideration to some open rectangular area $\mathcal{R} = (x^1_{\text{inf}}, x^1_{\text{sup}}) \times (x^2_{\text{inf}}, x^2_{\text{sup}})$ of $\mathfrak{M}$. Accordingly, the discrimination system $\langle \mathfrak{M}, \psi \rangle$ is restricted to $\langle \mathcal{R}, \psi \rangle$. The area $\mathcal{R}$ may be infinite in either or both dimensions (i.e., some or all of the symbols $x^1_{\text{inf}}, x^1_{\text{sup}}, x^2_{\text{inf}}, x^2_{\text{sup}}$ may stand for $\pm\infty$), and it may coincide with the entire $\mathfrak{M}$.

Definition B (Refer to Fig. 1.2). The dimension $\langle x^1 \rangle$ is *detachable* from the discrimination system $\langle \mathcal{R}, \psi \rangle$ if for any value of x^1 one can find an open vicinity $n_{x^1} \subseteq (x^1_{\text{inf}}, x^1_{\text{sup}})$ of x^1, such that whenever $x^1 + u^1 s \in n_{x^1}$, $\Psi_{\mathbf{x}}(\mathbf{x} + \mathbf{u}_1 s)$ does not depend on $x^2 \in (x^2_{\text{inf}}, x^2_{\text{sup}})$. In other words, whenever $\mathbf{x} \in \mathcal{R}$ and $x^1 + u^1 s \in n_{x^1}$,

$$\Psi_{\mathbf{x}}(\mathbf{x} + \mathbf{u}_1 s) = \Psi_{x^1}(x^1 + u^1 s). \tag{7}$$

Analogously for the detachability of $\langle x^2 \rangle$ from $\langle \mathcal{R}, \psi \rangle$: Whenever $\mathbf{x} \in \mathcal{R}$ and $x^2 + u^2 s \in n_{x^2}$,

$$\Psi_{\mathbf{x}}(\mathbf{x} + \mathbf{u}_2 s) = \Psi_{x^2}(x^2 + u^2 s). \tag{8}$$

The reason for confining the definition of detachability to a rectangular area $\mathcal{R}$ is simple: if $\mathfrak{M}$ is shaped differently, one can find $x^1, x^1 + u^1 s, x^2_1$, and x^2_2 such that $(x^1, x^2_1) \in \mathfrak{M}, (x^1 + u^1 s, x^2_1) \in \mathfrak{M}$, whereas $(x^1 + u^1 s, x^2_2) \notin \mathfrak{M}$. As a result, $\Psi_{\mathbf{x}}(\mathbf{x} + \mathbf{u}_1 s)$ would be defined for some and not defined for other values of x^2, which would mean that it does depend on x^2, contrary to the definition.

The following definition of perceptual separability is simply the conjunction of the previous two, except that the dimensional basis is now restricted to $\langle \mathcal{R}, \psi \rangle$.

Definition AB. The dimensions $\langle x^1 \rangle$ and $\langle x^2 \rangle$ are *perceptually separable* with respect to the discrimination system $\langle \mathcal{R}, \psi \rangle$ if $\langle x^1, x^2 \rangle$ forms a dimensional basis for $\langle \mathcal{R}, \psi \rangle$ and if both $\langle x^1 \rangle$ and $\langle x^2 \rangle$ are detachable from $\langle \mathcal{R}, \psi \rangle$.

Two aspects of this definition are significant for the subsequent development. First, one can readily verify that if $\langle x^1 \rangle$ and $\langle x^2 \rangle$ are perceptually separable, then so are all the smooth monotonic transformations ("recalibrations") thereof, $\langle \bar{x}^1 \rangle$ and $\langle \bar{x}^2 \rangle$. Second, the application of this definition to Lemma A immediately yields the following result.

LEMMA AB (Detachable additivity in the small). If $\langle x^1 \rangle$ and $\langle x^2 \rangle$ are perceptually separable with respect to $\langle \mathcal{R}, \psi \rangle$, then, within $\mathcal{R}$,

$$\Psi_{\mathbf{x}}(\mathbf{x} + \mathbf{u}s) \sim \Psi_{x^1}(x^1 + u^1 s) + \Psi_{x^2}(x^2 + u^2 s) \text{ (as } s \to 0+). \qquad (9)$$

I show in the next section that these two properties directly lead one to the Minkowski power-metric structure of the Fechnerian metric.

PERCEPTUAL SEPARABILITY: FECHNERIAN ANALYSIS

The theory of MDFS is based on four assumptions about the shapes of the psychometric functions $\psi_{\mathbf{x}}(\mathbf{y})$ (Dzhafarov, 2002a; Dzhafarov & Colonius, 2001). Rather than describing them here, I confine the discussion to those consequences of these assumptions that are relevant for the present analysis.

First, the assumptions of MDFS guarantee that the psychometric functions $\psi_{\mathbf{x}}(\mathbf{y})$ look more or less as shown in Fig. 1.3 (ignore for now the values of μ): For any $\mathbf{x}$, $\psi_{\mathbf{x}}(\mathbf{y})$ is continuous, attains its global minimum at some point, and increases as one moves a small distance away from this point in any direction. Note that $\psi_{\mathbf{x}}(\mathbf{y})$ is generally allowed to be different from $\psi_{\mathbf{y}}(\mathbf{x})$, and $\psi_{\mathbf{x}}(\mathbf{x})$ is allowed to vary with $\mathbf{x}$. By a certain procedure that eliminates constant error by "renaming" reference stimuli (Dzhafarov & Colonius, 1999, 2001) one can always ensure that the minimum of $\psi_{\mathbf{x}}(\mathbf{y})$ is attained at $\mathbf{y} = \mathbf{x}$, which in this chapter is assumed to be the case. This makes all psychometric differentials $\Psi_{\mathbf{x}}(\mathbf{x} + \mathbf{u}s)$ positive at $s > 0$ and continuously decreasing to zero as $s \to 0+$.

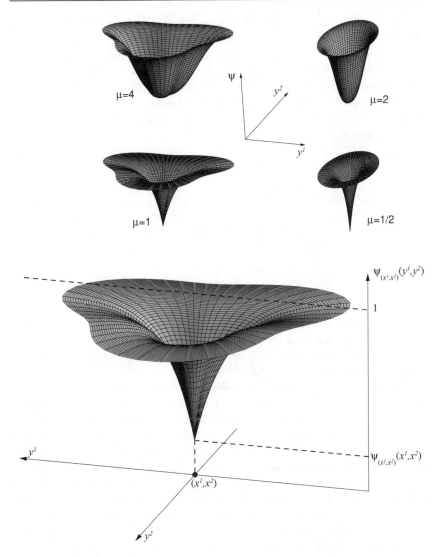

FIG. 1.3. Possible appearances of psychometric functions.

The assumptions underlying MDFS also ensure that all psychometric differentials can be asymptotically decomposed as

$$\Psi_{\mathbf{x}}(\mathbf{x} + \mathbf{u}s) \sim [F(\mathbf{x}, \mathbf{u})R(s)]^{\mu} \ (\text{as } s \to 0+), \tag{10}$$

with the following meaning of the right-hand terms. The constant $\mu > 0$, referred to as the *psychometric order* of the stimulus space, is one and the same for all reference stimuli **x** and directions of transition **u**, and it is determined by psychometric differentials uniquely. $R(s)$ is some function *regularly varying (at the origin) with a unit exponent.*[3] It, too, is one and the same for all psychometric differentials and is determined by them asymptotically uniquely. The latter means that $R(s)$ in Equation 10 can be replaced only with $R^*(s) \sim R(s)$ (as $s \to 0+$). Finally, $F(\mathbf{x}, \mathbf{u})$ in Equation 10 is the (Fechner–Finsler) *metric function*, also determined uniquely. $F(\mathbf{x}, \mathbf{u})$ is positive (for $\mathbf{u} \neq 0$), continuous, and Euler homogeneous, the latter meaning that, for any k,

$$F(\mathbf{x}, k\mathbf{u}) = |k| F(\mathbf{x}, \mathbf{u}). \tag{11}$$

This metric function is all one needs to compute Fechnerian distances. Briefly, the logic of this computation is as follows. When any two points (stimuli) **a** and **b** are connected by a smooth path $\mathbf{x}(t) : [a, b] \to \mathfrak{M}$, $\mathbf{x}(a) = \mathbf{a}$, $\mathbf{x}(b) = \mathbf{b}$, the *psychometric length* of this path is defined as

$$L[\mathbf{x}(t)] = \int_a^b F[\mathbf{x}(t), \dot{\mathbf{x}}(t)]\mathrm{d}t.$$

The *Fechnerian distance* $G(\mathbf{a}, \mathbf{b})$ is defined as the infimum of $L[\mathbf{x}(t)]$ across all smooth paths connecting **a** and **b**. The thus-defined $G(\mathbf{a}, \mathbf{b})$ is a continuous distance function, invariant with respect to all possible smooth transformations of coordinates (Dzhafarov & Colonius, 1999, 2001).

The metric function $F(\mathbf{x}, \mathbf{u})$ can be given a simple geometric interpretation in terms of the shapes of psychometric functions. This is achieved through the important concept of a *Fechnerian indicatrix*. For a given stimulus **x**, the Fechnerian indicatrix centered at **x** is the contour formed by the direction vectors **u** satisfying the equality $F(\mathbf{x}, \mathbf{u}) = 1$. The set of the indicatrices centered at all possible stimuli and the metric function determine each other uniquely. It turns out (Dzhafarov & Colonius, 2001) that the Fechnerian indicatrices are asymptotically similar to the contours formed by horizontally cross-secting $\psi_{\mathbf{x}}(\mathbf{y})$ at a small elevation h from their minima; the smaller the h, the better the geometric similarity (see Fig. 1.4).

Figure 1.4 and the top panel of Fig. 1.3 illustrate the geometric meaning of the psychometric order μ. As shown in Dzhafarov and Colonius (2001), if one cross-sects different psychometric functions by vertical planes passing through

---

[3]The unit-regular variation of $R(s)$ means that $R(ks)/R(s) \to k$ as $s \to 0+$. For example, $R(s) \equiv s$ is such a function, and in many respects any unit-regularly varying $R(s)$ is indistinguishable from s (Dzhafarov, 2002a). The reader who is willing to overlook technical details may, with no serious consequences for understanding this work, assume that $R(s) \equiv s$, and hence Equation 10 has the form

$$\Psi_{\mathbf{x}}(\mathbf{x} + \mathbf{u}s) \sim F(\mathbf{x}, \mathbf{u})^{\mu} s^{\mu} \quad (\text{as } s \to 0+).$$

This is the so-called *power-function version* of MDFS (Dzhafarov & Colonius, 1999). The more general theory adopted in the this chapter is called the *regular variation version* of MDFS (Dzhafarov, 2002a).

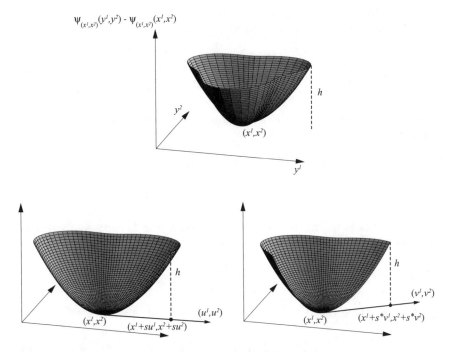

FIG. 1.4. A horizontal and two vertical cross sections of a psychometric function near its minimum.

their minima in various directions, then the cross sections confined between the minima and some small elevation h are horizontally scaled asymptotic replicas of each other. At the very minima of the psychometric functions these cross sections have a certain degree of flatness/cuspidality, and this degree is determined by the value of μ, from very flat (if μ is large) to pencil sharp ($\mu = 1$) to needle-sharp (if μ is close to zero). The fact that μ is one and the same for all psychometric differentials means that a specific degree of flatness/cuspidality is shared by all psychometric functions.[4]

We are now prepared to derive the main result of this work. Let the dimensions $\langle x^1 \rangle$ and $\langle x^2 \rangle$ be perceptually separable with respect to $\langle \mathcal{R}, \psi \rangle$. On applying Equation 10 to the coordinate projections $\mathbf{u}_1 = (u^1, 0)$ and $\mathbf{u}_2 = (0, u^2)$ of $\mathbf{u} = (u^1, u^2)$, one gets

$$\begin{cases} \Psi_{\mathbf{x}}(\mathbf{x} + \mathbf{u}_1 s) \sim [F(\mathbf{x}, \mathbf{u}_1) R(s)]^{\mu} \\ \Psi_{\mathbf{x}}(\mathbf{x} + \mathbf{u}_2 s) \sim [F(\mathbf{x}, \mathbf{u}_2) R(s)]^{\mu} \end{cases} \quad (\text{as } s \to 0+) \qquad (12)$$

---

[4] As indicated in footnote 2, certain basic properties of psychometric functions eliminate the possibility of $\mu > 1$ (see Dzhafarov, 2002d).

It follows from Equations 7 and 8 that $F(\mathbf{x}, \mathbf{u}_1)$ in Equation 12 cannot depend on x^2, whereas $F(\mathbf{x}, \mathbf{u}_2)$ cannot depend on x^1. Hence one can put

$$\begin{cases} F(\mathbf{x}, \mathbf{u}_1) = F[\mathbf{x}, u^1(1, 0)] = |u^1| F[\mathbf{x}, (1, 0)] = F_1(x^1) |u^1| \\ F(\mathbf{x}, \mathbf{u}_2) = F[\mathbf{x}, u^2(0, 1)] = |u^2| F[\mathbf{x}, (0, 1)] = F_2(x^2) |u^2| \end{cases},$$

where one makes use of the Euler homogeneity, Equation 11. Equation 12 now can be rewritten as

$$\begin{cases} \Psi_{\mathbf{x}}(\mathbf{x} + \mathbf{u}_1 s) = \Psi_{x^1}(x^1 + u^1 s) \sim F_1(x^1)^\mu |u^1|^\mu R(s)^\mu \\ \Psi_{\mathbf{x}}(\mathbf{x} + \mathbf{u}_2 s) = \Psi_{x^2}(x^2 + u^2 s) \sim F_2(x^2)^\mu |u^2|^\mu R(s)^\mu \end{cases} \quad (\text{as } s \to 0+).$$

Applying this to the right-hand side of Equation 9 in Lemma AB, and using Equation 10 for its left-hand side, one gets

$$F(\mathbf{x}, \mathbf{u})^\mu R(s)^\mu \sim F_1(x^1)^\mu |u^1|^\mu R(s)^\mu + F_2(x^2)^\mu |u^2|^\mu R(s)^\mu \quad (\text{as } s \to 0+),$$

which can only be true if

$$F(\mathbf{x}, \mathbf{u})^\mu = F_1(x^1)^\mu |u^1|^\mu + F_2(x^2)^\mu |u^2|^\mu. \tag{13}$$

To see that this structure of the metric function induces the Fechnerian metric with a Minkowski power-metric structure, choose an arbitrary point $\mathbf{o} = (o^1, o^2)$ and componentwise recalibrate (x^1, x^2) into

$$\bar{x}^1(x^1) = \int_{o^1}^{x^1} F_1(x) \mathrm{d}x, \quad \bar{x}^2(x^2) = \int_{o^2}^{x^2} F_2(x) \mathrm{d}x. \tag{14}$$

According to the remark immediately following Definition AB, the axes $\langle \bar{x}^1 \rangle$ and $\langle \bar{x}^2 \rangle$ are perceptually separable. Presenting $\mathbf{x} = (x^1, x^2)$ in Equation 13 as $\bar{\mathbf{x}} = (\bar{x}^1, \bar{x}^2)$, in new coordinates, the direction $\mathbf{u} = (u^1, u^2)$ attached to $\mathbf{x}$ also acquires new coordinates, $\bar{\mathbf{u}} = (\bar{u}^1, \bar{u}^2)$. From Equations 14, these new coordinates are

$$\bar{u}^1 = F_1(x^1) u^1, \quad \bar{u}^2 = F_2(x^2) u^2 \tag{15}$$

It follows that $F(\mathbf{x}, \mathbf{u})$ in Equation 13, when written in new coordinates as $\bar{F}(\bar{\mathbf{x}}, \bar{\mathbf{u}}) = F(\mathbf{x}, \mathbf{u})$, has the structure

$$\bar{F}(\bar{\mathbf{x}}, \bar{\mathbf{u}}) = \bar{F}(\bar{\mathbf{u}}) = \sqrt[\mu]{|\bar{u}^1|^\mu + |\bar{u}^2|^\mu}. \tag{16}$$

The Fechnerian indicatrices corresponding to this metric function,

$$|\bar{u}^1|^\mu + |\bar{u}^2|^\mu = 1, \tag{17}$$

have the same shape for all stimuli $\bar{x}$ at which they are centered. This shape is completely determined by the psychometric order μ, as shown in the lower panel of Fig. 1.5 (filled contours). Recall from the preceding discussion of indicatrices that these shapes describe the horizontal cross sections of the psychometric functions (Fig. 1.5, upper panel) at a small elevation above their minima. Recall also that μ has another geometric interpretation: It determines the shape (flatness/cuspidality) of the vertical cross sections of the psychometric functions in the vicinity of their minima (Fig. 1.5, middle panel). We see therefore that in the case of perceptually separable dimensions the shapes of the horizontal and vertical cross sections (generally completely independent) are interrelated, being controlled by one and the same parameter, μ.

Figure 1.5 demonstrates that the indicatrices for $\mu \geq 1$ are *convex* in all directions (*nonstrictly convex* if $\mu = 1$). A general theory of Fechnerian indicatrices is presented in Dzhafarov and Colonius (2001). Without recapitulating it here, I simply state the fact that if a Minkowskian indicatrix corresponding to $\bar{F}(\bar{u})$ is convex,[5] then the Fechnerian metric it induces is computed as $G(\bar{x}, \bar{y}) = \bar{F}(|\bar{x} - \bar{y}|)$. Applying this to Equation 16, with $\mu \geq 1$, one gets

$$G(\bar{x}, \bar{y}) = \bar{F}(|\bar{x} - \bar{y}|) = \sqrt[\mu]{|\bar{x}^1 - \bar{y}^1|^\mu + |\bar{x}^2 - \bar{y}^2|^\mu}. \tag{18}$$

That is, the Fechnerian metric induced by Equations 16 and 17 is a *Minkowski power metric*, with the exponent equal to μ, provided the latter is not less than 1.

One can also see in Fig. 1.5 that the Fechnerian indicatrix is not convex when $\mu < 1$ (in fact, it is then *concave* in all directions, except for the coordinate ones). The general theory (Dzhafarov & Colonius, 2001) stipulates that the metric induced by a nonconvex indicatrix is the same as the one induced by its *convex closure*, which is the minimal convex contour containing it. In our case it is obvious (see the enclosing contour in Fig. 1.5 for $\mu = \frac{1}{2}$) that the convex closure of an indicatrix corresponding to any value of $\mu < 1$ is the "diamond" described by $|\bar{u}^1| + |\bar{u}^2| = 1$. As a result, when $\mu < 1$, the Fechnerian metric induced by Equations 16 and 17 is

$$G(\bar{x}, \bar{y}) = \bar{F}(|\bar{x} - \bar{y}|) = |\bar{x}^1 - \bar{y}^1| + |\bar{x}^2 - \bar{y}^2|, \tag{19}$$

the city-block metric, which is familiar to psychophysicists.[6]

---

[5]Indicatrices and the corresponding metric function are called Minkowskian whenever $\bar{F}(\bar{x}, \bar{u}) = \bar{F}(\bar{u})$. The power-metric structure arrived at in Equation 16 is just a special case.

[6]See footnote 2.

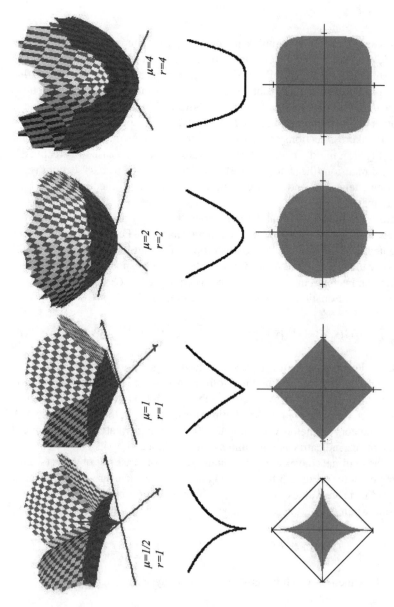

FIG. 1.5. Psychometric functions in the vicinity of their minima for different values of μ and corresponding r (upper row), their vertical cross sections (middle row), and horizontal cross sections (bottom row). The coordinate axes are calibrated in Fechnerian distances along these axes.

This equation can be combined with Equation 18 in the following statement. If $\langle x^1 \rangle$ and $\langle x^2 \rangle$ are perceptually separable, then they can be recalibrated (smoothly transformed) into $\langle \bar{x}^1 \rangle$ and $\langle \bar{x}^2 \rangle$ in such a way that

$$G(\bar{\mathbf{x}}, \bar{\mathbf{y}})^r = |\bar{x}^1 - \bar{y}^1|^r + |\bar{x}^2 - \bar{y}^2|^r, \tag{20}$$

with the exponent $r = \max\{\mu, 1\}$.

In essence, this statement fulfills the goal of the present analysis, except that it seems more satisfying to formulate the main result of this work without mentioning the recalibration procedure (or any specific calibration at all) for the dimensions $\langle x^1 \rangle$ and $\langle x^2 \rangle$. This can be readily achieved. Recall that the definition of perceptual separability is formulated for some rectangular area $\mathfrak{R} \subseteq \mathfrak{M}$. One consequence of this provision is that if one chooses a point of origin in $\mathfrak{R}$, $\mathbf{o} = (o^1, o^2)$, and draws through this point the coordinate lines $\{(x^1, x^2) \in \mathfrak{R}: x^2 = o^2\}$ and $\{(x^1, x^2) \in \mathfrak{R}: x^1 = o^1\}$, then, for any $\mathbf{x} = (x^1, x^2) \in \mathfrak{R}$ and $\mathbf{y} = (y^1, y^2) \in \mathfrak{R}$, their projections $\mathbf{x}_1 = (x^1, o^2)$, $\mathbf{y}_1 = (y^1, o^2)$ on the first axis and $\mathbf{x}_2 = (o^1, x^2)$, $\mathbf{y}_2 = (o^1, y^2)$ on the second axis are stimuli belonging to $\mathfrak{R}$. Observe now, in reference to Equation 20, that

$$|\bar{x}^1 - \bar{y}^1| = G(\mathbf{x}_1, \mathbf{y}_1), \quad |\bar{x}^2, y^2| = G(\mathbf{x}_2, \mathbf{y}_2).$$

With this, the development presented in this chapter can be summarized in the following theorem (see Fig. 1.6).

Theorem AB (Minkowski power-metric structure of Fechnerian metric). Let the dimensions $\langle x^1 \rangle$ and $\langle x^2 \rangle$ imposed on the stimulus space $\mathfrak{M}$ be perceptually

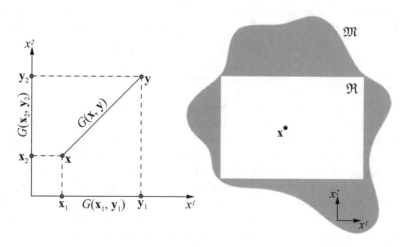

FIG. 1.6. A diagram for Theorem AB.

separable with respect to the discrimination system $\langle \mathcal{R}, \psi \rangle$. Then the Fechnerian metric G on this space is a Minkowski power metric with respect to the dimensions $\langle x^1 \rangle$ and $\langle x^2 \rangle$:

$$G(\mathbf{x}, \mathbf{y})^r = G(\mathbf{x}_1, \mathbf{y}_1)^r + G(\mathbf{x}_2, \mathbf{y}_2)^r, \qquad (21)$$

where $r = \max\{\mu, 1\}$, μ being the psychometric order of the space.

Note that the choice of the origin $\mathbf{o} = (o^1, o^2)$ used to define the coordinate projections of $\mathbf{x}$ and $\mathbf{y}$ need not be mentioned, because $G(\mathbf{x}_1, \mathbf{y}_1)$ and $G(\mathbf{x}_2, \mathbf{y}_2)$ are invariant with respect to this choice.

POSSIBLE EXTENSIONS

The definition of perceptual separability proposed in this work is mathematically unambiguous, based on observable or computable discrimination judgments, and leads to an interesting result within the framework of MDFS, the power-function Minkowski structure of the Fechnerian metric. The theory implies definite and nontrivial relationships between the horizontal and the vertical cross sections of the discrimination probability functions that can be subjected to experimental analysis. The theory is also readily extendible to an arbitrary number of perceptually separable dimensions or subspaces. None of these features, however, guarantees that the theory is empirically feasible. It is appropriate therefore to discuss in this concluding section some directions in which the theory could be generalized, if eventually found unsatisfactory in its present form.

One approach is to generalize the notion of a psychometric differential while preserving its basic properties and retaining the theory of perceptual separability as is. Specifically, one can define a generalized psychometric differential as

$$\Psi_{\mathbf{x}}^*(\mathbf{x} + \mathbf{u}s) = \Gamma^{-1}\{\Gamma[\psi_{\mathbf{x}}(\mathbf{x} + \mathbf{u}s)] - \Gamma[\psi_{\mathbf{x}}(\mathbf{x})]\},$$

where Γ is some smooth monotonic function. One could interpret this as the transformation of observable discrimination probabilities into "true" probabilities, implying thereby that the latter are "contaminated" by some extraperceptual biasing factors, whose influence can be made additive by an appropriately chosen Γ transformation. Alternatively (or equivalently, depending on one's approach), $\Psi_{\mathbf{x}}^*(\mathbf{x} + \mathbf{u}s)$ could be interpreted as a sensitivity index, on a par with the familiar d'.

A less radical approach from the standpoint of MDFS is to generalize the present theory by relaxing some of the defining properties of perceptual separability. One might argue, for example, that Definition A alone captures the essence of perceptual separability, whereas the detachability constraint can be relaxed or dropped altogether. Following this hypothetical suggestion, let us call dimensions $\langle x^1 \rangle$ and $\langle x^2 \rangle$ *weakly perceptually separable* if they form the dimensional basis for a discrimination system $\langle \mathfrak{M}, \psi \rangle$, in accordance with Definition A. The Fechnerian metric under weak separability does not have the Minkowski power metric structure. However, by applying Equations 10 and 12 to Lemma A, one can demonstrate the truth of the following statement.

Theorem A (Local Minkowski power-metric structure of Fechnerian metric). Let the dimensions $\langle x^1 \rangle$ and $\langle x^2 \rangle$ imposed on the stimulus space $\mathfrak{M}$ be weakly perceptually separable with respect to the discrimination system $\langle \mathfrak{M}, \psi \rangle$. Then the (Fechner–Finsler) metric function F on this space has the structure

$$F(\mathbf{x}, \mathbf{u})^\mu = F(\mathbf{x}, \mathbf{u}_1)^\mu + F(\mathbf{x}, \mathbf{u}_2)^\mu,$$

where μ is the psychometric order of the space. This in turn implies that the Fechnerian metric G is *locally* a Minkowski power metric with respect to the dimensions $\langle x^1 \rangle$ and $\langle x^2 \rangle$:

$$G(\mathbf{x}, \mathbf{x} + \mathbf{u}s)^r \sim G(\mathbf{x}, \mathbf{x} + \mathbf{u}_1 s)^r + G(\mathbf{x}, \mathbf{x} + \mathbf{u}_2 s)^r \, (\text{as } s \to 0+),$$

where $r = \max\{\mu, 1\}$.

This result is stronger than it might appear. The shapes of and the relationship between the vertical and the horizontal cross sections of the psychometric functions in the vicinity of their minima remain in the case of weak separability precisely the same as illustrated in Fig. 1.5, except that the calibration of the axes mentioned in the legend should now be understood in a local sense. The weak perceptual separability therefore may be sufficiently rich in consequences to be of interest.

These examples may suffice to demonstrate the generalizability of the perceptual separability theory. At this stage, however, the scientific value of the theory may to a greater extent depend on its development in the opposite direction, toward more specialized empirically falsifiable models, constructed by combining the theory's abstract and general premises with plausible constraints of a more technical and domain-specific nature.

ACKNOWLEDGMENTS

This research was supported by grant SES-0001925 from the National Science Foundation. I am indebted to Hans Colonius, Robin Thomas, and James Townsend for discussions and criticism, and to Damir Dzhafarov for his help in preparation of the manuscript.

REFERENCES

Ashby, F. G., & Townsend, J. T. (1986). Varieties of perceptual independence. *Psychological Review, 93*, 154–179.

Ashby, F. G., & Perrin, N. A. (1988). Towards a unified theory of similarity and recognition. *Psychological Review, 95*, 124–130.

Beals, R., Krantz, D. H., & Tversky, A. (1968). Foundations of multidimensional scaling. *Psychological Review, 75*, 127–142.

Dzhafarov E. N. (2001). Fechnerian psychophysics. In N. J. Smelser & P. B. Baltes (Eds.), *International encyclopedia of the social and behavioral sciences* (Vol. 8, pp. 5437–5440). New York: Pergamon.

Dzhafarov, E. N. (2002a). Multidimensional Fechnerian scaling: Regular variation version. *Journal of Mathematical Psychology, 46*, 226–244.

Dzhafarov, E. N. (2002b). Multidimensional Fechnerian scaling: Probability-distance hypothesis. *Journal of Mathematical Psychology, 46*, 352–374.

Dzhafarov, E. N. (2002c). Multidimentional Fechnerian scaling: Perceptual separability. *Journal of Mathematical Psychology, 46*, 564–582.

Dzhafarov, E. N. (2002d). Multidimensional Fechnerian scaling: Pairwise comparisons, regular minimality, and nonconstant self-similarity. *Journal of Mathematical Psychology, 46*, 583–608.

Dzhafarov, E. N., & Colonius, H. (1999). Fechnerian metrics in unidimensional and multidimensional stimulus spaces. *Psychological Bulletin and Review, 6*, 239–268.

Dzhafarov, E. N., & Colonius, H. (2001). Multidimensional Fechnerian scaling: Basics. *Journal of Mathematical Psychology, 45*, 670–719.

Garner, W. R. (1974). *The processing of information and structure.* Hillsdale, NJ: Lawrence Erlbaum Associates.

Helmholtz, H. von (1891). Versuch einer erweiterten Anwendung des Fechnerschen Gesetzes im Farbensystem. [An attempt at a generalized application of Fechner's Law to the color system.] *Zeitschrift für die Psychologie und die Physiologie der Sinnesorgane, 2*, 1–30.

Schrödinger, E. von (1920). Farbenmetrik. [Color Metrics.] *Zeitschrift für Physik, 12*, 459–466.

Shepard, R. N. (1987). Towards a universal law of generalization for psychological sciences. *Science, 237*, 1317–1323.

Tversky, A., & Krantz, D. H. (1970). The dimensional representation and the metric structure of similarity data. *Journal of Mathematical Psychology, 7*, 572–596.

Thomas, R. D. (1996). Separability and independence of dimensions within the same–different judgment task. *Journal of Mathematical Psychology, 40*, 318–341.

2

Subjective and Objective Scaling of Large Color Differences

Chingis A. Izmailov and Evgeni N. Sokolov
Moscow State University, Russia

The notion of "psychophysics beyond sensation" can be understood in at least two different ways: (a) as an extension of sensory psychophysics to complex psychological processes involving memory, semantics, etc. and (b) as an application of psychophysical methods to objective neurophysiological processes, such as event-related potentials and spike discharges. It is the second meaning that we focus on in this work. We think of psychophysics as being incorporated within the framework of generalized neuroscience, where both cognitive and executive processes are studied by both neurophysiological and psychophysical methods. The construction of color spaces by means of multidimensional scaling provides a good example of this integrated approach.

SPHERICAL MODEL OF COLOR DISCRIMINATION

The idea of measuring subjective distances among stimuli is one of the most fundamental ideas in psychophysics. There are two main approaches to this issue. One is to try to compute the subjective distances from some measure of an observer's ability to discriminate very similar stimuli, those that can be easily confused.

Fechner was the originator of this approach, and its modern version can be found in Dzhafarov and Colonius (1999, 2001). Another approach is to compute the subjective distances from various measures of dissimilarity obtained from people or animals facing pairs of clearly different stimuli, those that cannot be confused. With the second approach, irrespective of whether one uses direct numerical estimates of dissimilarities given by humans or amplitudes of evoked potentials obtained (in humans or in animals) in response to abrupt stimulus changes, the results can be presented in the form of a matrix whose rows and columns represent the same set of stimuli whereas the entries contain all pairwise dissimilarities among them. The technique for dealing with such matrices (which can be called matrices of large differences) is known as multidimensional scaling (MDS). The dissimilarity values within such a matrix are viewed as monotonically related (within statistical variation) to geometric distances among points representing stimuli in a psychophysical space. The goal of MDS is to reconstruct this space (Torgerson, 1958). In this chapter we describe how MDS leads to the reconstruction of the color-discrimination space.

The MDS analysis of dissimilarities among monochromatic lights varying in wavelength and luminance shows that, if these dissimilarities are interpreted as monotonically related to Euclidean distances, then the color points form a four-dimensional geometric configuration (Izmailov & Sokolov, 1991). An essential feature of this configuration is that the color points do not fill in the four-dimensional space densely, but rather form a surface of a constant positive curvature in this space, a four-dimensional sphere. The position of a point on this sphere is characterized by three spherical coordinates, each corresponding to one of the three subjective characteristics of color: hue, saturation, and brightness.

This is a remarkable finding when compared with the traditional view that only three Cartesian dimensions are sufficient to describe the color space and that color points comprise a three-dimensional solid in this space. This traditional model is based primarily on color-mixture data and threshold measurements. It has been noted, however (Izmailov, 1980; Judd, 1967), that estimated distances among co-linear points in the three-dimensional color solid are not additive. The spherical model shares with the color solid the traditional triad of subjective color characteristics (hue, saturation, and brightness), but their geometric status changes from that of Cartesian coordinates to that of spherical coordinates (Izmailov, 1995). Correspondingly, the number of the Cartesian coordinates in the spherical model increases from three to four. It is from these coordinates (rather than the three spherical ones) that one computes the intercolor differences as the Euclidean lengths of the chords connecting the color points lying on the four-dimensional spherical surface:

$$d(X, Y) = \sqrt{\sum_{k=1}^{4}(X_k - Y_k)^2}, \quad \sum_{k=1}^{4}X_k^2 = \sum_{k=1}^{4}Y_k^2 = 1, \qquad (1)$$

where $X_k, Y_k (k = 1, 2, 3, 4)$ are the Cartesian coordinates of the colors X, Y.

The first two Cartesian coordinates have a clear neurophysiological interpretation: They are interpreted as outputs of two color-opponent channels reacting to the spectral distribution of light (see Fig. 2.1). The first Cartesian coordinate (X_1) represents the output of the red-green channel, the second one (X_2) the output of the blue-yellow channel. Taken together, these two coordinates determine the color hue by the angle α on the chromatic plane $X_1 X_2$, defined as

$$\frac{X_2}{X_1} = \tan \alpha.$$

This interpretation agrees with the traditional view that the spectral distribution of light maps onto the color hue through the two color-opponent channels. Note that, when considered separately, the outputs of the red-green (X_1) and blue-yellow (X_2) channels change as cosine and sine functions, respectively, of the angle representing hue:

$$X_1 = a \cos \alpha, \quad X_2 = a \sin \alpha, \tag{2}$$

where a is a positive constant.

The interpretation of the remaining two Cartesian coordinates (X_3, X_4) is similar, although more subtle neurophysiologically (see Fig. 2.2). Clearly they encode the brightness of light, but this is not done by either of these coordinates taken separately. Rather, in a complete analogy with how the hue is encoded by the color-opponent channels, the brightness of a color is represented by the angle β of the color point in the brightness plane $X_3 X_4$, defined as

$$\frac{X_4}{X_3} = \tan \beta.$$

Taken separately, the coordinates X_3 and X_4 are assumed to represent the outputs of the nonopponent dark (X_3) and bright (X_4) channels, consisting of the off-cells and on-cells, respectively, of the visual system (Jung, 1973). Again, geometrically X_3 and X_4 change as cosine and sine functions, respectively, of the angle representing brightness:

$$X_3 = b \cos \beta, \quad X_4 = b \sin \beta, \tag{3}$$

where b is a positive constant.

To summarize, the visual system extracts from the light flow its two principal characteristics, the spectral distribution and the overall intensity. Each of these characteristics is encoded by a pair of channels that work in an interdependent fashion, so that the output of one of the dual channels is inversely related to the output of the other. Specifically, this reciprocity in the model works in the cosine–sine fashion, ensuring that the outputs of the dual channels form a circular trajectory in a plane (Izmailov, 1997; Sokolov & Izmailov, 1983, 1988).

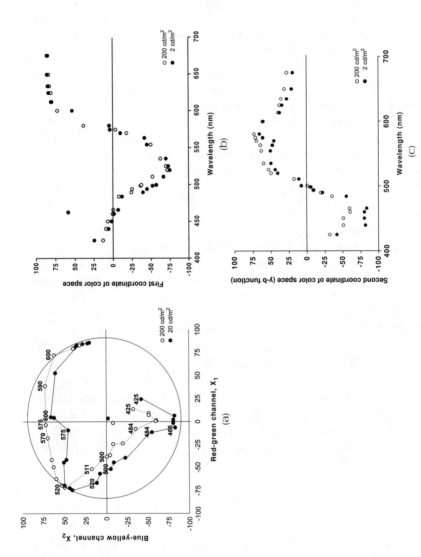

FIG. 2.1. (a) Projections of color points on the chromatic plane ($X_1 X_2$) of the four-dimensional color sphere. Filled and open circles represent monochromatic stimuli varying on two levels of luminance. (b), (c) Red-green (X_1) and blue-yellow (X_2) opponent functions derived from the spherical model of color discrimination.

30

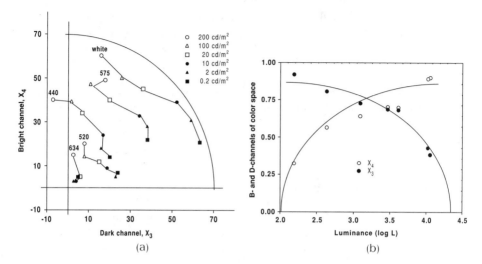

FIG. 2.2. (a) Projections of color points on the achromatic plane ($X_3 X_4$) of the four-dimensional color sphere. The colors shown are monochromatic and change on six levels of luminance, represented by six symbols connected by a solid curve, with the attached number indicating the wavelength in nanometers (b) Two achromatic coordinates of color space as functions of stimulus luminance. They are interpreted as dark (X_3) and bright (X_4) channels of visual system.

The reader may have noted that this description, although involving all four Cartesian coordinates of the color space, does not mention saturation. This is not an oversight, as we believe that saturation has a status different from that of hue and brightness. To produce the latter two is the primary function of the respective pairs of dual channels, $X_1 X_2$ for hue and $X_3 X_4$ for brightness, and they reflect separate physical properties of light, spectral distribution and luminance, respectively. In this sense one can consider these color characteristics as "natural" (or "primary") sensory phenomena. By contrast, we suggest that saturation results from a network interaction between the two color-processing dual mechanisms, and it does not reflect an independent physical property of light. In this sense saturation can be viewed as an "artificial" (or "secondary") characteristic of color. That is why its dependence on various physical parameters of light is very complex (Judd, 1951).

In the spherical model of color vision the network interaction between the two dual-channel mechanisms essentially emulates the reciprocal interaction within each of these mechanisms. Mathematically, this means that the constants a and b in Equations 2 and 3 are not arbitrary, but rather are related by

$$a^2 + b^2 = const.$$

Equivalently, on taking this constant for unity, one can represent saturation by the angle γ, defined by

$$a = \sin \gamma, \quad b = \cos \gamma. \tag{4}$$

Such a second-order reciprocal interaction manifests itself in the fact that the two primary color circles, the chromatic one $(X_1 X_2)$ and the brightness one $(X_3 X_4)$, unite within the structure of the single four-dimensional sphere:

$$X_1 = \cos \alpha \sin \gamma, \; X_2 = \sin \alpha \sin \gamma, \; X_3 = \cos \beta \cos \gamma, \; X_4 = \sin \beta \cos \gamma, \tag{5}$$

which is equivalent to Equation 1.

It is easy to see that if one fixes the level of brightness (β) and allows the color hue (α) to vary freely (i.e., if one considers a set of equally bright colors), then

$$\min\{X_3, X_4\} = c \max\{X_3, X_4\},$$

where c is a constant determined by the constant value of β. On denoting

$$\overline{X}_3 = \sqrt{X_3^2 + X_4^2} = \sqrt{1 + c^2} \, \max\{X_3, X_4\} \tag{6}$$

one readily derives from Equation 1 or from Equation 5 that the space of equally bright colors is described by the relationships

$$X_1 = \cos \alpha \sin \gamma, \; X_2 = \sin \alpha \sin \gamma, \; \overline{X}_3 = \cos \gamma, \; X_1^2 + X_2^2 + \overline{X}_3^2 = 1. \tag{7}$$

Thus the prediction of the spherical model of color discrimination is that the configuration of equally bright colors is a three-dimensional sphere. The MDS analysis of dissimilarities among colors of equal brightness corroborates this prediction completely (Izmailov, 1980; Shepard & Carroll, 1966). Note that in this reduced model the traditional two dimensionality (hue and saturation) of the equally bright colors is preserved, as the location of color points on the three-dimensional sphere is characterized by two spherical coordinates: the horizontal angle α representing the colors' hue and the vertical angle γ representing their saturation.

Considering the three Cartesian coordinates of this reduced model, the two color-opponent channels continue to be represented by the two axes X_1 and X_2, and $\overline{X}_3$ is simply one of the two brightness channels of the full model, X_3 or X_4, with the other channel's output varying in a compensatory fashion so that the brightness level remains constant. As $\overline{X}_3$ is inversely related to γ, the colors with low values of $\overline{X}_3$ (those closer to the chromatic plane $X_1 X_2$) are more saturated. Clearly $\overline{X}_3$ is also inversely related to $\sqrt{X_1^2 + X_2^2}$, the quantity that can be therefore viewed as an alternative measure of saturation. This is essentially the traditional measure of the saturation of a color: how far this color is from the center of the chromatic circle (corresponding to the "ideal white").

All this agrees with the results of the MDS analysis of experimental data: The white color has the highest value of $\overline{X}_3$ and the smallest distance from the $\overline{X}_3$ axis, whereas the opposite is true for the saturated monochromatic lights, red (620–660 nm), green (510–530 nm), and blue (450–470 nm). The less-saturated monochromatic lights, bluish-green (480–500 nm) and yellow (560–580 nm), fall in between, having intermediate values of both $\overline{X}_3$ and $\sqrt{X_1^2 + X_2^2}$. Finally, the MDS computations confirm that the coordinates X_1 and X_2 in the full four-dimensional model are related to $\overline{X}_3$ in the reduced three-dimensional model in accordance with Equation 6.

Izmailov and Sokolov (1991) also reported the results of the MDS reconstruction of the space of achromatic stimuli, based on estimated pairwise differences between various gray colors (presented in the disk–annulus paradigm). The prediction of the spherical model of color discrimination in this case is straightforward. The achromatic stimuli have a negligible amount of saturation, which means that $\gamma = 0$ in Equations 5 and a constant hue, which means that $\alpha = const.$ in Equations 5. With no loss of generality one can put $\alpha = 0$ for gray colors. The resulting reduced model is then

$$X_3 = \cos\beta, \quad X_4 = \sin\beta, \quad X_3^2 + X_4^2 = 1. \tag{8}$$

Thus the predicted spatial configuration is a planar circumference, and this is precisely what the MDS analysis results in. The angle β on the plane clearly represents brightness, and the two Cartesian axes represent the dark and the bright channels of the brightness encoding system.[1]

RECONSTRUCTION OF THE COLOR SPACE FROM VISUAL EVOKED POTENTIAL AMPLITUDES

We turn now to the reconstruction of the human color-discrimination space by means of applying MDS to neurophysiological data. The experimental paradigm that makes this possible consists of recording a neurophysiological response of the visual system to an abrupt replacement of one color by another: The magnitude of this response is interpreted as monotonically related to the neurophysiological difference between the two colors. In particular, the absence of a response indicates

---

[1] A striking prediction of the spherical model that as yet has not been tested is that the spatial configuration of equal-hue colors (e.g., green colors varying in brightness and saturation) has to be a three-dimensional sphere.

that the two colors are neurophysiologically identical, a logic used by Bongard (1955) to establish color-mixture equations for animals. As an example especially relevant to the present work, in Riggs, Blough, and Schafer (1972) the response to color changes is the electroretinogram of the pigeon's eye, and the amplitude of the b-wave is treated as monotonically related to color differences. The matrix of b-wave amplitudes thus obtained is analyzed by means of MDS, resulting in the reconstruction of a color space for the pigeon's retina. The geometric characteristics of this space turn out to closely match those of the trichromatic human color space.

The colors used by Riggs et al. (1972) were adjusted by the experimenters to appear equal in brightness, with the intent of interpreting the color differences measured by the b-wave as purely chromatic. This procedure, however, is logically flawed, as there is no assurance that the thus-defined equal brightness has the same meaning as equal brightness for a specific neurophysiological system (in this case, the retina) of an altogether different species. To solve the problem of obtaining a neurophysiological measure of purely chromatic color differences, Zimachev, Shekhter, Sokolov, and Izmailov (1986) and Izmailov, Isaychev, Korshunova, and Sokolov (1998) developed a different procedure.

Let C_0 and C_1 denote two colors (the reference color and the comparison color, respectively) with fixed spectral compositions S_0 and S_1. Let the intensity of the reference color C_0 be fixed at a level I_0. As the intensity I_1 of the comparison color C_1 varies, the neurophysiological response varies too, forming a V-shaped curve (see Fig. 2.3): It is large if I_1 greatly differs from I_0 in either direction, and it achieves a minimum level at some intensity

$$I_1 = f(S_0, S_1, I_0).$$

When $S_0 = S_1$ (Fig. 2.3, solid line), $f(S_0, S_1, I_0)$ coincides with I_0, the response then being at the background level. When $S_0 \neq S_1$ (Fig. 2.3, dashed line), the response to the change,

$$(S_0, I_0) \Rightarrow [S_1, f(S_0; S_1; I_0)],$$

should be taken to reflect the irreducible difference between the two colors that is due to the difference in their spectral compositions only. In this way one can obtain a set of stimuli that are equal from the point of view of a specific neurophysiological system in all respects but their chromaticity. The responses of this system to these stimuli then can be used to reconstruct a space of purely chromatic differences. Zimachev et al. (1991) used this technique to reconstruct the space of "equally bright" colors for the frog's retina. This space turned out to be similar to that for human trichromats, except for showing much coarser discrimination: Although spectral colors occupy positions different from each other and from that of the white color, less-saturated colors virtually coincide with the white color.

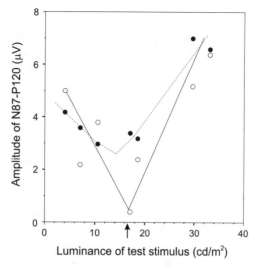

FIG. 2.3. N87–P120 interpeak amplitude of the visual evoked potential (site O1) obtained in response to abrupt color changes (from
a reference stimulus to a test one) as a function of the test-stimulus
luminance. The luminance of the reference stimulus is indicated
by the arrow on the horizontal axis. The open circles and solid line
represent a situation in which the two colors have identical spectral distributions (green colors), and the filled circles and dashed
line represent changes from a white reference color to a green
test one.

The significance of this technique is also due to the fact that the visual system,
on both the retinal and the cortical levels, is much more sensitive to brightness
differences than it is to chromatic ones: The V-shaped curves just described are very
sharply tuned at their minima, that is, even slight deviations from $I_1 = f(S_0, S_1, I_0)$
cause the retinal or the cortical response to increase dramatically (Izmailov et al.,
1998; Riggs & Sternheim, 1969; Zimachev et al., 1986, 1991).

The neurophysiological interpretation of the Cartesian coordinates in the spherical model of color discrimination implies that subjective estimates of color dissimilarities should be reflected in the electrical activity of the human brain. By
appropriately choosing the type of the electrical activity and by subjecting it
to MDS, one should be able to obtain a color space essentially identical to the
one obtained from psychophysical data. In our previous work (Izmailov, 1997;
Izmailov & Sokolov, 1991), the validity of this expectation was demonstrated
for the discrimination of achromatic lights. Here we present experimental data
that demonstrate the identity of the psychophysical and neurophysiological color
discrimination spaces for chromatic stimuli.

Method

Details of the presentation/recording procedure subsequently described can be found in Paulus, Homberg, Cuninghum, Halliday, and Ronde (1984), Zimachev et al. (1986), and Izmailov et al. (1998). Twelve combinations of the basic monitor colors, red, green, and blue (R, G, and B), were used as stimuli in both the psychophysical and the neurophysiological experiments, each stimulus covering the subject's entire visual field. Five colors (red, yellow, green, blue, and white) were made equal in brightness by means of the procedure already described (see Fig. 2.3), involving the minima of the V-shaped curves. As the resulting values of $I_1 = f(S_0, S_1, I_0)$ turned out to be sufficiently close to the brightness matches obtained by the conventional heterochromatic matching procedure, the latter was used to equate the remaining seven colors to the brightness of the white color. The resulting characteristics of the color stimuli are given in Table 2.1. The participants were normal trichromats who viewed the monitor with no head restraint, but with a fixation point preceding the presentation of stimuli.

In the neurophysiological experiment the presentation consisted of two colors interchanging 50 times: $C_0 \rightarrow C_1 \rightarrow \cdots \rightarrow C_0 \rightarrow C_1$, with the durations of the colors randomly varying between 800 and 1200 ms to avoid rhythm-related artefics. In response to each change we recorded occipital ($O1$, $O2$) and temporal ($T5$, $T6$) evoked potentials (for 340 ms following the change; the background electroencephalogram was recorded for 60 ms preceding the change). The visual evoked potentials (VEPs) were averaged over the 50 records after artifacts were removed.

TABLE 2.1
Characteristics of Color Stimuli Used in the Psychophysical and
Psychophysiological Experiments

Color	Chromatic Coordinates x	Chromatic Coordinates y	Luminance (cd/m²)	Wavelength (nm)
Red	0.612	0.342	14	610
Red-yellow	0.552	0.403	15	590
Yellow	0.484	0.446	14	580
Yellow-green	0.400	0.506	13	565
Green-yellow	0.306	0.575	14	550
Green	0.259	0.397	13	515
Green-blue	0.227	0.291	12	485
Blue-green	0.204	0.198	11	475
Blue	0.153	0.068	12	470
Blue-red	0.223	0.114	14	450
Red-blue	0.371	0.182	13	
White	0.299	0.295	13	

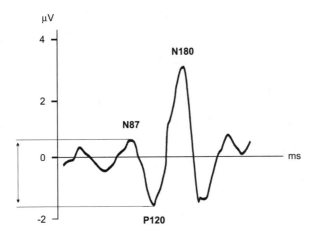

FIG. 2.4.   An example of VEP in response to a color substitution.

Three different measures of the averaged VEP magnitude were used (Fig. 2.4): the amplitude of the component N87 relative to the background level, the interpeak difference between N87 and P120, and the interpeak difference between P120 and N180.

The same 12 colors, under the same viewing conditions, were used in the psychophysical experiment, except that a presentation here consisted of a single change $C_0 \rightarrow C_1$, two 800-ms colors separated by a 1-s dark interval. Color pairs were randomized, each pair being presented 10 times in total. The participant's task was to numerically estimate the difference between the two colors on a 10-point scale, from 0 (identical colors) to 9 (most different colors).

Results and Discussion

All the subsequent results are shown for a single individual who participated in both the psychophysical experiment and the neurophysiological one. The results are presented as graphs of the averaged VEPs (Fig. 2.5) and as configurations of points in a color space (Fig. 2.6).

Below we discuss only the VEPs obtained from $O1$ and $T5$ recording sites, because those for the corresponding occipital ($O2$) and temporal ($T6$) sites are essentially the same. The analysis of the neurophysiological experiment therefore is based on six matrices, each corresponding to one of three measures of VEP (N87, N87–P120, or P120–N180) and one of two recording sites ($O1$ or $T5$). Together with the matrix of the numerical estimates of color dissimilarities obtained in the psychophysical experiment, these six matrices were subjected to MDS. In each case the goodness of fit for the MDS solutions was estimated by means of the conventional stress measure and by the coefficients of correlation between the

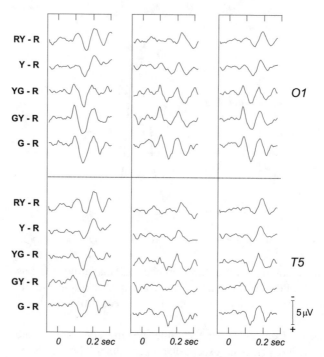

FIG. 2.5. VEPs recorded in response to changes from a test stimulus to a reference stimulus (first column) and vice versa (second column). The third column represents the average of the first two. The letters R, G, and Y stand for red, green, and yellow, respectively; the upper panel represents occipital VEPs (site O1), and the lower panel represents temporal VEPs (site T5).

interpoint distances and the matrix entries (numerical estimates or VEP amplitudes, respectively).

By these criteria a four-dimensional Euclidean space provides a good solution for all matrices. Although a three-dimensional solution was not significantly worse, we used the four-dimensional one to compare the VEP-based and psychophysical color configurations for the following reason. As mentioned in the method section, 5 of the 12 colors used in the experiments were matched in brightness by means of the procedure illustrated in Fig. 2.3, neurophysiologically, whereas the remaining 7 colors were matched in brightness to the white color psychophysically by means of the heterochromatic matching procedure. Although the two matching procedures do produce similar luminance values, these values are not identical. Consequently, the colors matched in brightness psychophysically were not precisely matched in brightness neurophysiologically, and vice versa. At the same time, the same set of 12 colors was used in both our experiments. As already explained, equally

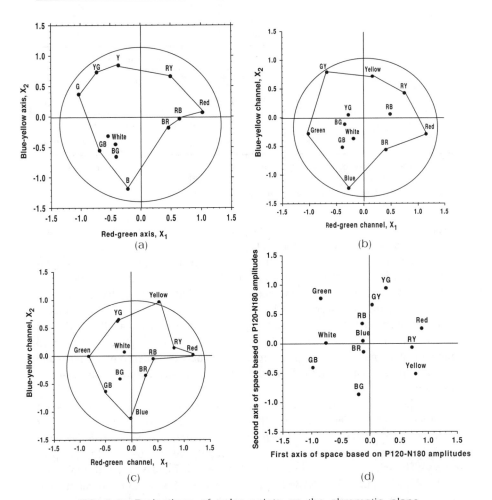

FIG. 2.6. Projections of color points on the chromatic plane ($X_1 X_2$) of the four-dimensional color sphere constructed on the basis of (a) numerical estimates of color dissimilarities and three measures of occipital VEPs (site O1): (b) N87 amplitude, (c) N87–P120 interpeak difference, and (d) P120–N180 interpeak difference.

bright colors lie on a three-dimensional sphere. If the brightness equality across the colors is only approximate, however, one should expect, in accordance with the spherical model of color discrimination, that the colors lie on the surface of a four-dimensional sphere but sufficiently close to one of its three-dimensional cross sections. This prediction agrees with the observed results.

The sphericity of the color configurations in the four-dimensional Euclidean solutions provided by MDS was tested by means of an iterative computational

TABLE 2.2
Two Goodness-of-Fit Indices

| | | MDS Based on | | | | | |
| | Numerical | N87 | | N87–P120 | | P120–N180 | |
Index	Dissimilarities	O1	T5	O1	T5	O1	T5
Pearson correlation	0.98	0.87	0.85	0.89	0.87	0.89	0.86
Coefficient of variation (%)	12	16	19	15	18	22	28

Note. The correlation between interpoint distances and initial matrix entries characterizes the quality of the four-dimensional MDS solution, whereas the coefficient of variation (sphere thickness) characterizes the sphericity of the configuration of color points.

procedure that searched for the center of the sphere, that is, the point in the space whose distances from all 12 colors had the smallest possible variance. The eventually achieved variation coefficient (the standard deviation of the radii as a proportion of their mean) serves as a measure of sphericity: The smaller this coefficient (the thickness of the sphere), the better the sphericity. The results are given in Table 2.2. Plainly, the overall quality of the four-dimensional Euclidean solution, as estimated by the Pearson correlation coefficients, is almost equally good in all cases. Note that the nonmetric MDS procedure used in our computations requires a monotonic but not necessarily linear relationship between interpoint distances and matrix entries. As a result, the Pearson correlation is only a crude goodness-of-fit measure.

The degree of sphericity, however, as measured by the coefficient of variation clearly differs for different matrices. It is best for the numerical estimates of color dissimilarities, with only 12% thickness of the sphere. For the occipital N87 and N87–P120 amplitudes the sphericity is only slightly worse (16% and 15%, respectively). The sphericity deteriorates for the temporal N87 and N87–P120 amplitudes of VEP, and for the P120–N180 amplitudes, both occipital and temporal, the coefficient of variation is so high that with a high degree of confidence here one can reject a spherical model as a reasonable approximation.

Figure 2.6 presents the projections of the color points on the chromatic plane X_1X_2 computed from the MDS solutions for the numerical estimates of color dissimilarities [Fig. 2.6(a)] and for the occipital N87, N87–P120, and P120–N180 amplitudes of VEP [Figs. 2.6(b), 2.6(c), and 2.6(d), respectively]. The configuration obtained for the numerical estimates is essentially a version of the one shown in Fig. 2.1(a). The colors form a classical Newtonian contour, from the red through orange to yellow and so on along the spectrum, until the contour is closed by the purple colors (blue-red and red-blue). The white color occupies a position near the origin of the X_1X_2 plane. (The blue-green color falls closer to the white than the other colors because of the well-known bleaching of the blue-green mixtures on all conventional monitor screens.)

The most important observation, however, is that essentially the same configuration of color points is obtained from the MDS analyses of the N87 and the N87–P120 amplitudes of VEP. The differences between the three configurations shown in panels (a), (b), and (c) of Fig. 2.6 are local and can be attributed to measurement errors as well as to real but second-order processing differences imposed on one and the same overall picture.

By contrast, the configuration of points obtained from the MDS analysis of the P120–N180 amplitudes of VEP is essentially random: Observe that the white color falls farther away from the origin than the more saturated blue, that the yellow has almost the same horizontal coordinate (which is supposed to represent the red-green opponent system) as the red, and that the order of the colors on the vertical axis is opposite to that consistent with its interpretation (as representing the blue-yellow opponent system). This justifies our rejection of the spherical model for this VEP component on the basis of the high sphere thickness and leads one to the conclusion that the late components of the cortical VEP may have little to do with color processing.

CONCLUSION

Although animal color vision has been extensively studied at the level of light receptors and individual neurons (Gouras & Padmos, 1974; Padmos & Van Norren, 1975; Zeki, 1980; Zrenner, 1983), analogous studies in humans are scarce because of obvious procedural limitations. The recording of the mass electrical activity of the brain therefore remains an indispensable tool in linking neurophysiological and psychophysical aspects of color vision. It seems, however, that the mass electrical activity, such as cortical or retinal evoked potentials, is truly informative only if it is recorded in response to an abrupt change of one stimulus to another, rather than, as is done traditionally, to a presentation of an individual stimulus (Ivanicsky & Strelecs, 1976; Regan, 1970; Shipley, Jones, & Fry, 1965; White, Kataoka, & Martin, 1977). The present results show that early components of the VEPs generated in the human striate cortex ($O1$ and $O2$ sites) in response to color changes contain essentially the same information about subjective differences among colors as one can extract from conscious estimates of these differences. In both cases the information extracted (by means of MDS) is in good compliance with the spherical model of color discrimination.

ACKNOWLEDGMENT

This work was supported in part by the INTAS grant 94-4064 and the RFBR grant 98-06-80064. The authors are grateful to Ehtibar N. Dzhafarov for critically editing the text of this work and greatly improving its mathematics and expository coherence.

REFERENCES

Bongard, M. M. (1955). Colororimetry on the animal's eye [in Russian]. *Annual Proceedings of the Academy of Science, USSR, 103,* 239–242.

Dzhafarov, E. N., & Colonius, H. (1999). Fechnerian metrics in unidimensional and multidimensional stimulus spaces. *Psychological Bulletin and Review, 6,* 239–268.

Dzhafarov, E. N., & Colonius, H. (2001). Multidimensional Fechnerian scaling: Basics. *Journal of Mathematical Psychology, 45,* 670–719.

Gouras, P., & Padmos, P. (1974). Identification of cone mechanisms in graded responses of foveal striate cortex. *Journal of Physiology (London), 238,* 569–582.

Izmailov, Ch. A. (1980). *A spherical model of color discrimination* [in Russian]. Moscow: Moscow University Press.

Izmailov, Ch. A. (1995). Spherical model of discrimination of self-luminous and surface colors. In R. D. Luce, M. D. D'Zmura, D. Hoffman, G. J. Iverson, & A. K. Romney (Eds.), *Geometric representations of perceptual phenomena* (pp. 153–168). Mahwah, NJ: Lawrence Erlbaum Associates.

Izmailov, Ch. A. (1997). Dual-channel sensory mechanism of stimulus discrimination. In *Proceedings of the XIIIth triannual congress of the International Ergonomics Association* (Vol. 5, p. 347–349). Tampere, Finland: International Ergonomics Association.

Izmailov, Ch. A., Isaychev, S. A., Korshunova, S. G., & Sokolov, E. N. (1998). Specification of color and brightness components of visual evoked potentials [in Russian]. *Journal of the Higher Nervous Activity, 48,* 777–787.

Izmailov, Ch. A., & Sokolov, E. N. (1991). Spherical model of color and brightness discrimination. *Psychological Science, 2,* 249–259.

Ivanicsky, A. M., & Strelecs, V. B. (1976). Evoked potential and psychophysical characteristics of perception [in Russian]. *Journal of the Higher Nervous Activity, 26,* 793–801.

Judd, D. B. (1951). Basic correlates of the visual stimulus. In S. S. Stevens (Ed.), *Handbook of experimental psychology* (Vol. 2, pp. 811–867). New York: Wiley.

Judd, D. B. (1967). Interval scale, ratio scale, and additive for the sizes of differences perceived between members of a geodesic series. *Journal of the Optical Society of America, 57,* 380–386.

Jung, R. (1973). Visual perception and neurophysiology. In R. Jung (Ed.), *Handbook of sensory physiology* (Vol.VII/3, pp. 3–152). New York: Springer.

Padmos, P., & Van Norren, D. (1975). Increment spectral sensitivity and colour discrimination in the primate, studied by means of graded potentials from the striate cortex. *Vision Research, 15,* 1103–1113.

Paulus, W. M., Homberg, V., Cuninghum, K., Halliday, A., & Ronde, N. (1984). Color and brightness components of foveal visual evoked potentials in man. *Electroencephalography and Clinical Neurophysiology, 58,* 107–119.

Regan, D. (1970). Evoked potential and psychophysical correlates of changes in stimulus colour and intensity. *Vision Research, 10,* 163–178.

Riggs, L. A., Blough, P. M., & Schafer, K. L. (1972). Electrical responses of the pigeon eye to changes of wavelength in the stimulating light. *Vision Research, 12,* 981–991.

Riggs, L. A., & Sternheim, C. E. (1969). Human retinal and occipital potentials evoked by changes of the wavelength of the stimulating light. *Journal of the Optical Society of America, 59,* 635–640.

Shepard, R. N., & Carroll, J. D. (1966). Parametric representation of nonlinear data structures. In P. R. Krishnaiah (Ed.), *Multivariate analysis* (pp. 561–592). New York: Academic Press.

Shipley, T., Jones, R. W., & Fry, A. (1965). Evoked visual potentials and human colour vision. *Science, 150,* 1162–1164.

Sokolov, E. N., & Izmailov, Ch. A. (1983). The conceptual reflex arc: A model of neural processing as developed for color vision. In H.-G. Geissler (Ed.), *Modern issues in perception* (pp. 192–216). Berlin: VEB Deutscher Verlag der Wissenschaften.

Sokolov, E. N., & Izmailov, Ch. A. (1988). Three-stage model of color vision. *Sensory Systems, 2,* 314–320.

Torgerson, W. S. (1958). *Theory and method of scaling.* New York: Wiley.

White, C. T., Kataoka, R. W., & Martin, J. M. (1977). Color evoked potential: Development of methodology for the analysis of the processes involved in colour vision. In J. E. Desmedt (Ed.), *Visual evoked potentials in man: New development* (pp. 250–272). Oxford, England: Clarendon.

Zeki, S. (1980). The representation of colours in the cerebral cortex. *Nature (London), 284,* 412–418.

Zimachev, M. M., Shekhter, E. D., Sokolov, E. N., & Izmailov, Ch. A. (1986). Chromatic component of frog's electroretinogram [in Russian]. *Journal of the Higher Nervous Activity, 36,* 1100–1107.

Zimachev, M. M., Shekhter, E. D., Sokolov, E. N., Näätänen, R., Nyman, G., & Izmailov, Ch. A. (1991). Discrimination of colors by frog's retina [in Russian]. *Journal of the Higher Nervous Activity, 41,* 518–527.

Zrenner, E. (1983). *Neurophysiological aspects of colour vision in primates.* Berlin: Springer.

3

Short-Term and Long-Term Frames of Reference in Category Judgments: A Multiple-Standards Model

Peter Petzold and Gert Haubensak
Justus-Liebig-University of Giessen, Germany

Numerous studies in psychophysical judgment have shown that the response depends not only on the current stimulus but also on previous stimulus-response events. In general, current responses are negatively correlated with the preceding stimuli and positively correlated with the preceding responses (e.g., Jesteadt, Luce, & Green, 1977; Petzold, 1981; Schifferstein & Frijters, 1992). In other words, there is assimilation toward the preceding responses and contrast with the preceding stimuli. These sequential effects can be explained by a process in which the response is adjusted to be consistent with the stimulus-response pair of the preceding trial. According to this view, the previous stimulus-response pair forms a frame of reference with which the current stimulus is compared. This implies that a relation between the internal representation $X(t)$ of the current stimulus and the trace $X^*(t - 1)$ of the preceding stimulus determines a relation between the current response $r(t)$ and the preceding response $r(t - 1)$.

On the other hand, there is an adjustment of the judgments to the total series of stimuli. The influence of the range suggests that stimuli are judged in relation to the subjective range that is defined by the lower extreme and the upper extreme of the stimuli presented (Parducci, 1965; Petzold, 1982; Witte, 1975). The essential operation then is to compare the representation of the stimulus with one or both of these extremes.

Thus two groups of experimental findings lead to different assumptions on the judgment process. Whereas sequential effects suggest that preceding stimuli serve as internal standards, the influence of the range suggests that it is the extremes that are used as standards.

Bringing sequential effects and range effects together, some models assume two types of frames of reference: (a) a trial-to-trial varying *short-term* system in which the preceding stimulus-response pair operates as referent and (b) a comparatively stable *long-term* system based on the stimulus set as a whole. A combination of these two systems is supposed to determine the judgments. The models suggested differ in their assumptions about the structure of short-term and long-term frames and the interplay between the two frames of reference.

In the first part of this chapter, we review some recent models of the combination of short-term and long-term frames of reference. In the later sections, these models are evaluated in the light of experimental findings on sequential dependencies. In particular, the inverted-V pattern for correlations between successive responses and interactions between events one and two trials back are analyzed.

MODELS OF THE INTERPLAY BETWEEN SHORT-TERM AND LONG-TERM FRAMES OF REFERENCE

Theory of Criterion Setting

The theory of criterion setting was formulated in the language of Thurstonian and signal-detection theories (Treisman, 1984; Treisman & Williams, 1984). According to this theory, stimuli are mapped onto a unidimensional continuum, and responses are selected by reference to criteria positioned along this continuum. The criterion-setting theory specifies mechanisms responsible for the locating the response criteria.

First, a long-term process determines initial values for the criteria that are affected by the overall parameters of the judgment situation, such as range and probability of stimuli. In the case of category judgment, the range of stimuli defines upper and lower limits. Then response criteria are placed at equal intervals or, according to other rules, between these limits.

Second, the criterion-setting theory assumes two kinds of short-term processes, stabilization and tracking. These processes provide fine adjustments to ensure that the criteria in use are optimally placed. The stabilization mechanism tends to maximize the information transmitted by the study participants' responses and leads to a shift of all criteria toward the trace of previous stimuli, which produces contrast. The tracking mechanism serves to match current changes in stimulus probabilities and results in a shift away from the previous response, which produces assimilation. The effective criteria in a trial are weighted combinations of the long-term values and the short-term adjustments.

DeCarlo Model

The response-ratio rule by Luce and Green (1974) postulates that in magnitude estimations the ratio of responses preserves the ratio of internal representations. This approach can be written as

$$r(t) = X(t) \frac{r(t-1)}{X^*(t-1)}, \tag{1}$$

From this rule it follows that the current response $r(t)$ increases with an increase of the preceding response $r(t-1)$. This corresponds to the assimilation effect found in experiments. Furthermore, the response also increases with a decrease in the internal representation of the preceding stimulus. This corresponds to contrast with the preceding stimulus $s(t-1)$.

Because some experimental findings are at variance with the response-ratio rule, DeCarlo (1989) proposed a generalization. According to his model, two frames of reference can influence the judgment: a short-term frame and a long-term frame. In the short-term frame, judgments are made relative to the previous sensation $X(t-1)$ and the previous response $r(t-1)$, whereas in the long-term frame, judgments are relative to stable references X_0 and r_0 that, for instance, might be the lower extreme of the range and the smallest response. To specify this approach, DeCarlo (1989) assumed that the short-term frame, $X(t-1)/r(t-1)$, and the long-term-frame, X_0/r_0, are weighted in the judgment as

$$r(t) = X(t) \left(\frac{r_0}{X_0}\right)^{1-\lambda} \left[\frac{r(t-1)}{X(t-1)}\right]^{\lambda} v(t), \tag{2}$$

where weight λ measures the relative influence of the short-term frame and $v(t)$ is a multiplicative error term. By a variation of λ, the relative influence of the two frames can be controlled by the participant. This assumption is supported by the finding that instructions affect the magnitude of sequential effects (DeCarlo, 1994; DeCarlo & Cross, 1990). The assimilation toward the preceding response is stronger when participants are instructed to use the preceding event as a referent than when they are asked to use a fixed reference point.

Judgment-Option Model

Another model that also specifies the interplay between short-term and long-term systems is the judgment-option model (Baird, 1997). According to this model, the response in trial t, $r(t)$, is a weighted average of the response k trials back, $r(t-k)$, and the judgment r^* that would be made if the prior event had no influence and only the long-term frame is operative. Thus

$$r(t) = \omega r(t - k) + (1 - \omega)r^*. \tag{3a}$$

The weight ω is given by

$$\omega = \text{sim}[s(t), s(t - k)] - \text{sim}(s_{max}, s_{min}), \tag{3b}$$

where $\text{sim}[s(t), s(t - k)]$ denotes the similarity between the current and the preceding stimulus and $\text{sim}[s_{max}, s_{min}]$ denotes the similarity between the two extreme stimuli. It is assumed that the largest of the similarity scores determines which of the previous responses will be integrated into the judgment. If, for instance, weight ω in Equation 3a is greater for $s(t - 2)$ than for $s(t - 1)$, then $r(t - 2)$ will be incorporated into the judgment and $r(t - 1)$ disregarded. This means that only one past event is involved in the judgment.

It follows from Equation 3a that the current response increases with an increase in the preceding responses. This means assimilation toward preceding responses. The effect of the similarity between $s(t)$ and $s(t - k)$ on the weight ω implies the contrast of $r(t)$ with the preceding stimuli.

Multiple-Standards Model

The multiple-standards model (Petzold & Haubensak, 2001a) is a generalization of range models according to which the judgment of a stimulus is determined by the proportion of the contextual range lying below it (Durlach & Braida, 1969; Parducci, 1965; Volkmann, 1951; Witte, 1975). More specifically, range models assume that judgments are based on a decision continuum Z, given by

$$Z = \frac{X - X_{min}}{X_{max} - X_{min}}, \tag{4a}$$

where X is the subjective value of the stimulus and X_{min} and X_{max} are minimum and maximum subjective values of the range defined by the extremes. In other words, judgments refer to two internal standard-response pairs: X_{min} is associated with the lowest response r_{min} and X_{max} is associated with the highest response r_{max}. The relative deviation of the current response from the lowest response,

$$\frac{r - r_{min}}{r_{max} - r_{min}}, \tag{4b}$$

is then determined by the relative deviation of X from X_{min} given by the value of Z.

The range model can be generalized with the assumption that not only the extremes of the range but also other standards may contribute to the formation of the subjective range. In particular, previous stimulus-response associations may serve as referents for the judgment. Then we have two types of standards: the extremes of the range as long-term standards and the traces of previous stimuli as short-term standards. Whereas the comparatively stable long-term standards are assumed to be permanently available in memory during an experiment, short-term standards will be forgotten and substituted by later ones after some trials (Haubensak, 1992). For simplicity, we assume a constant forgetting rate per trial.

Which of the standards available in memory are operative in a trial depends on their position relative to the representation X of the current stimulus. The next-lower standard serves as a lower referent X_l and the next-higher standard as an upper referent X_u. Then the process described by Equations 4 is generalized by a process in which the value of

$$\frac{r - r_l}{r_u - r_l} \tag{5a}$$

is determined by the value of

$$Z = \frac{X - X_l}{X_u - X_l}, \tag{5b}$$

where r_l and r_u are the responses associated with the standards X_l and X_u.

To illustrate this mechanism, let us consider the special case in which only the preceding event $X(t - 1)$ associated with $r(t - 1)$ is available in short-term memory. Then the trace of the preceding stimulus serves as one of the standards, and we have to distinguish two variants depending on the position of $X(t)$ relative to $X(t - 1)$:

1. If $X_{min} < X(t) < X(t - 1) < X_{max}$, we have

$$X_l = X_{min}, \qquad r_l = r_{min},$$
$$X_u = X(t - 1), \quad r_u = r(t - 1).$$

2. If $X_{min} < X(t - 1) < X(t) < X_{max}$, we have

$$X_l = X(t - 1), \quad r_l = r(t - 1),$$
$$X_u = X_{max}, \qquad r_u = r_{max}.$$

Using the next-lower and the next-upper standards leads to a minimal subjective range. Because the discriminability of two certain stimuli generally increases with a decrease in the range, the choice of the nearest standards can be regarded as the choice of best standards with respect to discriminability. This view resembles the single anchor model (Marley & Cook, 1984, 1986) according to which on each trial the subject uses the best available anchor. "Best" means the anchor that gives the smallest variability of the response.

To describe the process from the stimulus to the overt response in more detail, not only the comparison with internal standards, but also other processing stages are specified. From Thurstonian and detection theories, three stages are assumed for category judgment.

Internal Representation of Stimuli. Each stimulus results in an internal stimulus representation X that is modeled as a random variable that obeys a Gaussian distribution with mean $\mu(s)$ and standard deviation σ.

Comparison with Internal Standards. The internal representation X is transformed into a decision variable Z. The essential operation of this transformation is to refer to two internal standards, a lower standard X_l and an upper standard X_u. Then we have

$$Z = \frac{X(t) - X_l}{X_u - X_l}.$$

The choice of standards in a trial corresponds to the principle of nearest standards just described.

Selection of a Response. From the model by Torgerson (1958), it is assumed that the range of Z is subdivided into subranges by decision criteria. Each category between r_l and r_u corresponds to one subrange, where r_l and r_u are the responses associated with the standards X_l and X_u. To select a response, an examination must be made of which subrange the actual value of Z falls into (for illustration see fig. 3.2 in the next section).

Two characteristics of the multiple-standards model should be emphasized. First, two standards are operative in each trial, one as a lower standard and another as an upper standard. One or both of these standards may be traces of previous stimuli. Thus also the stimulus two trials back, $s(t - 2)$, may be included in the judgment process as a standard. Second, which of the standards available are operative in a trial depends on their positions relative to the current stimulus. From this it follows that the configuration of $s(t)$, $s(t - 1)$, $s(t - 2)$ along the dimension to be judged should affect the judgments. The prediction of such configurational effects is typical of the multiple-judgment model and distinguishes it from the other models.

In the following sections, we examine whether the models described are capable of explaining the inverted-V pattern of correlations between successive responses as a typical property of sequential dependencies. Then we consider which interactions between one and two events back are predicted by the models and whether these effects are reflected in the experimental data.

CORRELATIONS BETWEEN
SUCCESSIVE RESPONSES

The influence of the preceding response on the current response can be measured by the first-order autocorrelation of responses. This correlation turned out to depend on the distance between the stimulus $s(t)$ to be judged and the previous stimulus $s(t - 1)$ on the intensity dimension. Typically, an inverted-V pattern is obtained that indicates that the correlation is maximal for $s(t) - s(t - 1) = 0$ and declines with an increase in the distance between $s(t)$ and $s(t - 1)$ (Baird, Green, & Luce, 1980; DeCarlo & Cross, 1990; Green, Luce, & Duncan, 1977; Jesteadt et al., 1977). To demonstrate this relation, results from a category judgment task are shown in Fig. 3.1. In this task, the size of 12 squares were to be judged on a five-point rating scale.

The criterion-setting theory explains this distance effect by assuming that the magnitude of the changes in the response criteria decreases with an increase in their distance from the preceding stimulus. From this it follows that, if the current stimulus is farther away from the preceding stimulus, it falls into an area in which the changes of the criteria are small. Consequently the influence of the preceding response decreases.

The DeCarlo model can explain the inverted-V pattern if we assume that the weight of the short-term frame decreases with an increase in the distance between successive stimuli. Then the preceding response loses influence when the separation of stimuli increases.

The judgment-option model also predicts the inverted-V pattern. According to Equation 3b, the weight of the preceding response declines with a decrease in

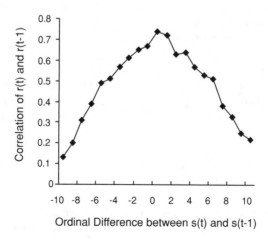

FIG. 3.1. Correlation of successive responses as a function of the difference between successive stimuli.

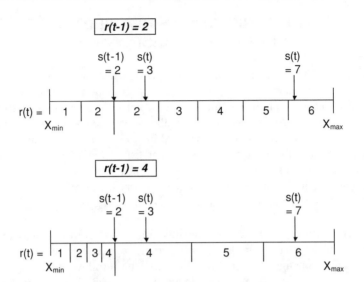

FIG. 3.2. Illustration of the distance effect by the multiple-standards model for a six-category scale. The division of the judgment dimension into subranges is presented for the preceding stimulus $s(t-1) = 2$ and two preceding responses, $r(t-1) = 2$ and $r(t-2) = 4$.

the similarity between successive stimuli. Consequently the correlation between successive responses is smaller for greater distances of successive stimuli.

To illustrate how the distance effect is produced within the framework of the multiple-standards model, we refer to the examples represented in Fig. 3.2. In this figure, a scheme of category judgment is depicted in which, for simplicity, the category limens are equally distant. First, we consider the case in which the current stimulus $s(t) = 3$ is highly similar to the preceding stimulus $s(t-1) = 2$. Comparing the upper and the lower part of the figure, we can see that $s(t)$ falls in different areas of the range for different previous responses. We have $r(t) = 2$ if $r(t-2) = 2$, but $r(t) = 4$ if $r(t-1) = 4$. Thus we find a strong influence of the previous response if $s(t)$ is near $s(t-1)$. However, in the case of the considerably remote stimulus $s(t) = 7$, the response is independent of the previous response. Both for $r(t-1) = 2$ and $r(t-1) = 4$ the current response $r(t)$ results to 6. More generally, the more distant $s(t)$ and $s(t-1)$ are, the lower the probability that the variation of the preceding response $r(t-1)$ affects the current response $r(t)$.

Taken together, all the models previously described are capable of accounting for the inverted-V pattern of the correlation between successive responses. Therefore additional findings are needed to decide among the models. To this end, we consider interactions between events one and two trials back.

INTERACTION BETWEEN THE EVENTS
ONE AND TWO TRIALS BACK

A variety of studies has shown that not only the immediately preceding event affects the judgment, but sequential effects extend over more than one trial. To determine the depth of sequential dependencies, Petzold and Haubensak (2001a) analyzed partial correlations. When, for instance, the partial correlation between $r(t-2)$ and $r(t)$ was calculated, the influence of all other variables was held constant. For category judgment, they found that stimulus-response events up to two trials back were included in the judgment process. The question arises as to whether the events one and two trials back operate independently of each other or if there is a joint action of both events. We examine which predictions can be derived from the preceding models. Then these predictions are compared with experimental findings.

Predictions of the Models

Theory of Criterion Setting. The effective criteria in a trial are obtained by a linear combination of the amounts indicated by the two mechanisms, stabilization and tracking, and by the stimulus-response events several trials back. Consequently the criterion-setting model does not predict an interaction between the stimuli more than one trial apart.

DeCarlo Model. The DeCarlo model as formulated in Equation 2 refers to only the immediately preceding event. This model can be generalized, however, with the assumption that the event two trials back can also serve as a referent. Then we have

$$r(t) = X(t) \left(\frac{r_0}{X_0} \right)^{\alpha} \left[\frac{r(t-1)}{X(t-1)} \right]^{\beta} \left[\frac{r(t-2)}{X(t-2)} \right]^{\gamma} v(t), \qquad (6)$$

with $\alpha + \beta + \gamma = 1$. As already mentioned, we can assume that the weight of the short-term frame decreases with in increase in the distance between the current stimulus and the previous stimulus (DeCarlo & Cross, 1990). From this follows an interdependence of the weights. When the distance between $s(t)$ and $s(t-2)$ increases, the weight γ will decrease and the influence of the stimulus-response event two trials back will be smaller. Because the sum of all weights is 1, a smaller γ is connected with a higher effective weight β. Consequently a smaller influence of the stimulus-response event two trials back leads to a higher influence of the event one trial back. Equivalently, we can conclude that a smaller impact of the event one trial back implies a higher influence of the event two trials back. This means that the DeCarlo model predicts an interaction between the events one and two trials back.

Judgment-Option Model.   According to Equation 3b, the weight of a previous response depends on the similarity between the current stimulus and the corresponding previous stimulus. The judgment-option model assumes that the largest
of the similarity score determines which of the previous responses will be integrated
into the judgment. If, for instance, the weight ω in Equation 3b is greater for $s(t - 2)$
than for $s(t - 1)$, then $r(t - 2)$ will be incorporated into the judgment and $r(t - 1)$
is disregarded. This means that *only one* past event is involved in the judgment.

From this it follows that interactions between the effects of the events one and
two trials earlier in the sequence should appear. If the distance between $s(t - 2)$
and $s(t)$ decreases, then the probability that $r(t - 2)$ is substituted into Equation 3a
increases. Consequently the probability that $r(t - 1)$ is included in the averaging
process decreases. This means that with a decrease in the distance between $s(t - 2)$
and $s(t)$ the correlation between $r(t)$ and $r(t - 2)$ increases and the correlation
between $r(t)$ and $r(t - 1)$ decreases. An analogous result is obtained when the
distance between $s(t)$ and $s(t - 1)$ is varied. Thus the model predicts an interaction
of the distance between $s(t)$ and $s(t - 1)$ and the distance between $s(t)$ and $s(t - 2)$
from both the correlations between $r(t)$ and $r(t - 1)$ and the correlations between
$r(t)$ and $r(t - 2)$.

Multiple-Standards Model.   This model assumes that the standards used
in a particular trial depend on their position relative to the representation of the
current stimulus. The smaller the distance between the previous and the current
stimulus, the higher the probability that the trace of the previous stimulus is used as
a standard. From this follows an interaction between the stimuli one and two trials
back. If the distance between $s(t)$ and $s(t - 2)$ increases, the probability that the
trace of $s(t - 2)$ operates as a standard decreases. As a consequence, the probability
of using the trace of $s(t - 1)$ increases. Accordingly, increasing distance between
$s(t)$ and $s(t - 1)$ leads to a decreasing probability of using the trace of $s(t - 1)$
and an increasing probability of using the trace of $s(t - 2)$.

In sum, whereas the theory of criterion setting implies no interaction between
the stimulus-response events one and two trials back, the other three models predict
an interaction concerning the distance between $s(t)$ and $s(t - 1)$ and the distance
between $s(t)$ and $s(t - 2)$.

Experimental Results

In an experiment reported elsewhere (Petzold & Haubensak, 2001a) we asked the
participants to judge 12 squares according to the size on a five-category scale.
The squares were presented on a 17-in. (43.18-cm) computer screen. Their width
varied from 50 to 83 mm in steps of 3 mm. Subjects were asked to make their
judgments by pressing the respective key on the computer keyboard. There was
no feedback. There were 31 paid observers who participated in the experiment.

For the analysis, we divided the stimuli into four groups of three adjacent stimuli
in order to have adequate sample sizes for each participant. Then individual mean

judgments were entered into a 4 [groups of the current stimulus $s(t)$] × 4 [groups of the stimulus one trial back $s(t - 1)$] × 4 [groups of the stimulus two trials back $s(t - 2)$] analysis with the previous responses $r(t - 1)$ and $r(t - 2)$ as covariants. What is most important is that there was a significant three-way interaction of $s(t)$, $s(t - 1)$, and $s(t - 2)$, $F(27, 6976) = 1.61$, $p < .05$. From this it follows that the stimulus-response events one and two trials back were included in the judgment process not independently of each other. This result is not consistent with the theory of response setting, but it is with the other three models described. For a further evaluation of these models we consider configural effects in which the position of $s(t)$, $s(t - 1)$, and $s(t - 2)$ relative to each other is relevant. These configural effects are specifications of the three–way interaction among these stimuli.

INTERACTION OF RANGE AND THE POSITION OF STIMULI

One kind of configurational effect concerns the influence of range as it depends on the relative position of the stimuli. We consider certain configurations of $s(t)$, $s(t - 1)$, and $s(t - 2)$, embedded in different ranges. For illustration, two configurations, A and B, and two ranges, 1 and 2, are shown in Fig. 3.3. In configurations A, $s(t)$ lies between $s(t - 1)$ and $s(t - 2)$, whereas in configurations B, $s(t)$ is located above $s(t - 1)$ and $s(t - 2)$. What are the consequences that this variation of the relative position has on the influence of the range?

Predictions of the Models

DeCarlo Model.   As suggested by DeCarlo and Cross (1990), the weights of the long-term and the short-term frames in Equation 6 depend on the distance between the current stimulus and the respective previous stimulus relative to the range of stimuli. From this it follows that the range affects the judgments of all stimuli in the same direction. Consequently, considering the configurations in Fig. 3.1, we can predict that there is a difference of judgments between both configurations 1A and 2A and configurations 1B and 2B. To specify this prediction, computer simulations were performed for several parameter combinations. The mean values of the results are shown in Fig. 3.4.

Judgment-Option Model.   Equation 3b implies that the weight of the preceding response is a linear combination of two terms: (a) the similarity between the current stimulus and a previous stimulus, and (b) the similarity between the extremes of all the stimuli presented. The first term is invariant for all configurations represented in Fig. 3.3, because the distance between the current stimulus and the nearest previous stimulus is held constant. The second term is smaller for the larger range than for the smaller range, because there is less similarity between the extreme stimuli for the larger range. From the negative sign of the second term

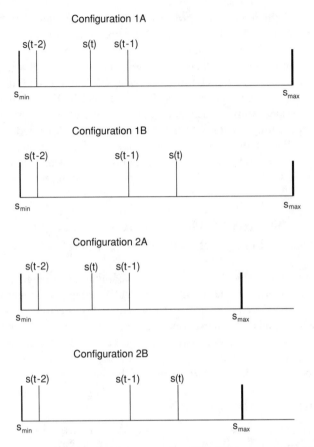

FIG. 3.3.   Stimulus configurations that differ in two respects. First, the current stimulus is within (1A and 2A) or outside (1B and 2B) the range formed by $s(t-1)$ and $s(t-2)$. Second, the range of all stimuli is wide (1A and 1B) or narrow (2A and 2B).

it follows that the weight of the previous response should be greater for larger ranges. Because of the linear combination of both terms, this effect of the range should be independent of the positions of the current stimulus and the previous stimuli. Consequently judgments should be equally affected by the range for configurations A and B. Thus the pattern of predictions resembles that one obtained for the DeCarlo model (Fig. 3.4).

Multiple-Standards Model.   According to the multiple-standards model, the influence of range should depend on the position of $s(t)$, $s(t-1)$, and $s(t-2)$. In configurations 1A and 2A, $s(t)$ lies between $s(t-1)$ and $s(t-2)$. Consequently $s(t-2)$ should serve as a lower standard and $s(t-1)$ as an upper standard. From this it follows that the extremes of the range are not used as standards and the range

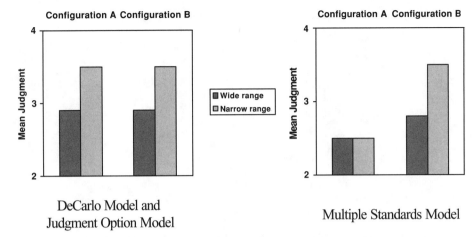

FIG. 3.4. Predictions of several models concerning mean judgments of the current stimulus for the configurations of $s(t)$, $s(t-1)$, and $s(t-2)$ shown in Fig. 3.3.

has no influence on the judgments. In configurations 1B and 2B, however, $s(t)$ lies above $s(t-1)$ and $s(t-2)$. Then, $s(t-1)$ as the nearest standard below $s(t)$ serves as a lower standard and the upper extreme of the range as an upper standard. Therefore in this case the variation of the range should affect the judgments. To illustrate the predictions, mean values of computer simulations are shown in Fig. 3.4.

Experimental Results

To study the interaction between range and position of stimuli, an additional experiment was performed. This experiment differed from that just described in the range of stimuli: only stimuli 1–6 were presented.

It was to be examined whether the range of stimuli affects the judgments in configurations such as those shown in Fig. 3.3. The following combinations were chosen:

1A $s(t) = 2$ or 3 1B $s(t) = 5$ or 6
    $s(t-1) = 4$ $s(t-1) = 4$
    $s(t-2) = 1$ $s(t-2) = 1$
    range: 1–12   range: 1–12

2A $s(t) = 2$ or 3 2B $s(t) = 5$ or 6
    $s(t-1) = 4$ $s(t-1) = 4$
    $s(t-2) = 1$ $s(t-2) = 1$
    range: 1–6   range: 1–6

Mean judgments for different configurations are shown in Fig. 3.5.

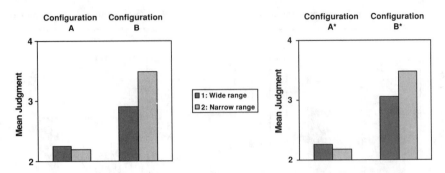

FIG. 3.5. Empirical values of mean judgments of the current stimulus for the configurations shown in Fig. 3.3 and described in the text.

As can be seen, there was no influence of range if the current stimulus was between $s(t - 1)$ and $s(t - 2)$. An effect of the range was found, however, if the current stimulus was located above $s(t - 1)$ and $s(t - 2)$. We also considered configurations in which $s(t - 1)$ and $s(t - 2)$ changed their position, which means that we have $s(t - 1) = 1$ and $s(t - 2) = 4$:

1A*	$s(t) = 2$ or 3	1B*	$s(t) = 5$ or 6
	$s(t - 1) = 1$		$s(t - 1) = 1$
	$s(t - 2) = 4$		$s(t - 2) = 4$
	range: 1–12		range: 1–12
2A*	$s(t) = 2$ or 3	2B*	$s(t) = 5$ or 6
	$s(t - 1) = 1$		$s(t - 1) = 1$
	$s(t - 2) = 4$		$s(t - 2) = 4$
	range: 1–6		range: 1–6

The results also given in Fig. 3.5 show once more that the range exerts an influence only if the current stimulus is located outside the range of $s(t - 1)$ and $s(t - 2)$. This finding corresponds to the prediction of the multiple-standards model and is at variance with the other models discussed here.

CONFIGURAL EFFECTS CONCERNING STIMULI ONE AND TWO TRIALS BACK

In the configurational effect described in the preceding section the position of $s(t - 1)$ and $s(t - 2)$ was constant, but the position of $s(t)$ varied. Now we consider another type of configural effect in which the current stimulus is constant, but the relative position concerning $s(t - 1)$ and $s(t - 1)$ changes. In particular, we

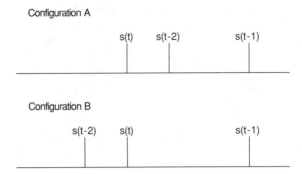

FIG. 3.6. Configurations of $s(t)$, $s(t-1)$, and $s(t-2)$ that differ in the positon of $s(t-2)$ relative to $s(t)$ and $s(t-1)$. In configuration A, $s(t-2)$ lies between $s(t)$ and $s(t-1)$; in configuration B, it lies outside.

compare configurations, as shown in Fig. 3.6. The distances between $s(t)$ and $s(t-1)$ as well as those between $s(t)$ and $s(t-2)$ are equal, but the position of $s(t-2)$ relative to $s(t)$ and $s(t-1)$ differs in these configurations. Whereas $s(t-1)$ and $s(t-2)$ lie on the same side of $s(t)$ along the dimension to be judged in configuration A, they are located on different sides in configuration B. What consequences has this variation for sequential effects?

Predictions of the Models

DeCarlo Model. In the extended DeCarlo model, the weights α, β, and γ are assumed to depend on the distances $\mid s(t) - s(t-1) \mid$ and $\mid s(t) - s(t-2) \mid$. Because these distances are constant in the configurations shown in Fig. 3.6, the correlation between $r(t)$ and $r(t-1)$ as well as that between $r(t)$ and $r(t-2)$ should be equal for configurations A and B.

Judgment-Option Model. According to this model, it is assumed that the largest of the similarity scores determines which of the previous responses will be integrated into the judgment. If, for instance, the weight ω in Equation 3a is greater for $s(t-2)$ than for $s(t-1)$, then $r(t-2)$ will be incorporated into the judgment and $r(t-1)$ will be disregarded. This means that *only one* past event is involved in the judgment.

From this model it follows that interactions between the effects of events one and two trials back should appear. If the distance between $s(t-2)$ and $s(t)$ decreases, then the probability that $r(t-2)$ is substituted into Equation 3a increases. Consequently, the probability that $r(t-1)$ is included in the averaging process decreases. This means that with a decrease in the distance between $s(t-2)$ and $s(t)$ the correlation between $r(t)$ and $r(t-2)$ increases and the correlation between $r(t)$ and $r(t-1)$ decreases. An analogous result is obtained when the distance between

$s(t)$ and $s(t - 1)$ is varied. Thus the model predicts an interaction of the distance between $s(t)$ and $s(t - 1)$ and the distance between $s(t)$ and $s(t - 2)$ from both the correlations between $r(t)$ and $r(t - 1)$ and the correlations between $r(t)$ and $r(t - 2)$. In the configurations of Fig. 3.6, the distance between $s(t)$ and $s(t - 1)$ as well as the distance between $s(t)$ and $s(t - 2)$ is invariant. Therefore there should be no difference in the sequential effects between configurations A and B.

Multiple-Standards Model. From the multiple-standards model it follows that, according to the principle of closest standards, the variation of the position of $s(t - 2)$ leads to different choices of the lower standard X_l and the upper standard X_u:

Configuration A, $X_{min} < X(t) < X(t - 2) < X(t - 1) < X_{max}$:
$$X_l = X_{min},$$
$$X_u = X(t - 2).$$

Configuration B, $X_{min} < X(t) < X(t - 2) < X(t - 1) < X_{max}$:
$$X_l = X(t - 2),$$
$$X_u = X(t - 1).$$

Note that the event one trial back is not included in the judgment process in configuration A. Therefore the correlation between successive responses should be zero, whereas a correlation greater than zero should exist between $r(t)$ and $r(t - 2)$. In configuration B, however, both $X(t - 1)$ and $X(t - 2)$ serve as internal standards and a significant correlation is to be expected between $r(t)$ and $r(t - 1)$ as well as between $r(t)$ and $r(t - 2)$.

In sum, whereas the DeCarlo model and the judgment option-model lead to no differences in sequential dependencies, the multiple-judgment model predicts that the correlation between successive responses is higher in configuration B.

Experimental Results

We refer to the experiment in which subjects had to assess the size of squares on a five-point rating scale: 12 stimuli were presented, ranging from 50 to 83 mm in steps of 3 mm.

We analyzed the following configurations:

3A	$s(t) = 4$ or 5		3B	$s(t) = 4$ or 5
	$s(t - 1) = 9, 10, 11,$ or 12			$s(t - 1) = 9, 10, 11,$ or 12
	$s(t - 2) = 6, 7,$ or 8			$s(t - 2) = 1, 2,$ or 3
4A	$s(t) = 8$ or 9		4B	$s(t) = 8$ or 9
	$s(t - 1) = 1, 2, 3,$ or 4			$s(t - 1) = 1, 2, 3,$ or 4
	$s(t - 2) = 5, 6,$ or 7			$s(t - 2) = 10, 11,$ or 12

TABLE 3.1
Partial Correlations for Configurations 3A, 3B, 4A, and 4B

Position	Configuration	A	B
$\rho[r(t), r(t-1)]$	3	0.23_a	0.46_b
	4	0.17_a	0.43_b
$\rho[r(t), r(t-2)]$	3	0.45	0.42
	4	0.46	0.51

In configurations 3A and 4A, $s(t-2)$ is located between $s(t)$ and $s(t-1)$. In this case, according to the multiple-standards model, $s(t-1)$ is not used as a standard when the trace of $s(t-2)$ is available. Therefore the correlation between $r(t)$ and $r(t-1)$ should be low. In configurations 3B and 4B, however, $s(t-2)$ is not located between $s(t)$ and $s(t-1)$, and consequently $s(t-2)$ will not displace $s(t-1)$ as a standard. Therefore a higher correlation between $r(t)$ and $r(t-1)$ is to be expected. The trace of $s(t-2)$, however, can serve as a standard in all configurations, in 3A and 4A as an upper standard and in 3B and 4B as a lower standard. Additionally, the mean distance between $s(t)$ and $s(t-2)$ is identical in all configurations. Consequently the correlation between $r(t)$ and $r(t-2)$ should be invariant.

Partial correlations obtained in the experiment are presented in Table 3.1. In accordance with the predictions of the multiple-standards model, the correlation between $r(t)$ and $r(t-1)$ is lower when $s(t-2)$ is located between $s(t)$ and $s(t-1)$, whereas the correlation between $r(t)$ and $r(t-2)$ does not differ between the configurations.

A further test is provided when $s(t-1)$ and $s(t-2)$ change their positions. Then we obtain the following configurations:

3A*	$s(t) = 4$ or 5	3B*	$s(t) = 4$ or 5
	$s(t-1) = 6, 7,$ or 8		$s(t-1) = 1, 2,$ or 3
	$s(t-2) = 9, 10, 11,$ or 12		$s(t-2) = 9, 10, 11,$ or 12
4A*	$s(t) = 8$ or 9	4B*	$s(t) = 8$ or 9
	$s(t-1) = 5, 6,$ or 7		$s(t-1) = 10, 11,$ or 12
	$s(t-2) = 1, 2, 3,$ or 4		$s(t-2) = 1, 2, 3,$ or 4

The predictions are analogous to those obtained for the latter configurations. In configurations 3A* and 4A*, $s(t-1)$ lies between $s(t)$ and $s(t-2)$. Consequently only a small correlation between $r(t)$ and $r(t-2)$ is to be expected. In configurations 3B* and 4B*, however, $s(t-1)$ is located on the other side of $s(t)$, and now $s(t-2)$ can serve as a standard, and a higher correlation between $r(t)$ and $r(t-2)$ should occur. The correlation between $r(t)$ and $r(t-1)$ should be invariant because $s(t-1)$ can act as a standard in all cases. These predictions are confirmed by the empirical findings represented in Table 3.2.

TABLE 3.2
Partial Correlations for Configurations 3A*, 3B*, 4A*, and 4B*

Position	Configuration	A*	B*
$\rho[r(t), r(t-1)]$	3	0.57	0.51
	4	0.55	0.61
$\rho[r(t), r(t-2)]$	3	0.03_a	0.35_b
	4	0.02_a	0.30_b

Taken together, the configural effects in the interaction between $s(t-1)$ and $s(t-2)$ confirm the multiple-standards model but are not consistent with the other models.

CONFIGURAL EFFECTS AND CATEGORY MEMBERSHIP OF STIMULI

It has been generally found that there is a tendency to judge stimuli relative to the category they are assigned to. For instance, when the loudness of pure tones is to be judged and tones of two frequencies are presented, there is a substantial effect of the stimulus category defined by the frequency (Luce & Green, 1978; Ward, 1990). Moreover, when the stimuli presented belong to different categories, there is a tendency for sequential effects to be stronger if the current stimulus and the previous stimulus belong to the same category. These findings indicate that short-term standards are also applied in a category-specific way as is well known for the extremes of the range as long-term standards (Hinz & Geissler, 1990; Marks, 1988; Parducci, Knobel, & Thomas, 1976).

What is striking is that the category membership of the stimulus *two* trials back affects the correlation between the current response and the response *one* trial back (Petzold & Haubensak, 2001b). If both $s(t-2)$ and $s(t-1)$ belong to the same category as $s(t)$, the correlation between $r(t)$ and $r(t-1)$ is lower than if only $s(t-1)$ shares the category with $s(t)$. This result suggests that $s(t-1)$ and $s(t-2)$ operate concurrently if both belong to the same category as $s(t)$, and consequently the probability that $s(t-1)$ serves as a standard is lower than if only $s(t-1)$ has the category in common with $s(t)$. The question arises as to whether such an interaction of $s(t-1)$ and $s(t-2)$ depends on their position relative to each other.

Predictions of the Models

DeCarlo Model. As shown in the preceding subsection, judgments are expected to depend on the distance between $s(t)$ and $s(t-1)$ as well as between $s(t)$ and $s(t-2)$. As long as these distances are constant, the correlation between successive responses should be invariant with respect to the relative positions of $s(t)$, $s(t-1)$, and $s(t-2)$.

Judgment-Option Model. From the judgment-option model, the same prediction follows as that from the DeCarlo model.

Multiple-Standards Model. According to the multiple-standards model, traces of previous stimuli can serve as a lower standard when they are located below the current stimulus on the judgmental dimension and they can be used as an upper standard when they lie above the current stimulus. Thus two previous stimuli can act concurrently only if they are positioned on the same side of the current stimulus. From this it follows that the correlation between $r(t)$ and $r(t-1)$ should be affected by the category membership of $s(t-2)$ only if $s(t-1)$ and $s(t-2)$ lie on the same side. Otherwise, the correlation should be invariant with respect to the category of $s(t-2)$.

Experimental Results

An experiment was performed in which participants had to rate the size of squares. Categories of stimuli were defined by the different colors of the squares. The set of stimuli consisted of 16 squares with an overlapping area of the two categories. The location of the 16 stimuli along the size dimension is shown in Fig. 3.7.

To examine whether configural effects concerning the category membership appear, the pairs of configurations presented in Table 3.3 were considered. The numbering of stimuli corresponds to that given in Figure 7. These pairs of configurations

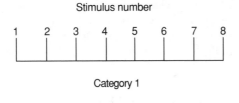

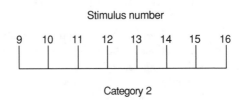

FIG. 3.7. Positions of the stimuli used in the experiment on the influence of categorization on sequential dependencies.

TABLE 3.3

Correlations Among Successive Responses for Different Configurations
of $s(t)$, $s(t-1)$, and $s(t-2)$

Side	Category of $s(t-1)$ and $s(t-2)$	$s(t)$	$s(t-1)$	$s(t-2)$	$\rho[r(t), r(t-1)]$
$s(t-1)$ and $s(t-2)$	Equal	4–5	1–3	6–8	0.65
on *different sides*	Different	4–5	1–3	10–12	0.69
of $s(t)$	Equal	12–13	14–16	9–11	0.59
	Different	12–13	14–16	5–7	0.67
$s(t-1)$ and $s(t-2)$	Equal	4–5	6–8	6–8	0.45
on the *same side*	Different	4–5	6–8	10–12	0.68
of $s(t)$	Equal	12–13	9–11	9–11	0.34
	Different	12–13	9–11	5–7	0.71

Note. These differ in the position of the preceding stimulus relative to the current stimulus and in the correspondence of the category membership of $s(t-1)$ and $s(t-2)$. For a more detailed description see text.

were selected according to the following principle. The positions of $s(t)$, $s(t-1)$, and $s(t-2)$ along the size dimension were identical, but the membership of $s(t-2)$ to categories was changed within one pair of configurations.

For illustration, let us consider the configurations in the first two lines of Table 3.3. In both configurations, $s(t)$ and $s(t-1)$ belong to category 1 and $s(t)=4$ or 5 and $s(t-1)=1$, 2, or 3. The position of $s(t-2)$ along the size dimension coincides in both configurations, but $s(t-2)$ belongs to category 1 in the first configuration [$s(t-2)=6$, 7, or 8] and to category 2 in the second configuration [$s(t-2)=10$, 11, or 12]. Using this pair of configurations, we can examine whether the category membership of $s(t-2)$ affects the correlation between $r(t)$ and $r(t-1)$. This is not the case for this special pair. Considering all pairs, Table 3.3 shows that the category membership of $s(t-2)$ exerts an influence only if $s(t-1)$ and $s(t-2)$ are positioned on the same side of $s(t)$ along the size dimension. This result confirms the prediction of the multiple-standards model.

EXTENSIONS OF THE
MULTIPLE-STANDARDS MODEL

As was shown, the multiple-standards model is capable of explaining the configural effects found for positions of the current stimulus and previous stimuli relative to each other including the category membership of stimuli. These configural effects confirm the assumption that (a) the extremes of the range and traces of preceding stimuli may serve as standards and (b) that the standards nearest to the current stimulus are operative in a trial. There are other experimental findings, however, that require some extensions of the model.

Control of Using Short-Term and Long-Term Standards

For purpose of simplicity, two factors were assumed to determine the choice of standards: (a) availability in memory and (b) nearness to the current stimulus. From this it follows that a standard is used when it is available and nearest to the current stimulus. However, subjects seem to be able to control to what extent short-term and long-term standards are applied. DeCarlo and Cross (1990) have shown that the magnitude of sequential effects is affected by the instruction. When individuals were instructed to make their judgments relative to the immediately preceding stimulus-response pair, sequential effects were stronger than in the case in which individuals were oriented on a fixed reference point. Thus the extent to which short-term and long-term standards are used is also determined by the demands of the judgmental task. Therefore we introduced a probability of using short-term standards that depends on both the forgetting rate of short-term standards (Haubensak, 1992) and on other factors such as the instruction.

Guessing as an Additional Component of the Judgment Process

According to the multiple-judgment model, sequential effects are caused by use of prior events as referents for judging current stimuli. This does not, however, exclude the possibility that other components may also contribute to sequential dependencies. In particular, a guessing strategy could also lead to sequential dependencies. In the case of low stimulus discriminability, more than one response might be acceptable after a stimulus representation. Which of the acceptable responses is finally selected may depend on the preceding response. Ward (1979) suggested within the framework of his fuzzy-judgment model that the less informative a stimulus is, the fuzzier its internal representation. From this it follows that sequential effects should be stronger in case of lower stimulus discriminability. This expectation is consistent with results from earlier studies (e.g. McGill, 1957; Mori & Ward, 1995; Ward & Lockhead, 1971).

What is important is that the guessing process is solely response driven and may bring about partial correlations only between successive responses but not between the current response and the preceding stimulus. Consequently the variation of the guessing behavior should affect only the partial correlation between successive responses. This was found in an experiment in which subjects had to judge the size of squares on a five-point rating scale. In one condition, the discriminability of stimuli was diminished by a background noise. Whereas the discriminability was $d' = 0.90$ in the condition without noise, the value decreased to $d' = 0.49$ when the noise was added. As a consequence of the lowered discriminability, the partial correlation between successive responses increased to 0.46, whereas the corresponding value in the condition without noise was 0.27. There was no significant difference, however, for the partial correlation between the current response and the preceding stimulus, -0.22 and -0.18, respectively. A similar result was obtained in a study by Mori (1998). In this study, the stimulus information affected only the dependency of the response on $r(t - 1)$, but not on $s(t - 1)$. Both findings suggest that a response-driven component is affected by the addition of noise. Perhaps this component is a guessing strategy that gained more influence when the stimuli were less discriminable.

Guessing behavior can be integrated into the multiple-standards model by variation of the processing stage "selection of responses." It may be assumed that the subranges of the decision variable Z do not determine the response unequivocally. Rather, subranges are characterized by different subsets of acceptable responses (Petzold, 1982). The final selection of the response within this subset of acceptable responses is brought about, then, by a guessing strategy that depends on the previous responses.

CONCLUDING REMARKS

We have considered some recent models that share the assumption of two frames of reference: a short-term frame referring to previous stimulus-response associations and a long-term frame based on the set of stimuli as a whole. The models described differ in specifying the structure and the interplay of the two systems. Considering some configural effects of sequential dependencies, we have seen that the multiple standards model is superior in explaining these effects. In particular, two characteristics of the multiple standards model are supported by the data:

1. The interaction between the range and the position of the recent stimulus relative to the stimuli one and two trials back has indicated that both the traces of former stimuli and the extremes of the range may serve as standards in one trial.

2. All the configural effects described provide evidence for the principle of nearness.

The standards operative in a trial are those that are nearest to the current stimulus along the judgmental dimension: the next lower standard as a lower referent and the next upper standard as an upper referent.

It should be emphasized, however, that the configural effects were found in studies of category judgment. So far the multiple-standards model is supported for category judgment only. The analysis of higher-order sequential dependencies for magnitude estimation has shown that in this case only the immediately preceding stimulus-response pair is included in the judgment process, but not events further back (Petzold & Haubensak, 2001a). From this it follows that the judgment process seems to differ in category judgment and magnitude estimation. Possibly the

DeCarlo model is more adequate for magnitude estimation. The task dependency of frames of reference needs further clarification.

ACKNOWLEDGMENTS

This study was supported by the Deutsche Forschungsgemeinschaft (Ha 936/6).

REFERENCES

Baird, J. C. (1997). *Sensation and judgment: Complementarity theory of psychophysics*. Mahwah, NJ: Lawrence Erlbaum Associates.

Baird, J. C., Green, D. M., & Luce, R. D. (1980). Variability and sequential effects in cross modality matching of area and loudness. *Journal of Experimental Psychology: Human Perception and Performance, 6*, 277–289.

DeCarlo, L. T. (1989). Sequential effects in magnitude scaling (Doctoral dissertation, State University of New York at Stony Brook, 1989). *Dissertation Abstracts International, 50*, 3730B.

DeCarlo, L. T. (1994). A dynamic theory of proportional judgment: Context and judgment of length, heaviness, and roughness. *Journal of Experimental Psychology: Human Perception and Performance, 20*, 372–381.

DeCarlo, L. T., & Cross, D. V. (1990). Sequential effects in magnitude scaling: Models and theory. *Journal of Experimental Psychology: General, 119*, 375–396.

Durlach, N. I., & Braida, L. D. (1969). Intensity perception: Prelimary theory of intensity resolution. *Journal of the Acoustical Society of America, 46*, 372–383.

Green, D. M., Luce, R. D., & Duncan, J. E. (1977). Variability and sequential effects in magnitude production and estimation of auditory intensity. *Perception & Psychophysics, 22*, 450–456.

Haubensak, G. (1992). The consistency model: A process model for absolute judgments. *Journal of Experimental Psychology: Human Perception and Performance, 18*, 303–309.

Hinz, A., & Geissler, H.-G. (1990). The influence of class membership of stimuli on judgment. In H.-G. Geissler (Ed.), *Psychophysical explorations of mental structures* (pp. 124–129). Toronto: Hogrefe.

Jesteadt, W., Luce, R. D., & Green, D. M. (1977). Sequential effects in judgments of loudness. *Journal of the Experimental Psychology: Human Perception and Performance, 3*, 92–104.

Luce, R. D., & Green, D. M. (1974). The response ratio hypothesis for magnitude estimation. *Journal of Mathematical Psychology, 11*, 1–14.

Luce, R. D., & Green, D. M. (1978). Two tests of the neural attention hypothesis for auditory psychophysics. *Perception & Psychophysics, 23*, 363–371.

Marley, A. A. J., & Cook, V. T. (1984). A fixed rehearsal capacity interpretation of limits on absolute identification performance. *British Journal of Mathematical Psychology, 37*, 136–151.

Marley, A. A. J., & Cook, V. T. (1986). A limited capacity rehearsal model for psychophysical judgment applied to magnitude estimation. *Journal of Mathematical Psychology, 30*, 339–390.

Marks, L. E. (1988). Magnitude estimation and sensory matching. *Perception & Psychophysics, 43*, 511–526.

McGill, W. J. (1957). Serial effects in auditory threshold judgments. *Journal of Experimental Psychology, 53*, 297–303.

Mori, S. (1998). Effects of stimulus information and number of stimuli on sequential dependencies in absolute identification. *Canadian Journal of Experimental Psychology, 52*, 72–83.

Mori, S., & Ward, L. M. (1995). Pure feedback effects in absolute identification. *Perception & Psychophysics, 57*, 1065–1079.

Parducci, A. (1965). Category judgment: A range-frequency model. *Psychological Review, 2*, 407–418.

Parducci, A., Knobel, S., & Thomas, Ch. (1976). Independent contexts for category ratings: A range-frequency analysis. *Perception & Psychophysics, 20*, 360–366.

Petzold, P. (1981). Distance effects on sequential dependencies in categorical judgments. *Journal of Experimental Psychology: Human Perception and Performance, 7*, 1371–1385.

Petzold, P. (1982). The edge effect of discriminability in categorical judgments. In H.-G. Geissler & P. Petzold (Eds.), *Psychophysical judgment and the process of perception* (pp. 222–232). Amsterdam: North-Holland.

Petzold, P., & Haubensak, G. (2001a). Higher order sequential effects. *Perception & Psychophysics, 63*, 969–978.

Petzold, P., & Haubensak, G. (2001b). The influence of category membership of stimuli on sequential effects. *Perception & Psychophysics*, Manuscript under review.

Schifferstein, H. N. J., & Frijters, J. E. R. (1992). Contextual and sequential effects on judgments of sweetness intensity. *Perception & Psychophysics, 52*, 243–255.

Torgerson, W. S. (1958). *Theory and methods of scaling*. Chicago: University of Chicago Press.

Treisman, M. (1984). A theory of criterion setting: An alternative to the attention band and response ratio hypotheses in magnitude estimation and cross modality matching. *Journal of the Experimental Psychology: General, 113*, 443–463.

Treisman, M., & Williams, T. C. (1984). A theory of criterion setting with an application to sequential dependencies. *Psychological Review, 91*, 68–111.

Volkmann, J. (1951). Scales of judgment and their implications for social psychology. In J. H. Rohrer & M. Sherif (Eds.), *Social psychology at the crossroads* (pp. 279–294). New York: Harper & Row.

Ward, L. M. (1979). Stimulus information and sequential dependencies in magnitude estimation and cross-modality matching. *Journal of Experimental Psychology: Human Perception and Performance, 5*, 444–459.

Ward, L. M. (1990). Critical bands and mixed frequency scaling: Sequential dependencies, equal-loudness contours, and power function exponents. *Perception & Psychophysics, 47*, 551–562.

Ward, L. M., & Lockhead, G. R. (1971). Response system processes in absolute judgment. *Perception & Psychophysics, 9*, 73–78.

Witte, W. (1975). Zum Gestalt- und Systemcharakter psychischer Bezugssysteme [About psychological frames of reference as Gestalt and Systems]. In S. Ertel (Ed.), *Gestalttheorie in der modernen Psychologie* [The theory of Gestalt in modern Psychology] (pp. 123–154). Darmstadt, Germany: Steinkopf.

4

Frame of Reference Models in Psychophysics: A Perceptual–Cognitive Approach

Viktor Sarris
J. W. Goethe-University, Frankfurt am Main, Germany

> *[There is] . . . the approach of the sensory scientist whose goal is to obtain unbiased scales of sensory magnitude to study sensory processes such as summation, inhibition, adaptation, and sensory channels. . . . The study by [other researchers], on the other hand, more represents the approach of the cognitive scientist whose goal is to understand the process of perception and judgment.*
>
> —Gescheider (1988, p. 183)

Central to the concern of modern psychophysics is the notion of perceptual–judgmental *relativity*, contrary to the mainstream of the more traditional approach of sensory psychophysics (cf. Baird, 1997; see, however, Blake, 1999; Ehrenstein & Ehrenstein, 1999; Farell & Pelli, 1999). Take, for instance, the loudness of familiar sounds varying in intensity, say from the absolute threshold of hearing to the painful noise of a jet-plane takeoff: Although the variable acoustic events are consciously experienced as absolute, they are in fact relative to their immediately given contextual surround (background). In this chapter, some basic conceptual aspects of frame-of-reference (FR) and contextual effects in psychophysics are illustrated, together with some major predictive FR models. Furthermore, the relevance of a behavioral psychophysics approach with human and animal subjects is shown.

The reader who is familiar with the more classic FR literature may easily skip the first part of this chapter.

FR EFFECTS IN PSYCHOPHYSICAL RESEARCH

The term *frame of reference*, originally stemming from Gestalt psychology, is understood here to denote a concept that has something to do with the perception of stimulus relations, which form the basis of most, if not all, of the so-called contextual effects in psychophysics. In contrast to the postulate that sensory psychophysics relies on the assumption of context-free subjective measurements, some other approaches start with the basic idea of a complex perceptual–cognitive processing in a given psychophysical setting (e.g., Lockhead, 1992; Sarris, 1975, 2000).

Perceptual–Cognitive Judgments

For many years there existed, not only in the realm of psychophysics, two contrasting major approaches in perceptual research: the sensory–neurophysiological research strategy, and the approach with a more perceptual–cognitive orientation. A critical state-of-the-art article by Weintraub published in 1975 in the *Annual Review of Psychology* introduced an ironic confrontation of these opposing research strategies in perception:

> Two large tribes ... there are neurophysiological theorists and [cognitive] psychological-process theorists.... The former deal in flesh and blood mechanisms [e.g., neural lateral interactions], the latter in descriptive labels for psychological functions ... there's a jungle down there, trails that lead nowhere overgrown with tangled roots, vegetation that is perceptually green but never flowers and these unfriendly tribes separated by nearly impenetrable forest. The tribes skirmish only occasionally because they seldom venture from their own clearings, which they stand ready to defend at a moment's notice.... The tribes can be distinguished by language, habits and lifestyle. (p. 263)

Nowadays, the more perceptual–cognitive perspective is preferred mainly by those scientists who emphasize the importance of *contextual* perceptual processing in psychophysics. The following quotation taken from the *Oxford Companion to the Mind*, illustrates Garner's (1954) classic finding of dramatic context effects in a loudness-estimation task:

> [The participants'] judgements depended on the immediate context rather than on the loudness of the stimulus. [Typically,] ... in experiments on the estimation of sensations the influence of context is very powerful and the accuracy of judgement

TABLE 4.1

Basic Problems in Psychophysics

Problem	Description
Measurement devices	Problem of scale convergence ("invalidity")
Instrumental precision	Problem of interindividual and intraindividual variability ("noise")
Contextual effects	Problem of scale distortion ("bias")

Note. These problems are of theoretical and practical importance. Usually, these three major psychophysical problems are confounded (Sarris, 2000).

is . . . poorer by one to two orders revealed in the measurement of just noticeable differences. (Laming, 1986, p. 657; cf. Laming, 1997)

Besides context effects on scaling, there are still other largely unresolved issues to be looked at, although they are not treated at length in this chapter (see Table 4.1).

Perhaps it is more than only of anecdotal interest to mention that some leading experts nowadays prefer the perceptual–cognitive approach to the sensory model of psychophysical reasoning. One particular case here would be the research work by Marks at Yale University. Whereas his psychophysical work published until the 1970s was almost exclusively devoted to the assumed sensory processes in psychophysics (cf. Marks, 1974), his more recent investigations emphasize the *cognitive* basis of psychophysical judgments. As a matter of fact, besides the explicit acknowledgment of the importance of context effects, this psychophysicist now considers even a theoretical FR approach for his research data (Marks, 1991, 1992; cf. Marks & Algom, 1998).

Relational Psychophysics

Whereas classical sensory psychophysics relies mainly on the (illusory) assumption of absolute, that is, invariant, stimulus-response laws, the relation-theory in psychophysics is based on the general premise that, in principle, one and the same stimulus may be perceived and judged very differently as a function of the variables implied by the total contextual situation at hand. For instance, the psychophysical scale values for pitch are strongly dependent on the respective stimulus range provided by the physical inputs; thus the slope of the stimulus-response curves varies inversely with the size of the stimulus range. This well-established fact is illustrated by a graphical representation of the findings taken from my own psychophysical work of almost 30 years ago (Fig. 4.1; Sarris, 1976).

The major types of contextual "shifts" of psychophysical scale values result from stimulus-range (see Fig. 4.1), stimulus-asymmetry ("anchoring"), and stimulus-frequency variations. Their theoretical relevance is illustrated by the fact that such shifts were ignored, if not bluntly denied, in the theoretical system of Stevens and his followers (see, e.g., Stevens, 1975). That is, such effects were downgraded as irrelevant "biases" of the assumed "true" psychophysical values.

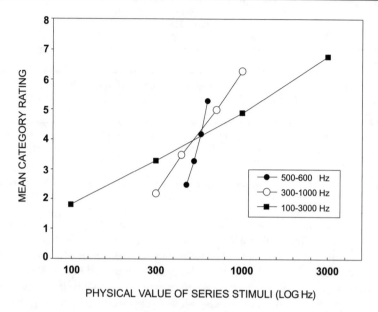

FIG. 4.1. Ratings of pitch as a function of the range with constant geometric mean (547.5 Hz): The slope varies inversely with the stimulus range of the three pitch series studied, that is, 500–600, 300–1000, and 100–3000 Hz (redrawn from Sarris, 1976).

Surely, Stevens and his followers were aware that context and expectations could alter the observer's sensory–perceptual experience (see, e.g., Stevens, 1975, chap. 9); however, they were looking at the "remedies" for rather than the "richness" of such effects for the development of cognitive psychophysics (cf. the Discussion section later in this chapter; for a lengthy treatment of this somewhat hotly debated issue, see Lockhead, 1992; Marks & Algom, 1998; also see the monographs by Baird, 1997; Laming, 1997; Sarris, 1975).

FR MODELS IN PSYCHOPHYSICS

In the following paragraphs, three FR models are briefly described, namely Helson's (1947, 1964) adaptation-level theory, my own similarity-classification model (Sarris, 1975, 2000) as a response to Helson's theory, and Parducci's (1965, 1983) range-frequency approach.

Adaptation-Level Model: A Sensory–Perceptual Approach

The so-called adaptation level (AL) is the central concept of Helson's context-effect theory. In this theory, the AL is conceived as the "neutral" stimulus that elicits psychological *zero* responses (e.g., neither soft nor loud), and it is assumed to function as the point of reference for all the other stimuli to be judged. In this FR theory the *relational* character of psychophysical ratings is expressed by the following mathematical equation:

$$R = F(S_i/AL), \tag{1}$$

where R is the rating-scale response on a given target or test stimulus S_i, and AL is the stimulus that elicits a neutral behavioral or perceptual response (zero response). Here F signifies a general mathematical log function. The AL results from the interaction of three classes of stimuli: (a) the focal stimuli (S_i) that are the center of attention, (b) the background stimuli, in Helson's experiments called the "anchor" or "contextual" stimuli (C), and (c) the residual stimuli, that is those stimuli that arise from previous experience (E), namely such stimulus representations stored in long-term memory and that produce various unspecified effects. Thus the following relation holds for the AL term:

$$AL = \bar{S}_{tot}^a C^b E^c. \tag{2}$$

The target or test stimuli enter into this relation as a *geometrical* mean, whereas exponents a, b, and c represent relative "weighting" constants that are to be empirically established $(a + b + c = 1)$. Because Helson omits the manipulation of past experience in his research paradigm, for practical purposes, Equation 1 should be rewritten as

$$R = F\left[\left(S_i/\bar{S}_{tot}^g\right)C^{(1-g)}\right], \tag{3}$$

where g and $(1 - g)$ are the new constant weighting factors adding up to 1. The multiplicative model predicts monotonic trends for context effects, that is, psychophysical contrast effects; thus each judgment is determined by the ratio of a given series stimulus to the AL.

Remarks. The basic assumption of a simple monotonic relationship between the variable context (anchor) stimulus and the quantity of the psychophysical contrast effect does not hold empirically; the real experimental trend is rather cubic ("tritonic") in nature (see the paragraphs that follow). This means that (a) at best, the AL model's main prediction holds only in the middle region of a given psychophysical dimension; (b) furthermore, AL theory rests on the ill-conceived assumption of the sensory nature of psychophysical judgments (instead, the conception of perceptual–cognitive stimulus classification seems more appropriate); and (c) Helson's postulate in which the AL represents a psychological zero point as an internal referent has not been supported. In contrast, Helson's AL approach has been fruitful in many subfields of psychological research, at least as a rule of thumb. This potential virtue of the theory has been acknowledged by many authors, and it continues to be of interest (cf. Zoeke & Sarris, 1983; see also Marks & Algom, 1998; Thomas, 1993).

Similarity-Classification Model: A Perceptual–Cognitive Theory

Whereas the AL approach is oriented on processes of sensory adaptation, my own similarity-classification (SC) model was intended as a theoretical alternative (Sarris, 1975; Zoeke & Sarris, 1983). The SC model can be characterized as a perceptual–cognitive theory of stimulus classification. In this model, the principle of perceptual classification explains both the presence and absence of context effects, as well as effects of the distance between the test-series stimuli and the prior contextual stimuli. These phenomena are attributed to the explicit categorization of "focal" (test) series stimuli in conjunction with the implicit categorization of the variable context (Fig. 4.2). At the same time, the SC model abandons the concept of a psychological zero. The point of subjective indifference (PSI) is regarded solely as a convenient psychometric value that must not be taken as the internal standard for judgment.

The quantitative SC model for individual stimuli comprehends judgment behavior as a function of the series stimulus S_i and of the contextual stimuli C, whereas the subjective similarity between C and S_i is introduced as a variable weighting

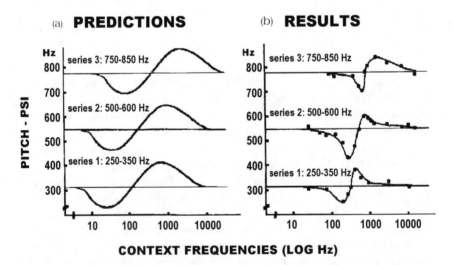

FIG. 4.2. (a) The SC model with predicted functions (see Equation 4); (b) empirical trends for a study of pitch context (anchor effectiveness), with data for three different stimulus series, 1, 2, and 3. Abscissa, physical values in log units; ordinata, PSI (data from Sarris, 1975; redrawn from Sarris, 2000).

parameter w and $(w + 1)$ for C and S_i, respectively:

$$R = S_i^{(1+w)}/C^w, \tag{4}$$

where $w_{c \geq s} = 1/(1 + C/S)$ and $w_{c \leq s} = 1/(1 + S/C)$.

Remarks. This nonadditive Equation 4 correctly predicts tritonic (cubic) trends for psychophysical contrast effects: small distances between the contextual stimulus and the series stimuli lead to strong context effects (maxima or minima of the trend curves), whereas large distances lead to a gradual disappearance of these effects (asymptotes of the tritonic curves; cf. Fig. 4.2; see also Sarris & Parducci, 1978).

Range-Frequency Model: A Perceptual–Judgmental Approach

According to Parducci's (1965, 1983) range-frequency (RF) model, psychophysical ratings are assumed to result as a compromise between two different cognitive tendencies of the subject; namely, (a) the tendency to divide the range into equal sections ("subranges"), and (b) the tendency to assign the same frequency (number) of stimuli to each category. This means that in the course of the test stimulus presentations, the judgment scale changes as a function of the range, on the one hand, and of the stimulus-frequency distribution, on the other. Thus the average judgment for a given stimulus S_i ensues according to the following prediction:

$$R_{S_i D} = m R_{iD} + (1 - m) F_{iD}, \tag{5}$$

where m is a constant weighting factor ($0 \leq m < 1$), and F_{iD} is the frequency value of S_i of the stimulus-frequency distribution D. Under the special consideration in which the subjective values R_i and F_{iD} have been calculated, the judgmental behavior R_{S_i} for a given stimulus S_i is predicted by an extension of Equation 5 as follows (Parducci, 1983, 1995):

$$R_{S_i} = m(S_i - S_{\min})/(S_{\max} - S_{\min}) + (1 - m)(r_i - 1)/(N - 1), \tag{5a}$$

where m is the aforementioned weighting factor, $S_{\min}$ is the lower-end stimulus, $S_{\max}$ is the upper-end stimulus of a given series, r is the rank of S, in the given contextual set, and N is the rank of the highest stimulus value.

Remarks. Like the SC model, Parducci's RF approach relies on the assumption of perceptual–cognitive classification in psychophysics. Contrary to the AL theory, the RF model correctly predicts higher overall mean judgments for periodically ascending series than for periodically descending series (cf. Parducci, 1983,

1995). In addition, in contrast to Helson's AL paradigm, Parducci proceeds without introducing special "background" stimuli. Typically, the series range as well as the frequency distribution of stimuli are varied systematically. The effects of variable stimulus distribution may, for example, be interpreted either in terms of learning processes or in terms of psychophysical contrast effects. If large stimuli are more frequently presented than "small" ones, then the presentation of a large stimulus will lead to underestimation and vice versa ("contrast"); however, a similar result is to be expected if the subject adapts the category scale to the frequency and range of the stimulus series increasingly better over time ("memory"; cf. Parducci, 1995).

BEHAVIORAL PSYCHOPHYSICS: CONTRASTING IDEAS AND SOME NEW DATA

Whereas the aforementioned three FR models were suggested and tested for so-called direct psychophysical methods (especially, ratings and category scales), there are other psychophysical techniques that are more appropriate for the case of nonverbal ("averbal") requirements. Consider, for example, an indirect method based on choice behavior (e.g., method of pair comparison) for the study of nonlinguistic or linguistically immature organisms (say, preverbal infants). An impressive illustration of auditory psychophysics in human infants was provided by Schneider and Trehub (1984), in which the psychometric curves were based on the amount of correct head turns as a function of varying decibel level for different test frequencies (for some brief introductions to animal and human infant psychophysics, see Atkinson & Braddick, 1999; Blake, 1999; Teller, 1983, 2000).

The comparative usage of behavioral psychophysical methods is important for the following reasons: (a) There has been a long-standing debate between Stevens and Helson and their students as to the so-called linguistic ("semantic") versus perceptual relativity of psychophysical scale-value shifts; (b) in basic research of comparative psychophysics (e.g., infant or animal psychophysics), behavioral methods are the only reasonable techniques at hand; and (c) in applied settings, for example, as for hearing-aid problems, the choice of simple behavioral assessment methods is usually indicated. Other behavioral techniques in psychophysics are, for instance, the method of adjustment or the matching-to-sample method, which also produce characteristic stimulus-response relationships. As described in detail elsewhere, in past context research there have been only a few attempts based on behavioral psychophysical techniques with humans as well as other animals (Dresp, 1999; Elfering & Sarris, 2003; Sarris & Zoeke, 1985; cf. Sarris, 1990, 1994).

A General FR Model in Behavioral Psychophysics

During the past 15 years my research group has developed and tested a comparative psychophysics paradigm for the investigation of contextual FR "shifts." This behavioral paradigm, which is based on a two-alternative two-forced-choice method (2A2FC), is described as follows.

The 2A2FC Task. Both in human and animal psychophysics, a successive discriminative task has been used; this task is illustrated by the following example. Consider two different cube sizes and discriminate them, during the training stage, according to the following rule: Push the left-hand response key when the smaller of the two cubes is presented; push the right key when the cube is the larger one. Next, during the test stage, the rule is as follows: Respond to the presentation of some additional cubes that are either smaller or larger than the training objects but use the same discrimination rule (see Fig. 4.3, which illustrates the investigated 2A2FC paradigm.)

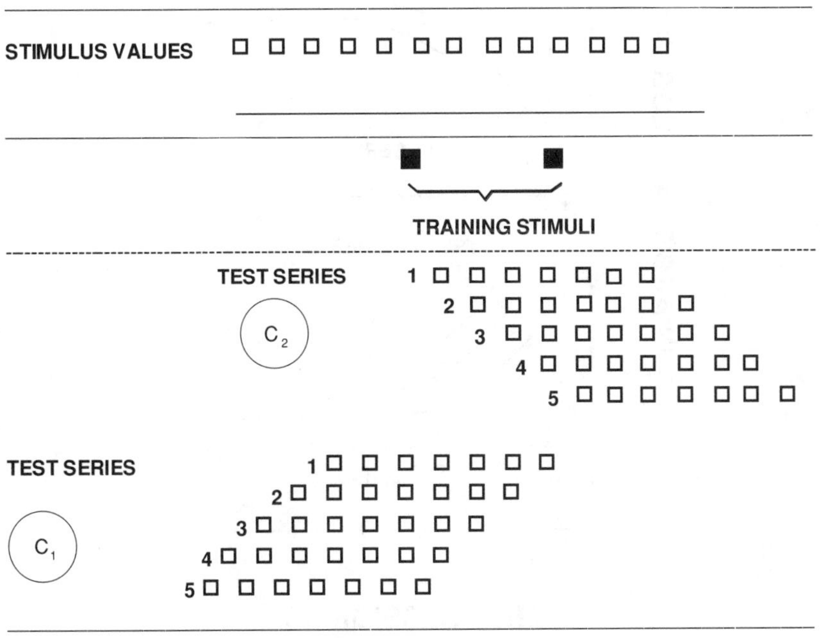

FIG. 4.3. Experimental designing for a behavioral psychophysics paradigm (2A2FC): Two training stimuli and five different sets of context test series, either in the ascending, C_2, or descending, C_1, order and consisting of seven test stimuli each (physical scale in arbitrary log units).

The PSI Process Model. Typically, the important factor "experience" (e.g., perceptual "practice") with the psychophysical stimuli used was largely ignored in earlier FR research; that is, the corresponding judgmental behavior following a given stimulus was predicted as a function of the given contextual conditions only (e.g., series vs. anchor stimuli, frequency distribution, etc.). However, when the SC model (see Equation 4) is combined with a stimulus-generalization approach, a simple process FR model is obtained that assumes that subjects change their choice behavior depending, first, on contextual conditions (e.g., relations of training stimuli to test stimuli) and, second, on the amount of practice with the test stimuli (see Fig. 4.4). According to this model, the PSI (i.e., the 50% rate of the two concurrent reactions) should shift in the direction of the respective new contextual test-series center (C_1, C_2), depending on the number of times the

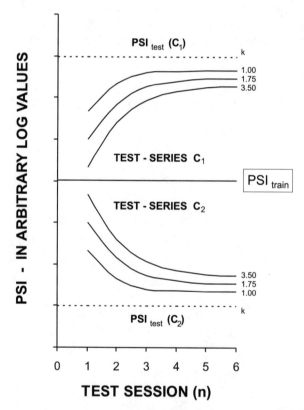

FIG. 4.4. Behavioral psychophysics paradigm: Predicted PSI functions, for different k values (1.00, 1.75, 3.50), depending on the contextual test-series conditions (C_1 or C_2) and the session practice ($n = 1, 2, 3, \ldots, 6$); see Equation 6 of the PSI process model.

series is presented. Specifically, the equation for the PSI process model reads as follows:

$$PSI_{(n)} = (k\,PSI_{train} + n\,PSI_{test})/(k + n), \tag{6}$$

where

PSI$_{(n)}$ is the PSI value for the nth test trial,
PSI$_{train}$ is the PSI value of the training stimuli,
PSI$_{test}$ is the PSI value of the test series,
k is the empirical weighting factor for the given training stimuli relative to the test series, and
n is the number of times the test series is presented.

Note that the empirical factor k, which expresses the relative weight caused by "experience" (perceptual memory), serves as an experimental weighting factor for the given training stimuli relative to the test stimuli (cf. Fig. 4.4).

Remarks. This behavioral psychophysics paradigm, together with its expanded PSI model, has been successfully tested with the use of different choice-behavior tasks (lifted weights, sizes, or durations), both with humans and animals. The general experimental designing used in these studies is illustrated in Fig. 4.3. The behavioral–dynamic approach to FR developmental psychophysics is related to the memory ("mnestic") processes involved, and it is based on an integration of discrimination training and stimulus generalization ("transposition") on the one hand and stimulus-context variations on the other. It is an extension of the classical transposition idea combined with a special quantitative application of the FR paradigm.

Human Psychophysics—Example I

According to the general experimental design outlined in Fig. 4.3, age-specific data were gathered on the basis of the behavioral–psychophysics paradigm used with human participants (size, weight, and duration judgments; see, e.g., Cangöz, 1999; Sander, 1998; Sander & Sarris, 1997). As an illustration, some empirical data stemming from size judgments made by kindergarten children are shown in Fig. 4.5.

Each data trend, established for the experimental test-context condition C1.3, C1.2, C1.1, ..., C2.2, C2.3, represents the respective shift caused by the six different asymmetry test series investigated (the C_0 trend, as a control, resulted from symmetric testing). Clearly, all these contextual shifts are in line with the overall prediction of lawful psychophysical "relativity" effects that are due to the variable test-series asymmetry (Dassler & Sarris, 1997; cf. Dassler, 2000).

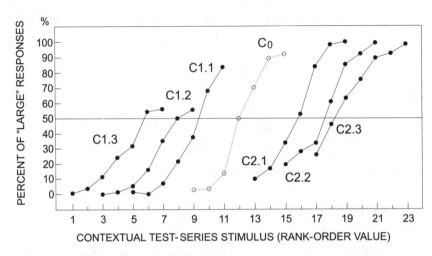

FIG. 4.5. Mean data trends for kindergarten children: Sets of experimental data trends stemming from the test phase of a behavioral psychophysics study. Each trend, C1.3, C1.2, C1.1, ..., C2.2, C2.3, represents the respective contextual shifts from the six different asymmetry test series investigated; the C_0 trend resulted from symmetric testing. Ordinata, the percent of large choice; abscissa, the test-series values used, in rank-order units (data from Dassler & Sarris, 1997; redrawn from Dassler, 2000).

Remarks. The ogival stimulus-response (S-R) curve as depicted in Fig. 4.5 for the control condition (dotted trend C_0, i.e., no test-series context) corresponds to the classic findings in human psychophysics. However, the left- and right-hand shifted curves, which are of main interest here, reflect the relative nature of psychophysical responding shown by the observation that one and the same physical stimulus is responded to as either "large" or "small," depending on the respective condition used. For example, the stimulus 12 is reacted to as neither small nor large in the control condition, but as large, for approximately 85%, under the context-test condition C.1; and so on. Note that the more extreme asymmetry conditions lead to somewhat fewer context shifts for children than for adults (cf. Cangöz, 1999; Dassler, 2000). Furthermore, for each S-R curve (Fig. 4.5), a respective PSI measure may be easily calculated. These inferred PSI values follow the theoretical trends as depicted in Fig. 4.4 for the different asymmetric test-series conditions.

Animal Psychophysics—Example II

The main argument in favor of my behavioral psychophysics approach stems from comparative investigations with subhuman subjects, namely chickens. In a series of experiments conducted with different groups of young hens, a

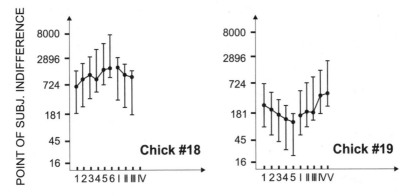

CONTEXT TEST SERIES (RANK-ORDER VALUE)

FIG. 4.6.   Mean PSI trends for two chickens, each tested under descending and ascending context conditions. The data points represent the respective contextual shifts from the different descending and ascending asymmetry context test-series investigated. (Ordinata, PSI values as derived from the respective percent-of-correct choice curves (the vertical bars illustrate the respective test-series range); abscissa, the number of the test-series conditions used, in rank-order units (redrawn from Sarris, 1990).

choice-discrimination procedure was used along with a postdiscrimination-generalization procedure that contained the variable contextual test series, in analogy with the human psychophysics investigations (see earlier text). The variable volume of different-sized cubes served as the physical continuum, both during the training and the testing phases. After reaching the learning criterion (at 95% correct choices after training), the chickens were tested with a variable context series of partly new cubes, with either increasingly larger or decreasingly smaller volumes. As shown in Fig. 4.6, marked contextual PSI effects were obtained with the variable context test-series used for two individual hens as an example.

Remarks.   Only after prolonged testing (Test Stages 2 and 3), not during the very first trials (Test Stage 1), the animals shifted their test responses gradually toward the new stimuli (asymmetric test series). In other words, this gradual S-R shifting occurred as a function of the volume size of the contextual test boxes, in line with the test-data trends found for human participants (cf. Fig. 4.5). However, the contextual shifting as observed for the chickens occurred at a much slower rate than that for the human subjects (Fig. 4.7). This finding is probably made because the *amount of training* needed to reach the respective learning criterion of 95% correct responding is much larger for the animals than for the human participants. The contextual test-series trends found may be considered as special transposition effects already observed, on a small-scale basis, with apes and chickens by

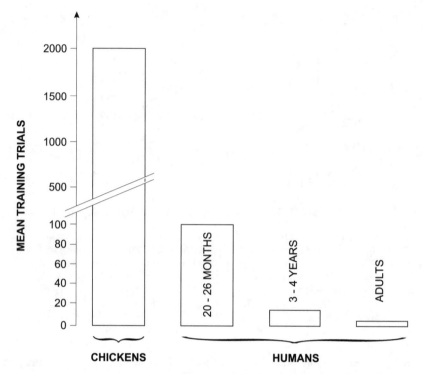

FIG. 4.7. Animal versus human training data compared (ordinata, amount of training trials needed). Left panel: Mean data for chickens ($n = 12$) trained to discriminate two cube sizes until reaching the learning criterion of 95% correct responses; right panel: mean data for humans, that is, for human infants ($n_1 = 6$), 3- to 4-year-old children ($n_2 = 6$), and adults ($n_3 = 10$), with the same stimulus-discrimination task (see text).

Köhler at the beginning of the former century (cf. Pearce, 1994; Wertheimer, 1959). Also note that the present data point to a convergence of classic FR reasoning (cf. Wertheimer, 1959) on the one hand and modern comparative psychophysical work on the other (for a modern account, see Pearce, 1994).

It is most likely that different perceptual–memory processes are involved for different animal species during the training and test phases. It is worth mentioning that the memory aspect of this comparative psychophysics paradigm has been further investigated in my laboratory by the more recent study of infant chickens (baby chicks), thus extending the previous research with young hens. The new findings illustrate the early ontogenetic development of relational psychophysical responding, thus pointing once again to the cognitive nature of the stimulus-information processing (Hauf, Arlt, & Sarris, 2000; Sarris, 1998; Sarris, Hauf, & Szczepanski, 1998).

GENERAL DISCUSSION
AND CONCLUSIONS

In past psychophysical research, relatively few investigations were directed toward the joint study of contextual effects in humans and animals, although, taking together the present evidence, it is clear that perceptual judgments as studied in psychophysics are basically relational in character. This holds true for humans as well as for animals such as birds, for example. Accordingly, the emphasis of this chapter has been mainly on two aims. The first goal was the consideration of the quantifiable evidence for FR effects in the light of a cognitive approach in psychophysics on the basis of earlier and recent comparative findings. The second goal was related to the fruitful application of a behavioral paradigm to both human and animal perception as studied in psychophysics. With respect to the latter aim, it is particularly important to note the relevance of memory processes underlying overt responses (e.g., Elfering & Sarris, 2003).

Perception and Judgment in Psychophysics

Gescheider (1988) emphasized the fact that the sensory scientist wants to obtain "unbiased" scales of sensory–perceptual magnitude, whereas the approach of the cognitive scientist is more devoted to a better understanding of the process of perceptual judgments (see the quote at the beginning of this chapter). Clearly, the contextual effects in psychophysics as described here point to the perceptual–cognitive nature of the information processing underlying human and animal (behavioral) responses. Because psychophysical responses depend, in general, on a host of contextual factors, one has to acknowledge that a given context can affect all the (sub)processes occurring at each of the following stages, namely (a) already in early sensory transduction, (b) in later perceptual encoding, (c) in higher-order cognitive recoding, and (d) at the decision–response level of processing. This general point was recently stressed by Marks and Algom (1998, pp. 148–158; also see the monograph on the same issue by Baird, 1997). Obviously, it is difficult, if not impossible, to disentangle all the different factors involved in the given human and other animal psychophysical responses.

Memory and Perceptual Processes

Whereas the animal studies described herein are concerned with only one particular type of contextual effects, namely the asymmetry of variable test series along with the respective training pair used, other investigations have also demonstrated marked test-stimulus range and frequency effects, that is, two further types of psychophysical context effects (cf. Sarris, 1990, for a summary). At the same time, it must be taken into account that the respective changes (or shifts) in the psychometric functions found for the chickens take place much slower than in humans. The main reason for this might be the amount of training animals require to learn the discrimination task (cf. Fig. 4.7); this particular memory feature is perhaps reflected by the empirical factor k of the FR (PSI) model that is expressed by Equation 6. In passing, it is worth mentioning that there has been additional research with some new corroborating findings as to the two-dimensional case in both human and animal psychophysics. The dimension of color (e.g., red vs. green cubes) was added to that of size in an attempt to understand the more complex issue of multidimensional FR effects in psychophysics (Hauf & Sarris, 1999; Sarris, Hofer, & Zoeke, 1990; cf. Hauf, 2001; Hauf et al., 2000).

Concerning the nature of the respective memory processes involved in comparative psychophysics, some characteristic features are most important. First, during the training phase, a successive two-stimulus two-response discrimination was chosen here, namely a unique task that avoids some basic confounding inherent in the classic Spence-type procedure of S+S− interactional effects caused by both perceptual–cognitive and motivational determinants (such as the well-known peak-shift effect). In contrast, my application of the successive S+S+ presentation method counterbalances motivational factors involved in both human and animal learning during the training phase. Second, during the testing stage, the relatively large number of test trials needed for chickens demonstrates the gradual, progressive establishment of the contextual effects in this species as compared with human participants. In other words, there are basic memory processes involved in this kind of psychophysical task, embedded in a postdiscrimination-stimulus generalization paradigm (for the still ongoing debate of the underlying cognitive processes during stimulus generalization in humans, see, e.g., Bouton, Nelson, & Rosas, 1999a, 1999b; Riccio, Richardson, & Ebner, 1999; cf. also Dewsbury, 1989, 1992; Sarris, 2001).

Toward a Neural-Network Model of Perceptual Learning

The assumed nonlinear dynamics of the cognitive processes in perceptual learning might be of considerable interest for the proper modeling of the contextual effects in comparative psychophysics (cf. Gregson, 1988, chap. 12). Although such a far-reaching approach might be felt to be premature, at least by some psychophysicists, nevertheless the attempt to better understand, say, the infant chick's psychophysical performing already seems worthwhile at the present stage of inquiry (see, e.g., Grossberg's adaptive resonance theory for a general account of the neural-network approach; Grossberg, 1999, 2000).

Perhaps the application and extension of the neural-network model suggested by Johnson (1997, 1999) for the baby chick and its transposition behavior might turn out to be fruitful. Johnson proposed a two-process theory for the chick's brain circuitry during the imprinting phase; this approach rests on the assumption of a basic linkage between imprinting and perceptual learning during infancy. The theory starts with the consideration of the functioning of a subcortical visual-pathway unit, on the one hand, and a forbrain (cortical) module in the so-called intermediate mediale hyperstriatum ventrale IMHV, on the other; this idea forms the basis of a connectionist model that consists of different layers with a detailed architecture designed around the neuroanatomical connectivity of the aforementioned two brain areas. Admittedly, even for the infant chick's brain and behavior, the respective neurobiological and psychological data are not complete (see, e.g., Bateson & Horn, 1994; Honey & Bolhuis, 1997; Honey, Horn, & Bateson, 1993; Honey, Horn, Bateson, & Walpole, 1995).

With his neural-network model, Johnson (1997, 1999) simulated some basic perceptual–learning phenomena associated with imprinting in the chick, especially with its sensitive or critical period. For future research it has to be seen if, and to which extent, such a model approach might be useful not only to simulate the chick's most elementary responses but also to allow some truly novel predictions, such as those concerning transposition and contextual effects during the postdis-crimination phase (of chickens and other animals). As should be evident from the preceding text, a cognitive psychophysics approach in the light of a FR paradigm has much to offer for the further development of our knowledge concerning information processing in human and animal perception, beyond the stage of sensation (Chun, 2000; Sarris 2001; Sarris & Parducci, 1984).

> ... no treatment of contemporary [animal psychophysics] is complete without at least some brief mention of cognition. The dramatic increase in interest in cognitive processes [may be viewed] as a return to the roots of comparative psychology. (Dewsbury, 1992, p. 215)

ACKNOWLEDGMENTS

Parts of my former research were funded by Deutsche Forschungsgemeinschaft (German Research Foundation) Grants Sa-143/4 and Sa-143/6. I am grateful to Birgitta Dresp, Petra Hauf, and Siegbert Reiss for reading and correcting an earlier version of the manuscript. The helpful comments by E. Schröger and two anonymous reviewers are also appreciated.

REFERENCES

Atkinson, J., & Braddick, O. (1999). Research methods in infant vision. In R. H. S. Carpenter & J. G. Robson (Eds.), *Vision research: A practical guide to laboratory methods* (pp. 161–186). Oxford, England: Oxford University Press.

Baird, J. C. (1997). *Sensation and judgment: Complementary theory of psychophysics.* Mahwah, NJ: Lawrence Erlbaum Associates.

Bateson, P., & Horn, G. (1994). Imprinting and recognition memory: A neural net model. *Animal Behaviour, 48*, 695–715.

Blake, R. (1999). The behavioral analysis of animal vision. In R. H. S. Carpenter & J. G. Robson (Eds.), *Vision research: A practical guide to laboratory methods* (pp. 137–160). Oxford, England: Oxford University Press.

Bouton, M. E., Nelson, J. B., & Rosas, J. M. (1999a). Stimulus generalization, context change, and forgetting. *Psychological Bulletin, 125*, 171–186.

Bouton, M. E., Nelson, J. B., & Rosas, J. M. (1999b). Resolution now! Reply to Riccio, Richardson, and Ebner (1999). *Psychological Bulletin, 125*, 190–192.

Cangöz, B. N. (1999). *Wahrnehmungs- und Urteilsrelativität bei Erwachsenen und Kindern: Psychophysikalische Bezugssystemeffekte in der Zeitwahrneh mung.* [Perceptual-judgmental relativity in grown-ups and children: Psychophysical frame-of-reference effects in time perception]. Frankfurt am Main, Germany: Lang.

Chun, M. M. (2000). Context as cueing of visual attention. *Trends in Cognitive Sciences, 4*, 170–178.

Dassler, K. (2000). *Altersspezifische Kontexteffekte bei der Wahrnehmung und Beurteilung von Reizgrössen.* [Age-related context effects in the perception and judgment of stimulus–sizes.] Unpublished doctoral dissertation, Universität Frankfurt.

Dassler, K., & Sarris, V. (1997, July). *Context effects in psychophysics: Size judgments with different age groups.* Paper presented at the Vth European Congress of Psychology, Dublin, Ireland.

Dewsbury, D. A. (1989). Comparative psychology, ethology, and animal behavior. *Annual Review of Psychology, 40*, 581–602.

Dewsbury, D. A. (1992). Comparative psychology and ethology: A reassessment. *American Psychologist, 47*, 208–215.

Dresp, B. (1999). Dynamic characteristics of spatial mechanisms coding contour structures. *Spatial Vision, 12*, 129–142.

Ehrenstein, W. H., & Ehrenstein, A. (1999). Psychophysical methods. In U. Windhorst & H. Johansson (Eds.), *Modern techniques in neuroscience research* (pp. 1211–1241). Berlin: Springer.

Elfering, A., & Sarris, V. (2003). Time-dependence of context effects in memory psychophysics: Evidence from a visual delayed-matching task. Manuscript in preparation.

Farell, B., & Pelli, D. G. (1999). Psychophysical methods, or how to measure a threshold, and why. In R. H. S. Carpenter & J. G. Robson (Eds.), *Vision research: A practical guide to laboratory methods* (pp. 129–136). Oxford, England: Oxford University Press.

Garner, W. R. (1954). Context effects and the validity of loudness scales. *Journal of Experimental Psychology, 48*, 218–224.

Gescheider, G. A. (1988). Psychophysical scaling. *Annual Review of Psychology, 39*, 169–200.

Gregson, R. A. M. (1988). *Nonlinear psychophysical dynamics.* Hillsdale, NJ: Lawrence Erlbaum Associates.

Grossberg, S. (1999). How does the cerebral cortex work? Learning, attention, and grouping by the laminar circuits of visual cortex. *Spatial Vision, 12*, 163–187.

Grossberg, S. (2000). The complementary brain: Unifying brain dynamics and modularity. *Trends in Cognitive Sciences, 4*, 233–246.

Hauf, P. (2001). Untersuchungen zum altersspezifischen mehrdimensionalen perzeptiv-kognitiven Urteilsverhalten in der Psychophysik. [Experiments on age-related multidimensional perceptual–cognitive behavior in psychophysics.] In F. Wilkening, O. Güntürkün, T. Rammsayer, V. Sarris, & F. Strack (Eds.), *Psychologia Universalis, Neue Reihe* (Bd. 26). Lengerich, Berlin: Pabst.

Hauf, P., Arlt, M., & Sarris, V. (2000, August–September). *Developmental visual psychophysics: New size-perception data from baby chicks.* Poster presented at the 16th Annual Meeting of the International Society for Psychophysics, Strasbourg, France (Abstract).

Hauf, P., & Sarris, V. (1999, November). *Age-related development of multidimensional judgment strategies in psychophysics: Size, color and brightness dimensions combined.* Poster presented at the 40th Annual Meeting of the Psychonomic Society, Los Angeles, CA (Abstract).

Helson, H. (1947). Adaptation-level as frame of reference for prediction of psychophysical data. *American Journal of Psychology, 60*, 1–29.

Helson, H. (1964). *Adaptation-level theory*. New York: Harper & Row.

Honey, R. C., & Bolhuis, J. J. (1997). Imprinting, conditioning, and within-event learning. *Quarterly Journal of Experimental Psychology, 50B*, 97–110.

Honey, R. C., Horn, G., & Bateson, P. (1993). Perceptual learning during filial imprinting: Evidence from transfer of training studies. *Quarterly Journal of Experimental Psychology, 46B*, 253–269.

Honey, R. C., Horn, G., Bateson, P., & Walpole, M. (1995). Functionally distinct memories for imprinting stimuli: Behavioral and neural dissociations. *Behavioral Neuroscience, 109*, 689–698.

Johnson, M. H. (1997). *Developmental cognitive neuroscience: An introduction*. Oxford, England: Blackwell.

Johnson, M. H. (1999). Developmental cognitive neuroscience. In M. Bennett (Ed.), *Developmental psychology: Achievements and prospects* (pp. 147–164). London: Psychology Press.

Laming, D. (1986). Psychophysics. In R. L. Gregory (Ed.), *The Oxford companion to the mind* (pp. 655–659). Oxford, England: Oxford University Press.

Laming, D. (1997). *The measurement of sensation*. Oxford, England: Oxford University Press.

Lockhead, G. R. (1992). Psychophysical scaling: Judgments of attributes or objects? *Behavioral and Brain Sciences, 15*, 543–601.

Marks, L. E. (1974). *Sensory psychophysics: The new psychophysics*. New York: Academic Press.

Marks, L. E. (1991). The dynamics of ratio scaling. In S. J. Bolonowski & G. A. Gescheider (Ed.), *Ratio scaling of psychological magnitude* (pp. 27–42). Hillsdale, NJ: Lawrence Erlbaum Associates.

Marks, L. E. (1992). The contingency of perceptual processing: Context modifies equal-loudness relations. *Psychological Science, 3*, 285–291.

Marks, L. E., & Algom, D. (1998). Psychophysical scaling. In M. H. Birnbaum (Ed.), *Handbook of perception and cognition: Measurement, judgment, and decision making* (2nd ed., pp. 81–178). New York: Academic Press.

Parducci, A. (1965). Category judgment: A range-frequency model. *Psychological Review, 72*, 407–418.

Parducci, A. (1983). Category ratings and the relational character of judgment. In H.-G. Geissler, H. F. J. M. Buffart, E. L. J. Leeuwenberg, & V. Sarris (Eds.), *Modern issues in perception* (pp. 262–282). Berlin: Deutscher Verlag der Wissenschaften.

Parducci, A. (1995). *Happiness, pleasure, and judgment: The contextual theory and its applications*. Hillsdale, NJ: Lawrence Erlbaum Associates.

Pearce, J. M. (1994). Discrimination and categorization. In N. J. Mackintosh (Ed.), *Animal learning and cognition: Handbook of perception and cognition* (pp. 109–134). New York: Academic Press.

Riccio, D. C., Richardson, R., & Ebner, D. L. (1999). Comment on Bouton, Nelson, and Rosas (1999). *Psychological Bulletin, 125*, 187–189.

Sander, K. (1998). Das "Two-Stimulus Two-Choice"-Paradigma für die Psychophysik: Range-Frequency-Modell und Adaptationsniveau-Theorie im Vergleich. [The two-stimulus two-choice paradigm in psychophysics: Range-frequency model and adaptation-level theory compared.] (Edition Wissenschaft, Reihe Psychologie, Bd. 57). Marburg, Germany: Tectum.

Sander, K., & Sarris, V. (1997). Das "Two-Stimulus Two-Choice"-Paradigma für die Psychophysik: Range-Frequency-Modell und Adaptation-Level-Theorie im Vergleich. [The two-stimulus two-choice paradigm in psychophysics: Range-frequency model and adaptation-level theory compared.] *Zeitschrift für Experimentelle Psychologie, 44*, 431–446.

Sarris, V. (1975). *Wahrnehmung und Urteil: Bezugssystemeffekte in der Psychophysik* [Perception and judgment: Frame-of-Reference Effects in Psychophysics.] (2nd ed.) Göttingen, Germany: Hogrefe.

Sarris, V. (1976). Effects of stimulus range and anchor value on psychophysical judgment. In H.-G. Geissler & Y. M. Zabrodin (Eds.), *Advances in psychophysics* (pp. 253–268). Berlin: Deutscher Verlag der Wissenschaften.

Sarris, V. (1990). Contextual effects in animal psychophysics: A comparative analysis of the chicken's perceptual relativity. *European Bulletin of Cognitive Psychology, 10*, 475–489.

Sarris, V. (1994). Contextual effects in animal psychophysics: Comparative perception. *Behavioral and Brain Sciences, 17*, 763–764.

Sarris, V. (1998). Frame-of-reference effects in psychophysics: New experimental findings with baby chicks. *Psychologia (Greece), 5*, 95–102.

Sarris, V. (2000). Perception and judgment in psychophysics: An introduction into the frame-of-reference theories. In A. Schick, M. Meis, & C. Reckhardt (Eds.), *Contributions to psychological acoustics* (pp. 39–62). Oldenburg, Germany: BIS.

Sarris, V. (2001). Frame-of-reference conceptions and context effects in psychophysics. In E. Sommerfeld, R. Kompass, & T. Lachmann (Eds.), *Fechner Day 2001. Proceedings of the International Society for Psychophysics* (pp. 155–160). Lengerich, Berlin: Pabst.

Sarris, V., Hauf, P., & Szczepanski, M. (1998, August). *The visual psychophysics of baby chicks: New context-dependent color and size data.* Poster presented at the 21st European Conference on Visual Perception, Oxford.

Sarris, V., Hofer, G., & Zoeke, B. (1990). The chicken's visual psychophysics: Two-dimensional effects. In F. Müller (Ed.), *Proceedings of the 6th Annual Meeting of the International Society for Psychophysics* (pp. 222–227). Würzburg, Germany: University Press.

Sarris, V., & Parducci, A. (1978). Multiple anchoring of category rating scales. *Perception and Psychophysics, 24*, 35–39.

Sarris, V., & Parducci, A. (Organizers). (1984, August). *Psychophysics beyond sensation.* Invited symposium at the XXIIIrd International Congress of Psychology, Acapulco, Mexico.

Sarris, V., & Zoeke, B. (1985). Tests of a quantitative frame-of-reference model: Practice effects in psychophysical judgments with different age-groups. In G. d'Ydewalle (Ed.), *Cognition, information processing, and motivation* (pp. 71–78). Amsterdam: North-Holland.

Schneider, B. A., & Trehub, S. E. (1985). Infant auditory psychophysics: An overview. In G. Gottlieb & N. A. Krasnegor (Eds.), *Measurement of audition and vision in the first year of postnatal life* (pp. 127–155). Norwood, NJ: Ablex.

Stevens, S. S. (1975). *Psychophysics: Introduction to its perceptual, neural, and social prospects.* New York: Wiley.

Teller, D. Y. (1983). Measurement of visual acuity in human and monkey infants: The interface between laboratory and clinic. *Behavioural and Brain Research, 10*, 15–23.

Teller, D. Y. (2000). Visual development: Psychophysics, neural substrates, and causal stories. In M. S. Gazzaniga (Ed.), *The new cognitive neurosciences* (2nd ed., pp. 73–81). Cambridge, MA: MIT Press.

Thomas, D. R. (1993). A model for adaptation-level effects on stimulus generalization. *Psychological Review, 100*, 658–673.

Weintraub, D. J. (1975). Perception. *Annual Review of Psychology, 26*, 263–269.

Wertheimer, M. (1959). On discrimination experiments: I. Two logical structures. *Psychological Review, 66*, 252–266.

Zoeke, B., & Sarris, V. (1983). A comparison of "frame of reference" paradigms in human and animal psychophysics. In H.-G. Geissler, H. F. J. M. Buffart, E. L. J. Leeuwenberg, & V. Sarris (Eds.), *Modern issues in perception* (pp. 283–317). Amsterdam: North-Holland.

5

Two Kinds of Global Perceptual Separability and Curvature

James T. Townsend
Indiana University, Bloomington

Jesse Spencer-Smith
University of Illinois, Urbana-Champaign

It is easy to appreciate that by moving the touching finger along objects, the sequence in which the impressions of the object are presented becomes known; that this sequence shows itself to be independent of whether one feels with this or with that finger; that, furthermore, it is not a single-channeled, determined series, whose elements one must again and again traverse forward or backward in the same order so as to go from one to another – thus is no linear series, but rather a surface-like coexistence, or in Riemann's terminology, a manifold of the second order.
—Helmholtz (1878/1995, p. 351)

In his 1878 lecture, "The Facts on Perception," Hermann von Helmholtz illustrates a mapping (i.e., function) between a physical object and its psychological representation. In describing the psychological representation arising from the experience of touching an object, Helmholtz calls on the mathematics of Bernhard Riemann. In this chapter, we appeal to the same framework—mapping from a stimulus space to a Riemannian manifold—to expand on the notion of perceptual separability (PS). We begin with a brief introduction of the mathematical milieu and place existing work on PS within this context. Next, we define new types of separability within the framework. We then examine some of the relationships among PS, the mapping between stimulus and psychological space, and the properties of the psychological manifold. Intuitively it might seem that an absence of perceptual distinctiveness (i.e., one or more kinds of separability) might be related to the geometric concept of curvature. However, we show in the penultimate section that the best known type of curvature is logically unrelated to one of our major varieties of separability. Although we try to minimize technicality, the reader should be able to ship these without harm to comprehension of our main results.

Roughly, a Riemannian manifold is a space that is locally Euclidean. Curves (e.g., on a plane or in a space) are manifolds of the first order, or one dimensional, whereas surfaces (e.g., the surface of a sphere, or a "wavy carpet" in space) are two dimensional. Manifolds can be of any dimension; the dimensionality relates to the number of parameters needed to specify a point (Lee, 2000). We have recently developed infinite-dimensional spaces that could be needed for research areas such as face perception (Townsend, Solomon, & Spencer-Smith, 2001).

A Riemannian manifold is a manifold on which a Riemannian metric, or way of measuring distance, is defined. The Euclidean plane is a particular type of two-dimensional Riemannian manifold that is flat, or, in other words, has a curvature of zero. However, globally non-Euclidean spaces that are flat exist; a cylinder (i.e., a rolled-up section of the Euclidean plane) is an example. Curvature is a local quantity, defined at each point of the manifold, that describes how much the manifold bends in the neighborhood of the point. The surface of a sphere is a Riemannian manifold with constant positive curvature, whereas the wavy carpet might have different measures of curvature at different points. The properties of non-Euclidean manifolds can vary greatly from those of Euclidean manifolds. On a Euclidean plane, the shortest path between two points is a line. On a sphere, the shortest path between two points is an arc of the great circle on which the two points lie. The study of these spaces is the subject of the branch of mathematics known as differential geometry.

Non-Euclidean mathematics played a significant role in the very beginning of psychology in the work of Helmholtz (1878/1995). Throughout his career, in fact, Helmholtz challenged the view that Euclidean geometry was the natural, privileged geometry, as argued by the followers of Kant. It is perhaps ironic that a substantial portion of the work in psychology since that time has used Euclidean (or similarly flat "power-metric") spaces. Except for isolated regions, such as theories of visual space (e.g., Indow, 1967; Pizlo, 1994), light and color perception (D'Zmura & Iverson, 1993; Suppes, Krantz, Luce, & Tversky, 1989), and occasional papers on perceptual scaling in nontraditional spaces (e.g., Cox & Cox, 1991; Drösler, 1979; Hoffman, 1968; Hoffman & Dodwell, 1985; Indow, 1982; Lindman & Caelli, 1978; Shepard & Carroll, 1966), there has been little penetration of more general metrics into most perceptual and cognitive domains. It is arguable that even the latter have not gained the attention they deserve. To be sure, applied (Carroll & Chang, 1970; Kruskal, 1964; Shepard, 1962) and foundational (e.g., Beals, Krantz, & Tversky, 1968; Suppes et al., 1989) multidimensional scalings have played enormous roles in modern cognitive psychology and cognate areas, with the purview including non-Euclidean spaces. However, we contend that not only should this work now be more integrated into process kinds of models (e.g., as in Ashby, 1992, 2000; Marley, 1992; Nosofsky, 1986), but there is still an immense and largely untouched set of mathematical tools that can greatly aid psychology in 21st-century multidimensional scaling (Townsend & Thomas, 1993).

Nevertheless, there are rays of light on the horizon. New and innovative work in psychophysical scaling (Dzhafarov & Colonius, 1999; Levin, 2000) and face or object perception (Hoffman, 1998; Townsend et al., 2001) offer positive examples. An emerging case in point is the recent innovative activity in scaling semantic spaces, primarily by principal-components analysis (Landauer & Dumais, 1997). Although undoubtedly much can be learned from this analysis, it would seem very surprising indeed if a linear, Euclidean space turned out to be all that was required for such a complex entity as semantic space.

In the following discussion, we denote the physical dimensions of a stimulus (e.g., frequency and amplitude of a sound wave) as X and Y. We label the corresponding psychological dimensions (e.g., the perceived pitch and loudness of a sound wave) as x and y (Fig. 5.1). X is the physical dimension most closely associated with x and Y with y (e.g., as is frequency with pitch and amplitude with loudness). We refer to X and Y as the domain and to x and y as the range of the mapping from the physical to the psychological spaces.

Our basic assumption is that the psychological manifold M, forming, for example, the space of percepts, is formed by smooth (e.g., no cusps or discontinuities) mappings of neighborhoods of $X \times Y$ into n-dimensional subsets of Euclidean space $\Re^n$, the latter being the cross product of n lines of real numbers. Because the resultant subset of points in $\Re^n$ may possess a non-Euclidean metric, we really need the designation M as an entity separate from subsets of $\Re^n$.

Furthermore, it is inherent in the very fundamentals of psychophysics that there exist numerical or at least mathematical correspondents to the psychological

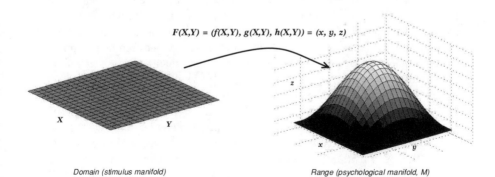

$F(X,Y) = (f(X,Y), g(X,Y), h(X,Y)) = (x, y, z)$

Domain (stimulus manifold)   Range (psychological manifold, M)

FIG. 5.1.   The function F maps a point (X, Y) on the stimulus manifold (domain) to a point (x, y, z) on the psychological manifold, M (range).

dimensions. Hence we can assume not only some type of coordinate system, but one that contains our psychological dimensions as two of the coordinates.

Note that we are in no way dependent on linear coordinates. In any case, no important limitations in what we have to offer now seem to be incurred by assuming that neighborhoods of $X \times Y$ are mapped into $\Re^3$; certainly the notation will be simplified. Of course, in many instances, it may be possible to form a representation of neighborhoods or all of $X \times Y$ mapped into $\Re^2$, instead of $\Re^3$, in general attended by a non-Euclidean metric. One consequence is that, although two-dimensional manifolds exist that cannot be placed in $\Re^3$, ours always can be, as will be subsequently discussed.

Additionally, it is often the case that surfaces or other manifolds are formed from mapping the same subsets of Euclidean space into the pertinent manifold M, where each component map is called a patch. All the patches are then collected into a mathematical object known as an atlas. (The actual facts are a little more complicated, but this description is sufficient for our exposition.) The fact that the same subset of Euclidean points, representing a physical stimulus, can map to distinct percepts would seem to imply a one-to-many function; that is, one stimulus can result in two or more percepts. A one-to-many function might indeed be useful for certain kinds of illusions and bistable perceptual figures (e.g., the face-vase figure), but it does not represent the typical situation. Hence we can assume a single one-to-one (one stimulus $\to$ one percept) and onto (all possible percepts are contained in the range of the function) map from $X \times Y$ to M. It follows that the psychological coordinates together "cover" M in the appropriate sense, and we are carried into elementary surface theory. Another sidelight is that, although much modern mathematical theory resides in placing the domain in M and forming maps to subsets of Euclidean space as the range (e.g., Boothby, 1986), the opposite and somewhat older tradition of mapping from $\Re^2$ to M is more natural here.

All of the following definitions and propositions are stated in a local (point-to-point) manner, but we always assume that they hold for all points in the map and refrain from repeating this assumption. Also, we note that, although differentiability conditions are important for much of the work in differential geometry (although there exist approaches to geometries other than Euclidean that do not require differentiability; see, e.g., Busemann, 1955), they must go unstated here (see any text on differential geometry; e.g., Boothby, 1986).

Let D be a rectangular domain in $\Re^2$, that is, $D = \{(X, Y)|a < X < b, c < Y < d\}$, where we shall assume that the limits may be infinite. We suppose then that our map consists of $F: D \to \Re^3$, such that $F(X, Y) = (f(X, Y), g(X, Y), h(X, Y)) = (x, y, z)$ (see Fig. 5.1). By definition, we make x and y the psychological coordinates of interest. F is assumed to be regular (O'Neill, 1997; this amounts to the derivative of F being one-to-one Boothby, 1986). Together with our point-to-point restriction, F is an embedding, that is, a one-to-one and onto (its range), and differentiable forward and backward.

The coordinate z (and potentially more coordinates) might in many cases be psychologically meaningful as when such psychological attributes as pitch, loudness and volume (or timbre, etc.) all are functions of the same major physical dimensions. However, in other cases, such coordinates might simply represent the varied dimensional (and in some cases curved) nature of the neural the cognitive, or both, space.

The simple upshot of the preceding discussion is that the perceptual manifold or surface in our special circumstances can be endowed with a set of coordinates representing the two psychological dimensions. It is within this framework that we approach our topic, which is a type of perceptual independence of psychological dimensions: How the psychological coordinates may be defined on the manifold will be of prime significance for these issues.

The major pioneering quantitative theoretical spadework on perceptual independence was accomplished by Shepard (e.g., Shepard, 1964) and Garner (e.g., Garner, 1974). More recently, Ashby and Townsend (1986) offered a general treatment of perceptual independence embedded in a multidimensional extension of signal detection theory, which we called general recognition theory (GRT). One thrust of this work was to establish a number of distinct notions of perceptual independence (Ashby & Townsend, 1986; Kadlec & Townsend, 1992; Maddox, 1992; Thomas, 1995) of two or more perceptual dimensions.

BASIC TYPES OF MANIFOLD-BASED SEPARABILITY AND RELATIONSHIPS

One major variety of perceptual independence is referred to as PS. Garner (e.g., 1974) proposed definitions of separability based on what kind of experimental results occurred in several experimental paradigms (traditionally, such definitions are known as operational definitions). Such definitions can be powerful tools in helping to uncover important qualitative aspects of phenomena like separability. Nonetheless, as Ashby and Townsend (1986) pointed out, operational definitions possess some deficits. For instance, when a theoretical underpinning is given to such notions as independence and separability, the several operational definitions may be unrelated or even contradictory. The definition of PS offered by Ashby and Townsend (1986) within GRT turns out, in fact, to be equivalent to the definition of perceptual independence by Garner, and Morton (1969). Notions of PS in GRT are defined within the context of probability theory.

In the present investigation, it is assumed that the stimuli are sufficiently far apart that probabilities play no role, so that the perceptual effects may be considered deterministic. Thus the behavior departs the arena of discriminability, or local psychophysics, and enters the arena of multidimensional psychophysical scaling, or global psychophysics. The most direct extension of the Ashby and Townsend (1986) PS notion is then to demand that, for its satisfaction, the perceptual scale of dimension X be unaffected by the manipulation of dimension Y. We thus begin the investigation of PS within the milieu of Riemannian manifolds. The basic approach can be extended to even more general spaces. Although we disregard probabilities here, the concepts immediately apply to the means of perceptual probability distributions.

An important distinction has become apparent in our initial examinations of more general spaces that might have been overlooked by other investigators in their concentration on Euclidean and power metric spaces. This distinction is between (a) experimental variations in X that cause changes in the psychological y or experimental variations in Y that cause changes in x, and (b) a relation between x and y after the physical-to-psychological mapping has already occurred. No theory of which we are aware exploits this distinction. Our approach initiates such explorations. We term notion (a) the *domain-range separability*. Domain range denotes the dependence on relations of the map connecting the physical with the psychological manifolds.

Domain-range separability has implicitly dominated theoretical efforts in the past. For instance, the Garner and Morton (1969) information-theory-based approach and the Ashby and Townsend (1986) GRT are of this type. Within the present deterministic account, domain-range separability can be captured by the very form of the mapping expressions: $x = f(X, Y)$, and $y = g(X, Y)$. If f is solely a function of X and g is solely a function of Y, domain-range separability holds. If f is a nondegenerate function of Y or g of X then perceptual nonseparability occurs.

On the other hand, questions about relationship (b) of x and y can be posed irrespective of the original map. We call this type of question simply *range alone*, as it takes place only within the range or psychological space.

DEFINITIONS OF GLOBAL PERCEPTUAL SEPARABILITY

We are now in a position to put forth our first definitions of global PS:

Definition 1. F is said to be utterly inseparable if $x = f(X, Y)$ and $y = f(X, Y)$.

Definition 2. F is said to be scalably inseparable if $x = f(X, Y)$ and $y = g[f(X, Y)]$.

Basically, Definition 2 means that either of the psychological dimensions is simply a rescaling of the other. For instance, suppose that $x = aX + bY$ and $y = \exp(x) = \exp(aX + bY)$. Then there is a perfect, if nonlinear, dependence between x and y even though they are not identical functions of X and Y. Now, one can imagine an alien being where even Definition 1 is satisfied and yet there are two different "sensations" simply because the signal terminates in distinct brain loci; an extreme case of "place theory." However, this possibility perhaps may be avoided presently, and we always assume that F satisfies neither Definition 1 nor Definition 2. Obviously, one can think of more types of inseparability (e.g., see Townsend & Thomas, 1993), but Definitions 1 and 2 suffice for our introductory examination. We are occupied with more stringent definitions that emphasize types of occurrence of separability, rather than inseparability.

Next, we begin to deal with an extension of the Ashby and Townsend (1986) and Garner and Morton (1969) separability notion.

Definition 3. F is weakly domain-range PS if $x = f(X)$ and $x = g(Y)$, but $h(X, Y)$ is a nontrivial function of both X and Y (see Fig. 5.2).

Definition 3 means that the psychological dimensions are functions of only their respective physical counterparts, but the other coordinate varies as a function of both X and Y. Definition 4 demands a stronger condition.

Definition 4. F is strongly domain-range PS if Definition 1 holds and also $h(X, Y) = h(X)$ or $h(Y)$, but not both (see Fig. 5.3).

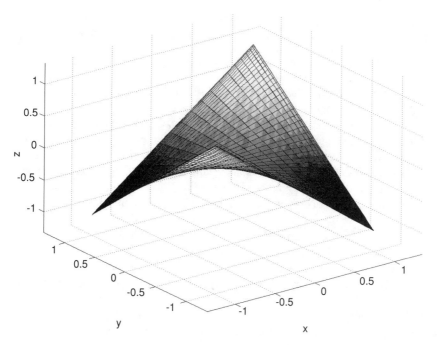

FIG. 5.2. The function $F(X, Y) = (\cos X, \sin Y, \sin Y \cos X)$ is weakly domain-range PS.

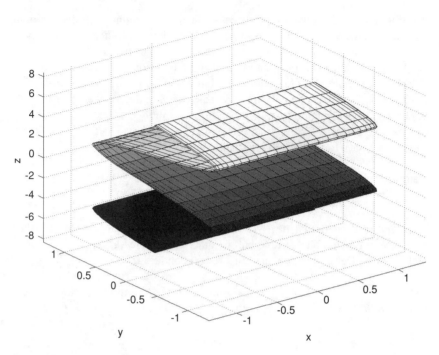

FIG. 5.3. The function $F(X, Y) = (\cos X, \sin Y, Y)$ is strongly domain-range PS.

Observe that a special case of Definition 4 would result if h were a constant function. Note also that utter inseparability and scalable inseparability both, naturally enough, violate both kinds of domain-range separability.

The idea of domain-range separability then seems straightforward enough. What about range-alone separability? What should it mean when range-alone separability does or does not hold? An instantiation of this notion is not so transparent, but one possibility is that range-alone separability would require local orthogonality. That is, the tangent vectors of the psychological coordinates at any point in the psychological space might be orthogonal (and thus noninteracting in a local sense).

The concept of orthogonality requires an inner product (a generalization of the familiar Euclidean dot product in Euclidean vector spaces), which will be garnered from the attendant Riemannian metric, as is subsequently discussed. We work primarily with the metric induced by the map itself and the Euclidean inner product taken on the tangent vectors on the surface. The induced inner product, given psychophysical function F, is given by $\langle \partial F / \partial X, \partial F / \partial Y \rangle$. Under the condition of orthogonality, it is required that $\langle \partial F / \partial X, \partial F / \partial Y \rangle = 0$, that is, the inner product of the tangent vectors to the image of F at any point in that image is 0. Local orthogonality and the induced Riemannian metric will be merged in what follows.

Definition 5.   The psychological dimensions x and y are locally orthogonal if and only if their tangent vectors at any point of M are orthogonal with regard to the appropriate metric. If this holds, range-alone local orthogonal PS is said to occur.

We now move back to a type of domain-range PS because the form of the map is intimately involved. Namely, consider a parameterization in which the psychological x dimension corresponds to varying X while holding Y constant and the y dimension corresponds to varying Y while holding X constant. An alternative way of thinking about matters here is that a constant-Y curve, varying X, is identified with a specific psychological y; similarly, a constant-X curve, varying Y, is identified with a psychological x.

Definition 6. F is said to be parameterization PS if the X and Y parameter curves (i.e., holding one constant while varying the other) correspond to the x and y perceptual dimensions, respectively. The term "correspond" is meant in the sense that when X is varied only x changes and not y and vice versa when Y is varied.

Observe that the essence of Definition 6 is that varying X for a fixed Y produces a trajectory in M that is unitarily associated with a particular value of y and similarly with regard to the psychological value x.

Note that, in Definition 6, x and y can each potentially be a function of both X and Y, negating weak and strong domain-range PSs. Note also that this extension of the idea that $x = f(X, Y)$ and $y = g(X, Y)$ nicely corresponds to a generalized notion of equiloudness contours (curves representing the same value of loudness), even though both sensory dimensions may be functions of both physical dimensions). Also, note that although the x parameter, say, is interpretable in some sense as a psychological dimension, by itself it cannot do the entire job because the actual psychological space is a two-dimensional manifold, including, for instance, the influence of the function h (e.g., in the case of sound, as in volume, timbre). As we also subsequently see, curvature requires taking into account the manifold itself, or at least a reparameterization of $X \times Y$ (for example) that involves a (typically) non-Euclidean metric.

On the other hand, it could be that $x = f(X)$ and $y = g(Y)$, that is, the psychological dimensions are exactly the original parameterizations. A special trivial case would be that $f(X) = aX = X = u$ and $g(Y) = bY = Y = v$, where a and b are positive constants, that is, the psychological dimensions are proportional to the physical dimensions themselves. This case seems to be the quintessence of domain-range PS. Nevertheless, even in such simple cases, the third dimension $z = h(X, Y)$, can play a nontrivial role, as just noted.

The sphere or parts thereof can provide further useful examples (see Fig. 5.4). Suppose that X and Y such that $\sqrt{X^2 + Y^2} < 1$ are mapped into the upper hemisphere by $F(X, Y) = (X, Y, \sqrt{1 - X^2 - Y^2})$. Then weak domain-range PS

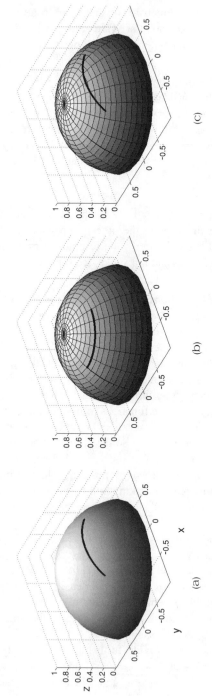

FIG. 5.4. (a) The unit disk in the plane is mapped to the upper hemisphere by $F(X, Y) = (X, Y, \sqrt{1 - X^2 - Y^2})$, which is weakly domain-range PS. The curve represents a mapping of $X: -0.5 < X < 0.5$, $Y = -0.5$. (b) A rectangular area of the plane representing angles is mapped to the upper hemisphere by $F(X, Y) = (\sin X \cos Y, \sin X \sin Y, \cos X)$. The curve represents $X = 0.2\pi$, $Y: -\pi < Y < -0.5\pi$. The light lines represent colatitude and longitude. (c) The disk is mapped to the upper hemisphere, as in (a). The light lines represent the psychological dimensions corresponding to colatitude and longitude.

obtains. This example is, of course, a member of the kind of map known as Monge patches, requiring the first two coordinates of the image to be identical to X and Y.

Next suppose that instead of the preceding mapping, X and Y are angles with X lying in the open interval between 0 and π and Y strictly between 0 and 2π, associated with $F(X, Y) = (\sin X \cos Y, \sin X \sin Y, \cos X)$. This forms the well-known parameterization in which X is the colatitude (complement of the latitude) and Y is the longitude. Suppose that the psychological dimension x can be identified with colatitude and y with the longitude. Then the X parameter curves (i.e., varying X with Y constant) become the equi-y (again, analogous to equiloudness) contours—the x percept is "independent" of the y percept, the latter corresponding to Y parameter curves on the sphere.

Now suppose that X and Y are again the usual coordinates of $\Re^2$ (rather than angles) with $\sqrt{X^2 + Y^2} < 1$ and $F(X, Y) = (X, Y, \sqrt{1 - X^2 - Y^2})$ as before. Then, even if x and y are the psychological dimensions on the sphere and are equivalent to the colatitude and longitude respectively, domain-range PS does not hold: In this case, x and y are not themselves the respective images of X and Y.

The definitions for perceptual separability are summarized in Table 5.1. Next we consider the mutual implications of the varieties of manifold separability (see Fig. 5.5): To start with, weak domain-range PS (Definition 3) does *not* imply range-alone local orthogonal PS (Definition 5), as can be seen by the simple map $F(X, Y) = (X, Y, X + Y)$, with $x = X$ and $y = Y$. Note that the tangents are simply the same as the coordinate curves because of linearity and that these coordinates are not perpendicular to each other. Strong domain-range PS (Definition 4) *does* imply range-alone orthogonal PS (Definition 5) because the z coordinate does not depend on both X and Y. We can prove this latter proposition by noting that the inner product of the partial derivatives of F with respect to X and Y of any map

TABLE 5.1

Summary of Definitions for PS

Definition Number	Definition Summary
1	F is said to be utterly inseparable if $x = f(X, Y)$ and $y = f(X, Y)$ also.
2	F is said to be scalably inseparable if $x = f(X, Y)$ and $y = g[f(X, Y)]$.
3	F is weakly domain-range PS if $x = f(X)$ and $x = g(Y)$, but $h(X, Y)$ is a nontrivial function of both X and Y.
4	F is strongly domain-range PS if Definition 1 holds and, also, $h(X, Y) = h(X)$ or $h(Y)$ but not both.
5	The psychological dimensions x and y are locally orthogonal if and only if their tangent vectors at any point of M are orthogonal with regard to the appropriate metric. If this holds, range-alone local orthogonal PS will be said to occur.
6	F is said to be parameterization PS if the X and Y parameter curves (i.e., holding one constant while varying the other) correspond to the x and y perceptual dimensions, respectively.

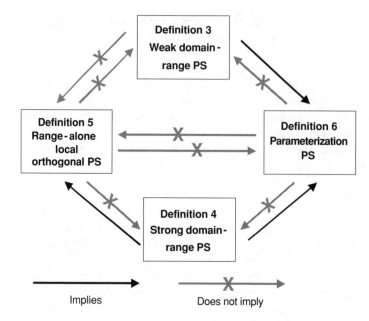

FIG. 5.5.   The logical relationships among Definitions 3, 4, 5, and 6 are shown in this implication graph.

of the form $f(X, Y) = [f(X), g(Y), h(X)]$, say, is identically 0. Both types of domain-range PS imply parameterization PS. This statement is apparent from the fact that any map of the form $F(X, Y) = [f(X), g(Y), h(X, Y)]$ has the property that varying X, for any fixed Y, produces a single trajectory in M associated with a unique value of X and vice versa for Y. From a philosophical point of view, it is intriguing that, in the case of domain-range PS, there is an ambiguity as to whether the percept is equal to $f(X)$ or is simply identified with the constant X curve.

Parameterization PS implies *none* of the other types of PS. First, it is obvious that a parameterization need not produce local orthogonality. For instance, just as we did previously, we could again define $f(X, Y) = (X, Y, X + Y)$ as producing x as associated with varying X and leaving Y constant and vice versa for y; clearly the pertinent inner product is not 0. Second, any map can be interpreted (hypothetically) as producing x and y through varying X and Y, respectively, and obviously need not satisfy weak or strong domain-range PS. (This broad argument works for local orthogonality as well.)

Moreover, local orthogonal PS implies *neither* kind of domain-range PS, nor does it imply parameterization PS. Obviously orthogonality of the tangents to x and y can occur even though they are not functions of the alternative Y or X physical variables. It is equally apparent that arbitrary x and y coordinates in M can be orthogonal without either being associated with the X and Y parameter curves, respectively. On the other hand, various maps can be adduced that satisfy various combinations of PS types.

As of now, there are precious few experimental examples for which we might begin to apply these concepts. Despite over a century of interest in non-Euclidean spaces and several recent decades of application of multidimensional scaling procedures, there simply are not many regions where multivariate psychological coordinates are tightly bound to physical variables, particularly in conjunction with an agreed-on spatial description. We discuss this somewhat surprising (given the long history) challenge in the discussion and conclusion section. For now, we content ourselves with mentioning a couple of possible psychophysical examples.

First, consider the tried and true example of loudness and pitch as functions of stimulus intensity and frequency. As far as we know, there have been no attempts to place the psychological space in any type of manifold, other than one with orthogonal coordinates, and there has been little discussion of which we are aware of the possibility of non-Euclidean or anyway, nonpower metric, distance functions. Nonetheless, it is well established that both loudness and pitch are mainly functions of intensity and frequency but nevertheless are indeed, affected significantly by the alternative physical variables. Hence, it seems safe to rule out weak and strong domain-range PS (Definitions 3 and 4). Likewise, parameterization PS (Definition 6) implies that whatever the coordinate for, say, loudness, is, it must be simply a function of intensity, thus precluding the notion that manipulating only intensity leads to its perceptual manipulation. With regard to local orthogonal PS (Definition 5), the conditions for embedding $x = f(X, Y)$ and $y = g(X, Y)$ for loudness and pitch or other dimensions in hearing, or other cognitive–perceptual contexts, into a manifold so that their coordinates are locally orthogonal is not so obvious. The issue clearly involves a mixture of a possible absence of domain-range PS with this kind of range-alone PS in some appropriate manifold.

CURVATURE AND SEPARABILITY

We now discuss the logical independence of Riemannian curvature of a two-dimensional manifold, also known as Gaussian curvature, and weak domain-range PS. Interestingly, notions of curvature cannot be mustered in the absence of a metric. Intuitively, curvature would seem to somehow reflect coordinate dependencies. For instance, a form of curvature was invoked in failures of a kind of separability (Gati & Tversky, 1982). However, we show here that at least Gaussian curvature is logically unrelated to weak domain-range PS in the sense that curvature may be 0 or not, independently of whether x and y are respectively functions of only X, Y. The structural generality in the $n = 3$ case appears to be present in higher-dimensional cases and permits an immediate extension to Riemannian curvature in general.

Proposition 1. Given a map F from $\Re^2$ to a two-manifold (surface) in $\Re^3$, weak domain-range PS and Gaussian curvature are logically unrelated: (a) weak domain-range PS may be violated while the manifold has a curvature other than 0.

(b) Weak domain-range PS may be violated while the manifold has curvature 0.
(c) Weak domain-range PS may hold while the manifold has a curvature other than 0. (d) Weak domain-range PS may hold while the manifold has 0 curvature.

Proof.   First, we show (a) the weak domain-range PS may be violated while the manifold has nonzero curvature, and (b) the weak domain-range PS is violated while the manifold has curvature 0.

Consider the patch $\mathbf{F} : U \subseteq (X \times Y) \rightarrow (f(X, Y), g(X, Y), h(X, Y))$. Assume that $x = f(X, Y)$, $y = g(X, Y)$, $z = h(X, Y)$, where x and y are the psychological dimensions of interest, and z may or may not have psychological relevance.

To produce a simple situation in which separability is violated, without loss of generality, let $x = f(X, Y)$, $y = g(Y)$, $z = h(X, Y)$. The psychological dimension x is then a function of both X and Y. We use the following formula for Gaussian curvature K, which, stated in its classical form, is

$$K = \frac{LN - M^2}{EG - F^2},$$

where L, M, and N are the coefficients of the second fundamental form relative to our mapping $\mathbf{F}$, and E, G, and F are the coefficients of the first fundamental form. The denominator is the determinant of the Riemannian coordinates from its metric form. (Note that more modern notation is used when one is dealing with cases that do not necessarily appeal to surfaces in a three-dimensional Euclidean embedding space: E, F, and G are denoted by g_{11}, g_{12}, and g_{22}.) The numerator can be thought of and produced in several ways. Our computation finds L, M and N through the dot product of a unit normal to the surface with the second partial derivatives of the map $\mathbf{F}$.

Thus, for our computation, a unit vector that is always orthogonal to the surface is needed. A natural calculation produces this by the cross product of the partial derivatives of $\mathbf{F}$ with respect to X and Y; we call these $\mathbf{F}_1$ and $\mathbf{F}_2$, respectively. (When called for, we make the obvious connection $X_1 = X$ and $X_2 = Y$.) Letting $F_i = \partial F / \partial Xi = (f_i, g_i, h_i)$, we find $F_1 = (a_1, 0, c_1)$, $F_2 = (a_2, b_2, c_2)$, where a_1, is the first partial derivative of $f(X, Y)$ with respect to X_1. In the present case then, $\mathbf{N} = \mathbf{F}_1 \times \mathbf{F}_2$:

$$\mathbf{N} = \begin{vmatrix} U_1 & U_2 & U_3 \\ a_1 & 0 & c_1 \\ a_2 & b_2 & c_2 \end{vmatrix} = -a_2 \begin{vmatrix} U_2 & U_3 \\ b_2 & c_2 \end{vmatrix} - c_1 \begin{vmatrix} U_1 & U_2 \\ a_2 & b_2 \end{vmatrix}$$

$$= -a_1(c_2 U_2 - b_2 U_3) - c_1(b_2 U_1 - a_2 U_2) = (-c_1 b_2, -a_1 c_2 + c_1 a_2, a_1 b_2),$$

where U_1, U_2 and U_3 are the unit vectors $(1, 0, 0)$, $(0,1,0)$ and $(0,0,1)$ respectively.

Next, to fully compute K, we should divide $\mathbf{N}$ by its magnitude; that is, $\mathbf{N}^* = \mathbf{N}/||\mathbf{N}||$. Then, $L = \mathbf{N}^* \cdot \mathbf{F}_{11}$, $M = \mathbf{N}^* \cdot \mathbf{F}_{12}$, $N = \mathbf{N}^* \cdot \mathbf{F}_{22}$, where again the index 1 indicates a derivative with respect to X and the index 2 indicates a derivative with respect to Y. However, we can dispense with the norming factor because we are mainly interested in when the denominator of the K function is 0 or not, rather than in its exact value. Hence we simply compute with $\mathbf{N}$ rather than with $\mathbf{N}^*$ for simplicity. We call the rescaled K, K', and the rescaled L, M and N in the numerator of K' L', M', and N', respectively.

Following this program in the present case, we let $\mathbf{F}_{11} = (a_{11}, 0, c_{11})$, $\mathbf{F}_{12} = (a_{12}, 0, c_{12})$, and $\mathbf{F}_{22} = (a_{22}, b_{22}, c_{22})$, where a_{11} is second partial derivative of $f(x, y)$ with respect to X_1.

Then, $E = \mathbf{F}_1 \cdot \mathbf{F}_1 = a_1^2 + c_1^2$, $F = \mathbf{F}_1 \cdot \mathbf{F}_2 = a_1 a_2 + c_1 c_2$, $G = \mathbf{F}_2 \cdot \mathbf{F}_2 = a_2^2 + b^2 + c_2^2$.

Next, $L' = \mathbf{N} \cdot \mathbf{F}_{11} = -a_{11} c_1 b_2 + c_{11} a_1 b_2$, $M' = \mathbf{N} \cdot \mathbf{F}_{12} = -c_1 b_2 a_{12} + c_{12} a_1 b_2$, $N' = \mathbf{N} \cdot \mathbf{F}_{22} = -a_{22} c_1 b_2 + b_{22}(c_1 a_2 - a_1 c_2) + c_{22} a_1 b_2$.

Now,

$$K' = \frac{L'N' - M'^2}{EG - F^2}.$$

Clearly the numerator of K' is just $b_2(-a_{11}c_1 + c_{11}a_1)[-a_{22}c_1 b_2 + b_{22}(c_1 a_2 - a_1 c_2) + c_{22}a_1 b_2] - (-a_{12}c_1 b_2 + c_{12}a_1 b_2)^2$. It is apparent that this does not have to be 0, and certainly the denominator can be non-0 whether the numerator is or not. This proves that violations of separability can occur without the curvature's being 0.

Furthermore, K' and $K = 0$ if $b_2(-a_{11}c_1 + c_{11}a_1)[-a_{22}c_1 b_2 + b_{22}(c_1 a_2 - a_1 c_2) + c_{22}a_1 b_2] - (-c_1 b_2 a_{12} + c_{12}a_1 b_2)^2 = 0$.

Suppose that $h(X, Y) = rX + sY$. Then the numerator is $-b_2 a_{11} r[-a_{22}rb_2 + b_{22}(ra_2 - sa_1)] - (-rb_2 a_{12})^2 = r^2(a_{11}a_{22}b_2^2 - a_{11}a_2 b_2 b_{22} - a_{12}^2 b_2^2) + rsb_2 a_{11}b_{22} a_1 = 0$. Obviously, if $r = 0$, that is, $z = h(X, Y) = sY$, then $K = 0$ and the denominator remains nonzero. Because this condition does not imply separability, which takes place in the f and g terms of the coordinate functions, this demonstrates that curvature can be 0 along with nonseparability.

Next, we demonstrate that (c) the weak domain-range PS is maintained while the manifold has curvature other than 0, and (d) the weak domain-range PS is maintained while the manifold has 0 curvature.

Let $x = f(X)$, $y = g(Y)$, $z = h(X, Y)$ so separability is in force.

Then, $\mathbf{F}_1 = (a_1, 0, c_1)$, $\mathbf{F}_2 = (0, b_2, c_2)$, $\mathbf{F}_{11} = (a_{11}, 0, c_{11})$, $\mathbf{F}_{12} = (0, 0, c_{12})$, and $\mathbf{F}_{22} = (0, b_{22}, c_{22})$. $E = a_1^2 + c_1^2$, $F = c_1 c_2$, $G = b_2^2 + c_2^2$.

$$\mathbf{N}' = \begin{vmatrix} U_1 & U_2 & U_3 \\ a_1 & 0 & c_1 \\ 0 & b_2 & c_2 \end{vmatrix} = -a_1(c_2 U_2 - b_2 U_3) - c_1(b_2 U_1) = (-c_1 b_2, -a_1 c_2, a_1 b_2).$$

Now, $L' = \mathbf{N}' \cdot \mathbf{F}_{11} = -a_{11}c_1b_2 + c_{11}a_1b_2$, $M' = \mathbf{N}' \cdot \mathbf{F}_{12} = c_{12}a_1b_2$, and $N' = \mathbf{N}' \cdot \mathbf{F}_{22} = -b_{22}a_1c_2 + c_{22}a_1b_2$ and

$$K' = \frac{(-a_{11}c_1b_2 + c_{11}a_1b_2)\,(-b_{22}a_1c_2 + c_{22}a_1b_2) - (c_{12}a_1b_2)^2}{\left(a_1^2 + c_1^2\right)\left(b_2^2 + c_2^2\right) - (c_1c_2)^2}$$

The necessary condition for K' and therefore $K = 0$ is $a_{11}b_{22}a_1c_1b_2c_2 - a_{11}c_{22}a_1c_1b_2^2 - c_{11}b_{22}a_1^2b_2c_2 + c_{11}c_{22}a_1^2b_2^2 - c_{12}^2a_1^2b_2^2 = 0$.

If h is a linear in X, Y, then the condition becomes $a_{11}b_{22}a_1c_1b_2c_2 = 0$. So at least f is linear in X or g is linear in Y. Obviously it is possible for the denominator to be nonzero while the numerator remains nonzero or vice versa so separability can be present, independently of the existence of nonzero Gaussian curvature, and the theorem is proved. □

It is clear from the definitions of parameterization PS and local orthogonal PS along with the structure of the proof to Proposition 1 that both of these types of PS are logically independent of Gaussian curvature. These results are stated in Proposition 2.

Proposition 2. Either parameterization PS or local orthogonal PS may exist with or without nonzero Gaussian curvature.

Needless to say, the sign of the Gaussian curvature is also independent of the logical format in Propositions 1 or 2.

DISCUSSION AND CONCLUSION

We briefly summarize our product in this chapter and then discuss a number of germane issues, both specific and general.

In the preceding sections, several definitions of separability that appear to capture strategic aspects of dimensional distinctiveness were proposed and their mutual relationships explored. We showed that one of the major types of domain-range separability is unrelated to Gaussian curvature. We strongly suspect that the other types of separability discussed here are also logically independent of curvature but we have not proved that.

What comes next? In particular, how can we apply these results to experimentation? A major problem in applying non-Euclidean concepts to psychology has undoubtedly been the difficulty in finding a key to a nontrivial interlocking between the mathematics and the empirical world. Some of these keys have been located in previous research, as briefly indicated in the introduction. Theories like those discussed call for some knowledge or at least hypotheses about the underlying space within some mental environ and then a set of independent and dependent variables that allow for the exploration of spatial concepts by means of implementation of these tools.

For instance, it is feasible to take a particular manifestation of color-perception space, under very stable conditions (e.g., Suppes et al., 1989) and, by use of findings about the way in which the various psychological dimensions, such as hue, chroma, and brightness, are functions of physical variables, investigate at least some of the kinds of separabilities proposed in this chapter. This was carried out in the preceding sections qualitatively in the case of loudness and pitch. However, it must be observed that it is possible to formulate the color space in different ways (e.g., Wyszecki, 1986), which might affect the answers to certain questions, particularly local orthogonal PS. These spaces will not generally be conformal (having equivalent angles of tangents to a point and its image) to one another and may not even be diffeomorphic (a very smooth 1–1 and onto map relating them). Which, if any, is the correct one? At this point, they seem to be convenient data reservoirs, but, in principle, one or more of them might carry critical information concerning a geometrically more constrained model. Can any space simultaneously capture all facets about the curves in the space representing psychological coordinates as well as other important aspects such as the laws of trichromacy, not to mention context and various adaptation effects?

On the other hand, once a good approximative model, including the coordinate system and curvature to the "true" space, is found, the intrinsic (i.e., pertaining to the properties of the space that a being living on the manifold could discover without departing) characteristics of the manifold would specify the fairly narrow class of mathematically equivalent models. The nature of the coordinate map from (X, Y) to (x, y), might also assist in constraining the space. This last remark brings up the intriguing question of whether visual scientists might ever be able to so fully confine the geometric model that only congruent manifolds (i.e., not only the geometrically intrinsic but also the extrinsic [e.g., discoverable by a being who has departed the manifold by, for instance, a rocket ship] features of the space would be determined) could encompass all the relevant data. Perhaps with the aid of crystal-clear physiology, such an ambitious goal might be attained.

Beyond these speculations, one fairly obvious region of potential implementation involves following up on the Lindman and Caelli (1978) construction of Riemannian spatial scaling programs. We are involved in extending these concepts and relating them to our separability theory.

It might be fruitful to make theoretical contact with the approaches of Levin (2000) and Dzhafarov and Colonius (1999). The former is in a spirit similar to that of this chapter, as it emphasizes supra-just-noticeable-differences (jnd) scaling and may be relatable to this chapter. The latter is a multidimensional extension of Fechnerian psychophysics, beginning with infra-jnd regions and their probability distributions and extrapolating through accumulation of jnd-like measures, the macroscopic psychophysical scales. We are currently developing a probabilistic

Riemannian version of our work in this chapter, which generalizes the Ashby and Townsend (1986) GRT. It may be possible to develop connecting links of the latter developments to the Dzhafarov and Colonius theory.

Another area of application is categorization. Ashby, Maddox, and their colleagues (e.g., Ashby & Maddox, 1996) have found that people can categorize most readily when the category boundaries are decisionally separable. We are exploring this possibility in non-Euclidean category environments by using the present theory.

There may also be applications of our theory in color perception (see references in Suppes et al., 1989), as already intimated, face perception, and other regions of cognition (see, e.g., Townsend et al., 2001; and discussion by O'Toole, Wenger, & Townsend, 2001). In particular, we believe that independence and separability are inherently antipodal to configurality, for instance, in face perception (Wenger & Townsend, 2001), so we expect models that predict configurality to conflict with separability and independence relationships.

Other open problem areas include extension to stochastic spaces that do not just include probability, but also the stochastic time course of the information processing aspects underlying the geometry discussed here (e.g., as a generalization of Ashby's stochastic general recognition theory; Ashby, 2000).

More generally, the discriminating reader may wonder whither geometry within psychology and cognitive science is heading. Research that intimately engages geometric notions may be roughly divided into three different categories: (a) ventures for which scaling procedures are used to unearth the presence of a geometry in a psychological task. These studies are legion, based especially on the Shepard–Kruskal (e.g. Shepard, 1962; Kruskal, 1964) line of methodology. (b) Information processing theories or models of a type of psychological behavior in which geometry inherently plays a vital role. This type of research is not extensive, but Nosofsky's (e.g., 1986) exemplar theory of categorization is a notable example of such effort in cognitive arenas in addition to the sensory-oriented type of study already mentioned. (c) Axiomatic investigations, especially from a measurement perspective, of how geometries may be related to underlying qualitative properties of data. These are less frequent still but of fundamental importance and exemplified by volume II of *Foundations of Measurement* by Suppes et al. (1989).

We have previously called for labor devoted to bringing together categories (a), (b), and (c) (Townsend & Thomas, 1993), and some of the earlier cited studies are showing a trend in that direction. One major lacuna in the literature that relates to the relative paucity of combinations of (a)–(c) is a set of phenomena demonstrated without question to be brought about through the presence of a *specific* geometry. The word specific was italicized because there seem to be few cases in which multidimensional scaling procedures, for instance, have reliably and cogently pointed to a specific space or metric. There is a plethora of examples, for instance in the associating of a particular power metric with psychological properties like separability (Shepard, 1964), in which a stimulus or task is purported to be paired with a certain metric. In some cases, except for certain dimensions such as orientation and shape (e.g., Kadlec & Hicks, 1998; Shepard & Farrell, 1985), these findings have turned out to be unreliable. Multidimensional scaling by itself may simply not be able to constrain the possibilities sufficiently, although indubitably it will continue to play a major role.

On the one hand it seems obvious that, if geometry matters at all in psychology, as Helmholtz argued over 100 years ago, all geometrics of psychological entities cannot be Euclidean. On the other hand, outside of a small cadre of areas, including perhaps that of the nature of visual space (e.g., see Suppes et al., 1989, for a fairly recent survey of this research), it is somewhat astonishing, and depressing, how few overwhelmingly convincing cases exist after all this time. We believe that such research as the present and several others mentioned herein may help to synthesize questions from the aforementioned various regions [(a)–(c)]. Too, we operate on the belief that, to some extent, the kind of wood used in construction depends on the types of hammers and nails available. The popularity of modern multidimensional scaling routines provides powerful evidence for that claim. Nonetheless, we feel that striking support for *any* particular geometry, even Euclidean, in any psychological research domain, remains a holy grail, but hopefully not so elusive.

ACKNOWLEDGMENTS

J. T. Townsend is indebted to the Hanse Institute for Advanced Study for a 10-month fellowship that facilitated this research, as well as for support by an National Institute of Mental Health research grant. J. Spencer-Smith thanks the Beckman Institute of University of Illinois at Urbana-Champaign for its support and the Cognitive Science Program for its support through the training grant in Modeling of Cognition.

REFERENCES

Ashby, F. G. (Ed.). (1992). *Multidimensional models of perception and cognition.* Hillsdale, NJ: Lawrence Erlbaum Associates.

Ashby, F. G. (2000). A stochastic version of general recognition theory. *Journal of Mathematical Psychology, 44,* 310–329.

Ashby, F. G., & Maddox, W. T. (1996). Perceptual separability, decisional separability, and the identification-speeded classification relationship. *Journal of Experimental Psychology: Human Perception and Performance, 22,* 795–817.

Ashby, F. G., & Townsend, J. T. (1986). Varieties of perceptual independence. *Psychological Review, 93,* 154–179.

Beals, R., Krantz, D. H., & Tversky, A. (1968). Foundations of multidimensional scaling. *Psychological Review, 75,* 127–142.

Boothby, W. M. (1986). *An introduction to differentiable manifolds and Riemannian geometry* (2nd ed.). San Diego: Academic Press.

Busemann, H. (1955). *The geometry of geodesics.* New York: Academic Press.

Carroll, J. D., & Chang, J. J. (1970). Analysis of individual differences in multidimensional scaling via an *n*-way generalization of "Eckart–Young" decomposition. *Psychometrika, 35,* 283–319.

Cox, T. F. R. & Cox, M. A. A. (1991). Multidimensional scaling on a sphere. *Communications in Statistics. A: Theory and Methods, 20,* 2943–2953.

Drösler, J. (1979). Foundations of multidimensional metric scaling in Cayley–Klein geometries. *British Journal of Statistical and Mathematical Psychology, 32,* 185–211.

Dzhafarov, E. N., & Colonius, H. (1999). Fechnerian metrics in unidimensional and multidimensional stimulus spaces. *Psychonomic Bulletin and Review, 6,* 239–268.

D'Zmura, M., & Iverson, G. (1993). Color constancy: I. Basic theory of two-stage linear recovery of spectral descriptions for lights and surfaces. *Journal of the Optical Society of America A, 10,* 2148–2165.

Garner, W. R. (1974). *The processing of information and structure.* Hillsdale, NJ: Lawrence Erlbaum and Associates.

Garner, W. R. & Morton, J. (1969). Perceptual independence: Definitions, models, and experimental paradigms. *Psychological Bulletin, 72,* 233–259.

Gati, I., & Tversky, A. (1982). Representations of qualitative and quantitative dimensions. *Journal of Experimental Psychology: Human Perception and Performance, 8,* 325–340.

Helmholtz, H. von (1995). The facts on perception. In D. Cahan (Ed. & Trans.), *Science and culture: Popular and philosophical essays* (p. 351). Chicago: University of Chicago Press. (Original work published 1878.)

Hoffman, D. D. (1998). *Visual intelligence: How we create what we see.* New York: Norton.

Hoffman, W. C. (1968). The neuron as a lie group germ and a lie product. *Quarterly of Applied Mathematics, 25,* 423–440.

Hoffman, W. C., & Dodwell, P. C. (1985). Geometric psychology generates the visual Gestalt. *Canadian Journal of Psychology, 39,* 491–528.

Indow, T. (1967). Two interpretations of binocular visual space: Hyperbolic and euclidean. *Annals of the Japan Association for the Philosophy of Science, 3,* 19–32.

Indow, T. (1982). An approach to geometry of visual space with no a priori mapping: Multidimensional scaling according Riemannian metrics. *Journal of Mathematical Psychology, 26,* 204–236.

Kadlec, H., & Hicks, C. L. (1998). Invariance of perceptual spaces and perceptual separability of stimulus dimensions. *Journal of Experimental Psychology: Human Perception and Performance, 24,* 80–104.

Kadlec, H., & Townsend, J. T. (1992). Signal detection analysis of multidimensional interactions. In F. G. Ashby (Ed.), *Multidimensional models of perception and cognition* (pp. 181–231). Hillsdale, NJ: Lawrence Erlbaum Associates.

Kruskal, J. B. (1964). Multidimensional scaling by optimizing goodness of fit to a nonmetric hypothesis. *Psychometrika, 29,* 1–27.

Landauer, T. K., & Dumais, S. T. (1997). A solution to Plato's problem: The latent semantic analysis theory of acquisition, induction, and representation of knowledge. *Psychological Review, 104,* 211–240.

Lee, J. M. (2000). *Introduction to topological manifolds.* New York: Springer.

Levin, D. N. (2000). A differential geometric description of the relations among perceptions. *Journal of Mathematical Psychology, 44,* 241–284.

Lindman, H., & Caelli, T. (1978). Constant curvature Riemannian scaling. *Journal of Mathematical Psychology, 17,* 89–109.

Maddox, W. T., (1992). Perceptual and decisional separabilty. In F. G. Ashby (Ed.), *Multidimensional models of perception and cognition* (pp. 147–180). Hillsdale, NJ: Lawrence Erlbaum Associates.

Marley, A. A. J. (1992). Developing and characterizing multidimensional Thurstone and Luce models for identification and preference. In F. G. Ashby (Ed.), *Multidimensional models of perception and cognition. Scientific psychology series* (pp. 299–333). Hillsdale, NJ: Lawrence Erlbaum Associates, Inc.

Nosofsky, R. M. (1986). Attention, similarity, and the identification/categorization relationship. *Journal of Experimental Psychology: General, 115*, 39–57.

O'Neill, B. (1997). *Elementary differential geometry.* (2nd ed.). San Diego: Academic Press.

O'Toole, A. J., Wenger, M. J., & Townsend, J. T. (2001). Quantitative models of perceiving and remembering faces: Precedents and possibilities. In M. J. Wenger & J. T. Townsend (Eds.), *Computational geometric and process perspectives on facial cognition: Context and challenges* (pp. 1–38). Mahwah, NJ: Lawrence Erlbaum and Associates.

Pizlo, Z. (1994). A theory of shape constancy based on perspective invariants. *Vision Research, 34*, 1637–1658.

Shepard, R. N. (1962). The analysis of proximities: Multidimensional scaling with an unknown distance function. Part I. *Psychometrika, 27*, 125–140.

Shepard, R. N. (1964). Attention and the metric structure of the stimulus space. *Journal of Mathematical Psychology, 1*, 54–87.

Shepard, R. N., & Carroll, J. D. (1966). Parametric representation of nonlinear data structures. In P. Krishnaiah (Ed.), *Multivariate analysis* (pp. 561–592). New York: Academic Press.

Shepard, R. N., & Farrell, J. E. (1985). Representation of the orientations of shapes. *Acta Psychologica, 59*, 103–121.

Suppes, P., Krantz, D. M., Luce, R. D., & Tversky, A. (1989). *Foundations of measurement: Vol. II. Geometrical, threshold, and probabilistic representations.* New York: Academic Press.

Thomas, R. D. (1995). Gaussian general recognition theory and perceptual independence. *Psychological Review, 102*, 192–200.

Townsend, J. T., Solomon, B. & Spencer-Smith, J. (2001). The perfect Gestalt: Infinite dimensional Riemannian face spaces, and other aspects of face perception. In M. J. Wenger & J. T. Townsend (Eds.), *Computational geometric and process perspectives on facial cognition: Context and challenges* (pp. 39–82). Mahwah, NJ: Lawrence Erlbaum Associates.

Townsend, J. T., & Thomas, R. D. (1993). On the need for a general quantitative theory of pattern similarity. In S. C. Masin (Ed.), *Foundations of perceptual theory* (Advances in psychology, Vol. 99, pp. 297–368). Amsterdam, Netherlands: North-Holland/Elsevier Science.

Wenger, M. J. & Townsend, J. T. (2001). Faces as Gestalt stimuli: Process characteristics. In M. J. Wenger & J. T. Townsend (Eds.), *Computational geometric and process perspectives on facial cognition: Context and challenges* (pp. 229–284). Mahwah, NJ: Lawrence Erlbaum Associates.

Wyszecki, G. (1986). Color appearance. In K. R. Boff, L. Kaufman & J. P. Thomas (Eds.), *Handbook of perception and human performance*, (Vol. 1, 9-1–9-57). New York: Wiley.

II

Timing and Dynamics
of Human Performance

Guest Editorial

Hans Colonius
Carl von Ossietzky Universität, Oldenburg, Germany

The eight chapters within this section encompass a wide variety of issues and experimental paradigms ranging from the dynamics of motor action to specific issues in visual perception (e.g., visual attention, visual awareness, and pattern recognition). Aschersleben, Gehrke, and Prinz are concerned with the links between perception and action, and they present evidence that the perceived time on an action is strongly determined by the sensory information arising from its execution. Elliott and Müller show that the detection of a visual target (a Kanizsa-type square) among a matrix of distractor items is facilitated by the prior presentation, at the subsequent target location, of four "premask" crosses presented "synchronously" within an oscillating matrix of otherwise asynchronized premask crosses, and they relate this intriguing finding to the well-known neurophysiological hypothesis of a feature-binding neural oscillatory synchronization mechanism. Geissler and Lachmann and van Leeuwen propose the memory-guided inference approach to the recognition process of complex stimuli explaining the representation of seemingly redundant information as a means to achieving economy within a more encompassing representational scheme based on mathematical group structures corresponding to the generation rules of the sets of objects. Müller, Krummenacher, and Heller present an attention-weighting account for the processing of basic stimulus dimensions in visual search and segmentation tasks according to which dimensional information is attentionally modulated according to task relevance and variability across trials.

Vorberg, Mattler, Heinecke, Schmidt, and Schwarzbach present findings from a series of metacontrast masking experiments suggesting that the time course of motor effects produced by the masked stimuli ("priming") is independent of the time course of their perceptual effects ("masking"). Watson, Humphreys, and Olivers review a number of experimental findings that present evidence for a top-down mechanism of inhibiting sets of items in a visual search array ("visual marking"), enabling selection to be directed more efficiently to relevant (e.g., new) items.

Neumann and Niepel contrast results from temporal-order judgment (TOJ) tasks with findings in reaction time (RT) studies. As this paper is closest to my own interests, I dwell on it here. They show that these two measures are differentially affected by sensory modality and stimulus intensity. For example, RTs to auditory stimuli is usually shorter than RTs to visual stimuli, whereas this relation is reversed in most TOJ studies, and stimulus intensity affects RT more strongly than TOJ. After ruling out a number of possible explanations for this dissociation, the authors suggest the existence of ". . . parallel pathways into which information flow separates after an initial stage of common processing, one feeding into the motor system and one leading to conscious perception. The effects of sensory modality and intensity on RT would then reflect processing in one of these pathways, and its effects on TOJ would be caused by processing in the other pathway." The direct pathway linking stimuli to responses is postulated to operate under Neumann's (1990) concept of "direct parameter specification" (DPS), according to which stimulus input information specifies motor action parameters without (or at least before) giving rise to conscious perception of the stimulus. The DPS concept is an elaboration of ideas going back to 19th-century work by Lange (1888) (from observing what he called "foreshortened reactions") and Münsterberg (1889), and the authors relate this concept to the influential distinction between a dorsal and a ventral stream in visual processing postulated in the work by Milner and Goodale (1995). Both streams have their origin in partially different areas of the occipital cortex. The dorsal stream projects by means of the parietal cortex into the motor system serving the sensorimotor control of actions, whereas the ventral stream projects into the inferotemporal cortex where stimuli are identified and represented in an allocentric frame of reference. Only the latter type of processing is necessarily associated with conscious experience. In an analogy to the functional role of "object constancy" in the Milner–Goodale theory, the authors make a convincing case that the dissociations between RT and TOJ relate to "time constancy": simultaneously presented stimuli differing in physical dimensions such as intensity will produce asynchronous activity in the primary cortical areas (i.e., different arrival times). This does not pose a problem for speeded motor responses to individual stimuli, but it precludes a veridical internal representation of the physical world as required for the TOJ task.

DPS seems to be a fruitful concept in domains beyond visual perception, such as the rapidly developing field of multisensory interaction. Take, for example, the classic phenomenon of "visual dominance" (Colavita, 1974): In a RT task, participants had to respond to a visual signal by pressing a key with one hand and to an auditory signal by pressing another key with the other hand. When participants were forewarned to modality, they produced the typical simple RT advantage for auditory over visual signals (179 vs. 197 ms, respectively). When auditory and visual signals were presented in an interspersed fashion without prior identification of signal modality for each trial, mean RTs for both modalities were approximately 100 ms longer, which is the typical simple versus choice RT difference. Most interestingly, however, when within the latter condition occasional trials on which both signals occurred were interspersed, the participants' reactions in those trials were made on the visual key almost always. This observation has been explained in terms of differential attention allocation (Posner, Nissen, & Klein, 1976), but DPS would, in my view, be a more natural concept to describe the dissociation between simple RT and the visual dominance in the choice trials.

A recent series of experiments in our laboratory (Kirchner, 2001; Kirchner & Colonius, 2003) provides evidence for the existence of DPS in saccadic responses to bimodal stimuli as well. The participants' task was to make an eye movement from the fixation point to a visual target appearing randomly left or right from fixation. Simultaneously with the target, an auditory accessory stimulus (which the participants were instructed to ignore) was presented either at the same position or opposite to the target position. In separate blocks of trials, the position of the accessory was either statistically uncorrelated with the position of the target or it was positively or negatively correlated with the position of the target. Saccadic RT was significantly shorter in both correlated conditions than in the uncorrelated condition (190 ms vs. 210 ms, with negligible gaze error rates), suggesting that participants can utilize the interstimulus contingency information at a very early stage of saccade programming without, however, this information being available for conscious report.

Although the paradigms differ completely, the latter result is consistent with the finding of a dissociation between masking and priming in the chapter by Vorberg et al., where the invariance of the priming function (under qualitative changes in masking) implies a visuomotor mechanism for which conscious perception is not a prerequisite. As the authors argue, the fact that the motor system seems to have access to shape information, possibly based on unfilled contours, is not consistent with central notions of Milner and Goodale's theory, however.

In summation, do the chapters in this section have more in common than the fact that all of them refer to some type of RT measure to assess performance? What does all this have to do with psychophysics? Let me start with the latter point: I do not see a foundational argument against using RT as a basic psychophysical measure of "sensation" comparable with, for example, the probability of a "same–different" judgment. In contrast, the approaches presented here certainly do not stand in the classical Fechnerian tradition of psychophysics, nor in that of representational measurement theory. Rather, the emphasis is on revealing mechanisms of how specific stimulus properties are coded by the sensory system, represented in certain brain structures, and translated into action. This search for mechanisms is well within the realm of classical psychophysics in the sense of Thurstone (1927). One common theme underlying these chapters is that they all— more or less explicitly—refer to the neural underpinnings of the behavior that is observed in the experiments. This is obviously a mainstream characteristic of current theorizing in cognitive psychology. The conspicuous lack of explicit reference to results from modern brain imaging techniques (such as functional magnetic resonance imaging) is probably due to the fact that these techniques are still at a very early level of development when it comes to the study of cognitive processes at a time resolution of a few milliseconds. Another common aspect of the chapters is that they all strive to either relate their findings to some general laws and principles or to develop explicit models to capture the postulated mechanisms. The final judgment as to the successful outcome of this enterprise stands out, but one would certainly hope that the approaches exemplified in this book bring us closer to Fechner's ultimate dream of an "inner psychophysics."

REFERENCES

Colavita, F. B. (1974). Human sensory dominance. *Perception & Psychophysics, 16*, 409–412.

Kirchner, H. (2001). *Visual-auditory interstimulus contingency effects in saccade programming.* Unpublished doctoral dissertation, Universität Oldenburg, Germany.

Kirchner, H., & Colonius, H. (2003). Saccadic responses in a bimodal go/no-go task show inter-stimulus contingency effects. Manuscript submitted for publication.

Lange, L. (1888). Neue Experimente über den Vorgang der einfachen Reaction auf Sinneseindrücke [New experiments on the process of simple reaction to sense impressions]. *Philosophische Studien, 4*, 479–510.

Milner, A. D., & Goodale, M. A. (1995). *The visual brain in action.* Oxford, England: Oxford University Press.

Münsterberg, H. (1889). *Beiträge zur experimentellen Psychologie. Heft 1: Über willkürliche und unwillkürliche Vorstellungsverbindungen* [Contributions to experimental psychology. Vol. 1: On voluntary and involuntary associations between ideas]. Freiburg, Germany: Mohr.

Neumann, O. (1990). Direct parameter specification and the concept of perception. *Psychological Research, 52*, 207–215.

Posner, M. I., Nissen, M. J., & Klein, R. M. (1976). Visual dominance: An information-processing account of its origins and significance. *Psychological Review, 83*, 157–171.

Thurstone, L. L. (1927). A law of comparative judgment. *Psychological Review, 34*, 273–286.

6

A Psychophysical Approach to Action Timing

Gisa Aschersleben, Jörg Gehrke, and Wolfgang Prinz
Max Planck Institute for Psychological Research, Munich, Germany

How do we perceive the timing of our own actions? Consider, as an example, an elementary, quasi-punctate act such as a keypress or a finger tap on a surface. Acts such as these are perceived as occurring at certain points in time. In this chapter, we explore functional sources on which the perceived timing of one's own actions is based. Even for a simple act such as a finger tap, a number of sources could contribute to the act's perceived time, ranging from its mental antecedents (e.g., action plans or intentions) through the motor outflow that generates the tap (say, central commands or peripheral activations) to the proprioceptive inflow arising from its execution (kinesthetic and tactile feedback)—perhaps even including the inflow arising from its consequences in the environment (e.g., the sound of a beep triggered by the tap).

Given the fact that all of these sources are neatly spread in time, the question of how they contribute to the perceived time of the action is by no means trivial. Yet, to the best of our knowledge, it has not been addressed in the literature thus far. There is, of course, a rich literature on how we perceive (evaluate or take into account) the *spatial characteristics* of our own actions. This literature goes back to Helmholtz's classical discussion of the basic issue of space constancy, that is, of taking one's own body movements into account in the perceptual evaluation of environmental information (e.g., Helmholtz, 1866; Mittelstaedt, 1990; Redding & Wallace, 1997).

117

However, there is no such literature referring to the *temporal characteristics* of one's own actions. This is quite surprising in view of the fact that we need to coordinate our actions with environmental events all the time, which implies that we need to anticipate and evaluate the times of our actions in exactly the same way as we need to evaluate and anticipate the times of environmental events. Some research has addressed the question of how the times of actions are coordinated with the times of both their mental and their physical antecedents (e.g., Haggard & Eimer, 1999; Libet, 1985, 1996; Libet, Gleason, Wright, & Pearl, 1983). However, this literature does not speak to the issue of how action times and event times are coordinated with each other.

In this chapter, we present some evidence in support of an inflow-based account of the perception of action times. Our evidence suggests that the perceived time of an action is strongly determined by the sensory and perceptual information arising from its execution. The evidence we discuss is derived from the sensorimotor synchronization task. In this task, participants are presented with isochronous sequences of auditory stimuli such as short beeps or metronome clicks, and they are required to perform simple movements (taps) in exact synchrony with those stimuli (clicks). The task is easy in the sense that everybody can do it. People first listen to three or four clicks before they start to accompany clicks with taps; soon they feel they are tapping in perfect synchrony.

One of the interesting observations with this task is that the feeling of synchrony requires that taps lead over clicks by approximately 20 to 80 ms. This lead interval is called the *negative asynchrony* (e.g., Aschersleben, 2001; Aschersleben & Prinz, 1995, 1997; Müller et al., 2000; Vos, Mates, & Van Kruysbergen, 1995). Interestingly, the size of the negative asynchrony does not decrease with practice. On the contrary, when one applies a feedback-based training procedure encouraging participants to perform taps in *physical* synchrony with clicks, they tend to lose the feeling of *mental* synchrony, believing that taps now lag behind clicks (Aschersleben, in press).

Most of the literature on this task is concerned with mechanisms underlying the occurrence of negative asynchronies (see, e.g., Aschersleben & Prinz, 1995, 1997; Billon, Semjen, Cole, & Gauthier, 1996; Mates, 1994a, 1994b; Mates & Aschersleben, 2000; Müller et al., 2000; Vos et al., 1995; for an overview, see Aschersleben, 2001) as well as the isochronous timing of the actions (e.g., Collyer, Broadbent, & Church, 1994; Hary & Moore, 1985; Repp, 2001; Vorberg & Wing, 1996; Wing & Kristofferson, 1973a, 1973b). In the present context, we consider a somewhat different, though related, aspect. What can we learn from the task about the way people perceive the times of their actions?

The task allows us to study how self-generated actions (taps) become synchronized with external events (clicks). As already mentioned, these actions are made up of a number of functional components that are extended over relatively long periods of time, such as the formation of the motor command in the brain, the execution of the physical movement, and the subsequent perception of reafferent information arising from the movement. Exactly what, then, is it in the tap that becomes synchronized with the click?

The direct way to approach this problem is to study which components of taps and clicks coincide in time. For instance, in one of the now classical models of the mechanisms underlying the occurrence of negative asynchronies, it is assumed that synchrony is achieved when the reafferent information arising from the tap arrives in the brain at the same time at which the information from the click arrives (*Paillard–Fraisse hypothesis*, Aschersleben & Prinz, 1995, 1997; Fraisse, 1966, 1980; Paillard, 1949). According to this account, negative asynchronies arise because the neural pathway from the fingertip to the brain is longer than the pathway from the ear to the brain, so that, in order to achieve synchrony of arrival times in the brain, a certain amount of asynchrony has to be maintained between their corresponding onset times in the world.

In this chapter we follow a more indirect approach. Its logic is to manipulate certain features of the actions to be performed and then study how this manipulation affects the size of the asynchrony.

THE SENSORY ACCUMULATOR MODEL

Before discussing our experiments, we introduce a simple model, called the sensory accumulator model (SAM). The SAM is based on three main assumptions. The first is that synchrony refers to *representations* of clicks and taps in the brain and not to the events in the world themselves. The second is that the relevant representations of taps are based on their reafferent *inflow* (i.e., somatosensory feedback) and not on the motor outflow generating them. The third assumption is that the representations of clicks and taps *unfold in time* and are not punctate events.

The SAM shares the first two of these assumptions with the Paillard–Fraisse hypothesis, which relies on conduction times. However, it differs from it with respect to the third assumption. The Paillard–Fraisse hypothesis is based on the fictitious assumption that quasi-punctate events in the world (such as clicks and taps) are represented as quasi-punctate events in the brain. However, as textbook wisdom suggests, this is certainly not true. Event-related brain potentials triggered by quasi-punctate stimuli, such as beeps and flashes, are extended over several multiples of these stimuli's effective exposure times (see, e.g., Birbaumer, Elbert, Canavan, & Rockstroh, 1990; Coles, 1986). Likewise, it has been shown for so-matosensory stimuli that the central representation of a discrete event may be much more complex temporarily than the event itself, involving coordinated cooperation between cortical and subcortical structures over a range of nearly 500 ms (Libet, Wright, Feinstein, & Pearl, 1979).

In the SAM, the unfolding of the sensory evidence for clicks and taps is captured by two corresponding accumulation functions. In accordance with both classical psychophysics (Fechner, 1860; Stevens, 1957) and neurophysiological evidence (Hanes & Schall, 1996), we assume that, for each event (i.e., each tap and each click), sensory evidence is accumulated over time. At some point, each accumulation function crosses a preset criterion. This criterion can be understood as a sensory threshold that determines the point in time at which the event is perceived (for a similar view, see Aschersleben, 1999; Aschersleben & Müsseler, 1999). Thus, we assume that the points at which the accumulation functions for clicks and taps reach their respective thresholds determine the times at which the two events are perceived.

The SAM posits that the sensory evidence for clicks and taps is accumulated in the same functional domain and that the same threshold applies to both of them. It is further assumed that, in order to achieve perceived synchrony, the two accumulation functions have to hit the threshold at the same point.

Given these two assumptions, it is the steepness of the two accumulation functions that determines to which extent the onsets of the two physical events must be offset to achieve perceived synchrony of the two mental events. For instance, as illustrated in Fig. 6.1, if one assumes that the accumulation function is steeper

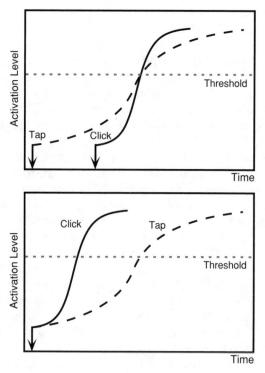

FIG. 6.1.   Illustration of the SAM.

for click-related evidence than for tap-related evidence, then tap onset has to lead over click onset to make sure that both functions hit the threshold at the same point (upper panel). Conversely, if physical onsets coincide, an asynchrony will emerge in the perceived times of the two events (lower panel). Thus, the SAM assumes that clicks and taps differ in the times required for the buildup of effective sensory representations (fast for taps and slow for clicks, as measured from their physical onsets). Unlike the Paillard-Fraisse hypothesis, which accounts for this difference in terms of peripheral conduction times, the SAM relies on central accumulation times. However, what both models have in common is that they regard differences in the times required for generating sensory codes as the functional basis of the asynchrony (code-generation times; cf. Müller, Aschersleben, Koch, Freund, & Prinz, 1999).

Evidence in support of the notion that clicks and taps may differ in the steepness of their respective accumulation functions can be derived from experiments on the temporal resolution for touch and audition. Gescheider (1966) showed that two tactile impulse stimuli that were applied to the same location on the fingertip with a duration of 1 ms each had to be separated by 10 ms in order to be perceived as distinct stimuli. In contrast, a separation of only 2 ms was necessary for two auditory clicks to be perceived as distinct (Gescheider, 1966; Hirsh, 1959). These observations suggest that temporal resolution is much higher in the auditory system than in the tactile system, implying faster accumulation rates for auditory information than for tactile information.

An obvious way to test the logic of the model is to manipulate factors that may affect the difference between the two functions. For example, if we were able to steepen the taps' accumulation function, this should act to shorten the time between their physical and their perceived onsets and produce a reduction in the size of the asynchrony. We reasoned that one way to achieve this might be to increase the amount of somatosensory feedback arising from the tap. For instance, an increase of the intensity of the stimulus arising from the tap should lead to such an increase in the amount of somatosensory information reaching the brain and, therefore, to a forward shift of the perceived time of the tap. As is known from physiological studies, stimulus intensity affects upstream information in terms of both the population code and the frequency code. The population code reflects the activity of a population of responding receptors (spatial summation of signals). Here, an increase in stimulus intensity is mirrored by an increase in the size of the responding receptor population (Hashimoto et al., 1991; Johansson & Vallbo, 1976, 1979). The frequency code refers to the temporal summation of signals, implying that strong stimuli lead to higher frequencies of action potentials within fibers as compared with weak stimuli. For instance, the discharge frequency of afferent signals arising from mechanoreceptors of the skin increases with the amplitude of indentation (Harrington & Merzenich, 1970; Knibestöl & Vallbo, 1980; Werner & Mountcastle, 1965). Further, the discharge frequency of joint receptors and muscle spindles increases when the movement velocity of the involved effectors increases

(Boyd & Roberts, 1953; Edin & Vallbo, 1990; Gandevia, McCloskey, & Burke, 1992; McKeon & Burke, 1983; Skoglund, 1956).

We ran three experiments to test the general logic of the SAM. In Experiment 1, we used different finger amplitudes to study the impact of the amount of tap-related feedback on synchronization performance. In Experiment 2, we tested the validity of the SAM for a task involving isometric force pulses. Finally, in Experiment 3, we tested the validity of some of the model's basic assumptions in a purely perceptual experiment.

EXPERIMENT 1

Experiment 1 tested the prediction that an increase in the amount of afferent feedback arising from the tap modulates the size of the asynchrony. The amount of feedback information was manipulated by instructing participants to produce finger movements with large versus small amplitudes. With constant tapping speed, large amplitudes result in a higher velocity of the downgoing finger and stronger indentation of the skin at the fingertip as compared with small amplitudes. This should increase the amount of somatosensory signals that are elicited by receptors contributing to kinesthetic and tactile sensation (receptors in joints and muscles and mechanoreceptors, respectively).

Therefore, according to the SAM, the accumulation of tap-related evidence should be faster under this condition. This should act to modulate the size of the negative asynchrony: it should be large for small amplitudes and small for large ones. In principle, if the accumulation of tap-related evidence becomes sufficiently steep, the asynchrony could even become positive (i.e., when its steepness exceeds that of the click-related accumulation).

We manipulated finger amplitudes in two ways. One group of participants could determine the size of large versus small amplitudes by themselves. Participants in the other group received precise instructions concerning the amplitudes of their finger movements.

Method

Participants.   The original sample consisted of 20 right-handed participants. Two participants were excluded from the final data analysis because they did not produce enough data according to the preset criteria (see the paragraphs that follow). Of the remaining participants, 10 were women and 8 were men. The mean age of the sample was 26 years. None of the participants reported any sensory defects. Participants were paid to serve in the experiment.

Apparatus and Stimuli.   Participants were asked to tap with their right-hand index fingers on a silent electrical contact switch while they sat at a table. An optical marker system (OPTOTRAK 3D motion measurement system, Northern Digital

Inc, Waterloo, Ontario, Canada) was used to record the movement of the index finger. An LED marker that signaled the position of the finger in space and time with a high precision was fixed laterally at the tip of the index finger. Finger movements were not impaired by the marker. The auditory pacing signal [400 Hz, 82 dB (A), and 10-ms duration] was presented binaurally through headphones (Sennheiser HD 250, Sennheiser Electronic, Wedamar, Germany), together with white noise [60 dB (A)] to mask external sounds. The auditory stimuli were produced by a personal computer (Pegasys 486/33, Pegasys Inc., Hatogaya Saitama, Japan) via a digital-to-analog converter (Data Translation Card DT2821, Data Translation Inc., Marlboro, MA, USA) and an amplifier (Philips FA 630, Royal Philips Electronics, Amsterdam, Netherlands). The onsets of the keypresses were registered with a resolution of 1 ms. Kinematic output data were collected at a sampling rate of 1 kHz.

Procedure.   One group of participants had to follow an explicit instruction that constrained the range of the amplitudes. In the condition with large amplitudes, maximum finger amplitudes had to lie between 50 and 80 mm; in the condition with small amplitudes, maximum finger amplitudes had to lie between 10 and 25 mm (i.e., constrained instruction). The second group was instructed to choose amplitudes for large and small finger displacements by themselves, in a way that was comfortable for them (i.e., unconstrained instruction). The only requirement for the latter group was that the amplitudes in the two conditions should be clearly distinguishable (10-mm difference at minimum). Participants were randomly assigned to one of the groups. The two amplitude conditions were presented blockwise with a balanced order between participants. Each block consisted of training trials and experimental trials. At the beginning of each block, training trials in which the finger displacements were controlled were presented. The training stopped after the participant had produced two successful trials, that is, trials in which at least 75% of the taps were performed with a correct amplitude. The training was followed by 10 experimental trials on which the experimental data were collected. All participants were instructed to tap as synchronously as possible with the pacing signal.

A trial included the following sequence of events: First, the beginning of the trial was indicated by a tone signal generated by the computer. After a delay of 1 s, a sequence of 25 auditory signals embedded in white noise was presented with an interstimulus interval of 800 ms. The participants' task was to synchronize the onset of the auditory signal with the onset of the tap. At the end of the trial, a second tone signal was generated by the computer. The next trial was started 5 s after the end of the previous one. Participants were instructed to tap with the index finger only, without any movement of the wrist, and with the other fingers resting on the surface on which the key was mounted. As a way to eliminate visual feedback, participants' eyes were covered throughout the experimental trials.

Data Analysis.   The first 5 taps of a trial were discarded from the data analysis because at least three to five signals are necessary to pick up the beat. The following dependent variables were obtained by averaging the corresponding values of the remaining 20 taps for each trial. First, as a way to check whether participants followed the instruction, mean finger displacement and mean peak velocity of the downward movement were computed per trial. Second, means and standard deviations of asynchronies between the tap onset and the click onset were computed (with negative values indicating a lead of tap onsets over click onsets). A trial was excluded from the final analysis if it contained fewer than 10 measurable finger movements or if the standard deviation of the asynchrony exceeded 100 ms. A participant was dropped from the analysis when more than 25% of his or her trials had to be rejected.

Mean finger displacements, mean peak velocities and mean asynchronies were entered into separate analyses of variance (ANOVAs) with mixed-factor designs. The between-subject factor was the instruction (constrained vs. unconstrained); the within-subject factor was the amplitude (large vs. small).

Results and Discussion

To determine whether participants performed the required movements at all, we first had to check the mean finger displacements in the two conditions. The corresponding ANOVA revealed a highly significant main effect of amplitude $[F (1, 16) = 335.72, p < .001]$, with the means being within the instructed range (large, 62 mm; small, 9 mm). The second significant source of variance was the Amplitude_Instruction interaction $[F (1, 16) = 5.96, p = .03]$. In the group with constrained amplitudes, participants maintained the instructed range of the large displacements (mean $= 68$ mm) while showing a slight undershoot in the condition with small amplitudes (mean $= 8$ mm). In the other group (unconstrained amplitudes), the difference between the amplitudes was somewhat reduced (large, 56 mm; small, 10 mm), although clearly substantial (see the upper panel of Fig. 6.2).

The same pattern of results was revealed by an ANOVA of the peak velocities of the downward movement. Two sources of variance were highly significant: the main amplitude $[F (1, 16) = 253.09, p < .001]$ and the interaction between instruction and amplitude $[F (1, 16) = 12.50, p = .01]$. Large finger displacements were accompanied by high peak velocities and vice versa.

Negative asynchronies between tap onsets and click onsets were observed under all conditions (see the lower panel of Fig. 6.2). In the corresponding ANOVA, only the main effect of amplitude reached significance $[F (1, 16) = 19.91, p < .001]$. As expected, the size of the asynchrony under conditions with large amplitudes (mean $= -24$ ms) was clearly reduced relative to conditions with small amplitudes (mean $= -50$ ms). The interaction between instruction and amplitude approached significance $[F (1, 16) = 2.35, p = .15]$, with asynchronies showing the same tendency as finger displacements: There was a greater difference between the amplitude conditions for the constrained instruction group than for the unconstrained instruction group.

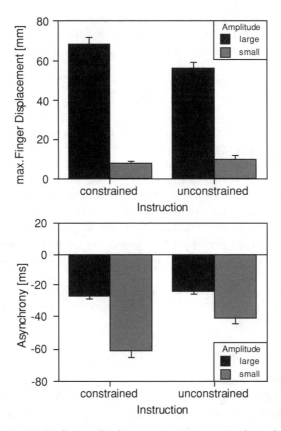

FIG. 6.2. Mean finger displacements (upper panel) and mean asynchronies (lower panel), and standard errors between participants, under two amplitude conditions (large vs. small) and two instructions (constrained vs. unconstrained).

According to the SAM, an increase in the amount of afferent feedback arising from the tap should lead to steeper accumulation functions, which, in turn, should lead to a decrease of negative asynchronies. To test this hypothesis, we asked participants to tap with different finger amplitudes. This manipulation should alter both the tactile and the kinesthetic component of the reafferent stimulation. Results showed that negative asynchronies were in fact reliably smaller for large movements than for small ones. Because this pattern was observed with both instructions (constrained vs. unconstrained), the SAM predictions were basically supported.

However, the question remains whether the conditions with different amplitudes are really as comparable as we thought they would be. Participants reported that performing small movements under constrained conditions was more difficult

than performing large movements. Therefore, amplitude size might have been confounded with task difficulty. In an attempt to avoid this problem, we ran the second
experiment with an isometric version of the tapping task.

EXPERIMENT 2

As a way to test whether the findings of the first experiment were restricted
to the standard tapping task, participants were required to exert isometric force
pulses instead of standard taps under some conditions in the second experiment.
Basically, we manipulated two factors. First, we tested participants in both the
isometric and the standard tapping task. Second, for both tasks we manipulated
the amount of somatosensory stimulation. We achieved this by instructing participants to apply strong versus weak pulses in the isometric task and finger
movements with large versus small amplitudes in the standard tapping task. The
SAM predictions are the same for both tasks: Large amounts of sensory evidence
(arising from strong force pulses or large movement amplitudes) should lead to
steeper accumulation functions than small amounts (weak pulses and small amplitudes, respectively), which should be reflected in a corresponding difference in the
asynchronies.

Method

Participants. Fourteen right-handed new participants participated for pay.
One of them had to be excluded from the final analysis because he failed to produce
sufficient data meeting the preset criteria (see Experiment 1). The remaining 13
participants, 8 men and 5 women, had a mean age of 23 years.

Apparatus and Stimuli. The apparatus and stimuli were the same as in
Experiment 1. In addition, the force applied to the key during contact was measured
by using a force transducer (Sensotec Load Cell, Sensotec Inc., Columbus, Ohio,
USA) with a sampling rate of 1 kHz.

Design and Procedure. The experimental design consisted of two factors,
task (isometric vs. standard) and force (weak vs. strong), resulting in four conditions. All conditions were performed by all participants. Each participant took
part in experimental sessions on 2 consecutive days. In one session, they produced
strong forces (isometric) and, in another condition, performed large amplitudes
(standard); in the other session, they produced weak forces (isometric) and, in
another condition, small amplitudes (standard). Sessions were subdivided into
two blocks of five trials each. In each block, participants were instructed either
to synchronize finger taps (standard tapping task) or, respectively, perform force

pulses (isometric task). For possible transfer effects to be avoided, four different orders of blocks were used. Participants were randomly assigned to one order of blocks.

They were trained to perform the correct amplitude or force at the beginning of each block. The kind of training and the instructed range of the finger amplitudes were identical to those used in Experiment 1. In the isometric task, participants were instructed to synchronize the maximum peak force of the isometric tap and not to release the key; that is, they were instructed to keep contact with the key during the whole sequence. A correct force pulse was defined by a force onset below 1 N and a peak force in the range between 2 and 4 N (weak force condition) or, respectively, in the range between 8 and 12 N (strong force condition). During training, participants received visual feedback of their produced force pulses. No feedback was provided after the training phase. The experimental procedure was identical to that in Experiment 1, except that each sequence now consisted of 35 auditory clicks presented at a rate of 800 ms.

Data Analysis. The data analysis was based on the last 30 clicks of a sequence. In contrast to the previous experiments, the asynchrony was computed as the temporal difference between the click onset and the peak force. This was done to obtain comparable data in both tasks, given that there was no tap onset in the isometric tapping task. The difference between peak force and tap onset in the standard tapping condition is usually below 5 ms (see Gehrke, 1996). For dependent variables, we analyzed the amplitude, the force applied to the key, and the asynchrony between peak force and click onset. Each variable was entered into an ANOVA with the two within-subject factors, task (isometric tapping task vs. standard tapping task) and force (strong vs. weak). The only exception concerned the amplitude of the finger movement, because there were no data in the isometric tapping task.

Results

The amplitudes performed in the two conditions under the standard tapping task differed significantly [F (1, 12) = 80.80, $p < .001$] and were within the predefined ranges (large amplitude, mean = 76 mm; small amplitude, mean = 38 mm). The analysis of the applied forces (including a comparison between the tasks) revealed three significant sources of variance. First, there was a main effect of task [F (1, 12) = 105.30, $p < .001$]; a substantially higher force was observed in the isometric tapping task (7 N) than in the standard tapping task (3 N). Second, there was a significant main effect of force [F (1, 12) = 94.21, $p < .001$]. The weak (3 N) and the strong (7 N) force conditions differed significantly in the instructed direction. Third, the interaction between task and force reached significance [F (1, 12) = 67.34, $p < .001$], indicating that in the isometric task

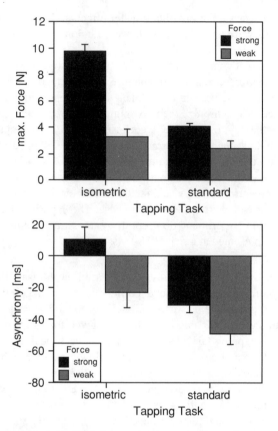

FIG. 6.3. Mean applied forces (upper panel), and mean asynchronies (lower panel), and standard errors between participants,
in two tapping tasks (isometric vs. standard) and two force conditions (instruction: strong vs. weak).

the difference between the force conditions was significantly greater than in the
standard tapping task (see the upper panel of Fig. 6.3).

The analysis of asynchronies between click onset and peak force revealed two
significant factors. The first was task [$F(1, 12) = 14.72$, $p < .001$]. Larger negative asynchronies were observed in the standard tapping task (-40 ms) than
in the isometric task (-7 ms). The main effect of force was also significant
[$F(1, 12) = 14.22$, $p = .01$]. Strong forces went along with smaller asynchronies
(-10 ms) as compared with weaker forces (-37 ms). The interaction of both task
and force factors approached significance [$F(1, 12) = 3.17$, $p = .10$], with asynchronies showing the same tendency as forces: A greater difference between the
force conditions in the isometric task ($+10$ ms vs. -31 ms) than in the standard tapping task (-23 ms vs. -49 ms) was observed (see the lower panel of

Fig. 6.3), with an even *positive* asynchrony in the isometric task with stronger forces [t (12) = 4.50; p < .01].

Discussion

Experiment 2 had two main results. First, we replicated our finding that asynchronies are modulated by finger amplitudes as predicted. Second, and what is more important, we could show that the same relation holds for isometric force pulses. Moreover, the results indicated that task difficulty cannot be responsible for the observed effects. Taken together, these results suggest that the critical factor that determines the time of a tap is the amount of feedback available: Irrespective of the tapping task, with increased sensory feedback the asynchrony decreases.

At the same time, the results also showed a striking difference between the two tasks with respect to both forces and asynchronies: In the isometric condition, forces are stronger than in the standard tapping task throughout; correspondingly, negative asynchronies are smaller and even tend to disappear (for similar results, see Aschersleben, Gehrke, & Prinz, 2001). This difference is in line with the SAM prediction that the amount of afferent feedback determines the steepness of the accumulation function and the time at which the tap is perceived relative to the click. With strong forces (10 N), the temporal order of the two events may even be reversed, indicating that the generation of the tap code may, under this condition, even be faster than the generation of the click code. In summary, we may thus conclude that the amount of afferent signals that are elicited by the peripheral stimulation and transmitted to the brain has a strong impact on the perceived time of the tap.

EXPERIMENT 3

The results of the first two experiments clearly support the SAM. There is an influence of the amount of feedback on the asynchrony for both standard taps and isometric force taps. Notably, although the synchronization task is primarily a motor task, the SAM's basic assumptions refer to the sensory aspects of this task. According to the model, the dependence of the asynchrony on feedback reflects an inflow-based, sensory effect, with no outflow-based, motor component involved. Accordingly, the model's scope is by no means restricted to sensory signals arising from motor acts. Instead, the SAM predicts that the timing of *any* sensory signal should be dependent on the rise time of the buildup of its central representation. Experiment 3 was designed to test this assumption by using a psychophysical method. We designed a perceptual experiment that mirrors as much as possible the tapping situation: Participants had to indicate the presentation order of an electrical stimulus applied to the fingertip and an auditory comparison stimulus. There were two electrical stimuli that were assumed to differ in the steepness of their accumulation functions, a weak and a strong stimulus, respectively. According to the logic of the SAM, one should expect that, in order to be judged as simultaneous with the auditory comparison stimulus, the weak electrical stimulus would have to be presented earlier than the strong electrical stimulus.

Method

Participants.   Twelve new participants took part for pay. The data of 1 subject were eliminated because of technical problems. The remaining 11 participants, 5 men and 6 women, had a mean age of 25 years.

Apparatus and Stimuli.   Participants were seated at a table in front of a computer monitor and a keyboard in a sound-absorbing room. The electrical stimulation electrode was applied at the right index finger. The stimulus consisted of a continuous sequence (5 Hz) of electrical pulses (300 V, 7–32 μA) with a duration of 10 ms. The auditory comparison signal [400 Hz, 82 dB(A), and 10-ms duration] was presented binaurally through headphones (Sennheiser HD 250). The auditory stimuli were produced by a personal computer (Pegasys 486/33) via a digital-to-analog converter (Data Translation Card DT2821) and an amplifier (Phillips FA 630).

Procedure.   The experiment consisted of two parts: in one part the weak electrical stimulus was applied; in the other, the strong electrical stimulus was applied. The order of these two parts was balanced across participants. The current through the skin electrodes for the electrical stimulation at the finger was adjusted for each participant. Because of the individual electrical resistance values of each participant's skin, we first determined the perceptual threshold by using the psychophysical method of limits. In the condition with weak stimulation, the electrical stimulus was 10% above threshold; in the conditions with strong stimulation, the stimulus applied to the participant's finger was 100% above threshold.

For temporal order judgments for the somatosensory and auditory stimulus to be obtained, the staircase method was applied (e.g., see Cornsweet, 1962; Levitt, 1971). Each experimental part (weak vs. strong electrical stimulation) consisted of four blocks. For each block, successive trials were selected from two randomly intermingled staircases, one starting with the sound preceding the electrical stimulus by a 200-ms stimulus onset asynchrony (SOA), the other with the sound following the electrical stimulus by the same SOA. When the "sound first" key was pressed, the sound for the next trial on the same staircase was delayed by one SOA step relative to the electrical stimulus, and vice versa after a "sound second" key press. At some point on each staircase, *reversals*, defined as responses different from the preceding one on the same staircase, began to occur. An exploration was stopped automatically as soon as 10 reversals had been recorded on each of the two staircases. Each staircase started with 20-ms steps and shifted to 10-ms steps once the SOA reached −100 ms or +100 ms. On each trial, the task was to indicate, by pressing one of two keys on a standard keyboard, whether the sound or the electrical stimulus was presented first.

Results and Discussion

The analysis was based on the SOAs at which the first 10 response reversals occurred on each staircase. For the point of subjective simultaneity (50% threshold) to be determined, means of the two intermingled presented staircases were calculated. Furthermore, means were calculated per condition across the last three blocks (the first block was treated as a practice block), the 10 reversals per block, and the 11 participants. A t test comparing the two conditions, weak versus strong electrical stimulation, revealed a significant difference [$t(10) = 4.92; p = .001$]. The weak electrical stimulus had to be presented 35 ms before the auditory stimulus to be judged as simultaneous with it; the strong stimulus had to precede the auditory stimulus by only 2 ms.

By using a psychophysical staircase method, we were able to gather additional evidence in favor of our model. The finding that, to be judged as occurring simultaneously with the auditory comparison stimulus, weaker somatosensory stimuli had to be presented earlier than stronger ones supports our assumption that the amount of evidence available from a perceptual event determines the steepness of the accumulation function at a central level and, thus, the time this event is dated. Therefore, we were able to validate the logic inherent in the SAM.[1]

GENERAL DISCUSSION

What can our results contribute to the issue raised in the introduction, that is, how do we perceive the times of our own actions? Our findings are in clear support of an inflow-based account of action perception. More specifically, the evidence suggests that the perceived time of an action is determined by the pattern of sensory and perceptual information arising from it.

---

[1]At first sight, it appears that an alternative explanation of this pattern of results can be derived from the prior entry account. Increasing the intensity of the feedback may attract more attention and, as a result, lead to faster processing; this in turn would decrease the asynchrony. However, if there was any implicit attentional manipulation at all (which would still have to be proved), it would have been rather small in comparison with typical prior entry experiments in which attention is manipulated explicitly through instructions. That is, the resulting difference in processing is likely to be negligible. Moreover, the SAM explains the observed effect by assuming only one hypothetical factor, whereas prior entry requires two. On the prior entry account, the difference in stimulus intensity leads to a difference in attention allocation, which in turn leads to a difference in processing speed. In contrast, the SAM assumes that the difference in stimulus intensity directly produces a difference in processing speed, without detour by means of the hypothetical factor of attention. In other words, the SAM is more parsimonious than prior entry.

The perception of an action's time could, in principle, be based on three sources of information: information arising in the brain, in the body, and in the world. The earliest information about an upcoming action is available in the brain, that is, in the outflow that takes care of action planning, action preparation, and action control. Outflow accounts of action perception assume that the perception of ongoing actions is based on this early information. Unlike the early outflow, which arises in the brain, inflow comes later and arises outside the brain. One source of action-related information is the actor's body, where sensory information about ongoing movements is generated (in muscles, joints, etc.). The other source of action-related inflow comes from the actor's environment, providing sensory information about the environmental consequences of ongoing movements.

The SAM suggests that the system uses inflow rather than outflow for action perception and timing; that is, it posits that an action's time is assessed on the basis of the sensory information available from it. Further, our findings suggest a stronger role for world-based inflow than for body-based inflow. We derive this tentative conclusion from the observation that exactly the same intensity-driven modulation as in tactile stimuli arising from self-generated taps is also observed in electrical stimuli driven by external sources.

A strong role for exteroceptive inflow for action timing is also supported from synchronization experiments with artificial feedback. In these studies we again had participants synchronize taps with clicks, but we added an artificial extrinsic feedback signal (beep) to the natural intrinsic feedback provided by propriocep-tive and tactile information (Aschersleben & Prinz, 1997; Mates & Aschersleben, 2000). This paradigm allows one to study the impact of inflow factors in isolation, that is, free from any possible confoundings with outflow factors. First consider the situation in which the delivery of that beep is triggered by the onset of the tap. In this situation, the occurrence of the combined tap–beep event is signaled to the brain via two pathways—somatosensory and auditory. Because the auditory path-way is shorter than the somatosensory one, the auditory information should arrive earlier than the tactile information. In fact, the size of the negative asynchrony was reduced under this condition, indicating that the occurrence of the combined tap–beep event was perceived slightly earlier than the occurrence of the tap-alone event in the control condition (where extrinsic feedback was absent).

In further experiments, we studied what happens when the delivery of the beep is shifted forward or backward in time, relative to tap onset. In the first study, the delivery of the auditory feedback signal was delayed up to 70 ms after tap onset—a range within which people still perceive the feedback signals in perfect synchrony with their taps (Aschersleben & Prinz, 1995, 1997). What we observed was that negative asynchronies increased with increasing delays in feedback delivery. More specifically, our results indicated that the two feedback signals—intrinsic and ex-trinsic, arising in the body and the environment, respectively—become integrated and that the time of the integrated signal is computed as a linear combination of the times of its two components.

A different picture emerged in the second study, where the beep *preceded* tap onset (to the effect that it coincided in time with the finger's downward stroke; Mates & Aschersleben, 2000). Under this condition, we found almost no effect of the beep on the size of the asynchrony. Thus, the integration of feedback information appears to be asymmetric. Feedback sources that precede the onset of the tap tend to be disregarded, whereas feedback sources that follow tap onset become integrated and determine the time at which the tap is perceived.

In summary, the evidence derived from both the present experiments and our earlier studies on the role of artificial extrinsic feedback converge on the conclusion that the time of an action is based on the inflow arising from it. The perception of one's own actions and the perception of environmental events appears to be made "of the same stuff." They are both based on sensory inflow arising from the action and its consequences.

If this is true, the question arises why the system does not make use of the earlier sources of ongoing actions, that is, the outflow arising from their early antecedents. Outflow accounts of action perception tend to emphasize that, via outflow, the perceptual system has direct, privileged access to action, whereas, via inflow, it has to action the same indirect, nonprivileged access as to any other event in the world. Why, then, should the privileged access not be used?

One possible answer is that it may be adaptive for the system to represent information about its own activity in exactly the same format as information about what is going on in the environment (Hommel, Müsseler, Aschersleben, & Prinz, 2001; Prinz, 1991). Because the system's main job is to coordinate actions with events, it may be advantageous to generate a common representational domain where they are both coded in terms of the same representational dimensions. According to this reasoning, the system does better without making use of outflow information: It dispenses with this information for the sake of supporting the coordination of actions and events through common coding.

ACKNOWLEDGMENT

We thank David Rosenbaum and Patrick Haggard for their helpful comments on an earlier draft of this paper.

REFERENCES

Aschersleben, G. (1999). Task-dependent timing of perceptual events. In G. Aschersleben, T. Bachmann, & J. Müsseler (Eds.), *Cognitive contributions to the perception of spatial and temporal events* (pp. 293–318). Amsterdam: Elsevier.

Aschersleben. G. (2001). Temporal control of movements in sensorimotor synchronization. *Brain and Cognition, 48*, 66–79.

Aschersleben, G. (in press). Effects of training on the timing of repetitive movements. In F. Columbus (Ed.), *Advances in psychology research*. Huntington, NY, US: Nova Science Publishers.

Aschersleben, G., Gehrke, J., & Prinz, W. (2001). Tapping with peripheral nerve block: A role for tactile feedback in the timing of movements. *Experimental Brain Research, 136*, 331–339.

Aschersleben, G., & Müsseler, J. (1999). Dissociations in the timing of stationary and moving stimuli. *Journal of Experimental Psychology: Human Perception & Performance, 25*, 1709–1720.

Aschersleben, G., & Prinz, W. (1995). Synchronizing actions with events: The role of sensory information. *Perception & Psychophysics, 57*, 305–317.

Aschersleben, G., & Prinz, W. (1997). Delayed auditory feedback in synchronization. *Journal of Motor Behavior, 29*, 35–46.

Billon, M., Semjen, A., Cole, J., & Gauthier, G. (1996). The role of sensory information in the production of periodic finger-tapping sequences. *Experimental Brain Research, 110*, 117–130.

Birbaumer, N., Elbert, T., Canavan, A. G., & Rockstroh, B. (1990). Slow potentials of the cerebral cortex and behavior. *Physiological Reviews, 70*, 1–41.

Boyd, I. A., & Roberts, T. D. M. (1953). Proprioceptive discharges from stretch-receptors in the knee-joint of the cat. *Journal of Physiology, 122*, 38–58.

Coles, M. G. H. (1986). *Psychophysiology*. New York: Guilford Press.

Collyer, C. E., Broadbent, H. A., & Church, R. M. (1994). Preferred rates of repetitive tapping and categorical time production. *Perception & Psychophysics, 55*, 443–453.

Cornsweet, T. N. (1962). The staircase-method in psychophysics. *American Journal of Psychology, 75*, 485–491.

Edin, B. B., & Vallbo, A. (1990). Dynamic response of human muscle spindle afferents to stretch. *Journal of Neurophysiology, 63*, 1297–1306.

Fechner, G. T. (1860). *Elemente der Psychophysik* [Elements of psychophysics]. Leipzig, Germany: Breitkopf & Härtel.

Fraisse, P. (1966). L'anticipation de stimulus rhythmiques, vitesse d'établissement et précision de la synchronisation [Anticipation of rhythmical stimuli, set-up speed and accuracy of synchronization]. *L' Année Psychologique, 66*, 15–36.

Fraisse, P. (1980). Les synchronisations sensori-motrices aux rythmes. [The sensorimotor synchronization of rhythms] In J. Requin (Ed.), *Anticipation et comportement* (pp. 233–257). Paris: Centre National.

Gandevia, S. C., McCloskey, D. I., & Burke, D. (1992). Kinesthetic signals and muscle contraction. *Trends in Neuroscience, 15*, 62–65.

Gehrke, J. (1996). *Afferente Informationsverarbeitung und die Synchronisation von Ereignissen* [Afferent information processing and the synchronization of events]. Unpublished doctoral dissertation, Ludwig Maximilians University, Munich.

Gescheider, G. A. (1966). Resolving of successive clicks by the ears and the skin. *Journal of Experimental Psychology, 39*, 378–381.

Haggard, P., & Eimer, M. (1999). On the relation between brain potentials and the awareness of voluntary movements. *Experimental Brain Research, 126*, 128–133.

Hanes, D. P., & Schall, J. D. (1996). Neural control of voluntary movement initiation. *Science, 274*, 427–430.

Harrington, T., & Merzenich, M. M. (1970). Neural coding in the sense of touch: human sensation of skin indentation compared with the responses of slowly adapting mechanoreceptive afferents innervating the hairy skin of monkeys. *Experimental Brain Research, 10*, 251–264.

Hary, D., & Moore, G. P. (1985). Temporal tracking and synchronization strategies. *Human Neurobiology, 4*, 73–77.

Hashimoto, I., Gatayama, T., Tamaki, M., Ushijima, R., Yoshikawa, K., Sasaki, M., Nomura, M., & Isojima, H. (1991). Multi-unit activity in sensory fibers is related to intensity of sensation evoked by air-puff stimulation of the glabrous hand in man. *Electroencephalography and Clinical Neurophysiology, 81*, 466–472.

Helmholtz, H. L. (1866). *Handbuch der physiologischen Optik* [Handbook of physiological optics] (Vol. 3, pp. 203–207). Hamburg, Germany: Voss.

Hirsh, I. J. (1959). Auditory perception of temporal order. *Journal of the Acoustical Society of America, 31,* 759–767.

Hommel, B., Müsseler, J., Aschersleben, G., & Prinz, W. (2001). The theory of event coding (TEC): A framework for perception and action planning. *Behavioral and Brain Sciences, 24,* 849–878.

Johansson, R., & Vallbo, A. (1976). Skin mechanoreceptors in the human hand. An inference of some population properties. In Y. Zotterman (Ed.), *Sensory functions of the skin* (pp. 171–184). Oxford, England: Pergamon Press.

Johansson, R. S., & Vallbo, A. (1979). Detection of tactile stimuli. Thresholds of afferent units related to psychophysical thresholds in the human hand. *Journal of Physiology, 297,* 405–422.

Knibestöl, M., & Vallbo, A. B. (1980). Intensity of sensation related to activity of slowly adapting mechanoreceptive units in the human hand. *Journal of Physiology, 300,* 251–267.

Levitt, H. (1971). Transformed up-down methods in psychoacoustics. *Journal of the Acoustical Society of America, 49,* 467–477.

Libet, B. (1985). Unconscious cerebral initiative and the role of conscious will in voluntary action. *The Behavioral and Brain Sciences, 8,* 529–566.

Libet, B. (1996). Neural processes in the production of conscious experience. In M. Velmans (Ed.), *The science of consciousness* (pp. 96–117). London: Routledge.

Libet, B., Gleason, C. A., Wright, E. W., & Pearl, D. K. (1983). Time of conscious intention to act in relation to onset of cerebral activity. *Brain, 106,* 623–642.

Libet, B., Wright, E. W., Jr., Feinstein, B., & Pearl, D. K. (1979). Subjective referral of the timing for a conscious sensory experience: A functional role for the somatosensory-specific projection system in man. *Brain, 102,* 193–224.

Mates, J. (1994a). A model of synchronization of motor acts to a stimulus sequence. I. Timing and error corrections. *Biological Cybernetics, 70,* 463–473.

Mates, J. (1994b). A model of synchronization of motor acts to a stimulus sequence. II. Stability analysis, error estimation and simulations. *Biological Cybernetics, 70,* 475–484.

Mates, J., & Aschersleben, G. (2000). Sensorimotor synchronization: The influence of temporally displaced auditory feedback. *Acta Psychologica, 104,* 29–44.

McKeon, B., & Burke, D. (1983). Muscle spindle discharge in response to contraction of single motor units. *Journal of Neurophysiology, 49,* 291–302.

Mittelstaedt, H. (1990). Basic solutions to the problem of head-centric visual localization. In R. Warren & A. H. Wertheim (Eds.), *Perception & control of self-motion* (pp. 267–287). Hillsdale, NJ: Lawrence Erlbaum Associates.

Müller, K., Aschersleben, G., Koch, R., Freund, H.-J., & Prinz, W. (1999). Action timing in an isochronous tapping task: Evidence from behavioral studies and neuroimaging. In G. Aschersleben, T. Bachmann, & J. Müsseler (Eds.), *Cognitive contributions to the perception of spatial and temporal events* (pp. 233–250). Amsterdam: Elsevier.

Müller, K., Schmitz, F., Schnitzler, A., Freund, H.-J., Aschersleben, G., & Prinz, W. (2000). Neuromagnetic correlates of sensorimotor synchronization. *Journal of Cognitive Neuroscience, 12,* 546–555.

Paillard, J. (1949). Quelques données psychophysiologiques relatives au déclenchement de la commande motrice [Some psychophysiological data relating to the triggering of motor commands]. *L'Année Psychologique, 48,* 28–47.

Prinz, W. (1991). *Why don't we perceive our brain states?* (Paper No. 1/1991). München: Max-Planck-Institut für Psychologische Forschung.

Redding, G. M., & Wallace, B. (1997). *Adaptive spatial alignment.* Mahwah, NJ: Lawrence Erlbaum Associates.

Repp, B. (2001). Phase correction, phase resetting, and phase shifts after subliminal timing perturbations in sensorimotor synchronization. *Journal of Experimental Psychology: Human Perception and Performance, 27,* 600–621.

Skoglund, S. (1956). Anatomical and physiological studies of knee joint innervation in the cat. *Acta Psychologica Scandinavica, 36*, 1–101.

Stevens, S. S. (1957). On the psychophysical law. *Physiological Review, 64*, 153–181.

Vorberg, D., & Wing, A. (1996). Modeling variability and dependence in timing. In H. Heuer & S. W. Keele (Eds.), *Handbook of perception and action: Motor skills* (Vol. 3, 181–261). London: Academic Press.

Vos, P. G., Mates, J., & Van Kruysbergen, N. W. (1995). The perceptual centre of a stimulus as the cue for synchronization to a metronome: Evidence from asynchronies. *Quarterly Journal of Experimental Psychology, 48A*, 1024–1040.

Werner, G., & Mountcastle, V. B. (1965). Neural activity in mechanoreceptive cutaneous afferents: Stimulus-response relations, Weber functions, and information transmission. *Journal of Neurophysiology, 28*, 359–397.

Wing, A. M., & Kristofferson, A. B. (1973a). Response delay and the timing of discrete motor responses. *Perception & Psychophysics, 14*, 5–12.

Wing, A. M., & Kristofferson, A. B. (1973b). The timing of interresponse intervals. *Perception & Psychophysics, 13*, 455–460.

7

Synchronization and Stimulus Timing: Implications for Temporal Models of Visual Information Processing

Mark A. Elliott and Hermann J. Müller
Ludwig-Maximilians-Universität, München, Germany

THE NATURE OF PERCEPTUAL ORGANIZATION AS A TEMPORAL PROCESS

In the visual system, objects and object groupings may be initially coded in terms of physically separable attributes or features, representing differential spatial frequencies, orientations, colors, directions of motion, and so on, which in combination come to define wholistic perceptual representations. Although it has been known for some time that visuocortical neurons can display quite specific response preferences for particular features, it is only recently that evidence has been gathered concerning the mechanisms by which these specific neural representations might become combined or "bound" to form a unified representation.

In a series of electrophysiological studies, Gray, König, Engel, and Singer (1989; see also Eckhorn et al., 1988) reported that, when the receptive fields of visuocortical cells in anesthetized cats were stimulated by separate bars of light moving in opposite directions (i.e., when the light bars were not apparently related), neural responses were unrelated. However, when bars were passed across the receptive fields in the same direction, a correlative relationship was observed between emergent oscillations within the 20- to 80-Hz frequency range. The strongest cross-correlations were obtained when a single, connected bar stimulated two separate neurons. The emergent oscillations and associated cross-correlations between neuronal firing patterns were only obtained for different cells when those cells responded to the parallel trajectories of the separate bar stimuli. Thus, the oscillatory and "synchronized" neuronal activity may be considered one important neurophysiological correlate with the processes by which independent stimulus activities may come to be bound within a unitary perceptual framework. By generalization, this idea has been extended to the perception of visual groupings, giving rise to the hypothesis that the perception of a Gestalt derives from the binding of separate feature-attributes by means of similar, if not identical, patterns of oscillatory neuronal synchronization.

The empirical support for this hypothesis of binding by synchronization by oscillation rests mainly on physiological experiments with anesthetized animals. However, convergent evidence has been provided by psychophysical experiments, which showed that detection of multielement target groupings (configurations) presented within a matrix of homogeneous distractor elements may be enhanced by the prior presentation of a temporally synchronized (target figure-neutral) priming stimulus (see Elliott & Müller, 1998, Experiments 1 and 3). Specifically, detection reaction times (RTs) to a display matrix containing a target Kanizsa-type square (an illusory square consisting of grouping 90° corner junctions) were expedited when the target was preceded by the presentation of four temporally synchronized crosses within a flickering matrix comprising multiple, asynchronized premask crosses (see Fig. 7.1).

The effects of the synchronized-cross (hereafter "synchronous premask") presentation were measured relative to a random-premask condition, in which one frame comprised four crosses that were pseudorandomly arranged in a nonsquare configuration; see Fig. 7.1(b).[1] In an examination of the difference between synchronous and random-condition RTs as a function of premask-presentation frequency (see Fig. 7.2), RTs were found to be expedited for synchronous relative to random premask presentation only when targets followed premask matrices presented at 40 Hz. Furthermore, these RT enhancements occurred only when the synchronous premask was presented across the locations in the premask matrix subsequently occupied by the target figure (Elliott & Müller, 1998, Experiment 3). That the RT enhancements were confined to target-present conditions (target specificity) in which the synchronous premask and target elements shared the same display locations (spatial specificity) was interpreted as evidence for the

---

[1] Additional findings of priming even when the premask matrix contained no local target-relevant inducer edges (i.e., when the edge-aligned premask crosses were replaced by circles; see Müller & Elliott, 1999) suggest a more precise, segregative function for neuronal synchronization. By this account, early synchronization might serve as a code by which activity representing the elements belonging to the figure can be easily differentiated from those across figurally unrelated, distractor elements (see von der Malsburg, 1981).

(a)

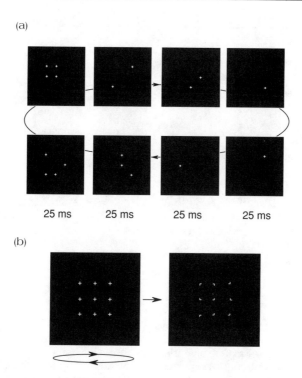

25 ms   25 ms   25 ms   25 ms

(b)

FIG. 7.1. (a) Example sequence of the four separate premask frames in the synchronous and random-premask conditions. Elliott and Müller (1998) used these seven premask-presentation frequencies: 25, 29, 33, 40, 50, 67, and 100 Hz. For the 40-Hz premask-presentation condition, frequency was defined as the frequency of occurrence of premask subsets per second; that is, the entire premask matrix was presented as 10 times the four premask frames per 1,000 ms, with a constant subset exposure duration of 25 ms and an interframe interval of < 1 ms. (b) The premask sequence was continually recycled for a period of time, after which the premask-matrix elements reduced to simple corner junctions. (In Elliott and Müller, 1998, priming effects were consistent across presentation times between 300 and 4,800 ms; in subsequent studies, presentation times were kept constant at either 600 or 1,200 ms.)

idea that synchronous premask presentation "primes" target coding by virtue of the organization of activity across the premask matrix in phases of the premask-matrix presentation rhythm. By this account, mechanisms responding to elements of the synchronous premask frame would become synchronized within a single phase, but they would be asynchronized relative to the mechanisms responding to other, nongrouping, distractor premask crosses, which would themselves become

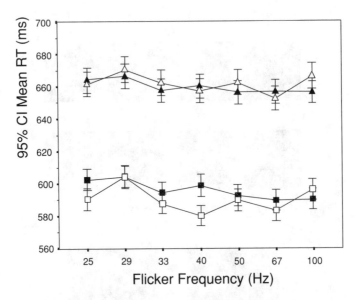

FIG. 7.2. Mean target-present RT synchronicity enhancements (random RTs minus synchronous RTs) as a function of premask-presentation frequency for frequencies across the 25- to 100-Hz range. The squares and triangles represent target-present and target-absent conditions, respectively, and the unfilled and filled symbols represent synchronous and random-premask presentation conditions, respectively. The target-present RTs reveal that significant priming occurred only for premask-matrix presentation at 40 Hz. CI = confidence interval.

synchronized across different spatial arrangements (when more than one cross is presented in a given distractor frame).

The spatial specificity of the priming effects provides some indication of the possible locus of prime activity. In particular, priming might arise as a result of the synchronization of mechanisms located in early visual areas, consisting of neurons with relatively small receptive fields. That synchronization occurs at a late stage of visual coding would appear to be precluded by observations that, in brain areas such as the temporal cortex, the receptive fields of single neurons are sufficiently large for the neurons to respond to stimuli anywhere within the premask matrix. If synchronization occurred late, then some effects of priming might be expected purely on the basis of synchronous premask presentation alone, irrespective of its precise location. A further argument against a late locus of prime formation derives from the finding that observers were unable to discern the composition of individual frames within the 40-Hz premask matrix (mean signal detection sensitivity parameter $A_z = 0.528$, $SD = 0.058$; chance level = 0.500; see Elliott & Müller, 1998, Experiment 2).

Implicit in the notion of stimulus-induced synchronization is the idea that the priming effects are likely to arise directly from transient properties of the stimuli. One possibility is that highly dynamic stimuli engage motion-coding mechanisms, which, it has been argued, could provide one account for demonstrations of temporally induced perceptual grouping with correlated stimulus motion (e.g., Alais, Blake & Lee, 1998). Temporally induced perceptual grouping would thus be explicable in terms of the spatiotemporal correlations ordinarily computed within motion-sensitive mechanisms (Gegenfurtner, 1998). However, inconsistent with this suggestion, Elliott and Müller (2001) found that the effects of priming by means of premask-matrix presentation were little influenced by possible motion signals induced by premask-matrix flicker or during the instantaneous transformation of the premask into the target matrix. Another possibility is that the development of an oscillatory structure to nonmoving dynamic stimulus presentations will closely follow the time course of local stimulus events. This possibility relates directly to the implicit notion of priming by means of the phase of premask presentation and, in the case of premask presentation, raises the question as to which stimulus frequency best explains the tendency for prime formation at 40 Hz: In particular, it has been noted (Müller, 1999) that the four-frame premask matrix used by Elliott and Müller (1998) results in local element repetitions at 10, rather than 40 Hz; see Fig. 7.1(b). This raises the question whether the temporal characteristics of the prime should be considered in terms of local 10-Hz (steady-state) responses in the neural substrate, rather than a 40-Hz response to the premask matrix as a whole.

A number of theoretical considerations (outlined in subsequent paragraphs) have offered support to the idea that when premask matrices flicker at 40 Hz, the resulting code that develops around the synchronous premask matches (in phase) the global frequency of the premask presentation. Nevertheless, for this idea to be examined more specifically, subsequent studies were designed to examine the temporal characteristics of prime activity (its oscillatory structure) by measuring priming effects at various interstimulus intervals (ISIs) between the premask-matrix offset and the target-matrix onset (e.g., Elliott & Müller, 2000). A prerequisite for these studies, which also offered an important indication of the type of mechanism at work during prime coding, was an examination of the duration of prime "persistence" in the absence of an inducing stimulus. As is illustrated in Fig. 7.3, the prime was reduced in efficiency between ISIs of 0 and 150–200 ms, which is consistent with the idea of persistence as a decaying visual trace with a duration of approximately 240–300 ms from prime-stimulus onset (taking into account that the onset of the final priming, i.e., synchronous premask, frame occurred 100 ms before the premask-matrix offset, so that the duration of synchronous prime persistence should be calculated as 100 ms + 150–200 ms). In a follow-up study (Wendt, 2000), the premask-presentation duration was set at 625 ms (rather than 600 ms, as in Elliott & Müller, 2000), permitting a more reliable estimate of the duration of prime persistence from the onset of the final (synchronous premask) frame

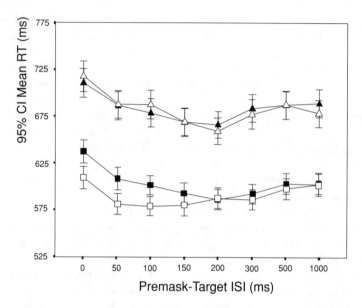

FIG. 7.3. Mean target-present and target-absent RTs (squares and triangles) for the synchronous and random-premask conditions (filled and unfilled symbols), as a function of premask-target ISI. The convergence of the lower functions at between 150 and 200 ms confirms that prime activity persists for up to 150 ms following premask-matrix termination. CI = confidence interval.

in the premask-presentation sequence (i.e., when the onset of the final synchronous premask frame occurred 25 ms before the premask-matrix offset). Consistent with the persistence estimate of Elliott and Müller (2000), that is, 250–300 ms, Wendt found evidence of prime persistence following premask-target ISIs of 300 ms, but not with ISIs of 400 ms and longer.

These estimates of approximately 300 ms correspond well with estimates of visual-stimulus persistence (i.e., 240 ms; see Efron, 1970a, 1970b, 1970c), which are described in terms of stimuli that are fully perceived by the observer (Coltheart, 1980). Thus, it may be concluded that the synchronous prime possesses a persistence duration consistent with that of visible stimuli, despite the fact that observers are unable to detect the presence of the synchronous premask frame within the premask matrix. A possible resolution to this apparent inconsistency is based on the idea that the synchronous prime is generated within the spatiotemporal context of the entire premask matrix (including the elements of the synchronous premask), which is, of course, fully visible. This entails that the synchronous prime inherits persistence properties from the premask matrix as a whole, which would account for why persistence extends beyond durations evoked by undetected stimuli (i.e., 80 ms; see Engel, 1970).

Concerning the presumed oscillatory structure of the synchronous prime, it remained an empirical issue whether the phase of any such code is better described in terms of a local 10-Hz rhythm or a global 40-Hz rhythm. Although visual mechanisms are commonly assumed to respond to local periodicities in the stimulus, there are several findings that cast doubt on this assumption with regard to the present paradigm. In particular, the absence of effects related to variations in local premask-feature specification and, indeed, the apparent redundancy of edge-aligned premask elements for generation of the priming effects (see Elliott & Müller, 2001; Müller & Elliott, 1999), suggest that priming works by means of the segregation of the synchronous premask frame from distractor frames (rather than element–element, i.e., feature–conjunction, binding). Given that segregation here refers to segregation in time (no spatial segregation is actually perceived), it is unlikely that segregated temporal codes develop independently across the local premask-matrix presentation frames (in the form of multiple local 10-Hz oscillations). Rather, more plausibly, if the synchronous prime is generated within the spatiotemporal context of the premask matrix as a whole, it follows that segregation of the synchronous premask must occur within the context of the global 40-Hz rhythm of premask presentation for which a common reference frequency is available for local phase adjustments.

In this respect it is important to note that, by this temporal-segregation account, entrainment would be expected to occur for all premask-matrix elements (irrespective of the Gestalt properties of a given premask frame). Under these circumstances, the pattern of activity across the premask matrix would come to take the form of multiple, separately oscillating neural clusters, each maintaining an internally synchronized and thereby specific pattern of activity across appropriate premask-matrix elements. In this way, the synchronous prime would develop and become maintained separately in time relative to other clusters of oscillatory neural activity. It is important that the notion of segmentation in time, or more specifically in phases, of the global premask-matrix presentation frequency makes quite clear the notion that the temporal characteristics of mechanisms coding local premask frames should be considered in terms of a 40-Hz response, with representations of the synchronous prime and of the three distractor frames located uniquely within different phases of this globally induced rhythm. Although this idea is consistent with computationally derived theories of information storage within different phases of a general processing rhythm (see, e.g., Lisman & Idiart, 1995), the empirical question remains as to whether or not, when premask matrices flicker globally at 40 Hz, the prime comes to possess a matching oscillatory structure.

To answer to this question, Elliott and Müller (2000) conducted a series of experiments with target presentation following at ISIs approximating a $0°$, $90°$, or $180°$ phase-angle extension to the global presentation rhythm of the premask-matrix frames. That is, phase angles were defined in terms of ISI duration relative to a hypothetical stimulus-locked 40-Hz rhythm. Thus, with the assumption of a

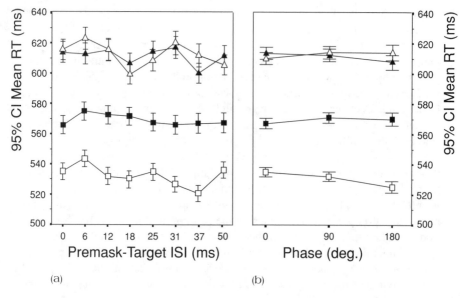

FIG. 7.4. Mean target-present and target-absent RTs (squares and triangles) for the synchronous and random-premask conditions (filled and unfilled symbols), as a function of (a) premask-target ISI and (b) phase angle. In (a), RTs are characterized by a modulatory (40-Hz) pattern across ISIs. In (b), priming effects are revealed to be maximal when target presentation followed ISIs corresponding to a 180° phase shift in the rhythm of the premask-matrix presentation.

periodic (temporal-impulse response) function of 25-ms duration with minima at 0 and 25 ms and maximum at 12.5 ms, the ISIs (within the range 0–50 ms) were 0, 25, and 50 ms for the 0° phase-angle condition, 6, 18, and 31 ms for the 90° condition, and 12 and 37 ms for the 180° condition. As shown in Fig. 7.4, by alternating 0°, 90°, and 180° phase-angle ISIs within the range 0–50 ms, there was indeed a significant phase-angle effect, which greater priming for targets presented at 180° phase-angle ISIs compared with 0° ISIs. This pattern was confirmed in another experiment using ISIs across the range 0–137 ms, and, as shown in Fig. 7.5, an experiment examining ISIs, in 4-ms steps, across the range from 25 (0° phase angle) to 49 ms (∼0°). In the latter experiment, priming was strongest for the 37-ms ISI (∼180°), with a significant difference between the 37-ms (∼180°) ISI and the 25-ms (0°) ISI. The nonlinearly changing priming effects at intermediate ISIs produced a quadratic enhancement–ISI function, providing strong support for the idea that synchronous prime persistence was maintained within a 40-Hz oscillation, with maximal RT enhancements to targets presented at a 180° phase angle relative to the rhythm established by premask-matrix presentation.

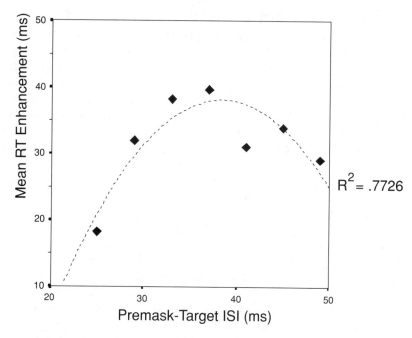

FIG. 7.5. Mean target-present RT synchronicity enhancements (random RTs minus the synchronous RTs) as a function of ISI. Also illustrated is the quadratic function that best fitted the RT priming effects, reaching its maximum at 37-ms ISIs, which corresponds to a phase angle of ~ 180° relative to the projected rhythm of premask-matrix presentation.

It is important that the modulatory pattern obtained in these experiments was confined to the synchronous premask (target-present) RTs, with no general pattern of periodicity evident for the target-absent or random-premask RTs. This pattern of results strongly supports the idea that the observed priming effects reflect the operation of an oscillatory segregative mechanism that becomes engaged by synchronous premask presentation, rather than the activity of other, more general, mechanisms related to stimulus encoding or response generation.[2]

---

[2] An analysis of the RT distributions from a number of experiments provides evidence of periodicities present in the RT data. Autocorrellograms derived from the RT distributions of individual observers indeed show peaks at between 3 and 4 ms and at 24 ms. These peak periods are invariant relative to changes in stimulus conditions, the type of response (target present or absent), the observer's handedness, and the phase of target presentation relative to the 40-Hz rhythm of premask-matrix presentation, and they are also invariant across subjects. Although this invariance is interesting in its own respect, in the present context it precludes a simple account of the 40-Hz modulation of synchronous target RTs in terms of a tendency for response preparation or generation to occur in phase with a stimulus-driven 40-Hz rhythm.

A RECURRENT MODEL
OF SYNCHRONOUS PRIME GENERATION

The ideas advanced herein to account for the evidence of premask persistence involve two apparently contradictory assumptions: Whereas priming is assumed to occur in early mechanisms where the spatial specificity of stimulus information is preserved, the oscillatory structure of prime activity is assumed to be generated by some mechanism capable of coding relations across the entire premask display. However, this contradiction can be resolved by consideration of how synchrony might be propagated within the brain.

It is reasonable to assume that the relative structure in the patterning of temporal-impulse responses to local premask-matrix elements is preserved with fidelity irrespective of the number of neural junctions through which this information passes. Furthermore, many visual areas will be involved in premask-matrix coding, including relatively late areas, because premask-matrix presentation has a direct conscious–perceptual consequence. Thus, the phase of premask-matrix presentations may be preserved, at least in relative terms, within the entire system responsible for perception of the premask matrix. However, the particular (late) mechanism responsible for rendering the premask matrix into consciousness is apparently unable to resolve the temporal asynchronies existing between premask frames, even to the extent that the first and last frames in the four-frame sequence (which are separated by some 50 ms) are perceived at the "same time." This cannot be attributed to certain fixed and relatively slow response frequencies of cells at later stages in the system. For example, inferotemporal (IT) cells, with receptive fields greater than 20° of visual angle (i.e., a diameter approximately three times the size of the premask matrix), are known to be capable of maintaining firing at 40 Hz. Instead, one could assume that, during the course of premask-matrix presentation at 40 Hz (globally), a later cell of this type does become active, responding to the rapid staccato of neural responses representing asynchronized premask-frame presentations. In this way, the 40-Hz structure of the premask matrix induces this neuron to oscillate at 40 Hz. However, because the individual premask frames follow each other effectively without lag, the response of this neuron to presentation of any particular frame might become integrated with identical responses to both preceding and subsequent frames. The neuron would thus maintain an average sustained response above the threshold for perception of the (whole) premask matrix, characterized by a relatively low-amplitude 40-Hz surface modulation that would never descend below the threshold and thereby permit the spatiotemporal structure of the premask display to be discerned.

As is suggested by anatomical evidence and supported by recent findings of Fries, Reynolds, Rorie and Desimone (2001), the pattern of 40-Hz activity generated by an IT neuron is fed back to earlier neurons that comprise the receptive field of that IT neuron, inducing them to oscillate at 40 Hz. In the present context, it is reasonable to assume that the response characteristics of earlier neurons would come to be determined by both recurrent 40-Hz activity and the repeated presentations of (local) premask elements at 10 Hz. Although it is not known precisely how, or with what modifications, information is relayed back to earlier stages, two possibilities emerge that might explain the phase shifting of local neurons within the context of a global 40-Hz rhythm. On one hand, on the basis of electroencephalogram evidence, it seems plausible to consider that there may be a mismatch in the amplitudes of the recurrent 40-Hz rhythm with local 10-Hz, stimulus-evoked, steady-state responses, such that the integration of the 10-Hz response with the induced 40-Hz code modifies the amplitude of the 40-Hz response, resulting in maxima of that response that become slightly amplified and at the same time temporally "shunted" relative to the 40-Hz rhythm universally fed back by the later neuron. On the other hand, the recurrent 40-Hz code might interact with the 10-Hz response via descending pathways that synapse on local interneural networks (see Whittington, Traub, Kopell, Ermentrout, & Buhl, 2000). As a consequence, the timing of interneural mechanisms, considered a critical determinant of the timing of long-range excitatory projections, might become altered such that the time of arrival at the IT neuron of locally mediated 10-Hz responses to premask-frame presentations becomes determined by the relationship between the regular timing of frame presentations and the developing temporal asynchronies at local interneural networks.

By either of these conjectures, the spatially and temporally distributed pattern of repeated interactions between the top-down induced 40-Hz rhythm with the stimulus-driven response to premask-frame presentations at 10 Hz would lead to a series of shifts in the phase of each set of neurons responding locally to a given subset of premask elements. These shifts in phase would occur relative to activity across other neurons that also receive 40-Hz modulation, but code asynchronized subsets of premask elements. Thus, over time, there develop highly dynamic and asynchronous patterns of 40-Hz activity across the entire set of lower-level neurons coding the premask matrix.

Consistent with these ideas concerning the phase-specific segregation of prime activity, within the pattern of asynchronous 40-Hz activity across early, spatially specific neurons, those neurons responding to the synchronous premask elements would occupy the same phase angle of a 40-Hz rhythm, but a different phase angle to neurons responding to other, temporally asynchronous premask-frame elements. In this way, a set of local and temporally precise coincidences in the early visuocortical activity would indeed result in the temporal segregation of activity, differentiating the prime from other premask-induced activity at 40 Hz.[3]

TIMING AND ITS RELATION TO STIMULUS-INDUCED SYNCHRONIZATION

Thus far, the effects of prime generation have been considered for just one frequency, 40 Hz. In fact, in initial experiments (Fig. 7.2), 40 Hz emerged as the

---

[3]See the chapter by Kompass (chap. 20, this volume) for a more detailed consideration of these issues.

only frequency at which priming effects were observed (priming was not found with other premask-matrix presentation frequencies, both higher and lower than 40 Hz), suggesting that priming at 40 Hz represents a special case of stimulus frequency-induced effects. This immediately led to the question of why, within an architecture of recurrent neural transmission between later and early visual processing mechanisms, primes should become generated at 40 Hz, but not at other premask-presentation frequencies. However, for the question to be posed properly, it became necessary to examine whether performance exhibits inherent regularities as a function of linear separations in frequency. In addition, analysis in the frequency domain promised to help separate true priming effects from the impact of other factors, such as conduction latencies or synaptic "gating" mechanisms that are known to influence the frequency characteristics of long-range, excitatory neuronal activity (e.g., Traub, Whittington, Buhl, Jefferys, & Faulkner, 1999; Whittington, Traub, & Jefferys, 1995).

Figures 7.6(a) and 7.6(b) present of the results of two experiments (briefly reported in Elliott & Müller, 1999) that examined the frequency dependence of priming effects (with premask-target matrix ISI = 0 ms). Consistent with the original findings of Elliott and Müller (1998), Fig. 7.6(a) reveals a priming effect in a narrow frequency range near 39–40 Hz, pointing to some degree of priming specificity centered on 39.5 Hz. However, Fig. 7.6(b) indicates that the notion of frequency-specific priming requires modification: Although the pattern of effects in the vicinity of 40 Hz (38–40 Hz) was similar to that represented in Fig. 7.6(a), further priming effects were revealed at 33 Hz and between 46 and 47 Hz, at local minima in the absolute RT-by-frequency functions (for all target-by-synchrony conditions). It is important that these frequencies are separated, across the 28- to 51-Hz bandwidth, by an interval of ~6.75 Hz, a fine-grained patterning hitherto unknown from the literature on visual perception.

On the basis of the finding of priming at 40 Hz and the corresponding 40-Hz modulation of the synchronous target RT by premask-target ISI function, it might be assumed that, for each frequency at which priming occurs, a corresponding pattern of prime activity develops with a characteristic modulatory pattern matching the frequency of premask-matrix presentation. It follows that an analysis of the RT by frequency relationships should proceed from the logically necessary relationship between ISI-dependent RT characteristics on one hand and frequency-dependent characteristics on the other. This implies that the family of possible empirical RT-by-ISI functions with frequency as a parameter represents the same data as the family of RT-by-frequency functions with ISI as a parameter. Another empirically based assumption is that priming as a function of ISI is characterized by a 180° phase shift such that priming is most efficient for ISIs that are out of phase with the projected rhythm of premask-matrix presentation (see Figs. 7.4 and 7.5) and that this "phase-angle rule" holds in general for any critical frequency.

Apart from the existence of more than one priming frequency, the graphs of Fig. 7.6(b) diverge in a second important respect from earlier expectations

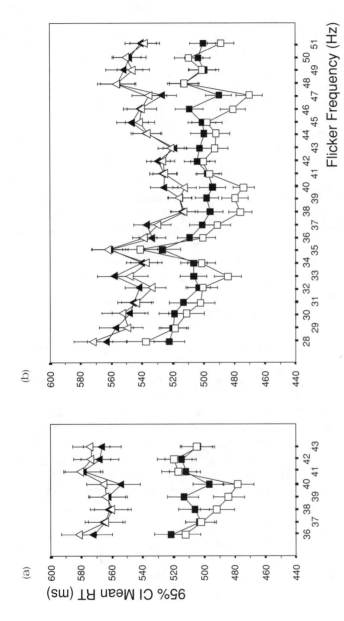

FIG. 7.6. (a) Mean target-present and target-absent RTs (squares and triangles) for the synchronous and random-premask presentation conditions (unfilled and filled symbols), as a function of premask-presentation frequency in the 36- to 42-Hz range. The target-present RTs revealed priming to be evident only between 38 and 40 Hz. (b) Mean target-present and target-absent RTs as a function of premask-presentation frequency in the 28- to 51-Hz range. Here, priming effects were revealed to be specific to frequencies of 33 Hz, 39–40 Hz, and 46–47 Hz. CI = confidence interval.

concerning the priming effect: There is a strong similarity of trends among all four of the depicted functions. In fact, the differences between maximum and minimum RTs within the basic trend of the target-present synchronous premask condition are up to three times larger than the maximum priming effect observed. Most strikingly, the trends of the target-present RTs for the synchronous premask and random-premask conditions show virtually the same maxima and minima (allowing for a constant upward shift and a shrinking by a constant scaling factor for the random-premask relative to the synchronous premask RTs) and are statistically indistinguishable; (synchronous, random) RT rank-order correlation $r_s = .791$). This strongly suggests that random premasks exert the same influence as synchronous premasks. The observation that priming occurs only at the minima of the basic trend suggests that priming is in some way dependent on this underlying trend.

Proceeding from these data-inherent regularities, we can address the first of the main issues raised herein concerning the consistency of the phase-angle rule with the observed (general) frequency trends. This issue can be resolved by assuming that the relevant time axis does not coincide with ISI itself, but represents an internal processing time differing from ISI in its zero point. The corresponding constant delay can be estimated from the data. Specifically, we assume the following generalized phase-angle hypothesis (GPAH) that, for a given priming frequency f and corresponding period duration $\tau = 1/f$, facilitation reoccurs at every time point

$$J(\tau) = \left(n\tau + \frac{1}{2}\right)\tau - T,$$

where $n\tau$ is a frequency-specific integer multiplier and T denotes a constant quantal time delay. The term $+ \frac{1}{2}$ accounts for the observation that, for $f = 40$ Hz, maximal facilitation occurred at phase angles of $180°$ relative to the rhythm of premask-matrix presentation.

A fit with the observed minima is obtained for $T = 138 \pm 2$ ms, where T and multiples of T correspond to those points in time at which the phases of all frequencies located at the minima of the RT-by-frequency function coincide. If this constant is conceived of as a time barrier, RTs may be assumed to reflect (on average) some delay in time proportional to the absolute deviation of the most proximal estimate of (the frequency-specific integer multiplier) $n\tau$ from the time window around this barrier.

IMPLICATIONS AND SPECULATIONS RELATED TO PHASE-SPECIFIC PROCESS TIMING

The analysis just given simultaneously refers to two directly observable aspects of premask-induced RT variation, namely the $180°$ phase shift of prime activity relative to the projected rhythm of premask-matrix presentation and the regular separations of priming frequencies across the range from 28 to 51 Hz. It is important that, by means of this analysis, a unified account can be presented for both. Moreover, stricter criteria are provided for relating the data presented to other known facts. One pertinent issue in this context concerns the open question of how frequency in the experiments should be considered. Against the 40-Hz range assumption, it has been objected that premask stimuli repeat locally with a frequency of 10 Hz. This objection could be resolved by the finding that the synchronous target RTs by premask-target ISI functions are indeed modulated at 40 Hz (Elliott & Müller, 2000). However, this evidence pertains only to 10 and, respectively, 40 Hz. The presence of additional priming frequencies, which, by virtue of adopting the phase shift characteristic of 40 Hz, share common interactions in time, strengthens our theoretically and empirically driven hypothesis: One fundamental consequence of repeating premask-matrix presentation is the generation of an identical rhythm in the brain, which, under certain specific temporal conditions, carries information of particular relevance for subsequent target detection.

On the assumption of stimulus-induced brain rhythms that carry target-relevant information at 40 Hz, these data suggest a strong relationship to induced 40-Hz oscillations revealed in physiological binding research, while also presenting a challenge to physiologically inspired theories of temporal coding. Most striking in this respect is the occurrence of several fine-tuned minima in the RT-by-frequency characteristics, which are strongly consistent across observers. The fact that frequency-dependent modulation is also observed under random-premask conditions suggests that even weak agreement with certain sharp frequencies is effective and, thus, that these frequencies should also be "preferred" under natural processing conditions.

To substantiate such a general proposal, the aforementioned analysis supports tentative conclusions as to the nature of the observed enhancement effects, which are consistent with notions of perceptual organization by means of frequency-specific synchronization. The target-absent characteristics and one of the target-present (random-premask) characteristics exhibit near-identical shapes, pointing to a premask-frequency effect that remains constant irrespective of target presence. [The Target × Frequency interaction was nonsignificant in an omnibus analysis of variance of the data in Fig. 7.6; $F (7,100) = 1.78$, $Ms_e = 1949$, $p = .17$; Huynh–Feldt epsilon correction applied]. This argues against the possibility that the observed frequency-specific priming effects arise in the decision or response-generating stages of the entire process; instead it suggests, as previously hypothesized, that they originate within processes responsible for perceptual organization. However, the similarity of RT-by-frequency trends for random-target and synchronous target conditions challenges the previous proposal that frequency specificity is developed only under synchronous premask conditions when targets are actually presented (see Fig. 7.4). Rather, this similarity strongly suggests that the frequency-dependent modulation of target detection revealed for synchronous premask target-present conditions is only one instance of some frequency-related, general-purpose mechanism that is active in all other conditions.

IMPLICATIONS AND SPECULATIONS
CONCERNING PRIMING BY SYNCHRONY

Thus, the account set out in the previous section provides a challenge to the notion of frequency-specific priming proposed to account for the 40-Hz specificity of the synchronicity enhancement effects (Elliott & Müller, 1998). Instead, the GPAH is more consistent with the idea that there is no specific resonance at any of the observed minima of the RT-by-frequency function. Rather, irrespective of which of the priming frequencies is concerned, priming will develop through generation of either a structurally homogeneous oscillation (which, on the basis of the RT-by-ISI functions described herein, is likely to be 40 Hz) or an oscillation with a structure matching the particular presentation frequency of the premask display. If, as assumed in the GPAH, all premask-presentation frequencies will engender neural resonance at a matching frequency (i.e., there is no specific priming frequency), the question naturally arises as to why certain frequencies prime (i.e., are functionally equivalent), whereas others do not. In this respect, the GPAH deviates from the idea that consideration of neural resonance alone may resolve the question of priming specificity. Instead, according to the GPAH, particular frequencies will come to prime by virtue of the phase angle of the induced oscillation after a defined time of internal transmission, that is, the phase angle of the presentation frequency relative to some constant time delay of the order of $T = 138$ ms, or, more tentatively, the relationship between the phase angle of the induced oscillation and the phase angle of a slower rhythm [i.e., $\sim$7.3 Hz (1,000 ms/138 ms)].

Given that a slower frequency is indeed involved in prime generation, the range of premask-induced oscillations may not be confined to the precise frequency of premask-matrix presentation. To illustrate, if the premask-induced oscillation at 40 Hz comes to prime because of phase coherence with a slower rhythm, the phase of the slower rhythm should also be determined by some temporal aspect of premask presentation (that is, e.g., the premask-presentation frequency itself or the time of premask-display onset). Otherwise, if one takes into consideration the relatively small time window specified by the GPAH within which successful phase interaction would have to take place (i.e., with an error of $\sim$2 ms relative to the critical phase of the slower frequency), priming would most certainly occur with a high degree of inconsistency, making it very difficult for reliable differences between the synchronous target and random-target detection RTs to be observed.[4]

The account presented herein suggests that priming occurs by virtue of the relationship between a stimulus-induced rhythm, adopting the frequency of premask

---

[4]If priming occurs by virtue of the phase angle of the induced oscillation after a defined time of internal transmission, then, by the same logic, the induced oscillation and time of transmission must ultimately relate to the same temporal reference. If this were not the case, the induced oscillation would appear to be unlikely to arrive at its critical phase angle at certain points in processing time with a sufficient degree of accuracy for prime generation to occur with any reliability.

presentation and carrying information related to the spatial composition of the individual premask frames, which is coordinated very precisely with a frequency-related general-purpose processing mechanism. This general-purpose mechanism is in some way responsible for the facilitation of information transmission at certain points in processing time.

Evidence in support of a frequency-related, general-purpose processing mechanism may also be taken from the additional assumption that the neural process by which the synchronous prime and target Kanizsa-type figure become integrated represents the only specific difference to the remaining conditions, while the effects continuously follow the same laws of transmission and processing. This leaves the difficult task of explaining why, for the target-present synchronous premask condition, the RT trend deviates from this regularity, that is, of providing a full and detailed explanation of "how" stimulus synchrony engenders a facilitatory effect on target trials. This question is the subject of current research.

RELATIONS TO OTHER TEMPORAL FACTORS

One additional consideration concerns the quantal delay parameter T and its relationship to other known quantal time constants. The value of $T = 138$ ms agrees nearly exactly with the upper bound of the smallest range of quantal time values in perception and cognition proposed by the taxonomic quantum model (Geissler, 1987). Specifically, for an assumed ideal value of the absolutely smallest quantal time unit of $T_0 = 4.57$ ms, the upper bound is predicted at $TM = 30 \times T_0 = 137$ ms. This value accounts for the empirical minima by 4.5/0.137 s = 32.9 Hz, 5.5/0.137 s = 40.2 Hz, and 6.5/0.137 s = 47.4 Hz (less marked minima are expected at 7.5/0.137 s = 53.4 Hz, 8.5/0.137 s = 62.0 Hz, and so on). This account gains some plausibility within the context of other results (based on item recognition tasks) that show a preference of 30 times a quantal period (e.g., 30 × 9 quantal periods; see Petzold & Edeler, 1996; Petzold, Edeler, & Geissler, 1999). Of course, the hypothetical relation given here is still to be regarded as "indirect" with reference to an assumed basic period of 4.57 ms. However, the existence of such a relation would imply that, although the common upper reference is a multiple of T_0, the critical period durations for each of the priming frequencies may show integer relations but need not be multiples of T_0. This, in turn, implies the emergence of nonlinearities by means of second-order relations to T_0, which, if substantive, extend the series of observed relations beyond the current framework of taxonomic quantum model predictions.

CONCLUSIONS

This chapter has been devoted to the examination, by means of psychophysical methods, of a physiological hypothesis concerning the organization of perceptual information. Thus, to conclude, it seems appropriate to refer back to physiology to assess the putative validity of our conclusions, in particular the idea that priming occurs by means of interactions between neural resonance that matches premask-presentation frequency and a constant time delay that may be related to the operation of much finer-scale timing of the order of 4.57 ms. Although the numerical relation between the priming frequencies, a constant delay of 138 ms, and the smallest hypothesized quantal timing unit of 4.57 ms can be assumed, and although very similar ideas of temporal interactivity have been used to successfully simulate certain, well-determined cognitive processing limitations (e.g., see the short-term memory storage model of Lisman & Idiart, 1995), to our knowledge, no concrete physiological evidence exists to specify perceptuocognitive operations as a function of the phase of an ongoing gamma-bandwidth oscillation relative to fixed points in process time. Consequently, the drawing of analogies between the psychophysical structures described here and the defining structures of neural resonance is not ultimately permissible. However, some indication of how best to approach the physiological questions that arise from the GPAH may be gathered from a combination of evidence relating to the temporal characteristics of visuocortical mechanisms and experimental evidence pointing to a possible link between activity within these mechanisms and the coding of stimulus synchrony within 40-Hz premask-matrix flicker.

With respect to neural timing, it is known that the timing of activity across interneural gap junctions occurs within a temporal range very close to 4.5 ms (specifically, $\sim$5 ms peak–peak intervals in the neocortex, equivalent to a frequency of activity varying in the range 200–250 Hz; X. W. Singer, personal communication, 17th March, 2000), and that this delay is critical for the rapid synchronization of inhibitory interneuron activity. Applied to the present paradigm, that inhibitory interneuron activity may be precisely related to priming is suggested by the finding of enhanced priming effects following treatment with the benzodiazepine lorazepam (Elliott, Becker, Boucart, & Müller, 2000). Lorazepam is known to enhance γ-aminobutyric acid-induced inhibition uniquely at receptors located at interneuron synapses, which in turn stabilize and reduce the frequency of postsynaptic, excitatory activity by synchronizing their own discharges at around 40 Hz. In the context of the recurrent model of prime activity outlined herein, this set of findings supports the idea that feedback projections would influence lower-level activity by means of interneural mechanisms. When both the frequency of interneural activity and the timing of activity at the interneuron synapse are taken into consideration, this idea allows for the further speculation that the coding of stimulus synchrony is indirectly but fundamentally determined by synaptic gating at times approximately equivalent to T_0 and multiples thereof.

Currently, these related speculations receive no direct empirical support. However, the careful modeling of the times and locations of temporal variability within recurrent networks, coupled with examination of the extent to which the RT-by-frequency and RT-by-ISI functions vary between γ-aminobutyric acid enhanced and control conditions, could provide results that are interpretable in terms of variability directly related to the behavior of internal timing parameters with firmly established neurophysiological correlates. This constitutes a promising proposal for corroborating the temporal patterning described here in terms of patterns of temporal activity in the brain.

ACKNOWLEDGMENTS

This contribution is dedicated to the work of Hans-Georg Geissler, Professor of Psychology at the University of Leipzig, who is responsible for the generalized phase-angle hypothesis set out herein. The research was supported by a Medical Research Council research grant (UK), and by Deutsche Forschungsgemeinschaft Project Grants SCHR 375/8-1 to H. J. Müller and A. Mecklinger and GE 678/12-1 to H.-G. Geissler and H. J. Müller (Germany). The authors are indebted to Stanislava Antonijević, Greg Davis, Raul Kompass, and Wolf Singer for insightful theoretical comments. The authors also express their thanks to C. Becker, L.-T. Boenke, D. Böttger, M. Conci, N. von Daaken, K. Meyer, and J. Wendt for their assistance in carrying out the experimental work.

REFERENCES

Alais, D., Blake, R., & Lee, S. H. (1998). Visual features that vary together over time group together over space. *Nature Neuroscience, 1,* 160–164.

Coltheart, M. (1980). Iconic memory and visible persistence. *Perception & Psychophysics, 27,* 183–228.

Eckhorn, R., Bauer, R., Jordan, W., Brosch, M., Kruse, W., Munk, M., & Reitböck, H. J. (1988). Coherent oscillations: A mechanism for feature linking in the visual cortex. *Biological Cybernetics, 60,* 121–130.

Efron, R. (1970a). Effects of stimulus duration on perceptual onset and offset latencies. *Perception & Psychophysics, 8,* 231–234.

Efron, R. (1970b). The minimum duration of a perception. *Neuropsychologia, 8,* 57–63.

Efron, R. (1970c). The relationship between the duration of a stimulus and the duration of a perception. *Neuropsychologia, 8,* 37–55.

Elliott, M. A., Becker, C., Boucart, M., & Müller, H. J. (2000). Enhanced GABA$_A$ inhibition enhances synchrony coding in human perception. *Neuroreport, 11,* 3403–3407.

Elliott, M. A., & Müller, H. J. (1998). Synchronous information presented in 40-Hz flicker enhances visual feature binding. *Psychological Science, 9,* 277–283.

Elliott, M. A., & Müller, H. J. (1999). On the role of 40-Hz, and evidence of faster-frequency oscillations during visual-object perception. In P. R Killeen & W. R. Uttal (Eds.), *Fechner Day 99. The end of*

20th century psychophysics. Proceedings of the 15th annual meeting of the International Society of Psychophysics (pp. 13–18). Tempe, AZ: The International Society for Psychophysics.

Elliott, M. A., & Müller, H. J. (2000). Evidence for a 40-Hz oscillatory short-term visual memory revealed by human reaction-time measurements. *Journal of Experimental Psychology: Learning, Memory and Cognition, 26,* 703–718.

Elliott, M. A., & Müller, H. J. (2001). Effects of stimulus synchrony on mechanisms of perceptual organization. *Visual Cognition, 8,* 655–677.

Engel, G. R. (1970). An investigation of visual responses to brief stereoscopic stimuli. *Quarterly Journal of Experimental Psychology, 22,* 148–160.

Fries, P., Reynolds, J. H., Rorie, A. E., & Desimone, R. (2001). Modulation of oscillatory neuronal synchronization by selective visual attention. *Science, 291,* 1560–1563.

Gegenfurtner, K. (1998). Visual psychophysics: Synchrony in motion. *Nature Neuroscience, 1,* 96–98.

Geissler, H.-G. (1987). The temporal architecture of central information processing: Evidence for a tentative time-quantum model. *Psychological Research, 49,* 99–106.

Gray, C. M., König, P., Engel, A. K., & Singer, W. (1989). Oscillatory responses in cat visual cortex exhibit inter-columnar synchronization, which reflects global stimulus properties. *Nature, 338,* 334–337.

Lisman, J. E., & Idiart, M. A. P. (1995). Storage of 7 ± 2 short-term memories in oscillatory subcycles. *Science, 267,* 1512–1515.

Müller, H. J., & Elliott, M. A. (1999). 40-Hz synchronicity priming of Kanizsa figure detection demonstrated by a novel psychophysical paradigm. In G. Aschersleben, T. Bachmann, & J. Müsseler (Eds.), *Cognitive contributions to the perception of spatial and temporal events* (pp. 323–340). Amsterdam: Elsevier.

Müller, K. (1999). Is 40-Hz-synchronicity priming demonstrated by a novel psychophysical paradigm indeed a 40-Hz phenomenon? Commentary on H. Müller & Elliott. In G. Aschersleben, T. Bachmann, & J. Müsseler (Eds.), *Cognitive contributions to the perception of spatial and temporal events* (pp. 341–343). Amsterdam: Elsevier.

Petzold, P., & Edeler, B. (1996). Organization of person memory and retrieval processes in recognition. *European Journal of Social Psychology, 25,* 249–267.

Petzold, P., Edeler, B., & Geissler, H.-G. (1999). Discrete clusters of processing time in a verbal item-recognition task. In P. R Killeen & W. R. Uttal (Eds.), *Fechner Day 99. The end of 20th century psychophysics. Proceedings of the 15th annual meeting of the International Society of Psychophysics* (pp. 25–30). Tempe, AZ: The International Society for Psychophysics.

Traub, R. D., Whittington, M. A., Buhl, E. H., Jefferys, J. G. R., & Faulkner, H. J. (1999). On the mechanisms of the $\gamma > \beta$ frequency shift in neuronal oscillations induced in rat hippocampal slices by tetanic stimulation. *Journal of Neuroscience, 19,* 1088–1105.

von der Malsburg, C. (1981). *The correlation theory of function* (Internal Rep. No. 81–2). Göttingen, Germany: Max-Planck-Institute for Biophysical Chemistry, Department of Neurobiology.

Wendt, J. (2000). *Masking the 40-Hz synchrony-priming effect by form and phase.* Unpublished master's thesis, Universität Leipzig, Germany.

Whittington, M. A., Traub, R. D., & Jefferys, J. G. R. (1995). Synchronized oscillations in interneuron networks driven by metabotropic glutamate activation. *Nature, 373,* 612–615.

Whittington, M. A., Traub, R. D., Kopell, N., Ermentrout, B., & Buhl, E. H. (2000). Inhibition-based rhythms: Experimental and mathematical observations on network dynamics. *International Journal of Psychophysiology, 38,* 315–336.

8

Functional Architectures in Structural Recognition and the Role of "Seeming Redundancy"

Hans-Georg Geissler
University of Leipzig, Germany

It is a commonplace in psychophysics that the performance of "sensory" tasks is a joint function of (mainly quantitative) stimulus attributes and task demands. "Beyond sensation," there is a shift of emphasis: Structural stimulus properties become dominant. The manifold of possible task demands expands strikingly, pushing the number of potentially relevant stimulus attributes practically beyond any limit. At the same time, the involvement of memory becomes virtually universal.

In perception, such complex determination holds for processes of recognition involved in goal-related classification. Despite the obvious complexity of these processes, psychology succeeds in formulating numerous rules of how recognition performance depends on stimulus structure and task demands. However, stimulus-related and intention-based organizational factors have only rarely been studied in their joint action. Therefore it is not surprising that no theoretical framework has emerged as yet that would permit an understanding of the general principles of this interplay.

Hope for progress on this issue derives from the fact that complex information systems, such as the brain, require the implementation of simplifications to keep processing manageable at all levels of organization. A preferred means of achieving this ought to be memory-based optimization. In this chapter a reanalysis of data is presented from the visual categorization of geometrical objects that form highly regular sets, which hitherto have not been systematically examined for superordinate rules governing the interaction of stimulus structure and intentional task demands in memory processing. The identification of such rules, even if within only a limited domain, appears to me to be an interesting step toward a theory of joint action, as it places sensory and intentional variations into one common reference frame.

My discussion of this issue refers to experiments on visual recognition that were carried out over a period between the mid-1970s and the late 1990s, in which regular sets of objects composed of clearly separated elements were used as stimuli. The results suggest that, in complex structural recognition, the overwhelming part of reaction-time (RT) variance can be attributed to top-down processing. The theoretical perspective put forward to account for the findings was labeled memory-guided inference (MGI) (Buffart & Geissler, 1984; Geissler & Buffart, 1985; see also Geissler & Puffe, 1983). Fundamental to MGI is the idea that flexible task-specific processing is based on the task-appropriate framing of representations of objects or sets of objects in memory, which "guides" the top-down inference of information required for decision making. Within this view, the processing routines themselves are not task specific, but rather exhibit a multipurpose character. Optimization of processing in memory is attributed exclusively to the generation of memory codes that are the simplest possible in a given situation. This proposal contrasts sharply with the intuitively appealing view that the number of decision steps necessary to solve a task is minimized.

Effective implementation of the structural-simplicity principle requires that constraints permitting strong analytical simplifications are taken into consideration. The existence of such constraints reflects universal regularities of processing, or, what I regard as equivalent, the existence of "functional architectures." Basically, there are three groups of relevant constraints. The first concerns the structures of processing in time. From the assumed nature of inference processes in recognition, it follows that processing must be recursive. In practice, recursive processing can often be approximated as serial processing. In this respect, the processing assumptions of MGI can be seen as extensions of Sternberg's (1966) model of item recognition, which easily generalizes to logically more complex versions of the same task (e.g., Naus, 1974; Okada & Burrows, 1978). Although parallel processing models (e.g., Ratcliff, 1978) can correctly describe data collected in the original Sternberg paradigm and even accommodate a greater number of empirical aspects than the Sternberg model, they do not offer similarly straightforward generalizations. Note, however, that, in MGI, seriality is considered primarily a technical approximation that must be specified for particular cases. For example, code constituents that are marked as irrelevant seem to be checked in parallel to the serial processing of relevant information. Furthermore, operations may be subject to simultaneous capacity limitations. Thus the actual procedures used are better referred to as "pseudoserial." Despite this reservation, in many tractable cases the relationships between predicted sequences of operations and RTs turn out to be sufficiently straightforward to justify the assumption that iterative refinements of process descriptions are possible.

The second type of constraint concerns the memory representations involved in top-down processing. At present, no sufficiently general formalism is available to provide a basis for deduction. To increase the deductive power of the MGI approach, one of the most broadly applicable formalisms, the string-code calculus of structural information theory (SIT) (Leeuwenberg, 1969), has been generalized to describe task-related memory codes of sets of objects (see Buffart & Geissler, 1984; Geissler & Puffe, 1983). As a simple example, consider the descriptions (a b) and (a c) of two objects represented by the memory references or "features" a, b, and c. This representation can be transformed into the shorter description a $\otimes$ (b, c), denoting a combinatorial product that generates the former two expressions. It is provisionally assumed that the linear sequences of symbols in expressions such as these, by permitting only either left–right or right–left processing, uniquely determine the possible orders of serial operation. (For the rules and detailed calculations underlying the data interpretations set out below, see the section "some formal considerations" and the appendix.)

The third aspect to be considered concerns indices of absolute timing. These emerge as a consequence of the implementation of operations in the brain, involving large numbers of neurons positioned and connected according to a definite anatomical structure. In the simplified serial model, absolute timing is assumed to become manifest in operation times taken to be characteristic of modular processes. The considerations subsequently set out are based on the fundamental assumption that operation times remain invariant within critical zones of variation in stimulus conditions and change discretely when the boundaries of these zones are crossed. If this is correct, (approximate) invariance of operation-time estimates across conditions would provide an additional means for ascertaining the validity of procedural assumptions. Judging from the results (which are discussed later), this approach appears to be successful. As the following examples show, comparatively small sets of data explored on the basis of operation time invariance may yield depictions of processing in such a detail that, to be attained with traditional techniques, would require large-scale experimental programs.

A PARADIGM TO START WITH: COMPLEX VISUAL SEARCH

For a more specific introduction to MGI-based procedures, it is useful to consider a visual-search experiment that served as a point of departure for the development of the approach (Scheidereiter, 1978; see Geissler, Klix, & Scheidereiter, 1978). Despite some technical imperfections, this experiment provides a good illustration of crucial points and potential benefits. The paradigm resembles figural test situations that differ from common visual-search paradigms by the importance of structural search criteria and stimulus complexity, excluding immediate perceptual "pop-out" and enforcing memory processing. Examples of test situations are shown in the upper row of Fig. 8.1. The task required the detection of repeating substrings within strings of figural elements. Subjects had to respond Yes or No, depending on whether a presented string contained a repetition of substrings. As leverage for strategy identification, three basic versions of the task were implemented. In subtask A, no additional information was given along with the test strings. In subtask B, subjects were informed about the lengths of possible repetitive strings. In subtask C, the precise string whose repetitive occurrence was to be detected, was presented together with the test string.

The families of mean RT functions obtained for each of the three subtasks are shown in the left-hand panels on the lower row of Fig. 8.1. Positive RTs are plotted against length m of repeating strings, with distance a between strings as a parameter. In addition, for subtasks B and C, the negative RTs are plotted against "instructed length" m^* of possible repeating strings. As can be seen, the results vary considerably among the three task versions. In particular, the functions for subtask C exhibit a reverse trend relative to those for tasks A and B, and the mean RTs are much shorter. Overall, two different characteristics emerge: In subtasks A and B, RTs increase with substring distance a according to a law of diminishing returns, and the dependence on m is roughly linear. In contrast, RTs in subtask C exhibit a negatively accelerated trend as a function of m and an approximately linear dependence on a.

From the nature of these differences, it is plausible to maintain that the experimental variation of the task did not give rise to fundamental changes in the processing regime. That is, the three families of functions can be represented by one and the same basic algorithm, with temporal processing parameters staying invariant across subtask conditions. If combined with the assumption of seriality, this requirement imposes a strong constraint on an account of the data.

To illustrate the principle underlying this argument, I begin with subtask C, where it is particularly simple. In this task, subjects are presented with cue strings, along with the test items, that are identical to the potential repeating (target) strings in the test items. A plausible strategy of memory processing would consist of searching for the presence of two identical substrings within the test string by a shift in a representation of the cue string stepwise along the test string and a comparison of it, at each successive position, elementwise with the corresponding elements of the test string. This process can be assumed to stop as soon as a second match is found, which yields a qualitatively correct nonlinear dependence of the number of required operations on the length m of repeating strings. The same basic rationale can be applied to negative decisions. In this case, because no match is found, comparison can stop $l - 2m + 1$ elements before the end of the target string, where l denotes the total number of elements in a string. To obtain a quantitative overall fit, it must be taken into account that, with positive decisions, $m - 2$ elements of the test string can be dropped from processing after the first match is found.

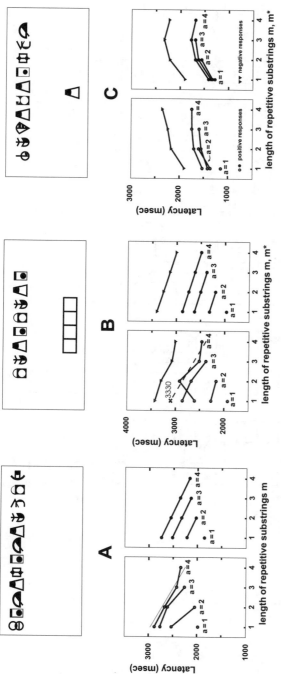

FIG. 8.1. Upper row, examples of test items in tasks A, B, and C (positive cases only). Subjects had to decide whether a string of pattern elements presented contained a repeating substring. As shown, in tasks B and C, the length of the potential repeating substring or the potentially repeating string itself was indicated below the test string. Lower row: Empirical mean RTs (left-hand graph) and model predictions (right-hand graph) for tasks A, B, and C plotted as functions of length m of repeating strings, with distance a between strings as parameter. For the purpose of model fitting, the "irregular" point at $a = 4$, $m = 1$ in subtask B, which is qualitatively inconsistent with the overall pattern of the data, was replaced with a value (represented by a cross) extrapolated from the three other points. In tasks B and C, RTs for negative decisions are plotted against "instructed" length m^*. Note the nonlinear dependence of RTs on a in tasks A and B and on m in task C. Note also that, for negative responses in subtask A, there is only one mean RT, which cannot be plotted against m.

161

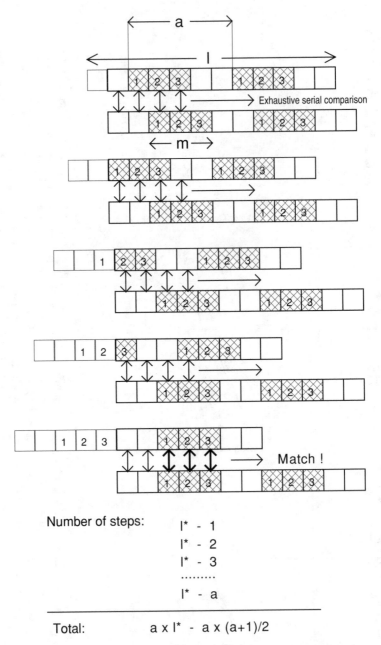

Number of steps: l* - 1

                    l* - 2

                    l* - 3

                    ....

                    l* - a

Total: a x l* - a x (a+1)/2

FIG. 8.2. Assumed first-stage comparison strategy in task A for
the example of repeating strings of length m= 3, distance a = 5,
and total string length l = 12. Upper strings depict copies that are

As shown on the right-hand side of the bottom panel of Fig. 8.1 for task C, the predictions of this model fit the data reasonably well. Although of no particular relevance to the present illustration, note that not all details in the data are correctly accounted for. In particular, the decreases in RT predicted from $m = 3$ to $m = 4$ do not have a counterpart in the data. Furthermore, directly adjacent repeating strings ($a = 1$) are detected considerably faster than predicted (presumably because detection is likely to rely on an entirely different "sensory" mechanism).

For subtasks A and B, it is plausible that a process of the same type is at work; however, this time it is using copies of the target strings themselves. As illustrated in Fig. 8.2, by such a strategy, a match will be found on positive trials after the copy is shifted by a steps along the representation of the test string. The detection of a match points to the existence of a repetition and would thus provide a secure basis for eliciting a positive response. However, for tasks A and B, unlike task C, this model does not yield a qualitatively correct description of the data, as it fails to account for the marked negative slope with m. When the dependence of the RT on m is statistically eliminated, however, the model can fit the data fairly well. As reported by Geissler et al. (1978), estimates of the operation times ($\sim$60 ms) closely agree with those from subtask C. Taken as an additional criterion, this finding supports the assumption that identical routines are involved in all subtasks. In terms of Sternberg's (1969) additive-stage logic, this argues for an independent stage of processing that causes the m dependence in tasks A and B.

These considerations leave us with an apparent paradox: From a purely logical point of view, one process, which is the same in all three tasks, would in principle suffice to account for the detection of repeating strings in each of the subtasks. However, what then could the function of another process be that, in subtasks A and B, produces a negative dependence of the RT on m, although there is no evidence of such a dependence in subtask C?

This question touches on a central issue of MGI. To understand this, note that there is a fundamental difference between the search processes assumed in task C on the one hand and those in tasks A and B on the other, which remains hidden as long as representational aspects of processing are not properly considered. While

---

←

(*Continued*) matched against the original strings by exhaustive serial comparison (indicated by vertical double arrows; right-pointing arrows indicate the continuation of comparison). The sequence of string pairs from top to bottom represents serial steps of processing involving a leftward shift of the copy string by one element. Analogous representations are also possible for tasks B and C (see text). Note that this representation is not to be taken literally. In an abstract, more generally applicable format, strategies can be represented by constrained scan paths in matrices containing, at column–row crossings, a_1 in the case of identical elements in the target and comparison strings and a_0 otherwise.

in subtask C, the cue string explicitly represents the (to-be-searched-for) target string; this critical piece of information is only implicitly given in tasks in A and B by the finding of a match. Assuming that explicit representation is essential for linking results of sensory analysis to task-related intentional processing, for a final response decision, the repeating strings must be made explicit in tasks A and B, too. This can be conceived of as a fast process of marking and chunking repetitions within the representation of a given test string. The final decision would then involve a serial check to verify whether the resulting representation agrees with the standard form of a test string that contains a repetition (see also Geissler & Buffart, 1985).

To account for the negative slope with m, a chunked substring must be assumed to be treated as one single element in this checking process, which yields a reduction by $m - 1$ operations. This two-stage view is supported by the fact that, in first-stage processing, no effect of the cue as to the length of possible repeating substrings is manifest in task B (consistent with the implicit nature of processing), whereas the dependence of RTs on instructed length m^* for negative decisions shows the sensitivity of the second stage to this information.

The preceding considerations support the following tentative conclusions. In complex memory-related tasks, the assumption of serial processing, together with the criterion of parameter invariance, provides a useful means for revealing procedural details in task-specific processing, such as the skipping of redundant information and termination of processing dependent on cue information. Under all conditions, intentional task demands operate on representations of stimulus objects in memory (short-term memory in the preceding experiments), which become restructured so as to make task-specific critical object properties explicit. Furthermore, depending on whether this restructuring is accomplished under direct intentional control or operating by means of intermediate links (such as operations that mark the critical information before being explicated), processing is revealed to involve one or two stages, respectively. This "optional" nature of processing suggests that principles of flexible functional organization, rather than hard-wired solutions, are at work.

Logically, the emergence of a two-stage architecture as a result of an interaction between stimulus and intentional task constraints implies that the same information is processed twice. In the next section, I attempt to demonstrate that this interaction also yields other cases of repeated processing of the same information, this time within one and the same stage. To denote the lawful nature of these phenomena, the term "seeming redundancy" was introduced (Geissler, 1985).

APPLICATION TO ITEM RECOGNITION

A possible objection to the interpretation set out in the previous section is that serial processing may be enforced by the sequential structure of the items. From the perspective of representational guidance, it is of considerable interest to ascertain whether (pseudo)serial processing extends beyond these special conditions. A well-known simpler paradigm that may serve as an example is item recognition (Sternberg, 1966). In item-recognition tasks, subjects are required to indicate whether a specified item is contained in a set of previously presented items. For solving this task, the sequential order of these memory items is clearly *not* relevant.

Common versions of the Sternberg task use lists of digits or words. This makes it difficult to reveal strategic processing details, such as the skipping of information, which would permit MGI operations to be identified unequivocally. To circumvent this difficulty, Puffe (1984; see Geissler, Puffe, & Stern, 1982) used sets of geometrical figures that consisted of clearly separated parts that formed feature dimensions of "outline contour," "inset contour," and "fill-in texture"; see the top row of Fig. 8.3 for examples. The experiments used a fixed-set procedure with memory-set sizes of $s = 1$, 2, and 3. Here, only RTs for negative decisions are considered, which are most straightforwardly explained in terms of feature checking. For memory sets without feature overlap between items, the mean RTs plotted against the number of relevant features exhibit nonlinear functions, as indicated by the solid lines in the graph on the left-hand side of Fig. 8.4. This nonlinearity can conveniently be modeled by two-stage serial processing. The dashed lines show, for $s = 1$, 2, and 3, predictions for one out of three

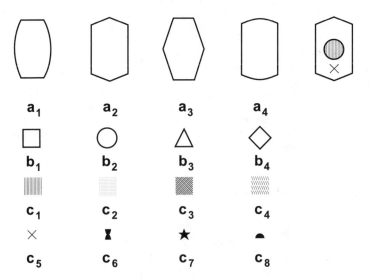

Fig. 8.3 Figure elements ("features") for the construction of items forming four configural dimensions, and an example of an item used in the item-recognition experiment. In the naming and verification experiments reported in the text, only three dimensions were used. In one of the experiments (experiment 1, tree structure RF), elements c_3–c_8 were used as additional filling-in patterns.

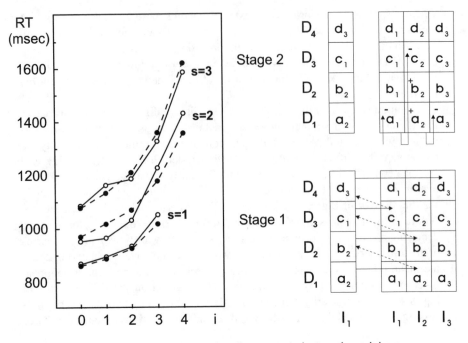

Fig. 8.4 Left, Empirical mean RTs (open circles) and model predictions (filled circles) for negative decisions and memory-set sizes $s = 1$, 2, 3, shown as functions of the number of matching features i (data from item-recognition experiment with objects as illustrated in Fig. 8.3). Right, Illustration of the two-stage model used for predictions in the example for a negative test item and memory-set size $s = 3$. a_i, b_i, c_i, and d_i denote geometrical features ordered in configural dimensions D_1, D_2, D_3, and D_4, respectively. In the model, serial self-terminating encoding of the test item is assumed along configural dimensions in the first stage of processing and itemwise self-terminating feature comparison in the second stage.

slightly differing models. As is illustrated on the right-hand side, in this model a first-stage self-terminating feature scan along the dimensions D_1 to D_4 marks the features that a given test item shares with memory-set items. The second stage involves a self-terminating scan along items. The best fit was obtained when operation times of 54 ms were assumed for both stages of processing, which may be taken as an indication of an identical neural basis.

To check for effects of feature redundancy, in separate experiments, the feature overlap R within the memory sets was varied between 0 and 2 features. Test items differed systematically in the number r of "redundant" features that they had in common with the set of overlapping features in the memory set. On the left-hand

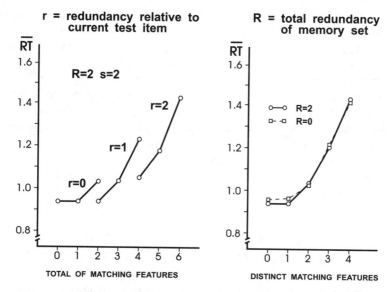

Fig. 8.5 Illustration of a representational contraction in item recognition. Mean RTs are shown for negative decisions with memory-set size $s = 2$ and number of redundant features within the memory set $R = 2$. Left, Plot of the negative-decision mean RTs as functions of the number of matching features, calculated on the assumption that redundant features are not dropped from the representation. The parameter r represents the number of features in the test items that match redundant features in the memory set. Right, Replot of the negative-decision mean RTs based on the assumption that redundant features are represented only once. The data for $R = 0$ are shown for comparison. Note the near identity of the two experimental curves.

side of Fig. 8.5, mean RTs for $R = 0$, 1, and 2 are plotted against the number of feature tests on the assumption that no tests can be skipped. On the right-hand side, the same data are plotted against the effective number of feature tests on the assumption that redundant features are tested only once. The resulting function almost perfectly matches that obtained for memory sets with no feature overlap ($R = 0$), which provides strong evidence that redundant features are indeed dropped from processing. The most economic account of this posits that redundant features are represented only once in the internal representation of the memory set.

In summary, the results of these experiments support the view that feature processing in this item-recognition paradigm can be approximated by a two-stage *serial* procedure. The first component process involves a dimensionwise reading-in of test item information, the second an itemwise check of the features marked at the first stage to determine the final response decision. This "double" processing of one and the same piece of information provides a further example of seeming redundancy, in the sense that logically identical information undergoes processing more than once, albeit in successive stages. This seeming "waste" of effort coexists with economical optimization of processing, which is manifest in the omission of redundant information from processing. In agreement with the former paradigm, the first stage can be interpreted as a reading-in of informational units at the lowest level (here, geometrical features), whereas the second stage mediates the final response decision based on a task-specific reconfiguration of this information (here in "item" units). In contrast to the former paradigm, however, shortcuts are found in both stages, because in the present case omission is a consequence of an explicit property of the memory set, which remains the same during the entire process, namely, that common features are represented only once.

NAMING AND VERIFICATION IN HIERARCHICALLY STRUCTURED SETS

The evidence discussed thus far concerns variations of stimulus-set structure. To include variations in task intention, multicategorical classification tasks are used in which category-defining representations are fixed in long-term memory. Such tasks provide an added advantage for analysis in that MGI-based procedural assumptions can easily be contrasted with intuitively plausible "pure-decision" accounts that attribute the task specificity of performance to decision procedures optimally adapted to the task. For categories of equal probability of occurrence, the latter accounts imply that the number of decisions approaches the logical minimum attained by dichotomization. If K is the number of categories, the number of operations is expected to increase with ld K (i.e., the dual logarithm of K). In contrast with serial category code checking according to MGI, the increase should be a linear function of K.

Some Formal Considerations

Before experiments are discussed, it is useful to make some considerations with an easy-to-handle formalism. As a simple example, consider a multicategorical classification of four objects: $O_1 = (a_1, b_1)$, $O_2 = (a_1, b_2)$, $O_3 = (a_2, b_1)$, and $O_4 = (a_2, b_2)$, where a_i and b_j denote binary features. Now, let T_1 represent a task in which these objects are to be assigned pairwise to response categories R_1 and R_2 according to $\{O_1, O_2\} \Rightarrow R_1$ and $\{O_3, O_4\} \Rightarrow R_2$. To follow this rule of assignment by dichotomization according to a pure-decision strategy, it would suffice to make a binary decision of whether an object presented contains a_1 or a_2. Depending on the outcome, either R_1 or R_2 can be initiated. This procedure is illustrated on the top left-hand side of Fig. 8.6. Suppose that, in task T_2, a different name is to be assigned to each of the four objects $O_1, O_2, O_3,$ and O_4. A procedure for this, based

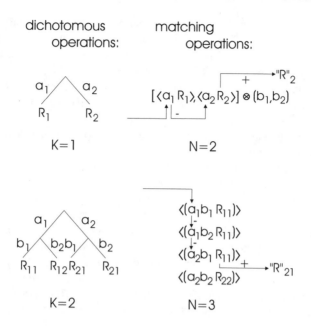

Fig. 8.6 Left, Examples of binary decision trees according to the pure-decision account. Right, Corresponding checking procedures according to the MGI account for the same task demands. For the purpose of illustration, here a check of the particular item $(a_2\ b_1)$ is assumed. For the arbitrarily fixed feature sequence of the assumed category codes in the task at the top, this implies first a mismatch for a_1 and then a match for a_2. For the task at the bottom, after two mismatches, both related to a_1, matches for a_2 and b_1 are obtained. K and N denote the numbers of operations predicted for the dichotomization and the serial strategies, respectively.

on dichotomies, is illustrated on the bottom left-hand side of Fig. 8.6. Here, after a binary decision on a_1 and a_2, a corresponding decision on b_1 and b_2 is to be made. Following this, the associated response can be elicited. This type of procedure can easily be generalized to objects constructed from k binary features. In this ideal case, the number of necessary binary operations will increase with the dual logarithm ld K of the number K of objects. A prerequisite of the pure-decision strategy in task T_2 is that, to produce the final response, the system needs "to keep in mind" the outcome of the preceding (the first) binary decision. (In more general cases of pure-decision strategies, the information to be kept in memory and the conditional rules of its usage will more complexly depend on the objects' properties and the task.)

In contrast, the MGI account assumes that the task-relevant information of a test object is to be made explicit and checked in a pseudoserial process. Unlike in item recognition, in the multicategorical classification task, no negative responses are involved. Thus classification may be assumed to be determined uniquely by one-stage top-down checking of explicit memory codes. These codes describe each of the categories in terms of their distinguishing features. Although feature redundancies within categories may lead to code contractions, the identity of the features necessary for discerning categories cannot be made explicit across codes. Thus no processing shortcuts are feasible.

Examples of code checking are illustrated on the right-hand side of Fig. 8.6. In task T_1, the object information of the category representations is given by the string code pairs $\langle (a_1\ b_1); (a_1\ b_2) \rangle$ and $\langle (a_2\ b_1); (a_2\ b_2) \rangle$. Within these codes, the feature shared between subcodes can be made explicit. To represent these, we use an operation $\otimes$ as defined in the introduction with the property $a \otimes (b, c) = (a\ b); (a\ c)$. To emphasize the mutual exclusivity of categories, we include the response symbols in the category codes with the denotation of markers indicating that, if a match is found, the corresponding response can be elicited. The proper "start codes" for representing within-category feature identities now read $\langle [(a_1\ b_1); (a_1\ b_2)]\ R_1 \rangle$ and $\langle [(a_2\ b_1); (a_2\ b_2)]\ R_2 \rangle$. Using the operation $\otimes$ for task T_1, we obtain as structural expressions that make these identities explicit $\langle a_1 \otimes (b_1, b_2)\ R_1 \rangle; \langle a_2 \otimes (b_1, b_2)\ R_2 \rangle$, or, separating the common irrelevant (nondistinctive) component, $[\langle a_1 R_1 \rangle; \langle a_2 R_2 \rangle] \otimes (b_1, b_2)$.

For a test item exhibiting feature a_2, the comparison procedure is illustrated on the top right-hand side of Fig. 8.6. Assuming (arbitrarily) left–right processing, the self-terminating procedure starts with a top-down check of a_1; after rejection, it proceeds to a_2, where a match is found and R_2 is elicited. The resulting number of operations is two. To ensure that no responses are made to items that do not exhibit the irrelevant features characteristic of objects assigned to R_1 and R_2, it is assumed that irrelevant features are checked in parallel without affecting the processing load.

For task T_2, the codes and procedures are illustrated on the bottom right-hand side of Fig. 8.6. In this task, both feature a_i and feature b_j are relevant and cannot be eliminated. Thus a possible final code sequence reads $\langle (a_1\ b_1)\ R_{11} \rangle; \langle (a_1\ b_2)\ R_{12} \rangle; \langle (a_2\ b_1)\ R_{21} \rangle; \langle (a_2\ b_2)\ R_{22} \rangle$. With $(a_2\ b_1)$ as an example test item, top-down matching yields mismatches for a_1 in the first and the second categories and a match for a_2 and b_1 in the third category, resulting in the activation of response R_{21}. This amounts to a total of four operations. Note that, to make a decision (in the example), test item a_1 needs to be checked twice. For the classification of $(a_2\ b_2)$, double checking is required of both a_1 and a_2. This constitutes a new case of seeming Redundancy, which arises as a consequence of representational constraints.

An important issue should be noted at this point: As the examples indicate, the order of serial category checking is *arbitrary*. Because of the very gist of MGI, this kind of (unavoidable) indeterminacy is an integral component of the approach. Consequently, unless a task poses additional constraints that lead to disambiguation, all possible sequences of category checks (i.e., here all possible permutations) are expected to occur with equal probabilities.

Experimental Comparison

Examination of the general and the specific predictions concerning category code processing requires more complex experimental conditions than have been considered hitherto. For examining the RT trends that are dependent on the number of categories and features, a minimum of three tasks with different numbers of categories is required. The demonstration of code-related intracategory omissions from processing also requires a minimum of three structures that differ sufficiently in the trends predicted. Such an experimental program was realized by Puffe. In planning these experiments, Puffe built on results by Hoffmann (see Hoffmann, Grosser, & Klein, 1987), who used similar geometrical materials. To collect a database large enough to permit parameter invariance to be considered, besides naming, Puffe's experiments included verification tasks in which subjects had to respond yes or no, depending on whether a previously presented category name applied to a given test object. In the following sections, I review findings by Geissler and Puffe (1983) as well as unpublished data of the same authors.

All experiments used sets of objects that were constructed from elements as shown in Fig. 8.3, with features c_5-c_8 corresponding to additional feature variants that, together with c_1-c_4, formed the third configural dimension (rather than constituting an independent fourth dimension). In the main series of experiments, these objects were grouped into categories on three hierarchical levels. At the top (t), there were two categories of four objects, to each of which a name (in most experiments a nonsense syllable) was assigned. On the intermediate level (i), there were four categories of two objects, each assigned to distinct names. At the bottom level (b), distinctive names were assigned to each single object. Subjects first learned to respond according to the name assignments on these three levels. Subsequently they performed blocks of naming and verification trials in different orders, depending on the particular experimental design. In naming, the required level of responding was indicated in advance (t, i, or b).

Figure 8.7 symbolically represents the category structures of objects in two experimental series. These series were designed to permit a simple comparison between the MGI and pure-decisions accounts. The hierarchy at the top represents an expansion of the second binary-feature hierarchy in Fig. 8.6 to three levels, involving the smallest possible number of distinctive features, the "minimal-feature" (MF) series. In the tree structure underneath, new features are introduced from top to bottom on each level of the hierarchy such that there are no features in common to categories on any level, the "redundant-feature" (RF) series.

According to the pure-decisions account, the number of necessary decision steps is expected to be the same for corresponding cases in both hierarchies. In

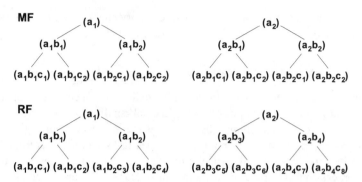

Fig. 8.7 Illustration of the minimal-feature (MF) and redundant-feature (RF) hierarchical category structures. See text for further explanation.

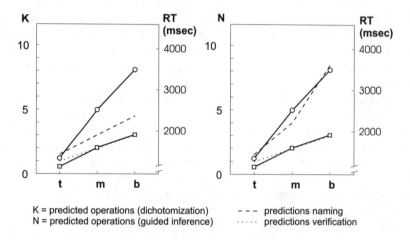

K = predicted operations (dichotomization)
N = predicted operations (guided inference)

– – – predictions naming
· · · · · predictions verification

Fig. 8.8 Mean RTs (solid lines) for the category structure MF and predictions (dashed and dotted lines for naming and verification, respectively) from the pure-decision (left) and MGI (right) accounts. Pure-decision predictions for classification are based on the assumption that one binary decision between two categories takes as long as 1.5 yes–no category checks (see text).

contrast, according to the MGI account, the conditions of the tree in series RF, but not in series MF, should permit shortcuts (see appendix).

Figure 8.8 permits the results for the category structure of series MF to be assessed against the predictions from the pure-decision (left-hand side) and the MGI (right-hand side) accounts. The solid lines denote the experimental data, the dashed lines the predictions. The comparative assessment is based on the fact that both models make identical predictions with regard to verification. With

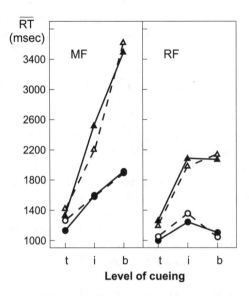

Fig. 8.9 Mean RTs for the category structures MF and RF as functions of the level of cueing (t, i, b), with task (naming, verification) as the parameter. See text for further explanation.

regard to naming, to make binary decisions comparable with MGI feature checks, it is assumed that one operation that yields a binary decision between two categories can be replaced with either one or two yes–no decisions in serial checking. On average, this amounts to 1.5 comparison operations to be considered as an upper limit. As Fig. 8.8 shows, the pure-decision account is qualitatively incompatible with the data, whereas the MGI account describes the data trends quite well.

A comparison between the MF and the RF series is given by Fig. 8.9, which shows that the MGI account correctly predicts the changes in the pattern of results between the two series. Simultaneous fitting of the naming and verification data yields operation times of 314 ms for both the MF and the RF series. This strongly suggests process implementation by identical underlying routines in both series, providing an additional validation of the model. Note that for both series the outcome is incompatible with the pure-decision account. Concerning the interaction between stimulus-set structure and intentional demand, the results suggest that both factors influence the same representational level: Intentional constraints restrict the action of stimulus-dependent structuring in memory to the subsets of objects corresponding to task-related categories while otherwise leaving the rules of structuring unaltered.

The intercept for the RF series is 222 ms lower than that for the MF series (953 versus 731 ms), corresponding to a facilitation effect of 37 ms per distinctive feature. This time is 1 order of magnitude below the operation times in top-down processing and thus points to the involvement of sensory-encoding operations.

MORE DETAILED EXAMINATION

In regard to the contrast between MGI and pure-decisions series, the outcome of the classification experiment in the preceding section is compelling. However, even when only stimuli of the type used are considered, several questions concerning the validity and range of application of the approach remain open. Of these, I briefly address three major issues: First, in the experiment, only one type of categorical structure was used, one referred to as a "conjunctive concept" in the literature on concept formation. This raises the question of whether MGI applies to other logical structures as well. Second, (pseudo)serial code processing was explored only with respect to cue-level mean RTs. This poses the question of whether MGI procedures may also be able to account for RT variances. Third, a common limitation of the preceding experiments was that subjects had received relatively little practice on the tasks. This raises the question of whether "flat" (nonhierarchical) code processing applies also after extensive practice or whether it might then give way to other strategies.

Inclusion of Disjunctive Structures

To examine the applicability of the approach to a broader range of structures, Puffe (1984) introduced some new categories, which are illustrated in Fig. 8.10. The structure represented by tree A is equivalent to that of MF, thus providing a baseline for comparisons across the experiments. Trees B and C represent disjunctive structures constructed such that objects cannot be classified by joint features. Nevertheless, the feature arrangements on some of the cue levels still allow for partial code contractions. A description of the formal codes, along with the corresponding numbers of operations, is given in the appendix. The predictions and data are presented in Fig. 8.11.

The MGI predictions agree in each case with the rank order of the mean RTs. To appreciate the overall result, note that, besides subtle qualitative differences in RT trends, even a trend reversal between verification in series A and C is correctly portrayed. Slopes for A and B of 356 and 350 ms, respectively, obtained by regression across naming and verification tasks, agree with the invariance assumption. With a slope of 331 ms in series C, that is, a deviation of ~6% from these estimates, the correspondence is slightly poorer than in the former experiment.

These findings corroborate, for identical sets of objects and responses and 2 × 3 task-demand conditions, the provisional conclusions set out in the preceding paragraph, namely, the patterns of results can be predicted by assuming that intentional constraints induce a task-specific partitioning of the set of objects in memory, and

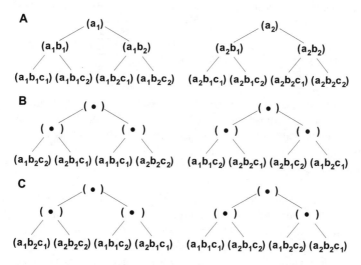

Fig. 8.10 Tree representations of the category structures in tasks A, B, and C. The filled circles indicate that no closed representation is possible. The model predictions are based on the fact that, nonetheless, partial compressions are possible (see appendix).

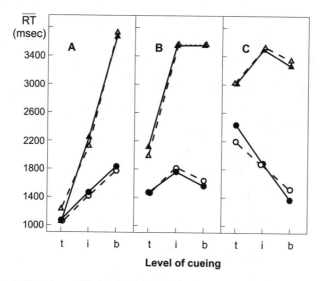

Fig. 8.11 Mean RTs for the hierarchical category structures A, B, and C as functions of the level of cueing (t, i, b), with task (naming versus verification) as the parameter.

stimulus-related structuring takes place within these sets in accordance with the generation rules that represent their regularities.

Examining Predictions About Reaction-Time Variances

A difficulty with examining MGI predictions about strong systematic changes of RT as a function of the position of a category within sequential category codes arises from the fact that category checking must be assumed to vary between subjects and that it could even change from test to test within subjects. A heuristic alternative is to assume that, after a few initial trials required for stabilization, individual checking sequences remain fixed. On this assumption, for each of the cueing levels (t, i, or b), individual rank orders of the mean RTs were determined. RTs of identical ranks were then averaged across subjects and cumulated across ranks. In regression analyses, the resulting cumulative means were treated as mean RTs for a given code sequence. Because the predicted numbers of operations depend only weakly on code sequence, values for an arbitrarily chosen sequence were used as predictors.

Series RF and MF may serve as instructive examples. In Table 8.1, the corresponding cumulative means are shown together with the numbers of operations calculated for the sequences illustrated in Fig. 8.7. Results of regression analyses are given in Table 8.2. Regression coefficients across level means (column 1) agree roughly with those based on the full set of rank-ordered data (column 2). The close agreement of the latter with estimates from ranked means at the b level

TABLE 8.1
Cumulated Mean Ranked RT_c and Number of Predicted Operations N for MF and RF Series

Series	Cue Level	Rank							
		1	2	3	4	5	6	7	8
MF	t	1252	1432						
		1	2						
	i	2176	2402	2750	2919				
		2	4	4	6				
	b	2353	2604	3105	3451	3718	4030	4355	5144
		3	6	7	7	10	10	11	14
RF	t	1172	1364						
		1	2						
	i	1668	1931	2204	2573				
		2	4	4	6				
	b	1248	1504	1713	1946	2166	2490	2752	3018
		1	2	3	4	5	6	7	8

Note. In each column–row set, the top number is the RT_c (in milliseconds) and the second number is the number of predicted operations.

TABLE 8.2

Results of Linear Regressions for MF and RF, Series

Series	Database According to Table 8.1		
	Level Means	Ranked RTs	Ranked RTs, Level b
MF	$t_0 = 1049.0$	$t_0 = 1285.2$	$t_0 = 1364.7$
	$T = 310.9$	$T = 272.4$	$T = 262.4$
	$R^2 = 0.96$	$R^2 = 0.95$	$R^2 = 0.95$
RF	$t_0 = 847.9$	$t_0 = 980.3$	$t_0 = 969.9$
	$T = 295.5$	$T = 255.0$	$T = 257.2$
	$R^2 = 0.98$	$R^2 = 0.97$	$R^2 = 1.00$

Note. These results are based on the data and predictors presented in Table 8.1. t_0 and T denote intercepts and operation times in milliseconds, respectively. See text for further explanation.

alone (column 3) indicates that the moderate, but consistent, differences between the estimates from level means and those based on the ranking procedure are due to an independent additional factor that produces an increase in RT with the number of level-specific categories. It is very likely that this factor reflects response generation, a major source of RT variation that has been neglected so far. Because this factor also enters into the slope estimates presented in the preceding paragraph, ranking analyses analogous to those presented here would provide corrected estimates of the order of 250–290 ms. These revised estimates should be of considerable interest for a theory of cognitive operation times, without, however, having an impact on the invariance assumption relevant for the present considerations.

The good agreement of parameter estimates between series RF and MF implies that the empirical ranges of RT variation agree nearly exactly with the 11:7 ratio predicted between these conditions.

Effects of Practice

A possible objection against the relevance of the serial-processing model is that flat (nonhierarchical) code processing might be restricted to the special "design and procedure" used in the experiments under consideration. This objection was addressed in several experiments. Among other factors, the influence of the training procedure was examined, which, in the preceding experiments, might have emphasized within-level (i.e., "horizontal") category ordering. To avoid this, procedures were introduced that oriented subjects explicitly toward "vertical" ordering of the categories in memory. However, neither this nor other measures produced changes in a direction expected on the basis of hierarchical processing according to pure-decision.

A remaining objection was that nonhierarchical processing might apply only as long as the level of practice was low. That is, early during practice, subjects might still be "searching" for the decision-relevant information, whereas this information

TABLE 8.3
Mean RTs for six Practice Blocks in Two Experimental Sessions for two Task
Demands (Verification, Naming) and Two Levels of Cueing (L_1, L_2)

Task	Session 1			Session 2		
	Block 1	Block 2	Block 3	Block 4	Block 5	Block 6
Verifying L_1	761	766	733	689	692	655
Verifying L_2	965	991	896	812	790	771
D_v	204	225	163	123	98	116
Naming L_1	1227	1150	1076	1055	1017	1035
Naming L_2	2405	2336	2036	1798	1662	1732
D_n	1178	1186	960	743	645	698
D_n/D_v	5.77	5.27	5.89	6.04	6.58	6.02

Note. D_v and D_n indicate the differences in RTs between L_1 and L_2 for verification and naming, respectively. According to the pure-decision account, RTs for naming should approach those for verification (disregarding the time required for verbal responding in the naming task). The nearly constantly high ratio of both between-level differences indicates that the processing mode does not change toward strategies that, over the course of practice, would permit the number of operations to approach the unconditional logical minimum.

might be immediately accessible after sufficient practice. To examine this objection, a practice experiment, consisting of two sessions of three experimental blocks each, was carried out. The category structures used were similar to those of the preceding structure A. To simplify the tasks, only two cue levels, L_1 and L_2, were included. Table 8.3 gives the time courses of the mean RTs across blocks for both cue levels, separately for verification and naming tasks. The scores D_v and D_n, which are given below the RT values indicating the differences in RTs between L_1 and L_2 for verification and naming, respectively, represent the expedition of processing across the six sequential blocks.

Note that, although D_v and D_n decrease with training by nearly 50%, there is no evidence at all of a decrease in the ratio $D_n:D_v$, which would have to occur in case of a transition to hierarchical (pure-decision) strategies. The absence of any decrease in this ratio strongly suggests that nonhierarchical pseudoserial processing is maintained even after extensive practice, although practice would also lead to further substantial decreases in operation times and consequently in the absolute differences D_n and D_v between RTs on different cue levels for naming and verification.

Two interesting implications concerning the action of intention derive from these findings, as well as from the evidence from the other experiments. The fact that variation of procedural conditions during acquisition has only little influence on the mode of processing suggests that the way on which framed representations emerge and the role they play in intentional perceptual–task performance may be universal. The practice experiment at the same time indicates that the format and the role of the representations do not change fundamentally over the course of the automatization of recognition. One is thus led to assume that, at least in normal human classification performance, even when highly practiced, no level of purely procedural optimization (as assumed by the pure-decision account) is inserted between internal object representations and control of task-specific action.

TRANSFORMATIONAL STRUCTURES AND SET-STRUCTURE ACQUISITION IN COMPLEX STRUCTURAL RECOGNITION

The feature-generated material that was used to disentangle stimulus-related and intention-related factors in the experiments reviewed thus far has its own limitations. The first arises from the fact that the precise properties of the figural elements do not enter into the category descriptions. As a consequence, the question of whether the sensory properties of these elements are somehow preserved in the memory representations cannot be addressed. Second, the rules of processing emerge as properties of ready, fully functioning architectures. Finding out how these architectures develop during acquisition appears to be a difficult undertaking. However, an understanding of this would be important for situations in which simple serial models fail to apply.

Both these issues can be addressed by use of stimulus materials consisting of regular geometrical objects that are interrelated by systematic transformations, thus permitting the study of relationships between structural properties of individual object representations and those of object-set representations in memory. As discussed in the next subsection, the fact that RTs vary as functions of transformational distances under these conditions can be exploited to depict processes of structure formation in memory.

The Role of Transformational Structures in Recognition: Basic Facts

For a study of the role of transformational structures in complex recognition, transformations that constitute groups in the mathematical sense are of particular interest. An example is the discrete group D_4, which is defined by transformations in the plane that result from any number of repeated rotations by $\pm 90°$ and vertical, horizontal, and diagonal reflections that represent the "generators" of the group. To see how this group "acts" on geometrical objects that obey related symmetries, consider, for example, the pattern $\ulcorner$, which, by any transformation belonging to the group, will turn into one of the elements of the pattern set $\{\ulcorner, \urcorner, \llcorner, \lrcorner\}$. Sets like these are referred to as equivalence sets and their number of elements as equivalence-set size (ESS). From a representational perspective, the members of an equivalence set can be considered as deriving from one prototypical member by an appropriate sequence of transformations. Within the context of MGI, it is important to note that, in general, this representation is not unique. Generation may start from any element of an equivalence set and can produce the remainder by using different transformational paths. In other words, an analog should hold to the ambiguity postulate for sequential category codes suggested.

It has been known since the work of Garner and collaborators (e.g., see Garner & Clement, 1963) that equivalence sets are psychologically relevant units and, in particular, that ESS is an effective predictor of performance in judgment and recognition tasks. Chekosky and Whitlock (1973) used the Garner and Clement set of five-point patterns constructed on a regular 3×3 grid in an item-recognition task. A reexamination of their data by Schmidt and Ackermann (1990) yielded results that were consistent with serial processing at the level of elements within equivalence sets of the memory-set items. In multiple naming, effects of ESS on RT were found for transformations of different types of pattern, such as arrays of black and white circles (Geissler, 1972, 1974) and angular patterns (see Geissler, 1980).

More recently, robust dependence on ESS was demonstrated in a delayed same–different comparison task in which the Garner–Clement patterns were used (Geissler & Lachmann, 1996, 1997; Schmidt & Ackermann, 1990; see also Lachmann & van Leeuwen, this volume, for an overview). In this task, "same" responses were required if the patterns could be brought to match by rotations, reflections, or both, and "different" responses otherwise. The evidence gathered under these conditions suggested that the MGI rationale extends to recognition of relations that cannot be stored in long-term memory, but must be temporarily held in working memory. Most remarkably, the "force" of representational guidance appears so strong that the instructed direct pairwise matching is being replaced with a serial search within internal representations of the equivalence sets of each of the compared patterns. Because this strategy is logically more complex than direct comparison, it reveals a special type of seeming redundancy.

Hypothesis on the Formation of Task-Related Set Representations

In the preceding studies, complete transformational structures are assumed as "given" by accounts of their function in judgment and classification. This does not, however, provide for an understanding of how transformations may become relevant to a task during acquisition, nor of how their influence will be modified by particular task demands. The approach suggested here is different: The set of relevant transformations is not to be considered as given or primary in any way. Rather, it emerges as a result of the embedding of concrete successive transformational relations among patterns into more comprehensive transformational structures. In a way that is analogous to the preceding "static" description, according to which intentional task demands are assumed to operate on the manifold of potential stimulus-set representations by those compatible with its constraints, latent transient representations of potential relations among objects in the actual

Fig. 8.12 Illustration of the successive constraining of expectations as a basis of the memory embedding of sets of objects. As
to the relationships among the patterns, in (a) the minimal representation is one by (the mathematical group of) horizontal reflections. Another, less restrictive, possibility is representation by 90°
rotations and integer multiples of 90°. In contrast, in (b), because
of the difference in leg lengths, only this latter representation is
possible. The horizontal-reflection interpretation is also ruled out
when, as in (a'), rotations are required later on in a sequence of
patterns. These illustrations do not yet show what memory embedding implies in relation to task specificity. For this, processes
of differential reinforcement and selection on the basis of task-
related constraints have to be assumed in addition (see text).

stimulus inputs are assumed to provide the raw material on which intentional
constraints operate.

A simple illustration of this idea is given in Fig. 8.12. The assumption is that,
from among a set of options built into the visual system, any embedding applying in a given case will be latently activated and will generate memory traces of
corresponding equivalence sets persisting over a short period and decaying thereafter. Accordingly, the relation between the two angular patterns of configuration
(a) in Fig. 8.12, with the exception of a displacement, can be seen as resulting
from alternative transformations that are elements of different transformational
groups. For example, this relation can be conceived of as a mirroring relative to
the vertical axis. This representation relates the patterns to the group of vertical
reflections R_v comprising right–left and left–right reflection, r_v and r_v^{-1}, and the
so-called neutral element obtained by carrying r_v and r_v^{-1} one after another. The
corresponding embedding includes exactly the two patterns under consideration.
Alternatively, the relation can be interpreted as resulting from a 90° rotation, which
is an element of the finite cyclical group of rotations R_{90} (consisting of rotations
by 90°, 180°, 270°, and 360° and their inverses). The "action" of this group upon
the patterns under consideration produces a set of four patterns, which is also
the equivalence set under the full group D_4 of rotations and reflections. As yet
another alternative, the relation between the two patterns may be interpreted as
an element from among the unconstrained set of possible rotations. The group
of continuous rotations R, which contains R_{90} as a subgroup, can be considered
as an admissible mathematical idealization of this set of transformations. In this
case, the patterns become embedded into a large set of patterns differing only in
orientation.

Which type of embedding becomes latently activated will, in general, depend on local pattern properties. This is illustrated by the pattern pair (b) in Fig. 8.12, for which only rotation is possible. In addition, each of the embeddings considered differentially constrains the expectations for further pattern presentations: In the mirroring interpretation, the "horizon" of expectation comprises only two patterns: In the finite cyclic-rotation interpretation, the horizon contains four patterns; in the (quasi-)continuous-rotation interpretation, there is no such limitation. Consequently, as the possible continuation (a') of (a) in Fig. 8.12 indicates, "perceptual" expectations may exert a selective influence on latent embedding. In the example, embedding according to the reflection interpretation would become immediately suppressed.

In the next section, experimental evidence is considered that concerns how latent embeddings may become framed by intentional task constraints. The underlying hypothesis is that, under the action of specific task demands, latent embeddings become selectively reinforced and transferred into memory-stabilized embeddings.

IRRELEVANT TRANSFORMATIONS AS A TOOL TO STUDY REPRESENTATIONAL DYNAMICS

The evidence reviewed in the preceding section indicates that the processing of "relevant" category information in transformationally generated sets of objects can be considered by analogy to the processing of feature-generated sets. However, for "irrelevant" transformations, there exists no such analogy (to the processing of irrelevant features), because these cannot, in general, be separated from relevant transformations. Consequently, there will be stable effects of irrelevant variation in the RT patterns. Fortunately these can be exploited to render processes of representational dynamics visible, which would otherwise remain hidden. In the following subsection, experiments are considered in which this was accomplished by systematic distortions applied to sets of regular geometric patterns (see Geissler, 1980).

Basic Design

In each of these experiments, a standard set of 16 angular patterns (shown at the top of Fig. 8.13) or subsets of this set were used. The standard set can be divided into two subsets: Subset I, consisting of eight angular patterns with legs of equal lengths oriented perpendicularly to one another; and subset II, consisting of eight patterns with legs including an angle of $45°$. The diagram in the row below provides an illustration of the transformational structuring of these subsets. Subset I includes four elements with horizontal and vertical legs (Ia) and four axis-symmetrical elements (Ib). Both subsets Ia and Ib transform into themselves under actions of group D_4 (see preceding section), but transition from one set to

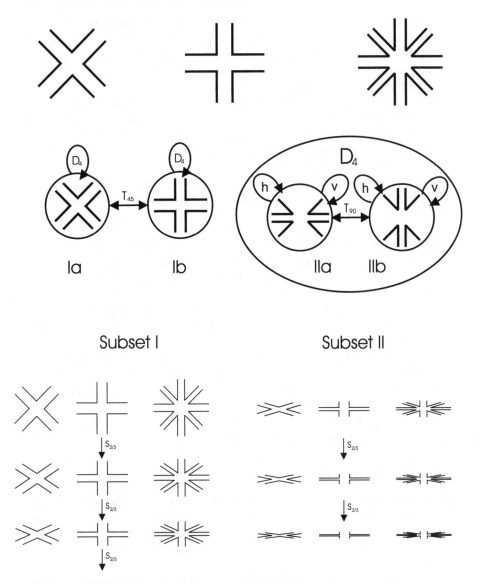

Fig. 8.13   Top, The 16 geometrical patterns of the standard set. Middle, Illustrations of the transformational group relations among the patterns (the letters h and v denote horizontal and vertical reflections, respectively). Bottom, The standard set of patterns and their appearance with degree of distortion ranging from 1 to 5. Note that the individual patterns are affected differentially by the same degree of distortion. Some patterns become more obtuse-angled, some more acute-angled; in others, only the length of a leg is changed. See text for the significance of these differential distortion effects.

the other requires odd multiples of rotations by $45°$ (T_{45}). Subset II turns into itself under D_4. It contains two subsets, one of patterns with one horizontal leg (IIa) and the other of patterns with one vertical leg (IIb), which both turn into themselves under horizontal and vertical reflections (denoted by h and v), whereas rotations by odd multiples of $90°$ mediate between both subsets.

To investigate recognition processes as a function of irrelevant transformations, five steps of vertical shrinking by $2/3$ were introduced and applied to all figures. This is illustrated in the lower part of Fig. 8.13. Mathematically, these transformations can be represented as elements of a group, $S_{2/3}$. Let $s_{2/3}$ represent one step of shrinking. An n-fold application can then be expressed by $s_{2/3}^n$. In the following discussion, n is referred to as the degree of distortion (DD). According to this convention, the steps of vertical shrinking correspond to DDs 1, 2, 3, and 5, whereas the undistorted state of the standard set patterns corresponds to a DD of 0. Note that shrinking caused by the repeated application of $s_{2/3}$ affects members of the original equivalence sets in different ways. For example, although the patterns of set Ia transform with either more obtuse or more acute angles as a result of repeated shrinking, the patterns of set Ib are all modified in identical ways by a shortening of one of the legs. The patterns of set II are subject to more complicated distortions: Those with one vertical edge (IIb) gradually become more similar to those of subset Ib, and those with one horizontal edge (IIa) become more similar to the acute-angled derivatives of subset Ia.

Concerning D_4 (the group generating the original standard set), note that groups $S_{2/3}$ and D_4 are noncommutable, that is, combining transformations from each of the groups in different orders may yield different results; formally, $S_{2/3} \times D_4 \neq D_4 \times S_{2/3}$. For example, a vertical shrinking of $\vee$ and subsequent rotation by $90°$ will lead to an obtuse-angled pattern, whereas the same pattern yields an acute-angled result if first rotated and then compressed.

Experiment I: The Basic U-Shaped Trend

How do the distortions enter into recognition? An initial hypothesis was that dynamic reference formation, along the lines of Helson's adaptation level (AL) (e.g., Helson, 1964), might take place. In this hypothesis, under the given conditions, ALs should function as centers of areas of generalization, that is, u-shaped trends would be expected.

In the first experiment considered (Experiment I), care was taken to distribute degrees of shrinking as uniformly among trials as possible. As in all other experiments, in an acquisition phase, subjects learned to respond to each of the 16 standard patterns with a special name. During this period, in order not to enforce the $2/3$ progression of distortion a priori, the patterns were presented with equal probabilities only in the DDs 0 and 5.

In Fig. 8.14, the mean RTs for the test series are plotted against DDs 0–5, which correspond to a logarithmic transformation of the original axis of shrinking.

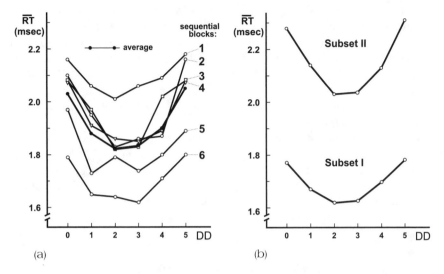

Fig. 8.14 Mean RTs as a function of the DD in Experiment I, in which DDs occurred with equal frequencies during testing. See text for further explanation.

Figure 8.14(a) shows the development of the mean RT across the subsequent six experimental blocks of the test series (open circles) and the average function (filled circles). Most striking is the lack of any systematic change in curve shape across experimental blocks and the nearly ideal symmetry of the u-shaped average function. In a continuous interpolation, the minimum of this function turns out to be close to the arithmetic mean of the levels of distortion. Note that the mean function loses its symmetry if plotted against the original s^k scale, with the minimum being close to the geometrical mean. This position of the minimum agrees well with expectations from AL theory. AL theory predicts that, for homogeneous sets of objects, the center of a range of categorical generalization is to be found at the geometrical mean of the scale values on the relevant dimension.

For the same data, Fig. 8.14(b) displays separately the mean trends for pattern subsets I and II. Both functions exhibit the same symmetrical shape, with a somewhat larger ground-to-edge distance for subset II than for subset I. In addition, the RTs for subset I are some 500 ms faster than those for subset II. This is approximately the same difference as that found in another experiment for the corresponding subsets of the undistorted standard-set patterns, suggesting that the basic procedure of category testing remains essentially unaltered by distortion.

There are two points worth noting: First, the graph of the mean RT as a function of DD implies that recognition is slowest for the standard set of the patterns and for their most strongly distorted derivatives. Because the standard set comprises elements of the highest figural goodness, this result provides clear evidence that it is not the perceptual appearance of the single patterns, considered as isolated elements, that primarily determines the speed of processing. Rather, it is a global reference frame related to the whole set of distorted and undistorted elements that is responsible for the observed effects. The difference of ~10 ms between the two poles of distortion, which is very small compared with the 150–250-ms lead for the center of the range of distortion, indicates how little a (presumably) sensory-processing component contributes to RT variation relative to memory-related intentional processing.

The second point to be made concerns the formation of memory structures. The presence of the constant u-shaped trend as early as in the first block of the test series indicates that its formation occurred already at the beginning of the block. As the entire block included only 64 out of 192 possible combinations of patterns and DDs, this implies that a relatively small fraction of the transformational space suffices for the memory mechanisms to anticipate its complete structure.

Stabilization of Framing Following a Change in Transformational Conditions

To explore the formation of the presumed global reference frames in more detail, the effects of shifts in the stimulus distributions were investigated in a further series of experiments. In two of these, only the patterns of the standard set were presented during acquisition and distortions were introduced at the start of the test series. In one version (Experiment II), all DDs were presented with equal probability. In the other version (Experiment III), distorted patterns were presented in balanced sequences of alternating blocks, each containing only DDs 0–3 or, respectively, 4–6. Figure 8.15 presents the results in an format analogous to Experiment II for the six subsequent experimental blocks.

The family of functions shown in the left-hand graph of Fig. 8.15 is consistent with the idea that, after the introduction of distortions by averaging-in of their scale values, the AL shifts smoothly from DD = 0 toward the long-term mean on the DD scale, 2.5. However, this is not the case for the right-hand graph of Fig. 8.15. In keeping with the notion of AL, to explain the occurrence of *two* dips from the beginning of the test series onward would require two internal referents, one for each of the partial DD ranges. However, to account also for the global initial upward trend, yet another referent would have to be assumed, which represents the undistorted patterns learned during acquisition as independent entities in memory and whose influence decays only very slowly. Further along these lines, a fourth referent would have to be introduced to accommodate the symmetry around the DD mean in the final, sixth, experimental block. The resulting description, albeit rather complicated, would still be incomplete logically, as it could not explain why the referent-related effects remain restricted to partial ranges.

These complications and ad hoc assumptions can readily be avoided if one dispenses with the AL approach altogether and resorts to the idea, already introduced,

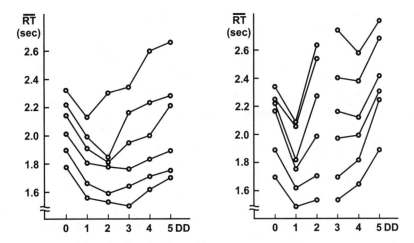

Fig. 8.15 Data from left, Experiment II and right, Experiment III in which distortions were introduced in the test phase. Empirical mean RTs are shown for each of the six successive blocks as a function of the DD. In Experiment II, patterns were presented in each DD with equal probability. In Experiment III, the distorted patterns were presented in balanced sequences of alternating blocks, each containing only DDs 0–3 or, respectively, DDs 4–6. See text for further explanation.

of successive transformational embedding. On this account, the real functional correlates and media of object-set representations are *transformational ranges* derived as abstractions from actual temporal stimulus sequences.

To incorporate task relatedness into this account, one would have to assume that only task demands act on the memory traces as selective reinforcement devices. Take the example of the right-hand part of Fig. 8.15. After an extended period without DD variation during acquisition, the introduction of distortions denotes the embedding of a constant state (preferred point on the DD axis) into a range that expands from that point in *one direction*. After a few trials, there arises a two-range embedding for DDs 0–2 and 3–5 as another independent range structure that stabilizes temporarily. DD variations within these ranges exhibit no preferred direction. On this account, the higher position of the minimum within the DD interval 3–5 relative to that within the interval 0–2 results from the fact that both embeddings coexist for a period of time with the representation of the standard set of patterns practiced originally. However, subrange division as well as the reference to the standard patterns is not reinforced by the task, as all DDs are equivalent for task-specific responding. After the subrange-related representations have been established, transitions between both ranges emerge as distinct events that span a symmetrical range of variation expanding from DD 0 to DD 5. Task-specific reinforcement is thus expected to amplify selectively the impact of the global DD 0–5 range at the expense of the other representations.

As I discussed (Geissler, 1980), a detailed description of distortion effects requires the additional assumption that the mean RTs are linear functions of the average weighted distances of a given probe stimulus to the total set of transformational states included in the range representations. This suggests a mechanism of cumulative parallel processing of similarity-based resonance values, analogously to that proposed by Ratcliff (1978). Weights herein may depend on several factors, particularly frequencies of occurrence. Apart from avoiding the difficulties just mentioned, this account has the advantage in that it automatically yields the parabolic shape of the basic trend found with uniform stimulation in experiment I.

The evidence reviewed thus far concerns the average impact of distortions, considered as irrelevant transformations of patterns, in relation to subsets I and II. It does not, however, permit statements about their impact on responding with respect to single categories. Experiment IV, in which only subset I of the standard set was used, turned out to be especially informative in this respect. In this experiment, after an acquisition phase with undistorted patterns, distortions were introduced uniformly, except for the particular case of the ∨-type standard pattern for which the presentation rate was increased in one of the DDs, specifically DD 4, to 15 times the normal value. Figure 8.16 shows the RT trends obtained after stabilization in the second half of the experiment. The results for the axis-symmetrical patterns, which are represented by solid lines, exhibit two main features: The RT minima for all elements of the equivalence set are shifted toward DD 4, although the presentation schedule was altered for only one of the elements. This result provides striking confirmation of a fundamental implication of the "embedding" view, namely, that processing is based on representations that represent the distortions for each of the set members in the same format of group action on the set of patterns as a whole. In other words, the results confirm that what matters is the common dimension of shrinking, rather than the changes in the appearance of individual patterns (which, depending on their orientations, are affected differentially by the distortions).

There is a further finding that goes beyond the mere fact of group coding: The mean RTs for patterns with axis-parallel legs (indicated by dashed lines), which exhibit a maximum in the vicinity of DD 4, show nearly exactly the reverse trend to the mean RTs for patterns with axis-symmetrical legs. A simple average-distance model cannot account for this trend. As I discussed (Geissler, 1980), an appropriate extension holds that RT effects are the net result of antagonistic components: RT increases as a function of within-category distance and decreases as a function of between-category distance.

Two Conclusions

The preceding evidence from the classification of transformationally related objects is consistent with the basic claims of MGI as proposed originally for feature-generated sets. Beyond this, the distortion experiments reveal two novel

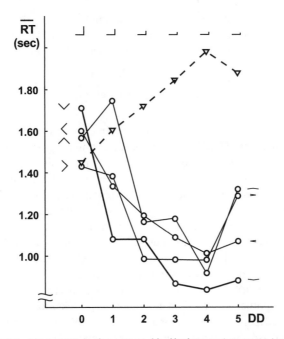

Fig. 8.16   Mean RTs in the second half of Experiment IV, in which only the patterns of subset I and their distortions are used. Each DD was presented with equal frequency, with one exception: One of the axes-symmetric patterns (that in the orientation of a V) was presented 15 times more frequently with DD = 4. RTs to all members of subset Ia (see Fig. 8.13), to which this exceptional pattern belongs, were affected in nearly the same way by this frequency manipulation. The reverse effect was obtained for the other subset, Ib. Note that the average effect for the entire set I was therefore much smaller than the subset-specific effects. See text for further explanation.

aspects: One is that process-guiding memory representations are "perceptual" in the sense that they are based on the same sensory information that is involved in the perception of structured objects. However, this information is configured differently. Similar to the Gestalt laws, the representational rules serve to eliminate redundancies by explicating regularities. Unlike the Gestalt laws, these rules do not represent the regularities of individual objects separately. In coordination with intentional task constraints, they make explicit regularities of sets of objects, such as the nesting of subsets and ranges of dimensional variation.

The second finding relates this result to cognitive faculties in a more general way: There is convincing evidence that intentional processing (which is fairly slow during early stages of practice) takes advantage, for its implementation, of competing fast processes of structure formation in memory. If the principle of embedding outlined in the preceding sections holds true, these processes involve, to a hitherto unprecedented degree, routines of implicit abstraction. In this regard, the investigations reviewed in this chapter relate to issues of human intelligence, marking a fascinating field of research in their own right.

FINAL REMARKS

The primary intent of the review of studies presented in this chapter was to address methodological issues of flexible intentional processing in perception. This and the focus on top-down processing preclude a detailed comparison with current domain-specific theories and models. However, a few remarks that relate the questions considered in this chapter to issues of current research appear to be in order here.

One limitation of the considerations given herein is the concentration on discrete structural properties. Certainly descriptions relevant to everyday situations have to include properties that are more adequately encompassed by continuous multidimensional formal representations. Thus the question arises of how a synthesis of these two representational modes, as a basis of task-related processing, might be accomplished. Important contributions to answering this question can be expected from approaches based on continuous representations, which attempt to implement task dependence. For a long time, continuous modeling was concerned with perceptual aspects independent of task demands, thus overemphasizing the role of decision processes. Recently, however, considerable progress in this regard was made by Maddox (2001), who developed an approach deriving from general recognition theory (Ashby & Townsend, 1986; see also Ashby & Lee, 1993). This theory assumes that a single multidimensional stimulus can be represented by a multivariate probability distribution. By separating perceptual and decisional components, Maddox (2001) was able to show that task-related selective attention reduces the perceptual variance along the relevant dimension relative to the irrelevant dimensions, a tendency that was found to increase with training in three of four observers.

As proposed, framed representations can be viewed as instances of common codes for perception and planned action. However, in mapping object-response relationships, the important case of dimensional covariation of stimuli and responses was not taken into consideration. This is exactly the focus of Prinz's "common-coding" approach (e.g., Nattkemper & Prinz, 2001; Prinz, 1997), which sets out to account for the relationships between dynamic and stationary aspects of stimulus information and motor actions specified in terms of spatiotemporal transformations. The latter approach, on the other hand, has not yet addressed representational dynamics, which, in the view of MGI, becomes relevant as soon as one action corresponds to several possible states in the dimensional variation of stimuli, that is, under conditions of many-to-one mapping. It thus appears that both approaches include complementary elements that should become explicit in the course of further developments.

A third issue to be considered here relates to the evidence already given that, although processing speed changes with practice, the structural principles of task-related processing remain invariant. The evolutionary value of this property may be that it ensures ultimate intentional control and reorganization at any level of practice. By virtue of this invariance, processing sequences remain structurally compatible and contents of processing may be translated between layers of different temporal resolution and processing speed. This flexibility of the flow of information places constraints on the temporal organization of the neural processes involved: Integration of object–action connections represented on different time scales into a unique architecture requires fixed temporal relations between layers. Therefore, to avoid unmanageable drifts, there should arise a fixed hierarchy of coupled processing epochs. This idea agrees with findings from an independent line of research on temporally discrete processing, which has led to a taxonomic system of invariant quantal epoch durations (e.g., see Geissler, 1987, 1992; Geissler, Schebera, & Kompass, 1999). In the present context, invariant epoch durations require attention, particularly as they may provide powerful cues for data analysis. For the methodological approach set out in this chapter, one such cue consists in a reversal of the parameter invariance criterion: In the preceding discussion, the invariance criterion was used *post festum* for additional validation. However, although straight cross-task parameter invariance may be violated as experimental conditions cross critical boundaries, the more general principle of invariance in the temporal organization may still hold. Therefore, given that a limited set of preferred temporal parameter values is known in advance, cross-task invariance could be replaced with the best fit of models for a selected subset of these parameter values. The criterion of parameter invariance in the former sense would then correspond to the special case that this set contains only one value.

APPENDIX: CODES AND CODE CALCULATIONS IN EXPERIMENTS 1 & 2

Expanding the notions introduced in the section "some formal considerations," Table 4 represents the formal category codes for each sub-series and cueing condition of the Experiments I and II. In the last two columns expected numbers of operations N and n for naming and (affirmative) verification responses, respectively, are shown which are calculated in a generalization of the scheme of Fig. 8.6.

In the codes, relevant constituents that are distinctive of task-related response categories are enclosed by $\langle \ \rangle$. The letter C denotes common irrelevant constituents or constituents partially correlated with relevant constituents. The attached indices are to allow assignment to the specific experimental conditions. T_i, I_j and B_k denote category-response symbols corresponding to the cueing levels t, i and b, respectively. For convenience, the same response symbols are used for each series. Note that the codes in Table 4 represent examples of arbitrarily chosen

TABLE 8.4

Examples of Formal Category Codes for Each Sub-Series and Cueing Condition of
the Experiments I and II. N and n Indicate Expected Numbers of Operations for
Naming and (Affirmative) Verification Responses, Respectively. Further
Explanation in the Text

Experiment	Series	Cueing Level	Code	Operations N	n
Exp I	MF	t	$[\langle a_1 T_1 \rangle, \langle a_2 T_2 \rangle] \otimes C^t_{MF}$	1.5	1.0
		i	$[\langle (a_1\,b_1) I_1 \rangle, \langle (a_1\,b_2) I_2, \rangle \langle (a_2\,b_1) I_3, \rangle \langle (a_2\,b_2) I_4 \rangle] \otimes C^i_{MF}$	4.0	2.0
		b	$\langle (a_1\,b_1\,c_1) B_1 \rangle, \langle (a_1\,b_1\,c_2) B_2 \rangle, \langle (a_1\,b_2\,c_1) B_3 \rangle,$ $\langle (a_1\,b_2\,c_2)\,B_4 \rangle, \langle (a_2\,b_1\,c_1) B_5 \rangle, \langle (a_2\,b_1\,c_2) B_6 \rangle,$ $\langle (a_2\,b_2\,c_1) B_7 \rangle, \langle (a_2\,b_2\,c_2) B_8 \rangle$	8.5	3.0
	RF	t	$\langle a_1 T_1 \rangle \otimes C^t_1, \langle a_2 T_2 \rangle \otimes C^t_2$	1.5	1.0
		i	$\langle (a_1\,b_1) I_1 \rangle \otimes C^i_1, \langle (a_1\,b_2) I_2 \rangle \otimes C^i_2, \langle (a_2\,b_3) I_3 \rangle \otimes C^i_3,$ $\langle (a_2\,b_4) I_4 \rangle \otimes C^i_4$	4.0	2.0
		b	$[\langle c_1 B_1 \rangle, \langle c_2 B_2 \rangle] \otimes C^b_1, [\langle c_3 B_3 \rangle, \langle c_4 B_4 \rangle] \otimes C^b_2,$ $[\langle c_5 B_5 \rangle, \langle c_6 B_6 \rangle)] \otimes C^b_3, [\langle c_7 B_7 \rangle, \langle c_8 B_8 \rangle] \otimes C^b_4$	4.5	1.0
Exp II	A	t	as for MF	1.5	1.0
		i	as for MF	4.0	2.0
		b	as for MF	8.5	3.0
	B	t	$\{\langle [(b_1\,c_1), (b_2\,c_2)] T_1 \rangle, \langle [(b_1\,c_2), (b_2\,c_1)] T_2 \rangle\} \otimes C^t_B$	4.0	2.5
		i	$\langle [(a_1\,b_2\,c_2), (a_2\,b_1\,c_1)] I_1 \rangle, \langle [(a_1\,b_1\,c_1), (a_2\,b_2\,c_2)] I_2 \rangle,$ $\langle [(a_1\,b_1\,c_2), (a_2\,b_2\,c_1)] I_3 \rangle, \langle [(a_1\,b_1\,c_2), (a_1\,b_2\,c_1)] I_4 \rangle$	8.5	3.5
		b	Equivalent to MF	8.5	3.0
	C	t	$\langle \{a_1 [(b_2\,c_1), (b_1\,c_2)], a_2[(b_2\,c_2), (b_1\,c_1)]\} T_1 \rangle,$ $\langle \{a_1[(b_2\,c_2), (b_1\,c_1)], a_2[(b_2\,c_1), (b_1\,c_2)]\} T_2 \rangle$	7.5	5.0
		i	$\langle [(a_1\,b_2\,c_1), (a_2\,b_2\,c_2)] I_1 \rangle, \langle [(a_1\,b_1\,c_2), (a_2\,b_1\,c_1)] I_2 \rangle,$ $\langle [(a_1\,b_1\,c_1), (a_2\,b_1\,c_2)] I_3 \rangle, \langle [(a_1\,b_2\,c_2), (a_2\,b_2\,c_1)] I_4 \rangle.$	9.0	4.0
		b	Equivalent to MF	8.5	3.0

Denotation of constituents:

$C^t_{MF} = [(b_1\,c_1), (b_1\,c_2), (b_2\,c_1), (b_2\,c_2)] = [(b_1, b_2) \times (c_1, c_2)]; C^i_{MF} = (c_1, c_2); C^t_1 = (b_1 \times (c_1, c_2),$
$b_2 \times (c_3, c_4)), C^t_2 = (b_3 \times (c_5, c_6), b_2 \times (c_7, c_8)); C^i_1 = (c_1, c_2), C^i_2 = (c_3, c_4), C^i_3 = (c_5, c_6), C^i_4 =$
$(c_7, c_8); C^b_1 = (a_1\,b_1), C^b_2 = (a_1\,b_2), C^b_3 = (a_2\,b_3), C^b_4 = (a_2\,b_4); C^t_B = (a_1, a_2).$
Note the conventions: $A \times (b, c) = (A\,b), (A\,c)$ and $(A, B) \times (b, c) = (A\,b), (A\,c), (B\,b), (B\,c).$

sequences of constituents. However, the number of operations calculated in accordance to the scheme of Fig. 8.6 will, in general, depend on the particular sequence of constituents. Given that there is no situational factor enforcing preference of a particular order, all possible orders are of equal 'rights'. Thus the expected numbers of operations across all possible permutations are the only possible representative predictions. Specifically, in counting operations two termination conditions are assumed: Termination based on feature mismatch and sub-category match at the feature and category levels. That is, processing is supposed to be self-terminating at the feature level and exhaustive at the sub-category (constituent) level. In naming, a response is assumed to be elicited as soon as a match is found for at least one sub-category representation positioned at the left side of the corresponding response symbol. In verification, after locating the response label corresponding to the cued name, only the respective code is assumed to be checked.

To avoid misinterpretations, I wish to emphasize that these code descriptions as well as processing rules are conceived as provisional approximations. The essence of the formalism is seen in a reflection of the ability of the brain to recognize regularities within sets of objects and to represent them in relation to specific task demands such that the processing load can be diminished. If and only if, on the basis of regularities, the representational mechanisms allow for separation of relevant and irrelevant constituents, the relevant constituents can be checked independently. Processing modes that mimic sequential code processing are assumed to arise under circumstances like those considered in the chapter mainly to ensure uniqueness of memory-guided top-down checking.

ACKNOWLEDGMENTS

This chapter is dedicated to my former students Martina Puffe, Klaus-Dieter Schmidt, Birgit Ackermann, Raul Kompass, and Thomas Lachmann by whose work it was made possible. I wish to thank Hanna Geissler, Hermann J. Müller and Mark A. Elliott for substantial help in the final wording; I also thank Wolf Schwarz for a stimulating discussion on related theoretical issues. Furthermore, the helpful comments of an anonymous reviewer which have led to a restructuring of the text are gratefully acknowledged.

REFERENCES

Ashby, F. G., & Lee, W. W. (1993). Perceptual variability as a fundamental axiom of perceptual science. In S. C. Massin (Ed.), *Foundations of perceptual theory* (pp. 369–399). Amsterdam: North-Holland.

Ashby, F. G., & Townsend, J. T. (1986). Varieties of perceptual independence. *Psychological Review, 93*, 154–179.

Buffart, H., & Geissler, H.-G. (1984). Task-dependent representation categories and memory-guided inference during classification. In E. Degreef & J. van Buggenhaut (Eds.), *Trends in mathematical psychology* (pp. 33–58). Amsterdam: North-Holland.

Chekosky, S. F., & Whitlock, D. (1973). The effects of pattern goodness on recognition time in a memory search task. *Journal of Experimental Psychology, 100*, 341–348.

Garner, W. R., & Clement, D. E. (1963). Goodness of pattern and pattern uncertainty. *Journal of Verbal Learning and Verbal Behavior, 2*, 446–456.

Geissler, H.-G. (1972). Recognition time and object composition. In H. Drischel & P. Dettmar (Eds.), *Biocybernetics* (Vol. IV, pp. 55–60). Jena, Germany: Gustav Fischer Verlag.

Geissler, H.-G. (1974). Issues of information processing in recognition tasks [in German]. In H.-G. Geissler & F. Klix (Eds.), *Psychologische Analysen geistiger Prozesse* (pp. 13–20). Berlin: Deutscher Verlag der Wissenschaften.

Geissler, H.-G. (1980). Perceptual representation of information: Dynamic frames of reference in judgment and recognition. In F. Klix & B. Krause (Eds.), *Psychological research Humboldt University 1960–1980* (pp. 53–83). Berlin: Deutscher Verlag der Wissenschaften.

Geissler, H.-G. (1985). Sources of seeming redundancy in temporally quantized information processing. In G. d'Ydewalle (Ed.), *Cognitive information processing and motivation. Selected/revised papers of the 23rd International Congress of Psychology* (Vol. 3, pp. 119–128). Amsterdam: North-Holland.

Geissler, H.-G. (1987). The temporal architecture of central information processing: Evidence for a tentative time-quantum model. *Psychological Research, 49*, 99–106.

Geissler, H.-G. (1992). New magic numbers in mental activity: On a taxonomic system for critical time periods. In H.-G. Geissler, S. W. Link, & J. T. Townsend (Eds.), *Cognition, information processing and psychophysics* (pp. 293–321). Hillsdale, NJ: Lawrence Erlbaum Associates.

Geissler, H.-G., & Buffart, H. (1985). Task-dependency and quantized processing in classification. In G. d'Ydewalle (Ed.), *Cognitive information processing and motivation. Selected/revised papers of the 23rd International Congress of Psychology* (Vol. 3, pp. 277–295). Amsterdam: North-Holland.

Geissler, H.-G., Klix, F., & Scheidereiter, U. (1978). Visual recognition of serial structure: Evidence of a two-stage scanning model. In E. L. J. Leeuwenberg & H. F. J. M. Buffart (Eds.), *Formal theories of perception* (pp. 299–314). New York: Wiley.

Geissler, H.-G., & Lachmann, T. (1996). Memory-guided inference in matching tasks: Symmetries and the case of inferred sets. In S. C. Masin (Ed.), *Proceedings of the 12th Annual Meeting of the International Society for Psychophysics* (pp. 119–124). Padua, Italy: International Society for Psychophysics.

Geissler, H.-G., & Lachmann, T. (1997). Processing spatial symmetry: Evidence of two distinct components in visual comparison. In A. Preis (Ed.), *Proceedings of the 13th Annual Meeting of the International Society for Psychophysics* (pp. 165–170). Poznań, Poland: International Society for Psychophysics.

Geissler, H.-G., & Puffe, M. (1983). The inferential basis of classification: From perceptual to memory codes. Part 2: Experiments on discrete feature processing. In H.-G. Geissler, H. F. J. M. Buffart, E. L. J. Leeuwenberg, & V. Sarris (Eds.), *Modern issues in perception* (pp. 106–124). Amsterdam: North-Holland.

Geissler, H.-G., Puffe, M., & Stern, W. (1982). Item recognition and no end: Representation format and processing strategies. In H.-G. Geissler & P. Petzold (Eds.), *Psychophysical judgment and the process of perception* (pp. 270–281). Amsterdam: North-Holland.

Geissler, H.-G., Schebera, F.-U., & Kompass, R. (1999). Ultra-precise quantal timing: Evidence from simultaneity thresholds in long-range apparent movement. *Perception & Psychophysics, 61*, 707–726.

Helson, H. (1964). *Adaptation level theory*. New York: Harper & Row.

Hoffmann, J., Grosser, U., & Klein, R. (1987). The influence of knowledge on visual search. In E. van der Meer & J. Hoffmann (Eds.), *Knowledge aided information processing* (pp. 81–100). Amsterdam: North-Holland.

Leeuwenberg, E. L. J. (1969). Quantitative specification of information in sequential patterns. *Psychological Review, 76*, 216–220.

Maddox, W. T. (2001). Separating perceptual processes from decisional processes in Identification and Categorization. *Perception & Psychophysics, 63*, 1183–1200.

Nattkemper, D., & Prinz, W. (2001). Der Einfluss von Aufgabenanforderungen auf Effekte räumlicher Reiz-Reaktionskompatibilität [Impact of task demands on spatial stimulus–response compatibility.] *Zeitschrift für Psychologie, 209* (3), 205–226.

Naus, M. J. (1974). Memory search of categorized lists: A consideration of alternative self-terminating strategies. *Journal of Experimental Psychology, 102*, 992–1000.

Okada, R., & Burrows, D. (1978). The effects of subsidiary tasks on memory retrieval from long and short lists. *Quarterly Journal of Experimental Psychology, 30*, 221–231.

Prinz, W. (1997). Perception and action planning. *European Journal of Cognitive Psychology, 9*(2), 129–154.

Puffe, M. (1984). *Visuelle Erkennung als anforderungsabhängige Inferenz über sequentiellen Kategorierepräsentationen* [Visual recognition as task-dependent inference upon sequential category representations]. Unpublished doctoral dissertation, Humboldt University, Berlin.

Ratcliff, R. (1978). A theory of memory retrieval. *Psychological Review, 85*, 59–108.

Scheidereiter, U. (1978). *Detection of sequential regularities in visual patterns: A systems approach toward recognition of structure* [in German]. Unpublished doctoral dissertation, Humboldt University, Berlin.

Schmidt, K.-D., & Ackermann, B. (1990). The structure of internal representations and reaction-time related matching task phenomena. In H.-G. Geissler (Ed.), *Psychophysical explorations of mental structures* (pp. 278–289). Göttingen: Hogrefe & Huber.

Sternberg, S. (1966). High-speed scanning in human memory. *Science, 153*, 652–654.

Sternberg, S. (1969). Memory-scanning: Mental processes revealed by reaction-time experiments. *American Scientist, 57*(4), 421–457.

9

Memory-Guided Inference in Same–Different Comparison Tasks

Thomas Lachmann
University of Leipzig, Germany and Brain Science Institute, RIKEN, Wako-shi, Japan

Cees van Leeuwen
Brain Science Institute, RIKEN, Wako-shi, Japan

Since the time of Gestalt psychology, it has been known that stimulus structure plays an important role in visual object recognition (e.g., Gottschaldt, 1926). Whereas the Gestaltists were largely concerned with the description of phenomena, more recent approaches have endeavored to discover the underlying information processes. For doing so, reaction time (RT) measures have proved to be a useful instrument (Lachman, Lachman, & Butterfield, 1979). It soon became clear that the influence of visual stimulus structure depends on the task to be performed (Ashby & Maddox, 1990; Pomerantz & Pristach, 1989). For instance, in a part–whole detection task, components of a complex figure were revealed to be part of its internal representation only if these components were relevant to the task (Stins & van Leeuwen, 1993). However, task-irrelevant aspects of visual structure are not always ignored, as evidenced in demonstrations of interference by irrelevant stimulus dimensions in Stroop and Garner tasks (Lockhead, 1972; Pomerantz & Pristach, 1989; van Leeuwen & Bakker, 1995). The influence of task-irrelevant aspects of structure is particularly striking with complex visual stimuli, which, by definition, are characterized by multiple stimulus dimensions.

Despite the importance of these issues, they have been addressed only rarely in a systematic manner. A noticeable exception is the work of Geissler, who, together with his coworkers, developed the framework of memory-guided inference

(Buffart & Geissler, 1984; Geissler, 1983, 1985, 1987; Geissler & Buffart, 1985; Geissler & Puffe, 1983; see also Geissler, Klix, & Scheidereiter, 1978; Geissler, Puffe, & Stern, 1982; and Geissler, Chap. 8, this volume). An application of this approach is considered in this chapter.

The framework of memory-guided inference describes the representational format in which a stimulus is coded in visual object memory as depending on the task. In this respect, it differs from theories that assume representational formats to be context free. In contrast, rather than the momentary stimulus or task, it is the broader context that determines the economy of representation and processing strategies. This context will encompass the specific stimuli and task at hand, but it usually also includes a family of related stimuli and tasks. As a consequence, the representation may be less than optimal for the specific task at hand. An important consequence of this notion is the concept of "seeming redundancy" (Geissler, 1985). According to this concept, representations can contain information that, although redundant in a specific task to be performed, serves to achieve economy of representation within a more encompassing scheme. From this point of view, by the redundant storing of multiple variants of a representation, uniform coding of a larger set of objects is possible. Similarly, task execution can have seemingly redundant steps. However, when the more encompassing demands of the situation are taken into account, economy emerges as the overall characteristic. For instance, when steps are taken that are redundant in a particular situation, a set of related task situations (the task as a whole) can be executed in a uniform way, which allows for automatization.

The concept of memory-guided inference has been used by Geissler and his coworkers to elucidate a number of unresolved issues concerning the *same–different task* (Geissler & Lachmann, 1996, 1997; Lachmann, 2000, 2001; Lachmann & Geissler, 2002; Schmidt & Ackermann, 1990). This task involves elements of both memory search and visual search. In a typical memory search task (Sternberg, 1966), a memory set (MS) consisting of a variable number of items $(MS = 2, 3, \dots)$ is first learned. Subsequently, a single probe is presented $(P = 1)$, which is to be compared with (i.e., to be detected among) the memory set items. Typically, the functions relating decision RT to memory set size are found to be linear, which has been taken to be indicative of a serial process (Sternberg, 1966). This interpretation was challenged, however, when RT effects consistent with serial search were shown to be explicable in terms of alternative processes (e.g., Townsend & van Zandt, 1990). Although the controversy remains unresolved, it is clear that serial processing cannot be simply inferred from linear increases in RT with the number of items in memory (van Zandt & Townsend, 1993). In a same–different task, however, the situation is different. In Sternberg terms, the MS in this task is fixed to 1, so that decision RTs cannot vary as a function of MS size. Nevertheless, (linear) increases in decision RTs *are* obtained in this task, as a function of the structural complexity of the items presented (Lachmann, 1996, 2000, 2001; Schmidt & Ackermann, 1990).

Normally in the memory search paradigm, a set of homogeneous items (i.e., items of equal structural complexity) is used. This is important for control purposes, as the data are usually presented as a function of the number of items processed. One notable exception is the work of Checkosky and Whitlock (1973), who systematically varied the role of stimulus complexity with MS. In more detail, they varied the complexity of the spatial layout of five-dot configurations (i.e., their "Goodness," as defined by Garner & Clement, 1963). In addition, they varied the intensity of the probe. Their aim was to decide, by using the additive factors logic (Sternberg, 1969), whether structural complexity (Goodness) affects the speed of encoding alone, retrieval alone, or both. In the first case, an effect of structural complexity on the intercept of the MS function was expected. In the second case, an effect was expected on its slope, as it was assumed that complexity "... influences the time to generate a visual representation for each of the memory set items" (p. 343). Checkosky and Whitlock found a 100-ms effect of the probe intensity manipulation on the intercept of the MS function. No interactions of configurational complexity with probe intensity were obtained. However, they did find an interaction between MS and complexity. In terms of the additive factors logic, this means that complexity influences the stage of memory retrieval, rather than that of stimulus encoding.

Schmidt and Ackermann (1990) replotted the data of Checkosky and Whitlock in the format of Fig. 9.1, with the x axis representing the product of MS $\times$ Complexity. The graphs reveal a striking regularity, suggesting an account in which retrieval depends on the complexity of the visual stimulus representation. Geissler's memory-guided inference theory provides such an account.

The role of structural complexity has also been examined in visual search studies. In this paradigm, a single predefined target ($N = 1$) has to be detected among a set of multiple probes ($P = 2, 3, \ldots$). Two results are typically obtained. One is that the spatial layout of the probes influences the search process. If they form a regular configuration, the regularity is used to simplify the search process (Bacon & Egeth, 1991; Banks & Prinzmetal, 1976; Duncan & Humphreys, 1989; Moraglia, 1989; Prinzmetal & Banks, 1977). From this it has been concluded that perceptual organization operates at an early stage to structure visual search (Cave & Wolfe, 1990). The other result is that how the layout of the probes is perceived may depend on the task to be performed (e.g., Hogeboom & van Leeuwen, 1997). Thus, it has been concluded that task dependency of perceptual organization is also operating in visual search.

Whereas some strategies depend on specific aspects of the task, others seem to depend on more general characteristics. For instance, in Hogeboom and van Leeuwen's study, some tasks that were optimized for a *holistic* and others for a more *analytic* perceptual organization strategy. It was expected that participants would organize the information according to whichever strategy was optimal for the performance of the specific task to be carried out. However, this turned out to be the case only for a minority of the participants. The majority stuck to either

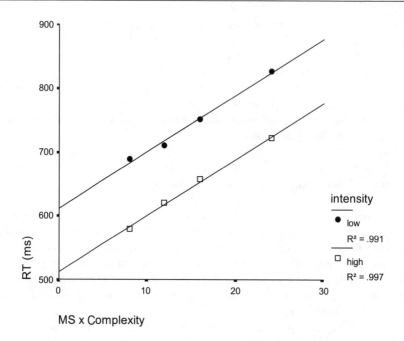

FIG. 9.1. Checkosky and Whitlock's (1974) RT data replotted as a function of the product of complexity and memory set.

one or the other strategy throughout the experiment; that is, they were performing a proportion of the tasks with a suboptimal strategy. This intriguing finding is at variance with the view that perceptual strategies are optimized automatically with respect to the particular task at hand.

The same–different task differs from visual search in that $P = 1$. As already mentioned, the work of Geissler and his associates demonstrated that effects of structural complexity could be obtained nevertheless. As in Hogeboom and van Leeuwen (1997), these effects reveal perceptual organization strategies that are not always optimal with respect to the specific task to be performed.

In the classical same–different task (Egeth, 1966; Nickerson, 1969; see Farell, 1985; and Sternberg, 1998, for reviews), one item is to be compared with an either simultaneously or subsequently presented single probe, in order to decide whether it is the same or different. When a *same* judgment is made, sometimes certain irrelevant features must be ignored, such as that the probe is rotated with respect to the item (see Posner, 1978, for a review).

Nickerson (1969) conceived of the comparison as a test of congruency between the representation of an item and a probe. In contrast to the memory search paradigm in which comparison processes always involve item comparisons within a single dimension, in same–different tasks the stimuli may differ in multiple dimensions (such as color, form, and position; see, e.g., Egeth, 1966). Whereas in memory search tasks the homogeneity of the stimulus set is necessary to control the procedure, in a same–different task the variation in dimensional structure is of central importance.

Theoretical accounts of same–different comparisons can be divided into two broad categories: analytic and configurational approaches. Analytic approaches assume that comparisons are made at the level of individual dimensions ("depending . . . on analysis into separate features, e.g. direction: up, and area: large, together with separate tests of those features," Sternberg, 1998, p. 371). A problem for this approach is the so-called *fast same effect*. None of these accounts can explain, without further assumptions, why *same* responses are made faster than *different* responses. Thus, for example, the more the item and the probe differ on relevant dimensions, the faster *different* responses are. For that reason, one would expect responses to be slowest when the items are the same in all dimensions. However, the opposite is true, as demonstrated, for instance, by Nickerson (1969). The other category of configurational approaches assumes that comparisons are made holistically ("patterns compared as wholes," Sternberg, 1998, p. 371). While this approach has no difficulty with the *fast same* effect, it encounters problems in explaining the increase in *different* response RTs as the number of relevant dimensions increases: If comparisons were made holistically across dimensions, no such increase would be expected.

Posner and Mitchell (1967; Posner, 1978) introduced a paradigm in which the same–different response may be based on other than visual aspects of the stimuli. For instance, in one condition, a pair of letters had to be responded to as *same* only when the letters were physically identical (e.g., B–B); in another condition, when they had the same "value" (a–A); and in a third condition, when they belonged to the same abstract category, such as vowels (a–e). Posner and Mitchell (1967) found a temporal hierarchy of decision processes depending on the instruction, which they interpreted as evidence for a theory of serial processing stages. According to this theory, at the lowest level, patterns are encoded in terms of their elementary physical characteristics (lines and curvatures). If a decision cannot be made at this level, memory information is used. In a terminology characteristic of the time, memory information was taken to consist of "templates" that are searched serially (Sternberg, 1969). If no match is found, comparison operations proceed to the next stage of "conceptual" processing, at which isolated concepts are used to tag the perceived objects. If comparison fails in this stage, semantic coding is used, which evokes rules and abstract categories to make identity decisions (e.g., vowel vs. consonant). Later, Posner (1978) revised the assumption of strictly serial levels of processing: The serial stage approach ". . . is simply too restrictive to use as a complete description of the processes involved," and "the temporal hierarchy . . . does not imply that the processes involved at the different levels represent a strict series" (p. 35). As a possible alternative, Posner considered a redundancy model in which all comparisons are made on the basis of a single memory code. This approach entails that comparison processes are facilitated by shared features between the items at different levels of abstraction. A second alternative, the pathway activation model, states that each comparison reaches the highest possible level but reaches this level the sooner the more lower-level features are being shared. In some respect, both models share features with Geissler's theory. Posner's preferred account is a race model. In this model, there are two types of codes—physical and categorical. These operate in separate, parallel systems, and they can influence each other only to a certain degree. According to Posner (1978), this account is well supported by the neuropsychological findings of those days (e.g., Geschwind & Levitsky, 1968). Numerous subsequent investigations have provided mixed evidence for or against the assumption that independent systems are working in parallel (see Lachmann, 2000, for a review). It was shown that categorical-level decisions can be facilitated by visual characteristics (e.g., Crist, 1981; Klatzky & Stoy, 1974), and that *different* responses on the physical level are strongly affected by an irrelevant categorical identity (Eviatar, Zaidel, & Wickens, 1994; Geissler & Lachmann, 1997; Lachmann, 2001).

An implication of Posner's (1978) approach is that mental rotation (Shepard & Metzler, 1971) and other mental transformations are conceived of as operations within the physical coding system. Klatzky and Stoy (1974), however, showed that mirror images are responded to as rapidly and accurately as identical images; furthermore, that, to decide whether two mirror-image stimuli are members of the same object category, one uses visual similarity rather than mental rotation. This would imply that mental rotation of visual representations only occurs under certain task demands (Jolicoeur, Corballis, & Lawson, 1998; Kuehn & Jolicoeur, 1994), and that mirror images are treated as visually rather than categorically invariant (Corballis & Beale, 1970; Lachmann, 2002). These findings support the view that visual coding can influence participants' task performance even when more abstract categorical information is needed to complete the response. The importance of visual structure for this task is consistent with its role in the other tasks considered herein, from visual search to memory retrieval. This applies to both stimuli as currently presented (the probe item) and stimuli as memorized (MS items).

GROUP CODE HYPOTHESIS

A common thread in memory search, visual search, and the same–different task is the persistent influence of visual structure. A particularly striking demonstration of this is obtained with a set of stimuli that are related by geometrical transformations. Several experiments have been performed by using such stimuli, which are reviewed in the following sections. These experiments used a same–different task, in which objects related through rotation or reflection transformations were to be responded to as *same*. According to Posner (1978), this task would be performed by using mental rotation of the stimuli's physical code. According to the guided inference approach, however, there is no mental transformation of a physical code; rather, there exists an abstract group code on which the search is being performed. As argued in the paragraphs that follow, each individual member of the group is coded with reference to all the other members. Thus, each individual member redundantly evokes all other patterns, but the code for the total category is optimally simple. For this reason, if two objects are presented for comparison that are orientation transformed, this does not involve a physical similarity but rather a categorical one. In this view, it is appropriate to attach the label *categorical* to sets of objects that are related to each other by transformation rules. Thus, pairs of stimuli with the same shape and orientation are considered as physically identical, and stimuli that are related in shape or orientation by a transformation rule are conceived of as categorically identical. Stimuli that differ in shape are considered as different.

To investigate the nature of the item representations involved, Schmidt and Ackermann (1990) and Lachmann and Geissler (Geissler & Lachmann, 1996; Lachmann, 1996, 2000; Lachmann & Geissler, 2002, Lachmann & van Leeuwen, subm.) used the pattern set first introduced by Garner and Clement (1963). This set consists of 90 five-dot patterns that can be constructed on a imaginary 3×3 grid without leaving a row or column empty. These stimuli have a set structure defined by transformation of rotation in $90°$ steps or of reflection (R & R; cf. Garner & Clement, 1963). The patterns differ in symmetry (see Fig. 9.2) and, thus, the degree of invariance according to R & R transformations. As a result, patterns that differ in symmetry belong to sets of different sizes (equivalence set size, ESS, of R & R subsets; cf. Garner & Clement, 1963). Eight sets contain four pattern elements, seven sets consist of eight elements, and two sets have only one pattern (see Fig. 9.1). Garner and Clement obtained goodness ratings for these stimuli, with ESS as independent variable. A strong and reliable effect of ESS on rated goodness was revealed. On this basis, ESS was taken as a direct measure for perceptual pattern goodness (Garner, 1962).

In Lachmann and Geissler (2002) participants performed a categorical same–different task in which patterns of the same equivalence, set had to be judged

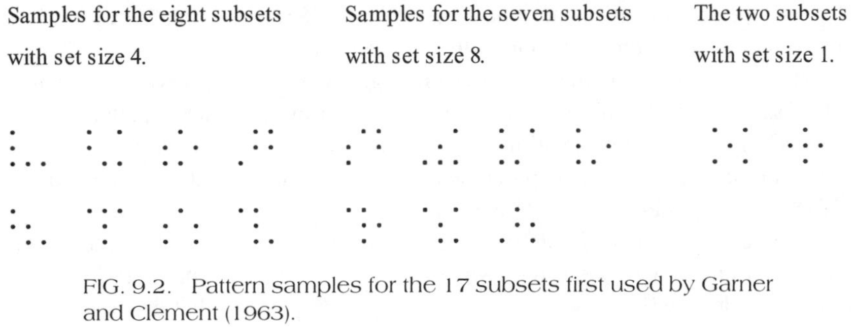

Samples for the eight subsets with set size 4.

Samples for the seven subsets with set size 8.

The two subsets with set size 1.

FIG. 9.2. Pattern samples for the 17 subsets first used by Garner and Clement (1963).

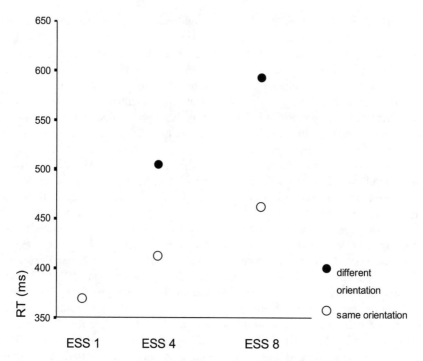

FIG. 9.3.   RTs (ms) for *same* responses as a function of the ESS of the sets to which the patterns to be compared belonged (data from Lachmann & Geissler, 2002).

as *same* and other pairs as *different*. The experiment tested the hypothesis of the guided inference approach that set structure elicits a corresponding group coding in the categorical task. If true, an effect of set size was expected. With ESS = 8, there are eight elements that have to be treated as *same*, so there will be eight elements represented in the visual code of the set. With ESS = 4 there will be four elements, and with ESS = 1 only one element in the respective visual codes. The results revealed RTs taken to judge two patterns as *same* to be dependent on ESS. A nearly perfect linear function between RT and ESS was found (see, Fig. 9.3), which was also evident in the individual participants' data.

Of special interest are the data shown in Fig. 9.3, which presents *same* response RTs for patterns of different orientations (transformation-related patterns) and, respectively, identical orientations. It is important that a linear function was obtained in the latter case. This precludes an explanation along the lines of Posner (1978), and it excludes a single explanation in terms of mental rotation. Moreover, generally in mental rotation, the RT delay is proportional to the difference in orientation between the two patterns (Cooper & Shepard, 1975; Shepard & Metzler, 1971). However, in this experiment, patterns that differed by 90°

exhibited the same RTs as those that differed by $180°$. Thus, there was no evidence for mental rotation function between the first and the second stimulus presented. Alternatively, a mental rotation might have been performed on a stored prototype rather than the first stimulus. However, no mental rotation functions were obtained with reference to prototypes that had been identified in separate control experiments.

An alternative explanation might assume that the ESS has its effect on encoding, rather than retrieval; that is, ESS, as a measure of perceptual goodness, influences the speed of encoding. The question whether perceptual goodness indeed has such an effect was debated in the 1970s (Bell & Handel, 1976; Checkosky & Whitlock, 1973; Clement & Varnadoe, 1967; Garner & Sutliff, 1974; Hock, 1973; Pomerantz, 1977) but remains unresolved (Biederman, Hilton, & Hummel, 1994). To explain the aforementioned data, a perceptual goodness account would have to make additional assumptions as to why stimuli identical in shape and orientation are responded to faster than those identical in shape but different in orientation. One possibility is to assume that encoding is facilitated when identical stimuli are presented, which would provide an account for the *fast same* effect (cf. Krueger, 1978; Lachmann, 2000; Proctor, 1981, 1986). However, again, the evidence for this assumption is mixed (Farell, 1985; Lachmann, 2000; Nickerson, 1975; Pachella & Miller, 1976).

Another attempt at an explanation might reintroduce the notion of mental transformation. In this view, stimuli that differ in orientation are responded to slower because a transformation has to be performed. It is crucial that the transformation cannot be performed in parallel with encoding. Ruthruff, Miller, and Lachmann (1995) provided evidence that mental rotation uses a central mechanism that is unlikely to share resources with encoding. Thus, encoding and rotation are independent and may operate in series (cf. Lachmann & Pataki, 2001; but see also Ruthruff & Miller, 1995). Miller (1978) and many others have argued, though, that sequential processing stages may overlap in time. However, even incomplete overlap of stages would be sufficient to explain the pattern of results in terms of combined encoding and mental transformation processes.

In our view, however, explanations based on encoding are unlikely to be true, as the stimuli were presented successively at a stimulus onset asynchrony of 750 ms and at separate locations. When participants move their eyes from one location to another to inspect the stimuli, location-specific traces of visual information will be "blanked out" (Irwin, 1993). Thus, if effects of ESS can still be demonstrated in this task, they must result from processes associated with more permanent traces than perceptual encoding. Furthermore, Lachmann and Geissler (2002) showed that an effect of ESS could also be obtained for *different* responses. This effect does not depend on the order in which the two patterns differing in ESS were presented on a trial. The encoding hypothesis would predict a larger effect of the ESS of the second stimulus. However, the effect depends equally on the ESSs of both stimuli.

Thus, neither mental rotation nor encoding can coherently account for the present results, whatever additional assumptions are being made. With the background of these considerations and findings, and with the observation that the RT–ESS slope for objects different in orientation was approximately twice that of objects of the same orientation (see Fig. 9.3), Lachmann and Geissler (2002) discussed possible models based on the guided inference approach. All these models assume that, when a particular pair of items is presented, the whole set of objects to which these items belong is activated and searched through.

The model that best fits the data assumes that a self-terminating search for the two patterns is performed. This search operates within the one (*same* responses) or, respectively, two (*different* responses) sets activated by stimulus presentation. The search starts from a random item within one of the evoked sets and proceeds in a manner that can be described best as serial. When a match has been found for one of the patterns after an average of $(\text{ESS}_1 + 1)/2$ search steps (with ESS_1 being the ESS of the first pattern that is being searched), the search for the other pattern starts. If both patterns are from the same set then the search continues, starting with the matching item. This means that, in the case of identical shapes and orientations, a second match is found immediately. In this case, the total number of search steps is, on average, $(\text{ESS}_1 + 1)/2 + 1$. In the case of identical shapes alone, a second search within the same set has to be carried out, and in the case of nonidentity (nonmatches), a second search within the other set, which takes another $(\text{ESS}_2 + 1)/2$ steps, on average, giving a total of $(\text{ESS}_1 + 1)/2 + (\text{ESS}_2 + 1)/2$ steps. The number of search steps expected according to this model is presented in Fig. 9.4. These expectations were then used to predict RTs. A single parameter was added to take account of "extra facilitation" for stimuli identical in both shape

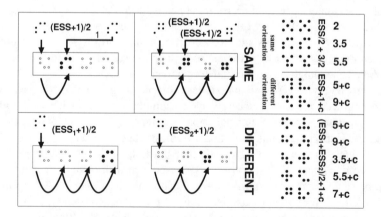

FIG. 9.4. Search model and RT predictions for the 10 the types of pattern comparisons. Both ESS_1 and ESS_2 are the equivalence set sizes elicited by the first and the stimulus, respectively (see text for further explanation).

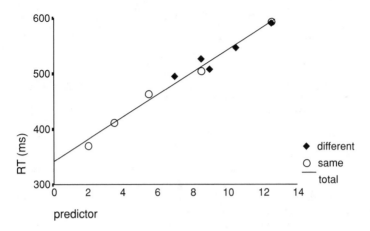

predictor

FIG. 9.5. RT (ms) as a function of the number of serial search
steps predicted by the model calculations set out in Fig. 9.4.

and orientation (this involved the addition of a constant value C to the prediction
for patterns differing in either shape or orientation).

Figure 9.5 reveals the fit of this model to the 10 empirical mean RTs ($C = 3.5$),
including both *same* and *different* responses, to be very good indeed ($R^2 = .98$;
$p < .001$). Separate calculations for the two types of responses also yielded very
good fits ($R^2_{same} = .99$ and $R^2_{different} = .96$; $p < .001$). The time required for each
search step was estimated to be 20.1 ms, and it was approximately equal for both
types of responses (*same*, 20.5 ms; *different*, 17.1 ms).

The good fit provides evidence in favor of a model according to which participants represent item information on the basis of entire equivalence sets. Processing
does not involve comparisons of features or configurational information; instead,
it is based on a collective code. This code is presumed to be involved even when
decisions have to be made on items identical in shape and orientation. Another
case for which this assumption is counterintuitive concerns nonmatching items,
which might, at first, seem easier to judge by using template matching or pointwise
correspondence testing. However, the collective code assumption is also supported
in such cases.

RELATIVE FREQUENCY EFFECTS

A direct test of the collective-code assumption was attempted in a subsequent
experiment by Lachmann and Geissler (1999; Lachmann, 2000), making use of a
relative frequency effect (e.g., Blackman, 1980; Hawkins & Friedin, 1972; Sanders,
1970). Increasing the presentation frequency of one pattern in a set was expected
to facilitate the response not just for that item but for the whole set to which it

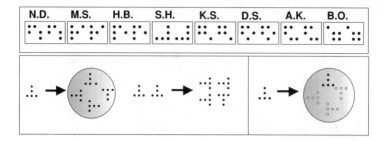

FIG. 9.6. Upper frame: Pattern pairs presented with increased frequency to individual participants (indicated by their initials). Lower frame, left: Effect of increased frequency on *same* responses at set level. The leftmost pattern activates a code for the whole set. As a result, all *same* combinations within this set are equally facilitated, even though their frequency is not increased. Lower frame, right: The effect of the frequency manipulation was examined for the standard members of the set, in comparison with that for the frequency-manipulated item.

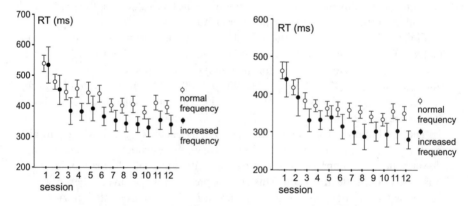

FIG. 9.7. Mean RT (ms) for *same* responses to pairs of the same shape and orientation (left) and the same shape only (right), for normal frequency patterns and patterns belonging to the increased-frequency set, excluding patterns actually increased in frequency. (From Lachmann & Geissler, 1999. Copyright by the International Society for Psychophysics. Reprinted with permission.)

belonged, and the facilitation for the items unchanged in frequency was expected to be of the same size. In more detail, the frequency of one pair of patterns, identical in shape and orientation, was increased by a factor of 10 relative to all other pairs in the categorical same–different comparison task. For each participant, a different pair was selected for this purpose (Fig. 9.6).

The results are presented in Fig. 9.7. A significant RT advantage ($p < .05$) was found for patterns that belonged to the equivalence set of the pattern whose frequency was increased. It is important that the advantage was the same for the increased-frequency pair and the other pairs within the set.

The results are in general agreement with the predictions from guided inference. In terms of the model, the facilitation could be understood as priming the pattern set by one of its members. Priming could, among others, strengthen the activation (cf. also Chechosky & Whitlock, 1973) of the set or facilitate search or response selection. The facilitation effects were restricted to *same* responses. For this reason, it is likely that at least response priming is involved. Regardless of which stage is primed, it is important that the priming affects only the members of the set. An explanation in which both the set members and the response are primed is consistent with the absence of an effect for *different* responses. For *same* responses, set activation and response priming would both facilitate the set; in contrast, for *different* responses, the positive effect of set activation and the (in this case) negative effect of response priming would cancel each other.

In the experiment by Lachmann and Geissler (2002), described earlier, each pattern set was presented with equal probability. This means that for instance, all items shown in Fig. 9.8 were included, and consequently, items with ESS = 1 were more frequent than, say, items with ESS = 4, to equate the frequencies of the various sets (see Fig. 9.8). A trivial explanation for the findings of the earlier experiments might, therefore, be the relative frequency of certain individual patterns.

Therefore, it was considered important to ascertain what happens when the probability of occurrence is equal for each individual pattern instead of each set. In this case the patterns are restricted to those depicted as solid circles in Fig. 9.8.

Such a design was used in Lachmann & van Leeuwen (2003). The results contrast sharply with those shown in Fig. 9.3. RTs for ESS = 1 patterns increased dramatically and were even higher than those for ESS = 8 patterns. This is the strongest evidence against an explanation based on the assumption that goodness facilitates encoding. The effect can be interpreted as a frequency effect operating at set level. Participants' reports suggest that the ESS = 1 stimuli in this experiment struck them as oddballs. This could never have occurred if the patterns were

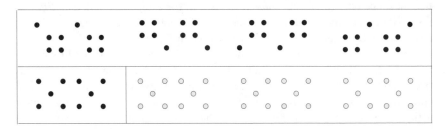

FIG. 9.8. Patterns from a set of ESS = 4 (upper row) and from a set of ESS = 1 (lower row). In the total figure, the frequency of members of both sets is equal. For the total set of solid patterns only, the frequency of occurrence of individual patterns is equal.

encoded on an individual basis. The experiment, therefore, favors an explanation along the lines of group coding.

TASK DEPENDENCE OF CODING
AND PROCESSING

We set out to consider the subtle interplay of stimulus structure and task demand in creating the representation that governs the execution of the task. The results reviewed thus far concerned effects of stimulus structure with categorical instruction. We now turn to the issue of physical instruction, that is, when participants respond *same* only when the patterns are identical in form and orientation. In this case, the set structure is not relevant for the task. One might, therefore, expect it to play no role at all. Another possibility would be that seeming redundancy in terms of Geissler operates between tasks, in which case one would expect the irrelevant group coding to occur nevertheless. For instance, Checkosky and Whitlock (1973) found strong effects of irrelevant ESS in a recognition task in which a physical identity match was required.

Berti, Geissler, Lachmann, and Mecklinger (2000) performed an electrophysiological study in which the instruction (physical vs. categorical) was varied between two sessions; it was counterbalanced within subjects by using a blocked design. A selection of six subsets was presented—three of ESS = 4 and three of ESS = 8. From the latter, only four patterns were actually used. These patterns were chosen such that it was necessary to include both transformations, rotation and reflection, to transform one into another. Berti et al. were interested in the effects of ESS and instruction on electrophysiological parameters. Evidence for group coding was found in both conditions. For the RTs, an interaction between ESS and instruction was obtained but not further analyzed. An analysis of these data was carried out for the current chapter, in which a distinction was drawn between patterns identical in shape and orientation (requiring *same* responses in both tasks), patterns identical in shape only (requiring *same* responses in the categorical task and *different* responses in the physical task), and patterns different in shape (requiring *different* responses in both tasks). The results are shown in Table 9.1.

For the categorical instruction condition, a relatively good model fit was obtained ($R^2 = .91$; $p < .01$; $C = 0$); for the physical condition, however, the fit was poor. Nevertheless, there was a noticeable effect of ESS on RTs in the physical condition. However, this effect was smaller and did not show the expected interaction with the type of matching; that is, the ESS effect appeared not to depend on whether the patterns agreed in shape and orientation, agreed in shape only (see Fig. 9.1), or differed in shape. The model explains the RT advantage for patterns of identical shape and orientation under the categorical instruction by assuming that, after finding a match in the set for the first item, the search then continues starting from that item. For such patterns, the same strategy can be adopted under

TABLE 9.1
RT Analysis in the Experiment of Berti et al. (2000)

		RT (ms)	
Matching	ESS	Categorical Instr.	Physical Instr.
Same shape and	4:4	547.12	482.85
orientation	8:8	620.11	519.45
Same shape;	4:4	592.11	551.33
different orientation	8:8	687.46	576.96
Different	4:4	621.71	536.12
	8:8	718.93	554.52
	4:8	629.26	531.17

Note. The RT data of 1 further participant were available for this analysis.

the physical instruction, so that a *same* response can be given after an average of $(ESS + 1)/2 + 1$ steps, as in the categorical task. Under the physical instruction, the remaining items are *different*. Therefore, in contrast to the categorical instruction, participants do not need to continue with the search. This means that a *different* response can be given, too, after $(ESS + 1)/2 + 1$ steps. With this assumption, a good model fit was also obtained for the physical instruction ($R^2 = .91$; $p < .01$; $C = 3.5$).

In an earlier study, Geissler and Lachmann (1997) had 22 participants perform a same–different task under physical instruction only. In this experiment, the complete pattern set was presented. Geissler and Lachmann identified two subgroups of participants. One subgroup of relatively slow performers exhibited strong ESS effects (see Fig. 9.9, Group 1). The second group of fast performers showed a much weaker dependency on ESS for *same* responses (i.e., patterns identical in shape and orientation) and no dependency at all for *different* responses (see Fig. 9.9, Group 2). With the use of a modified model for the physical instruction already outlined, a reanalysis of the RTs for Subgroup 1 yielded a good fit ($R^2 = .92$; $p < .01$; $C = 0$).

A similar distinction of subgroups was also found when the data of the experiment of Berti et al. (2000) was reanalyzed. More than half of the participants (6 of 11)[1] showed ESS effects, similar to Subgroup 1. An application of the modified model to this subgroup only yielded an improved data fit to $R^2 = .95$ ($p < .01$; $C = 2.8$). Figure 9.10 shows the data fit for the subgroups exhibiting ESS effects in both studies.

The performance of the other 5 participants was only a little faster and more heterogeneous. The participants showed a much weaker dependency on ESS for *same* responses and no dependency at all for *different* responses. In this respect, they are comparable with Subgroup 2 (Fig. 9.9) identified in Geissler and Lachmann (1997).

---

[1]In the original paper of Berti et al. (2000), the data of only 10 participants were presented. The data of 1 more participant was available for the analysis presented here.

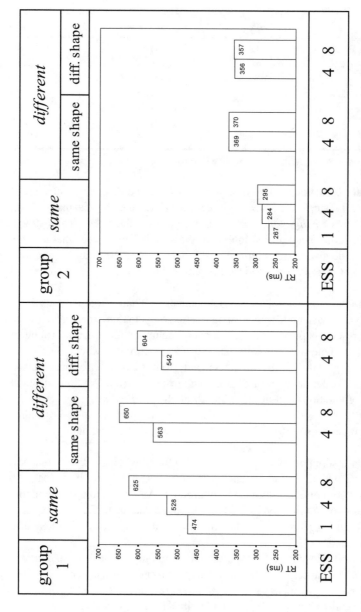

FIG. 9.9. RTs (ms) for *same* responses (patterns identical in shape and orientation) and *different* responses (patterns identical in shape but different in orientation, or patterns different in shape) for two subgroups of participants identified in Geissler and Lachmann (1997).

212

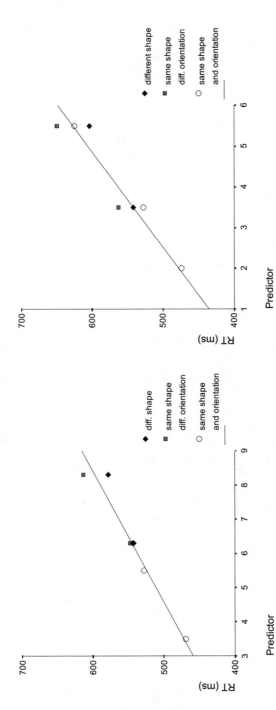

FIG. 9.10. Left: RT (ms) of 6 participants for the physical instruction condition in the experiment of Berti et al. (2000) as a function of the search model modified for physical instruction. Right: RT (ms) of a subgroup of participants in the experiment reported in Geissler and Lachmann (1997) as a function of the predictors resulting from the search model modified for physical instruction.

The data of this subgroup defy a clear explanation in terms of the model in both studies. Nevertheless, an effect of collective coding could still be observed for this subgroup. Their slowed RTs for patterns of the same shape but different orientation suggest a response conflict under this condition. Thus, a plausible explanation for the performance of this subgroup may be derived by referring to the literature on the *fast same* effect (see Farell, 1985, and Sternberg, 1998, for reviews). This effect has been explained by an extra operation of rechecking required for *different* responses (e.g., Krueger, 1978). Thus, because of the response conflict experienced by this subgroup, they will engage in more extensive rechecking. The independence of their performance from ESS might then be taken to suggest that rechecking is terminated on a time-based rather than a completion-based criterion.

Another theoretical approach is based on pattern similarity (e.g., Imai, 1977; Reed, 1974). This account can also be applied to the set level, by assuming that patterns are most similar when they belong to the same set (cf. Checkosky & Whitlock, 1973). This would provide another way to explain the response conflict for transformationally related patterns. Several other accounts, such as those assuming an identity "reporter" (Bamber, 1969), could be adapted to explain the effect. To account for the *fast same* effect, these theories assume a special, fast mechanism for reporting identity of a stimulus pair. If this mechanism operates at the level of sets, rather than of individual items, it will call for a *same* response in the case of same patterns that are different in orientation. This mechanism could also be invoked to explain the response conflict that occurs for these patterns. Finally, Eviatar et al. (1994) assumed the existence of two separate mechanisms that search the stimulus in parallel for evidence in support of *same* and, respectively, *different* responses. On this account, a response conflict would also occur if the mechanisms operate at the set level.

By assuming parallel mechanisms, some of these models represent a break with the assumption that memory search proceeds in a serial fashion. Whereas the categorical identity task seems to be best performed serially, the results for the physical identity task suggest that performance is faster when a serial strategy is not used (Subgroup 2 in Geissler & Lachmann, 1997). Analogous results were found in a visual search task in which participants had to detect a jigsaw puzzle fit between two patterns (Hogeboom & van Leeuwen, 1997). This task could either be performed in terms of a serial piecemeal search for mismatching notches, or a holistic, nonserial matching operation. It was found that, the more difficult the task, the more likely it was performed in a piecemeal fashion. When the task was relatively simple, participants tended to choose the nonserial, holistic strategy. Two different group strategies could even be observed for the simple tasks, for which the holistic group was faster.

For the search task of Hogeboom and van Leeuwen (1997), it could be shown that the two different strategies corresponded with different types of representations. The piecemeal strategy operates on a local representation, and the holistic strategy operates on a global representation (van Leeuwen, 1998). These analogies between the search and same–different tasks support the speculation that, in the same–different task, alternative local and global representations are also used by the two groups under physical same–different conditions (Fig. 9.9). This possibility would fully accord with the principle of memory-guided inference, which assumes that the nature of the representation is determined jointly by stimulus and task.

SUMMARY

A series of same–different experiments was described that used patterns related by rotation or reflection. Depending on symmetry, pattern sets of different sizes can be defined that consist of equivalent pattern elements transformable into each other by using rotation and reflection. This paradigm provides an instrument for investigating the effect of stimulus and task on the representation and processing of object information. The same material was used under different instructions in order to investigate effects of task demand.

When participants were instructed to judge two patterns as *same*, independent of their orientation, RTs for both *same* and *different* responses depended on the size of their equivalence sets. This was the case even when they were identical in form and orientation. This finding could be explained in terms of a model that was based on the principles of Geissler's memory-guided inference theory. The model assumes group coding; that is, the patterns are internally represented by their entire equivalence set. When an item is presented, its whole equivalence set is activated. For the comparison, memory search takes place within the activated set. The decision is made based on whether or not both stimuli are members of the same activated set. The best-fitting model was one in which the sets activated by both stimuli to be compared are searched serially, one after the other.

Direct evidence for the group code hypothesis was produced by increasing the frequency of presentation for a single pattern. As a result of this manipulation, frequency effects were obtained for all patterns that belonged to its equivalence set. Such frequency effects could also be invoked to explain the occurrence of oddball effects, even when individual items were presented with equal frequency.

Under instructions to judge patterns as the same only when they are identical in both shape and orientation, one group of participants still showed effects of ESS consistent with the model. The other group showed weak set size dependency of RTs for *same*, but not for *different*, responses. These results cannot be readily accommodated by the model. However, a response conflict was evident for this group with patterns identical in shape but different in orientation. In this case, a *different* response is required even though the items belong to the same set, which calls for a *same* response. The second group's performance, therefore, still accords with the general principle of group coding (though it could be interpreted in alternative ways).

The effects of group coding reviewed in this chapter clearly favor memory-guided inference over various alternative theoretical accounts. One of its basic concepts, that of seeming redundancy, predicts that representations may be generated that are redundant in specific task situations. Correspondingly, task execution has seemingly redundant steps. Both are strikingly demonstrated during group coding. To represent a single item by a collective code for its equivalence set is a clear case of redundant representation; to search the whole set to compare only two items is a similarly clear case of redundant processing.

However, when the more encompassing demands of the situation are taken into account (the task as a whole), economy emerges as the overall characteristic. This effect is also evident in the present study: the codes for equivalence sets are "general purpose devices" that can be used over and over again in different situations, such as to perform different comparisons. The stability of these sets is such that at least some participants even use them across different tasks (categorical and physical instruction). The intriguing suggestion is that those participants who show evidence of different processes do so on the basis of a different representational system for the set.

ACKNOWLEDGMENTS

This work was supported by Deutsche Forschungsgemeinschaft Grant La 1281/2-1 to Thomas Lachmann and Grant Gei 678/6-1 to H.-G. Geissler and T. Lachmann. The authors thank Scott Galvao, one anonymous reviewer and, especially, Mark Elliott and Hermann Müller for insightful comments on earlier versions of this chapter.

REFERENCES

Ashby, F., & Maddox, W. T. (1990). Integrating information from separable psychological dimensions. *Journal of Experimental Psychology: Human Perception and Performance, 16*, 598–612.

Bacon, W. F., & Egeth, H. E. (1991). Local processes in preattentive feature detection. *Journal of Experimental Psychology: Human Perception and Performance, 71*, 77–90.

Bamber, D. (1969). Reaction time and error rates for "same"-"different" judgments of multidimensional stimuli. *Perception & Psychophysics, 6*, 169–174.

Banks, W. P., & Prinzmetal, W. (1976). Configurational effects in visual information processing. *Perception & Psychophysics, 19*, 361–367.

Bell, H. H., & Handel, S. (1976). The role of pattern goodness in the reproduction of backward masked patterns. *Journal of Experimental Psychology: Human Perception & Performance, 2*, 139–150.

Berti, S., Geissler, H.-G., Lachmann, T., & Mecklinger, A. (2000). Event-related brain-potentials dissociate visual working memory processes under categorical and identical comparison conditions. *Cognitive Brain Research, 9*, 147–155.

Biederman, I., Hilton, H. J., & Hummel, J. E. (1994). Pattern goodness and pattern recognition. In G. R. Lockhead & J. R. Pomerantz (Eds.), *The perception of structure* (pp. 73–95). Washington, DC: American Psychological Association.

Blackman, A. R. (1980). Relative frequency effect on choice reaction time. *Perceptual & Motor Skills, 50*, 767–779.

Buffart, H., & Geissler, H.-G. (1984). Task-dependent representation of categories and memory-guided inference during classification. In E. Degreef & J. Buggenhaut (Eds.), *Trends in Mathematical Psychology* (pp. 33–58). Amsterdam: North-Holland.

Cave, K. R., & Wolfe, J. M. (1990). Modeling the role of parallel processing in visual search. *Cognitive Psychology, 22*, 225–271.

Checkosky, S., & Whitlock, D. (1973). The effects of pattern goodness on recognition time in a memory search task. *Journal of Experimental Psychology, 100*, 341–348.

Clement, D. E., & Varnadoe K. W. (1967). Pattern uncertainty and the discrimination of visual patterns. *Perception & Psychophysics, 2*, 427–431.

Cooper, L. A., & Shepard, R. N. (1975). Mental transformation in the identification of left and right hands. *Journal of Experimental Psychology: Human Perception & Performance, 1*, 48–56.

Corballis, M. C., & Beale, I. L. (1970). Bilateral symmetry and behavior. *Psychological Review, 77*, 451–464.

Crist, W. B. (1981). Matching performance and the similarity structure of the stimulus set. *Journal of Experimental Psychology: General, 110*, 269–296.

Duncan, J., & Humphreys, G. W. (1989). Visual search and stimulus similarity. *Psychological Review, 96*, 433–458.

Egeth, H. (1966). Parallel versus serial processing in multidimensional stimulus discrimination. *Perception & Psychophysics, 1*, 245–252.

Eviatar, Z., Zaidel, E., & Wickens, T. (1994). Nominal & physical criteria in same-different judgments. *Perception & Psychophysics, 56*, 62–72.

Farell, B. (1985). "Same-different"-judgments: A review of current controversies in perceptual comparisons. *Psychological Bulletin, 98*, 419–456.

Garner, W. R. (1962). *Uncertainty and structure as psychological concepts.* New York: Wiley.

Garner, W. R., & Clement, D. E. (1963). Goodness of pattern and pattern uncertainty. *Journal of Verbal Learning and Verbal Behavior, 2*, 446–452.

Garner, W. R., & Sutliff, D. (1974). The effect of goodness on encoding time in visual pattern discrimination. *Perception & Psychophysics, 16*, 426–430.

Geissler, H.-G. (1983). The inferential basis of classification: From perceptual to memory code systems. In H.-G. Geissler (Ed.), *Modern issues in perception* (pp. 87–105). Berlin: Deutscher Verlag der Wissenschaften.

Geissler, H.-G. (1985). Sources of seeming redundancy in temporally quantized information processing. In G. d'Ydewalle (Ed.), *Cognition, information processing, and motivation* (pp. 233–241). Amsterdam: North-Holland.

Geissler, H.-G. (1987). Guided inference: Components of task-dependence in human information processing. In E. van der Meer & J. Hoffmann (Eds.), *Knowledge aided information processing* (pp. 221–240). Amsterdam: North-Holland.

Geissler, H.-G., & Buffart, H. (1985). Task-dependency and quantized processing in classification. In G. d'Ydewalle (Ed.), *Cognition, information processing, and motivation* (pp. 277–294). Amsterdam: North-Holland.

Geissler, H.-G., Klix, F., & Scheidereiter, U. (1978). Visual recognition of serial structure: Evidence of a two-stage scanning model. In E. L. J. Leeuwenberg, & H. F. J. M. Buffart (Eds.), *Formal theories in perception* (pp. 299–314). Chichester: Wiley.

Geissler, H.-G., & Lachmann, T. (1996). Memory-guided inference in matching tasks: Symmetries and the case of inferred sets. In S. C. Masin (Ed.), *Proceedings of the International Society for Psychophysics* (pp. 119–124). Padua, Italy: International Society for Psychophysics.

Geissler, H.-G., & Lachmann, T. (1997). Processing spatial symmetry: Evidence of two distinct components in visual comparison. In A. Preis (Ed.), *Proceedings of the International Society for Psychophysics* (pp. 165–170). Poznan, Poland: International Society for Psychophysics.

Geissler, H.-G., & Puffe, M. (1983). The inferential basis of classification: From perceptual to memory codes. Part 2: Experiments on discrete feature processing. In H.-G. Geissler, H. F. J. M. Buffart, E. L. J. Leeuwenberg, & V. Sarris (Eds.), *Modern issues in perception* (pp. 106–124). Amsterdam: North-Holland.

Geissler, H.-G., Puffe, M., & Stern, W. (1982). Item-recognition and no end: Representation format and processing strategies. In H.-G. Geissler & P. Petzold (Eds.), *Psychophysical judgment and the process of perception* (pp. 270–281). Berlin: Deutscher Verlag der Wissenschaften.

Geschwind, N., & Levitsky, W. (1968). Human brain: Left-right asymmetries in temporal speech region. *Science, 161*, 186–187.

Gottschaldt, K. (1926). Über den Einfluss der Erfahrung auf die Wahrnehmung von Figuren. I. [About the influence of experience to the perception of objects] Über den Einfluss gehäufter Einprägung von Figuren auf ihre Sichtbarkeit in umfassenden Konfigurationen. *Psychologische Forschung, 8*, 261–283.

Hawkins, H. L., & Friedin, B. D. (1972). The relative frequency effect and S-R compatibility. *Psychonomic Science, 28*, 329–330.

Hock, H. S. (1973). The effects of stimulus structure and familiarity on same-different comparison. *Perception & Psychophysics, 14*, 413–420.

Hogeboom, M., & van Leeuwen, C. (1997). Visual search strategy and perceptual organization covary with individual preference and structural complexity. *Acta Psychologica, 95*, 141–164.

Imai, S. (1977). Pattern similarity and cognitive transformations. *Acta Psychologica, 41*, 433–447.

Irwin, D. E. (1993). Perceiving an integrated visual world. In D. E. Meyer, & S. Kornblum (Eds.), *Attention and Performance XIV* (pp. 121–142). Cambridge, MA: MIT Press.

Jolicoeur, P., Corballis, M. C., & Lawson, R. (1998). The influence of perceived rotary motion on the recognition of rotated objects. *Psychonomic Bulletin & Review, 5*, 140–146.

Klatzky, R. L., & Stoy, A. M. (1974). Using visual codes for comparisons of pictures. *Memory & Cognition, 2*, 727–736.

Krueger, L. E. (1978). A theory of perceptual matching. *Psychological Review, 85*, 278–304.

Kuehn, S. M., & Jolicoeur, P. (1994). Impact of quality of the image, orientation, and similarity of the stimuli on visual search for faces. *Perception, 23*, 95–122.

Lachman, R., Lachman, J. L., & Butterfield, C. (1979). *Cognitive psychology and information processing: An introduction*. Hillsdale, NJ: Lawrence Erlbaum Associates.

Lachmann, T. (1996). *Informationsverarbeitung beim visuellen Vergleich* [Information processing in visual matching performance]. Beitraege zur wissenschaftlichen Diskussion, Nr. 15. Munich: HSS.

Lachmann, T. (2000). *Erkennen und Vergleichen—Vorgaenge im Gedaechtnis bei der visuellen Relationserkennung* [Memory processes in recognition and comparison]. Psychologia Universalis, Nr. 22. Lengerich, Berlin: Pabst.

Lachmann, T. (2001). Strategies of coding and processing in a physical same-different-task. In E. Sommerfeld, R. Kompass, & T. Lachmann (Eds.), *Proceedings of the International Society for Psychophysics* (pp. 98–104). Lengerich, Berlin: Pabst.

Lachmann, T. (2002). Reading disability as a deficit in functional coordination. In E. Witruk, A. D. Friederici, & T. Lachmann (Eds.), *Basic functions of language, reading, and reading disability* (pp. 165–198). Boston: Kluwer.

Lachmann, T., & Geissler, H.-G. (1999). Frequency effects in a categorical same-different task point to collective pattern codes. In P. R. Killeen & W. R. Uttal (Eds.), *Proceedings of the International Society for Psychophysics* (pp. 138–143). Phoenix, AZ: The International Society for Psychophysics.

Lachmann, T., & Geissler, H.-G. (2002). Representation-guided inference in same-different performance. *Acta Psychologica, 111*, 283–307.

Lachmann, T., & Pataki, K. (2001). Does stimulus complexity affect central mechanisms? In E. Sommerfeld, R. Kompass, & T. Lachmann (Eds.), *Proceedings of the International Society for Psychophysics* (pp. 487–492). Lengerich, Berlin: Pabst.

Lachmann, T., & van Leeuwen, C. (2003). Representational Mechanisms and Pattern Goodness, Part I: Categorical Frequency Bias. Manuscript submitted for publication.

Lockhead, G. R. (1972). Processing dimensional stimuli: A note. *Psychological Review, 79*, 410–419.

Miller, J. O. (1978). Multidimensional same-different judgments: Evidence against independent comparisons of dimensions. *Journal of Experimental Psychology: Human Perception and Performance, 4*, 411–422.

Moraglia, G. (1989). Display organization and the detection of horizontal line segments. *Perception & Psychophysics, 45*, 265–272.

Nickerson, R. S. (1969). "Same-different"–response times: A model and a preliminary test. *Acta Psychologica, 30*, 257–275.

Nickerson, R. S. (1975). Effect of correlated and uncorrelated noise on visual pattern matching. In P. M. A. Rabbitt & S. Dornig (Eds.), *Attention and Performance V* (pp. 655–668). London: Academic Press.

Pachella, R. G., & Miller, J. O. (1976). Stimulus probability and same-different classification. *Perception & Psychophysics, 19*, 29–34.

Pomerantz, J. R. (1977). Pattern goodness and speed of encoding. *Memory & Cognition, 5*, 235–241.

Pomerantz, J. R., & Pristach, E. A. (1989). Emergent features, attention, and perceptual glue in visual form perception. *Journal of Experimental Psychology: Human Perception and Performance, 15*, 635–649.

Posner, M. I. (1978). *Chronometric explorations of mind*. Hillsdale, NJ: Lawrence Erlbaum Associates.

Posner, M. I., & Mitchell, R. F. (1967). Chronometric analysis of classification. *Psychological Review, 74*, 392–409.

Prinzmetal, W., & Banks, W. P. (1977). Good continuation affects visual detection. *Perception & Psychophysics, 21*, 389–395.

Proctor, R. W. (1981). A unified theory for matching task phenomena. *Psychological Review, 88*, 291–326.

Proctor, R. W. (1986). Response bias, criteria settings, and the fast-same phenomenon: A reply to Ratcliff. *Psychological Review, 93*, 473–477.

Reed, S. K. (1974). Structural descriptions and the limitation of visual images. *Memory & Cognition, 2*, 329–336.

Ruthruff, E., & Miller, J. O. (1995). Can mental rotation begin before perception finishes? *Memory & Cognition, 23*, 408–424.

Ruthruff, E., Miller, J. O., & Lachmann, T. (1995). Does mental rotation require central mechanisms. *Journal of Experimental Psychology: Human Perception and Performance, 21*, 552–570.

Sanders, A. F. (1970). Some variables affecting the relation between relative stimulus frequency and choice reaction time. *Acta Psychologica, 33*, 45–55.

Schmidt, K.-D., & Ackermann, B. (1990). The structure of internal representations and reaction time related matching task phenomena. In H.-G. Geissler (Ed., in collaboration with M. H. Mueller & W. Prinz), *Psychophysical explorations of mental structures* (pp. 278–289). Göttingen, Germany: Hogrefe & Huber.

Shepard, R. N., & Metzler, J. (1971). Mental rotation of three-dimensional objects. *Science, 171*, 701–703.

Sperling, G., & Dosher, B. A. (1986). Strategy and optimation in human information processing. In K. Boff, L. Kaufman, & J. Thomas (Eds.), *Handbook of perception and performance* (pp. 1–65). New York: Wiley.

Sternberg, S. (1966). High-speed scanning in human memory. *Science, 153*, 652–654.

Sternberg, S. (1969). The discovery of processing stages: Extensions of Donders' method. *Acta Psychologica, 30*, 276–315.

Sternberg, S. (1998). How we compare objects. In D. Scarborough & S. Sternberg (Eds.), *Methods, models and conceptual issues. An invitation to cognitive psychology IV* (pp. 365–454). Cambridge, MA: MIT Press.

Stins, J., & van Leeuwen, C. (1993). Context influence on the perception of figures as conditional upon perceptual organization strategies. *Perception & Psychophysics, 53*, 34–42.

Townsend, J. T., & van Zandt, T. (1990). New theoretical results on testing self-terminating vs. exhaustive processing in rapid search experiments. In H.-G. Geissler (Ed.), *Psychophysical explorations of mental structures* (pp. 469–489). Göttingen, Germany: Hogrefe & Huber.

van Leeuwen, C. (1998). Visual perception at the edge of chaos. In J. S. Jordan (Ed.), *Systems theories and apriori aspects of perception* (pp. 289–314). Amsterdam: Elsevier.

van Leeuwen, C., & Bakker, L. (1995). Stroop can occur without Garner interference: Strategic and mandatory influences in multidimensional stimuli. *Perception & Psychophysics, 57*, 379–392.

van Zandt, T., & Townsend, J. T. (1993). Self-terminating versus exhaustive processes in rapid visual and memory search: An evaluative review. *Perception & Psychophysics, 53*, 563–580.

10

Dimension-Based Visual Attention and Visual Object Segmentation

Hermann J. Müller
Ludwig-Maximilians-Universität, München,
Germany, and University of London, UK

Joseph Krummenacher
Ludwig-Maximilians-Universität, München, Germany

Dieter Heller
Rheinisch-Westfälische Technische Hochschule,
Aachen, Germany

VISUAL ATTENTION AND VISUAL OBJECT SEGMENTATION

Recent theories of selective visual attention have tended to favor the view that visual attention is essentially object based, selecting perceptually delineated and integrated "object" entities from the visual scene for further processing and action (e.g., Baylis & Driver, 1993; Bundesen, 1990; Duncan, 1984). On such object-based accounts, perceptual grouping is fundamental to visual scene segmentation and the formation of objects. Neisser (1967) proposed that visual scenes are segmented, initially, into groups (i.e., objects) based on the operation of the Gestalt principles of perceptual organization. Visual attention is then focused on separate objects sequentially for further processing.

This object-based view of visual attention has been contrasted with space-based accounts, according to which selection operates on whatever information is present within a circumscribed spatial region (e.g., Eriksen & Hoffman, 1973; Hoffman & Nelson, 1981; Posner, 1980; Posner, Snyder, & Davidson, 1980). Thus, for example, Duncan (1984) attempted to demonstrate object-based selection effects in the absence of space-based attentional factors by presenting two overlapping objects briefly within a central area of 1° of visual angle (which had been estimated to be the narrowest angle of the attentional "zoom lens"). Duncan compared two dual-judgment conditions: report of two attributes of a single object and report of two attributes each relating to a separate object. He observed an accuracy cost in making dual judgments to two objects, relative to dual judgments to one object, thus providing evidence for object-based selection.

Although Duncan's (1984) study has been widely accepted as supporting object-based selection, it has been argued, by Vecera and Farah (1994) and Kramer, Weber, and Watson (1997), that the two-object cost in Duncan's paradigm does involve spatial–attentional mediation. In particular, Kramer et al. argued that the initial selection of objects is essentially location-based, in terms of Marr's (1982) notion of a collection of place tokens grouped into an object-like array.

Baylis and Driver (1993) also attempted to demonstrate object-based effects while ruling out space-based factors. They showed that physically identical displays could be parsed as one or two objects, depending only on observers' feature-based perceptual set. In Baylis and Driver's study, observers made speeded, relative-height judgments of two apices on the outline contours of briefly presented solid shapes (a colored, e.g., red, hexagon flanked on either side by pentagons of a different, e.g., green, color). Observers had to make judgments involving a single shape, or two shapes, colored by a prespecified target hue (e.g., red) only. Observers had to respond left or right to indicate which apex was the lower of the two critical apices. In the critical condition, the central shape was joined horizontally to the flanking shapes, so that differences in judging one object versus two objects could be assessed by using physically identical stimuli. Regardless of the feature-based set for a given group of observers (red or green), a between-object reaction time (RT) cost was found when the two flanking objects were target colored relative to when the central object was target colored. Baylis and Driver concluded that determining the relative position of parts of the same object is direct because the parts are represented within a single, object-based system. In contrast, deriving the relative location of parts of two objects is indirect, requiring the computation of a (scene-based) relationship between object-based representations.

However, O'Grady and Müller (2003) have provided evidence that the two-object cost in Baylis and Driver's paradigm is in part attributable to dimension- or feature-based processes that segment the field into two salient loci of activation on some "overall activation," or "saliency," map representation of the scene determining the allocation priorities for spatial attention (e.g., Koch & Ullman, 1985; Treisman & Sato, 1990; Wolfe, 1994). That is, the two-object RT cost involves a spatial–attentional component: the time required to shift attention from one object locus to the second.

Thus, there is emerging evidence that visual selection involves functionally interrelated space-based and object-based processes, and that these processes are modulable by dimension-based segmentation processes (for reviews, see Müller & O'Grady, 2000; Schneider, 1993; and van der Heijden, 1993). Our purpose in this chapter is to develop this idea in greater detail by reviewing recent research on dimension-based visual selection in cross-dimensional visual searches for singleton feature and singleton conjunction targets and cross-dimensional object–attribute judgments under brief stimulus exposure conditions, and by developing the implications of this research for accounts of visual object segmentation.

DIMENSION-BASED VISUAL SELECTION

Whereas much research over the past two decades has been concerned with space-based and object-based selection and their integration, dimension-based selection has received relatively little interest. Dimension-based theories propose that selection is limited by the nature of the required discriminations between different stimulus attributes, more precisely, between categories or dimensions of attributes. One dimension-based theory is the "analyzer theory" deriving from Treisman (1969) and Allport (1971, 1980). They assumed independent systems of analyzers, each processing a particular dimension of stimulus attributes (e.g., form or color). According to analyzer theory, two simultaneous discriminations relying on the same analyzer will give rise to mutual interference. However, Duncan (1984) concluded in his critical consideration of this theory that "as things stand, evidence for the analyzer theory does not seem especially strong" (p. 503).

However, recent studies of simple visual searches for singleton (odd-one-out) feature targets under conditions in which the target-defining dimension varied across trials have led to an alternative account to analyzer theory, called a "dimension-weighting account" (Found & Müller, 1996; Müller, Heller, & Ziegler, 1995). According to this account, there is a limit to the total attentional weight available to be allocated at any one time to the various dimensions of the target object, with potential target-defining dimensions (i.e., dimensions in which the target might differ from nontarget objects) being assigned weight in accordance with their instructed importance and their variability across trials. The greater the weight allocated to a particular dimension, the faster the presence of a target defined in that dimension can be discerned. By this account, dimensional weighting should not only modulate target detectability in odd-one-out feature search tasks; there should also be a limitation in how multidimensional features are bound into a coherent object representation. The evidence for this account, from cross-dimensional singleton searches as well as object judgment tasks, and its implications for theories of visual object segmentation are considered in the following sections.

CROSS-DIMENSION COSTS AND INTERTRIAL TRANSITION EFFECTS IN A SINGLETON FEATURE SEARCH

The experiments considered in this section are concerned with a seemingly simple problem, namely how an odd-one-out object, a single-feature target, is segmented from a background of homogeneous nontarget objects when the target-defining dimension is not known in advance, that is, when the critical dimension varies from trial to trial, resulting in cross-dimensional target uncertainty. Our experiments argue that, under such conditions, the target does not simply "pop out" of the field on the basis of some early, preattentive, segmentation mechanism operating in a purely bottom-up fashion. Rather, target segmentation involves an attentional mechanism that modifies the processing system by allocating a limited "selection weight" to the various dimensions that potentially define the target.

Visual Search for Odd-One-Out Feature Targets

It is well established that targets that differ from distractors in certain single salient attributes, or *features*, can be rapidly discerned irrespective of the number of items in the display (the set size). Phenomenally, the target appears to pop out of the display (pop-out effect). Visual features that support set-size-independent searches are generally assumed to be registered in parallel across the visual field. Such features are regarded as primitive image descriptors organized along a set of feature dimensions (e.g., color and orientation). Feature coding within dimensions is considered to be mutually exclusive such that a simple display item cannot exhibit two features in the same dimension (e.g., be both red and blue) but can possess a number of features in different dimensions (e.g., be red and tilted to the right). A number of feature dimensions have been shown to support parallel search, including orientation, size, color, stereo depth, and motion (see Wolfe, 1998, for a review).

There are various accounts of how salient feature differences in the field may be detected. One influential account is guided search (GS) (Cave & Wolfe, 1990; Wolfe, 1994, 1998). GS assumes that the visual field is initially represented, in parallel, as a set of basic stimulus attributes in different dimension-specific "modules" (such as color or orientation). Each module computes saliency signals for all stimulus locations, indicating the feature contrast between one particular item relative to the various other items represented within the same module: The more dissimilar an item is compared with the others, the greater its saliency. Maps of saliency signals are computed in parallel in all modules, and then these signals are summed onto a master map of activations. The activity on the master map guides focal attention, the most active location being sampled with priority. Focal attention gates the passage of information to higher stages of processing (visual object recognition and response systems). Thus, any odd-one-out feature target will generate a strong contrast signal within its own dimension. Even given some variability caused by noise, the target's saliency signal on the master map should always be larger than that of distractor items, and attention should always be deployed first to its location. However, recent work in our laboratories demonstrates that bottom-up models such as GS are, in a crucial respect, incomplete as an account of a singleton feature search, in particular when the dimension defining the target is uncertain (i.e., variable) on a trial. Dimensional uncertainty produces a cost in discerning the presence of a target (see also Treisman, 1988), which is inconsistent with the assumption that saliency signals from relevant dimensions are integrated by the master map units in a parallel and equally weighted fashion.

Visual Search for Singleton Feature Targets Across Dimensions

We (Found & Müller, 1996; Müller et al., 1995) recently investigated a search for singleton feature targets within and across stimulus dimensions. In an initial experiment, a search for three possible targets all defined *within* the orientation dimension (left-tilted, horizontal, and right-tilted small gray bars) was compared with a search for three possible targets defined *across* three different—orientation, color, and size—dimensions (a right-tilted gray small bar, a vertical black small bar, or a gray vertical large bar). The distractors in both uncertainty conditions, within-dimension (intradimension) and cross-dimension conditions, were the same: small gray vertical bars; for an illustration of the target conditions, see Fig. 10.1(a). There was also a no-uncertainty control condition in which the target was always known to be a small gray right-tilted bar among small gray vertical bars. Observers were instructed to simply respond to the detection of any heterogeneity in the display, without processing its source any further. According to bottom-up accounts, search performance ought to be unaffected by whether or not observers can predict the dimension and the feature value defining the target on a particular trial.

However, although the search was parallel in all conditions, detection of the common right-tilted target was 60 ms slower in the cross-dimension condition relative to both the intradimension condition and the control condition—a considerable RT cost in view of the fast base RTs; see Fig. 10.1(b). That there was a RT cost only in the cross-dimension condition but not the intradimension condition suggests that, to detect the presence of a target, observers had to determine in which dimension a feature difference was present: orientation, color, or size.

A follow-up experiment (Müller et al., 1995, Experiment 2) confirmed that detecting a target requires determination of its defining dimension (e.g., color) but not necessarily of its feature value in that dimension (e.g., red). In this experiment, observers were forced to identify the target before they could make a positive

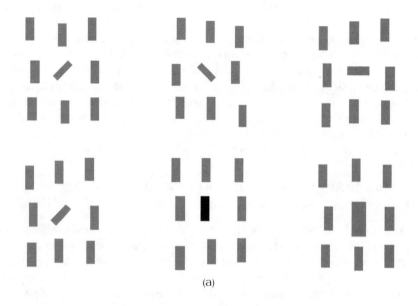

(a)

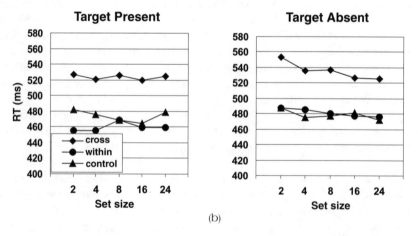

(b)

FIG. 10.1. Müller et al. (1995), Experiment 1: (a) illustration of possible target displays in the intradimension (upper displays) and cross-dimension search conditions (lower displays); (b) RTs to displays with a right-tilted orientation target (target present) and displays without a target (target absent) as a function of set size in the control, within-dimension, and cross-dimension search conditions.

response. There was again an intradimension and a cross-dimension condition. In the intradimension condition, observers responded "present" to a right-tilted or horizontal bar, but a left-tilted bar required an "absent" response. Thus, to reject the left-tilted bar, observers had to determine the precise orientation of the odd-one out stimulus. Analogously, in the cross-dimension condition, observers responded "present" to a right-tilted or black bar, but a large bar required an "absent" response. Thus, to reject the large bar, observers had to know the dimension of the odd-one-out stimulus.

If a positive response indeed requires determination of the target dimension, one should expect performance in the cross-dimension condition to be little affected by the explicit requirement to know in which dimension the target is present. However, there ought to be a large cost in the intradimension condition because the featural identity of the target would have to be determined in a further, time-consuming process. This prediction was confirmed in Experiment 2. RTs were increased by only 20 ms in the cross-dimension condition, but by 70 ms in the intradimension condition (see Fig. 10.2).

Two further aspects of cross-dimension search performance are noteworthy: (a) there was a RT advantage for a target on a given trial if the previous trial contained a target on the same dimension relative to when it was defined on a different dimension (i.e., the dimension-specific intertrial transition effect); (b) the variability of each observer's RTs was increased (relative to the intradimension and control conditions). However, the increase tended to be less than expected if the checking and elimination of dimensions were serial and self-terminating.

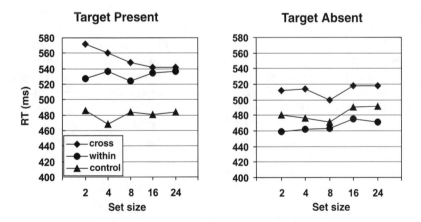

FIG. 10.2. Müller et al. (1995), Experiment 2: RTs to displays with a right-tilted orientation target (target present) and displays without an odd-one-out item (target absent) as a function of set size in the control, within-dimension, and cross-dimension search conditions.

Dimension-Specific Intertrial Transition Effect

A further experiment (Found & Müller, 1996, Experiment 1) demonstrated that the intertrial facilitation (ITF) is indeed dimension specific rather than feature specific in nature. Displays [see Fig. 10.3(a)] in these experiments contained, for positive trials, one of four possible targets: either a left- or a right-tilted white bar (orientation target) or a red or a blue vertical bar (color target). If the intertrial effect is dimension specific, it should always be evident when the target dimension (e.g., color) is repeated on consecutive trials irrespective of whether or not the target feature value (e.g., red) is repeated.

The results showed clear ITF of 30 to 40 ms when consecutive trials contained targets defined in the same dimension, relative to targets defined in different dimensions [see Fig. 10.3(b), right-hand scale]. This was the case irrespective of whether a target (on trial N) was preceded by a featurally identical target (on trial $N - 1$) or by a dimensionally identical, but featurally nonidentical, target. For example, there was a RT advantage for a red target preceded by either a red or a blue target, relative to a preceding orientation target; however, there was little (extra) advantage for a red target preceded by a red target, relative to a preceding blue target.

DIMENSIONAL WEIGHTING

We (Found & Müller, 1996; Müller et al., 1995) took the cross-dimension cost and ITF observed in our experiments to argue for a dimension-weighting account of visual search for feature targets. Similar to GS, for a feature target to generate a fast parallel search requires it to rapidly attract focal attention. Focal attention operates on a master map of integrated (summed) saliency signals derived separately in dimension-specific input modules. However, unlike (earlier versions of) GS, intradimensional saliency processing is attentionally "weighted" prior to signal integration by the master map units. The greater the weight assigned to the target dimension, the greater the rate at which evidence for a feature difference within this dimension accumulates at the master map level. In the intradimension conditions already described, the target dimension was always constant and so weighted consistently, permitting rapid search. However, in the cross-dimension condition, the search involved a time-consuming "weight-shifting" process to determine the target's dimension and render it salient at the master map level. The weight setting established in this process persists into the next trial, producing a dimension-specific RT advantage for a target defined within the same dimension as the preceding target. The crucial assumption is that there is a limit to the total attentional weight available to be allocated at any one time to the various dimensions of the target object, with potential target-defining dimensions being

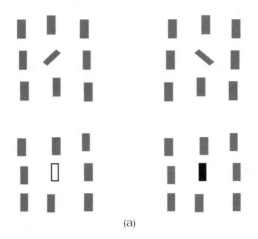

(a)

Dimension-Specific Intertrial Effects

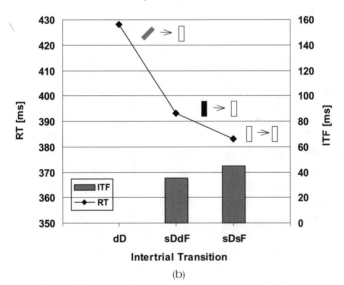

(b)

FIG. 10.3. Found and Müller (1996), Experiment 1: (a) illustration of orientation-defined, left- and right-tilted targets (upper displays) and of color-defined, red and blue, targets (lower displays); (b) RTs to a target on trial n dependent on the dimensional and featural identity of the target on trial $n-1$ (intertrial transition: dD = different dimension; sDdF = same dimension, different feature; sDsF = same dimension, same feature). Also presented is the ITF for sDdF and sDsF targets relative to dD targets.

assigned weight in accordance with their instructed importance (intentionally) or
their variability across trials (automatically).

TOP-DOWN WEIGHTING OF DIMENSIONS

One important question concerns the extent to which the weighting of dimensions is, or can be, top-down controlled. There is behavioral evidence that, in
simple singleton feature search tasks of the type just described (pop-out tasks),
the target-defining dimension is determined and weighted relatively automatically,
without involving deliberate (top-down) control operations. For example, Müller,
Krummenacher, and Heller (in press) found that, in a cross-dimensional search,
observers did not explicitly encode and retain the target-defining dimension (or the
target feature) on a given trial, and yet they showed dimension-specific inter-trial
effects. In contrast, there is evidence that observers can modulate the dimensional
weight setting in a top-down fashion in response to symbolic precues indicating the
dimension within which the target is likely to be defined on a given trial. (Müller
et al., 1995, Experiment 3).

We (Müller, Reimann, & Krummenacher, 2003) have recently followed up this
finding using trial-by-trial (rather than block-wise) cueing of the likely target-
defining dimension (by the cue words "color" or "orientation"). Precueing produced RT benefits for valid-cue trials, on which the target was defined in the cued
dimension, and costs for invalid-cue trials, on which the target was defined in an
uncued dimension, relative to a neutral-cue condition [with the cue word "neutral";
see Fig. 10.4(a)]. Furthermore, the dimension-specific intertrial effects were reduced for valid (and invalid) trials relative to neutral trials [see Fig. 10.4(b)]. Note
that, even when a specific target feature (e.g., red) was precued to be likely, while
other features in the same dimension (i.e., color: e.g., blue or yellow) were unlikely,
the cueing effects were dimension specific in nature; that is, there were benefits
of the cueing even for unlikely features within the same dimension as the cued
features (whereas there were costs only for features in a different dimension). This
was the case even when an uncued feature within the dimension of the cued feature
was extremely rare. This pattern of results is consistent with the idea that observers
can use the advance cue to set themselves for (i.e., allocate attentional weight to)
the likely target dimension. However, the fact that there remained a residual intertrial transition effect even with 100% valid precues suggests that top-down control
processes cannot be completely overcome by automatic priming processes (which
last for several seconds).

Taken together, these results suggest that dimension switching can operate relatively automatically, in a largely stimulus-driven manner, once the basic operating
parameters are set (e.g., between which dimensions switches must be carried out).
However, dimension switching may also be top-down controlled when there is an
advantage, or a need, to do so.

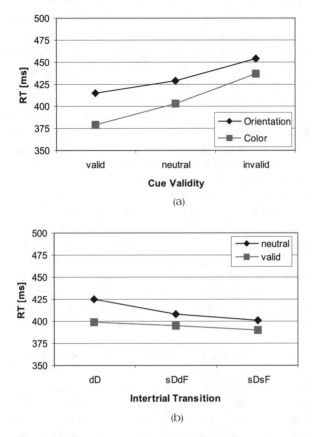

FIG. 10.4. Müller et al. (in press), Experiment 1: (a) RT as a function of cue validity, separate for color-defined and orientation-defined targets; (b) RT as a function of intertrial transition, separate for neutral and valid-cue trials (intertrial transition: dD = different dimension; dDdF = same dimension, different feature; sDsF = same dimension, same feature).

PARALLEL OR SERIAL WEIGHTING OF DIMENSIONS?

Although there is convergent evidence as to the existence of dimensional weighting, how does the weighting process actually work? Does it operate in a parallel, continuous fashion across dimensions, or in a serial, all-or-none fashion? Although some theorists have advocated serial processing of dimensions (e.g., Grossberg, Mingolla, & Ross, 1994; Treisman, 1988), other evidence such as the increased variability of observers' RTs in a cross-dimension search (Müller et al., 1995) points toward parallel processing. The dimension-weighting account as such makes no prediction as to whether a singleton feature search across dimensions is serial in nature or parallel, and, if the latter, whether a parallel-race model is true (a parallel race of independent redundant target signals to activate the detection mechanism) or a parallel-coactivation model (coactivation of the detection mechanism by redundant target signals). Thus, the issue of serial versus parallel processing of dimensions is an empirical one. Krummenacher, Müller, and Heller (2001) recently investigated this issue by examining visual searches for singleton feature targets *redundantly* defined in multiple dimensions; more specifically, they adapted the redundant-target detection paradigm (e.g., Mordkoff & Yantis, 1993; Mordkoff, Yantis, & Egeth, 1990) to a cross-dimension search, permitting Miller's (1982) "race model inequality" (RMI) to be tested.

Normally in redundant-target search, there can be one or two targets in the display (on present trials). Serial search models predict a redundancy gain such that mean RTs should be faster when there are two targets than when there is only one, simply because one of two targets has a higher chance of being encountered early in the search than a single target. However, when the entire distributions of RTs are analyzed (rather than just mean RTs), a form of redundancy gain may be revealed that is inconsistent with any strictly serial model. Miller (1982) demonstrated that all models that assume that each target produces an independent, separate activation must satisfy the following RMI:

$$P(\text{RT} < t/T_1 \,\&\, T_2) \leq P(\text{RT} < t/T_1) + P(\text{RT} < t/T_2),$$

where t is the time since display onset and T_1 and T_2 are targets 1 and 2, respectively. It is important that this inequality entails that the fastest RTs to displays with redundant targets be no faster than RTs to displays with single targets; however, fast RTs may occur more often with redundant targets. Violations of this inequality constitute evidence against serial processing, in favor of parallel-coactive processing.

In a cross-dimension search, Krummenacher, Müller, and Heller (2002, Experiment 1) varied the number of dimensions in which a single target is defined (instead of varying the number of targets in a display), such as color only or orientation only (singly defined targets, e.g., a red target or a 45° tilted target), or color and orientation simultaneously [redundantly defined target, e.g., a red 45° tilted target; for an illustration of the target conditions, see Fig. 10.5(a)]. They could then examine, by testing for violations of the RMI, whether only one dimension (dimension-specific saliency signal) at a time can activate a response-relevant (e.g., master map) representation, or whether there is coactivation from multiple dimensions.

Krummenacher et al. found that not only were RTs to redundantly defined targets on average faster than RTs to singly defined targets (mean RT redundancy gain), but also that the fastest RTs to redundantly defined targets were faster than the fastest RTs to singly defined targets, violating the RMI; see Fig. 10.5(b) and Table 10.1. The second finding constitutes strong evidence in favor of dimension-specific saliency signals' coactivating, or being integrated by, a common response-relevant (output) unit. The implication is that a cross-dimension search for singleton feature

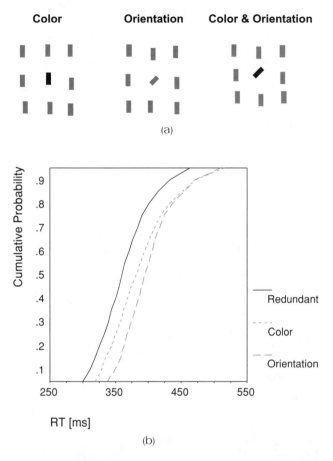

FIG. 10.5. Krummenacher et al. (2001), Experiment 1: (a) illustration of singly defined and redundantly defined color and orientation targets; (b) cumulative RT distribution functions (CDFs) for singly defined and redundantly defined color and orientation targets (singly: dotted and dashed CDFs; redundantly: solid CDF)

targets does indeed proceed in parallel in multiple dimensions (e.g., Mordkoff & Yantis, 1993; Müller et al., 1995), rather than serially, in only one dimension at a time (e.g., Grossberg et al., 1994; Treisman, 1988).

Krummenacher et al. (2002) went on to show that there is no evidence of coactivation when there are dual (redundant) saliency signals, at separate locations, defined within the same dimension (e.g., a red and a blue color target), which is consistent with the findings of Mordkoff and Yantis (1993). Furthermore, when there are dual (redundant) signals defined in different dimensions (e.g., a red color target and a 45° tilted orientation target), evidence for coactivation is found only when the two signals are spatially adjacent, and even in this case the evidence tends

TABLE 10.1
Test for Violation of RMI

p_r	t_r	p_c	p_o	p_c & p_o	T_9	P
5	300.50	1.61	1.26	2.87	2.28	0.024
10	310.95	4.01	2.16	6.17	1.70	0.0615
15	318.65	6.68	3.47	10.15	1.97	0.040
20	324.90	9.93	5.41	15.34	1.58	0.0745
25	332.45	12.31	7.31	19.62		
30	338.60	16.47	10.16	26.63		
35	343.95	20.47	11.35	31.82		
40	349.60	25.11	13.24	38.35		
45	355.00	29.73	15.52	45.25		
50	359.70	34.13	18.60	52.73		
55	364.00	38.19	20.73	58.92		
60	370.20	44.24	26.95	71.19		
65	375.95	48.68	31.39	80.07		
70	383.35	54.11	37.19	91.30		
75	390.70	59.67	43.90	103.57		
80	400.65	64.75	52.65	117.40		
85	414.85	72.16	62.67	134.83		
90	434.10	79.72	72.19	151.91		
95	463.55	87.84	82.79	170.63		

Note: From Krummenacher et al. (2001), Experiment 1 (red-color, constant-dimension condition). Here $P(\text{RT} < t/C \ \& \ O) > P(\text{RT} < t/C) + P(\text{RT} < t/O)$, where p_r is the quantile of redundant-target RT distribution, t_r is the time corresponding to quantiles of redundant-target RT distribution, $p_c = P(\text{RT} < t/C)$, $p_o = P(\text{RT} < t/O)$, $p_c \ \& \ p_o = P(\text{RT} < t/C) + P(\text{RT} < t/O)$, T_9 is the Student's $t(df = 9)$, and P is the one-tailed probability associated with Student's t.

to be weaker compared with when there is a single target redundantly defined on two dimensions (e.g., a red 45° tilted orientation target), that is, with two saliency signals at the same location. This pattern of effects suggests that there is signal integration only for saliency signals from separate dimensions and the integration is spatially specific. This is consistent with the dimension-weighting account, according to which saliency signals from multiple dimensions can combine to raise the activation of the master map unit signaling the presence and location of the target above the value achieved by a single dimensional saliency signal.

CROSS-DIMENSIONAL VISUAL SEARCH FOR SINGLETON CONJUNCTION TARGETS

One interesting question concerns whether our evidence for differential weighting of dimensions generalizes to a cross-dimensional singleton conjunction search, that is, a search for odd-one-out targets defined by a particular combination of features in separate dimensions. It is reasonable to assume that a cross-dimensional conjunction search is based on (at least some of) the same mechanisms that have evolved to support the rapid pop out of simple feature targets. However, although little top-down control may be required in singleton feature searches, top-down control processes may have to come into play in singleton conjunction searches.

We (Weidner, Pollmann, Müller, & von Cramon, 2002) recently examined this issue by requiring observers to detect a target defined by a conjunction of size with either color or motion. Displays contained items, filled-in squares, that were either large or small in size, red versus blue or green in color, and sinusoidally oscillating diagonally (lower right–upper left vs. lower left–upper right) or horizontally in the motion direction. In this way, cross-dimension and intradimension conditions could be realized analogously to the simple singleton feature search tasks already described. In the cross-dimension singleton conjunction search, the target was defined, unpredictably on a given trial, either by a unique combination of size with color (the only large red target) or a unique combination of size with motion (the only large target oscillating in the lower right–upper left direction). In the intradimension singleton conjunction search, the target was consistently defined by a conjunction of size with color, but the target color was unpredictable on a trial (the target was the only large target that was either red or blue), or it was consistently defined by a conjunction of size with motion, but the motion direction was unpredictable (the target was the only large target that was oscillating in either the lower right–upper left or lower left–upper right direction). In terms of Kahneman and Treisman (1984), this task may be referred to as a *filtering* task, in that the search had to be directed effectively to large items (i.e., small items had to be filtered out). However, it was a singleton search task in that, in the intradimension and cross-dimension conditions, the secondary target attribute was variable either within or across dimensions.

As expected (on the assumption that the dimension-weighting processes that were revealed in simple singleton feature search tasks extend to this more complex singleton conjunction search task), the results revealed an RT cost for cross-dimension search relative to intradimension search and an RT cost for dimension change (relative to no-change) trials, but not for feature change (relative to no-change) trials; see Figs. 10.6(a) for mean RTs and 10.6(b) for change costs. However, these effects were greatly increased relative to the singleton feature search for the same, color and motion-defined, targets (Pollmann, Weidner, Müller & von Cramon, 2000). The cross-dimension search cost was increased from 26 ms (feature search) to 161 ms (conjunction search), and the dimensional change effect was increased from 48 ms to 155 ms, whereas the overall RTs were markedly slower for the conjunction search relative to a simple feature search: 873 ms versus 428 ms for the intradimension search and 1033 ms versus 454 ms for the cross-dimension search. However, the search rates were shorter than 10 ms per item, the conventional criterion for a serial search, suggesting that the search involved a spatially parallel search (instead of a serial scanning of display items).

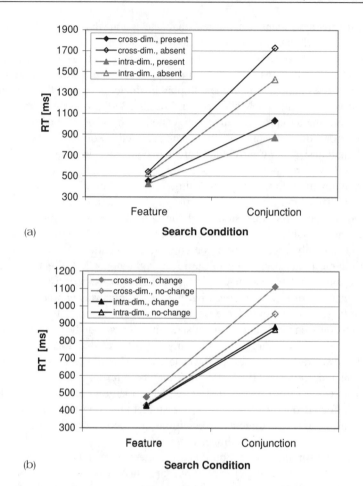

FIG. 10.6. Comparison between a singleton feature search (Pollmann et al., 2000) and a singleton conjunction search (Weidner et al., in press): (a) target-present and target-absent RTs in intradimension and cross-dimension searches; (b) RT intertrial change effects in intradimensional (feature change vs. no-change) and cross-dimensional (dimension change vs. no-change) searches.

It is likely that the search involved two successive processing stages, each operating spatially in parallel across the display: the first would be a filtering stage (cf. Kahneman & Treisman, 1984), selecting items by their (large) size, the primary target-defining dimension, and the second would involve search within or across the secondary target-defining dimension(s) of the items selected in the first stage. Size-based filtering might work by weighting the size dimension so that there would be less attentional weight available for processing the secondary dimension (assuming that the total attentional weight is limited). This would have two consequences: First, it would take longer to ascertain whether or not a (target) saliency signal is present in the secondary dimension (the assumption being that the rate at which evidence for a feature difference accumulates within a dimension is a direct function of the attentional weight allocated to that dimension). Second, in a cross-dimension search, if there is no saliency signal in the secondary dimension checked first, switching over to the alternative secondary dimension would be correspondingly delayed and, again, it would take longer to ascertain whether or not a saliency signal is present in this dimension. Thus, the need for a filtering stage would explain why target detection RTs are generally slowed in a singleton conjunction search relative to those in a singleton feature search (even for an intradimension search), and the reduced attentional weight available to be allocated to any secondary target-defining dimension could explain why the switch costs are increased in a cross-dimensional singleton conjunction search relative to a cross-dimensional singleton feature search.

With the assumption that feature difference computation within secondary dimensions (color or motion) is restricted to, or at least biased toward, items selected by the initial filtering process in the size dimension (large items), the primary dimension would have to somehow "guide" the processing in potential secondary dimensions to the relevant items (i.e., to mark these items either by increasing the activity of units coding secondary features of large items or by decreasing the activity of units coding secondary features of small items). This would involve top-down control to set the appropriate cross-dimensional processing links.

FUNCTIONAL IMPLEMENTATION
OF DIMENSION WEIGHTING

However, these findings do not tell what is actually weighted attentionally in dimension weighting: the computation of dimension-specific saliency signals within the respective visual input modules, or the transfer of dimension-specific saliency signals to the integration stage. That is, does dimensional weighting influence (e.g., enhance) early saliency signal computation or (e.g., amplify) the subsequent signal transfer? Evidence in favor of the former is provided by recent functional imaging studies, which showed that dimension-based attention modulates neuronal activity in extrastriate visual areas involved in the processing of features of the respective dimensions.

For example, Corbetta, Miezin, Dobmeyer, Shulman, and Petersen (1991) compared two conditions in a positron emission tomography study. In the first, observers could allocate their "undivided" attention to a constant dimension, such as motion. In contrast, in the second, "divided attention" baseline, condition, observers could not predict the target dimension (form, color, or motion) with certainty. Corbetta et al. found that, when observers could consistently allocate their attention to a single dimension, the blood flow to the task-relevant cortical processing area (e.g., V5 in the case of motion) was increased relative to the baseline condition. Interestingly, the latter condition also involved increased dorsolateral–frontal activation coupled with activation of the anterior cingulate, which may play a role in controlling the allocation of attention across dimensions.

We (Pollmann et al., 2000) recently confirmed and extended these findings in a functional magnetic resonance imaging (fMRI) study of singleton feature searches, which examined event-related activation changes accompanying changes in the target-defining dimension across trials, specifically changes from color to motion and vice versa. Changes in the target-defining dimension (but not changes in the target feature within a constant dimension) led to increased activation in a frontoposterior network consisting of left frontopolar cortex (BA 10) and inferior frontal gyri, high-level visual processing areas in the parietal cortex and temporal cortex, and dorsal occipital visual areas. When attention was shifted to a new target-defining dimension, activation increased in the visual areas involved in the processing features of this dimension. Pollmann et al. hypothesized that the frontopolar cortex is involved in controlling attentional weight shifting and that inferior frontal gyri and high-level parietal and temporal areas mediate attentional weighting by means of feedback to extrastriate visual areas that process the features of the new target dimension.

Another frontal structure that showed increased activation when the target-defining dimension was variable, compared with when it was fixed, was located in the frontomedial wall of the anterior border of the anterior cingulate cortex (BA 24/32). However, the anterior cingulate cortex exhibited increased activation throughout the cross-dimensional search block, whether a dimension change occurred or not (it showed only a weak increase of activation following actual dimension changes). In contrast, the frontopolar (BA 10) activation was increased when the target dimension changed, compared with when it remained unchanged. Pollmann et al. took this to suggest that the anterior cingulate cortex activity represents a continuous divided-attention set that enables attentional weight to be shifted to the relevant feature dimensions, whereas the frontopolar cortex is involved during the actual shifting of attentional weight.

In a further fMRI study, we (Weidner et al., 2002) examined cross-dimensional singleton conjunction searches (see earlier paragraphs). An event-related analysis revealed increased activation in fusiform gyrus at the location of V4 when color became the (secondary) target-defining dimension, and in lateral occipital cortex, in the area of V5, when motion became the (secondary) target-defining dimension. This essentially replicates the findings with the singleton feature search. Furthermore, consistent with the aforementioned proposal of greater top-down control in singleton conjunction as compared with singleton feature search, different frontal brain structures were revealed to be involved in dimension changes across trials.

There were significant activation increases in right F1, the most posterior covering its medial surface and extending into the anterior third of the superior frontal sulcus (BA 9), and in the dorsal and medial division of the right superior frontal gyrus as well as bilaterally in the pregenual anterior cingulate cortex (BA 10/32). Although the left lateral frontopolar activation in the singleton feature search (Pollmann et al., 2000) and the anterior frontomedian activation in the conjunction search are separated by only a few millimeters, they clearly belong to different parts of BA 10. This dissociation may be interpreted as frontopolar involvement in stimulus-driven dimension switching versus anterior frontomedian, along with anterior superior frontal sulcus, involvement in top-down controlled switching (see also Koechlin, Corrado, Pietrini, & Grafman, 2000; Rogers, Andrews, Grasby, Brooks, & Robbins, 2000).

In summary, the functional imaging evidence suggests that dimension weighting is mediated by separable frontal-lobe mechanisms, dependent on whether task performance is bottom-up or top-down controlled, and involves the modulation of neuronal activity in extrastriate visual areas specialized in the processing of features of the respective dimensions. The latter is consistent with the view that dimension weighting is perceptual in nature, influencing (enhancing) the computation of dimension-specific saliency signals.

THE RELATIONSHIP BETWEEN OBJECT-BASED AND DIMENSION-BASED VISUAL ATTENTION

That there is a dimension-based limitation in how separate dimensional attributes become accessible is also suggested from a recent study by Müller and O'Grady (2000), in which observers had to make dual discrimination judgments to independent features (attributes) of two separate objects or a single object.

Duncan (1984), who presented two overlapping objects (a line and a box) for a limited exposure duration, asked observers to direct dual judgments to either one and the same object (line tilt and line texture or box size and box gap-side) or the two separate objects (line tilt and box size, line tilt and box gap, line texture and box size, or line texture and box gap). He found that dual judgments directed to a particular object were as accurate as single judgments directed to that object. However, there was an accuracy cost for dual judgments directed to two different objects. Duncan argued from this that attention is object based rather than space based, that is, allocated to integrated objects rather than spatial location.

Our experiments (Müller & O'Grady, 2000) extended Duncan's study by introducing an intradimension–cross-dimension judgment variable. For example, in Experiment 3, observers were briefly presented with two overlapping objects

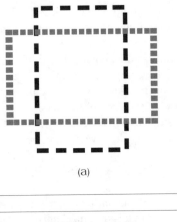

(a)

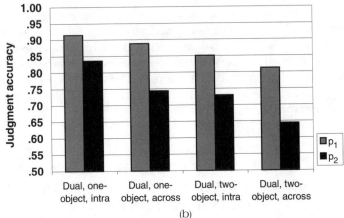

(b)

FIG. 10.7. Müller and O'Grady (2000), Experiment 3: (a) illustration of an overlapping-object display consisting of a large dashed saturated red (= black) vertical box and a large dotted saturated yellow (= gray) horizontal box; (b) dual-attribute judgment accuracy for intradomain and cross-domain judgments directed to one and two objects, respectively (p_1 = average probability of one judgment correct; p_2 = joint probability of both judgments correct).

(a vertical and a horizontal rectangular outline box) that were masked immediately after their exposure; see Fig. 10.7(a). The box attributes to be judged were hue and saturation (color attributes) and texture and size (form attributes). In dual-judgment conditions, observers had to report any combination of these attributes, so that there were various intradimension (hue + saturation; texture + size) and cross-dimension judgments (hue + texture; hue + size; saturation + texture; saturation + size) to be performed, and these dual judgments were to be directed either to a single object or to separate objects. The results are summarized in Fig. 10.7(b) and Table 10.2.

TABLE 10.2
Judgment Accuracy for the Conditions of Müller and O'Grady

	Single	Dual, One Object		Dual, Two Object	
		Within	Across	Within	Across
p_1	.892	.915	.888	.851	.813
p_2	—	.836	.774	.730	.644

Note. Judgment conditions are single-attribute, dual-attribute one-object (within-domain), dual-attribute one-object (cross-domain), dual-attribute two-object (within-domain), and dual-attribute two-object (cross-domain) judgment conditions, from Müller and O'Grady 2000, Experiment 3). For dual-attribute judgments, the average probability of one judgment being correct is given in the top half of the table (p_1) and the joint probability of both judgments being correct is given in the bottom half (p_2).

In agreement with Duncan (1984), dual-judgment accuracy was reduced when observers had to report attributes of two objects (average probability of one judgment being correct, $p_1 = .832$; joint probability of both judgments being correct, $p_2 = .687$) rather than of just one object (.902; .805). (In fact, relative to the single-object report condition, there was a dual-judgment cost in terms of p_1 only when observers had to report attributes of two objects, consistent with Duncan.) However, the size of the dual-judgment cost was dependent on whether observers had to report attributes from the same dimension (intradimension judgments) or from different dimensions (cross-dimension judgments): they were significantly reduced for dual cross-dimension judgments relative to dual intradimension judgments (.883/.783 vs. .850/.709). An analysis of variance of the dual-judgment accuracies revealed the main effects for both object condition (one vs. two objects) and dimension condition (intra vs. across) to be significant. However, the Object × Dimension interaction was nonsignificant, which is consistent with the idea that the object-based and dimension-based limitations of visual selection are additive, independent, effects.

Another experiment (Experiment 2) revealed a dimension-based effect for dual judgments directed to one object, even when only one object was displayed (instead of two overlapping objects), that is, when there was no need for object-based selection (which requires prior object segmentation and foregrounding of the target object). This confirms that dimension-based selection operates in addition to and independently of object-based selection.

The dimension-based effects demonstrated by Müller and O'Grady (2000) emphasize the importance of dimensional boundaries for visual selection, consistent with the dimension-weighting account. In particular, the finding of an added cross-dimension cost when dual judgments were directed to one and the same object points to a capacity limitation in how multidimensional features become available (for binding into a coherent object representation), that is, in terms of the dimensional-weighting account, a limit to the total weight available to be allocated to the object's dimensions.

DIMENSION-BASED VISUAL ATTENTION
AND VISUAL OBJECT SEGMENTATION

Recently, Duncan (1996) attempted to account for object-based selection within the framework of his integrated competition hypothesis. According to this hypothesis, "Of the many brain systems responding to visual input, perceptual, motor, cortical, subcortical, many and perhaps most are *competitive*.... Within each system, ... representations of different objects may be mutually inhibitory.... Between systems, however, competition is *integrated*. As an object gains ascendancy in one system, this ascendancy tends also to be transmitted to others. 'Attention' is the state that emerges as different brain systems converge to work on the same dominant object" (pp. 551–552). In summary, Duncan proposes a strong "late" object-based theory of selection according to which the different attributes of an object are selected together for control of behavior.

The findings just reviewed, especially those by Müller and O'Grady (2000), are in accord with Duncan's integrated competition view. However, the dimension-based effects observed in the present experiments question the strong assumption that all object attributes are selected together. Instead, the present findings argue that an object may be selected, and become reportable, on the basis of some dominant attribute(s), before all attributes become available—where selection is more strongly integrated for attributes from the same dimension than for attributes from different dimnesions. This would make adaptive sense, as there are situations in which objects would have to take control of behavior before all object properties are fully analyzed. Besides conferring an adaptive advantage (of increased behavioral flexibility), a system operating along these lines would also be simpler. According to Duncan's "strong" object-based selection account, the selection system would somehow need to know that all object attributes are available. In contrast, according to a weak object-based selection account, selection could take place as soon as any object attributes have gained dominance, perhaps with selection involving a temporally extended process that passes other object attributes as they become available.

A possible account of how dimension-based and object-based selection processes interrelate is as follows: Dimension-based selection, considered to be a form of segmentation, is assumed to occur first, followed by object-based selection. Objects become available for selection as soon as a response-critical attribute dimension drives segmentation of the display into separable entities (e.g., segmentation driven by a weighted dimension, d_1, allows one object, o_1, to be passed on for further processing, making the dimension-specific attributes of o_1 available for report). In case of dual judgments directed to separate objects, if the response-critical attribute dimension is the same for both objects (e.g., d_1), then a switch from one dimension to another (e.g., from d_1 to d_2) is unnecessary; only a switch from o_1 to o_2 is required. In contrast, if the attributes involved are from different dimensions, then dimension switching becomes necessary, resulting in a dimension-based processing cost. If only one object is response critical (e.g., o_1) but the relevant attributes are from different dimensions (d_1 and d_2), then a dimension-based switching cost is still incurred. This scheme is in accord with Duncan's (1996) integrated competition view, but it permits that all object attributes are not necessarily selected together. Rather, by this weak object-based selection account, an object may be selected on the basis of some weighted (response-critical) attribute(s) before all attributes become available.

It is important that, on this account, object selection is based on a mere spatial object array rather than a spatially invariant object representation, with the array being formed by dimension-based segmentation processes (cf. Kramer et al., 1997).

REFERENCES

Allport, D. A. (1971). Parallel encoding within and between elementary stimulus dimensions. *Perception & Psychophysics, 10*, 104–108.

Allport, D. A. (1980). Attention and performance. In G. Claxton (Ed.), *Cognitive psychology: New directions* (pp. 112–153). London: Routledge & Kegan Paul.

Baylis, G. C., & Driver, J. (1993). Visual attention and objects: Evidence for hierarchical coding of location. *Journal of Experimental Psychology: Human Perception and Performance, 3*, 451–470.

Bundesen, C. (1990). A theory of visual attention. *Psychological Review, 97*, 523–547.

Cave, K. R., & Wolfe, J. M. (1990). Modelling the role of parallel processing in visual search. *Cognitive Psychology, 22*, 225–271.

Corbetta, M., Miezin, F. M., Dobmeyer, S., Shulman, G. L., & Petersen, S. E. (1991). Selective and divided attention during visual discriminations of shape, color and speed: Functional anatomy by positron emission tomography. *Journal of Neuroscience, 11*, 2382–2402.

Duncan, J. (1984). Selective attention and the organization of visual information. *Journal of Experimental Psychology: General, 114*, 501–517.

Duncan, J. (1996). Cooperating brain systems in selective perception and action. In T. Inui & J. L. McClelland (Eds.), *Attention and performance XVI. Information integration in perception and communication* (pp. 549–578). Cambridge, MA: MIT Press.

Eriksen, C. W., & Hoffman, J. E. (1973). The extent of processing of noise elements during selective encoding from visual displays. *Perception & Psychophysics, 14*, 155–160.

Found, A., & Müller, H. J. (1996). Searching for unknown feature targets on more than one dimension: Investigating a "dimension-weighting" account. *Perception & Psychophysics, 58*, 88–101.

Grossberg, S., Mingolla, E., & Ross, W. D. (1994). A neural theory of attentive visual search: Interaction of boundary, surface, spatial, and object representations. *Psychological Review, 101*, 470–489.

Hoffman, J. E., & Nelson, B. (1981). Spatial selectivity in visual search. *Perception & Psychophysics, 30*, 283–290.

Kahneman, D., & Treisman, A. (1984). Changing views of visual attention and automaticity. In R. Parasuraman & D. R. Davies (Eds.), *Varieties of attention* (pp. 29–61). New York: Academic Press.

Koch, C., & Ullman, S. (1985). Shifts in selective visual attention: Towards the underlying neural circuitry. *Human Neurobiology, 4*, 219–227.

Koechlin, E., Corrado, G., Pietrini, P., & Grafman, J. (2000). Dissociating the role of the medial and lateral anterior prefrontal cortex in human planning. *Proceedings of the National Academy of Sciences, USA, 97*, 7651–7656.

Kramer, A. F., Weber, T. A., & Watson, S. E. (1997). Object-based attentional selection—grouped arrays or spatially invariant representations?: Comment on Vecera and Farah (1994). *Journal of Experimental Psychology: General, 50*, 267–284.

Krummenacher, J., Müller, H. J., & Heller, D. (2001). Visual search for dimensionally redundant pop-out targets: Evidence for parallel-coactive processing of dimensions. *Perception & Psychophysics, 63*, 907–917.

Krummenacher, J., Müller, H. J., & Heller, D. (2002). Visual search for dimensionally redundant pop-out targets: Parallel-coactive processing of dimensions is location-specific. *Journal of Experimental Psychology: Human Perception & Performance, 28*, 1303–1322.

Marr, D. (1982). *Vision. A computational investigation into the human representation and processing of visual information.* New York: Freeman.

Miller, J. (1982). Divided attention: Evidence for coactivation with redundant signals. *Cognitive Psychology, 14*, 247–279.

Mordkoff, J. T., & Yantis, S. (1993). Dividing attention between color and shape: evidence of coactivation. *Perception & Psychophysics, 53*, 357–366.

Mordkoff, J. T., Yantis, S., & Egeth, H. E. (1990). Detecting conjunctions of color and form in parallel. *Perception & Psychophysics, 48*, 157–168.

Müller, H. J., Heller, D., & Ziegler, J. (1995). Visual search for singleton feature targets within and across feature dimensions. *Perception & Psychophysics, 57*, 1–17.

Müller, H. J., Krummenacher, J., & Heller, D. (in press). Dimension-specific intertrial facilitation in singleton feature search: An implicit visual short-term memory effect. *Visual cognition.*

Müller, H. J., & O'Grady, R. B. (2000). Dimension-based visual attention modulates dual-judgment accuracy in Duncan's (1984) one versus two-object report paradigm. *Journal of Experimental Psychology: Human Perception and Performance, 26*, 1332–1351.

Müller, H. J., Reimann, B., & Krummenacher, J. (2003). Visual search for singleton feature targets across dimensions: stimulus- and expectancy-driven effects in dimensional weighting. Manuscript submitted for publication.

Neisser, U. (1967). *Cognitive psychology.* New York: Appleton-Century-Crofts.

O'Grady, R. B., & Müller, H. J. (2003). *Object-based selection in the Baylis and Driver (1993) paradigm is subject to space-based attentional modulation.* Manuscript submitted for publication.

Pollmann, S., Weidner, R., Müller, H. J., von Cramon, D. Y. (2000). A fronto-posterior network involved in visual dimension changes. *Journal of Cognitive Neuroscience, 12*, 480–494.

Posner, M. I. (1980). Orienting of attention. *Quarterly Journal of Experimental Psychology, 32*, 3–25.

Posner, M. I., Snyder, C. R. R., & Davidson, B. J. (1980). Attention and the detection of signals. *Journal of Experimental Psychology: General, 109*, 160–174.

Rogers, R. D., Andrews, T. C., Grasby, P. M., Brooks, D. J., & Robbins, T. W. (2000). Contrasting cortical and subcortical activations produced by attentional-set shifting and reversal learning in humans. *Journal of Cognitive Neuroscience, 12*, 142–162.

Schneider, W. X. (1993). Space-based visual attention models and object selection: Constraints, problems, and possible solutions. *Psychological Research, 56*, 35–43.

Treisman, A. (1969). Strategies and models of selective attention. *Psychological Review, 76*, 282–299.

Treisman, A. (1988). Features and objects. The fourteenth Bartlett Memorial Lecture. *Quarterly Journal of Experimental Psychology, 40A*, 201–236.

Treisman, A. M., & Sato, S. (1990). Conjunction search revisited. *Journal of Experimental Psychology: Human Perception and Performance, 16*, 459–478.

van der Heijden, A. H. C. (1993). The role of position in object selection in vision. *Psychological Research, 56*, 44–58.

Vecera, S. P., & Farah, M. (1994). Does visual attention select objects or locations? *Journal of Experimental Psychology: General, 123*, 146–160.

Weidner, R., Pollmann, S., Müller, H. J., & von Cramon, D. Y. (2002). Top down controlled visual dimension weighting: An event-related fMRI study. *Cerebral Cortex, 12*, 318–328.

Wolfe, J. M. (1994). Guided search 2.0: A revised model of visual search. *Psychonomic Bulletin & Review, 1*, 202–238.

Wolfe, J. M. (1998). Visual search. In H. Pashler (Ed.), *Attention* (pp. 13–73). Hove, England: Psychology Press.

11

Timing of "Perception" and Perception of "Time"

Odmar Neumann and Michael Niepel
Bielefeld University, Germany

One problem with the psychological study of time is that time is not a single, unitary dimension. First, there is the physical time in which brain processes take place and in which we measure response latency (reaction time, or RT) or the latency of event-related potentials. This is time as defined by physics. Second, there is the concept of psychological time in the sense of a particular "fine structure" (Stroud, 1955) of processing in the brain, as suggested in Geissler's theory of time quanta (e.g., Geissler, 1985, 1990). Third, there is phenomenal time—the dimension in which perceived events take place and which can be assessed by psychophysical methods such as temporal-order judgments (TOJs). In this chapter, we are concerned with two of these time dimensions, that is, the physical time in which processing takes place and the phenomenal time in which perceived events succeed each other. Both time dimensions have traditionally been used to estimate how long it takes a stimulus to cause a perception, a span variously called "sensory latency", "perception time", "sensation time", or "perceptual lag" (Berger, 1886; Cattell, 1886; Exner, 1873, 1875; Hirsch, 1863; Szili, 1892; for surveys, see Jaskowski, 1996, 1999; Roufs, 1974). Interestingly, the results of these two research traditions do not converge.

LOGIC OF USING RT AND TOJ TO MEASURE PERCEPTUAL LATENCY[1]

The usage of RT as a measure of sensory-processing time is straightforward: Because sensory processing is one stage in the chain of events leading from stimulus to response, any factor that affects the speed of sensory processing should also exert an influence on RT. Under the assumption that this factor affects only the sensory stage, the resulting RT differences should be equal to the difference in sensory-processing time. On the basis of this reasoning, RT has been used since the late 19th century as a major method for assessing sensory latency as a function of stimulus variables such as intensity (e.g., Berger, 1886; Burkhardt, Gottesman, & Keenan, 1987; Cattell, 1886; Chocholle, 1940–1941; Exner, 1873; Hirsch, 1863; Mansfield, 1973; Neumann, Koch, Niepel, & Tappe, 1992; Piéron, 1920; Roufs, 1974; for surveys see Nissen, 1977; Teichner & Krebs, 1972). The estimation of sensory latency by psychophysical measurement is based on a more indirect logic. The faster a stimulus is processed, the earlier should it produce a conscious (i.e., reportable) sensation. Hence, an observer's judgment about the moment in time when he or she experienced a sensation should reflect the processing time of the stimulus that gave rise to that sensation. The usual way to obtain such a judgment has been to ask observers to determine the temporal order of the test stimulus and a standard comparison stimulus. Like the RT approach, this TOJ method has been utilized for more than a century (e.g., Exner, 1875; Hamlin, 1895; Jaskowski, Jaroszyk, & Hojan-Jezierska, 1990; Neumann et al., 1992; Roufs, 1974; Rutschmann & Link, 1964; Scharlau & Neumann, in press; Smith, 1933; Whipple, 1899; review in Roufs, 1974). Note that both methods can only assess time differences, not the absolute timing of sensory processing. They (purportedly) reflect changes in processing time as a result of some experimental manipulation (e.g., a variation of stimulus intensity or sense modality), but they do not provide a measure of processing time itself. This is obviously true for the TOJ method, but it is also true for RT measurement, because RTs do not provide an estimate of the absolute duration of any of the stages intervening between stimulus and response (see Scharlau, Ansorge, & Neumann, in press).

When different methods are used to assess what is assumed to be the same internal process or variable, the question of course arises whether that which they measure is actually the same. In other words, are RT and TOJ converging operations

---

[1]There have been other methodological approaches to the measurement of perceptual latency. Some are based on the simultaneous stimulation of the retina with stimuli of different intensities. If either the stimuli (Hess, 1904; Prestrude & Baker, 1968; Pulfrich, 1922) or the eyes (Hazelhoff & Wiersma, 1924) are in motion, then latency differences should translate into retinal disparities that can be measured. A second approach uses visual backward masking by a very bright flash to determine the maximal interval at which a stimulus can still be retroactively erased, that is, barred from conscious perception (Exner, 1868; Piéron, 1925). Third, it has been claimed that sensory latency can be computed from the position at which a stimulus, that enters a window and moves in it, is first perceived (Fröhlich, 1929; for a recent comprehensive review of Fröhlich's work as well as current research on this effect see Carbone, 2001). These methods are essentially restricted to the visual modality and depend on specific properties of the visual system. We will therefore not include them in the present review.

that operationalize one identical hypothetical construct, "sensory latency"? This is an important question for at least two reasons. The first is methodological. If these measures can be shown to converge, then they will cross-validate each other. Taken in isolation, both have their methodological difficulties that are, however, different in each case. For example, a factor such as stimulus intensity might affect not only sensory processing but also the decision or motor stage (e.g., Ulrich & Stapf, 1984), leading to an additional effect on RT that is absent in TOJ. Similarly, factors such as decision bias might influence TOJ but leave RT unaffected (e.g., Sternberg & Knoll, 1973). If the results from RT and TOJ measurements should turn out to be essentially the same, then it would be very unlikely that they are seriously contaminated by any of these sources of artifact. Conversely, the opposite result could be of potential interest for theoretical reasons. If it could be shown that RT and TOJ measures do not converge, even under conditions where the aforementioned factors are unlikely to be responsible for the divergence, then this would point to a dissociation. Dissociations between motor performance and explicit verbal report have been reported from several areas, the best known of which is probably implicit memory (see Schacter, 1987). Closer to our present topic are dissociations that have been found between RT and verbal report in metacontrast masking (Fehrer & Raab, 1962; Klotz & Neumann, 1999; Neumann & Klotz, 1994; for overviews see Bernstein, Amundson, & Schurman, 1973; Neumann, Ansorge, & Klotz, 1998) and between manual pointing and verbal report under conditions of induced motion (Bridgeman, Kirch, & Sperling, 1981). Various similar dissociation effects seem to exist (see Neumann, 1989, 1990). A systematic difference between TOJ and RT estimates of sensory-processing time could constitute a further demonstration of such a dissociation.

EMPIRICAL FINDINGS

Stimulus Intensity

RT Data. The available evidence on whether RT and TOJ data on sensory-processing time converge stems from two sources. First, there are the (relatively few) studies that have directly compared the two methods under identical or comparable conditions. This is, of course, the most desirable kind of evidence. Second, some further, more tentative conclusions can be drawn from a comparison of experiments that have used either only RT or only TOJ measures. We begin with the latter kind of comparison.

Experiments that have investigated the effect of intensity on simple RT have been performed since the second half of the 19th century. The finding that RT decreases as a function of stimulus intensity dates back to Hirsch (1861–1864) and Exner (1873) and was systematically investigated in Wundt's laboratory (Berger, 1886; Cattell, 1886). The size of this effect is quite substantial. RTs to the onset of very intense visual stimuli are usually near or somewhat below 200 ms, whereas RTs to the onset of near-threshold stimuli typically range well above 300 ms and may be as high as 400 to 600 ms for short durations (e.g., Berger, 1886;

Burkhardt et al., 1987; Piéron, 1920; Sticht, 1969; see Teichner & Krebs, 1972, for a systematic analysis). Roughly the same values have been found for RTs to stimulus offset (e.g., Burkhardt et al., 1987; Piéron, 1927; Sticht, 1969). The curve that relates RT to luminance is negatively accelerated and has been variously approximated by an exponential function (Hull, 1949), a logarithmic function (Roufs, 1963), or, most often, a power function (Burkhardt et al., 1987; Mansfield, 1973; Piéron, 1920, 1927; Teichner & Krebs, 1972; Ueno, 1977; Vaughan, Costa, & Gilden, 1966). Similar findings have been reported for auditory stimuli (e.g., Angel, 1973; Berger, 1886; Chocholle, 1940–1941; Kohfeld, 1971; McGill, 1961).

TOJ Data. The effect of stimulus intensity on TOJ has been investigated less systematically. Smith (1933) used visual and auditory stimuli of different intensities in a bisensory TOJ task and reported effects on the point of subjective simultaneity (PSS), which indicated that stimuli of higher intensity were perceived earlier than stimuli of lower intensity. We have reanalyzed his data with probit analyses (Finney, 1971) and found that this effect was of the order of between 20 and 30 ms, for intensity differences of between 2 and 3 logarithmic units (Fig. 11.1, left panel). Very similar results were reported by Roufs (1963, Fig. 6; a PSS shift

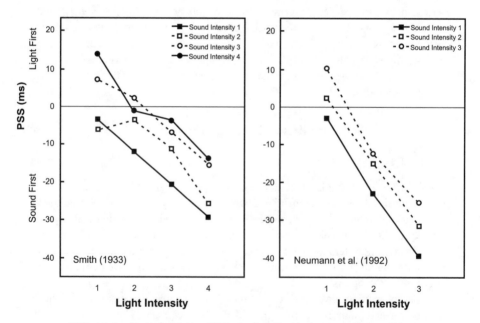

FIG. 11.1. Data from two TOJ studies that have varied sound intensity and light intensity orthogonally. The PSS is shown as a function of light intensity, with sound intensity as the parameter. The PSSs from the Smith (1933) experiment were estimated from the published data (Table 11.1) by probit analyses.

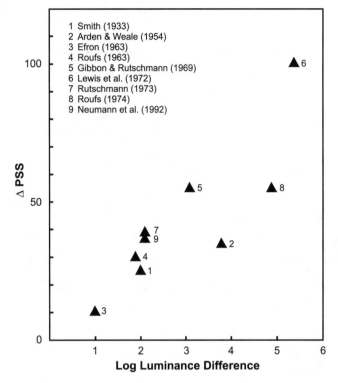

FIG. 11.2. PSS differences as a function of log luminance difference from seven studies in which either intrasensory (visual–visual) or intersensory (visual–auditory) PSSs were determined for visual stimuli of different luminances. If more than two intensities were investigated in a study, only the data from the smallest and largest intensities are shown. Data for peripheral stimulation are not included.

of approximately 30 ms when luminance was increased over a range of roughly 2 logarithmic units). In an intramodal visual TOJ task, Rutschmann (1973) reduced the luminance of a foveal flash by 2 logarithmic units and found that this shifted the PSS by approximately 30–40 ms, which corroborates the results from the other studies. Arden and Weale (1954) reported an effect in the same order of magnitude for an intensity range of 4 logarithmic units with foveal stimuli, whereas the effect was much larger for extrafoveal stimuli (approximately 70 and 110 ms, respectively, for two subjects). When Roufs (1974) varied luminance over 5 logarithmic units, this produced a PSS shift of approximately 60–70 ms. In the study of Lewis, Dunlap, and Matteson (1972), the average effect of a luminance variation over 5 logarithmic units was approximately 90 ms. Efron's (1963) data from an intramodal TOJ task show a PSS shift of approximately

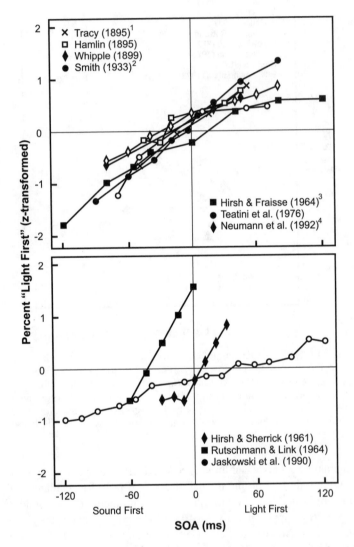

FIG. 11.3. Psychometric functions for visual–auditory TOJ from 10 studies. Data were either taken from tables or estimated from figures. Results from different subjects that were published separately in the original papers have been averaged. Superscripts: [1]Data of F. Tracy, reported in Hamlin (1895); [2]averaged over four

10 ms as a result of reducing the intensity of a visual stimulus by 1 logarithmic unit.

These findings fit quite well together. First, there is ample evidence that stimulus intensity does affect TOJ. Second, there are clear indications that the size of this effect is a positive function of the intensity difference between the stimuli (Fig. 11.2). Third and most important, there is no evidence that intensity effects of the order of magnitude that can be found in RT tasks (i.e., differences of several hundred milliseconds) occur in TOJ experiments. At least for foveal stimuli, none of the obtained differences exceeded 100 ms.

This points to a possible dissociation effect. However, procedural differences and, in particular, differences in the range of intensities investigated render it impossible to draw any firm conclusions. In principle, such conclusions should be possible on the basis of experiments that have directly compared the two methods.

Combined RT–TOJ Data. There are a few studies that seem to demonstrate a close correspondence between RT and TOJ data. Gibbon and Rutschmann (1969) found an almost perfect agreement between the slopes of their psychometric functions and the slopes that were predicted by RT data over an intensity range of approximately 3 logarithmic units, suggesting that RT variability was essentially determined by visual latency as measured by TOJ. Although there were reliable differences between the empirical PSSs and the predictions computed from RT data, the deviation differed for the two subjects, suggesting that it was due to response bias. Similarly, Roufs (1963) compared RT measurement with intrasensory and bisensory TOJ and found that all three tasks yielded almost identical effects of a variation of visual intensity over 2 logarithmic units. However, this is a small range as compared with the intensity differences that were investigated in typical RT studies. Hence it is not surprising that the RT differences in Roufs' (1963) study did not exceed 40 ms—much less than the usual intensity effect on RT when a broader range of intensities is used.

When Roufs (1974) used a larger luminance range, his results duplicated those from previous studies that had examined either RT or TOJ alone. In both bisensory (auditory–visual) and intrasensory (visual) TOJ tasks, the maximal PSS shift as a result of varying stimulus intensity was approximately 60–70 ms (Roufs, 1974, Figs. 2 and 3), whereas maximal RT differences were of the order of 130–180 ms

---

(Continued) sound and four light intensities; [3]curve based on medians from the 8 subjects that were presented with SOAs from −120 to +120 ms and that had to judge "light first" or "sound first" (there were various other conditions in the experiment); [4]averaged over three sound and three light intensities. Upper panel: Data from 7 studies that show similar psychometric functions. Lower panel: Data from the 3 studies with deviant results

(Roufs, 1974, Figs. 5 and 6). This dissociation seemed to be mainly due to very long RTs to very low-intensity stimuli. More recently, Neumann et al. (1992) compared TOJ and RT to stimuli that varied over a little more than 2 logarithmic units in both the visual and the auditory modality. Numerically, intensity had stronger effects on RT than on TOJ for both modalities. However, this interaction was (marginally) reliable for the auditory stimuli alone and did not reach significance for the visual stimuli.

Thus, the evidence from direct comparisons is in general agreement with the data from experiments that have investigated either RT or TOJ alone, or at least it does not contradict them. To summarize, the data suggest that (a) both RT and TOJ are susceptible to the influence of stimulus intensity, but (b) there is a tendency for RT to show a stronger intensity effect, especially in the lower range of intensities.

Sensory Modality

Like the literature on stimulus intensity, studies on the effect of sensory modality can be subdivided into those that investigated either RT or TOJ alone and those that were explicitly aimed at a comparison.

RT Data. The dependence of RT on stimulus modality was among the earliest topics in RT research. The Swiss astronomer Hirsch (1861–1864; 1863) may have been the first author to study this relationship. Two decades later, Berger (1886) included sensory modality as a second factor in his study on the relationship between stimulus intensity and RT. He found that RT to visual stimuli varied between 198 and 338 ms for one subject (the author), depending on stimulus intensity, whereas RTs to auditory stimuli of different intensities ranged from 123 to 151 ms for the same subject.[2] These values are fairly representative of later estimates, with the exception that auditory RTs to near-threshold stimuli— which Berger did not include—may be as high as 400 ms (Chocholle, 1940– 1941). Thus, the RT to very soft auditory stimuli approaches the RT to dim visual stimuli. However, the "irreducible minimum" seems to be clearly different.[3] It

---

[2]Berger did these experiments in Wundt's laboratory together with James McK. Cattell, who published some of them separately in a short note (Cattell, 1886). The auditory data and many other tables are missing from Cattell's report. Mysteriously, all his values for the visual and the electric stimulation experiments are exactly 30 ms shorter than those published by Berger! (See Piéron, 1920, who discovered this strange discrepancy.) Possibly because of this error, later authors have often assumed that Berger and Cattell published data from different studies.

[3]The common assumption that RT to auditory stimuli is shorter than RT to visual stimuli and that this is due to different peripheral transmission latencies (e.g., Woodworth & Schlosberg, 1954) has been challenged by experiments that found similar RTs to stimuli from the two modalities when their intensities were equated in terms of decibels (regarding a reference value slightly below threshold; see Stevens, 1955) and when the visual stimuli were made larger in order to "fill" large parts of the visual "channel," as auditory stimuli are assumed to do (e.g., Kohfeld, 1971; Niemi & Lethonen, 1982). However, these results with low- and medium-intensity stimuli do not invalidate the fact that

has been found to be approximately 110–120 ms for auditory stimuli (Chocholle, 1940–1941, in an extremely careful study; for a survey see, e.g., Woodworth & Schlosberg, 1954) and approximately 150–160 ms for visual stimuli (survey in Teichner & Krebs, 1972).

TOJ Data.   As with stimulus intensity, the effect of sensory modality on TOJ is less clear-cut than its effect on RT. In what was probably the first study of bisensory TOJ, Exner (1875) found a longer latency for visual than for auditory stimuli, which would be qualitatively in accordance with the RT findings. However, later studies show a different picture.

Figure 11.3 presents the data from 10 studies. The upper panel contains the data from seven reports that show remarkably similar slopes of the psychometric function. The differential threshold is of the order of 40 ms throughout, which is a close agreement that justifies confidence in the validity of these studies. The lower panel exhibits the three remaining psychometric functions, whose slope diverges from this value. Two (Hirsh & Sherrick, 1961; Rutschmann & Link, 1964) are much steeper; the third (Jaskowski et al., 1990) is much flatter.

As to the Hirsh and Sherrick (1961) study, these experiments were carried out under particular conditions, as was later pointed out by Hirsh and Fraisse (1964). Subjects were highly trained, and each stimulus presentation was repeated as often as the subject desired before a response had to be given. These conditions differ substantially from those in the other experiments, and as shown by Gengel and Hirsh (1970), they fully account for the discrepancy. For the remaining two data sets in the lower panel of Fig. 11.3, the cause of the deviation is less clear. There were only 2 subjects in the Rutschmann and Link (1964) experiment and only 3 subjects in the Jaskowski et al. (1990) study. Because it is a common experience in investigations of bisensory TOJs that individual differential thresholds differ vastly, the most probable explanation may be sampling variability.

From the data in the upper panel of Fig. 11.3 it is clear that there is no tendency for auditory stimuli to have a shorter latency than visual stimuli. On the contrary, the majority of the studies yielded a PSS at negative stimulus onset asynchronies

---

the irreducible minimum is different. RTs as low as 120–140 ms, which can be easily obtained with loud tones, do not seem to be attainable even with the most efficient visual stimuli. For example, Elliott (1968, Experiment 2) found visual RTs of 160–180 ms to a very high-energy, large visual stimulus (an extremely bright light from an electronic flashgun with an area of 80°), whereas the RTs of the same subjects to a 80-dB (A) tone ranged from 135 to 152 ms, yielding a mean difference of 24 ms in favor of the tone. Furthermore, it is doubtful that visual and auditory stimuli that are equalized with respect to intensity in decibels are indeed of "equal intensity" in a functional sense. Given the many factors that influence RT and that cannot be equated for the two modalities (visual area, visual spectral composition, sound frequency, critical intervals for temporal summation, etc.), and in view of the much larger dynamic range of vision (approximately 12 logarithmic units of luminance) as compared with audition (approximately 7 logarithmic units of sound pressure; see, e.g., Trincker, 1977), such attempts at a cross-modality matching are of limited value.

(SOAs; according to the convention that we adopt in this paper). That is, the auditory stimulus had to be presented before the visual stimulus in order to obtain 50% "light first" responses. The only exception are the data of Hirsh and Fraisse (1964). However, the fact that their PSS falls to the right of the zero SOA is essentially due to a single data point. Moreover, this is the only study in which the data are based on the medians rather than the arithmetic means of 13 subjects, rendering the comparison somewhat problematic. On the whole, these studies clearly suggest a negative PSS as the rule.

The data in the lower panel present a more confusing picture. Although we have separated them from the rest because of their atypical slopes, these psychometric functions also show deviant positions of the PSS. The PSS in the Rutschmann and Link (1964) experiment is strongly negative, that in the Hirsh and Sherrick (1961) study is slightly positive, and the study of Jaskowski et al. (1990) yielded a definitely positive SOA. This sheds some doubt on the generality of the finding that the PSS is situated at a negative SOA. Furthermore, there is at least one additional study, not included in Fig. 11.2 because the paper did not provide the necessary data, that likewise reported a positive PSS (Roufs, 1963). The experiments of Hirsh and Sherrick (1961) and of Roufs (1963) are among the most careful in the field. Hence these deviations must be taken seriously.

One possible reason for the discrepancy can be read off from Fig. 11.1. It exhibits the results of two studies in which sensory modality and stimulus intensity were varied orthogonally (Neumann et al., 1992; Smith, 1933). Both experiments show the same kind of effect: For the majority of the intensity combinations, the auditory stimulus has to be presented before the visual stimulus to obtain the perception of subjective simultaneity. However, this effect shrinks in size and may finally be reversed to the degree to which auditory intensity increases or visual intensity decreases. If the light is dim and the sound is loud, then subjective simultaneity will be perceived when the light is presented before the sound. In other words, the modality effect in favor of the visual stimulus can be compensated or even reversed by an intensity effect in favor of the auditory stimulus.

There is some evidence that this trade-off between modality and intensity is the major cause of the diverging results. The positive PSS reported in Roufs (1963) was obtained with a moderate range of light intensities. In later research (Roufs, 1974), the same author investigated a more extended intensity range. Whereas the original result was replicated for low flash intensities, the PSS shifted to negative values for the higher intensities (see Roufs, 1974, Fig. 2), which is in perfect accordance with our interpretation. In the experiment by Jaskowski et al. (1990), the auditory stimulus had the considerable intensity of 70 dB, whereas the visual stimulus was a patch with a luminance of only 12 cd/m^2. Although this intensity difference may have been partially compensated by different exposure durations, these are conditions that may well have been equivalent to the loud sound–dim flash combinations in the experiments by Smith (1933) and Neumann et al. (1992).

The remaining studies in which the PSS was found to be positive do not contain full information about the intensities that were used. Hence it must remain open whether they can be interpreted in the same way. What can be stated with confidence is that intensity effects may counteract the modality effect that normally favors the visual stimulus in TOJ experiments. It cannot be ruled out that there are further, still unidentified factors that may also cause such a reversal.

Combined RT–TOJ Data. Among the studies that have directly compared bisensory TOJ data with RTs to the same stimuli are those whose data are shown in Fig. 11.3 (Jaskowski et al., 1990; Neumann et al., 1992; Rutschmann & Link, 1964). The corresponding RTs exhibit an unambiguous pattern: In none of the three studies did the RT differences correctly predict the PSS. RTs to auditory stimuli were shorter than visual RTs, and they accordingly predicted a positive PSS. In contrast, the PSS was negative in the experiments of Rutschmann and Link (1964) and Neumann et al. (1992). In the study by Jaskowski et al. (1990), it was positive but still closer to zero than predicted by the RTs; thus these data do not contradict our conclusion from the studies that have separately investigated either RT or TOJ.

Conclusion. Our review has revealed two interesting empirical trends. The first concerns stimulus intensity, which has a strong and well-investigated influence on RT. Its effect on TOJ has received much less attention. Nevertheless, the data that we have reviewed suggest that TOJ is less susceptible to the effect of intensity than RT, especially in the lower-intensity range. The second trend pertains to the effect of sensory modality. As has been established for more than a century, simple RT to auditory stimuli is shorter than RT to visual stimuli, at least for the stimuli that have normally been used in laboratory studies. If this disparity reflects a difference in sensory latency, as has commonly been assumed, one would expect it to affect RT and TOJ equally. Our survey of the available data has suggested a different picture: The TOJs are clearly not generally based on the latency differences that the RT data predict. The majority of the experiments even show a reversal of the predicted modality-based difference, and the few discrepant findings can at least in part be explained as hidden intensity effects.

Taken together, these data suggest that neither stimulus intensity nor sensory modality affect RT and TOJ equally. We have meanwhile replicated the results from the Neumann et al. (1992) study in three experiments that varied various stimulus parameters (e.g., exposure duration, stimulus area, and percent catch trials in the RT task), and in which possible artifacts (in particular, a conceivable intersensory facilitation in the TOJ task) were eliminated (Neumann & Niepel, 2003). Strong modality and intensity dissociations were obtained in all three experiments. Taken together, this evidence is solid enough to warrant the consideration of possible functional implications.

THEORETICAL CONSIDERATIONS

The existence of intensity and modality dissociations speaks against the assumption that RT and TOJ measurements are simply two operationalizations of the same construct, that is, perceptual lag or sensory latency. In principle, this could be the result of either of two kinds of flaws in this assumption. First, there is the possibility that the construct itself is mistaken and that there is no unitary sensory latency upon which the different measures could converge. Second, the assumption might be wrong that the stimulus variables "intensity" and "modality" exert their effect exclusively on the sensory-processing stage. If they also affect other stages that differ for RT and TOJ, then dissociations between these measures would of course be trivial. In the rest of the chapter, we elaborate these possibilities and discuss them in the light of the data. Space does not permit consideration of all variants of these explanations. For an excellent treatment of some of the issues that we have to omit, see Jaskowski (1996, 1999).

Three Possible Causes for the Intensity and Modality Dissociations

Three Assumptions. Somewhere in the course of events initiated by a sensory signal, a state of the brain may occur that is associated with the onset of a conscious (i.e., reportable) perception. Further, somewhere in this course of events a state of the brain may occur that contains the information about the various sensory aspects of the stimulus and that leads to processes that may trigger a motor response. The classical concept of sensory latency and its operationalization by RT and TOJ measurements comprise three assumptions about these events.

First, it is assumed that the two brain states—the one that underlies the onset of the conscious perception and the one that triggers the processes that lead to the motor response—are identical; in other words, it is assumed that the pathway from stimulus to response is mediated by the same sensory state that also underlies the conscious sensation. This is the general basis for using both RT and the PSS as measures of sensory latency. Let us call this the *single-pathway assumption.*

The second assumption may be termed the *critical-moment assumption.* It postulates that there is not only a common underlying brain state but also that it has a measurable latency, that is, that it is punctiform in time or at least comprises a well-defined and sufficiently small critical region that determines both the onset of the conscious perception and the perceptual processes that later lead to the motor response. If no such critical moment exists, or if it is different for these two events, then there is no reason for expecting RT and PSS measures to produce identical estimates of differences in sensory latency. For example, RT might reflect the state of sensory processing at an early stage, and TOJ might reflect its state at some later stage that is associated with conscious perception.

The third assumption does not concern the construct of sensory latency as such but the effect of the stimulus variables that have been found to produce dissociations. These dissociations would be trivial if intensity and modality had their locus at processing stages other than sensory processing, that is, stages that are likely to be different for RT and for TOJ. If, for example, stimulus intensity had part of its effect on decision or motor processes subsequent to sensory processing, then there would be no reason to expect RT and TOJ data to converge with respect to the effect of this variable. The TOJ involves decision processes that are absent in a simple RT task, and the RT involves motor processes that do not play any role in psychophysical judgments. Therefore, using RT and TOJ as converging operations for sensory latency rests on the assumption that the variables whose effects are measured exert their influence exclusively on the sensory-processing stage. Let us call this the *uncontaminated-measurement assumption*.

The Uncontaminated-Measurement Assumption. According to this assumption, sensory variables such as stimulus intensity and sensory modality exclusively affect the sensory- and perceptual-processing stages. Studies in the psychophysical research tradition have often taken this for granted (for references see, e.g., Ulrich & Stapf, 1984), and stage analyses within information-processing research have yielded evidence in favor of it (e.g., Massaro, 1990; Sanders, 1980; Sternberg, 1969). However, there are grounds for doubting that it is generally true.

One finding that is difficult to reconcile with this assumption has been reported by Ulrich and Stapf (1984). They used a task that required participants to respond with both hands simultaneously in a simple RT task. Stimuli were either visual or auditory and varied in intensity. For both sensory modalities, the variance of the RT differences between the two hands increased as stimulus intensity was reduced. Because the input into the motor system came from the same stimulus for both hands and hence the same sensory processing was involved, this finding strongly suggests that postperceptual processes that are at least partially independent for the two hands were influenced by stimulus intensity.

Second, there have been various reports that factors that presumably affect postperceptual processing stages may produce statistical interactions with the intensity factor. Thus, the intensity of an auditory stimulus has been reported to interact with foreperiod duration and foreperiod variability (Bernstein, Chu, Briggs, & Schurman, 1973; Niemi & Lehtonen, 1982; Niemi & Näätänen, 1981; Sanders, 1977; for reviews see Nissen, 1977; Sanders, 1990). For example, the effect of foreperiod duration became smaller when the imperative stimulus had a high intensity, that is, one approximately above 70 dB. This has been interpreted as evidence that an intensive stimulus increases alertness (Nissen, 1977) or immediate arousal (Sanders, 1977, 1990), which may have a direct effect on motor adjustment, bypassing central decision mechanisms (Sanders, 1977, 1983, 1990). The finding that stimulus intensity may affect response force further supports this interpretation (e.g., Jaskowski, Rybarcyk, & Jaroszyk, 1994; Jaskowski, Verleger, &

Wascher, 1994). Such a mechanism should affect RT by speeding up its motor component. In contrast, it would leave the TOJ unaffected, because this task does not require a speeded response. Moreover, any possible effect of arousal on processing speed would affect both the standard and the comparison stimulus and therefore not change the TOJ.

At first sight, it thus seems that the intensity dissociation could be the result of the differential effect of high-intensity stimuli on postperceptual processes in the RT task as compared with the TOJ task. The modality dissociation could also be interpreted along these lines, because auditory stimuli seem to be more effective than visual stimuli in causing immediate arousal.

However, data from Neumann and Niepel (2003) contradict this explanation. They found intensity dissociations for auditory stimuli although all intensities studied were well below the 70 dB (A) that, according to Sanders' (1990) review of the literature, is the minimum value required for immediate arousal. Second, although immediate arousal should be more pronounced with auditory than with visual stimuli, the intensity dissociations in all three experiments reported in this study were at least as large in the visual as in the auditory modality. Further, auditory stimuli of 45 dB (A) and 68 dB (A) produced an intensity dissociation (i.e., the difference between the PSS measured in the TOJ task and the PSS predicted by RTs was larger for the louder stimulus). However, in a visual RT task in which these same two tones were added as accessory stimuli, they had identical effects on visual RT. This is a clear indication that the faster RTs to louder stimuli were due to a specific effect of intensity on processing in the auditory pathway rather than to an unspecific arousal, which should have also acted on RT to a visual stimulus. Finally, in another experiment reported by Neumann and Niepel (2003), the degree of response preparation was varied when different proportions of catch trials were introduced. According to the findings just cited, an effect on immediate arousal should interact with response preparation. However, the effects of catch trials and stimulus intensity on RT were strictly additive.

These findings warrant the conclusion that the intensity and modality dissociations are not due to postperceptual effects, that is, to a violation of the uncontaminated-measurement assumption.

The Critical-Moment Assumption.   Suppose that the presentation of a sensory stimulus produces an internal response whose activation level initially grows as a function of time. If there is no single critical moment, then there will be one point in time when the internal response exceeds the threshold for triggering a motor response, and another moment when it is sufficiently strong to produce a conscious sensation. The threshold for triggering a motor response might be lower than the threshold for producing the onset of a conscious sensation or, alternatively, the motor response might require a higher level of activation than the conscious sensation. If a stimulus parameter such as intensity is manipulated, this is unlikely to simply produce a linear shift of the activation function. Rather it will probably affect the rate of accrual of the internal response, with faster accrual for more intense stimuli. Hence the different thresholds will be affected differently, which offers a basis for an explanation of the intensity dissociation.

To account for the intensity dissociation, one has to assume that either (a) the RT threshold is lower than the TOJ threshold and intensity has a larger effect in the lower portion than in the higher portion of the growth function, that is, the growth functions for different intensities converge, or (b) the RT threshold is higher than the TOJ threshold and intensity has a larger effect in the higher part than in the lower part, that is, the growth functions for different intensities diverge. In both cases, the points in time where the growth function reaches threshold will be closer together for TOJs than for RTs. Both patterns should manifest themselves as a statistical interaction between intensity and response threshold. Neumann and Niepel (2003, Experiment 2) tested this prediction in an RT experiment in which the response threshold was manipulated by comparing RTs in experimental blocks with different proportions of catch trials. It was expected that increasing the proportion of trials in which subjects had to withhold their response (no-go trials) would lead to an upward shift of the response threshold. This manipulation was successful, as evidenced by longer RTs and smaller error rates as the number of catch trials was increased. Although this pattern was found for visual as well as auditory stimuli of different intensities, there was no interaction between stimulus intensity and proportion of catch trials. In other words, the intensity dissociation was unaffected by a shift in response criterion. This is strong evidence against the hypothesis that this dissociation is related to a simple difference in response threshold between RT and TOJ tasks.

A further problem with this interpretation is how to extend it to modality dissociations. This would require the assumption that (for stimuli of the kind used in the present experiments) the auditory internal response reaches the motor response threshold approximately 40 ms earlier than the visual internal response, but that the latter then catches up and attains the threshold for the TOJ up to 40 ms before its auditory counterpart. If this is not to remain a purely ad hoc assumption, the hypothetical faster processing of visual stimuli at later processing stages requires an explanation that can be empirically tested. One possibility could be that it is due to visual dominance at the level of attentional selection, resulting in faster processing of visual stimuli at that level. This is essentially the classical idea of "prior entry" (Minnemann, 1911; Peters, 1905; Titchener, 1908). However, modern attempts to demonstrate prior entry have produced contradictory results (Cairney, 1975; Frey, 1990; Jaskowski, 1993; Vanderhaeghen & Bertelson, 1974). What is more important is that data from our laboratory directly contradict this hypothesis. In three studies (Neumann, Esselmann, & Klotz, 1993; Scharlau & Neumann, in press; Steglich & Neumann, 2000), we investigated how a visual localization cue (prime) affected TOJ and RT. In all three studies, the effect of the cue on RT was *larger* than its effect on TOJ. In the most recent series of experiments (Scharlau & Neumann, in press), special care was taken to make sure that the cue's effect was indeed attentional and not the result of some other kind of interaction (e.g., sensory facilitation). Thus, it is RT and not TOJ that is more strongly affected by attention, directly contradicting the hypothesis that the modality dissociation is due to an attentional effect that affects the TOJ to visual stimuli more strongly than RT to them.

The Single-Pathway Assumption.   According to this assumption, the information flow from stimulus to response in the RT task is funneled by means of a conscious sensation (or, more precisely, by the brain state that underlies a conscious sensation). Alternatively, there could be parallel pathways into which the information flow separates after an initial stage of common processing, one feeding into the motor system and one leading to conscious perception. The effects of sensory modality and intensity on RT would then reflect processing in one of these pathways, and its effects on TOJ would be caused by processing in the other pathway. In other words, the dissociations as empirical patterns would be based on a functional dissociation in the sense of a splitting up into parallel processing streams.

This idea dates back to the 19th century, when Lange (1888), working in Wundt's laboratory, described what he called "foreshortened reactions" (verkürzte Reaktionen), in which the response seemed to occur before the stimulus was consciously perceived. Although Wundt (e.g., Wundt, 1903) believed that this direct pathway from stimulus to response, without a prior conscious perception of the stimulus, was restricted to simple reactions, his student Münsterberg (1889) claimed that even complex choice reactions (e.g., the vocal classification of verbal stimuli) could be produced in this forshortened mode, which, he believed, was indeed the normal way in which sensory information determined motor responses (cf. Neumann & Prinz, 1987). When one of us revived this idea more than a decade ago by introducing the concept of direct parameter specification (DPS) (Neumann, 1989, 1990; see also Neumann & Müsseler, 1990), this was based on a tentative survey of findings from various fields. Most of these data were by-products of research endeavors that had mainly been directed at other issues.

In the meantime, the picture has changed. Since the publication of Milner and Goodale's seminal work on the dorsal and ventral processing streams (e.g., Goodale & Milner, 1992; Milner & Goodale, 1995), the view has rapidly gained support that conscious stimulus identification and sensorimotor control are partially based on different processing pathways, such as the ventral and dorsal streams in the case of visual processing. Both streams have their origin in (partially different) areas of the occipital cortex. The dorsal stream projects via the parietal cortex into the motor system and serves the sensorimotor control of actions such as pointing and grasping. The ventral stream projects into the inferotemporal cortex, where stimuli are identified and represented in an allocentric frame of reference. Presumably, this latter type of processing, but not necessarily the former, is associated with a conscious (reportable) experience.

This theoretical approach has stimulated a wealth of research. One paradigm that has proven fruitful is the metacontrast dissociation in which congruent or incongruent primes are completely masked by metacontrast. On the basis of earlier work by Neumann (1982), recent research with this paradigm shows conclusively that conscious discrimination of a stimulus is not required in order for this stimulus to affect RT and error rate (e.g., Ansorge, Klotz, & Neumann, 1998; Ansorge & Neumann, under revision; Eimer & Schlaghecken, 1998, 2001; Klotz & Neumann, 1999; Klotz & Wolff, 1995; Leuthold & Kopp, 1998; Neumann & Klotz, 1994; Schlaghecken & Eimer, 1997, 2001, in press; Vorberg, Mattler, Heinecke, Schmidt, & Schwarzbach, chap. 12, this volume).

The data from Neumann et al. (1992) and from Neumann and Niepel (2003), already cited, were collected in a research project in which RT data were compared to TOJ data in various experimental paradigms in an attempt to validate the concept of DPS with a second, independent experimental logic. The basic finding from this research was that almost all stimulus properties that we investigated had differential effects on RT and TOJ. Dissociations were found not only for intensity and modality but also for stimulus size (Neumann & Niepel, 2003), spatial frequency (Carbone, Niepel, & Neumann, 2003; Tappe, Niepel, & Neumann, 1994), and the effect of a masked cue (prime) preceding the target stimulus (Neumann & Esselmann, 1992; Neumann et al., 1993; Scharlau & Neumann, in press; Steglich & Neumann, 2000). In all cases, a manipulation that has long been known to speed up sensory processing (low vs. high spatial frequency, large vs. small stimulus size, and presence of a location cue) had the expected effect on RT, whereas a corresponding effect on TOJ was either attenuated or absent. Together with the notion of DPS, this pattern of results suggests an account of these dissociations that refers back to the concept of psychological time.

DPS and Psychological Time

We began this chapter with the remark that psychological time is not a unitary dimension. In RT measurement, we measure the duration of processes that occur in physical time, whereas the TOJ task refers to a sequence of events in phenomenal time. From a biological point of view, there is a fundamental difference between these two time dimensions. The timing of motor responses has to be tailored to the requirements of actions in physical reality. One of the major requirements is probably to respond as fast as possible, that is, as soon as the relevant information is available. In contrast, the way in which events are ordered in phenomenal time should, from a functional point of view, reflect the objective time relations as they exist independent from the organism and its momentary action.

An analogy to space will make this clearer. As Milner and Goodale (1995) have pointed out, sensorimotor control by visual stimuli requires spatial coding in an egocentric frame of reference, because the direction of grasping and similar object-directed actions depend on where the target object is located relative to the body and effector, not on where it is in absolute space. Similarly, it matters how far away it is, whether it is seen from the front or from behind, and so on. In other words, *object constancy* is *not* functionally appropriate for the task of sensory guidance of motor actions. It is, however, required when it comes to identifying and categorizing an object. We should be able to recognize an oyster, whether it is placed at the near or the far end of the plate; however, the movements to pick it up should be controlled by the retinal projections that differ in the two cases. Milner and Goodale relate this to the dorsal–ventral stream differentiation: Whereas neurons in the dorsal stream do not seem to show size or orientation constancy, neurons have been found in the inferotemporal cortex that exhibit this kind of constancy; that is, they continue responding to an object even if it is moved away or turned around.

Similarly, the dissociations between RT and TOJ data may be related to *time constancy*. Intensive and large stimuli are processed faster than dim or small stimuli, because of energy summation. Low spatial frequency stimuli are processed faster than high spatial frequency stimuli, because transient channels are faster than sustained channels. The lag from acoustical stimulation to the beginning activity in the acoustical nerve is shorter than the lag from an optical stimulus to the start of firing in the optical nerve because transduction in the cochlea takes less time than the biochemical processes in the retina. Thus, the time of arrival of the sensory signal in the primary cortical areas depends on these factors. For speeded responses to individual stimuli or stimulus dimensions this does not pose a problem. On the contrary, just as changes in retinal projection when an object is moved or turned around provide useful information for the task of grasping it, so the fast processing of intensive stimuli or stimuli of low spatial frequencies (which provide information, e.g., about the gross shape of objects) may be functionally helpful for triggering quick responses to these stimuli. The fast processing of acoustical as compared with visual signals may be especially helpful, because auditory information often serves an alerting function (see Neumann, van der Heijden, & Allport, 1986).

However, the fact that simultaneous physical stimuli that differ in intensity and so on will produce asynchroneous activity in the primary cortical areas does produce a problem for a veridical internal representation of the world. Time constancy is required at the level of object identification and classification, just as size or form constancies are necessary in the spatial domain, in order to create a veridical representation of the world. The dissociations between RT and TOJ suggest that the processing that leads to conscious perception—probably involving the ventral stream for visual stimuli—encompasses mechanisms that attenuate or completely obliterate these differences in arrival times. By contrast, the pathways to motor activation do not need—and indeed do not seem to involve—such corrective mechanisms.

CONCLUSION: PERCEPTION OF "TIME" AND TIME OF "PERCEPTION"

It will be clear by now why we have placed the terms "time" and "perception" in quotation marks in the title of this chapter. If the aforementioned considerations are correct, there is no perception of a sensory stimulus that can be associated with a particular point in time. Sensory and perceptual processing proceeds along parallel pathways that produce different results, with no sharp transition from sensory–perceptual processes to "central" or motor processes (see, e.g., Neumann, 1990, for a discussion of this point as related to the functions of the posterior parietal cortex; see also the theoretical work of Prinz and his associates on the concept of common coding, e.g., Müsseler, 1999; Prinz, 1990, 1992, 1997). As one of us has argued (Neumann, 1990), it is therefore unwise to use the term "perception" with respect to particular processes in the brain. It is the organism that perceives, not the occipital or the parietal or the inferotemporal cortex or whatever systems may be involved in stimulus processing.

This act of perceiving has the subjective aspect that conscious perceptual experiences are created, that is, experiences that can be reported, commented on, and measured with psychophysical methods such as TOJs. We have stressed that the temporal order that the TOJ refers to is located in phenomenal time, not in the physical time in which we measure RTs. One might therefore argue that the dissociation between RT and TOJ data does not require an explanation, because they do not refer to the same dimension. However, although it is true that confounding the perception of time with the time of perception would involve a logical mistake (Dennett, 1991; Neumann, 1982), it is likewise true that TOJs are normally quite exact (e.g., Hirsh & Sherrick, 1961; Scharlau & Neumann, in press); that is, the order of stimuli is closely reflected in the perceived temporal order. In other words, *empirically*, there is a close correspondence between phenomenal order and the physical order of stimuli, although *logically* we cannot equate phenomenal order with the order in which brain processes take place.

The mechanisms that underlie this close correspondence between perceived temporal order and the order of events in the physical world are not yet well understood. This correspondence could be based on the timing of brain processes or on some other kind of information ("time marks" or "tags"). If it is based on the timing of brain processes, then the dissociation between RT and TOJ data suggests that differences in the order of arrival caused by factors such as intensity and spatial frequency are somehow compensated for on the way from the primary sensory areas to those areas whose activity has its counterpart in conscious perception. Alternatively, it is conceivable that there is no such compensation at the purely temporal level, but the processes that construct conscious perceptions combine temporal information with other kinds of information to create a (almost) veridical representation of the timing of events in the outside world.

ACKNOWLEDGMENTS

This chapter is partially based on the unpublished manuscript "The effect of stimulus intensity and sensory modality on reaction time and temporal order judgment: A survey and an appraisal," by O. Neumann, T. Tappe, and M. Niepel. This research was supported by Grants Ne 366/1-1 and Ne 366/2-1 from the Deutsche Forschungsgemeinschaft to O. Neumann.

REFERENCES

Angel, A. (1973). Input-output relations in simple reaction time experiments. *Quarterly Journal of Experimental Psychology, 25*, 193–200.

Ansorge, U., Klotz, W., & Neumann, O. (1998). Manual and verbal responses to completely masked (unreportable) stimuli: Exploring some conditions for the metacontrast dissociation. *Perception, 27*, 1177–1189.

Ansorge, U., & Neumann, O. (under revision). Intentions determine the effect of metacontrast-masked primes: A test of direct parameter specification in a peripheral cueing task. *Journal of Experimental Psychology: Human Perception and Performance.*

Arden, G. B., & Weale, R. A. (1954). Variations of the latent period of vision. *Proceedings of the Royal Society of London, Series B: Biological Sciences, 142*, 258–267.

Berger, G. O. (1886). Über den Einfluß der Reizstärke auf die Dauer einfacher psychischer Vorgänge mit besonderer Rücksicht auf Lichtreize [On the influence of stimulus intensity on the duration of simple mental processes with a special consideration of light stimuli]. *Philosophische Studien, 3*, 38–93.

Bernstein, I. H., Amundson, V. E., & Schurman, D. L. (1973). Metacontrast inferred from reaction time and verbal report: Replication and comment on the Fehrer-Biederman experiment. *Journal of Experimental Psychology, 100*, 195–201.

Bernstein, I. H., Chu, P. K., Briggs, P., & Schurman, D. L. (1973). Stimulus intensity and foreperiod effects in intersensory facilitation. *Quarterly Journal of Experimental Psychology, 25*, 171–181.

Bridgeman, B., Kirch, M., & Sperling, A. (1981). Segregation of cognitive and motor aspects of visual function using induced motion. *Perception & Psychophysics, 29*, 336–342.

Burkhardt, D. A., Gottesman, J., & Keenan, R. M. (1987). Sensory latency and reaction time: Dependence on contrast polarity and early linearity in human vision. *Journal of the Optical Society of America, A4*, 530–539.

Cairney, P. T. (1975). Bisensory order judgement and the prior entry hypothesis. *Acta Psychologica, 39*, 329–340.

Carbone, E. (2001). *Die Rolle von Aufmerksamkeitsprozessen bei der Fehlwahrnehmung dynamischer Reize.* Unpublished doctoral dissertation, University of Bielefeld. (Accessible at Elena.carbone@uni-bielefeld.de)

Carbone E., Niepel, M., & Neumann, O. (2003). *Producing short intervals: Temporal limits of direct parameter specification in an unspeeded task.* Manuscript submitted for publication.

Cattell, J. M. (1886). The influence of the intensity of the stimulus on the length of the reaction time. *Brain, 8*, 512–515.

Chocholle, R. (1940–1941). Variation de temps de réaction auditifs en fonction de l'intensité de diverses fréquences [Variation of auditory reaction time as a function of the intensity of different frequencies]. *Année Psychologique, 41/42,* 65–124.

Dennett, D. C. (1991). *Consciousness explained.* Boston: Little, Brown.

Efron, R. (1963). The effect of stimulus intensity on the perception of simultaneity in right- and left-handed subjects. *Brain, 86,* 285–294.

Eimer, M., & Schlaghecken, F. (1998). Effects of masked stimuli on motor activation: Behavioral and electrophysiological evidence. *Journal of Experimental Psychology: Human Perception and Performance, 24,* 1737–1747.

Eimer, M., & Schlaghecken, F. (2001). Response facilitation and inhibition in manual, vocal, and oculomotor performance: Evidence for a modality-unspecific mechanism. *Journal of Motor Behavior, 33,* 16–26.

Elliott, R. (1968). Simple visual and simple auditory reaction time: A comparison. *Psychonomic Science, 10,* 335–336.

Exner, S. (1868). Über die zu einer Gesichtswahrnehmung nöthige Zeit [On the time necessary for a visual perception]. *Sitzungsberichte der kaiserlichen Akademie der Wissenschaften zu Wien, Mathematisch-naturwissenschaftliche Classe, 58* (2), 601–632.

Exner, S. (1873). Experimentelle Untersuchung der einfachsten psychischen Prozesse. I. Abhandlung. Die persönliche Gleichung [Experimental examination of the most simple psychological processes. I. Treatise. The personal equation]. *Pflüger's Archiv für die gesamte Physiologie der Menschen und der Thiere, 7,* 601–660.

Exner, S. (1875). Experimentelle Untersuchung der einfachsten psychischen Prozesse. III. Abhandlung. Der persönlichen Gleichung zweiter Teil [Experimental examination of the most simple psychological processes. III. Treatise. Second part of the personal equation]. *Pflüger's Archiv für die gesamte Physiologie der Menschen und der Thiere, 11,* 403–432.

Fehrer, E., & Raab, D. (1962). Reaction time to stimuli masked by metacontrast. *Journal of Experimental Psychology, 63,* 143–147.

Finney, D. J. (1971). *Probit analysis* (3rd ed.). Cambridge, England: Cambridge University Press.

Frey, R. D. (1990). Selective attention, event perception and the criterion of acceptability principle: Evidence supporting and rejecting the doctrine of prior entry. *Human Movement Science, 9,* 481–530.

Fröhlich, F. W. (1929). *Die Empfindungszeit. Ein Beitrag zur Lehre von der Zeit- Raum- und Bewegungsempfindung* [Sensation time. A contribution to the doctrine of the sensation of time, space, and motion]. Jena, Germany: Fischer.

Geissler, H.-G. (1985). Zeitquantenhypothese zur Struktur ultraschneller Gedächtnisprozesse [A time quanta hypothesis about the structure of ultra fast memory processes]. *Zeitschrift für Psychologie, 193,* 347–362.

Geissler H.-G. (1990). Foundation of quantized processing. In H.-G. Geissler, M. H. Müller, & W. Prinz (Eds.), *Psychophysical explorations of mental structures* (pp. 303–310). Göttingen, Germany: Hogrefe.

Gengel, R. W., & Hirsh, I. J. (1970). Temporal order: The effect of single versus repeated presentations, practice, and verbal feedback. *Perception & Psychophysics, 7,* 209–211.

Gibbon, J., & Rutschmann, R. (1969). Temporal order judgment and reaction time. *Science, 165,* 413–415.

Goodale, M. A., & Milner, A. D. (1992). Separate visual pathways for perception and action. *Trends in Neurosciences, 15,* 20–25.

Hamlin, A. J. (1895). On the least observable interval between stimuli addressed to disparate senses and to different organs of the same sense. *American Journal of Psychology, 6,* 564–573.

Hazelhoff, F. F., & Wiersma, H. (1924). Die Wahrnehmungszeit I [Perception time I]. *Zeitschrift für Psychologie und Physiologie der Sinnesorgane, 96,* 171–188.

Hess, C. (1904). Untersuchungen über den Erregungsvorgang im Sehorgan bei kurz- und bei längerdauernder Reizung [Examinations of the process of excitation in the visual organ during short and longer lasting stimulation]. *Pflüger's Archiv für die gesamte Physiologie der Menschen und der Thiere, 101*, 226–262.

Hirsch, A. (1861–1864). Expériences chronoscopiques sur la vitesse des différentes sensations et de la transmission nerveuse [Chronoscopic examinations of the velocity of different sensations and nervous transmission]. *Bulletin de la Societé des Sciences Naturelles, 6*, 100–114 (as cited in Exner, 1875, and Woodworth & Schlosberg, 1954).

Hirsch, A. (1863). Chronoskopische Untersuchungen über die Geschwindigkeit der verschiedenen Sinneseindrücke und der Nervenleitung [Chronoscopic examinations of the velocity of different sensations and nervous transmission]. *Moleschotts Untersuchungen, 9*, 182 (as cited in Fröhlich, 1929).

Hirsh, I. J., & Fraisse, P. (1964). Simultanéité et succession de stimuli hétérogènes [Simultaneity and succession of heterogeneous stimuli]. *Année Psychologique, 64*, 1–19.

Hirsh, I. J., & Sherrick, C. E. (1961). Perceived order in different sense modalities. *Journal of Experimental Psychology, 62*, 423–432.

Hull, C. L. (1949). Stimulus intensity dynamism (V) and stimulus generalization. *Psychological Review, 56*, 67–76.

Jaskowski, P. (1993). Selective attention and temporal-order judgment. *Perception, 22*, 681–689.

Jaskowski, P. (1996). Simple reaction time and perception of temporal order: Dissociations and hypotheses. *Perceptual and Motor Skills, 82*, 707–730.

Jaskowski, P. (1999). Reaction time and temporal order judgment as measures of perceptual latency: The problem of dissociations. In G. Aschersleben, T. Bachmann, & J. Müsseler (Eds.), *Cognitive contributions to the perception of spatial and temporal events* (pp. 265–282). Amsterdam: Elsevier.

Jaskowski, P., Jaroszyk, F., & Hojan-Jezierska, D. (1990). Temporal-order judgments and reaction time for stimuli of different modalities. *Psychological Research, 52*, 35–38.

Jaskowski, P., Rybarcyk, R., & Jaroszyk, F. (1994). On the relationship between latency of auditory evoked potentials, simple reaction time and stimulus intensity. *Psychological Research, 56*, 59–65.

Jaskowski, P., Verleger, R., & Wascher, E. (1994). Response force and reaction time in a simple reaction task under time pressure. *Zeitschrift für Psychologie, 202*, 405–413.

Klotz, W., & Neumann, O. (1999). Motor activation without conscious discrimination in metacontrast masking. *Journal of Experimental Psychology: Human Perception and Performance, 25*, 976–992.

Klotz, W., & Wolff, P. (1995). The effect of a masked stimulus on the response to the masking stimulus. *Psychological Research, 58*, 92–101.

Kohfeld, D. (1971). Simple reaction time as a function of stimulus intensity in decibels of light and sound. *Journal of Experimental Psychology, 88*, 251–257.

Lange, L. (1888). Neue Experimente über den Vorgang der einfachen Reaction auf Sinneseindrücke [New experiments on the process of simple reaction to sense impressions]. *Philosophische Studien, 4*, 479–510.

Leuthold, H., & Kopp, B. (1998). Mechanisms of priming by masked stimuli: Inferences from event-related brain potentials. *Psychological Science, 9*, 263–269.

Lewis, J. H., Dunlap, W. P., & Matteson, H. H. (1972). Perceptual latency as a function of stimulus onset and offset and retinal location. *Vision Research, 12*, 1725–1731.

Mansfield, R. J. W. (1973). Latency functions in human vision. *Vision Research, 13*, 2219–2234.

Massaro, D. W. (1990). An information processing analysis of perception and action. In O. Neumann & W. Prinz (Eds.), *Relationships between perception and action: Current approaches* (pp. 133–166). New York: Springer.

McGill, W. J. (1961). Loudness and reaction time. *Acta Psychologica, 19*, 193–199.

Milner, A. D., & Goodale, M. A. (1995). *The visual brain in action.* Oxford, England: Oxford University Press.

Minnemann, C. (1911). Untersuchungen über die Differenz der Wahrnehmungsgeschwindigkeiten von Licht- und Schallreizen. [Experiments on the difference of perceptual latencies for light and sound stimuli]. *Archiv für die gesamte Psychologie, 20,* 227–259.

Münsterberg, H. (1889). *Beiträge zur experimentellen Psychologie. Heft 1: Über willkürliche und unwillkürliche Vorstellungsverbindungen* [Contributions to experimental psychology. Vol. 1: On voluntary and involuntary associations between ideas]. Freiburg, Germany: Mohr. (Reprinted from *Hugo Münsterberg. Frühe Schriften,* H. Hildebrandt & E. Scheerer, Eds., 1990, Berlin: Deutscher Verlag der Wissenschaften).

Müsseler, J. (1999). How independent from action control is perception? An event-coding account for more equally-ranked crosstalks. In G. Aschersleben, T. Bachmann, & J. Müsseler (Eds.), *Cognitive contributions to the perception of spatial and temporal events* (pp. 265–282). Amsterdam: Elsevier.

Neumann, O. (1982). *Experimente zum Fehrer-Raab-Effekt und das 'Wetterwart'-Modell der visuellen Maskierung* [Experiments on the Fehrer-Raab effect and the weather station model of visual masking] (Bericht Nr. 24/1982). Bochum, Germany: Arbeitseinheit Kognitionspsychologie, Psychologisches Institut der Ruhr-Universität Bochum.

Neumann, O. (1989). Kognitive Vermittlung und direkte Parameterspezifikation. Zum Problem mentaler Repräsentation in der Wahrnehmung [Cognitive mediation and direct parameter specification. On the problem of mental representation in perception]. *Sprache und Kognition, 8,* 32–49.

Neumann, O. (1990). Direct parameter specification and the concept of perception. *Psychological Research, 52,* 207–215.

Neumann, O., Ansorge, U., & Klotz, W. (1998). Funktionsdifferenzierung im visuellen Kortex: Grundlage für motorische Aktivierung durch nicht bewußt wahrgenommene Reize? [Functional differentiation in the visual cortex: Basis for motor activation by not consciously perceived stimuli?]. *Psychologische Rundschau, 49,* 185–196.

Neumann, O., & Esselmann, U. (1992). Visual attention, response latency, and temporal order judgment. *International Journal of Psychology, 27,* 13.

Neumann, O., Esselmann, U., & Klotz, W. (1993). Differential effects of visual-spatial attention on response latency and temporal order judgment. *Psychological Research, 56,* 26–34.

Neumann, O., & Klotz, W. (1994). Motor responses to nonreportable, masked stimuli: Where is the limit of direct parameter specification? In C. Umiltà & M. Moscovitch (Eds.), *Attention and performance XV. Conscious and nonconscious information processing* (pp. 123–150). Cambridge, MA: MIT Press.

Neumann, O., Koch, R., Niepel, M., & Tappe, T. (1992). Reaktionszeit und zeitliches Reihenfolgeurteil: Übereinstimmung oder Dissoziation? [Reaction time and temporal order judgment: Correspondence or dissociation?]. *Zeitschrift für Experimentelle und Angewandte Psychologie, 39,* 621–645.

Neumann, O., & Müsseler, J. (1990). "Judgment" vs. "response": A general problem and some experimental illustrations. In H.-G. Geissler, M. H. Müller, & W. Prinz (Eds.), *Psychophysical explorations of mental structures* (pp. 445–455). Göttingen, Germany: Hogrefe.

Neumann, O., & Niepel, M. (2002). A dissociation between temporal order judgment and reaction time: Evidence for direct parameter specification. Manuscript submitted for publication.

Neumann, O., & Prinz, W. (1987). Kognitive Antezedenzien von Willkürhandlungen [Cognitive antecedents of voluntary actions]. In H. Heckhausen, P. M. Gollwitzer, & F. E. Weinert (Eds.), *Jenseits des Rubikon: Der Wille in den Humanwissenschaften* [Beyond the Rubicon: The will in the humanities] (pp. 195–215). New York: Springer.

Neumann, O., van der Heijden, A. H. C., & Allport, D. A. (1986). Visual selective attention: Introductory remarks. *Psychological Research, 48,* 185–188.

Niemi, P., & Lehtonen, E. (1982). Foreperiod and visual stimulus intensity: A reappraisal. *Acta Psychologica, 50,* 73–82.

Niemi, P., & Näätänen, R. (1981). Foreperiod duration and simple reaction time. *Psychological Bulletin, 89,* 133–160.

Nissen, M. J. (1977). Stimulus intensity and information processing. *Perception & Psychophysics, 22*, 338–352.

Peters, W. (1905). Aufmerksamkeit und Zeitverschiebung in der Auffassung disparater Sinnesreize [Attention and time shift in the perception of disparate sensory stimuli]. *Zeitschrift für Psychologie und Physiologie der Sinnesorgane, 39*, 401–428.

Piéron, H. (1920). Nouvelles recherches sur l'analyse du temps de latence sensorielle et sur la loi qui relie ce temps à l'intensité de l'excitation [New research on the analysis of sensory latency and about the law that relates this latency to the intensity of excitation]. *Année Psychologique, 22*, 58–142.

Piéron, H. (1925). Recherches expérimentales sur la marge de variation du temps de latence de la sensation lumineuse (par une méthode de masquage) [Experimental research on the amount of variation of the latency of light sensations (by a method of masking)]. *Année Psychologique, 26*, 1–30.

Piéron, H. (1927). L'influence de l'intensité sur le temps de réaction à la cessation d'un stimulus lumineux [The influence of intensity on reaction time to the cessation of a light stimulus]. *Compte Rendu de la Societé de Biologie, 97*, 1147–1149.

Prestrude, A. M., & Baker, H. D. (1968). New method of measuring visual-perceptual latency differences. *Perception & Psychophysics, 4*, 152–154.

Prinz, W. (1990). A common coding approach to perception and action. In O. Neumann & W. Prinz (Eds.), *Relationships between perception and action: Current approaches* (pp. 167–201). Berlin: Springer.

Prinz, W. (1992). Why don't we perceive our brain states? *European Journal of Cognitive Psychology, 4*, 1–20.

Prinz, W. (1997). Perception and action planning. *European Journal of Cognitive Psychology, 9*, 129–154.

Pulfrich, C. (1922). Die Stereoskopie im Dienste der isochromen und heterochromen Photometrie [Stereoscopy in the service of isochromical and heterochromical photometry]. *Die Naturwissenschaften, 10*, 553–564, 569–574, 714–722, 735–743, 751–761.

Roufs, J. A. J. (1963). Perception lag as a function of stimulus luminance. *Vision Research, 3*, 545–558.

Roufs, J. A. J. (1974). Dynamic properties of vision—V. Perception lag and reaction time in relation to flicker and flash thresholds. *Vision Research, 14*, 853–869.

Rutschmann, J., & Link, R. (1964). Perception of temporal order of stimuli differing in sense mode and simple reaction time. *Perceptual and Motor Skills, 18*, 345–352.

Rutschmann, R. (1973). Visual perception of temporal order. In S. Kornblum (Ed.), *Attention and performance IV* (pp. 687–701). New York: Academic Press.

Sanders, A. F. (1977). Structural and functional aspects of the reaction process. In S. Dornic (Ed.), *Attention and performance VI* (pp. 3–25). Hillsdale, NJ: Lawrence Erlbaum Associates.

Sanders, A. F. (1980). Stage analysis of reaction time. In G. E. Stelmach & J. Requin (Eds.), *Tutorials in motor behavior* (pp. 331–354). Amsterdam: North-Holland.

Sanders, A. F. (1983). Towards a model of stress and human performance. *Acta Psychologica, 53*, 61–67.

Sanders, A. F. (1990). Issues and trends in the debate on discrete vs. continuous processing of information. *Acta Psychologica, 74*, 123–167.

Schacter, D. L. (1987). Implicit memory: History and current status. *Journal of Experimental Psychology: Human Learning and Memory, 13*, 501–518.

Scharlau, I., Ansorge, U., & Neumann, O. (in press). Reaktionszeitmessung: Grundlagen und Anwendungen. [Reaction time measurement. Foundations and applications]. In G. Rickheit, T. Herrmann, & W. Deutsch (Eds.), *Psycholinguistik* (pp. 190–202). Berlin: de Gruyter.

Scharlau, I., & Neumann, O. (in press). Perceptual latency priming by masked and unmasked stimuli: Evidence for an attentional explanation. Psychological Research.

Schlaghecken, F., & Eimer, M. (1997). The influence of subliminally presented primes on response preparation. *Sprache und Kognition, 16*, 166–175.

Schlaghecken, F., & Eimer, M. (2001). Partial response activation to masked primes is not dependent on response readiness. *Perceptual and Motor Skills, 92*, 208–222.

Schlaghecken, F., & Eimer, M. (in press). Motor activation with and without inhibition: Evidence for a threshold mechanism in motor control. *Perception & Psychophysics.*

Smith, W. F. (1933). The relative quickness of visual and auditory perception. *Journal of Experimental Psychology, 16*, 239–270.

Steglich, C., & Neumann, O. (2000). Temporal, but not spatial, context modulates a masked prime's effect on temporal order judgment, but not on response latency. *Psychological Research, 63*, 36–47.

Sternberg, S. (1969). The discovery of processing stages: Extension of Donders' method. *Acta Psychologica, 30*, 276–315.

Sternberg, S., & Knoll, R. L. (1973). The perception of temporal order: Fundamental issues and a general model. In S. Kornblum (Ed.), *Attention and performance IV* (pp. 692–685). New York: Academic Press.

Stevens, S. S. (1955). Decibels of light and sound. *Physics Today, 8* (10), 12–17.

Sticht, T. G. (1969). Effects of intensity and duration on the latency of response to brief light and dark stimuli. *Journal of Experimental Psychology, 80*, 419–422.

Stroud, J. M. (1955). The fine structure of psychological time. In H. Quastler (Ed.), *Information theory in psychology* (pp. 174–207). Glencoe, IL: The Free Press.

Szili, A. (1892). Zur Erklärung der "flatternden Herzen" [On the explanation of "fluttering hearts"]. *Zeitschrift für Psychologie und Physiologie der Sinnesorgane, 3*, 359–387.

Tappe, T., Niepel, M., & Neumann, O. (1994). A dissociation between reaction time to sinusoidal gratings and temporal-order judgment. *Perception, 23*, 335–347.

Teichner, W. H., & Krebs, M. J. (1972). Laws of the simple visual reaction time. *Psychological Review, 79*, 344–358.

Titchener, E. B. (1908). *Lectures on the elementary psychology of feeling and attention.* New York: Macmillan.

Trincker, D. (1977). *Taschenbuch der Physiologie* [Manual of physiology] (Vol. III/2). Stuttgart: Gustav Fischer.

Ueno, T. (1977). Reaction time as a measure of temporal summation at suprathreshold levels. *Vision Research, 17*, 227–232.

Ulrich, R., & Stapf, K. H. (1984). A double-reponse paradigm to study stimulus intensity effects upon the motor system in simple reaction time experiments. *Perception & Psychophysics, 36*, 545–558.

Vanderhaeghen, C., & Bertelson, P. (1974). The limits of prior entry: Nonsensitivity of temporal order judgments to selective preparation affecting choice reaction time. *Bulletin of the Psychonomic Society, 4*, 569–572.

Vaughan, H. G., Costa, L. D., & Gilden, L. (1966). The functional relation of visual evoked response and reaction time to stimulus intensity. *Vision Research, 6*, 645–656.

Whipple, G. M. (1899). On nearly simultaneous clicks and flashes. *American Journal of Psychology, 10*, 880–886.

Woodworth, R. S., & Schlosberg, H. (1954). *Experimental psychology.* New York: Holt, Rinehart & Winston.

Wundt, W. (1903). *Grundzüge der physiologischen Psychologie* [Outlines of physiological psychology] (5th ed.). Leipzig, Germany: Engelmann.

12

Invariant Time Course of Priming With and Without Awareness

Dirk Vorberg, Uwe Mattler, Armin Heinecke,
Thomas Schmidt, and Jens Schwarzbach
Technische Universität Braunschweig, Germany

It is customary in all branches of psychophysics to determine the limits of sensory systems from perceptual judgments. As an example, in the psychophysics of visual masking, responses in forced-choice tasks are conventionally considered as reports of the subjective experience arising from the masked stimulus. Such reports are supposed to summarize all information that is available to the visual system and to reflect the system's limits of resolution for stimuli in close temporal vicinity. This assumption, however, is unwarranted to the degree that perception is possible without awareness, and dissociations between perceptual judgments and motor responses (e.g., grasping) presumably not based on awareness have in fact been demonstrated recently (Aglioti, DeSousa, & Goodale, 1995; but see Franz, Gegenfurtner, Bülthoff, & Fahle, 2000).

The issue of perception without awareness, or subliminal perception, has a long history in psychology. For decades, researchers have sought to demonstrate that judgments or actions can be affected by stimuli of which we are not aware without reaching unanimous consensus on definitional and methodological issues (Holender, 1986; Reingold & Merikle, 1993). However, a wealth of recent studies with neurological patients suffering, for example, from hemispatial neglect or from blindsight (see Köhler & Moscovitch, 1997; Weiskrantz, 1997), and with normal subjects (see He, Cavanagh, & Intriligator, 1996; MacLeod, 1998; Merikle &

Daneman, 2000) document behavioral effects of stimuli that truly remain outside conscious awareness. Current research focuses on whether unconscious and conscious processes produce qualitatively different effects, following the assumption that conscious perception allows voluntary control, whereas information registered without awareness leads to automatic reactions at best. It is well known that conscious experience does not arise instantaneously with the stimulus but lags behind by some 100 ms (e.g., Libet, 1996; Nijhawan, 1994, 1997). Speeded motor responses are therefore unlikely to be exclusively based on visual awareness. This brings us to the question that guided the research reported here: Can stimuli that are not available for visual awareness be used to control fast motor responses, and is the temporal dynamics of their effects different from that of consciously perceived stimuli?

We used metacontrast masking to manipulate awareness of stimuli. Metacontrast masking is a form of backward masking in which the visibility of a briefly flashed stimulus is reduced if it is followed by a spatially flanking stimulus (Breitmeyer, 1984). Metacontrast can prevent stimuli from being noticed that would otherwise be clearly seen. However, masked stimuli ("primes"), even though invisible, can influence responses to masking stimuli ("masks"). For example, simple reactions to the mask are speeded up by undetected primes (Fehrer & Raab, 1962). Moreover, unrecognized primes facilitate or inhibit choice reactions to the mask if they share stimulus attributes with the mask that are critical for the correct or the alternative response (Klotz & Neumann, 1999; Neumann & Klotz, 1994). Our experiments extend these findings and show that conscious perception and unconscious behavioral effects of masked primes obey different temporal dynamics.

EXPERIMENT 1

We studied perceptual masking and priming in tasks that differed only with respect to which stimulus served as target but that left stimulus conditions identical. On each trial, a prime arrow was presented briefly, followed after a variable stimulus-onset asynchrony (SOA) by a mask arrow at the same location; see Fig. 12.1(a). Perceptual masking was studied in a recognition task that asked subjects to report the orientation of the prime stimulus. The *time course of masking* was determined by measuring prime recognition at different SOAs. Priming was studied in a task in which subjects had to produce choice reactions to the mask. Whether primes, although masked, affect responses to the mask is revealed by the effects of prime–mask congruence on response time (RT). Prime and mask are congruent if they have identical orientation, and they are incongruent otherwise. The amount of priming was assessed by the RT advantage on congruent as compared with incongruent trials. We determined the *time course of priming* by the net advantage at different SOAs. The goal of Experiment 1 was to dissociate masking and priming by their

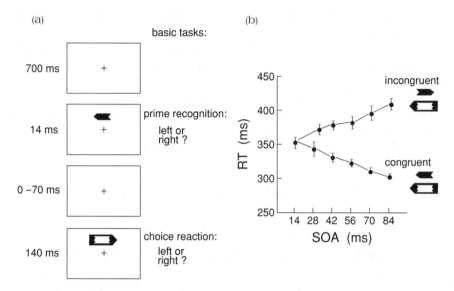

FIG. 12.1. (a) Temporal sequence of a typical experimental trial. Left- and right-oriented arrows served as prime and mask stimuli. The orientation of prime and mask varied unpredictably from trial to trial. (b) Effects of congruent and incongruent primes on choice RT as a function of the SOA, in the first session of Experiment 1. Error bars indicate ± SE around means. From Vorberg et al. (2003). © 2003 National Academy of Sciences, U.S.A.

time courses. We wanted to show an increase in priming over an SOA range where masking is complete and its time course virtually flat. To check the generality of our findings, we used several variants of the two basic tasks described herein.

Method

Subjects. Six students from the University of Braunschweig, aged 20–42 years, were tested in nine 1-hr sessions each.

Stimuli. Left and right arrows served as prime and mask stimuli (see Fig. 12.1). They were presented black on white, on an Atari SM 124 monitor Atari Corporation, Sunnyvale, CA at a refresh rate of 70 Hz. Primes subtended visual angles of 0.8° × 1.86°, masks 1.09° × 3.47°, and were positioned 1.38° above or below the fixation cross. The outer contour of the prime stimuli coincided with the inner contour of the central cutout of the masks. The prime duration was 14 ms; the mask duration was 140 ms. Prime–mask SOA varied randomly from trial to trial, in steps of 14 ms, from 14 to 70 ms in Tasks b, c, and d, and between 14 and 84 ms in Tasks a and e (see the paragraphs that follow).

Design. Perceptual and behavioral effects of the prime stimuli were assessed by both direct and indirect tasks. Direct tasks were used for testing how well subjects could detect or recognize the prime stimulus. In a detection task, subjects decided whether a prime was present or absent; in recognition tasks, they reported the prime's orientation. Indirect tasks were used to assess effects of the primes on the speed of responding to the mask. In a simple RT task, subjects reacted bimanually to the onset of the mask; in choice RT tasks, they responded to the mask's orientation. Direct and indirect tasks were administered, either separately or jointly, in the following sequence:

a. Choice RT only (Session 1; 612 trials).

b. Choice RT and detection combined (Sessions 2 + 3; 1,224 trials). For each trial, subjects reacted to the orientation of the mask and then indicated whether they had detected a prime. Detection responses had to be delayed by 250 ms from their choice response. Primes were present on 5/6 of the trials.

c. Simple RT and recognition combined (Sessions 4 + 5; 1,512 trials). Subjects gave a bimanual simple reaction to the onset of the prime–mask compound, and after a delay of 600 ms they reported on the prime's orientation. Left, right, and neutral masks (with a rectangular outer contour) occurred equally often; the type of mask was either random or fixed within blocks.

d. Recognition only (Sessions 6 + 7; 1,512 trials). Subjects reported the orientation of the prime, disregarding the shape of the mask (left, right, or neutral). To prevent indirect priming effects of recognition, subjects were instructed to respond after a delay of 600 ms after the mask. Other details are as in Task c.

e. Choice RT only (Session 9; 612 trials).

Data from an additional task (prime recognition under speed stress; Session 8) are not reported.

Procedure. Trials started with the fixation cross, followed after 700 ms by the prime either above or below, and the mask at the same position; in Task e, prime and mask appeared at the center of the screen in half of the trials. Responses were given by pressing the appropriate response button with the left or right index finger. Visual feedback was provided on choice RT error trials; auditory feedback was provided on recognition error trials. Summary feedback (mean RT; percentage correct) was given at the end of each block. Subjects were not informed about the existence of primes before Session 2.

Statistical Methods. Detection and recognition performances were analyzed by use of signal-detection methods (Macmillan & Creelman, 1991), which gave essentially the same results as the percentage-correct measure reported here. Performance indices were estimated separately per subject and condition, and they were tested for significance by means of Pearson's χ^2 calculated from the corresponding prime $\times$ response cross-table. Global tests are based on the χ^2 statistics summed across subjects and conditions (see Fleiss, 1981).

Choice RTs were summarized by trimmed means on correct trials, determined per subject and condition. RT difference scores were analyzed by repeated-measures analyses of variance (ANOVAs). Errors bars in graphs are based on the standard error of the difference between two means, estimated from the corresponding ANOVA interaction error term (Loftus & Masson, 1994).

Results

Detection and Recognition Performance. Figure 12.2 (top) shows that metacontrast masking precluded recognition of the primes, as in Figs. 12.2(c) and 12.2(d), but not their detection, as in Fig. 12.2(b). In the detection task, Task b, the probability of a correct detection increased from .023 at SOA = 14 ms to .810 at SOA = 70 ms, compared with an overall false-alarm rate of .026 on blank trials. These values correspond to detection ds of -0.05 and 2.82, respectively. However, at no SOA from 14 to 70 ms could subjects report the orientation of the primes, neither when recognition was administered separately (Task d) nor jointly with choice reaction (Task c). Recognition performance remained at chance level across these more than 3,000 trials with error feedback (Task c, $\chi^2_{180} = 186.63$, $p = .352$; Task d, $\chi^2_{180} = 200.61$, $p = .139$).

Response Priming. Even though perfectly masked, the primes strongly affected the speed of choice responses to the mask. Figure 12.1(b) provides a typical example: congruent primes sped up, and incongruent primes slowed down, responses to the orientation of the mask. These effects strongly depended on the SOA between prime and mask, as shown by the *priming function*, that is, the net effect $RT_{incong} - RT_{cong}$ at a given SOA (bottom of Fig. 12.2). The empirical priming function remained invariant in three different phases of the experiment: in Task a before subjects had been informed about the occurrence of the primes, in Task b where the combined choice RT and detection task required subjects to focus their attention on both mask and prime, and in Task d, after five sessions of prime recognition. Neither intercept nor slope (mean 1.54) of the priming function varied across sessions [F (2,10) = .007, $p = .993$].

Controlling Bias in Recognition Judgments. To ensure that the observed lack of ability to report the critical prime features was real and not due to subtle influences of the mask on recognition judgment, we analyzed the data in greater detail and sorted trials according to type of mask (left, right, or neutral). It is important to note that mask orientation biases recognition reports, which may produce spurious effects unless controlled. There is no agreement on the proper treatment of this problem in the literature. We sketch the different approaches and their merits, from the perspective of signal detection theory (SDT).

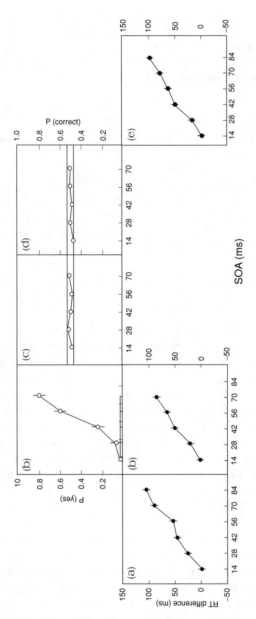

FIG. 12.2. Masking and priming as a function of the SOA in Experiment 1. The sequence of panels corresponds to the order in which the tasks were performed. Top row: Detection and recognition of masked primes: (b) hit rate (open circles) and false-alarm rate (solid curve) in prime detection; (c)–(d) probability of correct prime recognition. Dotted lines indicate the region where performance does not significantly differ from chance. Bottom row: Effect of prime–mask congruence on choice RT: (a) initial, (b) middle, and (e) final sessions. Error bars are based on the SE of the difference between two means: nonoverlapping error bars indicate that the corresponding means differ with $\alpha = .05$. From Vorberg et al. (2003). © 2003 National Academy of Sciences, U.S.A.

We arbitrarily define hit and false-alarm rates by the proportion of "left" reports to a left and right prime, respectively, and allow these rates to depend on which mask was presented on a trial (see Table 12.1). In Exp. 1, recognition responses were in fact strongly influenced by the type of mask, and we suspect that this effect was largely strategic. For example, a subject in Schmidt's study (2000) claimed to have given the response complementary to the mask whenever she had noticed some flicker, but chose the response matching the mask otherwise.

TABLE 12.1
Alternative Ways of Analyzing Recognition Performance

Stimulus-response matrices in prime recognition, sorted according to (a) type of mask, (b) prime-mask congruence, or (c) neither. L, R: "left" or "right" response; H, F: hit and false-alarm rates, respectively, where $H = P(L \mid \text{left prime})$ and $F = P(L \mid \text{right prime})$. Subscripts indicate type of mask, dark and light shading congruent and incongruent trials, respectively.

(a)

	left mask			right mask	
	L	R		L	R
left prime	H_l	$1 - H_l$	left prime	H_r	$1 - H_r$
right prime	F_l	$1 - F_l$	right prime	F_r	$1 - F_r$

(b)

	congruent			incongruent	
	L	R		L	R
left prime	H_l	$1 - H_l$	left prime	H_r	$1 - H_r$
right prime	F_r	$1 - F_r$	right prime	F_l	$1 - F_l$

(c)

	L	R
left prime	$(H_l+H_r)/2$	$1 - (H_l+H_r)/2$
right prime	$(F_r+F_l)/2$	$1 - (F_r+F_l)/2$

Pooling data across mask type (Table 12.1c) is the approach most frequently taken (e.g., Neumann & Klotz, 1994; Leuthold & Kopp, 1998; Klotz & Neumann, 1999). But it is well known that computing sensitivity measures like d' from averaged hit and false alarm rates underestimates sensitivity unless bias did not vary across mask types (Macmillan & Creelman, 1991, p. 276–277). Obviously, d's close to zero computed from pooled data cannot refute the claim that true sensitivity might have been above chance.

Sorting trials by prime-mask congruence, and subsequently computing separate recognition d's has been suggested to us by several researchers. This approach, also used by Klotz and Neumann (1999), seems intuitively appealing but severely confounds sensitivity with bias, as we now demonstrate. Let recognition performance of primes followed by a type m mask be summarized by hit and false-alarm rates (H_m, F_m). In the Gaussian equal-variance SDT model, $d'_m = z(H_m) - z(F_m)$. Assume that the mask changes the response criterion on the trial, but leaves sensitivity unaffected, i.e. $d'_l = d'_r = d'$. What does this imply for the sensitivity measure when assessed separately for congruent and incongruent trials? Table 1b illustrates that congruent hits occur on trials with left prime followed by left mask, but congruent false-alarms occur on trials with right prime followed by right mask. Thus, recognition performance gives (H_l, F_r) for congruent, and, by analogy, (H_r, F_l) for incongruent mask. Therefore,

$$d'_{\text{cong}} = z(H_l) - z(F_r) = [z(H_l) - z(F_l)] + [z(F_l) - z(F_r)] = d' + \Delta\beta,$$

and

$$d'_{\text{incong}} = z(H_r) - z(F_l) = [z(H_r) - z(F_r)] + [z(F_r) - z(F_l)] = d' - \Delta\beta,$$

where $\Delta\beta = z(F_l) - z(F_r)$ is the differential effect of the mask on response bias (in z units). This shows that true sensitivity is misestimated unless $\Delta\beta = 0$. As an example, consider the case when left and right masks induce "left" responses with probability .7 and .3, respectively, independent of prime orientation. Assessing sensitivity by congruence gives $d'_{\text{congruent}} = 1.05$ and $d'_{\text{incongruent}} = -1.05$, in spite of true sensitivity $d'_l = d'_r = 0$.

The obvious way to remove response bias effects of the mask is to follow the recommendation given by SDT: When estimating sensitivity, keep conditions constant that affect response bias. Therefore, we computed separate d's for each mask type, and averaged the resulting estimates d'_l and d'_r.

In the analysis reported above, trials were sorted according to task (c or d), SOA, mask (left, right, or neutral), and whether mask shape varied or was constant within a block. For each single subject × trial type stimulus-response matrix, we tested by (two-sided) χ^2-test whether hit rate deviated from false-alarm rate. Just 24 out of the 360 Pearson-χ_1^2 statistics altogether exceeded the critical value at

$\alpha = .05$, a mere excess of 6 over the 18 to be expected by chance. To counter the objection that sample size was too small (each response rate was based on 24 observations per stimulus) to be approximated well by the χ^2-distribution, and that d' might be estimated more efficiently from pooled data in this case (Macmillan & Creelman, 1991, p. 280–281), we performed additional analyses based on response rate pooled across subjects. With right or left masks, recognition performance gave mean $d' = -.003$ under varied conditions ($\chi^2_{20} = 21.52$, $p = 0.367$) and mean $d' = .003$ when mask was blocked ($\chi^2_{20} = 19.10$, $p = 0.515$). Even with neutral masks, performance was not reliably better than chance, although there were minimal improvements (varied: $d' = .078$, $\chi^2_{10} = 15.17$, $p = 0.126$; blocked: $d' = .111$, $\chi^2_{10} = 14.17$, $p = 0.165$). The conclusion was the same as before: No evidence was found that on critical trials (left or right masks within mixed blocks), subjects were able to report the orientation of the primes any better than chance.

Experiment 1 thus provides strong evidence for subliminal priming and demonstrates a clear dissociation between masking and priming. RTs to the mask showed large priming effects that increased with SOA, in spite of total masking of the primes, evidenced by the flat masking function that never exceeded chance level. Note that detection performance was better than chance, except at the shortest SOA. Here the priming effect was also zero, which may indicate that primes can become effective only if visual information is sufficient for detecting their presence.

EXPERIMENT 2

Although Experiment 1 succeeded in showing large priming effects within an SOA range in which recognition performance was at chance, one might nevertheless argue that our findings are just due to different sensitivity ranges of the direct and the indirect measures and do not truly reflect separate mechanisms underlying perceptual and motor effects. To counter this objection, we studied the time course of priming under conditions in which masking effects followed a time course that was either monotonically decreasing or nonmonotonic with SOA. With this manipulation, we could also assess whether the dissociation between masking and priming, if still existent, holds for supraliminal primes as well. To this end, we varied the critical stimulus durations in Experiment 2 to render the primes more visible.

Method

Subjects. Six students from the University of Braunschweig, aged 21–29 years, were tested in seven 1-hr sessions each. The students had not participated in Experiment 1.

Design. Stimuli and procedure were identical to those of Experiment 1. Choice reaction and prime recognition (corresponding to Tasks a and d already described) were tested separately, administered in the order a-d-a per session, each of which consisted of 504 choice reaction and 252 recognition trials. In recognition, only left and right masks were used, which occurred equally often within blocks. Prime and mask durations varied randomly, with values of 14 ms or 42 ms each. The prime–mask interstimulus interval (ISI) varied between 0 and 70 ms in steps of 14 ms; therefore, SOA varied between 14 and 84 ms for 14-ms primes, and between 42 and 112 ms for 42-ms primes.

Statistical Methods. Recognition performance was analyzed by repeated-measures ANOVAs of the arcsine-transformed frequencies of correct responses; signal-detection analyses gave essentially the same results. Statistical analysis methods of the RT priming were the same as in Experiment 1. Data reported are from Sessions 3–7.

Results and Discussion

As expected, reducing mask duration and increasing prime duration improved recognition performance (see Fig. 12.3, top row). Varying mask duration produced almost additive effects, with short masks giving rise to less perceptual masking than long ones [mask, $F(1, 5) = 96.35$, $p < .0005$; Prime $\times$ Mask, $F(1, 5 = .941$, $p = .377$; Mask $\times$ ISI, $F(5, 25) = 2.67$, $p = .046$]. Varying prime duration, in contrast, produced qualitative changes in masking dynamics; see Figs. 12.3(a) and 12.3(b). Whereas short primes were recognized better the later the mask appeared, recognition of long primes was best at the shortest SOA [prime, $F(1, 5) = 33.91$, $p = .002$; Prime $\times$ ISI, $F(5, 25) = 7.92$, $p < .0005$]. In the masking literature, such monotonously increasing and U-shaped time courses are known as "Type A" and "Type B" functions, respectively (Breitmeyer, 1984).

This qualitative change of the masking function with the physical stimulus parameters is in stark contrast to the RT effects (Fig. 12.3, bottom row). Again, congruent primes led to faster responding to the mask than incongruent primes, and the effect increased with SOA. The shape of the priming function is very similar to that observed in Experiment 1, and it remains invariant across conditions that strongly affect perceptual masking. Although primes followed by long masks were clearly less visible than those followed by short masks, they produced equal effects on RT [mask, $F(1, 5) = .30$, $p = .606$). Even more striking is the finding that priming was identical under Type A and under Type B masking conditions [prime, $F(1, 5) = .67$, $p = .450$; Prime $\times$ ISI, $F(5, 25) = .73$, $p = .543$]. This suggests that the critical stimulus attributes of the prime are fully processed whether they reach visual awareness or not.

This conclusion is supported by an analysis of the errors in the RT task. On congruent trials the error rate was below 3%, at any SOA and in both experiments. On incongruent trials, however, the error rate increased dramatically with

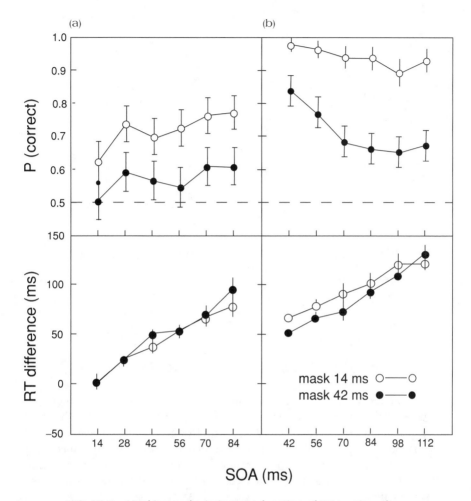

FIG. 12.3. Masking and priming as a function of SOA, prime duration, and mask duration in Experiment 2: (a) prime 14 ms; (b) prime
42 ms. Error bars indicate ±*SE* around means. Top row: Probability of correct prime recognition. Bottom row: Effect of prime–mask
congruence on choice RT. From Vorberg et al. (2003). © 2003
National Academy of Sciences, U.S.A.

SOA; see Fig. 12.4. Such an error pattern rules out interpretations in terms of
fast guessing triggered by the mere detection of the prime (Yellott, 1971). These
data seem also at odds with the hypothesis that primes remain unprocessed
yet exert their effects by facilitating or inhibiting the processing of the mask
(Bachmann, 1984; Neumann & Klotz, 1994). Contrary to these views, primes seem
to fully activate their corresponding response, eliciting incorrect responses on incongruent trials unless countermanded, but correct responses on congruent trials.
This interpretation is also supported by recent neurophysiological evidence for

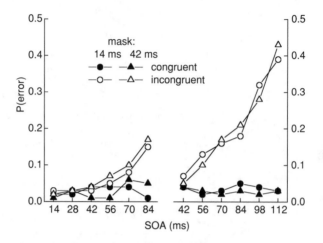

FIG. 12.4. Error rates a function of prime-mask congruence, SOA, prime duration, and mask duration in Experiment 2. Left: Error rates for 14 ms primes. Right: Error rates for 42 ms primes.

prime-related activation of the motor cortex (Dehaene et al., 1998; Leuthold & Kopp, 1998).

THE SLOPE OF THE PRIMING FUNCTION

How can one account for the detailed time courses of masking and priming? The complex dynamics of metacontrast masking seems well understood with regard to its perceptual aspects (Francis, 1997, 2000). However, priming phenomena and the dissociation of priming from masking seem out of reach to current theorizing on masking. As a preliminary to a quantitative model of priming, we analyzed the RT data from Experiment 2 more closely. They are fit surprisingly well by the linear function

$$RT_{incong} - RT_{cong} = SOA + b,$$

with slope equal to 1, and intercept b equal to 0 except for the 42-ms primes. Within the overlapping SOA range from 42 to 84 ms, the slope of the empirical priming functions did not differ from 1 [mean = 0.96; $F(1, 5) = 0.12$, $p = 0.74$]. At shorter SOAs, the slope slightly exceeded 1, as in Experiment 1.

Why should prolonging SOA by 20 ms, say, increase the net priming effect by about the same 20 ms? Most current models do not predict the unit slope except for particular parameters. We have proposed a model (Vorberg, Mattler, Heinecke, Schmidt, & Schwarzbach, 2003) that predicts the slope nonparametrically. Our model modifies and extends the accumulator model proposed Hanes and Schall (1996), but differs in the details of the stochastic accumulation process and by assuming saturation, which turns out to be crucial. Separate accumulators are assumed to collect neural evidence for stimuli that require left or right responses, initiating a response when the accumulated neural for it exceeds that for the alternative response by some a critical value.

According to our model, priming effects arise because primes bias the accumulators, driving their difference towards the target threshold on congruent trials, and away from it on incongruent trials. The bias induced by the prime keeps growing until the mask occurs, which implies that the difference $RT_{incong} - RT_{cong}$ increases almost linearly with SOA. Analysis of the model has revealed that the effective slope of the priming function is insensitive to the value of the accumulation rates, but the degree of saturation is crucial. The slope of the theoretical priming function is bounded between 1 and 2, approaching the limit 1 as SOA increases, which accounts well for our findings.

The characteristic linear priming function with slope near one that we found for Exps. 1 and 2 has been found for other types of stimuli and responses as well, e.g., color (Schmidt, 2000), symbolic stimuli (Vorberg, 2002), pointing (Schmidt, 2002), saccadic eye-movements and vocal responses. Figure 12.5 shows the results of an experiment that contrasted manual with vocal responding (Vorberg, unpublished), under the same conditions as in Exp. 1 (task a). Although vocal responses, as measured by voice key, were slower by about 130 ms than manual responses, the net priming effects were indistinguishable from each other on statistical grounds. As seen, both priming functions were almost perfectly linear, with slope slightly larger than 1.

Schwarzbach (1999) studied saccadic eye movements to one of eight target positions indicated by a central cue the was preceded by a masked prime. Primes and cues were arrow-shaped; as in the other experiments presented here, the imperative stimulus also served as mask (Fig. 12.6a). Congruence between prime and cue was defined by the absolute angular difference $|\phi_{cue} - \phi_{prime}|$. Saccadic reaction times differed as a function of congruence and SOA (Fig. 12.6b), showing facilitation if prime and cue were fully congruent ($0°$) and inhibition if prime and cue orientation differed by $180°$. Except for the $135°$ condition, priming effects were ordered by congruence, and increased with SOA. For comparison with the two-response findings, Schwarzbach computed the difference $RT_{180°} - RT_{0°}$ as a function of SOA, and also found a linear priming function, but with slope .8.

These results indicate that the findings reported here generalize across widely different stimulus and response attributes, which has theoretical implications that are discussed below.

GENERAL DISCUSSION

Our experiments have revealed two types of dissociation between masking and priming:

Subliminal priming refers to the finding that the priming function increases with the SOA, in spite of perfect masking. Subliminal priming provides compelling

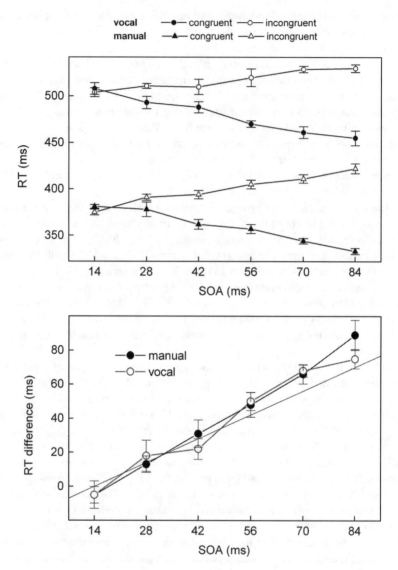

FIG. 12.5. Priming of manual and vocal choice-response times by masked primes (Vorberg, unpublished). Experimental details as in Exp. 1, task a, except that subjects responded to the target stimuli by naming the words "left" or "right" in half of the sessions. Top: Mean RT on congruent and incongruent trials. Bottom: Net priming effects and slope 1 prediction. Error bars give critical range around means, constructed such that non-overlapping bars indicate significant difference between means at a given SOA ($\alpha = .05$).

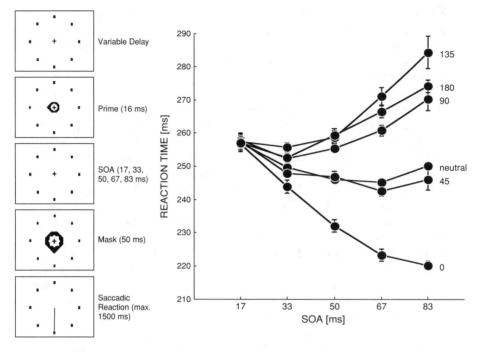

FIG. 12.6. Priming of saccadic latencies (Schwarzbach, 1999). Left: Trial events. Subjects started trials by key press. After a delay a prime pointing to one of eight target positions appeared for 17ms, followed by a target presented for 50 ms with a variable SOA. The task was to direct gaze to the position indicated by the target. The angle between prime and target direction varied between 0° and 180°. Right: Mean saccadic reaction times as a function of congruence and SOA. Error bars indicate ± SE around means.

evidence for behavioral effects of stimuli that do not access awareness, and it suggests that metacontrast masking abolishes conscious perception of a prime but not its motor effect. Obviously, masking and priming reflect different mechanisms.

Invariant priming with and without awareness concerns the finding that the priming function is shape invariant in spite of qualitative changes in masking. This major new finding held for perfect masking, and for Type A and Type B masking. Invariant priming under such a wide range of conditions implies a visuomotor mechanism for which conscious perception is not a prerequisite. One possible implementation of such a mechanism is the neural accumulator model proposed here.

At first sight, invariant priming seems to contradict the qualitative difference in the effects of unconscious and conscious prime stimuli reported recently (Greenwald, Draine, & Abrams, 1996; Merikle & Joordens, 1997a, 1997b). We believe that those findings reflect effects of conscious control of action, which arise relatively late in the processing chain. In contrast, the invariance of priming with and without awareness is a characteristic of early processing stages, and it is typically found in experiments with prime–target SOAs that are shorter than 100 ms (Vorberg, 2000).

The reported dissociations are consistent with the notion of separate action and perception systems (Milner & Goodale, 1995). To account for them, we assume that, within the perception system, visual stimuli are not processed further and thus remain invisible if they are overwritten by new input before their boundary contours have been computed and filled in (Francis, 1997; Grossberg & Mingolla, 1985). This view is backed by neurophysiological and psychophysical evidence (Jeffreys & Musselwhite, 1986; Bridgeman, 1975; 1980; 1988). In single-cell recordings, Macknik and Livingstone (1998) have observed an after-discharge of cells in the primary visual cortex some 100 ms after the offset of the prime stimulus, which is suppressed when a mask follows. From the similarity of the temporal dynamics of neural suppression and perceptual masking, these authors concluded that the after-discharge is crucial for perception. The action system, in contrast, seems to have access to shape information of unseen stimuli, possibly from their unfilled contours, and to integrate rather than overwrite evidence from prime and mask. Such information integration across prime and mask is the crucial assumption in our accumulator model.

The generality of our priming findings across stimulus and response types, described above, seems to be in opposition with central notions of Milner and Goodale's theory, such as the role of color processing in the action system, and the importance of hard-wired connections to effectors. These observations are consistent with our model, however, which may be seen as reflecting either a general principle of response priming that different local mechanisms obey, or the operation of a single central decision module, probably located within the prefrontal cortex, which is programmable to link arbitrary sensory output to action.

The findings reported in this paper show that perceptual measures based on conscious reports do not suffice to determine whether some information is or is not available to the visual system at large. Instead, motor and perceptual effects can be become perfectly dissociated. This indicates that relevant stimulus attributes are fully processed up to the level of response control but remain unavailable for conscious report. It is also clear that classical psychophysical measures do not necessarily reflect all information available to the visual system, and they should be supplemented by performance measures that do not tap perceptual awareness. We believe that our approach of contrasting direct and indirect performance measures and of dissociating perception and action by their time courses may provide, in conjunction with neurophysiological and functional brain imaging approaches, a more complete picture of information processing within the visual system.

ACKNOWLEDGMENTS

We thank Marianne Wunderow for testing the subjects and preparing the figures, and we thank Ulrich Mayr, Peter Wolff, Werner Klotz, Angelika Lingnau, Ernst Niebur, and especially Pienie Zwitserlood for their discussions and helpful suggestions.

REFERENCES

Aglioti, S., DeSouza, J. F., & Goodale, M. A. (1995). Size-contrast illusions deceive the eye but not the hand. *Current Biolology, 5*, 679–685.

Bachmann, T. (1984). The process of perceptual retouch: Nonspecific afferent activation dynamics in explaining visual masking. *Perception & Psychophysics, 35*, 69–84.

Breitmeyer, B. (1984). *Visual masking: An integrative approach.* Oxford, England: Oxford University Press.

Bridgeman, B. (1975). Correlates of metacontrast in single cells of the cat visual system. *Vision Research, 15*, 91–99.

Bridgeman, B. (1980). Temporal response characteristics of cells in monkey striate cortex measured with metacontrast masking and brightness discrimination. *Brain Research, 196*, 347–364.

Bridgeman, B. (1988). Visual evoked potentials: Concomitants of metacontrast in the late components. *Perception & Psychophysics, 43*, 401–403.

Dehaene, S., Naccache, L., Le Clec'H, G., Koechlin, E., Mueller, M., Dehaene-Lambertz, G., van de Moortele, P. F., & Le Bihan, D. (1998). Imaging unconscious semantic priming. *Nature, 395*, 597–600.

Fehrer, E., & Raab, D. (1962). Reaction time to stimuli masked by metacontrast. *Journal of Experimental Psychology, 63*, 143–147.

Fleiss, J. L. (1981). *Statistical methods for rates and proportions.* New York: Wiley.

Francis, G. (1997). Cortical dynamics of lateral inhibition: Metacontrast masking. *Psychological Review, 104*, 572–594.

Francis, G. (2000). Quantitative theories of metacontrast masking. *Psychological Review, 107*, 768–785.

Franz, V. H., Gegenfurtner, K. R., Bülthoff, H. H., & Fahle, M. (2000). Grasping visual illusions: No evidence for a dissociation between perception and action. *Psychological Science, 11*, 20–25.

Greenwald, A. S., Draine, S. C., & Abrams, R. L. (1996). Three cognitive markers of unconscious semantic activation. *Science, 273*, 1699–1702.

Grossberg, S., & Mingolla, E. (1985). Neural dynamics of form perception: Boundary completion, illusory figures and neon color spreading. *Psychological Review, 92*, 173–211.

Hanes, D. P., & Schall, J. D. (1996). Neural control of voluntary movement initiation. *Science, 274*, 427–430.

He, S., Cavanagh, P., & Intriligator, J. (1996). Attentional resolution and the locus of visual awareness. *Nature, 383*, 334–337.

Holender, D. (1986). Semantic activation without conscious identification in dichotic listening, parafoveal vision and visual masking: A survey and appraisal. *Behavioral and Brain Sciences, 9*, 1–66.

Jeffreys, D., & Musselwhite, M. (1986). A visual evoked potential study of metacontrast masking. *Vision Research, 26*, 631–642.

Köhler, S., & Moscovitch, M. (1997). Unconscious visual processing in neuropsychological syndromes: A survey of the literature and evaluation of models of consciousness. In M. Rugg (Ed.), *Cognitive neuroscience* (pp. 305–373). Hove, England: Psychology Press.

Klotz, W., & Neumann, O. (1999). Motor activation without conscious discrimination in metacontrast masking. *Journal of Experimental Psychology: Human Perception and Performance, 25,* 976–992.

Leuthold, H., & Kopp, B. (1998). Mechanisms of priming by masked stimuli: Inferences from event-related brain potentials. *Psychological Science, 9,* 263–269.

Libet, B. (1996). Neural processes in the production of conscious experience. In M. Velmans (Ed.), *The science of consciousness. Psychological, neuropsychological and clinical reviews* (pp. 96–117). London: Routledge.

Loftus, G. R., & Masson, M. E. J. (1994). Using confidence intervals in within-subject designs. *Psychonomic Bulletin & Review, 1,* 476–490.

Macknik, S. L., & Livingstone, M. S. (1998). Neural correlates of visibility and invisibility in the primate visual system. *Nature Neuroscience, 1,* 144–149.

MacLeod, C. (1997). Implicit perception: Perceptual processing without awareness. In K. Kirsner (Ed.), *Implicit and explicit mental processes* (pp. 57–78). Mahwah, NJ: Lawrence Erlbaum Associates.

Macmillan, N. A., & Creelman, C. D. (1991). *Detection theory: A user's guide.* Cambridge, England: Cambridge University Press.

Merikle, P. M., & Daneman, M. (2000). Conscious vs. unconscious perception. In M. S. Gazzaniga (Ed.), *The new cognitive neurosciences* (pp. 1295–1303). Cambridge, MA: MIT Press.

Merikle, P. M., & Joordens, S. (1997a). Measuring unconscious influences. In J. D. Cohen & J. W. Schooler (Eds.), *Scientific approaches to consciousness* (pp. 109–123). Mahwah, NJ: Lawrence Erlbaum Associates.

Merikle, P. M., & Joordens, S. (1997b). Parallels between perception without attention and perception without awareness. *Consciousness & Cognition, 6,* 219–236.

Milner, A. D., & Goodale, M. A. (1995). *The visual brain in action.* Oxford, England: Oxford University Press.

Neumann, O., & Klotz, W. (1994). Motor responses to nonreportable, masked stimuli: Where is the limit of direct parameter specification? In C. Umiltà & M. Moscovitch (Eds.), *Attention & Performance XV* (pp. 124–150). Cambridge, MA: MIT Press.

Nijhawan, R. (1994). Motion extrapolating in catching. *Nature, 370,* 256–257.

Nijhawan, R. (1997). Visual decomposition of color through motion extrapolation. *Nature, 386,* 66–69.

Reingold, E. M., & Merikle, P. M. (1993). Theory and measurement in the study of unconscious processes. In M. Davies & G. W. Humphreys (Eds.), *Consciousness* (pp. 40–57). Oxford, England: Blackwell.

Schmidt, T. (2000). Visual perception without awareness: Priming responses by color. In T. Metzinger (Ed.), *Neural correlates of consciousness: Empirical and conceptual questions* (pp. 157–169). Cambridge, MA: MIT Press.

Schmidt, T. (2002). The finger in flight: Real-time motor control by visually masked color stimuli. *Psychological Science, 13,* 112–118.

Schwarzbach, J. (1999). *Priming of eye movements by masked stimuli.* Unpublished doctoral dissertation, Technical University, Braunschweig, Germany.

Vorberg, D. (2000). Wann wirken unbewusste Reize anders als bewusste? In H. H. Bülthoff, M. Fahle, K. R. Gegenfurtner, & H. Mallot (Eds.), *Beiträge zur 3. Tübinger Wahrnehmungskonferenz* (p. 133). Kirchentellinsfurt, Germany: Knirsch.

Vorberg, D. (2000). Gibt es unbewusste Wahrnehmung, und wenn ja, warum nicht? In M. Baumann, A. Keinath, & J. F. Krems (Eds.), *Experimentelle Psychologie. Abstracts der 44. Tagung experimentell arbeitender Psychologen* (p. 8). Regensburg: Roderer Verlag.

Vorberg, D., Mattler, U., Heinecke, A., Schmidt, T., & Schwarzbach, J. (2003). Different time courses for visual perception and action priming. *Proceedings of the National Academy of Sciences, 100,* 6275–6280.

Weiskrantz, L. (1997). *Consciousness lost and found.* Oxford, England: Oxford University Press.

Yellott, J. I., Jr. (1971). Correction for fast guessing and the speed-accuracy tradeoff in choice reaction time. *Journal of Mathematical Psychology, 8,* 159–199.

13

Visual Marking: Using Time as Well as Space in Visual Selection

Derrick G. Watson
University of Warwick, UK

Glyn W. Humphreys
Birmingham University, UK

Christian N. L. Olivers
Vrije Universiteit, Amsterdam, The Netherlands

One of the main functions of the visual system is to allow an internal representation of the external world to be developed in order for us to interact efficiently and successfully with our environment. However, the visual world typically contains vast amounts of information, far more than can possibly be processed by our limited sensory and cognitive capabilities. Such limitations are readily demonstrated when we fail to detect even large changes that occur between sequentially presented visual scenes or even in real-world interactions (Simons, 1996; Simons & Levin, 1997; 1998) or when we fail to notice new stimuli while attending to other stimuli (Mack & Rock, 1998). Even if a stimulus is attended, the details of its visual representation may fade rapidly, perhaps even to a level no greater than that before attention was applied (Wolfe, Klempen, & Dahlen, 2000). Indeed, visual attention may be required to become conscious of even the most simple of features (Joseph, Chun & Nakayama, 1997; see also Mack, Tang, Tuma, Kahn, & Rock, 1992; Rock, Linnett, Grant, & Mack, 1992). We are thus greatly limited in the number of objects that we can attend to, process, or link to actions at any particular moment in time (e.g., Allport, 1987; Duncan, 1980). Fortunately, much of the information represented in the visual array may often be irrelevant to our particular current or future needs. However, it is clearly of great importance to be able to control effectively and prioritize the types of stimuli that receive preferential processing depending on our current behavioral needs. Consider, for instance, the predator's goal of detecting its prey. In this situation, the predator needs to detect the prey as soon as it appears from a background of other largely irrelevant items. The irrelevant items need to have little impact for selection to be efficient. Likewise, not all the visual information available to an air traffic controller or a pilot may need to be processed. Traditionally, theories of visual attention have emphasized selection through space. That is, attention is said to act like a spotlight or a zoom lens (e.g., Eriksen & St. James, 1986; Posner, 1980), with objects falling within the "illuminated" area receiving the greatest processing. Indeed, Neisser (1976) argued that, if picking apples from a tree, you simply "select" the one that you want without needing a mechanism to suppress other apples, to prevent them from being picked. In contrast to selection based on spatial parameters as previously described, here we consider how the visual system can also use time to prioritize selection.

In contrast to spatial selection, little attention has been paid to selection over time.[1] Clearly the visual world is not static; objects continuously appear and disappear as they and ourselves move throughout the environment. As a result we are often faced with the task of detecting and selecting something that is perhaps not yet visible but which is nonetheless anticipated: for instance, awaiting the appearance of a predator (or prey) or important data on a complex instrumentation panel whose location may often not be known in advance. Here the stimulus cannot simply be selected by some type of "spotlight of attention" because it is not yet visible and its location is not predictable. Rather, there needs to be a way to increase the efficiency of selecting "new" stimuli that appear. In fact, much evidence suggests that new objects can capture attention automatically over changing objects also in the field, although such an advantage may be limited to approximately four new objects (e.g., Watson & Humphreys, 1995; Yantis & Hillstrom, 1994; Yantis & Johnson, 1990; Yantis & Jones, 1991; Yantis & Jonides, 1984; for an overview, see Yantis, 1998). The new objects appear to be detected faster overall and there is often no or only a weak effect of the number of older objects (which change when the new stimulus appears). Also it may be possible to prime the visual system to bias itself to the selection of stimuli, depending on their characteristics, such as whether they possess color or luminance discontinuities (e.g., Folk, Remington, & Johnston, 1992; Folk, Remington, & Wright, 1994; see also Chelazzi, Miller, Duncan, & Desimone, 1993).

However, the efficient selection of new objects could be further enhanced if it were possible to voluntarily inhibit or deprioritize old objects already in the visual field that are known to be irrelevant to current goals. In this chapter we describe evidence for the existence of such a mechanism, which we have called

---

[1] We note here the exception of work using the rapid serial visual presentation paradigm (e.g., Raymond, Shapiro, & Arnell, 1992; Shapiro & Raymond, 1994) in which individuals typically have to select a target stimulus and those that follow it from a single stream of rapidly presented digits.

visual marking (Olivers, Watson, & Humphreys, 1999; Theeuwes, Kramer, & Atchley, 1998; Watson, 2001; Watson & Humphreys, 1997, 1998, 2000; Watson, Humphreys & Olivers, in press).

VISUAL MARKING

In outline, visual marking operates, by the active inhibition of old stimuli in the visual field, thereby conferring an additional selection advantage for new stimuli when they appear. We proposed that the intention to ignore old items results in the development of a goal state that initializes and maintains an inhibitory template. This template coordinates inhibition applied to the locations or features of old items. The development and maintenance of the goal state and its associated template is both on-line and resource demanding and is therefore subject to competition from rival goal states set up to perform other tasks.

Evidence for such a mechanism that serves to facilitate selection over time was originally obtained with a modified visual search procedure (Watson & Humphreys, 1997). Typically in visual search tasks, individuals indicate the presence or absence of a target item among a varying number of distractors (for an overview, see Wolfe, 1998). If the target differs from the distractors by the possession of a unique feature such as colour, shape, or size, then reaction times (RTs) are generally fast and vary little as the number of distractors increase. In contrast, if the target is uniquely defined by the possession of a combination of two or more features shared with the distractors (conjunction search), then RTs are slower and usually increase as the number of distractors increase. Often the absent to present RT to display-size search slope is 2:1, consistent with a serial and self-terminating search through the stimuli (Treisman & Gelade, 1980; but see Humphreys & Müller, 1993; Townsend, 1972, for alternative accounts). Generally, as the target becomes more similar to the distractors or as the distractors become more heterogeneous, then search becomes slower and less efficient (see Bundesen, 1998; Duncan & Humphreys, 1989, 1992; Treisman & Sato, 1990; Wolfe, 1994; Wolfe, Cave, & Franzel, 1989, for general and computational accounts of visual search).

We compared a standard conjunction search and a single-feature search task with a "preview" condition in which we presented one set of distractors (defined on the basis of color) before the remaining items[2] (which contained the target when present—see also Kahneman, Treisman, & Burkell, 1983, for use of a similar procedure). Our conjunction condition consisted of a blue H target among blue A and green H distractors. The single-feature condition contained just the blue items

---

[2]In previous papers we used the term gap condition because there was a temporal "gap" between the presentation of the old items and the onset of the new. However, recently we have instead used the term preview condition because it is a more accurate description and less likely to be misinterpreted.

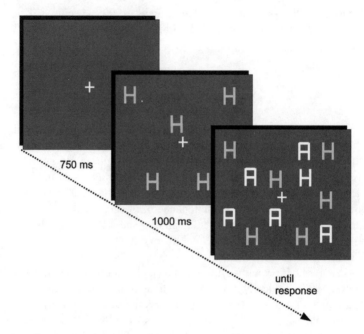

FIG. 13.1.   An example trial from the preview condition of Watson
and Humphreys (1997). A single trial consisted of a blank screen,
followed by a white central fixation cross, after which green H distractors (shown in gray) were added. After a further 1000 ms, blue
A distractors (shown in white) and a blue H (on target present trials) were added. This final display remained until the participant
responded, which blanked the screen and initiated the start of the
next trial. The fixation cross stayed on throughout the trial and participants were instructed to maintain fixation on the cross during
the period in which the green distractors were presented alone
(the preview interval).

from the conjunction task (blue H target among blue A's). In the preview condition
we presented the green H's for 1000 ms and then added the remaining blue items
(see Fig. 13.1). If participants were able to ignore the old (green) items, then search
efficiency in the preview condition should have matched that in the single-feature
baseline in which only the blue items were presented. In contrast, if they could
not ignore the old items, then search should have matched that of the conjunction
baseline in which all items were presented at the same time. The extent to which
search fell between the two baselines would indicate the degree to which the old
items could be ignored.

The results showed that, measured in terms of search slopes, search efficiency
in the preview condition did not differ significantly from that of the single-feature

baseline but was significantly more efficient than in the conjunction baseline[3] (Fig. 13.2). Thus search was as efficient in the preview condition as when only the blue items were presented alone.

This suggests that people were able to selectively attend to the new blue items and totally exclude the old green items from their search. At least for stationary stimuli the preview advantage does not require that there be a simple feature difference (e.g., color) between the old and the new stimuli (Olivers et al., 1999) and has been shown to occur even when there are 15 new items (Theeuwes et al., 1998) with no upper limit for either old or new items yet determined. In comparison, studies showing automatic attentional capture for the appearance of multiple new objects have found a limit of approximately four new items (e.g., Yantis & Jones, 1991). We have argued that the additional benefit for the selection of new objects found in our studies is a result of the involvement of an additional process that we called visual marking.

In the preceding visual search experiments, the inhibition of the old stimuli was inferred from the lack of an effect of the old distractors on subsequent search through the new stimuli. More direct evidence for the role of inhibition was provided by a probe-dot detection paradigm similar to that initially developed by Klein (1988). In Watson and Humphreys (2000), individuals had to perform a search task (detect the presence of a blue H target among blue A's and green H's) in a briefly presented display in most (76%) of the trials. In the remaining trials (probe trials), a brief tone presented at the same time as the new items indicated that, rather than search for the blue H target, the participants instead had to indicate the presence or the absence of a small probe dot. The dot, present in 50% of the probe trials, appeared simultaneously with the onset of the new items and equally often at the location of an old item or a new item (see Fig. 13.3).

Relative to a conjunction baseline (where the green H's were not presented before the blue items), detection accuracy was much worse when the probe fell at the location of an old marked item compared with the location of a new item. In addition, poorer probe detection on old items occurred only when participants

---

[3]A common finding in most visual marking experiments is a raised overall RT in the preview condition relative to the single-feature baseline, despite there being no difference in the search slopes. This might have been caused by a decrease in arousal (Posner & Boies, 1971) in the preview condition (when the old distractors were displayed alone) compared with the single-feature baseline in which the search display appeared immediately following the fixation cross. Alternatively, the allocation of attentional resources to the task of deprioritizing the old items might have delayed the initial onset of the search when the new items appeared. When differential arousal effects were controlled for, however, the difference in overall RTs was still observed, supporting the latter explanation for this effect (Watson & Humphreys, 1997). Recent experiments suggest that there may be some transfer of inhibition from old to new items on the basis of similarity. For instance, if the target shares its orientation with the old items it is harder to find than when it has a different orientation. This might also contribute to the intercept raise, to the extent that the target (blue H) shares features with the old items (green H's; Olivers & Humphreys, in press). The exact determination of the causes of this intercept effect awaits future research.

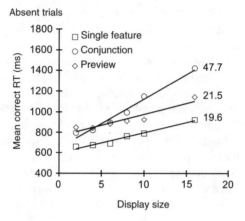

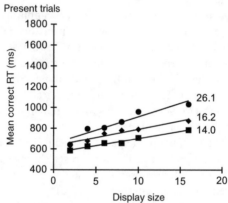

FIG. 13.2. Mean correct RTs as functions of condition and display size for absent trials (top) and present trials (bottom). The lines indicate the best-fitting linear function and the numbers indicate the search rate in milliseconds per item. Adapted from "Visual marking: Prioritizing selection for new objects by top-down attentional inhibition" by D.G. Watson and G.W. Humphreys, 1997, Psychological Review, 104, 90–122. Copyright 1997 by the American Psychological Association.

adopted the "intention" or "set" to search through the new items, ignoring the old. In a further experiment, with the same preview condition participants had to detect the probe dot on all the trials and never had to search for a blue H target. In this situation, the sequence of displays was identical to those described earlier except that, because subjects did not have to selectively search the new blue stimuli, there was no rationale for them to mark (inhibit) the old stimuli. Now there was relatively little difference between the detection of probes that fell on an old or on a new item (see Fig. 13.4).

Preview Condition - Search trial (76%)

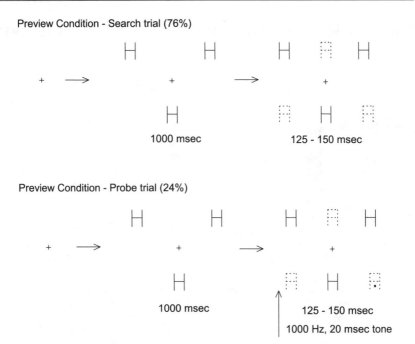

Preview Condition - Probe trial (24%)

FIG. 13.3. Example displays from the preview condition of the probe-dot detection experiment of Watson and Humphreys (2000). Solid lines, green; dotted, blue. In one condition, participants had to search for and indicate the presence or the absence of a blue H target in the majority (76%) of trials. In the remaining trials, a brief tone presented when the new items were added signaled that they instead had to indicate the presence or absence of a small dim probe dot. The probe dot, which was present in 50% of the probe trials, appeared simultaneously with the new items and appeared at either the location of an old item or that of a new item. A conjunction version of the task was also examined in which the green and the blue search items appeared simultaneously (thereby removing the chance to mark the old items). [From "Visual Marking: Evidence for Inhibition Using a Probe-Dot Detection Paradigm," by D. G. Watson and G. W. Humphreys, 2000, *Perception & Psychophysics, 62*, pp. 471–481. Copyright 2000 by the Psychonomic Society, Inc. Reprinted with permission.]

This converging operation directly implicates the role of inhibition in the prioritization of new stimuli (see also Olivers and Humphreys, 2002). Furthermore, it demonstrates that people can apply or withhold visual marking flexibly according to the current task demands. When it was advantageous to inhibit the old stimuli, then marking was applied; when it was of no benefit, it was not applied. This set of findings cannot be explained based on the automatic capture of attention by new stimuli nor is it due to the old items' acting as more effective forward masks because of their longer presentation time.

(a) **76% search trials, 24% probe trials**   (b) **100% probe trials**

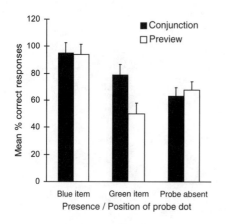 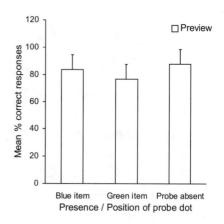

FIG. 13.4. Some results from the probe-dot experiment. In the preview condition, when the majority of trials were search trials, probe-dot detection was much worse when the probe fell at the location of an old green item compared with when it appeared at the location of a new blue item (white bars in panel (a)). In contrast, in other conditions there was much less difference when either marking was prevented by a display of a conjunction version of the task in which all the items appeared simultaneously (black bars in panel (a)) or when the rationale for marking was removed by making all the trials in the preview condition probe trials (panel (b)). Error bars indicate +95% confidence intervals. (From "Visual Marking: Evidence for Inhibition Using a Probe-Dot Detection Paradigm," by D. G. Watson and G. W. Humphreys, 2000, *Perception & Psychophysics, 62*, pp. 471–481. Copyright 2000 by the Psychonomic Society, Inc. Adapted with permission.

The flexibility to mark old objects only when needed makes visual marking a particularly adaptive mechanism. It also further distinguishes it from other, more automatic processes of temporal prioritization that are not under direct control of the observer, including inhibition of return (Maylor, 1985; Posner & Cohen, 1984; Tipper, Driver, & Weaver, 1991) or negative priming (Tipper, 1985; see Watson & Humphreys, 1997 and Olivers et al., 2002, for further discussion).

MARKING MOVING ITEMS

Clearly the world is not static and so it would be advantageous if marking were also able to be applied to moving items. This was tested by Watson and Humphreys (1998), who used the same type of visual search paradigm described previously, except that the old items moved down the screen within a virtual window. When an item reached the bottom of the window it disappeared and reappeared at the top of the window at the same horizontal location. In the preview condition, after 1000 ms the new blue items appeared and continued to move with the old items. Search in the preview condition was again found to be equivalent to that in an appropriate moving single-feature baseline and more efficient than the equivalent conjunction baseline. This demonstrated that old moving as well as stationary items could be inhibited, although, as we discuss later, the way in which moving items are marked appears to differ from that of stationary items in some circumstances.

RECAPTURING ATTENTION

The ability to ignore old objects is clearly a highly adaptive process and will serve to improve the efficiency with which new stimuli can be detected. However, it is also true that changes to old stimuli might signal important events to which we must potentially attend. For instance, an ignored piece of foliage might change shape as a previously unnoticed animal emerges from it. A change in shape or motion might indicate important changes in an object's heading. In these situations it will be advantageous for old ignored objects to recapture our attention. We (Watson & Humphreys, 1997) assessed the effects of changes to old objects by presenting a preview condition in which the initial old distractors were incomplete. When the new blue items appeared, then the old items changed into green H's by the addition of the missing line segments (producing both a shape and a luminance change). Now the search rate in the preview condition was much less efficient than that in the single-feature baseline and did not differ significantly from that of the conjunction baseline. We found the same result when the initial distractors changed by the removal of redundant line segments (luminance decrement) or if the old items were briefly (250 ms) blinked before the appearance of the new items. With moving stimuli, abrupt changes in motion (such as an abrupt stop) were likewise found to be sufficient to reset marking (Watson & Humphreys, 1998). Thus a change in shape and luminance, the brief disappearance and reappearance of an old item, or an abrupt change in motion was enough to reset marking, causing that item to recapture attention and compete for selection with the new stimuli.

Recent work (Watson & Humphreys, 2002) has shown that, despite the power of luminance and shape changes to reset visual marking, a substantial (red to green) isoluminant color change does not. Furthermore, a luminance change alone was not always sufficient to reset marking. This is informative regarding the possible neurophysiological implementation of visual marking (see subsequent sections) and its functional roles in attentional guidance. For instance, luminance changes may be quite common as lighting conditions vary and shadows are cast. However, these types of "surface feature" change most often do not signal an important change in the status of the object, such as its identity or directional heading, and so should be less likely to require our attention. Likewise natural objects rarely change color in isolation of other changes, and so there may be little survival advantage in responding to such events.

NATURE OF THE INHIBITION

There are a number of ways in which old stimuli might be ignored. These range from inhibition applied to the locations of the old items to inhibition applied to their features — perhaps by inhibition being applied at the level of whole "feature maps" (see Treisman & Sato, 1990). To test these accounts for stationary stimuli, Watson and Humphreys (1997) presented a "subset" preview condition in which some new green items were also presented along with the new blue items. Old green H's (either 7, 4 or 1) were presented for 1000 ms followed by either 1, 4, or 7 (respectively) new green H's that appeared along with 8 new blue items. Thus the final display size was always 16 items. If the old items were being inhibited by feature-map inhibition then the new green items should also have become inhibited because they would be represented in the inhibited feature map. This predicts that RTs should not vary as the ratio of old to new green H distractors changed. Alternatively, if the locations of the old items were inhibited, then the RTs should have decreased as the number of old green Hs increased. The results showed a significant and systematic decrease in RTs as the number of initial old green H's increased. Thus for stationary stimuli this finding is consistent with inhibition that is applied to the locations of the old items rather than to their features.

In contrast, when the same experiment was performed with moving stimuli (Watson & Humphreys, 1998), there was no consistent decrease in RTs as the number of old green items increased. Rather, the appearance of the new green items appeared either to disinhibit the old items (if there were a sufficiently large number) or they themselves became inhibited. For moving stimuli the inhibition appeared to be based on whole map inhibition of a critical feature (in this case color) that distinguished the old distractors from the new items. Thus, marking of stationary items appears to be location based and for moving stimuli feature based. These findings were further supported by additional work that showed that a feature difference between old and new stationary stimuli was not necessary for the marking of stationary items (Olivers et al., 1999; Theeuwes et al., 1998), but was necessary for the successful marking of moving stimuli (Olivers et al., 1999 see also Kunar, Humphreys & Smith, in press).

Thus stationary stimuli appeared to be marked by inhibition applied to their locations, whereas for moving stimuli inhibition was applied at the level of whole feature maps. Watson and Humphreys (1998) argued that feature-based inhibition for moving stimuli was adaptive because it allowed all old items containing a particular feature to be inhibited simultaneously regardless of their motion. Thus this method removed the need for a computationally expensive method of tracking multiple moving items and applying inhibition to their locations continuously. Indeed, Pylyshyn and Storm (1988) have shown that the ability to track a subset of moving items that do not have distinguishing features may be limited to approximately four or five items and that this process is both effortful and attention demanding (Pylyshyn et al., 1994). The disadvantage of whole map inhibition is that new items sharing the inhibited feature could themselves become inhibited, making them hard to detect. Alternatively, if there was a sufficiently large increase in the activity of an inhibited feature map, then this might be sufficient to reset or override the inhibition, reestablishing the old previously inhibited distractors as candidates for attentional selection. As is often the case, one advantage is traded for another. However, the displays previously described used continuous translational motion. This procedure was necessary to allow the displays to remain visible and centered on the display for an unlimited amount of time during search. However, it also meant that the local spatial relations between the items were not constant over time. They were continually disrupted as a result of the "wraparound" procedure. To address this issue, Watson (2001) presented moving displays in which there was no feature difference between old and new stimuli but in which the local spatial relations between old stimuli remained constant over time. This was achieved by use of common rotational motion as opposed to translation. Interestingly, in these displays, the old moving items could be marked despite the lack of a feature difference between old and new stimuli. When the local spatial relationships were no longer constant, achieved by having the stimuli rotate in different directions, then marking again failed to occur.

One possibility suggested by Watson (2001) was that when the local spatial relationship between items remained constant, then the stimuli could be grouped to form a single virtual object (see Yantis, 1992) with an associated marking template, as may be the case with stationary stimuli. Inhibition could then be aligned and maintained on the individual stimuli by a motion transformation of this single inhibitory template. Thus the representation used to coordinate, and the implementation of, visual marking appears to be highly flexible and able to exploit whatever features of the old stimuli are available. The extent to which these different methods of marking are used independently or can be selectively impaired through neurological damage awaits future research. However, recent work (Watson & Maylor, 2002) showed that the marking of old moving items may be especially vulnerable to the effects of old age. We found that older participants (mean age, ~70 years) showed a full marking effect with stationary stimuli (see also Kramer & Atchley, 2000). However, with moving stimuli there was no evidence of marking. This held regardless of whether there was a feature difference between the old and the new items or whether they could be grouped to form a virtual object. The results were not consistent with any straightforward account in terms of generalized slowing and instead suggested a process-specific deficit.

THE PROCESS OF SETTING UP AND
MAINTAINING VISUAL MARKING

According to the account that we are proposing, old objects are ignored in part by the application of inhibition which is coordinated by means of an inhibitory template. The template specifies the locations or features to which inhibition is to be applied. The template itself is set up and maintained by a goal state that is created as a result of the intention to inhibit the old objects (see Watson & Humphreys, 1997, 1998). We further propose that the maintenance of the inhibitory goal state and template is an on-line and resource-demanding process. This argument is based on the finding that marking is susceptible to interference from competing tasks similar to those used in previous studies of dual task interference in visual search (e.g., Braun, 1994; Braun & Julesz, 1998; Braun & Sagi, 1991; Joseph et al., 1997). For instance, we showed that when participants had to perform an attentionally demanding secondary task (shadowing a rapidly presented stream of visual digits) throughout the period when the old distractors were displayed, then visual marking was reduced. Specifically, search efficiency in the preview condition fell between that of the single feature and conjunction baselines. This effect occurred regardless of whether the load task appeared at the same time as the old distractors or even whether it appeared 750 ms later (i.e., even when participants were given a chance to inhibit old items before having to attend to the load task).

Interestingly, the load task increased the search slope in the preview condition but the search slopes were still highly linear. This suggests that marking is applied simultaneously to items in parallel across the field (see also Watson & Humphreys, 2000). Alternatively, if marking was applied in an all-or-none fashion to individual stimuli independently, then reducing resources required for marking would have reduced the maximum number of items that could be marked. This would have resulted in a dog-leg RT to display-size function because, for small display sizes, all old items would be inhibited, leading to efficient search. In contrast, at larger display sizes only a subset of the old items would be inhibited, leading to an inefficient search.

More recently, we (Humphreys, Watson, & Jolicoeur, 2002) examined the setting up and maintenance of visual marking more closely. We presented visual or auditory shadowing load tasks either at the onset of the initial set of old distractors or a little time later. As in Watson and Humphreys (1997), the visual load task interfered with marking both when it was presented simultaneously with the old items or when it was delayed relative to the onset of the old items. However, for the auditory load task, interference occurred only when it was presented at the same time as the old distractors were presented. In the case in which the old distractors appeared before the load task, there was no interference. This suggests that visual marking can be fractionated into at least two components. One component may be responsible for setting up the marking goal state and template, whereas the other is responsible for maintaining it once initialized. The initial setting up of the goal-state and template appears to require modality-independent resources and so any attentionally demanding secondary task causes interference. In contrast, the maintenance component seems to rely more on visual resources and is therefore immune to nonvisual competing tasks from other modalities.

NEUROPHYSIOLOGY

In our original work (Watson & Humphreys, 1997), we suggested that the prefrontal cortex, which in primates is heavily involved in working memory (e.g., Goldman-Rakic, 1987), might be involved in the maintenance of the inhibitory template. Consistent with this, Olivers and Humphreys (2002) found visual marking to be disrupted under so-called attentional blink conditions (Raymond, Shapiro, & Arnell, 1992). Electrophysiological studies have indicated that the attentional blink involves a temporary disruption of the updating of working memory (thought to be a prefrontal process), making post blink items unavailable for selection (Vogel & Luck, 2002; Vogel, Luck, & Shapiro, 1998). The fact that visual marking is affected by the blink may thus reflect a disruption of memory consolidation of the previewed items. Together with superior parietal areas, the same prefrontal areas are thought to be involved in a fronto-parietal network biasing attention towards relevant (or away from irrelevant) visual stimuli, by modulating activation in visual areas (see Kastner & Ungerleider, 2000, for a review). For instance, Motter (1994a,b) demonstrated in monkey cortex, that cells in area V4 were modulated by attention on the basis of stimulus color and that such modulation could occur even with only a memory of the target color. We speculate that the fronto-parietal network might be responsible for maintaining the inhibitory goal state and for coordinating inhibition. This inhibition might then give rise to the inhibitory effects found for distractor items represented within more visual areas like V4. Consistent with this, recent functional MRI studies of visual marking (Olivers, Humphreys, Smith & Mathews, 2002; Pollman, Weidner, Humphreys, et al. 2003) found increased superior parietal activation during preview search (compared with the equivalent conjunctive and single feature baselines). In addition, there is evidence from ERP work for a sustained negative waveform when an active bias is held against old items and this is most pronounced over fronto-parietal regions (Jacobsen, Humphreys, Schröger, & Roeber, 2002). Moreover, Olivers et al. found decreased activation in more visual areas (in occipital cortex) during previews. This decrease may serve to reduce the visual salience of the old items resulting in a higher signal-to-noise ratio for the subsequent new stimuli. It follows that the maintenance of visual marking may be more susceptible to interference from secondary tasks that activate the more visual areas as opposed to tasks that are auditory in nature, as was found by Humphreys, Watson, and Jolicoeur (2002).

IS INHIBITION REALLY NECESSARY FOR TEMPORAL PRIORITIZATION?

Donk and Theeuwes (2001) examined whether the benefit from presenting old items before new items still occurred even if the new items did not result in a luminance transient at their locations. This was achieved by the presentation of old and new stimuli that were isoluminant with the display background. With this manipulation, search efficiency differed both as a function of the number of new items and also as a function of the number of old items displayed. They proposed that the prioritization of luminance changes occurring at the locations of new items was sufficient to account for the prioritization of new stimuli without the need for an inhibitory mechanism. This account is consistent with the finding that briefly blinking the old items and then presenting them at the same time as the new items abolished visual marking (Watson & Humphreys, 1997). In these situations, a luminance transient would not distinguish old from new items. However, there are a number of problems with the onset account when one is trying to explain the full set of findings based on the visual marking paradigm.

First, Watson and Humphreys (1997) found that luminance changes caused by adding or removing features from old objects were sufficient to abolish marking. In contrast, in previous studies that examined automatic capture by onset stimuli (e.g., Yantis & Jonides, 1984, 1990), onsets that formed new objects captured attention at the expense of onsets formed by changing existing objects. It is not therefore clear why new objects should not also have dominated (even to a partial degree) in the visual marking task. Instead, changing old objects totally abolished any benefit for the new items just as effectively as when the old items momentarily disappeared and reappeared with the new items. In addition, we have found that marking is not fully abolished even when old items totally disappeared and reappeared due to occlusion cues (Kunar, Humphreys, Smith, & Watson, 2002). In contrast, an onset account would predict a lack of marking whenever old and new items cannot be distinguished on the basis of transients alone. Finally, luminance increments that are not also accompanied by a shape change in the old objects may have no impact on marking (Watson & Humphreys, 2002). Again, according to the onset account, such increments ought to have some effect and act to reduce the selection advantage for the new stimuli.

Second, the onset account has difficulty in explaining results that show that ignoring old items becomes more difficult when a secondary load task has to be simultaneously performed (Humphreys et al., 2002; Watson & Humphreys, 1997). It might be argued that participants need to adopt an attentional "set" to respond to new stimuli and that this set is compromised under dual task conditions. However, even with this extension, the onset account does not explain why the detection of probe dots should be reduced at the locations of old items when participants adopt a set for prioritizing new transients. Olivers and Humphreys (2002) have further shown that the detection of probes at old locations is improved under dual task conditions, consistent with less inhibition being applied under these circumstances.

Third, the time course required for optimal automatic attentional capture by new objects differs from that required for optimal selection in the marking paradigm. Studies of attentional capture caused by new object transients show that a temporal separation between old and new objects of ~100 ms is sufficient for maximal capture effects (e.g., Yantis & Gibson, 1994). In contrast, the time course for optimal marking effects appears to be much longer (about 400 ms; Watson and Humphreys, 1997). This greater time course may reflect the time required for the operation of an additional prioritization process that we suggest functions to inhibit old items already in the field.

Fourth, attentional capture by new objects has been previously demonstrated to be limited to approximately four new objects (e.g., Yantis & Johnson, 1990). In contrast, Theeuwes et al. (1998) demonstrated selective prioritization for up to at least 15 new items in the marking paradigm with no limit yet determined. The ability to be able to prioritize more than four new items is likely the result of the involvement of an additional mechanism that is brought into play when there is the adaptive rationale and temporal opportunity to inhibit old irrelevant items already in the field.

In addition to providing an explanation for the preceding results, prioritization based on the inhibition of old items (visual marking) can be reconciled with the results of Donk and Theeuwes (2001), provided that the applied inhibition serves to optimize selection within a system that is sensitive to luminance changes. In this way, visual marking may operate by providing a way to enhance the signal- (new items) to-noise (old distractors) ratio within a luminance-sensitive system. Indeed, recent neurophysiological evidence with stationary stimuli suggests that marking may operate by enhancing the detection of items within dorsal visual areas that are sensitive to dynamic changes (see preceding sections). By this account, marking might not be effective when either (a) the new items are not accompanied by a luminance signal or (b) the old items are not strongly represented within visual areas that represent the location of items based on luminance differences. Finally, we note too that the idea of some prioritizing of selection on the basis of onsets is not incompatible with the idea of inhibitory visual marking. It may well be that a limited set of new items is prioritized by onset capture. However, in addition to this, we suggest that the selection of new items is optimized by inhibitory marking too.

SUMMARY AND CONCLUDING COMMENTS

In this chapter we have tried to provide an overview of research that has illustrated the huge importance that temporal factors can play in the controlled selection of visual information. We have proposed the existence of a mechanism that we

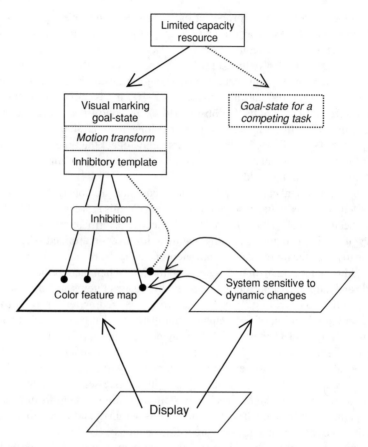

FIG. 13.5. Schematic representation of visual marking. Visual marking proceeds by means of the development of the goal state or the intention to inhibit items currently in the field. This goal state initializes and maintains an inhibitory template. For stationary stimuli the template specifies the locations of the old items to which inhibition should be applied. Inhibition might be applied to the locations within a specific feature map(s) or to locations within a master map, coding only object locations. For moving stimuli that maintain fixed spatial relationships, a motion transform might be incorporated to maintain the inhibition aligned with the location of the old items. When old moving items do not maintain a fixed spatial arrangement, inhibition must be applied at the level of a whole feature map. Changes to old marked items can reset the inhibition. For location-based visual marking, changes occurring at the locations of old items feed back to the inhibitory template to remove inhibition at those locations. In the case of feature-based inhibition of moving stimuli, sufficiently large changes of activity within the inhibited feature map are sufficient to reset the map-based inhibition.

have called visual marking that serves to facilitate and enhance the selection of new stimuli by the inhibition of old stimuli already visible. In summary, we have argued that the intention to inhibit old items results in a visual marking goal state. This goal state initializes and maintains an inhibitory template that coordinates inhibition of the old items. The development of the goal state and template requires general limited-capacity resources, whereas their maintenance draws on modality-specific resources. Other tasks selectively interfere with the various stages of setting up and maintaining marking to the extent that they draw on those same resources. The inhibitory template specifies the inhibition of individual locations or whole feature maps. A motion transform may be used to maintain and align the inhibition to old moving items, provided they maintain a constant configuration. Despite being top-down in nature, salient bottom-up events such as shape or motion changes can feed back to remove or reset the inhibition either at the level of individual locations or at the level of whole feature maps (see Fig. 13.5 for a schematic representation).

A number of features suggest that visual marking is a highly adaptive process: First, the ability to voluntarily apply marking only in those circumstances in which it will provide an overall benefit to task performance. In situations in which there is no incentive (or a disincentive) to visual marking, then it is not applied. Second, although a top-down process, potentially important changes (e.g., shape or motion) that occur to old marked items are sufficient to remove or reset the inhibition, allowing those items to compete for current selection. Third, marking appears to be able to exploit numerous characteristics of the old objects in order to inhibit them. Such characteristics include their locations, features, and ability to group into virtual objects. Although a highly robust phenomenon, many issues remain unresolved, and there are many unanswered questions regarding the nature of visual marking, its role in real-world situations, and its relationship to other selection mechanisms, all of which await future research.

ACKNOWLEDGMENTS

This work has benefited from funding by the Medical Research Council and the Economic and Social Research Council of Great Britain. We are most grateful to Hermann Müller, Mieke Donk, and Adrian von Mühlenen for many valuable comments and suggestions.

REFERENCES

Allport, D. A. (1987). Selection for action: Some behavioral and neurophysiological considerations of attention and action. In H. Heuer & A. F. Sanders (Eds.), *Perspectives on perception and action* (pp. 395–419). Hillsdale, NJ: Lawrence Erlbaum Associates.

Braun, J. (1994). Visual search among items of different salience: Removal of visual attention mimics a lesion in extrastriate area V4. *Journal of Neuroscience, 14*, 554–567.

Braun, J., & Julesz, B. (1998). Withdrawing attention at little or no cost: Detection and discrimination tasks. *Perception & Psychophysics, 60*, 1–23.

Braun, J., & Sagi, D. (1991). Texture-based tasks are little affected by second tasks requiring peripheral or central attentive fixation. *Perception, 20*, 483–500.

Bundesen, C. (1998). Visual selective attention: Outlines of a choice model, a race model and a computational theory. *Visual Cognition, 5*, 287–309.

Chelazzi, L., Miller, E. K., Duncan, J., & Desimone, R. (1993). A neural basis for visual search in inferior temporal cortex. *Nature (London), 363*, 345–347.

Donk, M., & Theeuwes, J. (2001). Visual marking beside the mark: Prioritizing selection by abrupt onsets. *Perception & Psychophysics, 63*, 891–900.

Duncan, J. (1980). The locus of interference in the perception of simultaneous stimuli. *Psychological Review, 87*, 272–300.

Duncan, J., & Humphreys, G. W. (1989). Visual search and stimulus similarity. *Psychological Review, 96*, 433–458.

Duncan, J., & Humphreys, G. W. (1992). Beyond the search surface: Visual search and attentional engagement. *Journal of Experimental Psychology: Human Perception and Performance, 18*, 578–588.

Eriksen, C. W., & St. James, J. D. (1986). Visual attention within and around the field of focal attention: A zoom lens model. *Perception & Psychophysics, 40*, 225–240.

Folk, C. L., Remington, R. W., & Johnston, J. C. (1992). Involuntary covert orienting is contingent on attentional control settings. *Journal of Experimental Psychology: Human Perception and Performance, 18*, 1030–1044.

Folk, C. L., Remington, R. W., & Wright, J. H. (1994). The structure of attentional control: Contingent attentional capture by apparent motion, abrupt onset, and color. *Journal of Experimental Psychology: Human Perception and Performance, 30*, 317–329.

Goldman-Rakic, P. S. (1987). Circuitry of primitive prefrontal cortex and regulation of behavior by representational knowledge. In F. Plum & V. Mountcastle (Eds.), *Handbook of physiology* (Vol. 5, pp. 373–417). Bethesda, MD: American Physiological Society.

Humphreys, G. W., & Müller, H. J. (1993). Search via recursive rejection (SERR): A connectionist model of visual search. *Cognitive Psychology, 25*, 43–110.

Humphreys, G. W., Watson, D. G., & Jolicoeur, P. (2002). Fractionating the preview benefit in search: Dual task decomposition of visual marking by timing and modality. *Journal of Experimental Psychology: Human Perception and Performance, 28*, 640–660.

Jacobsen, T., Humphreys, G. W., Schroger, E., & Roeber, U. (2002). Visual marking for search: behavioral and event-related potential analyses. *Cognitive Brain Research, 14*, 410–421.

Joseph, J. S., Chun, M. M., & Nakayama, K. (1997). Attentional requirements in a "preattentive" feature search task. *Nature (London), 387*, 805–807.

Kahneman, D., Treisman, A., & Burkell, J. (1983). The cost of visual filtering. *Journal of Experimental Psychology: Human Perception and Performance, 9*, 510–522.

Kastner, S., & Ungerleider, L. G. (2000). Mechanisms of visual attention in the human cortex. *Annual Review of Neuroscience, 23*, 315–341.

Klein, R. (1988). Inhibitory tagging system facilitates visual search. *Nature (London), 334*, 430–431.

Kramer, A. F., & Atchley, P. (2000). Age-related effects in the marking of old objects in visual search. *Psychology and Aging, 15*, 286–296.

Kunar, M. A., Humphreys, G. W., & Smith, K. J. (in press). Visual change with moving displays: More evidence for color feature map inhibition during preview search. *Journal of Experimental Psychology: Human Perception and Performance*.

Kunar, M. A., Humphreys, G. W., Smith, K. J., & Watson, D. G. (2002). When a re-appearance is old news: Visual marking survives occlusion. *Journal of experimental Psychology: Human Perception and Performance, 29*, 185–198.

Mack, A., & Rock, I. (1998). *Inattentional blindness*. Cambridge, MA: MIT Press.

Mack, A., Tang, B., Tuma, R., Kahn, S., & Rock, I. (1992). Perceptual organization and attention. *Cognitive Psychology, 24*, 475–501.

Maylor, E. A. (1985). Facilitatory and inhibitory components of orienting in visual space. In M. I. Posner & O. S. M. Marin (Eds.), *Attention and performance: Vol. 11. Mechanisms of attention* (pp. 189–204). Hillsdale, NJ: Lawrence Erlbaum Associates.

Motter, B. C. (1994a). Neural correlates of attentive selection for color or luminance in extrastriate area V4. *Journal of Neuroscience, 14*, 2178–2189.

Motter, B. C. (1994b). Neural correlates of feature selective memory and pop-out in extrastriate area V4. *Journal of Neuroscience, 14*, 2190–2199.

Neisser, U. (1976). *Cognition and reality: Principles and implications of cognitive psychology*. San Francisco: Freeman.

Olivers, C., & Humphreys, G. W. (2002). When visual marking meets the attentional blink: More evidence for top-down limited capacity inhibition. *Journal of Experimental Psychology: Human Perception and Performance, 28*, 22–42.

Olivers, C. N. L., & Humphreys, G. W. (in press). Visual marking and singleton capture: Fractionating the unitary nature of visual selection. *Cognitive Psychology.*

Olivers, C. N. L., & Humphreys, G. W., Heinke, D., & Cooper, A. C. G. (2002). Prioritization in visual search: Visual marking is not dependent on a mnemonic search. *Perception & Psychophysics, 64*(4), 540–560.

Olivers, C. N. L., Humphreys, G. W., Smith, P., & Mathews, P. (2002). Optimising selection of new objects: Neural substrates of visual marking. Manuscript Submitted for Publication.

Olivers, C. N. L., Watson, D. G., & Humphreys, G. W. (1999). Visual marking of locations versus feature maps: Evidence from within-dimension defined conjunctions. *Quarterly Journal of Experimental Psychology, 52A*, 679–715.

Pollmann, S., Weidner, R., Humphreys, G. W., Olivers, C. N. L., Müller, K., Lohmann, G., Wiggins, C. J., & Watson, D. G., (2003). Separating segmentation and target detection in posterior parietal cortex-an event-related fMRI study of visual marking. *NeuroImage*, 310–323.

Posner, M. I. (1980). Orienting of attention. *Quarterly Journal of Experimental Psychology, 32*, 3–25.

Posner, M. I., & Boies, S. J. (1971). Components of attention. *Psychological Review, 78*, 391–408.

Posner, M. I., & Cohen, Y. (1984). Components of visual orienting. In H. Bouma & D. G. Bouwhuis (Eds.), *Attention and performance: Vol. 10. Control of language processes* (pp. 531–556). Hillsdale, NJ: Lawrence Erlbaum Associates.

Pylyshyn, Z., Burkell, J., Fisher, B., Sears, C., Schmidt, W., & Trick, L. (1994). Multiple parallel access in visual attention. *Canadian Journal of Experimental Psychology, 48*, 260–283.

Pylyshyn, Z. W., & Storm, R. W. (1988). Tracking multiple independent targets: Evidence for a parallel tracking mechanism. *Spatial Vision, 3*, 179–197.

Raymond, J. E., Shapiro, K. L., & Arnell, K. M. (1992). Temporary suppression of visual processing in an RSVP task: An attentional blink? *Journal of Experimental Psychology: Human Perception and Performance, 18*, 849–860.

Rock, I., Linnett, C., Grant, P., & Mack, A. (1992). Perception without attention: Results of a new method. *Cognitive Psychology, 24*, 502–534.

Shapiro, K. L., & Raymond, J. E. (1994). Temporal allocation of visual attention. In D. Dagenbach & T. H. Carr (Eds.), *Inhibitory processes in attention, memory and language* (pp. 151–188). San Diego, CA: Academic Press.

Simons, D. J. (1996). In sight, out of mind: When object representations fail. *Psychological Science, 7*, 301–305.

Simons, D. J., & Levin, D. T. (1997). Change blindness. *Trends in Cognitive Sciences, 1*, 261–267.

Simons, D. J., & Levin, D. T. (1998). Failure to detect changes to people during a real-world interaction. *Psychonomic Bulletin & Review, 5*, 644–649.

Theeuwes, J., Kramer, A. F., & Atchley, P. (1998). Visual marking of old objects. *Psychonomic Bulletin & Review, 5*, 130–134.

Tipper, S. P. (1985). The negative priming effect: Inhibitory priming by ignored objects. *Quarterly Journal of Experimental Psychology, 37A*, 571–590.

Tipper, S. P., Driver, J., & Weaver, B. (1991). Short report: Object-centred inhibition of return of visual attention. *Quarterly Journal of Experimental Psychology, 43A*, 289–298.

Townsend, J. T. (1972). Some results on the identifiability of parallel and serial processes. *British Journal of Mathematical and Statistical Psychology, 25*, 168–199.

Treisman, A. M., & Gelade, G. (1980). A feature-integration theory of attention. *Cognitive Psychology, 12*, 97–136.

Treisman, A., & Sato, S. (1990). Conjunction search revisited. *Journal of Experimental Psychology: Human Perception and Performance, 16*, 459–478.

Vogel, E. K., & Luck, S. J. (2002). Delayed working memory consolidation during the attentional blink. Psychonomic Bulletin & Review, 9, 739–743.

Vogel, E. K., Luck, S. J., & Shapiro, K. L. (1998). Electrophysiological evidence for a postperceptual locus of suppression during the attentional blink. *Journal of Experimental Psychology: Human Perception and Performance, 24*, 1656–1674.

Watson, D. G. (2001). Visual marking in moving displays: Feature-based inhibition is not necessary. *Perception & Psychophysics, 63*, 74–84.

Watson, D. G., & Humphreys, G. W. (1995). Attention capture by contour onsets and offsets: No special role for onsets. *Perception & Psychophysics, 57*, 583–597.

Watson, D. G., & Humphreys, G. W. (1997). Visual Marking: Prioritizing selection for new objects by top-down attentional inhibition. *Psychological Review, 104*(1), 90–122.

Watson, D. G., & Humphreys, G. W. (1998). Visual marking of moving objects: A role for top-down feature based inhibition in selection. *Journal of Experimental Psychology: Human Perception and Performance, 24*, 946–962.

Watson, D. G., & Humphreys, G. W. (2000). Visual marking: Evidence for inhibition using a probe-dot detection paradigm. *Perception & Psychophysics, 62*, 471–481.

Watson, D. G., & Humphreys, G. W. (2002). Visual marking and visual change. *Journal of Experimental Psychology: Human perception and performance, 28*, 379–395.

Watson, D. G., & Maylor, E. A. (2002). Aging and visual marking: Selective deficits for moving stimuli. *Psychology and Aging, 17*, 321–339.

Watson, D. G., Humphreys, G. W., & Olivers. C. N. L. (2003). Visual marking: Using time in visual selection. *Trends in Cognitive Sciences, 7*, 180–186.

Wolfe, J. M. (1994). Guided search 2.0: A revised model of visual search. *Psychonomic Bulletin & Review, 1*, 202–238.

Wolfe, J. M. (1998). Visual search. In H. Pashler (Ed.), *Attention* (pp. 13–74). Hove, England: Psychology Press.

Wolfe, J. M., Cave, K. R., & Franzel, S. L. (1989). Guided search: An alternative to the feature integration model for visual search. *Journal of Experimental Psychology: Human Perception and Performance, 15*, 419–433.

Wolfe, J. M., Klempen, N., & Dahlen, K., (2000). Post attentive vision. *Journal of Experimental Psychology: Human Perception and Performance, 26*, 693–716.

Yantis, S. (1992). Multielement visual tracking: Attention and perceptual organization. *Cognitive Psychology, 24*, 295–340.

Yantis, S. (1998). Objects, attention and perceptual experience. In R. D. Wright (Ed.), *Visual attention* (pp. 187–214). Oxford, England: Oxford University Press.

Yantis, S., & Gibson, B. S. (1994). Object continuity in apparent motion and attention. *Canadian Journal of Experimental Psychology, 48*, 182–204.

Yantis, S., & Hillstrom, A. P. (1994). Stimulus-driven attentional capture: Evidence from equiluminant visual objects. *Journal of Experimental Psychology: Human Perception and Performance, 20,* 95–107.

Yantis, S., & Johnson, D. N. (1990). Mechanisms of attentional priority. *Journal of Experimental Psychology: Human Perception and Performance, 20,* 812–825.

Yantis, S., & Jones, E. (1991). Mechanisms of attentional selection: Temporally-modulated priority tags. *Perception & Psychophysics, 50,* 166–178.

Yantis, S., & Jonides, J. (1984). Abrupt visual onsets and selective attention: Evidence from visual search. *Journal of Experimental Psychology: Human Perception and Performance, 10,* 601–621.

Yantis, S., & Jonides, J. (1990). Abrupt visual onsets and selective attention: Voluntary versus automatic allocation. *Journal of Experimental Psychology: Human perception and performance, 16,* 121–134.

III

Psychophysics of Memory

Guest Editorial

Nelson Cowan
University of Missouri, Columbia

Writing an essay on the psychophysics of memory is like clearing a doorway in a wall separating adjoining apartments inhabited by Gustav Fechner (1801–1887) and Hermann Ebbinghaus (1850–1909) or, given that they actually lived in different cities, perhaps like installing network connectivity between them. Fechner had the idea of examining the relation between the physical world and the psychological effects that result from our experiencing that world; Ebbinghaus had the idea of tracing the diminishing availability of some psychological effects over time (Boring, 1957). Put them together, and you get the concept of exploring the nature of the effects of physical stimuli that persist following the disappearance of the actual stimuli. There were fundamental similarities between Fechner and Ebbinghaus that could assist in this union. For example, both men grasped the potential of systematic research on the human mind and both understood the need to develop research methods that could deal with considerable trial-to-trial variability.

I would like to consider a possible taxonomy of the psychophysics of memory and ask which parts of it pertain to the following chapters. There actually are at least two ways in which psychophysics and memory can interact. First, in what could be called *memory endurance*, the physical stimulus can cause a sense impression, and the sense impression can result in a memory trace or representation of the stimulus. Then the integrity and accessibility of the trace can be queried at a later

313

point in time. As a trace is partly forgotten, there may be several subcategories under memory endurance. The trace may change over time in its *veridicality*, or adherence to the original percept; in its *precision*, or level of completeness; and in it *accessibility*, or conditions necessary to evoke the memory again.

Second, in what could be called *memory influence*, a preexisting memory can influence the perceptual effect that a stimulus elicits when it is first presented. For example, if one has never before seen even a picture of an elephant, one's next encounter with a real elephant will evoke quite a different (more emotionally intense, yet confusing) psychological effect than if one is familiar with elephants. Let me define two subtypes of memory influence. There can be a *remote* influence from well-learned information or there can be a *local* influence from immediately preceding stimuli.

Most, though not all, of the evidence presented in the excellent chapters within this section of the book relates to what I have broadly termed memory endurance. Bredenkamp (chap. 14, this volume) presents a mathematical model that describes short-term memory in terms of bits or features of each item, the capacity for those features, and the time it takes to search through those features. However, underneath this surface another important question lurks: the question of how we know the composition of an item that determines its retention. Bredenkamp specifies items in terms of their presumed informativeness in bits but, ordinarily at least, we must consider how preexisting learning affects how new information is encoded; in present terms, we must consider memory influence.

Miller's (1956) famous article suggested that people typically can recall approximately seven items in serial order, but that does not imply that seven independent chunks are retained; the items may have been grouped into a smaller number of chunks, as he also described. I (Cowan, 2001) suggested looking at situations in which the items are familiar to begin with and in which grouping of these familiar items into higher-level chunks is prevented in one way or another. A wide variety of such situations showed that adult humans could recall approximately 4 items in such situations, which presumably reflected only four chunks. However, I am currently looking for ways to extend our understanding to the more typical situation in which it is difficult to know how the material is chunked. In many situations, chunks may not even exist. Instead, there can be sets of items that are too strongly associated to be considered independent chunks, yet too weakly associated to be considered a single chunk. What is needed as a first start toward relating intermediate levels of association between items to capacity is a psychophysical type of mapping between the history or strength of associations between items (memory influence) and the amount of a limited-capacity focus of attention that is taken up by the items (memory endurance).

Kaernbach (chap. 15, this volume) examines whether the types of short-term memory described as *sensory* and *categorical* may actually operate according to closely analogous mechanisms, as I (Cowan, 1988) suggested. Sensory memory refers to memory of how an item appears to the senses and categorical memory refers to the meaning it has. However, both may be carried by activated circuits within a larger long-term memory network. Kaernbach's investigation focuses on the two main ways in which a memory representation can become inaccessible: through the passage of time, or *decay*, and through displacement by, or interference from, other memory representations. In the latter case, one can ask whether the memory representations could be displaced by any other representations or only by others that are very similar in nature. If the interference is rather general and depends on the number of items in total that are being held in a readily accessible form at once, that is basically what is commonly meant by a *capacity* limit, which Kaernbach discusses. In the present taxonomy, the paper deals primarily with memory endurance generally and memory accessibility specifically (i.e., what elements are retained or lost). However, if a multisegment stream of noise is taken to be a unit in memory and some segments are lost in memory, then memory for the multisegment stream can be said to suffer a loss of precision, too.

Lass, Lüer, Becker, Fang, and Chen (chap. 16, this volume) cover the relation between encoded items and the mechanisms that allow memory representations of these items to be retrieved shortly afterward. What is under study is the speeds of various mnemonic processes. There appear to be two types of processes whose speeds enter into recall separately: rehearsal processes, emphasized in the most prominent theory of short-term or working memory (Baddeley, 1986), and retrieval processes, as suggested by Cowan et al. (1998) to supplement rehearsal. This work emphasizes a careful examination of the processes that take place after the initial sensory encoding of items and therefore seems to focus on memory endurance generally, and memory accessibility specifically.

The final two papers in the series can be said to combine both memory endurance and memory influence. Roeber and Kaernbach (chap. 17, this volume) show how a memory-search function does not depend much on rehearsal and does not have a fixed limit in terms of how many items can be searched; the slope function flattens out gradually. This is taken as support for the notion of a large pool of activated, rather accessible representations of items persisting after the presentation of a stimulus set. Thus the memory endurance from list item presentations provides a local memory influence on a following test probe item presentation.

Schröger, Tervaniemi, and Huotilainen (chap. 18, this volume) examine the properties of auditory sensory memory and its endurance, but they also suggest that there is a long-term or remote memory influence on auditory sensory memory from previous, attended discrimination learning sessions that use those stimuli.

The work that has been discussed primarily deals with what information is remembered or forgotten. It does not deal much with how information is distorted or, in present terms, memory veridicality. Of course, false memories are a hot topic in cognitive psychology today, and some of the recent research on false memories is even related to sensory factors (Gallo, McDerbott, Percer, & Roediger, 2001; Kellogg, 2001). More specifically related to psychophysics, though, is a small area termed *memory psychophysics* (e.g., Algom, 1992; Hubbard, 1994; Petrusic,

Baranski, & Kennedy, 1998). Research from that area shows that the basic laws of psychophysics, such as Stevens' power law, are preserved when one must recall, rather than presently experiencing, the stimuli to be judged. However, they are preserved with a change in exponents; there is compression of the range of judged intensities. Bright lights when remembered do not seem quite as bright as they did when they were actually presented, and so on. In relying on persisting memories of events there is not only a loss of memory precision, but also a loss of veridicality. In a similar vein, Cowan and Morse (1986) found that memory of a cardinal vowel not only becomes less precise but also seems to slide toward a more neutral vowel representation as it is forgotten in the seconds following its presentation.

The taxonomy that I have suggested is just a first approximation. For one thing, unstated by the taxonomy, veridicality of the percept may depend on memory influence. For example, an uninterrupted short auditory memory trace of a brief sound is needed to reach the full intensity of the auditory percept (Cowan, 1987).

As yet, there is not much integration between the methods used in sensory psychophysics and memory. For example, Miller (1956) brought up absolute identification of items as a psychophysical method and pointed out a limit in how many unidimensional stimuli can be included in the set of items to be identified; approximately six or seven, a severe informational capacity limit. The research in memory psychophysics has used similar techniques but seems to keep the number of stimuli to be identified under the capacity limit, so that the problems of long-term memory of the percepts to be judged and short-term memory of the categories assigned to these items do not affect the results simultaneously. It would seem that there is still much to be gained from studies in which a standard set of experimental procedures is applied to the joint exploration of psychophysics and memory.

ACKNOWLEDGMENTS

This chapter was written with support from grant R01 HD-21338 from the National Institutes of Health. I thank Jeffrey Rouder for discussions on the method of absolute identification.

REFERENCES

Algom, D. (1992). Memory psychophysics: An examination of its perceptual and cognitive prospects. In D. Algom (Ed.), *Psychophysical approaches to cognition* (Advances in Psychology No. 92, pp. 444–513). Amsterdam: North-Holland.

Baddeley, A. D. (1986). *Working memory* (Oxford Psychology Series No. 11). Oxford: Clarendon Press.

Boring, E. G. (1957). *A history of experimental psychology* (2nd ed.). Englewood Cliffs, NJ: Prentice-Hall.

Cowan, N. (1987). Auditory sensory storage in relation to the growth of sensation and acoustic information extraction. *Journal of Experimental Psychology: Human Perception and Performance, 13,* 204–215.

Cowan, N. (1988). Evolving conceptions of memory storage, selective attention, and their mutual constraints within the human information processing system. *Psychological Bulletin, 104,* 163–191.

Cowan, N. (2001). The magical number 4 in short-term memory: A reconsideration of mental storage capacity. *Behavioral and Brain Sciences, 24,* 87–185.

Cowan, N., & Morse, P. A. (1986). The use of auditory and phonetic memory in vowel discrimination. *Journal of the Acoustical Society of America, 79,* 500–507.

Cowan, N., Wood, N. L., Wood, P. K., Keller, T. A., Nugent, L. D., & Keller, C. V. (1998). Two separate verbal processing rates contributing to short-term memory span. *Journal of Experimental Psychology: General, 127,* 141–160.

Gallo, D. A., McDerbott, K. B., Percer, J. M., & Roediger, H. L., III. (2001). Modality effects in false recall and false recognition. *Journal of Experimental Psychology: Learning, Memory, and Cognition, 27,* 339–353.

Hubbard, T. L. (1994). Memory psychophysics. *Psychological Research, 56,* 237–250.

Kellogg, R. T. (2001). Presentation modality and mode of recall in verbal false memory. *Journal of Experimental Psychology: Learning, Memory, and Cognition, 27,* 913–919.

Miller, G. A. (1956). The magical number seven, plus or minus two: Some limits on our capacity for processing information. *Psychological Review, 63,* 81–97.

Petrusic, W. M., Baranski, J. V., & Kennedy, R. (1998). Similarity comparisons with remembered and perceived magnitudes: Memory psychophysics and fundamental measurement. *Memory & Cognition, 26,* 1041–1055.

14

Cavanagh's Hypothesis Within the Context of Other Invariance Hypotheses: Theory and Data

Jürgen Bredenkamp
University of Bonn, Germany

This chapter concerns the experimental tests of a hypothesis by Cavanagh (1972) within the context of other invariance hypotheses. These invariance hypotheses are a refined version of the total-time hypothesis (TTH) (Cooper & Pantle, 1967), Nevelski's hypothesis of a constant long-term memory span in terms of bits of information (Kintsch, 1970; Nevelski, 1970), and Baddeley's phonological loop hypothesis (Baddeley, 1997). The original version of the TTH states that the total learning time needed to obtain the performance criterion of a perfect recitation of material is independent of its presentation time. Therefore, if the presentation time is 10 s and six learning trials are required, the number of learning trials should be two if the presentation time is 30 s. In both cases, the total learning time is 60 s. However, experimental results do not confirm this version of the TTH. Therefore it had to be modified (Bredenkamp, 1993). The refined TTH states that the number of learning trials minus a constant a multiplied by the presentation time is a time constant b. We come back to these constants when considering Equation 1.

The refined TTH was connected to Nevelski's (1970) hypothesis of a constant long-term memory span (Bredenkamp, 1993). It states that the information in terms of bits processed in one learning trial (r) is independent of the total amount of information (I) to be processed. For example, if $I = 40$ bits and 10 learning trials are needed, then 5 learning trials will suffice to process 20 bits. The amount of information processed in one learning trial is 4 bits in both cases. r is called the long-term memory span that depends on only the presentation time.

As can be shown, the refined TTH and Nevelski's hypothesis together imply that the information in terms of bits processed in one learning trial increases with presentation time of the items according to a hyperbolic function (Bredenkamp & Hamm, 2001; Bredenkamp & Klein, 1998). The hyperbolic function was already chosen by Thurstone (1919) to describe the acquisition of typing speed. Within the theory that connects various invariance hypotheses (Bredenkamp, 1993), the following hyperbolic function can be derived from the refined version of the TTH and Nevelski's hypothesis:

$$r_j = \frac{I_v \, a_v^{-1}}{1 + b_v \, a_v^{-1} t_j^{-1}}, \tag{1}$$

where r_j denotes the information in terms of bits processed in one learning trial, I_v is the total amount of information of material v to be processed, t_j is the presentation time, and a_v and b_v are material-specific constants that denote the number of learning trials in short-term memory (STM) and the total learning time in long-term memory, respectively. Note that the information processed in one learning trial depends on the presentation time only. According to Equation 1, the manipulation of I_v affects the constants a_v and b_v in such a way that for a given presentation time t_j the information processed in one learning trial remains constant. The validity of Equation 1 has been experimentally tested under various conditions by Bredenkamp and Klein (1998) and Bredenkamp and Hamm (2001). In all experiments, consonant–vowel bigrams that differed with respect to their information value were used as learning materials. The experiments confirmed the validity of Equation 1 under the condition of articulatory suppression of the items required to be learned in a correct order, under the condition of irrelevant speech, under the condition of an attention demanding secondary task, and under a control condition.

These conditions were chosen to test a further assumption of the theory. According to that theory, the asymptote of the hyperbolic function equals the immediate memory span in bits if the span is not affected by long-term memory. Baddeley's working-memory model (WMM) (Baddeley, 1997) explains the deteriorating effect on immediate span of the preceding conditions compared with a control condition. The experiments by Bredenkamp and Klein (1998) and Bredenkamp and Hamm (2001) showed this deterioration not only on the immediate span but also on the asymptote of the hyperbolic learning curve. Thus the theory connecting the refined version of the TTH and Nevelski's hypothesis to Baddeley's WMM has been experimentally corroborated. It holds if the total amount of information to be processed exceeds the STM span in terms of bits.

This chapter concerns the question of whether Cavanagh's hypothesis (1972) can be added to the aforementioned ones. According to his hypothesis, multiplying the immediate memory span by the STM search time for one item results in a constant C that is independent of the material:

$$g_v \, s_v = C, \tag{2}$$

where g_v is the immediate span in terms of items for the material v and s_v is the search time for one item of the material v in a Sternberg task (Sternberg, 1966). Because the asymptote of the hyperbolic learning curve (A) is equivalent to the immediate span in bits ($m_v \, g_v$), it can be predicted that the following equation holds:

$$A = C \, m_v \, s_v^{-1}, \tag{3}$$

where m_v is the information value of one item of material v. According to Cavanagh (1972), C is 243 ms. However, Puffe (1990) has shown that there are interindividual differences with respect to C (see also Geissler & Kompass, 1999).

This chapter seeks to answer mainly two questions:

1. Does Cavanagh's hypothesis hold for the bigrams used in the experiments by Bredenkamp & Klein (1998) and Bredenkamp & Hamm (2001)?
2. Can the asymptote of the learning curve be predicted according to Equation 3?

These questions were examined under the condition of articulatory suppression and a control condition with the possibility of articulating the items to be processed. As far as I know, not a single experiment has yet been performed to test the validity of Cavanagh's hypothesis under the condition of articulatory suppression. However, such a test would be informative. According to the WMM, visually displayed items whose articulation is suppressed are not processed in the phonological loop. Hence, if Cavanagh's hypothesis holds under this condition, it must refer to another system of working memory. If the latter is the case, it can be expected that only the memory span, not the search time, is affected by articulatory suppression. This is the third question examined in this article.

Methodologically, the connection of various hypotheses has the advantage in that the empirical content of the resulting theory is larger than the empirical content of each single hypothesis belonging to this theory (Gadenne, 1994). The empirical content is defined as the set of data that is not in accordance with a hypothesis or theory. The larger the empirical content, the more empirical outcomes are forbidden by the theory (Popper, 1982). Therefore the connection of various hypotheses reduces the probability of false empirical confirmations and increases the strength of hypothesis testing (Erdfelder & Bredenkamp, 1994). In this chapter Cavanagh's hypothesis is focused on as part of a theory with a larger empirical content.

OVERVIEW OF EXPERIMENTS

To check the validity of Cavanagh's hypothesis, a Sternberg experiment and an immediate-span experiment must be conducted. Connecting Cavanagh's hypothesis to the asymptote of the learning curve requires an additional learning experiment. Because the learning experiments and span experiments were described in detail elsewhere (Bredenkamp & Hamm, 2001; Bredenkamp & Klein, 1998), only their results are reported in this chapter and connected to the Sternberg experiments described in the subsequent subsections. These Sternberg experiments were performed under a control condition (Experiment 1) with the possibility of articulating the items and under the condition of articulatory suppression (Experiment 2).

Material

In both Sternberg experiments, the same material as in the corresponding span and learning experiments was used. It consisted of consonant–vowel bigrams whose information value varied between $m_1 = 2$ bits and $m_3 = 4$ bits. The construction of the material is described in detail by Bredenkamp and Klein (1998). The bigrams were chosen to minimize the influence of long-term memory on immediate span. Only in this case it can be expected that the immediate span in bits is equivalent to the asymptote of the learning curve.

Participants

The participants in all experiments were first-year psychology students and students of other fields of specialization. They were either paid for participation or received credits in partial fulfilment of an exam requirement. The participants were randomly assigned to materials with $m_1 = 2$ bits, $m_2 = 3$ bits, and $m_4 = 4$ bits of information per item with the restriction of equal subsample sizes. Each subject participated in a Sternberg experiment and an immediate-span experiment. The order of the experiments was chosen randomly for each participant.

Sternberg Experiment

The participants were presented with a memory set of bigrams to hold in STM. The size of the memory set was varied from one bigram to three for the students assigned to the m_1 bigrams and from one bigram to four for the participants assigned to the other bigrams. The bigrams were displayed horizontally on a computer screen in ASCII code, black characters on a white background. Each item in the memory set was displayed once (random sampling without replacement) for 1 s, and after an interstimulus interval of 0.2 s, the next item appeared to the right of the previous item. The first item of the memory set was always signaled by a tone (400 Hz, 50 ms) followed by the sign "!" (950 ms). 950 ms after the last item of the memory set had been displayed, a tone (400 Hz 50 ms) followed by the sign "*" (200 ms) signaled the test item that was presented after 800 ms (empty screen). The presentation of this stimulus started the timer. The participants were required to determine as fast as possible whether the test item was in the memory set by pressing a "right" or "wrong" key. The time between the start of the test item and the pressing of the key was measured with the algorithm of Bovens and Brysbaert (1990), which compares favorably with other procedures (Graves & Bradley, 1991). For each participant the test items were positive in 60 out of 120 cases. Positive and negative test items were presented with equal frequencies in each size condition, and the order of the treatment combinations (size of memory set by quality of test item) was completely randomized for each participant.

Statistical Analysis

The statistical analysis of the individual mean times per treatment combination excluded false decisions and outside values. Following Tukey (1977), an outside value was defined as a time faster than $2.5\ Q_1–1.5Q_3$ or slower than $2.5\ Q_3–1.5Q_1$, where Q_1 and Q_3 designate the first and the third quartile, respectively. The individual corrected mean times were analyzed with three trend analyses, with repeated measures on both factors (size of memory set and quality of test item). Three trend analyses were used because the memory set of m_1 bigrams varied between one and three items whereas the memory set of the other items varied between one and four.

To test Cavanagh's hypothesis, the individual memory spans and the individual search times were logarithmically transformed. The sums of these logarithms per subject served as the dependent variable in a one-way analysis of variance (ANOVA) with the factor "amount of information per item." A result in favor of the null hypothesis is in accordance with Cavanagh's hypothesis if the power of the statistical test is high. The reason for using logarithmically transformed variables is explained as follows. If Cavanagh's hypothesis, stated in Equation 2, holds for each subject with different values for g, s, and C, then the same equation cannot hold for the arithmetic means but only for the geometric means of these variables (Bredenkamp, 1993). The null hypothesis of the aforementioned ANOVA is equivalent to the hypothesis of equal geometric means.

A procedure described in the appendix of the article by Bredenkamp & Klein (1998) was used to test the hypothesis that the asymptote of the learning experiment can be predicted by Equation 3.

EXPERIMENT 1 (CONTROL CONDITION)

There were 75 students who participated in the Sternberg experiment, with $n = 25$ participants in each condition. The three trend analyses with the factors "size of memory set" and "quality of test item" confirmed without any exception that response time increases linearly with the size of memory set. Thus the regression coefficients estimate the times needed for the comparison of a test item with one bigram in the memory set. The individual regression coefficients were logarithmically transformed and added to the subject's logarithmic span value. The sums of these logarithms were analyzed with a one-way ANOVA as described in the preceding section. According to Cohen (1988), the power of the $F(2,72)$ test to detect large effects ($f^2 = 0.16$) is 0.93 when $\alpha = 0.10$. The resulting F value was insignificant ($F = 0.36$). This result is in accordance with Cavanagh's hypothesis. The antilogarithm of the grand mean of all sums of logarithms estimates the constant C. Its value is 434 ms.

The results of the span experiment were published by Bredenkamp and Klein (1998; Experiment 3). The spans are shorter the higher the information value per item is. Because Cavanagh's hypothesis holds, the search times also covary with the amount of information per item.

When Equation 3 with $C = 434$ ms is used, the asymptote of the learning curve can be estimated. The estimate is 15.35 bits. The analysis of a corresponding learning experiment, in which the presentation time and the information value per item were independently manipulated, resulted in an estimate of the asymptote whose value is 15.63 bits (Bredenkamp & Hamm, 2001). Both values do not differ significantly [$F(8,171) < 1$].

Discussion

The Sternberg experiment and a corresponding immediate-span experiment confirmed Cavanagh's hypothesis. Both experiments used bigrams with different information values. Thus the results could be connected to a learning experiment in which the same bigrams are used. The asymptote of the resulting learning curve could be successfully predicted from the results of both STM experiments. The implications of these results are considered in relation to further findings in the general discussion section.

EXPERIMENT 2 (ARTICULATORY SUPPRESSION)

There were 105 students who participated in the Sternberg experiment, with $n = 35$ participants in each condition. It was a replication of Experiment 1 with the exception that the items had to be processed under the condition of articulatory suppression. The participants had to speak aloud the German word *drei* (three) simultaneously with a tone (30 Hz; 100-ms duration) that was presented once every 600 ms. The presentation of the tones started 3.6 s before the first item of the memory set was displayed. Thus each participant had to speak the word *drei* six times before the presentation of the bigrams started. The presentation of the tones stopped when the test item appeared. The students also participated in an immediate memory span experiment under the condition of articulatory suppression. This experiment is described in detail by Bredenkamp and Klein (1998; Experiment 4). Before the experiments, the participants had to practice speaking the word *drei* in unison with the tone.

The response times of correct decisions were analyzed with three trend analyses, with repeated measures on both factors (size of memory set and quality of test item). All analyses confirmed the prediction that response time increases linearly with the memory set size. The interactions were insignificant. Thus the regression coefficients estimate the search times. However, there were 20 participants in the condition of a negative test stimulus whose regression coefficients were negative for the 2-bit items. They were excluded from further data analyses. The same applies to another five participants with negative regression coefficients (see website, Chapter 14, Table 1).

To test Cavanagh's hypothesis, the positive individual regression coefficients were logarithmically transformed and added to the participant's logarithmic span value. These sums were computed separately for positive and negative test stimuli. Therefore Cavanagh's hypothesis was tested twice. The first test concerned the positive test stimuli. The $F(2, 97)$ value was insignificant ($F = 2.18$; $p = 0.12$). The power of this test to detect large effects ($f^2 = 0.16$) on the basis of an average group size of $n = 33$ (see Cohen, 1988) and $\alpha = 0.10$ is 0.98. The second test concerned the negative test stimuli. The $F(2,82)$ value was also insignificant ($F = 2.05$; $p = 0.14$). The power of this test to detect large effects on the basis of an average group size of $n = 28$ (see Cohen, 1988) and $\alpha = 0.10$ is 0.95. Thus both results are in accordance with Cavanagh's hypothesis. The estimates of the constant C are 293 ms (positive test stimuli) and 278 ms (negative test stimuli), respectively. The analysis of a corresponding learning experiment performed under the condition of articulatory suppression resulted in an estimate of the asymptote whose value is 10.60 bits (Bredenkamp & Klein, 1998). The procedure described by Bredenkamp and Klein (1998) was used to test whether the asymptote can be successfully predicted from the results of the STM experiments. The predicted values of the asymptote are 12.21 bits and 12.53 bits for positive and negative test stimuli, respectively. They do not differ significantly from the obtained value of 10.60 bits.

Discussion

The Sternberg experiment and a corresponding immediate-span experiment confirmed Cavanagh's hypothesis under the condition of articulatory suppression. In addition, the asymptote of a learning experiment performed under this condition matched the prediction derived from the Sternberg experiment and the immediate-span experiment. Thus the same structure of results was obtained under the condition of articulatory suppression and the control condition.

However, there is a substantive difference between both experiments with respect to the 2-bit items. Out of 35 participants, 20 seemed to have applied a special strategy in Experiment 2 when a negative test stimulus was displayed. As the set of possible items comprises only four bigrams, the "strategic" subjects might have simply identified the missing items in the memory set. In this case, a negative correlation between size of memory set and response time would be expected. Whether such a strategy was used in Experiment 2 but not in Experiment 1 is uncertain. Of importance is that the data of the subjects with negative regression coefficients (see website, Chapter 14, Table 1) had to be excluded from further data analyses. Thus a selection bias may jeopardize the interpretation of the results of Experiment 2. However, if there is such a bias, it is small with respect to the immediate-span values of the participants.

GENERAL DISCUSSION

Cavanagh (1972) considered three possible explanations of Equation 2. One hypothesis was that the representation of a stimulus in memory is composed of a list of features. For deciding in Sternberg's task whether the test item is a member of the memory set, the item must be compared feature by feature against each stored stimulus according to that hypothesis. The STM can hold only a limited number of features. If each stimulus representation is composed of q_v features, the maximum number of features to be held in STM is $q_v \ g_v$. If the time per feature test is a constant z, then the following equation holds:

$$z \ q_v \ g_v = C. \tag{4}$$

In Cavanagh's approach, the meaning of the features is left open. Because the asymptote of the learning curve in terms of bits could be predicted by Equation 3, it may be hypothesized that the number of features per item, q_v, equals the amount of information, m_v (see Bredenkamp, 1993). If this assumption is correct, then z can be estimated by the following equation because the immediate span in bits ($m_v \ g_v$) equals the asymptote A:

$$z = C \ A^{-1}. \tag{5}$$

When this equation is applied by use of the asymptote values of both learning experiments ($A_1 = 15.63$ bits; see Bredenkamp & Hamm, 2001; $A_2 = 10.60$ bits; see Bredenkamp & Klein, 1998), the estimates of z are 27.76 ms for Experiment 1 and $z = 26.98$ ms for Experiment 2. The latter estimate results if a weighted geometric mean for positive test stimuli ($C = 293$ ms) and negative test stimuli ($C = 278$ ms) is computed ($C = 286$ ms). Thus articulatory suppression does not affect the time per feature test, z. The reduction of C through articulatory suppression is solely due to the reduction of the number of features that can be held in STM. As only g but not z is reduced by articulatory suppression, the feature-by-feature comparison assumed by Cavanagh (1972) cannot be carried out in the phonological loop. Another part of the working memory must be responsible for these comparisons. However, the reported experiments cannot answer the question of which part of working memory is involved.

If the results reported in this chapter are considered in the context of the whole theory connecting various invariance hypotheses (Bredenkamp, 1993), the following statement may be made. If the information value of the learning material exceeds the immediate memory span in bits, the upper bound of the information processed in one learning trial is that immediate span in bits. The longer the presentation time of the items, the more bits per trial are processed. The upper bound can be predicted by STM experiments. It is equivalent to the number of information units the STM can hold. This number depends on the condition under which the items are processed. Articulatory suppression reduces the capacity but does not affect the time per feature test according to Cavanagh (1972). Therefore it may be concluded that it is not only the phonological loop that contributes to span and learning tasks. In accordance with the results presented, Hulme, Newton, Cowan, Stuart, and Brown (1999) have shown that certain variables (lexicality, length of words or nonwords) affect the immediate span but not the search time measured in a Sternberg task. According to these authors, "these findings contradict the empirical generalization (based on between-subjects comparisons) suggested by Cavanagh (1972) that memory span is higher for materials with higher scanning rates" (Hulme et al., 1999, p. 460). Indeed, according to Cavanagh (1972), differences in immediate span should be associated with differences in search time or search rate. Does the conclusion follow that Cavanagh's hypothesis does not hold if this association cannot be observed?

This query may be answered with Geissler's time quantum model (TQM) (see Geissler, 1990; Puffe, 1990). TQM assumes an elementary time quantum T that is claimed to be an universal parameter. "T is supposed to represent an absolute lower bound of temporal resolution, hence the smallest possible lower bound of an operative interval" (Geissler, 1990, p. 196). Experimental results from different sources converge to an estimate of the time quantum of $\sim$4.5 ms (Geissler, 1990; Geissler, Schebera, & Kompass, 1999). Integer multiples of T can be the shortest lower bound, too. Applied to the estimates of z of both experiments, the integer multiple would be 6. The elementary time period T (or z as a multiple of T) and the number of storable units are conceived as independent of each other by the TQM. Therefore results showing that a variable affects the number of storable units but not the multiple of the elementary time quantum do not contradict the TQM. They imply, however, that C cannot be conceived as a universal time constant. It depends on the multiple of the elementary time quantum and on the number of storable information units. However, the TQM puts constraints on the variability of C. According to that model, the upper bound of storable units in STM is 30. Thus C should be an integer multiple of 30 T. Both estimates of C (434 and 286 ms) come close to these constraints, with multiples of 3 and 2 for the first and the second experiment, respectively (H.-G. Geissler, January 29, 2001, personal communication).

The invariant part of Cavanagh's hypothesis seems to be that C divided by z remains constant if only the integer multiple of T is affected through experimental manipulations. As Puffe (1990) has shown for Sternberg experiments, the multiple of the time quantum varies between subjects and task demands. On the other hand, if the number of storable units is affected, the ratio $C z^{-1}$ also varies between different experimental conditions although it corresponds to the immediate span in bits within each condition. The influence on immediate span of the various conditions is explained by the WMM. The relation between the immediate span and the asymptote of the learning curve is the subject of a model that connects further hypotheses to the aforementioned ones. Within the context of Cavanagh's hypothesis, the asymptote can be interpreted as the maximum number of features the STM can hold. The model presented by Bredenkamp (1993) and tested by Bredenkamp and Klein (1998), Bredenkamp and Hamm (2001), and by the experiments described in this chapter defines these features as information units.

ACKNOWLEDGMENT

The work on this chapter was supported by grants of the Deutsche Forschungs-gemeinschaft to the author (Br 301/9). The author thanks Klaus-Martin Klein for programming the experiments and statistically analyzing the results. He is also indebted to Hans-Georg Geissler and Edgar Erdfelder for helpful remarks on a previous version of chapter.

REFERENCES

Baddeley, A. (1997). *Human memory. Theory and practice* (Rev. ed.). Hove, England: Lawrence Erlbaum Associates.

Bovens, N., & Brybaert, M. (1990). IBM PC/XT/AT and PS/2 Turbo Pascal timing with extended resolution. *Behavior Research Methods, Instruments & Computers, 22*, 332–334.

Bredenkamp, J. (1993). Die Verknüpfung verschiedener Invarianzhypothesen im Bereich der Gedächtnispsychologie [The connection of different invariance hypotheses in the field of the psychology of memory]. *Zeitschrift für experimentelle und angewandte Psychologie, 40*, 368–385.

Bredenkamp, J., & Hamm, S. (2001). Further experimental tests of invariance hypotheses on learning and memory processes. *Zeitschrift für Psychologie, 209*, 227–244.

Bredenkamp, J., & Klein, K. M. (1998). Experimental tests of a model connecting three invariance hypotheses on learning and memory processes. *Zeitschrift für Psychologie, 206*, 107–124.

Cavanagh, J. P. (1972). Relation between the immediate memory span and the memory search rate. *Psychological Review, 79*, 525–530.

Cohen, J. (1988). *Statistical power analysis for the behavioral sciences* (2nd ed.). Hillsdale, NJ: Lawrence Erlbaum Associates.

Cooper, E. H., & Pantle, A. J. (1967). The total time hypothesis in verbal learning. *Psychological Bulletin, 68*, 221–234.

Erdfelder, E., & Bredenkamp, J. (1994). Hypothesenprüfung [Hypothesis testing]. In T. Herrmann & W. Tack (Eds.), *Enzyklopädie der Psychologie, Themenbereich B: Methodologie und Methoden:*

Serie I, Vol. 1. Methodologische Grundlagen der Psychologie [Encyclopedia of Psychology, Subject B: Methodology and Methods: Series I, Vol. 1. Methodological Foundations of Psychology] (pp. 604–648). Göttingen, Germany: Hogrefe.

Gadenne, V. (1994). Theoriebewertung [Theory assessment]. In T. Herrmann & W. Tack (Eds.), *Enzyklopädie der Psychologie, Themenbereich B: Methodologie und Methoden: Serie I, Vol. 1. Methodologische Grundlagen der Psychologie* [Encyclopedia of Psychology, Subject B: Methodology and Methods: Series I, Vol. 1. Methodological Foundations of Psychology] (pp. 295–342). Göttingen, Germany: Hogrefe.

Geissler, H.-G. (1990). Foundations of quantized processing. In H.-G. Geissler (Ed.), *Psychological explorations of mental structures* (pp. 193–210). Toronto: Hogrefe & Huber.

Geissler, H.-G., & Kompass, R. (1999). Diskrete Zeitstrukturen in Wahrnehmungs- und Gedächtnisvorgängen [Discrete temporal structures in perceptual and memory processes]. In E. Witruk & H.-J. Lander (Eds.), *Informationsanalysen* [Information analyses] (pp. 21–54). Leipzig: Leipziger Universitätsverlag.

Geissler, H.-G., Schebera, F.-U., & Kompass, R. (1999). Ultra-precise quantal timing: Evidence from simultaneity thresholds in long-range apparent movement. *Perception & Psychophysics, 61*, 707–726.

Graves, R. E., & Bradley, R. (1991). Millisecond timing on the IBM PC/XT/AT and PS/2: A review of the options and corrections for the Graves and Bradley algorithm. *Behavior Research Methods, Instruments & Computers, 23*, 377–379.

Hulme, C., Newton, P., Cowan, N., Stuart, G., & Brown, G. (1999). Think before you speak: Pauses, memory search, and trace redintegration processes in verbal memory span. *Journal of Experimental Psychology: Learning, Memory, and Cognition, 25*, 447–463.

Kintsch, W. (1970). *Learning, memory, and conceptual processes*. New York: Wiley.

Nevelski, P. B. (1970). Comparative Investigation of the short-term and long-term memory span. In K. H. Pribram & D. E. Broadbent (Eds.), *Biology of memory* (pp. 21–28). New York: Academic Press.

Popper, K. R. (1982). *Logik der Forschung* [The logic of scientific discovery]. Tübingen, Germany: Mohr.

Puffe, M. (1990). Quantized speed-capacity relations in short-term memory. In H.-G. Geissler (Ed.), *Psychological explorations of mental structures* (pp. 290–302). Toronto: Hogrefe & Huber.

Sternberg, S. (1966). High speed scanning in human memory. *Science, 153*, 652–654.

Thurstone, L. L. (1919). The learning curve equation. *Psychological Review Monograph Supplement, 26*(3) 1–51.

Tukey, J. W. (1977). *Exploratory data analysis*. Reading, MA.: Addison-Wesley.

15

Auditory Sensory Memory and Short-Term Memory

Christian Kaernbach
Universität Leipzig, Germany

Since the days of the multiple-components theory of memory (Atkinson & Shiffrin, 1968), it has become common practice to characterize or differentiate memory systems by specifying their lifetime, capacity, and susceptibility to interference. The concept of independent structural components had to be given up; the one-store model by Shiffrin and Schneider (1977) and many later models defined short-term memory as activated long-term memory, that is, as a process rather than as a component. However, comparing the aforementioned three parameters is still a useful approach to gain evidence on common or different mechanisms of memory systems or processes.

It is now well established that storage of sensory information is at least twofold. Massaro and Loftus (1996) differentiated between sensory and perceptual storage, with the latter lasting much longer than the former. An early classification into short and long sensory stores was done by Cowan (1984) in the auditory realm. He gave an extensive review of many studies relevant to auditory memory, but often dealing primarily with other topics, such as masking or periodicity detection. He classified them into two groups: those revealing time constants of 200 ms or less, and those revealing time constants of 10–20 s. For the short store (phenomena up to 200 ms) Cowan cites data from masking experiments, auditory persistence, and temporal integration. The aftertone found by Zwicker (1964) fits well with this account. These phenomena are not perceived as memory but form part of sensation. The long store accounts for phenomena of up to 20 s. In contrast to the phenomena of the short sensory storage, these are perceived as memory. Therefore the term auditory sensory memory henceforth denotes the long auditory store.[1] The methodological analogy to the visual partial report (Sperling, 1960), the auditory partial report (Darwin, Turvey, & Crowder, 1972), falls into this category as well as dichotic listening experiments (Glucksberg & Cowen, 1970) and the perception of periodic random waveforms as introduced by Guttman and Julesz (1963).

In his memory model Cowan (1988, 1995) extended this distinction between short and long sensory stores to all modalities. According to this model, long sensory storage and short-term memory are both activated parts of long-term memory. Although the lifetime of traces in long sensory stores is compatible with the assumption of a close relation to short-term memory, the capacity of sensory stores is often thought of as being much higher than that of short-term memory, and sensory stores are thought of as being much more susceptible to interference. Although this seems to be true for short sensory stores, it need not be so for long sensory stores. The goal of the research presented here was to examine all three parameters for the long auditory store by use of a single class of stimuli and by this means to avoid unjustified synopses across tasks and material.

Periodic random waveforms represent an excellent test of auditory sensory memory. They do not offer clues to categorical storage as most other auditory materials do. The following section introduces this little-known stimulus. The sections thereafter address the issues of lifetime, capacity, and susceptibility to interference of auditory sensory memory for random waveforms; the lifetime section also addresses the issue of categorical storage. The final section discusses similarities and differences between sensory and categorical information storage.

PERIODIC RANDOM WAVEFORMS

Auditory white noise is a random waveform. It is perceived as a homogeneous, featureless stimulus. It can be generated by the feeding of a sequence of random numbers to a sound card. One sequence of random numbers sounds just like any other: It is impossible to make the difference between, say, the digits of π

---

[1]The term long auditory store might be confusing because it could be associated with long-term memory. "Echoic memory" is a correct name for long auditory storage phenomena. The term echo was originally coined by Neisser (1967) as an auditory analog to the term icon, both specifying sensory registers. Although the icon is a phenomenon of the short visual store, it would be a misnomer to apply the term echo to the short auditory store: Echo perception starts exactly for delays where phenomena of the short auditory store end, i.e., at 200 ms. However, to avoid confusion with short sensory storage, the term auditory sensory memory is used throughout this chapter. In the discussion section I propose auditory short-term memory as a naming alternative in light of the similarities between auditory sensory memory and classical short-term memory.

and the digits of e (both π and e are considered good pseudorandom number generators) once they are converted to sound and hit our ear. It is impossible to remember the sound of the amplitude values 3, 1, 4, 1, 5, 9, . . . , and to distinguish it from the sound of the amplitude values 2, 7, 1, 8, 2, 8, . . . This property of noise differentiates it from most other auditory material used in memory tasks. It is easy to remember a syllable or a word. In many situations it is not evident how far this memory performance is based solely on a sensory representation of the stimulus or at least partially on a semantic, categorical representation of the stimulus. The indistinctness of noise is due to the fact that for this stimulus there are no semantic categories available that could ease remembering. If, however impossible it seems, a listener remembers white noise, this can be done only on the basis of the sensory representation of this stimulus. Therefore white noise represents an excellent material to test auditory *sensory* storage.

The seeming impossibility of remembering white noise is due to the short lifetime of auditory sensory storage. To enable auditory sensory memory to detect the reoccurrence of a certain segment of a random waveform this segment is compelled to reoccur within a few seconds, and no other strong perceptual cues such as onsets and offsets should intervene. If one wants to test memory for noise, the random waveform should be repetitive. Indeed, the indistinctness of random waveforms ceases dramatically if the random waveform starts to repeat itself after a second or less (Guttman & Julesz, 1963). Even naive listeners perceive a striking difference between periodic and continuous random waveforms as long as the cycles are shorter than 1 or 2 s. Periodic random waveforms are perceived as rhythmically structured and filled with perceptual events such as "clanks" and "rasping." These perceptual events are the outcome of a memory process: If (and only if) the auditory system detects the reoccurrence of those random numbers (say, 3, 1, 4, 1, 5, 9, . . .), it can by "relistening" confirm small irregularities that in a single nonperiodic presentation would be drowned out by those thousands of other small features of the noise stimulus to follow. Evidently the form of the memory representation is not simply the waveform itself: The repetition seems to prime early auditory feature codes (Kaernbach, 2000, 2004a; Kaernbach, Schröger, & Gunter, 1998).

It is important to distinguish periodic random waveforms from other types of frozen-noise stimuli. Separately presented segments of frozen noise play an important role in studies of masking (see, e.g., Hanna & Robinson, 1985). Iterated with onset and offset ramps, the stimulus sounds similar to a steam engine. In this case, the amplitude modulation dominates perception and the faint percepts characteristic of periodic random waveforms are suppressed.

In contrast, if repetitions of a single segment of white noise are connected seamlessly, no major amplitude modulations are introduced. No artifacts are introduced at the connection points that could give rise to clicks or other artificial percepts: A sequence of random numbers does not feature any coherence that could be disrupted by this cut-and-paste operation. In consequence, cycles longer than 1 or 2 s sound on first, inattentive listening just as featureless as continuous white noise. If periodic random waveforms elicit rhythmical perceptual events, this can be due to only the detection of the reoccurrence of parts of the waveform. These perceptual events are to a certain degree reproducible across different sessions of the same listener (Kaernbach, 1992). However, they vary from listener to listener. This variation is further evidence that the origin of the perceptual events is not artificial but stems from the analysis performed by the auditory system of the listener. The temporal extent of the physical basis of these perceptual events is restricted to ~100 ms (Kaernbach, 1993). Gerbils have been demonstrated to be able to discriminate periodic and continuous noise up to cycle lengths of 400 ms (Kaernbach & Schulze, 2002), and cats show a similar performance (Frey, Kaernbach, & König, in press). Periodic noise has been used as a signal in masking experiments (Pollack, 1990), its perception has been compared with pitch perception (Guttman & Julesz, 1963; Warren & Bashford, 1981; Warren & Wrightson, 1981; Warren, Wrightson, & Puretz, 1988), and it has been used to study time order processing (Warren & Bashford, 1993). The relevance of periodic noise stimuli to memory was already noted by Pollack (1972). For a review on periodic-noise research see Warren (1998). A demonstration of periodic noise stimuli can be found at www.periodic-noise.de

LIFETIME OF SENSORY AND CATEGORICAL INFORMATION

The lifetime of short-term memory for syllables, words, or letters can be reliably assessed only if measures are taken to prevent rehearsal. In the classical Brown–Peterson paradigm (Brown, 1958; Peterson & Peterson, 1959), participants were prevented from rehearsing by articulatory tasks such as counting backwards. In this case, categorical information in short-term memory is known to last several seconds.

Memory for auditory random waveforms does not seem to qualify for the same decay range. Guttman and Julesz (1963) reported that for periods longer than 1 or 2 s it would become difficult to detect the periodicity of periodic noise. Nevertheless, Cowan (1984) ascribed periodic noise perception to the long auditory store (time constants 10–20 s). He is strengthened in this view by an informal observation reported in a footnote of a study by Warren and Bashford (1981): One of their highly trained listeners could detect cycles as long as 10 s. Warren, Bashford, Cooley, and Brubaker (2001) showed that cross-modal cueing could help experienced listeners to detect the periodicity in cycles of 10, 15, or even 20 s. In my own pilot studies it became obvious that only a small amount of training is needed for naive listeners to perceive long cycles without cross-modal cueing.

In an experiment with 20 participants (Kaernbach, 2004b), the relation between training and maximum cycle length in naive listeners was quantified. Different

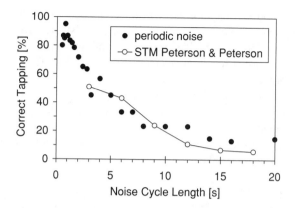

FIG. 15.1. Percentage of participants with correct tapping as functions of the cycle length. The filled circles represent data from Kaernbach (2004b). The open symbols represent data on categorical storage (STM, short-term memory) by Peterson and Peterson (1959) for comparison.

samples of Gaussian noise were generated for each single trial. Participants performed 66 trials of periodic noise detection, cycling 3 times through 22 different cycle lengths ranging from 0.5 to 20 s, with 10 participants proceeding in ascending order and the other 10 participants proceeding in descending order. Success or failure was determined from the participant's ability to correctly tap the rhythm of the periodic-noise stimulus on a computer keyboard.

Figure 15.1 shows the results as a function of the cycle length, averaged over all participants regardless of presentation order and run. Periodic-noise cycles of several seconds can be correctly detected. The performance decays monotonically with increasing cycle length, but there is a certain performance for naive participants even at cycle lengths of 10, 15, or 20 s.

In total, there was not much training during this experiment. The entire session lasted only 30 min. Although there was a significant training effect (performance first run: 205/440, third run: 276/440 correct detections/total trial number), a remarkable performance was found already during the first run: Four participants could correctly tap a 20-s cycle after less then 10 min of training. Two participants of the second group (descending periodicities) successfully tapped a cycle of 12 s after ~6 min of exposure to longer cycles. This can hardly be called training as they did not hear any periodicities in these longer cycles. This experiment demonstrates that naive listeners can with only a little training detect random waveform cycles of 10 s and more. To this end they must have memorized parts of the waveform, and this memory must have survived several seconds.

Figure 15.1 illustrates the time course of sensory memory for random waveforms. For comparison, Fig. 15.1 shows also classical data from Peterson and

Peterson (1959) on the retention of consonant trigrams. The match of these two sets of data is almost too good to be true. Please note that the data of Peterson and Peterson depend on the cutoff criterion for the response latency: With a later cutoff criterion, higher correct recall values would have resulted. The main purpose of the inclusion of these data in Fig. 15.1 was, however, to compare the approximate range of temporal decay for sensory versus categorical information. In the face of Fig. 15.1 one could conclude that the temporal decay is quite similar for these two types of information.

One might, however, argue that in experiments dealing with categorical storage the material to be memorized is somehow presented to the senses; therefore it might not be obvious that the data collected are really relevant to categorical storage. For instance, Peterson and Peterson presented their stimuli auditorily. It might well be that the similarity of the decay observed in their data and in those of auditory sensory memory for random waveforms (see Fig. 15.1) is due to the fact that both experiments deal with sensory storage. Experiments with random waveforms are aimed at evaluating parameters of sensory storage, excluding categorical coding as far as possible. It might be worthwhile to consider the opposite approach: design experiments that assess categorical storage while excluding sensory coding. This would imply testing short-term memory for categorical information that has not been presented to the senses.

Munka and Kaernbach (2001) tested memory for self-generated information. To our knowledge this is the first attempt to assess categorical short-term memory bereft of sensory traces. Participants had to add two 4-digit numbers that were presented for 3 s (short presentation) or for 7 s (long presentation). They were instructed to do so silently and without articulatory movements, and the experimenter paid attention that they followed this instruction. The retention interval lasted 3, 6, 9, 12, or 15 s. During this interval, participants had to perform a distraction task that prevented rehearsal: They had to alternately recite the alphabet in a 1.5-s rhythm, starting from two given letters (e.g., given D and J, recite E, K, F, L . . .). Figure 15.2 shows the percentage of correct recall for long and short presentations (self-generated is indicated by the filled symbols) for 10 participants. Also shown are data from conditions that were modeled after the Brown-Peterson paradigm (visual B-P is indicated by the open symbols) for the same participants. For these conditions participants had to memorize visually presented consonant trigrams (presentation time 2 or 4 s) while counting backward during the retention interval.

Although the performance level was somewhat different for these four conditions, the decay of information occurred in the same temporal range of ~5–10 s. This is so for purely sensory information (periodic random waveforms), for a visual replication of the Brown–Peterson paradigm in which both sensory and categorical codes were available, and even for self-generated categorical information that was never presented to the senses. Obviously sensory and categorical information decay at a comparable speed.

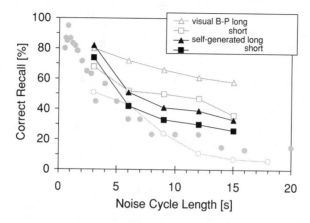

FIG. 15.2. Percentage of correct recall in a memory experiment (Munka & Kaernbach, 2001) in which the information to be memorized had to be generated by the participant and was never presented to the senses (filled symbols). As a control condition, a visual Brown–Peterson (B-P) paradigm was performed (open symbols). For both types of task the presentation time was either long (triangles) or short (squares). For comparison, the data of Fig. 15.1 are indicated by the light gray shading.

CAPACITY FOR SENSORY INFORMATION

Short-term memory for categorical information is known to be limited in capacity. This limitation is mostly specified as the number of items that can maximally be stored, be it seven or four (Cowan, 2001; Miller, 1956; but see Baddeley, 1986, for a time-limiting account). The early concepts of sensory registers (Neisser, 1967) implied that they should have a high capacity so as to store all details of the sensory input. The finding that a 10-s repetition of a random waveform can be detected could mislead one into assuming that some hundred thousands of random amplitude values (depending on the sample rate) were stored. Not only is the form of the memory representation quite different from the waveform itself, comprising low-level features of auditory signals such as frequency edges and transients (Kaernbach, 2000, 2004a), but it is also not evident that these features cover the entire cycle, that is, it is questionable whether a major part of the cycle is recoded and memorized. On the contrary, from introspective observation it was clear that only small parts of a long cycle, but not all of it, elicit distinct perceptual features. The rest of this section describes three experiments that were designed to determine the amount of the cycle that a participant memorized while listening to periodic noise and to estimate the maximum item number of memorized pieces of auditory information.

In the first two experiments, five participants had to judge in a yes–no task whether a certain test cycle of an ongoing periodic-noise stimulation had been changed or not. These changes consisted of the substitution of small segments of this test cycle by new random numbers that would not correspond to the memory content and could thus trigger a change detection—if and only if the substitution would concern the memory content.

The cycle (length 1.2–6 s in the first experiment) was virtually segmented into 300-ms segments (resulting in 4–20 segments for the 1.2–6-s cycles). A small number of these segments were exchanged. This number was increased after a miss (no change detected) and increased after a hit (change detected) so as to obtain 50% change detections. A session comprised 60 test cycles, and participants performed three to four sessions per condition. In 20% of the trials no segment was exchanged. Participants were aware that more than two false alarms would lead to a rejection of the data. In 120 sessions, this occurred four times. The periodic-noise stimuli were different from session to session.

On the basis of the detection data, the "change-sensitive length" was determined by means of a maximum-likelihood algorithm. This algorithm evaluated the probability for each single virtual segment that its exchange would have triggered a detect response. Most segments did not contribute to detect responses: Their exchange passed unnoticed. Figure 15.3(a) shows the change-sensitive length as a function of the cycle length for the first of these two experiments. Only 500 ms of the noise cycle were sensitive to exchanges, and this did not depend on the cycle length. The independence of cycle length is evidence that the change-sensitive length is no surrogate for lifetime. The change-sensitive length was found to be rather small, setting an upper limit to the capacity of auditory sensory memory. However, the real capacity might have been much smaller: Even in the case in which the memorized portion of the waveform was infinitely small, the change-sensitive length would have come out to be at minimum 300 ms, that is, the length of the virtual segments of the noise cycle that were exchanged in this experiment.

The second experiment of this series tested segment lengths of 200 and 400 ms at two cycle lengths (2.4 and 4.8 s). Figure 15.3(b) shows that there is a marked influence of the segment length: The change-sensitive length increases linearly with the length of the segments. The y-axis intercept of this linear trend can be interpreted as an estimate of the true capacity of the auditory sensory memory for random waveforms, and the slope reveals the fragmentation of the stored information (Kaernbach, 2003b). From the data presented in Fig. 15.3(b), the total capacity of auditory sensory memory for random waveforms can be estimated to be 130 ms, with a fragmentation of ~1.4. This indicates that usually one (but sometimes two; on average 1.4), segment of ~90 ms was memorized.

A χ^2 analysis was performed to obtain a confidence interval for the y-axis intercept and the slope. The upper limit of the 95% confidence interval for the slope was 1.9, that is, the average number of disjoint waveform segments that

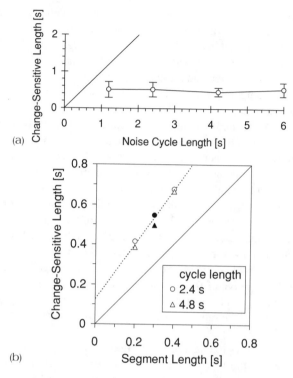

FIG. 15.3. (a) Change-sensitive length of periodic white-noise cycles as determined by the change of 300-ms segments as a function of the cycle length. The error bars indicate the standard deviation of the data. (b) Dependence of the change-sensitive length on the segment length for two different cycle lengths. The standard deviations are similar to those in (a) and are not shown. The solid symbols are taken or interpolated from (a).

the participants memorized was at maximum two. The upper limit for the y-axis intercept (and hence for the total capacity) was 260 ms. Although the confidence interval was rather large, it is still remarkable that the upper limit for the capacity measure was as small as 260 ms.

These experiments demonstrated that the capacity of auditory sensory memory is rather limited. It is not the entire waveform of a 10-s cycle that is memorized but only a small part of it. However, the capacity estimate might have come out too small because of some methodological details of these experiments. First, the yes–no task required the participants to maintain a criterion, and the instruction given (two false alarms would require a repetition of the session) encouraged a rather severe criterion, leading to more misses and fewer hits than a neutral criterion would have induced. Second, participants were neither instructed nor required to retain as much information as possible. To detect the periodicity, it was sufficient to memorize one or two features. Third, the choice of the material was suboptimal: Some of these cycles might just not have contained enough significant features that could be memorized by a certain participant. An additional problem is that the data analysis was too complicated and indirect. It seems especially disadvantageous to try to evaluate the temporal extent of the stored items as well as their fragmentation from the same set of data.

In the third experiment of this series (Kaernbach, 2004b) the focus was entirely on the number of items that can be stored in auditory sensory memory. The stimulus was no longer strictly periodic. It was composed of a cycle of several 200-ms segments of frozen white noise, with 100-ms segments of new random noise between these segments. This detached presentation aimed at isolating the percepts elicited by each of the frozen segments while avoiding undesirable amplitude modulations. Participants selected their 20 favorites out of 80 segments of white noise. They did so by rating the clearness of the percept in such a detached periodic presentation. Instead of a yes–no task, participants had to decide in a two-alternative forced-choice paradigm which of two test cycles was changed. The cycles were composed of three to five of their favorite segments, and the changed cycle had one to all of these segments replaced with new random noise. The sequence of the segments either stayed the same between trials (regular) or was permuted between trials (random).

Figure 15.4(a) shows the data of ten participants. The more elements that are exchanged (x axis), the better the performance of the participants. For a fixed number of exchanged elements, performance is better in cycles with a small total

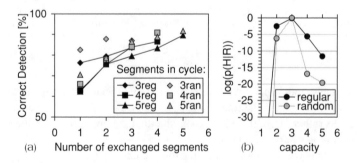

FIG. 15.4. (a) Percentage of correct change detection in a capacity experiment in which a two-interval forced-choice task was used (Kaernbach, 2004b). Cycles were composed of a certain number of individually selected frozen-noise segments (see legend) for regular or random sequences. The data are plotted as functions of the number of segments that were exchanged (x axis). (b) Likelihood for the observed results as functions of the capacity parameter of a simple memory model.

number of elements than in a cycle with many items. All this is to be expected in the case of a capacity limit: The higher the percentage of exchanged elements, the higher the chance to exchange a sensitive item, that is, one that has been memorized.

A simple model of a capacity limit (in terms of the number of items to be memorized), plus lapse rates (a single-item lapse rate and a total-response lapse rate) can predict curves similar to those in Fig. 15.4(a). The likelihood of the exact outcome of the experiment can be calculated, and it depends clearly on the setting of the parameters (capacity, lapse rates). These can be optimized to give the highest possible likelihood for the experimental data. Figure 15.4(b) shows the likelihood for the experimental data for various values of the capacity parameter. It peaks at three, regardless of whether the sequence of the segments was permuted or not. The immunity of this capacity measure against permutation indicates that chunking did not play a role in this experiment.

This second approach to evaluate the capacity of auditory sensory memory is promising. The two-alternative forced-choice paradigm frees the participant of the need to maintain a criterion, allowing him or her to evaluate the slightest cues that might indicate a change of the random waveform. The choice of favorite segments improves significantly the ability of the participant to focus on several items at a time. As a result, the data clearly indicate a higher estimate of the capacity than would follow from the fragmentation index of the previous experiments. This estimate comes close to the often-mentioned capacity limit of short-term memory of four items (for an extensive discussion of evidence that point to this capacity limit, see Cowan, 2001). Apparently, auditory sensory memory for random waveforms and short-term memory for categorical information are subject to the same capacity limitations.

SUSCEPTIBILITY TO INTERFERENCE

Sensory storage is in general considered to be prone to strong interference effects. The short visual storage can, for instance, be overwritten by subsequent visual input, as has been demonstrated by Averbach and Coriell (1961). As for the short auditory store, one of the classes of experiments cited by Cowan (1984) as evidence for this type of storage was masking experiments. Long sensory storage can also be afflicted by interference: Sensory memory for single-input dimensions such as pitch will be impaired by a similar input during the retention interval (Deutsch, 1973). This interference is, however, not as absolute as the interference in short sensory stores: Although tones adjacent in the musical scale interfere strongly with the retention task, distant tones interfere to a lesser degree. Another example of interference in long auditory storage is the suffix effect found in the auditory modality (Crowder & Morton, 1969): To-be-ignored list-final items interfere with list recall. This is again a weaker interference than that observed for short sensory stores, as in this case it is the capacity for the relevant information that is afflicted. The list-final item enters the store even if it was to be ignored, and this memory load reduces the amount of relevant information that can be stored.

It appears that interference in the long auditory store is not as absolute as interference in short stores, as long as the capacity limit is kept and there is no similarity between the memorized stimulus and the interfering stimulus. This was tested in an experiment with a distractor task during the retention interval (Kaernbach, 2004b). The experiment again used random waveforms, the same stimulus material that served for the evaluation of the lifetime and capacity parameters. It was tested whether it was possible to solve both a main task with a long retention interval based on random waveforms and at the same time an interfering task that was also based on random waveforms but with a different repeating segment.

Participants had to decide whether a 250-ms segment of a random waveform that occurred 14 times at the beginning of a 17-s noise stimulus did reoccur at the end of this stimulus. These 250-ms segments were presented "detached" (compare third experiment of capacity series), that is, new random noise (250 ms) was inserted so that the relevant segment reoccurred twice per second. After the 14 initial presentations (i.e., 7 s) the noise stimulus continued for another 10 s: a 9-s retention interval and 1 s during which the relevant segment might or might not reoccur twice. A visual cue indicated the occurrences of the segment at the beginning of the stimulus, as well its potential reoccurrence at the end. The frozen segment was different from trial to trial.

The leftmost data point of Fig. 15.5 shows the performance in this main task averaged across three well-trained participants in case that there was no further interfering task. It is often suggested that silence be used instead of ongoing white noise during the retention interval for the no-interference condition. It is, however, much more difficult to solve the main task if the noise is switched off during the

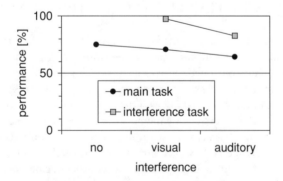

FIG. 15.5. Performance in main and interference tasks of an interference experiment with random waveforms (Kaernbach, 2004b), averaged across participants, as a function of the interference task type.

retention interval. This is due to the strong interference resulting from the offset and onset ramps needed to switch the noise off and on again. The performance in the no-interference condition is halfway between perfect and random performance. This threshold performance is due to the fact that the retention interval is rather long (compare Fig. 15.1).

Apart from this no-interference condition there were two different interference conditions: In these, participants had to perform a visual or an auditory task during the retention interval. The auditory interference task was also based on recurring segments of a random waveform (different from that of the main task) and again facilitated by a visual cue. The visual interference task concerned a visual cue that flashed in a 500-ms rhythm. The difficulty of the two types of interference tasks was not matched, as can be seen in Fig. 15.5: The auditory interference task was more difficult than the visual interference task. With both interference tasks, performance dropped in the main task. This drop was slightly more marked in the auditory interference condition. This might well be due to the greater difficulty of the auditory interference task. The important observation is that the performance in the main task, being already close to threshold even without any interference, remained still significantly better than chance when a difficult interference task had to be performed during the retention interval. These results demonstrate that interference in the long auditory store is less absolute than in short sensory stores.

DISCUSSION

Long sensory memory shares many features with categorical short-term memory. The studies summarized in this chapter assessed lifetime, capacity, and susceptibility to interference for the long auditory store by use of the same type of stimulus material, periodic random waveforms. With respect to all three parameters, the long auditory store showed similarities to storage phenomena for categorical information. This strengthens the view of Cowan (1988, 1995) who described long sensory stores as activated parts of long-term memory. According to this view, the difference between long sensory stores and categorical short-term memory is the code (sensory or categorical) that is memorized, whereas the process of maintaining a high level of activation for some seconds could be the same.

It has been questioned whether the decay observed in Brown–Peterson paradigms (Brown, 1958; Peterson & Peterson, 1959) is due to the decay of a trace or due to interference. Keppel and Underwood (1962) emphasized the role of proactive interference by previous trials. Another approach to explain the decay in Brown–Peterson paradigms is by retroactive interference from stimulus material presented during the retention interval (see, e.g., Waugh & Norman, 1965). The decay/interference debate is somewhat intractable as it is possible to mimic decay by retroactive interference by internal states, that is, even in absence of external interfering stimuli. In the case of periodic-noise perception it is not plausible to assume that the retention of a piece of waveform over several seconds is impaired by external interference by the ongoing noise. The reoccurrence of a segment of the random waveform can be detected after several seconds (compare Fig. 15.1). During the rest of the cycle plenty of potentially interfering items are present. If the decay in performance would be due to interference, it would be questionable as to why it would need so many interfering items before performance goes down. Decay of the trace, even if mediated by ongoing internal activity, remains a valid option.

The long sensory stores can be clearly differentiated from the early concepts of sensory registers (Neisser, 1967) that were thought of as storing huge amounts of information and being highly susceptible to interference. The comparatively low susceptibility to interference (Fig. 15.5) as well as the low capacity (Figs. 15.3 and 15.4) can be considered as evidence that the long sensory storage is more closely related to short-term memory than to the traditional notion of sensory register.

It could be questioned whether the capacity limit of the long sensory store and of short-term memory for categorical information is inherent to the storage system or whether it stems from the capacity limit of the attentional processes (Cowan, 2001) that are needed to report the stored information. In the case of the short visual store, it was this question which led Sperling (1960) to apply the partial-report method, by which he could prove that more information was available than could be reported. It could be argued that the report procedure interferes with the retained information, thereby decreasing the measure of the capacity found per report. This argument would be valid only for experiments that depend on report of many items such as the Waugh–Norman paradigm. It would not apply to periodic-noise perception, in which the successful memorization will alter perception in the first place. According to introspective reports, it is impossible to perceive a long cycle as being filled with distinct events. Only two or three events become audible. Conscious attention cannot be involved in this process, as the features that are memorized pass unnoticed during the first few cycles, and when they become audible this is due to the retention of their occurrence in an earlier cycle in which they were not audible. For instance, if a periodic noise signal of 4-s length is made up of four identical segments of 1-s length, even a well-trained participant will hear at most three cycles of such perceptual events. The first cycle will sound as homogeneous as continuous noise does.

If attentional processes are at the origin of the capacity limit observed in periodic-noise experiments, one would have to attribute it to a kind of "precon-scious attention." The maximum cycle length is at least an order of magnitude larger than the capacity of auditory sensory memory. Only by instruction are lis-teners able to store a certain signal portion in their auditory sensory memory for several seconds that has not yet produced any conscious percept. In this "locked" state of auditory sensory memory, new signal information does not interfere with its content. This locking appears to be a deliberate action for long cycles, and it appears that this strategy can be learned quite quickly.

The memory model of Cowan (1988, 1995) stands the test with noncategorical stimulus material such as white noise. Given the correspondence of lifetime, the narrow capacity limit, and the low susceptibility to interference, auditory sensory memory for random waveforms can well be considered a specialized module of short-term memory. In the light of our data it seems quite appropriate to speak of auditory short-term memory. There seems to be, however, a major difference between categorical and sensory storage that deserves consideration: Categorical storage can be enhanced with rehearsal techniques, whereas it seems that this is not the case for sensory storage. Consider, for example, the difference between the paradigms that led to the results shown in Figs. 15.1 and 15.2: For categorical information (Fig. 15.2) it is essential that there is an articulatory task during the retention interval that prevents participants from rehearsing. Otherwise there would be no decay at all. With random waveforms, however, there was no need to suppress rehearsal. This is supportive evidence for the claim that periodic random waveforms do not offer clues for categorical storage.

Formal evidence for the failure of rehearsal in sensory memory comes from cueing experiments. Demany, Clément, and Semal (2001) used an S1–S2 paradigm, with S1 being a three-component chord and S2 one single tone of these three, being either slightly higher or lower than the corresponding one in S1. A cue early or late during the retention interval would prepare the participant as to which tone was to be compared. They found no improvement that was due to early cueing. Early information did not activate a rehearsal, or if so, rehearsal did not help to maintain a better memory representation of pitch. Pilot data (Hahn & Kaernbach, 2004) demonstrated that rehearsal (at least, overt rehearsal) might even be detrimental to the quality of the pitch trace. A first analysis of the data indicates why this is so: The errors of the participants in a S1–S2 pitch memory paradigm were predictable from their singing during the retention interval. Rehearsal of noncategorical information might be detrimental because it adulterates the trace while attempting to rehearse it. Categorical information, on the other hand, tolerates small tampering with the original trace as it can be recategorized.

It is interesting to consider the difference between sensory memory experiments in which single stimulus dimensions (pitch, brightness, etc.) are used and experiments in which a complex stimulus such as a random waveform is used. Both types of experiments test sensory memory: There is no possibility of categorizing random waveforms. On first hearing one might think that it should be possible to "name" the percepts elicited by periodic noise, that is, to compare them to everyday sound events such as the sound of a windshield wiper or a washing machine. This naming is purely associative and does not help a participant to maintain the trace, for example by means of rehearsal. In vision, experiments with random block patterns (Mohr, 2002) correspond most closely to auditory random waveform experiments. A major difference between single-dimension and complex sensory experiments seems to be the higher susceptibility to interference in the case of a single dimension: In single-dimension experiments interference is found to depend on the similarity of the interfering stimulus to the memory trace (Deutsch, 1973). It is much harder to elicit interference with complex stimuli. These vary on a multitude of dimensions, and two separately generated stimuli are in general all but similar.

It might well be that the practicability of rehearsal is the only essential difference between short-term memory for categorical and noncategorical information—apart from the different type of information that is stored. Studies on sensory storage would then provide a valuable cross check to studies on storage of categorical information, with predictable differences in cases in which rehearsal plays a role.

ACKNOWLEDGMENTS

The author thanks Laurent Demany, who introduced him to periodic-noise stimuli and who was always ready to discuss experimental ideas and results, Jan Vorbrüggen for early discussions of the methods used in these studies, and Nelson Cowan, Laurent Demany, Mark A. Elliott, Randall W. Engle, Hans-Georg Geissler, and Erich Schröger for valuable discussions and comments concerning the manuscript.

REFERENCES

Atkinson, R. C., & Shiffrin. R. M. (1968). Human memory: A proposed system and its control processes. In K. W. Spence & J. T. Spence (Eds.), *The psychology of learning and motivation: Advances in research and theory* (Vol. 2, pp. 89–195). New York: Academic Press.

Averbach, E., & Coriell, A. (1961). Short-term memory in vision. *Bell System Technical Journal, 40*, 309–328.

Baddeley, A. D. (1986). *Working memory*. Oxford, England: Clarendon.

Brown, J. (1958). Some tests of the decay theory of immediate memory. *Quarterly Journal of Experimental Psychology, 10*, 12–21.

Cowan, N. (1984). On short and long auditory stores. *Psychological Bulletin, 96*, 341–370.

Cowan, N. (1988). Evolving concepts for memory storage, selective attention, and their mutual constraints within the human information processing system. *Psychological Bulletin, 104*, 163–191.

Cowan, N. (1995). *Attention and memory: An integrated framework*. Oxford, England: Oxford University Press.

Cowan, N. (2001). The magical number 4 in short-term memory: A reconsideration of mental storage capacity. *Behavioral and Brain Sciences, 24*, 87–114.

Crowder, R. G., & Morton, J. (1969). Precategorical acoustic storage. *Perception & Psychophysics, 5*, 365–373.

Darwin, C., Turvey, M., & Crowder, R. (1972). An auditory analog of the Sperling partial report procedure: Evidence for brief auditory storage. *Cognitive Psychology, 3*, 255–267.

Demany, L., Clément, S., & Semal, C. (2001). Does auditory memory depend on attention? In D. J. Breebaart, A. J. M. Houtsma, A. Kohlrausch, V. F. Prijs, & R. Schoonhoven (Eds.), *Physiological and psychophysical bases of auditory function* (pp. 461–467). Maastricht, The Netherlands: Shaker Publishing BV.

Deutsch, D. (1973). Interference in memory between tones adjacent in the musical scale. *Journal of Experimental Psychology, 100,* 228–231.

Frey, H.-P., Kaernbach, C., & König, P. (2003). Cats can detect repeated noise stimuli. *Neuroscience Letters, 346,* 45–48.

Glucksberg, S., & Cowen, G. N., Jr. (1970). Memory for nonattended auditory material. *Cognitive Psychology, 1,* 149–156.

Guttman, N., & Julesz, B. (1963). Lower limits of auditory periodicity analysis. *Journal of the Acoustical Society of America, 35,* 610.

Hahn, K., & Kaernbach, C. (2004). Pitch memory with and without rehearsal. Manuscript submitted for publication.

Hanna, T. E., & Robinson, D. E. (1985). Phase effects for a sine wave masked by reproducible noise. *Journal of the Acoustical Society of America, 77,* 1129–1140.

Kaernbach, C. (1992). On the consistency of tapping to repeated noise. *Journal of the Acoustical Society of America, 92,* 788–793.

Kaernbach, C. (1993). Temporal and spectral basis of the features perceived in repeated noise. *Journal of the Acoustical Society of America, 94,* 91–97.

Kaernbach, C. (2000). Early auditory feature coding, in contributions to psychological acoustics. In A. Schick, M. Meis, & C. Reckhardt (Eds.), *Results of the 8th Oldenburg Symposium on Psychological Acoustics* (pp. 295–307). Oldenburg, Germany: University of Oldenburg.

Kaernbach, C. (2004a). Elementary auditory percepts revealed by a behavioral reverse-correlation technique. Manuscript submitted for publication.

Kaernbach, C. (2004b). The memory of noise. Manuscript submitted for publication.

Kaernbach, C., Schröger, E., & Gunter, T. C. (1998). Human event-related brain potentials to auditory periodic noise stimuli. *Neuroscience Letters, 242,* 17–20.

Kaernbach, C., & Schulze, H. (2002). Auditory sensory memory for random waveforms in the Mongolian gerbil. *Neuroscience Letters, 329,* 37–40.

Keppel, G., & Underwood, B. J. (1962). Proactive inhibition in short-term retention of single items. *Journal of Verbal Learning and Verbal Behavior, 1,* 153–161.

Massaro, D. W., & Loftus, G. R. (1996). Sensory and perceptual storage: Data and theory. In E. L. Bjork & R. A. Bjork (Eds.), *Memory* (pp. 67–99). San Diego, CA: Academic Press.

Miller, G. (1956). The magical number seven plus minus two. *Psychological Review, 63,* 81–97.

Mohr, G. (2002). Delayed discrimination: Passive storage vs. active processing. In M. Baumann, A. Keinath, & J. F. Krems (Eds.), *Experimentelle Psychologie. Abstracts der 44. Tagung experimentell arbeitender Psychologen* [Experimental psychology. Abstracts of the 44th conference on experimental psychology] (p. 11). Regensburg, Germany: S. Roderer Verlag.

Munka, L., & Kaernbach, C. (2001). Lifetime of memory for self-generated information. In E. Sommerfeld, R. Kompass, & T. Lachmann (Eds.), *Proceedings of the Seventeenth Annual Meeting of the International Society for Psychophysics* (pp. 541–546). Lengerich, Germany: Pabst Science Publishers.

Neisser, U. (1967). *Cognitive psychology.* New York: Appleton-Century-Crofts.

Peterson, L. R., & Peterson, M. J. (1959). Short-term retention of individual items. *Journal of Experimental Psychology, 58,* 193–198.

Pollack, I. (1972). Memory of auditory waveforms. *Journal of the Acoustical Society of America, 52,* 1209–1215.

Pollack, I. (1990). Detection and discrimination thresholds for auditory periodicity. *Perception & Psychophysics, 47,* 105–111.

Shiffrin, R. M., & Schneider, W. (1977). Controlled and automatic human information processing: II. Perceptual learning, automatic attending, and a general theory. *Psychological Review, 84,* 127–190.

Sperling, G. (1960). The information available in brief visual presentations. *Psychological Monographs, 74* (Whole No. 498).

Warren, R. M. (1998). *Auditory perception, A new synthesis.* Cambridge, England: Cambridge University Press.

Warren, R. M., & Bashford, J. A. (1981). Perception of acoustic iterance: Pitch and infrapitch. *Perception & Psychophysics, 29,* 395–402.

Warren, R. M., & Bashford, J. A. (1993). When acoustic sequences are not perceptual sequences: The global perception of auditory patterns. *Perception & Psychophysics, 54,* 121–126.

Warren, R. M., Bashford, J. A., Cooley, J. M., & Brubaker, B. S. (2001). Detection of acoustic repetition for very long stochastic patterns. *Perception & Psychophysics, 63,* 175–182.

Warren, R. M., & Wrightson, J. M. (1981). Stimuli producing conflicting temporal and spectral cues to frequency. *Journal of the Acoustical Society of America, 70,* 1020–1024.

Warren, R. M., Wrightson, J. M., & Puretz, J. (1988). Illusory continuity of tonal and infratonal periodic sounds. *Journal of the Acoustical Society of America, 84,* 1338–1342.

Waugh, N. C., & Norman, D. A. (1965). Primary memory. *Psychological Review, 72,* 89–104.

Zwicker, E. (1964). "Negative afterimage" in hearing. *Journal of the Acoustical Society of America, 36,* 2413–2415.

16

Encoding and Retrieval Components Affecting Memory Span: Articulation Rate, Memory Search, and Trace Redintegration

Uta Lass, Gerd Lüer, and Dietrich Becker
University of Göttingen, Germany

Yunqiu Fang, and Guopeng Chen
East China Normal University, Shanghai, China

THEORETICAL INTERPRETATIONS OF THE LIMITS OF MEMORY SPAN

A person's memory span is measured by the number of items (usually digits) that can be reproduced in the correct order immediately following stimulus presentation. Performance in this task is subject to strict limitations—for adults it is defined by the Miller parameter of 7 ± 2 (Miller, 1956). Memory span is seen as a traditional measure of short-term-memory or working-memory capacity, and it is also used as a subtest in intelligence test routines (i.e., Wechsler, 1956, 1958). In stark contrast to the fact that this parameter is so commonly used as a means of defining short-term-memory performance, our knowledge over the mechanisms that ultimately limit memory span is, as yet, highly incomplete. This has led to an intense discussion in recent years (i.e., Cowan et al., 1998; Dosher & Ma, 1998; Hulme, Newton, Cowan, Stuart, and Brown, 1999). With the present study, we aim to contribute to this discussion by reexamining data we have published since 1997 and analyzing data gathered specifically for the purpose of furthering the quest for the mechanisms that limit memory span.

It is a question that has led to the formulation of different theoretical approaches. Probably the most popular model is that developed by Baddeley (e.g., Baddeley, 1997; Baddeley & Hitch, 1974), which supposes that memory span is defined by item articulation rates. In contrast, the multicomponent model, proposed by authors such as Cowan and Hulme (Cowan et al., 1998; Hulme et al., 1999), assumes that, as the name indicates, memory span is determined by more than one factor.

Baddeley's approach links memory-span limits to characteristics and functions of the so-called phonological loop, which is a subsystem of working memory dedicated to processing language-based input. The phonological loop comprises a processing and a storage component. Although the latter can store memory traces for only a very short time (approximately 1.5–2 s), such representations can be refreshed with the help of the processing component by means of rehearsal, thereby being preserved beyond the critical interval of 1.5–2 s. This rehearsal process can be equated to subvocal articulation. The phonological loop is able to process not only verbal input but visual input as well, if it is transformed into a phonological format.

Baddeley can draw on a number of robust experimental effects to support the phonological loop he proposes. In the search for factors limiting memory span, the word-length effect appears to be the most interesting piece of evidence. The subjects in experiments are usually able to correctly recall 6–7 monosyllabic words immediately following stimulus presentation. Memory span decreases if polysyllabic words are used. Baddeley, Thomson, and Buchanan (1975) have shown that there is a systematic relation between memory span and articulation rate: Memory span roughly corresponds to the number of items that can be articulated in the space of two seconds. It follows that memory span may vary, not only depending on the items used but also depending on the subjects taking part in the experiment. There is substantial empirical support for both of these aspects. A number of studies have shown that memory span for digits varies depending on subjects' first language—if the words for digits are relatively short in a given language, subjects exhibit longer memory spans (Chincotta & Underwood, 1997; Ellis & Hennelly, 1980; Hoosain, 1979, 1984; Lüer, Becker et al., 1998; Naveh-Benjamin & Ayres, 1986). This also provides an explanation for the fact that memory span increases in young subjects with age. Articulation rate follows this pattern as well. Hulme, Thomson, Muir, and Lawrence (1984) proved this correlation with a study establishing articulation rate and memory span for children of different age levels. In accordance with Baddeley's model, a relatively high memory span can be expected whenever items can be articulated particularly quickly, that is, whenever a large number of memory traces can be refreshed within the critical interval of 1.5–2 s.

Cowan and Hulme (Cowan et al., 1998; Hulme et al., 1999) claim that the phonological loop model is not sufficient to explain memory span. Although articulatory rehearsal does play an important role in span tasks, they reason, other processing mechanisms such as rapid search processes and mechanisms designed to reconstruct partially degraded item traces are equally relevant, particularly during output.

The inclusion of processes for the latter type derives particular support from experiments comparing memory span for words and nonwords (letter sequences with the phonotactical characteristics of words). Hulme, Maughan, and Brown (1991) found that memory span for nonwords is lower than that for words. In both cases, memory span decreases as articulation times increase. The word-length effect just described is therefore evident for both types of stimuli. In addition to this, the familiarity of items apparently plays a role. Familiar items such as words are recalled more successfully than unfamiliar items such as nonwords. This is where processes designed to reconstruct item traces that have already partially degraded in short-term memory come in. Long-term memory, in contrast to words, holds no representations of nonwords. It is therefore much more difficult to reconstruct incomplete item traces of nonwords for recall purposes (Hulme et al., 1997).

The assumption that retrieval factors play a role in determining memory-span performance derives particular support from studies that have shown that the size of memory span is not correlated with the time required for articulating the items themselves, but with characteristics of the interitem pauses evident during output (Cowan, 1992). The multicomponent model assumes that items yet to be recalled are reactivated during these pauses. As the interitem pause durations are considerably shorter than the time required for articulating the items in question, verbal rehearsal is excluded as a means of reactivation. This reactivation is apparently achieved by a much faster process such as the memory scanning outlined by Sternberg (1966). Cowan et al. (1994) studied the memory span of children and carried out fine-grained temporal analyses of the output. They found that, as expected, older children (8 years old) exhibited higher memory spans than younger ones (4 years old). There was no difference between the two groups with regard to articulation time per item, but there was a difference with respect to the length of interitem pauses—these were shorter with the older children. Furthermore, the preparatory interval (the elapsed time between the end of stimulus presentation and the onset of a spoken response) was shorter in the older children compared with that of the younger ones. Their task was to recall lists of items corresponding in length to their memory span, that is, they were exercising their faculties to capacity. This led the authors to conclude that the search and reactivation processes to be performed during the pauses were achieved more effectively by the older children than by the younger ones. Both groups remembered more shorter words than they did longer ones. This study therefore also points to the presence of further processing components apart from the word-length effect that, for its part, indicates the importance of articulatory processes in determining memory-span performance.

From these and similar results, Cowan and Hulme (Cowan et al., 1998; Hulme et al., 1999) conclude that the phonological loop model has merit, but is an oversimplification. They propose the multicomponent model as an alternative. According to this model, cognitive processing in memory-span tasks take place as follows: The items that are to be recalled are encoded phonologically. To be reproduced, these phonological representations must be retrieved from memory. This retrieval comprises at least two types of processes. The first is a rapid search mechanism, similar to Sternberg's memory scanning. This is referred to as trace selection. However, traces activated by this search process will frequently be incomplete because of degradation. These traces are subject to a form of erosion whose main cause is assumed to be output interference. Reproduction of early items in the list leads to interference and thereby partial destruction of traces of items further down the list. Incomplete traces have to be restored for items to be reproduced. This second process is referred to as trace redintegration. These two retrieval processes find expression in the length of the interitem pauses during reproduction. The results of their own studies provide Cowan and Hulme with support for their hypothesis, namely, that there are two quite separate factors determining an individual's memory span: rehearsal efficiency and short-term-memory retrieval efficiency.

Finally, the output-time model of Dosher and Ma (1998) ought to be placed into context in its relation to the two models previously outlined. The criticism by Dosher and Ma of Baddeley's model is similar to that brought forward by the proponents of the multicomponent model. In the authors' view, the phonological loop model disregards an important factor relevant to memory span, namely, that stored information can get lost in the course of the response output. According to Dosher and Ma, the overall time for which a subject spoke when recalling the lists should therefore allow for a better prediction of memory span than traditional variables such as list-reading duration. The data they have gathered support this hypothesis. Reading times are a particularly good means of predicting stimulus-specific differences in memory span, but output times are still slightly better predictors. Interestingly, this relation is evident both in oral reproduction and in responses registered by a keyboard.

The reported ability of overall output times to closely predict memory span could, at first glance, be seen as contradicting the results of Cowan (1992; Cowan et al., 1994) as previously cited, who found that reproduction time per item did not differ between subjects exhibiting different memory spans. However, Cowan equally found that there was a significant correlation between overall reproduction times and short-term-memory performance. If, however, reproduction times were adjusted for interitem pause durations, only these pause durations correlated with memory span, not the mean word durations. Therefore, in this respect, the results of Dosher and Ma were in agreement with the assumptions of the multicomponent model. It should be noted that the study of Dosher and Ma also established Sternberg scanning rates. They were not, however, used to predict memory span, rather to parallellize varying item sets with regard to their interference characteristics.

PREDICTING MEMORY SPAN FROM REPRODUCTION AND MEMORY SCANNING TIMES—A SUMMARY OF OUR OWN DATA

In cooperation with colleagues from Shanghai and Hangzhou, we conducted a German–Chinese joint project that examined the influence of language on short-term-memory performance. Several experiments yielded results that can be seen as supporting the phonological loop model (see Table 16.1). For one, Chinese participants exhibited higher memory spans for digits than, did their German counterparts of the same age (Lass, 1997; Lüer, Becker et al., 1998). This superior performance by Chinese participants was also in evidence where, instead of digits, corresponding words denoting digits in the subjects' native language were used as items. The Chinese participants also achieved better results with other item sets made up of words denoting colors and the names of simple geometric shapes such as arrow, star and circle (Lass, 1997; Lass et al., 2000; Lass, Fang, Chen, Becker, & Lüer, 1999; Lüer, Becker et al., 1998). At the same time, mean verbal reproduction times per item were shorter for Chinese items than for German ones across all categories of material. Assuming that verbal reproduction times are a valid indicator of subvocal rehearsal, the larger memory spans exhibited by the Chinese participants compared with their German counterparts can be traced back to their more effective rehearsal.

As documented in the studies cited, and unexpected from us, no significant difference occurred in the language-specific memory effect, whether the items were presented as verbal stimuli (names of colors and shapes) or nonverbal stimuli (color stimuli or drawings of geometric shapes). We interpret this as showing that even the nonverbal stimuli used were memorized either wholly or at least with significant participation from the phonological loop. Therefore, for example, if the picture of an arrow is presented, this not only triggers the corresponding concept in memory, but, because of the associative mode characterizing our knowledge structures (see, for instance, Anderson, 1995), the corresponding verbal expression is simultaneously activated. As the items used (color stimuli and geometric shapes) represent highly familiar concepts, their names can be expected to be highly over-learned and the corresponding memory links between the concepts and their verbal expressions characterized by great associative strength. According to this model, the latter goes hand in hand with fast automatic retrieval.

The suggested interpretation of our results within the framework of Baddeley's model is reinforced by the discovery that the Chinese participants failed to perform better than their German counterparts in trials in which random shapes were used—irregular four-point shapes after Vanderplas and Garvin (1959)—(Lass et al., 1999, 2000). Memory holds no representations of verbal expressions that describe these shapes that might be spontaneously activated. Therefore they cannot be grasped and processed by the phonological loop.

TABLE 16.1

Memory Span, Sternberg Scanning Time per Item, and Verbal Reproduction Time per Item for Different Stimulus Categories Measured for German and Chinese Participants

Stimulus Category	Participants	Memory Span		Verbal Reproduction Time per Item (ms)		Sternberg Scanning Time per Item (ms)	
Digits	German	6.10	$(N = 96)^a$	363	$(N = 21)^b$	41.27	$(n = 48)^a$
		6.22	$(N = 48)^b$			35.30	$(n = 48)^c$
		6.16		*363*		*38.29*	
	Chinese	7.83	$(N = 96)^a$	236	$(N = 48)^b$	31.52	$(n = 48)^a$
		7.33	$(N = 48)^b$			27.80	$(n = 48)^c$
		7.58		*236*		*29.66*	
Words denoting digits	German	5.79	$(N = 96)^a$	377	$(N = 18)^b$	43.49	$(n = 48)^a$
		5.88	$(N = 48)^b$			38.70	$(n = 48)^c$
		5.84		*377*		*41.05*	
	Chinese	7.70	$(N = 96)^a$	232	$(N = 48)^b$	29.76	$(n = 48)^a$
		7.48	$(N = 48)^b$			28.40	$(n = 48)^c$
		7.59		*232*		*29.08*	
Colors	German	4.56	$(N = 96)^a$	454	$(N = 12)^b$	52.50	$(n = 48)^a$
		4.56	$(N = 48)^b$			48.80	$(n = 48)^c$
		4.56		*454*		*50.65*	
	Chinese	5.55	$(N = 96)^a$	302	$(N = 48)^b$	38.61	$(n = 48)^a$
		5.38	$(N = 48)^b$			35.20	$(n = 48)^c$
		5.47		*302*		*36.91*	
Words denoting colors	German	4.71	$(N = 96)^a$	423	$(N = 13)^b$	44.95	$(n = 48)^a$
		4.80	$(N = 48)^b$			38.50	$(n = 48)^c$
		4.76		*423*		*41.73*	
	Chinese	6.45	$(N = 96)^a$	278	$(N = 48)^b$	33.73	$(n = 48)^a$
		6.06	$(N = 48)^b$			34.70	$(n = 48)^c$
		6.26		*278*		*34.22*	
Geometric shapes	German	3.70	$(N = 48)^d$	519	$(n = 20)^e$	95.67[f]	$(N = 48)^d$
		3.98	$(N = 48)^g$			94.04[f]	$(N = 48)^g$
		3.56	$(n = 24)^e$			53.67[f]	$(n = 24)^e$
		3.94	$(n = 24)^e$			61.74[f]	$(n = 24)^e$
		3.80		*519*		*76.28*	
	Chinese	4.44	$(N = 48)^d$	495	$(n = 24)^e$	73.85[f]	$(N = 48)^d$
		5.06	$(N = 48)^g$			75.73[f]	$(N = 48)^g$
		4.96	$(n = 24)^e$			58.17[f]	$(n = 24)^e$
		4.10	$(n = 24)^e$			62.18[f]	$(n = 24)^e$
		4.64		*495*		*67.48*	
Words denoting geometric shapes	German	4.04	$(n = 24)^e$	468	$(n = 20)^e$	47.08[f]	$(n = 24)^e$
		4.08	$(n = 24)^e$			57.07[f]	$(n = 24)^e$
		4.06		*468*		*52.08*	
	Chinese	5.79	$(n = 24)^e$	456	$(n = 24)^e$	51.10[f]	$(n = 24)^e$
		4.52	$(n = 24)^e$			51.77[f]	$(n = 24)^e$
		5.16		*456*		*51.44*	

TABLE 16.1

(Continued)

Stimulus Category	Participants	Memory Span		Verbal Reproduction Time per Item (ms)		Sternberg Scanning Time per Item (ms)	
Random	German	1.98	$(N = 48)^d$			103.82[f]	$(N = 48)^d$
four-point		3.28	$(N = 48)^g$			136.98[f]	$(N = 48)^g$
shapes		*2.63*				*120.40*	
	Chinese	1.82	$(N = 48)^d$			100.29[f]	$(N = 48)^d$
		3.13	$(N = 48)^g$			133.40[f]	$(N = 48)^g$
		2.48				*116.85*	

Note. Mean values refer to either the whole sample (number of participants indicated by *N*) or parts of the sample subject to specific variation in conditions (number of participants indicated by *n*). Mean values in italics refer to the overall mean value per stimulus category and language group.

Data sources: [a]Lass (1997); [b]Lüer, Becker et al. (1998), Exp. 2; [c]Lüer, Lass et al. (1998); [d]Lüer, Becker et al. (1998), Exp. 3; [e]Lass et al. (2000); [f]So far unpublished data gathered from individuals who also took part in the experiments cited; [g]Lass et al. (1999).

We used linear regression to test the ability of verbal reproduction rates to predict the memory span values measured in our experiments. To this end, we aggregated the mean group values per stimulus category and language group derived from the various experiments into one overall mean value (in Table 16.1) if there was more than one value. We think it justifiable to use this aggregate as the experimental setup was similar with regard to essential characteristics throughout the various experiments, as is detailed in what follows.

To measure memory span, the items of a list were presented in sequence on a screen. Each item remained visible for 1 s. The interitem interval was 200 ms. An acoustic signal indicated the end of each list to the subject and triggered reproduction. The item lists were constructed by random selection with certain limitations. To start with, short sequences were presented. After four trials with a sequence of a given length, the number of items in a sequence was increased by one, provided the subject had recalled at least one of the four sequences correctly. All individuals taking part in an experiment were presented with the same lists. Reproduction was either done by spoken recall or by a recognition test with a touch screen. Memory span (g) was calculated as $g = K + 0.5\ N$, where K is the number of items in the longest sequence of which all four lists were recalled correctly and N the number of sequences longer than K of which at least two lists were reproduced correctly.

The participants' verbal responses were recorded on tape to establish reproduction rates. With the aid of a computer program (Sound Edit 16 for Apple Macintosh), the total duration of each reply was measured by marking the first and last visible sound in the oscillographic display. Rarely found reproduction pauses produced by slips of the tongue, coughs, and so forth, were removed. The mean verbal reproduction time per item was calculated on the basis of all error-free responses produced by a subject. Reproduction rate, measured in items per second, was then used as an independent variable for the regression analysis.

As can be seen from Table 16.1, high memory spans go hand in hand with short reproduction times per item. Correspondingly, the regression analysis confirms a close relationship between memory span and reproduction rate. The correlation coefficient of $r = .93$ and $p < .0001$ differs significantly from zero. Reproduction rates account for 86% of variance in memory span ($R^2 = .86$). The regression equation is as follows: $y = 1.67 + 1.36x$ (where x is the verbal reproduction rate and y is the memory span). The standard error of the regression coefficient ($SE\ B$) amounts to 0.17. Figure 16.1 shows memory span as a function of reproduction rate.

Alongside the question of the extent to which memory span is determined by variables that indicate subvocal rehearsal, we have always been interested in a possible relationship between memory span and memory scanning time, as established by Sternberg's (1966) item-recognition task (Lass, 1997). In this task, the individual is first presented with a number of items that have to be memorized. The size of this memory set usually varies from one to seven items. The individual then has to decide whether a test item presented subsequently was part of the memory set or not. The time required for reaching this decision is typically a linear function of the size of the memory set (Kintsch, 1977). The slope of this function can be seen as a measure of the time per item needed to scan memory. This parameter is also referred to as scanning time.

The relationship between the two variables, memory span and scanning time, was first made the subject of a study by Cavanagh (1972), who presented a summarizing analysis of previously published data. He found a high correlation between memory span and scanning time in that, where there were high memory spans for a stimulus category, the corresponding scanning times were short and vice versa. Brown and Kirsner (1980) have questioned whether such a relationship could be found on an individual-subject level. Puckett and Kausler (1984), however, found evidence that it could. On the basis of their own results, Cowan and Hulme (Cowan et al., 1998; Hulme et al., 1999) even reach the conclusion that scanning rate and articulation rate are both independent predictors of memory span.

We also gathered Sternberg item-recognition data from our experiments. Some of this is published here for the first time (see Table 16.1). Using the same method previously described, we used linear regression to test the ability of scanning rates to predict the memory-span values established in our experiments.

The different experiments were comparable with respect to all significant characteristics of the item-recognition task. The subjects had to memorize a new memory set for each trial. The items of the memory set were presented on screen, one after another, for a duration of 1 s each and an interitem interval of 200 ms. The test item presented subsequently remained visible on screen until the participant had registered a response by pressing a key on a keyboard. Mean scanning time per item was calculated on the basis of all correct responses given by a subject. Table 16.1 contains data derived only from participants working under reward conditions, that is, they were paid a certain amount of money for rapid correct responses and

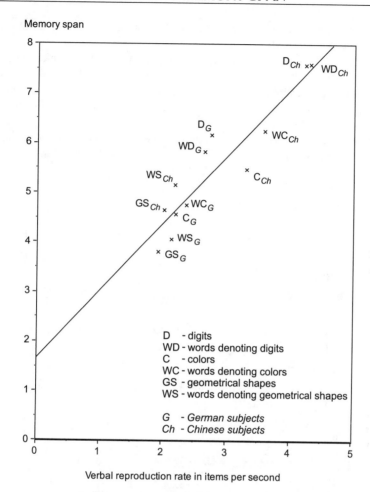

FIG. 16.1. Relation between verbal reproduction rate in items per second and memory span for different stimulus categories for German and Chinese participants. Mean values per stimulus category and language groups were derived from various experiments and aggregated into an overall mean value.

wrong answers carried corresponding penalties—we discovered that, unlike their Chinese counterparts, German participants performed to the limit of their abilities only when they were given a reward as an added incentive (Lüer, Lass, et al., 1998).

Again, mean values per stimulus category and language group derived from the various experiments were aggregated into an overall mean value (in Table 16.1). The results detailed in Table 16.1 show that the relationship between memory span and scanning time per item turns out to be analogous to that between memory span and reproduction time per item. The higher the memory span, the shorter the memory scanning time.

We used the scanning rate as an independent variable for the regression analysis. The correlation coefficient proved highly significant: $r = .96$ and $p < .0001$. Scanning rate during memory search accounts for 92% of the variance in memory span ($R^2 = .92$). The regression equation is as follows: $y = 1.20 + 0.18x$ (where x is the memory scanning rate and y is the memory span). The standard error of the regression coefficient is $SE\ B = 0.015$. Figure 16.2 shows memory span as a function of memory scanning rate.

To sum up, it should be noted that in our experiments both verbal reproduction rate and memory scanning rate proved to be good predictors of memory span.

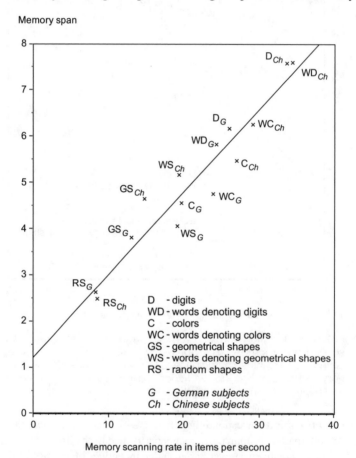

FIG. 16.2. Relation between memory scanning rate in items per second established with the item-recognition task (Sternberg, 1966) and memory span for different stimulus categories for German and Chinese participants. Mean values per stimulus category and language groups were derived from various experiments and aggregated into an overall mean value.

Do our results support the criticism directed at the phonological loop, that is, claims regarding the participation of processing components other than articulatory rehearsal?

The indicator for subvocal rehearsal in our experiments was the mean verbal reproduction time per item or reproduction rate. As already outlined, this indicator was calculated from the length of spoken responses within the span task that had been adjusted for interruptions in speech flow. The resulting reproduction rate displays a high correlation with memory span. In contrast to this, proponents of the multicomponent model rarely found significant correlations between memory span and reproduction time adjusted for pauses (e.g., Cowan, 1992; Hulme et al., 1999). This contradiction appears to be due to the two approaches differing in what was seen as pauses. In the studies of Cowan and Hulme, interitem intervals occurring in between the articulation of individual words during reproduction were measured. These are pauses on a much higher level of resolution than the rougher ones, measured in our experiments, caused by slips of the tongue, coughs, and so forth. It is therefore conceivable that those processing mechanisms indicated by interitem intervals as defined by the multicomponent model were still contained in the reproduction time variables as we defined them. The high correlation between memory span and reproduction rate that we found in our experiments could therefore be due to the very processing mechanisms pinpointed by Cowan and Hulme as taking effect during interitem intervals. If we follow this reasoning, the reproduction rate that are used would not be a suitable indicator of subvocal rehearsal. The finding of the second regression analysis, that memory span can be predicted quite accurately by scanning rates, also supports the assumption that output-related processing components may be relevant in determining memory span as scanning rates can be seen as indicators of rapid memory search during output.

Taken together, our results would seem to support the multicomponent model. In the experiment outlined in the next section, we have tried to differentiate the variables relevant to the model more clearly than has been possible in the preceding post hoc analyses. We also wanted to test their ability to predict differences in memory span on an individual-subject level.

PREDICTING MEMORY SPAN FROM INPUT- AND OUTPUT-RELEVANT PROCESSING COMPONENTS—AN EXPERIMENTAL STUDY

Method

The people taking part in this experiment were comparable with those who had taken part in earlier experiments with regard to important characteristics. They were German students ($N = 48$) from various departments with a mean age of 23 years (range: 20–25 years). The subjects completed a total of three tasks. Memory span was measured for digits, words denoting digits, colors, and words denoting color. Verbal responses were recorded on tape. The same stimulus material was used for the Sternberg (1966) item-recognition task. The setup of these two tasks, as well as the measurement of memory span and scanning time, was the same as in our previous experiments (see the section on predicting memory span from reproduction and memory scanning times—a summary of our own data). We introduced a new task to determine articulation times for the items used. To this end, the students had to read (words denoting digits or colors) or name (digits, color stimuli) sequences comprising five items each as rapidly as possible, three times in a row. During the recitation, an index card with the respective item sequence was placed in front of the subject.

Timing measurements for the span-task responses and for responses in the rapid articulation task were made through tape recordings of the test session and the computer program as outlined in the previous section. This time, however, not only were the pauses during the flow of speech caused by slips of the tongue and coughing noted, but all identifiable silent periods between words were also taken into account.

Two variables for the span-task responses, the verbal reproduction time per item and the length of the so-called preparatory interval, were calculated on the basis of verbal reproductions of lists containing three items each. (We chose this list length as it was the one for which there were still complete data for all subjects across all stimulus categories.) The preparatory interval comprised the time elapsing between the start signal that indicated to the participant that the reproduction of items was to begin and the actual onset of the response. Proponents of the multicomponent model see the two interval variables, preparatory interval and interitem interval, as indicators for the presence of retrieval processes (Cowan, 1992; Cowan et al., 1994, 1998; Hulme et al., 1999). However, it was difficult to define an interval variable corresponding to interitem intervals, as very few intervals between individual words actually occurred with the stimulus material used. An interval variable of the interitem interval type would therefore certainly not be a valid indicator for the presence of retrieval processes. With this in mind, we defined the interval variable as the length (i.e., number of items) of the first list during whose reproduction a subject paused for the first time. The reasoning behind this is as follows: Measurable pauses occurring during output indicate that additional processing mechanisms such as the reactivation and redintegration of memory traces take up considerable time. Participants with higher memory spans will only have to start using these mechanisms for longer lists. Intervals will therefore appear in only longer lists, compared with those intervals used for participants with more limited memory spans.

As previously stated, the scanning time per item was used as an indicator for rapid search processes. In addition, overall reaction time was measured in the item-recognition task to establish the general processing speed of each subject (see Hulme et al., 1999).

Unlike in our previous experiments, in these experiments the articulation time per item was used as an indicator for the effectiveness of rehearsal. These were calculated from the tape recordings of the rapid articulation task.

Results of the Correlation Analyses

We followed a two-step approach to be able to compare our findings with those of Hulme et al. (1999). The first step was to calculate the correlations between the dependent variables established by us (see Table 16.2; Table 16.3 shows mean values and standard deviations). For the second step we examined, by means of regression analyses, how well the variation in memory span can be predicted by the other variables. We begin by presenting the most interesting results of the correlation analyses.

Articulation time per item was the only variable correlating significantly with memory span across all four stimulus categories. This once again replicated a result frequently found in the past: High articulation rate goes hand in hand with high memory span and vice versa (for example, Baddeley et al., 1975; Schweickert & Boruff, 1986). In contrast to this, Hulme et al. (1999) found a significant correlation for only one of the four stimulus categories (trisyllabic nonwords), but not for monosyllabic nonwords or for words. In the study by Hulme et al., a participant's task was to repeatedly articulate sequences comprising two items, whereas we used five-item sequences in our experiment. The repeated rapid articulation of two-item sequences consisting of familiar or very short items (such as monosyllabic nonwords) may represent too simple a task to yield adequate indications of the speed of subvocal rehearsal.

There was no significant correlation between memory span and reproduction time per item, even though the two variables, articulation time and reproduction time per item, exhibited a significant correlation. The latter is probably due to the shared influence of motoric processes involved in speech utterance, whereas it apparently was the explicit time pressure in the articulation task that led to a significant correlation with memory span.

Furthermore, our study showed that, as expected, there was a significant correlation between the interval variable or the length of the first item list containing a pause and the memory span. The longer the list within which a given participant first paused, the higher the memory span achieved by the participant. This relationship was apparent between the interval variable, in which words denoting numbers had to be reproduced, and memory span across all four stimulus categories. This result can be seen as indicating the importance of retrieval processes during output, as proposed by the multicomponent model. Individuals who can reactivate and repair partially degraded memory traces quickly and economically achieve higher memory spans. It remains to be seen why the interval variable deriving from the reproduction of words denoting digits correlated particularly highly with memory span across all four stimulus categories. It is possible that an individual's

TABLE 16.2

Correlations of Memory Span, Articulation Time, and Response Timing in the Memory Span Task and the Sternberg Memory Scanning Task

Variable	1	2	3	4	5	6	7	8	9	10	11	12	13	14
1 MS A														
2 MS B	.66**													
3 MS C	.71**	.52**												
4 MS D	.69**	.52**	.63**											
5 PREPI A	-.16	-.08	.00	-.04										
6 PREPI B	-.04	-.09	-.05	.02	.33*									
7 PREPI C	-.18	-.14	-.15	-.02	.17	.58**								
8 PREPI D	.03	-.10	.13	.04	.44**	.39**	.49**							
9 REP A	-.12	-.04	-.04	-.08	.50**	.28	.04	.07						
10 REP B	-.01	.00	.09	.03	.31*	.48**	.14	.05	.83**					
11 REP C	-.09	-.12	.02	-.03	.29*	.31*	.24	.08	.66**	.72**				
12 REP D	-.02	-.14	.05	-.08	.44**	.28	-.01	.24	.65**	.63**	.73**			
13 PAUSE A	.14	.08	.20	.05	.03	-.16	-.03	.11	.07	-.10	-.14	-.05		
14 PAUSE B	.55**	.58**	.52**	.49**	-.35	-.33	-.08	-.26	.00	-.02	.04	-.03	.44*	
15 PAUSE C	.50**	.26	.50**	.29	-.13	-.20	-.29	-.02	.06	.20	.12	.28	-.21	.12
16 PAUSE D	.07	-.09	.13	-.01	.03	-.04	-.08	-.11	-.21	-.10	-.24	-.23	-.16	.16
17 ART A	-.45**	-.43**	-.37**	-.33*	-.04	.02	.00	-.30*	.41**	.43**	.46**	.35*	-.07	.14
18 ART B	-.34*	-.35*	-.40**	-.22	.15	.09	.06	-.12	.54**	.50**	.56**	.48**	-.03	.04
19 ART C	-.31*	-.33*	-.37**	-.32*	-.13	-.03	.06	-.23	.29*	.36*	.36*	.21	.01	.21
20 ART D	-.39**	-.41**	-.39**	-.32*	-.13	-.10	.02	-.20	.35*	.35*	.29*	.26	.05	.12
21 SCAN A	.02	.08	-.14	.00	-.02	.00	.09	.08	-.35*	-.38**	-.41**	-.46**	-.05	-.31
22 SCAN B	-.03	.04	-.05	.00	.10	.23	.13	.13	-.06	.05	-.02	-.07	-.36*	-.25
23 SCAN C	-.02	.03	-.07	-.09	-.18	-.02	-.10	-.18	-.09	-.07	.00	-.06	-.37*	.06
24 SCAN D	.04	.08	.19	.03	-.05	.13	.02	.02	-.08	.03	.07	-.04	-.10	.10
25 RT A	-.17	-.08	-.25	-.11	.17	-.10	.14	.02	.04	.03	.13	.00	-.23	-.24
26 RT B	-.10	-.25	-.30*	.00	.12	.25	.17	.09	-.03	.14	.16	.06	-.41*	-.35
27 RT C	-.15	-.17	-.35*	-.11	-.02	.00	.22	.04	-.02	-.08	.17	.06	-.34*	-.05
28 RT D	-.14	-.18	-.33*	-.23	.02	-.02	.07	-.07	-.01	-.01	.28	.16	-.39*	-.14

TABLE 16.2
Table A.1 (Continued)

Variable	15	16	17	18	19	20	21	22	23	24	25	26	27
1 MS A													
2 MS B													
3 MS C													
4 MS D													
5 PREPI A													
6 PREPI B													
7 PREPI C													
8 PREPI D													
9 REP A													
10 REP B													
11 REP C													
12 REP D													
13 PAUSE A													
14 PAUSE B													
15 PAUSE C													
16 PAUSE D	.12												
17 ART A	.05	−.14											
18 ART B	−.02	−.34	.80**										
19 ART C	.05	−.22	.73**	.60**									
20 ART D	.04	−.27	.77**	.66**	.82**								
21 SCAN A	−.33	−.25	−.52**	−.37*	−.21	−.17							
22 SCAN B	−.21	−.33	−.30*	−.14	−.01	−.11	.52**						
23 SCAN C	−.03	−.26	−.02	−.04	.01	−.09	.24	.26					
24 SCAN D	−.31	−.19	−.21	−.23	−.09	−.12	.40**	.46**	.19				
25 RT A	−.19	−.39*	.01	.29*	.16	.10	.41**	.38**	.19	.04			
26 RT B	−.12	−.32	−.03	.18	.15	.10	.41**	.67**	.16	.15	.54**		
27 RT C	−.13	−.37*	.03	.22	.11	.00	.20	.35*	.27	−.08	.58**	.60**	
28 RT D	−.14	−.19	.21	.33*	.30*	.23	.18	.35*	.07	.09	.58**	.58**	.57**

Note. MS = memory span; PREPI = preparatory interval; REP = reproduction time per item; PAUSE = length of the first-pause list; ART = articulation time per item; SCAN = scanning time per item in the Sternberg task; RT = overall reaction time in the Sternberg task; A = digits; B = words denoting digits; C = colors; D = words denoting colors.
*p < .05. **p < .01.

363

TABLE 16.3

Number of Cases, Means, and Standard Deviations of the Variables Used
in the Experiment

Variable	Cases	M	SD
Memory span (number of items)			
Digits	48	5.99	1.01
Words denoting digits	48	5.92	0.91
Colors	48	4.78	0.79
Words denoting colors	48	4.91	0.76
Preparatory interval (ms)			
Digits	48	680	179
Words denoting digits	48	647	166
Colors	48	686	211
Words denoting colors	48	653	167
Reproduction time per item (ms)			
Digits	48	346	91
Words denoting digits	48	338	78
Colors	48	376	62
Words denoting colors	48	377	66
Length of the first-pause list (number of items)			
Digits	36	6.17	1.28
Words denoting digits	29	6.62	1.92
Colors	35	4.71	1.66
Words denoting colors	30	5.40	1.43
Articulation time per item (ms)			
Digits	48	236	44
Words denoting digits	48	243	48
Colors	48	351	66
Words denoting colors	48	300	48
Scanning time per item (ms)			
Digits	48	49	20
Words denoting digits	48	50	20
Colors	48	56	18
Words denoting colors	48	50	22
Overall reaction time in the Sternberg task (ms)			
Digits	48	583	88
Words denoting digits	48	633	101
Colors	48	630	98
Words denoting colors	48	631	96

ability to reactivate and repair memory traces found particularly clear expression in relation to words denoting digits. As far as items such as digits or color stimuli were concerned, recoding into a phonological format could possibly have played an additional role. Regarding colors and words denoting color, it is possible that the comparatively unusual sequentialization of the task "obscured" an individual's abilities with regard to the reactivation and redintegration of memory traces.

Contrary to expectations suggested by the multicomponent model, there was no significant correlation between the preparatory interval and memory span. Hulme et al. did not find any correlation of this sort either, as far as word items were concerned. They did, however, for nonwords. It is conceivable that this relationship becomes apparent only when the task to be completed reaches a certain level of subjective difficulty. For adults, this may be the case in which nonwords have to be recalled (Hulme et al., 1999); for children this may apply even to words (Cowan, 1992; Cowan et al., 1994).

Memory span for color stimuli furthermore correlated significantly with overall reaction time in the Sternberg task (with the exception of reaction time for digits). Individuals who displayed fast reactions in the Sternberg task also had high memory spans for color stimuli. It is likely that this relationship becomes apparent with regard to color stimuli because this is the only case in which uttering the term denoting the concept is not a completely automated process. This therefore leaves scope for individual differences, with regard to general processing speeds, to exercise a strong influence on generating output, and thus on memory span.

It should be noted that, contrary to Hulme et al., we did not find any significant correlation between scanning time per item in the Sternberg task and memory span. The scanning time for digits correlated significantly with articulation time per item for digits and words denoting digits, as well as with reproduction time per item across all four stimulus categories. In addition, we found significant correlations for digits and words denoting digits between scanning time and overall reaction time in the Sternberg task. It seems therefore that a certain speed component was indicated by scanning time per item, but apparently not one that was directly relevant to memory span—at least not in the present study.

To summarize, it can be said that our data yield support for both the phonological loop and the multicomponent model. The finding of individual differences in articulation rate as significantly correlated with individual differences in memory span suggests that rehearsal plays an important role in memory span tasks. However, the occurrence of intervals during output, which can be seen as indicating the involvement of further processing mechanisms such as trace reactivation and redintegration, has proved to play a role in memory-span tasks as well.

Results of the Regression Analyses

To assess the relative power of the variables that we considered to be predictors of memory span, we conducted four simultaneous regression analyses by using each of the memory-span measures (digits, words denoting digits, colors, words denoting color) as the dependent variable. There were five stimulus type-specific predictors in each equation: duration of preparatory interval, reproduction time per item, scanning time per item, articulation time per item, and overall reaction time in the Sternberg task. An interval variable was included in all four regression analyses as a sixth predictor, this being the length (i.e., number of items) of the

TABLE 16.4
Summary of Four Stimultaneous Regression Analyses Predicting Memory Span

Predictor	Digits		Words Denoting Digits		Colors		Words Denoting Colors	
	Beta	c^a	Beta	c^a	Beta	c^a	Beta	c^a
Preparatory interval	−.17	−.23	−.05	−.14	−.09	−.21	.04	.07
Reproduction time per item	.18	−.16	.25	.00	.26*	.02	.01	−.15
Length of first-pause list for words denoting digits	.47***	.67	.43**	.71	.45***	.57	.43**	.74
Articulation time per item	−.65***	−.62	−.4*	−.55	−.50***	−.54	−.33*	−.58
Scanning time per item	−.15	.03	.22	.07	−.02	−.10	−.03	.05
Overall reaction time	.01	−.24	−.22	−.40	−.29*	−.50	−.10	−.42
Multiple R	.72***		.63**		.70***		.55*	
R^2	.52		.40		.49		.30	

[a] Structure coefficient ($c_i = r_{ci}/R$).
*$p < .05$, **$p < .0$, ***$p < .001$.

list during which a participant first exhibited a pause, as established for words denoting digits. This was done because this interval variable correlated highly with memory span across the board.

Table 16.4 contains a summary of the relevant results. All four regression analyses yielded a significant multiple correlation coefficient. The total variance accounted for ranged from 30% for words denoting color to 52% for digits. Each regression analysis yielded a significant regression coefficient for both the variable articulation time per item and the interval variable. In addition, the regression coefficients of the two variables reproduction time per item and overall reaction time in the Sternberg task significantly differed from zero where color stimuli were concerned. Structure coefficients ($c_i = r_{ic}/R$) were calculated to assess the extent to which each of the six independent variables made a unique contribution to the prediction of memory span, independent of the effect from other variables. As can be seen from Table 16.3, structure coefficients for the variable articulation time per item and the interval variable were much higher than those for the remaining variables. Only in the case of color stimuli did the variable overall reaction time provide a contribution of comparable extent with the prediction of memory span.

In our opinion, these results are straightforward. They support the criticism leveled against Baddeley's model by proponents of the multicomponent model with regard to rehearsal efficiency being only one of the factors determining memory span. Retrieval mechanisms, which operate mainly during output intervals, are at least as important. As shown in Table 16.3, the interval variable (established for words denoting digits) was just as good a predictor for the memory span as the articulation time variable. However, in the data gathered from this experiment, we did not find any support for the suggestion that a process similar to the rapid memory search proposed by Sternberg (1966) might be one of the relevant processes during output. These findings are expanded in the next section.

GENERAL DISCUSSION

In the second section of this article (predicting memory span from reproduction and memory scanning times—a summary of our own data), we reported results of two post hoc analyses for which we used data from different experiments carried out within the last few years (see Table 16.1). Both the verbal reproduction rate and the memory scanning rate were highly correlated with span measures. The verbal reproduction rate accounted for 86% of the variance in span and the memory scanning rate accounted for 92% of the variance in span. In the new experiment that was reported next (see the section on predicting memory span from input- and output-relevant processing components—an experimental study), these two variables were not related to memory span. Important predictors in this experiment were the articulation time per item, which was determined in a rapid articulation task, and an interval variable, which was determined with the help of the recorded verbal responses in the memory span task: the length (i.e., number of items) of the first list during which a subject paused for the first time.

As to the reproduction time variable, we do not see any contradiction in its varying power as predictor of memory span. The variable in the post hoc analysis still encompasses the interitem intervals that were theoretically thought of as decisive when, in our later experiment, it was taken out of the calculation of the mean reproduction time per item in the responses of the subjects.

In the multicomponent model by Cowan and Hulme (Cowan et al., 1998; Hulme et al., 1999), the relevance of the interitem intervals is explained as follows: Pauses during output encompass retrieval processes such as reactivation and redintegration of memory traces, which determine the reproduction performance in addition to the .rehearsal. With the data from our new experiment, we can support the assumption that the size of the memory span is systematically influenced by the extent of necessary additional processing. The data do not confirm, however, the assumption that the processes in the pauses during output are of the type of memory search described by Sternberg (1966).

Why does the measure of scanning not play a role for the prediction of the memory span in the last experiment presented, but does so in the post hoc analysis? The reason for this can be seen in the methodical procedure in which mean values drawn from subject groups were aggregated and used in the post hoc analysis. This might be subject to the critique by Brown and Kirsner (1980) in which it is stated that the measure of scanning is not very suitable as a means of diagnosing individual differences in memory span.

Altogether, our results from the post hoc analysis and from our new experiment support the core assumption of the multicomponent model: namely, that both the rehearsal efficiency (as indexed by the articulation time) and the retrieval efficiency (as indexed by the interval variable) are important determinants of the memory span (see Cowan et al., 1998).

It remains to be clarified as to why in our experiment the measure of scanning was no powerful predictor of memory span, but was so in the experiment of Hulme et al. (1999). This discrepancy cannot be explained with greater standard errors of the memory search measure in our sample. As was expected, because of the greater number of participants in our experiment ($N = 48$), in comparison with the number of participants in the experiment of Hulme et al. ($N = 24$), the standard errors turned out lower in our experiment (digits, $SEM = 2.8$; words denoting digits, $SEM = 2.95$; colors, $SEM = 2.65$; words denoting colors, $SEM = 3.25$; versus one-syllable words, $SEM = 12.09$; five-syllable words, $SEM = 9.38$; one-syllable nonwords, $SEM = 7.71$; three-syllable nonwords, $SEM = 11.05$). The discrepancy in question between the two studies cannot be attributed to poor reliability of the memory search measure in our experiment. The reliabilities (Cronbach's α) obtained in our experiment were similar to what Hulme et al. reported (digits, $\alpha = .72$; words denoting digits, $\alpha = .41$; colors, $\alpha = .60$, words denoting colors, $\alpha = .55$; versus one-syllable words, $\alpha = .77$; five-syllable words, $\alpha = .48$; one-syllable nonwords, $\alpha = .60$; three-syllable nonwords, $\alpha = .56$).

It is conceivable, as indicated in the work of Hulme et al., that there may be a trade-off between memory search and rehearsal processes. If phonological rehearsal is selected and used in a particular situation, evidence for memory search will be reduced within that situation and vice versa. Does this hypothesis suggest a plausible reason why the results of scanning were so different in the two studies? We do not think so. The items that we used can be marked as well-known units, which, moreover, affected the capacity of the phonological loop relatively little. Of the 10 words denoting digits, 9 were monosyllabic, 1 word had two syllables, 8 of the 10 color names were monosyllabic, and 2 names had two syllables. In the experiment from Hulme et al., the item set with the one-syllable words comes closest to our stimuli—and of all four stimulus categories used in that experiment, the measure of memory search turned out to be the most powerful predictor of memory span just with this stimulus category.

In addition, a comparison of the two experiments with regard to the execution mode of the Sternberg task and the subjects used yielded, in our eyes, no further information. We have to agree with Cowan and Hulme (Cowan et al., 1998; Hulme et al., 1999), who claim that the processes that contribute to the coming about of the memory span are too simplified in the model of the phonological loop and that retrieval processes play an additional important role during the output. A more exact identification of these retrieval processes is, however, still needed.

AUTHOR NOTE

This research was supported by the Volkswagen Foundation, Hanover, Germany. Data collection was carried out with the participation of Song Yan and Claudia Wilimzig, Göttingen, and Zhongming Wang, Hangzhou, PR China. We thank Nelson Cowan for helpful comments. We are grateful to Christina Sarembe for her help in preparing the English version of our article.

REFERENCES

Anderson, J. R. (1995). *Cognitive psychology and its implications* (4th ed.). New York: Freeman.

Baddeley, A. D. (1997). *Human memory: Theory and practice* (rev. ed.). Hove, England: Psychology Press.

Baddeley, A. D., & Hitch, G. (1974). Working memory. In G. A. Bower (Ed.), *The psychology of learning and motivation* (Vol. 8, pp. 47–89). New York: Academic Press.

Baddeley, A. D., Thomson, N., & Buchanan, M. (1975). Word length and the structure of short-term memory. *Journal of Verbal Learning and Verbal Behavior, 14*, 575–585.

Brown, H. L., & Kirsner, K. (1980). A within-subjects analysis of the relationship between memory span and processing rate in short-term memory. *Cognitive Psychology, 12*, 177–187.

Cavanagh, J. P. (1972). Relation between the immediate memory span and the memory search rate. *Psychological Review, 6*, 525–530.

Chincotta, D., & Underwood, G. (1997). Digit span and articulatory suppression: A cross-linguistic comparison. *European Journal of Cognitive Psychology, 9*, 89–96.

Cowan, N. (1992). Verbal memory span and the timing of spoken recall. *Journal of Memory and Language, 31*, 668–684.

Cowan, N., Keller, T. A., Hulme, C., Roodenrys, S. J., McDougall, S., & Rack, J. (1994). Verbal memory span in children: Speech timing clues to the mechanisms underlying age and word length effects. *Journal of Memory and Language, 33*, 234–250.

Cowan, N., Wood, N. L., Wood, P. K., Keller, T. A., Nugent, L. D., & Keller, C. V. (1998). Two separate verbal processing rates contributing to short-term memory span. *Journal of Experimental Psychology: General, 127*, 141–160.

Dosher, B. A., & Ma, J. J. (1998). Output loss or rehearsal loop? Output time versus pronunciation time limits in immediate recall for forgetting-matched materials. *Journal of Experimental Psychology: Learning, Memory, and Cognition, 24*, 1217–1232.

Ellis, N. R., & Hennelly, R. A. (1980). A bilingual word-length effect: Implications for intelligence testing and the relative ease of mental calculation in Welsh and English. *British Journal of Psychology, 71*, 43–52.

Hoosain, R. (1979). Forward and backward digit span in the languages of the bilingual. *Journal of Genetic Psychology, 135*, 263–268.

Hoosain, R. (1984). Experiments on digit spans in the Chinese and English languages. In H. S. R. Kao & R. Hoosain (Eds.), *Psychological studies of the Chinese language* (pp. 23–38). Hong Kong: The Chinese Language Society of Hong Kong.

Hulme, C., Maughan, S., & Brown, G. D. A. (1991). Memory for familiar and unfamiliar words: Evidence for a long-term memory contribution to short-term memory span. *Journal of Memory and Language, 30*, 685–701.

Hulme, C., Newton, P., Cowan, N., Stuart, G., & Brown, G. (1999). Think before you speak: Pauses, memory search, and trace redintegration processes in verbal memory span. *Journal of Experimental Psychology: Learning, Memory, and Cognition, 25*, 447–463.

Hulme, C., Roodenrys, S., Schweickert, R., Brown, G. D. A., Martin, S., & Stuart, G. (1997). Word frequency effects on short-term memory tasks: Evidence for a redintegration process in immediate recall. *Journal of Experimental Psychology: Learning, Memory, and Cognition, 23*, 1217–1232.

Hulme, C., Thomson, N., Muir, C., & Lawrence. A. L. (1984). Speech rate and the development of short-term memory span. *Journal of Experimental Child Psychology, 38*, 241–253.

Kintsch, W. (1977) *Memory and cognition.* New York: Wiley.

Lass, U. (1997). Einfluß von Sprache auf Verarbeitungsprozesse im Kurzzeitgedächtnis—eine vergleichende Untersuchung mit deutschen und chinesischen Probanden. [Language effects on short-term memory-experiments on the Chinese and German languages]. In G. Lüer & U. Lass (Eds.), *Erinnern und Behalten. Wege zur Erforschung des menschlichen Gedächtnisses* [Storage and retrieval. Strategies in memory research] (pp. 244–268). Göttingen, Germany: Vandenhoeck & Ruprecht.

Lass, U., Fang, Y., Chen, G., Becker, D., & Lüer, G. (1999). Is memory for shapes subject to language-specific effects? An experimental study of memory span in German and Chinese subjects. *Zeitschrift für Sprache & Kognition, 18*, 136–145.

Lass, U., Lüer, G., Becker, D., Fang, Y., Chen, G., & Wang, Z. (2000). Kurzzeitgedächtnisleistungen deutscher und chinesischer Probanden mit verbalen und figuralen Items: zur Funktion von Phonologischer Schleife und visuell-räumlichen Notizblock. [Short-term memory performance of Germans and Chinese with verbal items and geometrical figures: On the functions of phonological loop and visuo-spatial sketch pad]. *Zeitschrift für Experimentelle Psychologie, 47*, 77–88.

Lüer, G., Becker, D., Lass, U., Fang, Y., Chen, G., & Wang, Z. (1998). Memory span in German and Chinese: Evidence for the phonological loop. *European Psychologist, 3*, 102–112.

Lüer, G., Lass, U., Becker, D., Fang, Y., Chen, G., & Wang, Z. (1998). Zum Einfluß von Belohnung auf die Geschwindigkeit von Suchprozessen im Kurzzeitgedächtnis. [Effect of reward on the speed of memory scanning]. In K. C. Klauer & H. Westmeyer (Eds.), *Psychologische Methoden und soziale Prozesse* [Psychological methods and social variables] (pp. 352–371). Lengerich, Germany: Pabst Science Publishers.

Miller, G. A. (1956). The magical number seven, plus or minus two: Some limits on our capacity for processing information. *Psychological Review, 63*, 81–97.

Naveh-Benjamin, M., & Ayres, T. J. (1986). Digit span, reading rate, and linguistic relativity. *Quarterly Journal of Experimental Psychology, 38A*, 739–751.

Puckett, J. M., & Kausler, D. H. (1984). Individual differences and models of memory span: A role for memory search rate? *Journal of Experimental Psychology: Learning, Memory, and Cognition, 10*, 72–82.

Schweickert, R., & Boruff, B. (1986). Short-term memory capacity: Magic number or magic spell? *Journal of Experimental Psychology: Learning, Memory, and Cognition, 12*, 419–425.

Sternberg, S. (1966). High-speed scanning in human memory. *Science, 153*, 652–654.

Vanderplas, J. M., & Garvin, E. A. (1959). The association value of random shapes. *Journal of Experimental Psychology, 57*, 147–154.

Wechsler, D. (1956). *Die Messung der Intelligenz Erwachsener* [Measurement of adult intelligence]. Bern: Huber.

Wechsler, D. (1958). *The measurement and appraisal of adult intelligence.* Baltimore: Williams & Wilkins.

17

Memory Scanning Beyond the Limit—If There Is One

Urte Roeber and Christian Kaernbach
Universität Leipzig, Germany

Memory is essential for human information processing. Retrieval is the process of remembering something when you want to. How the retrieval from memory works can be studied by recall and recognition tasks. Performance errors and reaction times (RTs) are useful in elucidating underlying structures and processes and in constructing memory theories. Despite more or less fundamental differences between memory theories, most of them distinguish some kind of a transient short-term store containing information for immediate projects from a permanent long-term store in which our lifetime experiences are stored and updated when needed. Traditional theories of memory (e.g. Atkinson & Shiffrin, 1968) propose a sharp distinction between capacity-limited short-term memory (STM) that holds and processes activated information and a long-term memory that contains inactivated information. In contrast to this, Cowan (1995) extended the one-store model of Shiffrin and Schneider (1977) and suggested that memory is more continuous. Whereas only information that is activated in the capacity-limited focus of attention can be processed, more (long-term) information is in a temporarily heightened state of activation that can easily be transferred into the focus of attention. Regarding memory retrieval beyond a certain capacity limit, these two approaches would predict a different outcome. If STM is a distinct structural component, quite different from long-term memory, there should be remarkable performance discontinuities at the capacity limit because extra mechanisms have to be used to activate additional information. For Cowan's approach, however, the retrieval mechanisms do not necessarily differ, because the relevant information can already be activated.

The nature of retrieval in recognition memory is a classic issue in memory research. The item-recognition paradigm (Sternberg, 1966) has led to much of our current understanding of recognition processes. In this paradigm participants study a (usually short) list of items. Hereafter, they have to decide whether a probe item was on the memorized list. The pioneering studies of Sternberg (Sternberg, 1966; Sternberg, Knoll, and Nasto, 1969) first documented that the RTs for positive and negative responses were both linearly related to list length (LL), with approximately equal slopes. From these data, Sternberg drew two inferences: (a) the linearity of the recognition function implied a serial scanning of the list and (b) the equal slope for positive and negative responses suggested that the scanning was exhaustive. In following studies these linear recognition functions were—on the whole—found to be a good generalization and robust to variations of the type of material to be memorized (see Sternberg, 1975).

Sternberg's inferences were questioned by other investigators. For instance, parallel-search algorithms have been shown to produce similar results. From the recognition functions alone it cannot be decided whether memory search is serial or parallel (for an extensive discussion of this issue, see Townsend, 1971, 1990). In the next section we briefly sketch some alternative models of (short-term) memory scanning. One possibility to obtain additional information is to extend the paradigm to memory lists that are not (totally) represented in the attentional focus either because of their length (Burrows & Okada, 1975) or because of a distractor task (Sternberg et al., 1969). However, these two studies reported inconsistent results, which are outlined in the following sections. Following this, an experimental variant combining both approaches is introduced and predictions are contrasted and subsequently tested. Finally, a modified parallel-search model is presented that can account for the data.

MODELS OF MEMORY SEARCH

The validity of a serial exhaustive scanning model was especially challenged by analysis of RT distributions and recency effects. In the pushdown stack model of Theios, Smith, Haviland, Traupmann, and Moy (1973), a serial and self-terminating mechanism was suggested that was compatible with the basic finding of linear recognition functions of identical slope for yes and no responses. The stack contains the positive list and all previously presented probes, that is, the whole stimulus ensemble and their response records. Scanning through that stack predicts effects of frequency and position: More frequently presented items as well as the latter items in the list are recognized faster. However, the model appears to be too paradigm specific because it applies only to small, known stimulus ensembles.

Direct-access models are less paradigm specific. Murdock (1971) assumed in his parallel-processing model that, with short lists, presentation of a probe initiates a self-terminating scanning process that operates across all members of the list, but the rate at which each item is processed varies with its serial position. Townsend (1974) and Taylor (1976) proposed a parallel and exhaustive scanning process with the additional assumption that the processing capacity of the memory system is limited and fixed. This limited capacity has to be distributed over the parallel comparisons. Therefore a single comparison takes longer the longer the positive list is. Still another direct-access model was proposed by Ratcliff (1978). The scanning process operates in parallel across all members of the list, with the single comparisons being random walks going on continuously. The scanning terminates when the relatedness value of a probe and an element in the list exceeds a matching threshold (positive response) or when all comparisons terminate at a nonmatch threshold (negative response). The time needed for a response depends on the LL because the thresholds increase with longer lists.

The studies mentioned so far refer to rather short positive lists for which linear recognition functions were found. The scanning is assumed to occur within the activated information in the short-term store, and no additional effort to transfer or activate relevant information is needed. However, what happens to the scanning process when the positive list cannot be entirely activated for immediate processing? The question can be addressed in two ways: either by the introduction of a capacity-consuming secondary distractor task (Sternberg et al., 1969) or by the introduction of lists long enough to exceed the capacity limit (Burrows & Okada, 1975).

EXTENDING THE PARADIGM:
INTRODUCING A DISTRACTOR TASK

In the study of Sternberg et al. (1969) participants had to recognize items of a memorized *list of digits* in a distracted condition and in an undistracted control condition. In the distracted recognition condition each trial started with the presentation of an additional *list of letters* that had to be recalled in some trials. The slope of the recognition function was approximately doubled in this distracted condition as compared with the undistracted control condition (Fig. 17.1). The doubled slope of the recognition function indicates that the scanning time per item increases when the positive list is (presumably) not held in activated memory due to a secondary task. For the distracted condition, Sternberg et al. (1969) proposed two unrelated serial processes: At first, the long-term store is scanned for the whole positive list and its elements are serially activated. Thereafter, the reactivated list is scanned serially and exhaustively, just as in the control condition. Both processes consume time proportionally to the length of the list, and therefore the RT increases also

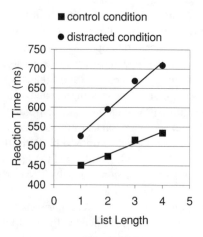

FIG. 17.1.   Mean RT as a function of LL for the distracted condition (filled circles) and the control condition (filled squares) averaged over positive and negative responses (after Sternberg et al., 1969).

linearly with LL, but at a higher slope as in the control condition in which there is no need for activation.

In summary, Sternberg et al. infer from their study that there are different mechanisms at work when one is scanning highly activated material of short lists entirely in the focus of attention versus scanning in a distracted condition.

EXTENDING THE PARADIGM: USING LONG LISTS

Burrows and Okada (1975) studied item recognition by using short and long positive lists of words. For long lists, they reported a flattened slope of the RT as a function of LL (Fig. 17.2) as compared with the slope for short lists. In other words, the scanning time per item was less when the positive list exceeded a certain limit. It should be noted, however, that although a bilinear fit was better, the authors admit that a logarithmic fit did also represent the data satisfactorily. Burrows and Okada explained their results in terms of optimized (long-term) memory processing: Beyond a certain number of items a second type of scanning process can be used that needs longer to initiate, but, once operating, it allows faster searching. In another explanation, a two-stage mixture of processes for long lists, some dependent and others nondependent on LL, was proposed.

Again, an essential part of the explanation given by Burrows and Okada is the assumption of a limited capacity of short-term storage and of additional mechanisms in case this limit is exceeded. Regarding the speed of this second scanning

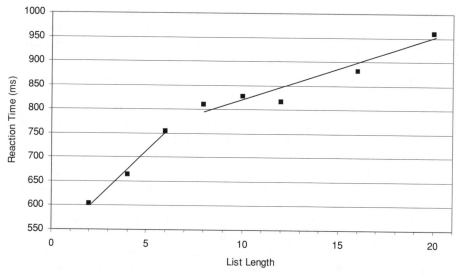

FIG. 17.2. Mean RT as a function of LL averaged over positive and negative responses. The lines represent the lower and the upper limbs of the best-fitting bilinear function (after Burrows & Okada, 1975).

mechanism, however, the results of both studies are contradictory: Sternberg et al. (1969) obtained an increase in the slope of the recognition function, whereas Burrows and Okada (1975) found a decrease.

EXTENDING THE PARADIGM: COMBINING BOTH APPROACHES

The experiment reported here was motivated by that contradiction. Its objective was twofold: We wanted to examine the results of both studies and based on that we intended to test whether these results necessitate the assumption of a limit of information storage and a second mechanism in cases in which this limit is exceeded. We used the item-recognition paradigm (Sternberg, 1966) with short as well as long positive lists in two conditions: with and without a distractor task. Okada and Burrows (1978) described a similar study in which they used two different variations to increase the memory load (ML). In one experiment participants had to perform a counting-backward task after the positive list was presented. In another experiment participants had to combine a fixed positive list (2 to 16 words) with a varying positive list on a trial-by-trial basis. Both variations produced an increase in RT that was constant across short and long lists; that is, the slope of the recognition function did not increase for short lists as reported by Sternberg et al. (1969). In comparing these results it must be noted that Sternberg et al. increased the memory load by means of a distractor task with alternative material. Accordingly, the distractor task in our experiment corresponded closely to the one of Sternberg et al.: Each trial started with the presentation of a list of distractor items that had to be recalled in some trials.

However, to extend the paradigm to long lists we had to change the material. For the recognition task, instead of digits, words were used as stimuli (see Burrows & Okada, 1975) because the available vocabulary was large enough to avoid unwelcome repetitions. The typical linear parallel recognition functions can also be obtained with words (Sternberg, 1975). For the distractor task, digits were used instead of the letters used by Sternberg et al. (1969), because digits should be better distinguishable from the words to recognize but are still alphanumeric signs.

Considering the empirical findings, we expected that LL as well as distractor task would influence the recognition process. For the LL factor, we expected a constant increase in RT with each additional item at first, which should flatten with increasing LLs. The presence of the distractor task should also cause prolonged RTs. For the interaction of both factors, at least three different outcomes seemed possible, as shown in Fig. 17.3.

- First, according to Sternberg et al. (1969), the slope of the recognition function of the condition with a distractor task could be steeper compared with the condition without a distractor task—at least for short lists. This would be a mere reproduction of their data. Their model makes no prediction as to what should happen for long lists. For short lists it assumes that after a distraction task the list would have to be reactivated in its entirety, which is consuming time proportional to the LL. A long list would not fit into short-term storage anyway, and the model would have to specify how long lists are scanned by sequential activation. Only then it would be possible to predict the effect of a distractor task on the scanning of long lists.
- Second, the distractor task could influence processes that do not depend on LL but only produce a general offset of the recognition function across all list lengths. Such a finding would be compatible with the results of Okada and Burrows (1978), this time with a distractor task used à la Sternberg et al. (1969). The recognition functions of both conditions would then be parallel.
- Third, in the condition with a distractor task, there could be a linear recognition function over all LLs with a relatively flat slope. This prediction would be consistent with the reasoning of Burrows and Okada (1975): Even for short lists the positive list would not stay in short-term store, which would be blocked by the distractor task, and its scanning in long-term memory would need a long activation time but little scanning time per item. In that case, each list should be scanned with the same scanning time per item as the long lists in the condition without a distractor task.

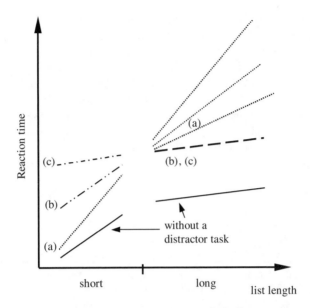

FIG. 17.3. Possible outcomes for RT as a function of LL and distractor task. The solid lines indicate the expected outcome in the condition without distractor task according to Burrows and Okada (1975). For the condition with distractor task, different outcomes were conceivable: (a) an increase in scanning time per item (according to Sternberg et al., 1969) at least for short lists (dotted lines), (b) the same slope of the recognition function as without a distractor task but with a general RT offset (dash–dot–dot and dashed lines), (c) a shallow slope for both short and long lists, i.e., the same slope as for the long lists without distractor task (dash–dotted and dashed lines). See the text for further explanations.

Method

Participants. A total of 16 undergraduate psychology students (11 women) participated in the experiment after they had passed the training criterion (out of 18 initial participants; see procedure subsection). Their mean age was 20 years (age range 18 to 23 years). Participants served for course credit or were paid (€5.80/hr).

Material. For the recognition task, items were selected from a total of 640 German one-syllable nouns consisting of four or five letters. The vocabulary was built from a German dictionary found on the World Wide Web (ftp.informatik.uni-kiel.de/pub/kiel/dicts/hk2-deutsch.tar.gz), from which relatively unknown or offensive words as well as words with presumably emotional impact had been deleted. For the distractor task, digits served as stimuli. All stimuli appeared in black, centered on a white background.

Procedure. Each participant had to pass a training session successfully. During this session only the distractor task (i.e., recalling series of digits) was taught. It started with series of four digits. The length of the series was increased stepwise up to seven digits, depending on correct recalls of all digits in the correct serial order. Two participants failed to properly recall series of seven digits and therefore were excluded from the experiment. Following this, participants performed a familiarization session that resembled an experimental session (see subsequent discussion) but with a positive list of letters instead of words. It aimed at acquainting the participants with the experimental design and its demands.

The experiment was subdivided into eight sessions, to be performed on eight different days. In each session every participant got a positive list of a different length (1, 3, 5, 7, 9, 11, 13, or 15 items). The conditions without (−) and with (+) a distractor task were presented blockwise by turns, two blocks each per LL. The sequence of these four blocks (+ − + − or − + − +) was counterbalanced across participants. The eight participants following a certain sequence (say, + − + −) were randomly assigned to eight different sequences of the eight LLs according to a balanced Latin square. The Latin square fulfilled the following two constraints in order to avoid sequential effects and to control potential effects of training: (a) each LL (say, 7) was tested with the same frequency at each serial position of the sequence (say, day 3); (b) any direct succession of two LLs occurring in one participant would never occur for any other subject of the same group of eight subjects. Positive lists and negative probes were formed by random selection from the vocabulary under the restrictions that a positive word was not repeated in another session and that a negative word appeared only once per session and was not repeated in the following four sessions. The series forming the distractor task comprised seven different digits and were randomly generated on-line.

An experimental session for a certain LL started with a learning phase. During this phase the participant's task was to memorize the words of the positive list in the sequence they appeared in spite of a distracting digit-recall task. Presentation of the single words was self-paced by the participant. After studying the last word the participant had to perform a distracting digit-recall task. Then the words of the positive list had to be recalled in the correct serial order. This procedure was repeated until the series of digits and the positive list were correctly recalled twice in a row.

Then the positive list was tested for recognition with (+) or without (−) distraction. These two conditions were presented in four alternating blocks (+ − + − or − + − +) and announced at the beginning of each block.

- In the condition without a distractor task, a test trial started 0.67 s after a participant's key press with a screen-centered digit zero that remained there for 0.33 s. A probe followed immediately that a participant had to respond to as quickly as possible by pressing the yes or the no key, depending on whether the probe was positive or negative. For false responses, auditory feedback was given.

- In the condition with the distractor task, a test trial started 0.67 s after a participant's key press with a screen-centered presentation of a series of seven digits at a 0.33-s rate. Immediately after presentation of the last digit either a probe word or a question mark was presented. Following the question mark, the participant had to recall the digits in their correct sequence, with a feedback given about the number of correct recalls. Following the probe word the participant had to respond to it as quickly as possible by pressing the yes or the no key, depending on whether it was positive or negative. For false responses, auditory feedback was given.

A block of the condition without a distractor task consisted of 50 trials with an identical number of positive and negative probes. A block of the condition with a distractor task consisted of 100 trials, half of them involving the distractor task and the other the recognition task, with an identical number of positive and negative probes. In an entire session, each LL was tested with 100 positive and 100 negative probes per participant. The trials within a block were randomly interleaved.

Results

Distractor Task. Of the series of digits, 90.6% were correctly recalled. A repeated-measures analysis of variance (ANOVA) revealed no significant effect of the LL factor ($p > .5$).

Item-Recognition Task. The mean percentages of errors were 1.8% in both distractor and no-distractor tasks. A two-factor ANOVA with errors as the dependent variable yielded neither main effects of condition ($p > .5$) and LL ($p > .1$) nor a significant interaction ($p > .5$).

Correct no responses were on average 49 ms slower than yes responses in the condition without a distractor task and 26 ms slower in the condition with a distractor task. Figure 17.4 shows mean RTs for correct responses (averaged over yes and no responses) for both conditions separately (see website, chapter 17, table 1). An ANOVA for the mean RTs revealed significant main effects of condition ($p < .0001$) and list length ($p < .0001$), but yielded no significant interaction ($p > .1$). RTs were slower with a distractor task than without a distractor task, and longer positive lists had a shallower RT slope in each condition.

Bilinear and logarithmic fits for the relationship between mean RT and list length were applied for both conditions separately (Table 17.1) (see Burrows & Okada, 1975). The goodness of the fit was tested by computing root-mean-square deviation (*RMSD*).

For the bilinear functions, "short lists" were defined as lists of 1, 3, and 5 items, and "long lists" as lists of 7–15 items. The distinction was made in accordance with the analysis proposed by Burrows and Okada (1975). In both conditions the logarithmic function fits the empirical data better than the bilinear function

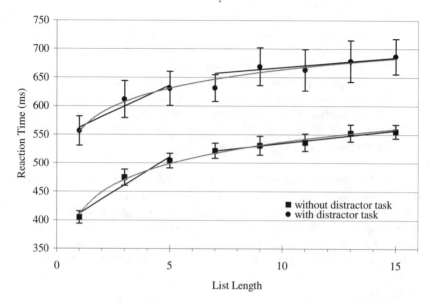

FIG. 17.4. Mean RTs and standard errors as functions of LL for the conditions without and with distractor task. The black lines indicate bilinear fits, and the gray lines represent logarithmic fits of the recognition functions. The error of the mean is approximately four times smaller than the standard error.

($p < .05$ and $p < .01$, respectively). There is a slight decrease in slope in the condition with distractor task: The slope values of the bilinear fits are smaller in this condition, as is the "stretch" value b of the logarithmic fits. This interaction between LL and condition is not significant (but see next paragraph).

Finally, we analyzed whether practice could have affected our results. For each experimental day (e.g., the first day, regardless of LL tested at this first day) the "day effect" was calculated: The mean RT of an individual participant was calculated and compared with the mean RT over all participants for the same LL (regardless of day of test). This day effect was averaged over all participants as a function of the experimental day. Separate ANOVAs for the mean RT differences revealed no significant effect of the experimental day ($p > .05$) in the condition without a distractor task, but did yield a significant effect of the experimental day ($p < .01$) in the condition with a distractor task. In this condition, the day effect was ~136 ms at the first day, decaying exponentially with a decay time of ~2 days. It should not have affected the result, as the relation between LL and day of test was perfectly balanced by means of a Latin square (see methods subsection). However, it could have increased the variance and thereby reduced the significance of the effects observed. Therefore this day effect was subtracted from the individual mean RT of each experimental day. These corrected RTs were reanalyzed for effects of

TABLE 17.1

Parameter Values of the Best-Fitting Bilinear and Logarithmic Recognition Functions and Their *RMSDs* for the Conditions Without and With a Distractor Task

Condition	Bilinear Fits					Logarithmic Fits		
	Short Lists (ms)		Long Lists (ms)			$RT = a + b * log_2$ (List Length) (ms)		
	y Intercept	Slope	y Intercept	Slope	RMSD (ms)	a	b	RMSD (ms)
Without a distractor task	387.01 (±15.54)	24.77 (±4.29)	489.93 (±39.63)	4.49 (±3.25)	6.13	410.27 (±11.37)	38.11 (±3.94)	4.23
With a distractor task	543.63 (±35.25)	18.61 (±10.32)	632.80 (±91.74)	3.46 (±7.52)	10.97	555.58 (±25.58)	32.57 (±8.86)	7.16

Note. Standard errors are given in parentheses. The estimated value for LL 7 was derived from the equation for long lists, because both limbs meet at approximately six items in either condition.

LL and condition. As expected, slight increases in significance were obtained. The interaction between LL and condition is especially significant ($p < .05$) if evaluated from the corrected RTs.

Discussion

The purpose of this study was to examine the speed of recognition for varying degrees of memory load. We measured response latencies during an item-recognition task for various lengths of positive lists in the presence or absence of a distractor task. A simple summary of the results is that LL as well as a distractor task influences the recognition performance: Longer lists produce an increase in RT, and recognition is slower in conditions with a distractor task as compared with conditions without a distractor task. Both effects seem to be largely independent: The distractor task produced an RT offset with the slope of the recognition function changing only slightly. These findings also hold for short lists, and thereby seem to contradict the results of Sternberg et al. (1969), who reported a nearly doubled slope when participants were involved in a distractor task. They are, however, compatible with the results of Burrows and Okada (1975), despite the differences in the methods to increase the memory load. The major difference from the experiment of Sternberg et al. is the choice of the material for the positive lists (words in our case, digits in their experiment), imposed by the need to include long lists in the design of our study. It is not clear how this difference could be at the origin of the discrepancy of the results.

The results are compatible with the assumption that the additional task does not influence processes that depend on LL, but has a general effect [see hypothesis (b) in Fig. 17.3], which can loosely be interpreted in terms of costs of task switching at an early stage of processing. This switching process would involve a decision about the task for a given trial and possibly an increase of activation of the information needed. All subsequent processing stages for eventual item recognition are common to distractor and nondistractor tasks. The presence of the distractor task would not influence the actual recognition process, because after task switching the positive list is proposed to be in the same state as without a distractor task.

Bilinear recognition functions fit our data reasonably well, with a steeper slope for short than for long lists. This difference could be understood to represent a change in strategy that allows a faster recognition in long positive lists. This comparison process would need longer to initiate but would operate faster (Burrows & Okada, 1975). An alternative explanation for the difference in slope was given by Puffe (1990). She suggested that long positive lists are chunked into categories and the reduced slope of the recognition function is due to a combination of scanning the categories first, and the items of the relevant category after that, and not due to an increase of the scanning rate itself (see also Franklin, Okada, Burrows, & Friendly, 1980).

These explanations are based on the assumption that there is some limit at which the processing changes abruptly. It is debatable where the break in performance should be expected. Although Burrows and Okada based their model on the classical value of seven given by Miller (1956), it has, since then, often been stated that the capacity for attentional processes is much smaller. Cowan (2001) argues that the capacity of the focus of attention is only four. Given the sparse data sampling for LLs below four in our study as well as in that of Burrows and Okada, it is impossible to demonstrate or falsify a break at such a low value. Even for lists with seven or fewer elements the linearity of the recognition function is based on only three data points. Looking closely at these three data points (Fig. 17.4) reveals that the deviation from linearity concurs with the general trend of the data: a shallower slope for longer LLs (3 & 5) than for shorter LLs (1 & 3). In line with this observation, logarithmic recognition functions provide a better fit to our data than bilinear functions do. Therefore it cannot be excluded that there is no such limit at which the processing changes abruptly. This notion is supported by a recent functional MRI study (Zysset, Müller, Lehmann, Thöne-Otto, & von Cramon, 2001) in which the authors did not find an activation of additional brain regions for recognition in long compared with short lists. At present, there is no neurophysiological evidence for different processes for short compared with long lists.

A PARALLEL-SEARCH MODEL

On the basis of our data, there is little reason to conclude that the recognition process changes because of the presence of a secondary task or that different recognition processes are set up for short compared with long lists. If short and long lists are scanned in the exact same manner, then our results speak against a simple serial scanning, which would have resulted in a linear slope for the recognition function over all LLs: We found a decrease in slope for long lists. However, a serial model that assumed a warm-up or speedup of processing as the person scans their list could make exactly this qualitative prediction. Such a model would go without any capacity limit.

As an alternative, we tested a parallel and exhaustive scanning model as proposed by Townsend (1974) and Taylor (1976). According to this model, the recognition for a probe is processed by simultaneous comparisons of the probe with all members of the positive list, and it ends when all of the comparisons are finished. Because of variations in the processing time of the single items, the total amount of time increases with LL. It does so in a saturating nonlinear fashion. Taylor assumed that the linearity of the recognition function for short lists (the only ones he considered) is due to the capacity limit of STM, with LLs close to the capacity limit, straining the resources available for each single item. If—in line with our data—one skips the presumption of linearity, the model can be simplified and formulated without any capacity assumption. Townsend and Ashby (1983) demonstrated that any unlimited-capacity independent parallel model must predict negatively accelerated (i.e., concave-down) curves, whatever the exact model and distribution. In his memory model, Cowan (1995) proposed that only information that has to be reproduced has to be in the focus of one's attention. Much more information can be in a temporarily heightened state of activation without our being aware of it. Perhaps memory span tells us only something about the limit of this focus of attention. Although long positive lists cannot be totally reproduced in immediate recall tasks, because they exceed the limit of the focus of attention, they would be as easily accessible by scanning processes as short lists, because they are in that heightened state of activation. Cowan's approach encourages the modeling of a recognition paradigm with a parallel and exhaustive scanning model that is not restricted by a limited capacity.

We have modified the parallel-search model and applied it to our data. The original model assumes an exponential distribution for the scanning time of a single item. The advantage of this distribution is that the scanning times for lists of a certain length can be predicted from analytical analysis. Today's computational power permits us to evaluate list scanning times numerically for arbitrary distributions of item scanning times. In consequence, we assumed a normal distribution for the single-item scanning times. Gamma distributions might have been even more appropriate (McGill & Gibbon, 1965), but they need an additional parameter and approach normal distribution for certain parameter values. For simplicity, we decided not to truncate the normal distribution. For each LL we drew 100,000 times LL random values from the normal distribution $N(0, 1)$. From each drawing we chose the maximum of these LL values, which indicates the normalized time for the hindmost finishing comparison process per scan. The mean maximum values (see the upper part of the second table at the website, chapter 17) were linearly transformed to fit them to our empirical data. This corresponds to transforming the underlying distribution from $N(0, 1)$ to $N(\mu, \sigma)$, that is, the single-item scanning time would on the average be μ ms, with a standard deviation of σ ms. The value

TABLE 17.2
Parameter Values of the Best-Fitting Linear Transformations and their *RMSDs*
for the Conditions Without and With a Distractor Task

Condition	Separate Fits (ms)			Memory-Loaded Fits (ms)		
	μ	σ	*RMSD*	μ	σ	*RMSD*
Without a distractor task	403.90	86.41	2.59	398.15		3.71
					91.31	
With a distractor task	551.11	73.06	8.79	515.72		8.98

Note. The left-hand side shows the values for independent transformations for both conditions, the right-hand side for an identical σ, with an additional memory load of 1 in the condition with a distractor task.

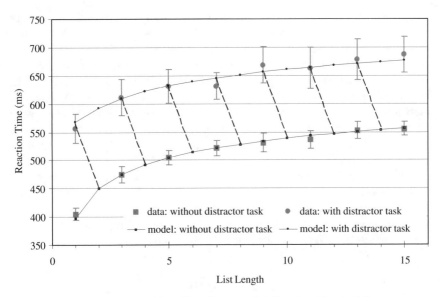

FIG. 17.5. Recognition functions (solid lines) estimated by a model of parallel and exhaustive scanning for the conditions without and with distractor task. Both conditions were modeled with the same value σ for the variation of the single-item scanning time. For the condition with distractor task we assumed an additional ML of one item to be added to the number of items in the positive list. The dashed lines show the corresponding LLs for both conditions: In the condition with distractor task a list of length 1 is processed like a list of length 2 would be in the condition without distractor task. The data points represent the empirical RTs and their standard errors (error bars).

for LL = 1 of the transformed mode data corresponds to the mean scanning time μ for a single item.

In the first step, the recognition functions were modeled for both conditions separately (Table 17.2). In this case one would have to assume that the scanning process does not change as a function of LL but changes as a function of the presence of a distractor task. The resulting *RMSD* values are better than those for the bilinear fits and comparable with those of the logarithmic fits (see Table 17.1). Again the σ parameter is smaller for the condition with distractor task, indicating a slightly compressed recognition function in this condition.

Up to now all fits (bilinear, logarithmic, parallel model) have been performed separately for the conditions without versus with distractor task. This approach is unsatisfying in that comparable psychophysical tasks are modeled with different sets of parameters of the same model, and no explanation is given as to why this should be so. Although it is possible to force identical slope parameters on the fits, the *RMSD* values would increase because of the slight differences in slope for these two conditions. The parallel model offers the possibility of fitting both sets of results with an identical base parameter (variation σ of single-item scanning times) and at the same time reflect these slope differences. This is possible because we may assume that the distractor task represents an additional ML. Given a LL, the scanning process would have to wait for LL + ML processes to complete. Accordingly, the linear transformations of the mean maximum values per LL were performed with σ held constant for both conditions and the offset parameter μ allowed to differ because of task-switching costs. Additionally, for the condition with distractor task, different MLs were considered as additional items in the positive list. The best fit was found for an additional ML of 1 in the condition with a distractor task (see Table 17.2 and website, chapter 17, table 2). The modeled recognition functions for both conditions are shown in Fig. 17.5. The total *RMSD*s for these functions are in the same range as the logarithmic fits (with two separate parameter sets! See Table 17.1) and smaller than bilinear fits.

CONCLUSION

We tested scanning of memorized lists for short and long lists, in conditions with and without distractor task. Our data put into question the need to postulate different scanning mechanisms in the presence of distractor tasks or for long lists. Data with gradually decreasing slopes are better explained by models that assume a single scanning mechanism for all these conditions. These can be variants of serial search models or parallel models. We presented a very simple parallel model that not only reflects this gradual decrease of the slope of the recognition function, but also the slight difference in slope between the conditions with versus without distractor task. It supplies a fairly good description of the obtained empirical data. Moreover, the advantage of the proposed model is its simplicity in terms of necessary assumptions. It assumes the same processing mechanism in conditions with and without a distractor task, and the scanning is not subjected to capacity limits of short-term storage. If there is no change in the mechanism beyond a certain limit of stored information, this might be due to the fact that there is no such limit.

The model has been derived in a post hoc fashion, and further testing is required. There are a number of questions left unanswered. In particular, we do not know where the relatively large standard deviations of the response latencies in the condition with distractor task might come from. Presumably, the task-switching stage contributes to it. In addition, one would like to know why the difference between no and yes responses is smaller in the condition with distractor task than without. Thus we have not yet developed a detailed understanding of the recognition process itself. These issues notwithstanding, our empirical data support the results reported by Burrows and Okada (1975) and Okada and Burrows (1978), indicating that distractor tasks applied do not influence the recognition mechanism itself. They are also compatible with the memory model of Cowan (1995) and its assumption that there is no limit for the amount of activated information in short-term memory.

ACKNOWLEDGMENTS

We thank Hans-Georg Geissler and Stephen A. Madigan for valuable assistance with the design of the experimental procedure, Carsten Bogler for his contributions to the model, and Stephen W. Link, Stephen A. Madigan and James T. Townsend for thoughtful discussions of the manuscript.

REFERENCES

Atkinson, R. C. & Shiffrin. R. M. (1968). Human memory: A proposed system and its control processes. In K. W. Spence & J. T. Spence (Eds.), *The psychology of learning and motivation: Advances in research and theory* (Vol. 2, pp. 89–195). New York: Academic Press.

Burrows, D., & Okada, R. (1975). Memory retrieval from long and short lists. *Science, 188*, 1031–1033.

Cowan, N. (1995). *Attention and memory: An integrated framework.* (1st ed.). New York: Oxford University Press.

Cowan, N. (2001). The magical number 4 in short-term memory: A reconsideration of mental storage capacity. *Behavioral and Brain Sciences, 24*, 87–114.

Franklin, P. E., Okada, R., Burrows, D., & Friendly, M. L. (1980). Retrieval of information from subjectively organized lists. *Journal of Experimental Psychology: Human Learning and Memory, 6*, 732–740.

McGill, W. J. & Gibbon, J. (1965). The general-gamma distribution and reaction times. *Journal of Mathematical Psychology, 2*, 1–18.

Miller, G. (1956). The magical number seven plus minus two. *Psychological Review, 63*, 81–97.

Murdock, B.B., Jr. (1971). A parallel-processing model for scanning. *Perception & Psychophysics, 10*, 289–291.

Okada, R., & Burrows, D. (1978). The effects of subsidiary tasks on memory retrieval from long and short lists. *Quarterly Journal of Experimental Psychology, 30*, 221–233.

Puffe, M. (1990). Quantized speed-capacity relations in short-term storage. In H. Geissler (Ed.), *Psychophysical explorations of mental structures* (pp. 290–302). Toronto: Hogrefe & Huber.

Ratcliff, R. (1978). A theory of memory retrieval. *Psychological Review, 85*, 59–108.

Shiffrin, R. M., & Schneider, W. (1977). Controlled and automatic human information processing: II. Perceptual learning and automatic attending. *Psychological Review, 84*, 127–190.

Sternberg, S. (1966). High-speed scanning in human memory. *Science, 153*, 652–654.

Sternberg, S. (1975). Memory scanning: New findings and current controversies. *Quarterly Journal of Experimental Psychology, 27*, 1–32.

Sternberg, S., Knoll, R. L., & Nasto, B. A. (1969). *Retrieval from long-term vs. active memory.* Paper presented at the annual meeting of the Psychonomic Society, St. Louis, MO.

Taylor, D. A. (1976). Stage analysis of reaction time. *Psychological Bulletin, 83*, 161–191.

Theios, J., Smith, P. G., Haviland, S. E., Traupmann, J., & Moy, M. C. (1973). Memory scanning as a serial self-terminating process. *Journal of Experimental Psychology, 97*, 323–336.

Townsend, J. T. (1971). A note on the identification of parallel and serial processes. *Perception & Psychophysics, 10,* 161–163.

Townsend, J. T. (1974). Issues and models concerning the processing of finite number of inputs. In B.H. Kantowitz (Ed.), *Human information processing: tutorials in performance and cognition* (p. 133–68). Hillsdale, NJ: Lawrence Erlbaum Association.

Townsend, J. T. (1990). Serial and parallel processing: Sometimes they look like Tweedledum and Tweedledee but they can (and should) be distinguished. *Psychological Science, 1,* 46–54.

Townsend, J. T., & Ashby, F. G. (1983). *The stochastic modeling of elementary psychological processes.* New York: Cambridge University Press.

Zysset, S., Müller, K., Lehmann, C., Thöne-Otto, A. I. T., & von Cramon, D. Y. (2001). Retrieval of long and short lists from long term memory: A functional magnetic resonance imaging study with human subjects. *Neuroscience Letters, 314,* 1–4.

18

Bottom-up and Top-down Flows of Information Within Auditory Memory: Electrophysiological Evidence

Erich Schröger
University of Leipzig, Germany

Mari Tervaniemi
University of Leipzig, Germany, and University of Helsinki, Finland

Minna Huotilainen
University of Helsinki, Finland

SENSORY MEMORY

Different views about the nature of human memory have resulted in conceptualizations, which may be categorized in multistore models, single store models, and hybrid models. They all postulate some kind of sensory memory and more or less explicitly assume that this sensory memory is informationally encapsulated from other memory stores.

In their multistore model, Atkinson and Shiffrin (1968) postulate the existence of three separate stages of memory. These stages have been identified in terms of capacity for the number of items to be included and for the duration for which this information is held in an active state. The sensory register may contain a large amount of information for a very brief period of approximately 100–200 ms. The short-term store has a capacity of approximately three to nine that which survive for approximately 10–20 s. The long-term store has an almost unlimited capacity and its duration is mainly restricted by the functionality of the brain in which it is held. The flow of information between these separate stores is assumed to happen from the sensory register to the short-term and then to the long-term store or directly from the sensory register to the long-term store. Feedback loops are confined from long-term back to the short-term store; the sensory register does not receive input from other memory stores. In their single-store model, Shiffrin and Schneider (1977) claimed the existence of only one memory system consisting of different levels of processing. The role of the sensory register is taken as an initial, automatic encoding process that reflects early levels of processing within this unitary memory-storage system. These early encoding levels do not receive input from higher levels. In his hybrid memory model, Cowan (1988, 1995) postulated two different sensory stores. One exists within the long-term store and is regarded as activated sensory features of the long-term store. The other precedes processing occurring in the long-term store and is assumed to operate rather automatically, in the sense that the information computed in this store can be delivered to the long-term store but not vice versa.

Taken together, the memory models introduced here agree more or less concerning the functional role of sensory memory for subsequent processing that occurs at higher memory stores (in multistore accounts) or at higher levels within a long-term store (in single-store accounts). Accordingly, sensory memory

a. automatically establishes neural representations of the sensory input and
b. automatically holds these representations available for a brief period,
c. enables that information to be transferred toward subsequent, higher-level systems, and
d. is informationally encapsulated from higher-level memory representations.

In this chapter, we focus on auditory memory, and we present an event-related brain response, the mismatch negativity (MMN), which taps into auditory memory functioning; we then examine these assumptions in more detail.

AUDITORY MEMORY

Sensory memory can be distinguished from other forms of memory by two main criteria (cf. Cowan, 1988). First, it is characterized by a modality-specific encoding of information. This means that representations in sensory memory of one modality can (usually) not be transformed to representations of sensory memory from another modality. Second, the contents of sensory memory are noncategorical.

That is, two slightly differing stimuli belonging to the same conceptual category (e.g., two versions of the vowel /a/) may be distinguished on the basis of their representational format in sensory memory. Additional characteristics of sensory memory are (a) that it can mainly be inhibited retroactively, that is, proactive inhibition (which is typical for other forms of memory) is rather weak in sensory memory or does not even exist, and (b) that its contents are activated exogenously while rehearsal (keeping representations of short-term memory actively alive) is not possible (see the paragraphs that follow).

Other phenomena belonging to this concept are *integration*, for example, loudness estimation depends on a stimulus duration up to 200 ms (e.g., Stevens & Hall, 1966) and frequency discrimination improves with increasing stimulus duration up to 200–500 ms (e.g., Doughty & Garner, 1948); *persistence*, that is, sounds that are shorter than 100 ms are estimated to be longer (e.g., Efron, 1970); and *echo or perseveration* (we can somehow "listen" to representations of auditory memory). Evidence for the existence of auditory sensory memory from behavioral studies is the finding that backward masking impoverishes the identification of a tone (e.g., Massaro, 1970) and that task-irrelevant, interfering items reduce the suffix effect (e.g., Crowder & Morton, 1969).

The two main functions of auditory memory are the integration of information within brief periods of time and the perseveration of information for further processing. Integration is, for example, utilized for the identification of consonants; perseveration is utilized for sentence comprehension, for the discrimination of successive sounds according to particular criteria (e.g., pitch), and for the usage of information in unattended channels (one may think of the situation in which he or she was not attentive to the question of his or her partner but could recollect the information needed to answer to question from auditory memory). According to these two functions, two different phases of auditory memory have been distinguished—a short phase (Cowan, 1984) or preperceptual store (Massaro, 1970), and a long phase (Cowan, 1984) or synthesized store (Massaro, 1970). The short phase of sensory memory has a lifetime of approximately 100–300 ms and is responsible for integration, whereas the long phase with a duration of approximately 10–20 s is in the service of perseveration of information.

Some recent evidence from cognitive neuroscience research performed in the auditory modality is reviewed that suggests that these assumptions do generally hold. However, assumption (a) has to be modified because the establishment of such representations is not necessarily fully automatic but may be modulated by attention. Moreover, assumption (d) is challenged by recent evidence showing that information can not only be transferred in a bottom-up way from sensory-memory stages to higher processing levels but that also information from short- and long-term stores may influence sensory-memory operations. We believe that the bottom-up transfer represents the main road in information transfer between different memories but that the top-down transfer can assist sensory-memory operations and that this feedback may improve the quality of information that is fed from sensory memory to subsequent processing stages.

Auditory memory is regarded as automatic in the sense that the encoding, transformation, and storage of information occurring in this type of memory takes place irrespective of whether the person intends to perceive the acoustic input or not. As already mentioned, sensory memory is regarded as automatically establishing representations that can be read out by subsequent processes. However, classical research on auditory memory involves attentional processing of the acoustic input because it relies on overt, behavioral responses given by the subject. Verbal reports, reaction times, hit rates, false-alarm rates, d' and the like are helpful measures to unravel the nature of auditory memory, but they may possibly be contaminated by attention-related processes that are not indicative for sensory-memory functioning per se. Thus some additional tool that taps into auditory memory that does not rely on the attentive processing of the respective sounds would be valuable. The MMN of the event-related potential (ERP) or the event-related magnetic field, which is introduced in the next section, represents such a tool in cognitive neuroscience.

MMN: AN INDICATOR OF AUDITORY MEMORY

The MMN is elicited by an irregularity in discrete, repetitive auditory stimulation (for a review, see Näätänen, 1992; Näätänen, Alho, & Schröger, 2002). This preattentive brain response is generated by the outcome of a comparison process that registers a difference between the neural representation of the actual input and the memory trace of the invariances inherent to the recent standard stimulation. In addition to general benefits of ERP recordings (providing knowledge on psychological and physiological levels, having good time resolution, being noninvasive, and directly reflecting electrophysiological brain activity), MMN is of special interest because it can be measured even when participants are not attending to the auditory stimulation. That is, it is not contaminated by task-related processing.

There is evidence that the neural processing underlying MMN plays a causal role in the elicitation of involuntary attention shifts. Furthermore, the MMN is often followed by the P3a (reflecting an attention switch to deviant or novel stimuli) when large deviants are presented (for an overview, see Escera, Alho, Schröger, & Winkler, 2000). According to a related but slightly different interpretation, MMN does not reflect an initial state of an orienting response but rather the updating of the neural trace that encodes the invariances in the acoustic environment (Winkler, Karmos, & Näätänen, 1996). That is, whenever a deviancy occurs, our mental model about the acoustic invariances has to be modified; depending on the experimental circumstances, an attention switch may also be triggered.

MMN can best be identified in the deviant minus standard difference waves in which the ERP elicited by the standard sound is subtracted from the ERP elicited

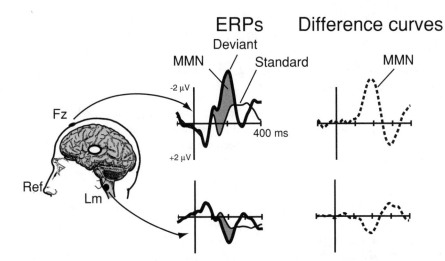

FIG. 18.1. Typical MMN response. Left column: Indication of the recording sites (Fz and left mastoid, shown as Lm) and the reference electrode (nose). The white area symbolizes the supratemporal plane where the main generator location of the MMN is located. Middle column: ERPs elicited by frequent standard and infrequent deviant sounds at Fz and at the left mastoid. The difference between the two traces (shaded area) corresponds the MMN. Right column: The resulting difference curves (dotted curves) when the ERPs elicited by the standard sounds are substracted from those elicited by the deviant sounds.

by the deviant sound. MMN reveals a frontocentral, often right-hemispheric preponderant distribution and peaks between 100 and 250 ms from stimulus onset. When nose reference is used, it usually inverts polarity at leads positioned below the sylvian fissure (Fig. 18.1).

The presence of MMN in a particular experimental setting implies the existence of a sensory-memory trace in which the features of the frequently occurring standard sound are represented. One can probe this trace by presenting deviants in different experimental conditions and thus indirectly determine features of auditory memory. Notably, as shown by several recent studies, the representations underlying the elicitation of MMN govern attentive auditory-discrimination ability in humans (e.g. Amenedo & Escera, 2000; Tiitinen, May, Reinikainen, & Näätänen, 1994). This close resemblance of the features of MMN to that of the previously behaviorally observed auditory memory strongly suggests that the MMN provides a noninvasive, objective, task-independent measurable physiological correlate of stimulus-feature representations in auditory sensory memory.

EVALUATION OF THE ASSUMPTIONS
ABOUT AUDITORY MEMORY

Automaticity of the Establishment of Sensory-Memory Representations

The elicitation of MMN by a particular deviancy implies that the respective feature of the acoustic input has been extracted and encoded into a short-lived memory representation, R. In addition, not only the actual stimulus information must have been encoded but also invariants inherent in the recent stimulation must have been detected and encoded into a memory representation R'. Finally, the discrepancy between R and R' must have been detected by some memory-comparison operation (cf. Schröger, 1997). As the MMN does not rely on the explicit intention of a person to detect irregularities in the acoustic input and may be elicited even in the absence of attention, the underlying memory operations may be regarded as automatic or preattentive. Several studies have shown that the MMN elicited by a frequency change is not only present in the absence of attention but also is not modulated by attention even with highly demanding primary tasks such as dichotic listening or visual tracking (e.g., Alho, Woods, & Algazi, 1994; Harmony et al., 2000; Paavilainen, Tiitinen, Alho, & Näätänen, 1993; for an exception, see Trejo, Ryan-Jones, & Kramer, 1995). The automaticity hypothesis of the respective memory processing is strengthened by the finding that MMN is elicited in sleeping infants (e.g., Cheour, Leppänen, & Kraus, 2000; Cheour-Luhtanen et al., 1995), in REM sleep and during Stage 2 sleep in adults (e.g, Atienza, Cantero, & Gomez, 2000; Loewy, Campbell, & Bastien, 1996; Nashida et al., 2000; Sallinen, Kaartinen, & Lyytinen, 1994), and even in coma patients (Fischer, Morlet, & Giard, 2000; Fischer et al., 1999; Kane, Butler, & Simpson, 2000; Kane et al., 1996).

However, strong automaticity (Hackley, 1993) is not necessarily provided in all circumstances, as several studies have shown that attention may modulate some forms of MMN. For example, although MMN to an intensity change is also elicited when participants are reading during stimulus presentation, it has been found that it can be largely reduced when attention is strongly focused to a demanding primary task (Woldorff, Hackley, & Hillyard, 1991; Woldorff, Hillyard, Gallen, Hampson, & Bloom, 1998). Similarly, Alain and Woods (1997) found a distinct attenuation of MMN to deviations in spectrotemporal patterns in dichotic listening tasks, that is, when the participants' attention was strongly focused on the contralateral ear. Other studies have demonstrated top-down control effects on the MMN for phonemic deviants (Szymanski, Yund, & Woods, 1999), for deviances in duration (Dittmann-Balcar, Thienel, & Schall, 1999), and for deviances relying on attentive auditory-stream segregation (Sussman, Ritter, & Vaughan, 1998a).

It has to be asked whether these attentional modulations on MMN amplitude do affect the deviance-detection mechanism per se or, alternatively, reflect modification of the memory traces entering the memory-comparison process underlying

MMN. The finding that MMN is not modified when the occurrence of a deviant is perfectly predictable supports the latter alternative (Rinne, Antila, & Winkler, 2001; Sussman, Ritter, & Vaughan, 1998b; Sussman, Winkler, & Schröger, in press). In the studies by Scherg et al. (1989), a pattern of standards (S) and deviants (D) was delivered in a predictable fashion ($SSSSD$) in one condition and at random in another condition. Although the deviant is perfectly predictable in the former condition and unpredictable in the latter condition, MMN was not different between the two conditions. This result was replicated by Sussman et al. (1998b). In this study, the patterns were presented at two different speeds (1.3 s and 100 ms). An MMN was obtained at the D position tone at the slow but not the fast pace. The absence of MMN with the fast stimulation rate suggests that the input is organized in a pattern-like manner so that D stimuli are not treated as deviants; thus, the absence of MMN in this situation does not mean that the predictability of a deviant does abolish MMN. Moreover, in a study by Ritter, Sussman, Deacon, Cowan, and Vaughan (1999), perfectly predictably deviants (indicated by a visual cue) elicited the MMN despite the fact that they were expected. This suggests that the preattentive sensory-memory operations underlying the MMN are unaffected by the information available to the higher-order system. This finding has been replicated and partly extended in a study by Sussman et al. (in press) in which the MMN was again found to be unaffected by the knowledge about a forthcoming deviant. Moreover, it was found that the P3a (indicating an attention shift toward a perturbating event) and the behavioral distraction effect (consisting of a reaction time increase in a primary task when the target information was preceded by a deviant) were abolished when the auditory deviant was indicated by a visual cue. Thus, the distraction about the knowledge of a forthcoming deviancy can be avoided but the preceding preattentive deviance-detection system cannot be turned off.

Automaticity of the Maintenance of Sensory-Memory Representations

The elicitation of MMN to a particular deviancy not only implies that a representation R' about the invariances inherent to the acoustic input must have been established but also that they are still active when the deviancy is encountered. Otherwise, no discrepancy between R and R' could have been detected and, therefore no MMN could be elicited. When no attention is devoted to the auditory stimuli, the respective maintenance of the memory representation may be regarded as automatic or preattentive. It has been found that MMN for changes in frequency in passive listening conditions is relatively stable with offset-to-onset interstimulus intervals (ISIs) ranging from approximately 0.3 to 10 s (e.g., Böttcher-Gandor & Ullsperger, 1992; Imada, Hari, Loveless, McEvoy, & Sams, 1993; Winkler, Schröger, & Cowan, 2001). In the study by Imada et al. (1993), approximately half of the subjects revealed MMN in their longest ISI condition, that is, with 12 s. However, it has to be considered that the critical lower limit of the maximal ISI still eliciting full-amplitude MMN can be shorter for particular groups of subjects such as children (Gomes et al., 1999), elderly people (Pekkonen, Jousmäki, Partanen, & Karhu, 1993), Alzheimer patients (Pekkonen, Jousmäki, Kononen, Reinikainen, & Partanen, 1994), and schizophrenic patients (Javitt, Doneshka, Grochowski, & Ritter, 1995; Shutara et al., 1996).

It should also be noted that the absence of MMN in a long-ISI condition does not necessarily prove that there is no memory for the respective feature. An alternative account is that the memory R' for the regularity is dormant but still accessible. In a study by Cowan, Winkler, Teder, and Näätänen (1993), trains of tones with short stimulus onset asynchronies (SOAs) were presented containing identical standards from train to train and 11–15 s of silence between trains. It was found that a frequency deviant in Position 1 of the train did not elicit a MMN. However, a frequency deviant at Position 2 did elicit a MMN in a condition in which the standards were constant across trains, whereas it did not in a roving condition in which the frequency of the standards changed from train to train. The absence of an MMN in the latter condition was explained by the hypothesis that the occurrence of a single tone does not yet give rise to a rule. The presence of MMN in the former condition was explained as a carryover effect of the invariancy representation of the previous train for the frequency of standard tones in previous trains that became dormant during the long ISI but could be reactivated by one reminder. Another explanation of the absence of MMN with long ISIs is that there the memory for R' is still present but not applied because the present deviancy falls out of context. This hypothesis was confirmed in a study by Winkler et al. (2001) in which trains of six standard tones were presented with a short, 0.5-s SOA between tones in the train followed by a variable 7-s SOA between the last standard and the deviant tone in one condition (the irregular presentation condition). In the other condition, the tones were presented at a regular SOA of 7 s. MMN was elicited in 9 out of 16 participants in the irregular presentation condition, whereas MMN was elicited in all participants in the regular presentation condition.

These results cannot be explained on the basis of memory-strength decay but can be interpreted in terms of automatic, auditory preperceptual grouping principles. In the irregular presentation condition, the close grouping of standards may cause them to become irrelevant to the mismatch process when the deviant tone is presented after a long silent break. Because the MMN indexes preattentive auditory processing, the present results provide evidence that large-scale preperceptual organization of auditory events occurs even though attention is directed away from the auditory stimuli. A similar finding was reported by Gaeta, Friedman, Ritter, and Cheng (2001) for two groups of participants: young and elderly adults. In both groups all subjects had MMNs for a frequency deviant in Position 1 of the trains with 1 s of silence between trains, but only some had a MMN for 8 s of silence. However, in a behavioral active condition in which subjects had to press a key whenever a deviant was delivered, both groups had near 100% accuracy for the

1 and 8 s of silence between trains, showing that there was still a memory for the invariancy after 8 s.

Although the elicitation of MMN with SOAs of up to 10 s when the stimuli are ignored demonstrates that the respective memory trace for the invariance is maintained for at least 10 s, it is still an open question whether the allocation of attention may enhance the lifetime of auditory memory. Electrophysiological experiments directly testing this question have (to our knowledge) not yet been performed and behavioral results are ambiguous. Keller, Cowan, and Saults (1995) reported improved performance in a two-tone S1–S2 comparison task when participants were instructed to rehearse the pitch of the first tone covertly during the intertone interval relative to conditions when such rehearsal was prevented by a distractor task. Results suggest that auditory imagery can be used strategically to slow the rate of decay of auditory information for tone pitch. In contrast, Demany, Clément, and Semal (2001) did not find effects of attention on the duration of auditory memory.

Auditory Memory Creates the Informational Basis for Subsequent Processing Stages

The hypothesis claiming that the output of the preattentive deviance-detection system is utilized for the conscious detection of deviants is supported by the fact that the latencies and amplitudes of MMN elicited by frequency changes (measured in the ignore condition) correlate with the latencies and amplitudes of N2b and P3 components (measured in the attend condition), reflecting conscious stimulus processing, and with behavioral discrimination performance (e.g., Novak, Ritter, & Vaughan, 1992a, 1992b; Novak, Ritter, Vaughan, & Wiznitzer, 1990; Paavilainen, Jiang, Lavikainen, & Näätänen, 1993; Ritter, Simson, Vaughan, & Friedman, 1979; Tiitinen et al., 1994; Winkler, Reinikainen, & Näätänen, 1993), as shown in Fig. 18.2.

Moreover, Amenedo and Escera (2000) studied the accuracy of the human brain in detecting differences in sound duration (indicated by MMN) and the subject's ability to perceive the same differences (indicated by the distance between the distributions of false alarms and hits, i.e., d'), respectively. It was found that the accuracy of the human auditory system to represent sound-duration information is related to the duration context in which the sounds are heard, and that these contextual representations determine the accuracy of perception at the behavioral level. Correspondingly, Desjardins, Trainor, Hevenor, and Polak (1999) showed that the presence of occasional silent gaps between short tone pips elicits MMN in young adults and that gap-detection thresholds with MMN agree well with behavioral thresholds; that is, near threshold, the MMN increased as the gap size increased millisecond by millisecond. In contrast, in a study by Bertoli, Heimberg, Smurzynski, and Probst (2001), there was no clear relation between psychoacoustical and MMN

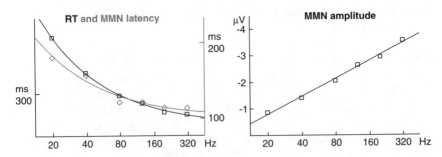

FIG. 18.2. The relationship between the MMN parameters and behavioral measures. The repetitive tone of 1000 Hz (standard) was randomly replaced by a tone of 20, 40, 80, 160, and 320 Hz higher in frequency (deviants). These sounds were presented to individuals who first concentrated on reading a book of their own choice and second were asked to indicate when they detected a pitch-deviant tone. Left: The reaction time and the MMN latency decreased logarithmically as a function of increasing deviancy. Right: The MMN amplitude increased linearly as a function of increasing deviancy.

thresholds; however, in this study, MMN did occur with gaps that were slightly larger than the mean behavioral gap-detection threshold, suggesting that MMN and behavior are not completely unrelated.

Finally, particular patient groups revealing deficits in auditory-discrimination performance were often found to reveal reduced MMN amplitudes in the passive oddball condition, confirming that the traces used in preattentive auditory memory are utilized for conscious processing. For example, Deouell, Bentin, and Soroker (2000) studied patients with right-hemisphere damage resulting in contralesional neglect. They compared the MMN elicited by right- and left-sided deviant stimuli with left unilateral neglect (all showing signs of auditory extinction and neglect) and healthy volunteers. Across dimensions, the MMN elicited by deviance occurring to the left of the patients was reduced relative to that elicited by deviance occurring to the right. This effect was robust for spatial location, and less so for pitch, and the processing of stimulus duration was not significantly affected by the side of stimulation. Corroborating evidence was obtained by Ilvonen et al. (2001), who compared the duration discrimination of left- versus right-ear sound stimulation between a control group and aphasic patients, with the receptive (Wernicke) aphasia resulting from a left middle-artery infarct. The data indicate that the patients' behavioral performance and the MMN were significantly deteriorated when compared with control group only when the stimulation was delivered to their right ear, with the majority of the information being then projected to the left hemisphere. In contrast, the intact neural circuits within the right auditory cortex properly encoded the sound duration with left-ear stimulation in patients.

INFLUENCE OF LONG-TERM EXPERIENCE
ON AUDITORY SENSORY MEMORY

It was previously mentioned that MMN may be modulated by attention and that this effect is most probably the result of the attentional modification of the memory traces entering the memory-comparison process underlying MMN. That is, this attentional effect is related to the way neural representations used in sensory-memory operations are established, accessed, or activated. Indeed, there is evidence for the hypothesis that attention can affect the basic encoding of features in central auditory processing (e.g., Woldorff & Hillyard, 1991) and even at the cochlea (Giard, Collet, Bouchet, & Pernier, 1994; for a converse result, see Michie, LePage, Solowij, Haller, & Terry, 1996). These results relate to the effects of attention of the current stimulus. However, it has to be asked whether experience acquired by means of previous long-term stimulus exposure or active training may have effects on sensory-memory operations of acoustic input presented subsequent to the previous exposure or training. That is, it has to be asked whether representations kept in more durable memory stores (long-term memory) can influence sensory-memory operations indicated by MMN or whether those operations are informationally encapsulated from such representations.

Training-Related Short-Term Effects in Passive Listening

A transfer effect of training performed in an active listening condition on sensory-memory processing in a closely spaced passive listening condition was obtained in a study by Näätänen, Schröger, Karakas, Tervaniemi, and Paavilainen (1993) in which an unfamiliar sound pattern consisting of consecutive tones was repeatedly presented to reading individuals. In deviant patterns, one segment was shifted in frequency for an illustrations see website. In those participants who could not discriminate the patterns before they were trained to do so, no MMN was elicited at the early phase of the experiment. However, when the participants learned to behaviorally discriminate the patterns (Improvers) after one or two training sessions, (middle- and late-phase) deviant patterns elicited the MMN even when participants did not pay attention to the sounds. This result suggests the development of a memory trace for a complex sound; it seems that, with training, the memory trace for a standard stimulus became precise enough to enable the cortical change-detector mechanism to detect a slightly different stimulus.

Training-Related Long-Term Effects on Sensory-Memory Processing

This previous finding was replicated and fundamentally extended by Atienza and Cantero (2001). They measured MMN and behavioral performance before participants learned to consciously discriminate between the two patterns and just after the training and 12, 24, 36, and 48 hr later. Similar to the study by Näätänen, Schröger, et al. (1993), participants who learned to discriminate deviant from standard patterns in the active condition applied this "knowledge" in the passive condition as indexed by the elicitation of MMN. It is important that the data of Atienza and Cantero also demonstrated a long-term effect of training on sensory-memory operations indexed by MMN. Relative to the posttraining recording, they found additional enhancement of MMN amplitude and a decrease in reaction time 36 and 48 hr after the training phase. Kraus, McGee, and Koch (1998) also reported long-term effects on sensory memory. They examined the effect of training in speech-contrast discrimination on MMN. Behavioral training in the discrimination of those speech stimuli resulted in a significant change in the duration and magnitude of the cortical potential.

In a very effortful study, Menning, Roberts, and Pantev (2000) measured MMNm elicited by sequences of pure tones of 1000 Hz and deviant tones of 1050, 1010, and 1005 Hz before, during, and 3 weeks after participants were trained at frequency discrimination for 15 sessions (over 3 weeks). The participants' task was to detect deviants differing by progressively smaller frequency shifts from the standard stimulus. Frequency discrimination improved rapidly in the first week and was followed by small but constant improvements thereafter. The MMNm and also the N1m to the deviant stimuli increased in amplitude during training. This enhancement persisted until training was finished, but it decreased 3 weeks later. Pantev and Lütkenhöner (2000) suggested that the cortical representation of tones may change within hours after a reversible "functional deafferentation," and they took this as a mechanism of short-term plasticity.

The results reported in these studies suggest a reorganization of the cortical representation for the trained tonal patterns and frequencies. It is not known whether the training effect is confined to the patterns or frequencies that have been trained or whether there is a transfer to other patterns or frequencies. The following paragraphs show that some form of generalization is possible, although it may be questioned whether this is the case for the examples presented so far.

Long-Term Effects in Language-Specific Phoneme Processing

It is assumed that long-term exposure to a particular language creates language-dependent memory traces that are already activated in the early processing of speech. Evidence for this hypothesis was obtained in an electroencephalographic and magnetoencephalographic MMN study (Näätänen et al., 1997) in which a native-language-specific enhancement of the MMN amplitude for phonemes belonging to the participant's native language while he or she was ignoring speech sounds was shown. In this study, Finnish individuals were presented the Finnish prototypes /e/ as the frequent stimulus and other Finnish phoneme prototypes, [e/ö], [ö], [o], or the Estonian prototype /õ/ (which is a nonprototype for Finns) as the infrequent stimulus. It was found that the MMN was enhanced when the infrequent stimulus was the Finnish /ö/ (a prototype) relative to when it was the Estonian /õ/. In contrast, /õ/ caused enhancement of MMN in Estonians. This shows that these phonemic traces, revealed by MMN, are language specific. Moreover, this demonstrates effects of long-term experience with one's native language on auditory-memory operations underlying the elicitation of MMN (cf. Huotilainen, Kujala, & Alku, 2001).

Effects of long-term experience with one's own language was also demonstrated in a study by Winkler, Lehtokoski, et al. (1999), in which a Finnish and a Hungarian language group were presented with identical stimuli. One standard–deviant pair represented an across-vowel category contrast in Hungarian but a within-category contrast in Finnish, with the other pair having the reversed role in the two languages. Both within- and across-category contrasts elicited the MMN speakers of either language. However, the MMN amplitude was larger in across-than within-category contrasts in both language groups, suggesting that the preattentive change-detection process utilized both auditory (sensory) and phonetic (categorical) representations of the test vowels, with the latter demonstrating an effect of long-term experience on sensory-memory operations. A similar finding was obtained by Winkler, Kujala, et al. (1999) with Finnish and Hungarian individuals. The Hungarian group consisted of a naive (no knowledge of Finnish) and a fluent (in Finnish) subgroup. It was found that the MMN for a contrast between two Finnish phonemes was elicited in the fluent Hungarians but not in the naive Hungarians, indicating that the fluent Hungarians developed cortical memory representations for the Finnish phoneme system that enabled them to preattentively categorize phonemes specific to this language.

Passive Long-Term Effects in the Processing of Musical Information

Another realm where long-term effects can be expected is the processing of musical information in highly trained musicians. It is known that musical information can be discriminated better by musicians than by nonmusicians. However, it is unknown whether this superiority of musicians is located at more cognitive levels or whether processing already at early stages involving sensory memory is improved in musicians relative to nonmusicians. The study by Koelsch, Schröger, and Tervaniemi (1999) aimed to provide evidence for influences of musical experience in highly trained professional violinists on auditory sensory-memory mechanisms. Professional violinists and musical novices were presented with a frequent standard perfect major chord (a triad comprising tone frequencies of 396, 495, and 596 Hz) and an infrequent deviant chord (396, 491, and 596 Hz). MMN was enhanced in musical experts but almost absent in novices, independent of whether stimuli were attended to or ignored. When stimuli were ignored, deviant chords elicited a distinct MMN in experts but no MMN in novices, reflecting improved sensory-memory processing in experts compared with novices. When chords were attended to, slightly impure chords were clearly discriminable for experts but virtually undetectable for musical novices. These results provide evidence for superior preattentive auditory processing in musicians, that is, that the superior discrimination performance of musicians is not only due to processing at higher cognitive levels but also to preattentive memory-based processing. Because attentive auditory discrimination performance can be improved by training, the present data are in accordance with the hypothesis that long-term training is able to modify even preattentive neural memory mechanisms. These mechanisms are located on the earliest physiologically measurable level of auditory-comparison processes in the human brain.

Moreover, passive musical exposure might also influence the way pitch is processed at a preattentive level. In a study by Brattico, Näätänen, and Tervaniemi (2002), the pitch MMN to a change in a familiar scale context was compared with that in an unfamiliar context (not following the rules of Western musical system). The data showed that both musicians and nonmusicians showed an enhanced MMN to the pitch change embedded in the familiar context. This might suggest that automatic pitch-change discrimination is influenced by long-term memory traces for those sounds commonly used in our musical structure also in subjects without active participation in music training. Moreover, the pitch MMN had a shorter latency in musicians than in nonmusicians, suggesting that expertise in music may further facilitate preattentive sound-change processing.

Passive Long-Term Effects in the Processing of Musical Information Involving Active Training

Improved sensory-memory processing for musical information in musicians relative to nonmusicians was also obtained in a recent study by Tervaniemi, Rytkönen, Schröger, Ilmoniemi, and Näätänen (2001). There, participants were presented with melody-like sound patterns consisting of five tones for an illustration see website. Those were played at 12 different frequency levels. Deviants differed from standards in the melody contour of the pattern. During electroencephalographic recording, participants watched a silent movie with subtitles. The recordings were interspersed three times with an active discrimination task in which subjects should detect deviant melody contours. According to their behavioral performance, participants were divided in two groups. The best 8 participants (all of them professional musicians) detected on average 91% of the deviants (accurate individuals), whereas the rest of the participants (7 nonmusicians and 5 musicians) had a hit rate of 41% only (inaccurate individuals). In the first passive phase of the experiment (before participants ran an intervening discrimination block), neither group showed MMN. In the second and third passive phases (when intervening active blocks had been run), only the accurate participants showed MMN. This finding suggests that the abstract sound features needed for detecting the deviant melody contour can be reactivated in passive listening conditions when adequate memory traces were formed in an active discrimination task (a finding related to the short-term effects of training of the Näätänen, Schröger, et al., 1993 study). However, only professional musicians receiving many years of musical training who also preferred to play without a musical score were able to establish such traces. Thus this result not only shows short-term effects of auditory sensory-memory operations but also top-down effects involving long-term experience with musical information.

CONCLUSION

Four assumptions about auditory sensory-memory processing were extracted here. Assumptions (a) and (b) relate to the automaticity of the establishment and the maintenance of sensory-memory representations. Assumptions (c) and (d) relate to the way information is transferred between sensory memory and subsequent processing systems, stating that sensory-memory operations are in the service of higher-level systems but that they may, in turn, not be affected by higher-level operations. Electrophysiological data were delivered suggesting that these assumptions are valid over a broad range of phenomena. However, there are important exceptions challenging the general validity of assumption (a) that postulates strong automaticity of the establishment of sensory-memory representations and of assumption (d) that postulates a purely unidirectional flow of information from sensory-memory processing to processing in subsequent memory stages. Although the exact nature of the top-down effects on auditory sensory-memory processing is not yet understood, it seems that there are different ways these can be implemented. A better understanding of the flow of information within sensory memory and between preceding and subsequent stages of processing may be achieved by a more detailed specification, which requires further research. In particular, the joint consideration of neurobiological and behavioral data will, one would hope, be fruitful for our theories on the flow of information into, within, and from sensory memory.

ACKNOWLEDGMENT

This research was supported by a grant from the Deutsche Forschungsgemeinschaft, by the Deutscher Akademischer Austauschdienst (DAAD), and by a European Union (EU) grant (Marie-Curie Fellowship) to Dr. Tervaniemi.

REFERENCES

Alain, C., & Woods, D. L. (1997). Attention modulates auditory pattern memory as indexed by event-related brain potentials. *Psychophysiology, 34*, 534–546.
Alho, K., Woods, D. L., & Algazi, A. (1994). Processing of auditory stimuli during auditory and visual attention as revealed by event-related potentials. *Psychophysiology, 31*, 469–479.

Amenedo, E., & Escera, C. (2000). The accuracy of sound duration representation in the human brain determines the accuracy of behavioural perception. *European Journal of Neuroscience, 12*, 2570–2574.

Atienza, M., & Cantero, J. L. (2001). Complex sound processing during human REM sleep by recovering information from long-term memory as revealed by the mismatch negativity (MMN). *Brain Research, 901*, 151–160.

Atienza, M., Cantero, J. L., & Gomez, C. M. (2000). Decay time of the auditory sensory memory trace during wakefulness and REM sleep. *Psychophysiology, 37* (4), 485–493.

Atkinson, R. C., & Shiffrin, R. M. (1968). Human memory: A proposed system and its control processes. In K. W. Spence & J. T. Spence (Eds.), *The psychology of learning and motivation: Advances in research and theory* (Vol. 2, pp. 89–195). New York: Academic Press.

Bertoli, S., Heimberg, S., Smurzynski, J., & Probst, R. (2001). Mismatch negativity and psychoacoustic measures of gap detection in normally hearing subjects. *Psychophysiology, 38* (2), 334–342.

Böttcher-Gandor, C., & Ullsperger, P. (1992). Mismatch negativity in event-related potentials to auditory stimuli as a function of varying interstimulus interval. *Psychophysiology, 29* (5), 546–550.

Brattico, E., Näätänen, R., & Tervaniemi, M. (2002). Context effects on pitch perception in musicians and non-musicians: Evidence from ERP recordings. *Music Perception, 19*, 199–222.

Cheour, M., Leppänen, P. H., & Kraus, N. (2000). Mismatch negativity (MMN) as a tool for investigating auditory discrimination and sensory memory in infants and children. *Clinical Neurophysiology, 111* (1), 4–16.

Cheour-Luhtanen, M., Alho, K., Kujala, T., Sainio, K., Reinikainen, K., Renlund, M., Aaltonen, O., Eerola, O., & Näätänen, R. (1995). Mismatch negativity indicates vowel discrimination in newborns. *Hearing Research, 82* (1), 53–58.

Cowan, N. (1984). On short and long auditory stores. *Psychological Bulletin, 96*, 341–370.

Cowan, N. (1988). Evolving conceptions of memory storage, selective attention, and their mutual constraints within the human information-processing system. *Psychological Bulletin, 104*, 163–191.

Cowan, N. (1995). *Attention and memory: An integrated framework*. Oxford, England: Oxford University Press.

Cowan, N., Winkler, I., Teder, W., & Näätänen, R. (1993). Memory prerequisites of mismatch negativity in the auditory event-related potentials (ERP). *Journal of Experimental Psychology: Learning, Memory, and Cognition, 19*, 909–921.

Crowder, R. G., & Morton, J. (1969). Precategorical acoustic storage. *Perception & Psychophysics, 5* (6), 365–373.

Demany, L., Clément, S., & Semal, C. (2001). Does auditory memory depend on attention? In D. J. Breebaart, A. J. M. Houtsma, A. Kohlrausch, V. F. Prijs, & R. Schoonhoven (Eds.), *Physiological and Psychophysical Bases of Auditory Function* (pp. 461–467). Maastricht, The Netherlands: Shaker.

Deouell, L., Bentin, S., & Soroker, N. (2000). Electrophysiological evidence for an early (pre-attentive) information processing deficit in patients with right hemisphere damage and unilateral neglect. *Brain, 123*, 353–365.

Desjardins, R. N., Trainor, L. J., Hevenor, S. J., & Polak, C. P. (1999). Using mismatch negativity to measure auditory temporal resolution thresholds. *NeuroReport, 13*, 2079–2082.

Dittmann-Balcar, A., Thienel, R., & Schall, U. (1999). Attention-dependent allocation of auditory processing resources as measured by mismatch negativity. *NeuroReport, 10*, 3749–3753.

Doughty, J. M., & Garner, W. R. (1948). Pitch characteristics of short tones: II. Pitch as a function of tonal duration. *Journal of Experimental Psychology, 38*, 478–494.

Efron, R. (1970). The relation between the duration of a stimulus and the duration of a perception. *Neuropsychologia, 8*, 57–63.

Escera, C., Alho, K., Schröger, E., & Winkler, I. (2000). Involuntary attention and distractibility as evaluated with event-related brain potentials. *Audiology & Neuro-Otology, 5*, 151–166.

Fischer, C., Morlet, D., Bouchet, P., Luaute, J., Jourdan, C., & Salord, F. (1999). Mismatch negativity and late auditory evoked potentials in comatose patients. *Clinical Neurophysiology, 110*, 1601–1610.

Fischer, C., Morlet, D., & Giard, M. (2000). Mismatch negativity and N100 in comatose patients. *Audiology & Neuro-Otology, 5*(3–4), 192–197.

Gaeta, H., Friedman, D., Ritter, W., & Cheng, J. (2001). The effect of perceptual grouping on the mismatch negativity. *Psychophysiology, 38*, 316–324.

Giard, M. H., Collet, L., Bouchet, P., & Pernier, J. (1994). Auditory selective attention in the human cochlea. *Brain Research, 633*, 353–356.

Gomes, H., Sussman, E., Ritter, W., Kurtzberg, D., Cowan, N., & Vaughan, H. G. Jr. (1999). Electrophysiological evidence of developmental changes in the duration of auditory sensory memory. *Developmental Psychology, 35* (1), 294–302.

Hackley, S. A. (1993). An evaluation of the automaticity of sensory processing using event-related potentials and brain-stem reflexes. *Psychophysiology, 30* (5), 415–428.

Harmony, T., Bernal, J., Fernandez, T., Silva-Pereyra, J., Fernandez-Bouzas, A., Marosi, E., Rodriguez, M., & Reyes, A. (2000). Primary task demands modulate P3a amplitude. *Cognitive Brain Research, 9*, 53–60.

Huotilainen, M., Kujala, T., & Alku, P. (2001). Long-term memory traces facilitate short-term memory trace formation in audition in humans. *Neuroscience Letters, 310*, 133–136.

Ilvonen, T. M., Kujala, T., Tervaniemi, M., Salonen, O., Näätänen, R., & Pekkonen, E. (2001). The processing of sound duration after left hemisphere stroke: event-related potential and behavioral evidence. *Psychophysiology, 38*, 622–628

Imada, T., Hari, R., Loveless, N., McEvoy, L., & Sams, M. (1993). Determinants of the auditory mismatch response. *Electroencephalography & Clinical Neurophysiology, 87* (3), 144–153.

Javitt, D. C., Doneshka, P., Grochowski, S., & Ritter, W. (1995). Impaired mismatch negativity generation reflects widespread dysfunction of working memory in schizophrenia. *Archives of General Psychiatry, 52*, 550–558.

Kane, N. M., Butler, S. R., & Simpson, T. (2000). Coma outcome prediction using event-related potentials: P(3) and mismatch negativity. *Audiology & Neuro-Otology, 5* (3–4), 186–191.

Kane, N. M., Curry, S. H., Rowlands, C. A., Manara, A. R., Lewis, T., Moss, T., Cummins, B. H., & Butler, S. R. (1996). Event-related potentials—neurophysiological tools for predicting emergence and early outcome from traumatic coma. *Intensive Care Medicine, 22* (1), 39–46.

Keller, T. A., Cowan, N., & Saults, J. S. (1995). Can auditory memory for tone pitch be rehearsed? *Journal of Experimental Psychology: Learning, Memory, and Cognition, 21*, 635–645.

Koelsch, S., Schröger, E., & Tervaniemi, M. (1999). Superior pre-attentive and attentive auditory processing in musicians. *NeuroReport, 10*, 1309–1313.

Kraus, N., McGee, T. J., & Koch, D. B. (1998). Speech sound representation, perception, and plasticity: A neurophysiologic perspective. *Audiology & Neuro-Otology, 3*, 168–182.

Loewy, D. H., Campbell, K. B., & Bastien, C. (1996). The mismatch negativity to frequency deviant stimuli during natural sleep. *Electroencephalography & Clinical Neurophysiology, 98* (6), 493–501.

Massaro, D. W. (1970). Preperceptual auditory images. *Journal of Experimental Psychology, 85*, 411–417.

Menning, H., Roberts, L. E., & Pantev, C. (2000). Plastic changes in the auditory cortex induced by intensive frequency discrimination training. *NeuroReport, 11*, 817–822.

Michie, P. T., LePage, E. L., Solowij, N., Haller, M., & Terry, L. (1996). Evoked otoacoustic emissions and auditory selective attention. *Hearing Research, 98*, 54–67.

Näätänen, R. (1992). *Attention and brain function.* Hillsdale, NJ: Lawrence Erlbaum Associates.

Näätänen, R., Alho, K., & Schröger, E. (2002). Electrophysiology of attention. In H. Pashler & J. Wixted (Eds.), *Steven's handbook of experimental psychology, vol. 4: Methodology in experimental psychology* (3rd ed., pp 601–653). New York: Wiley.

Näätänen, R., Lehtokoski, A., Lennes, M., Cheour, M., Huotilainen, M., Iivonen, A., Vainio, M., Alku, P., Ilmoniemi, R. J., Luuk, A., Allik, J., Sinkkonen, J., & Alho, K. (1997). Language-specific phoneme representations revealed by electric and magnetic brain responses. *Nature, 385*, 432–434.

Näätänen, R., Schröger, E., Karakas, S., Tervaniemi, M., & Paavilainen, P. (1993). Development of a memory trace for a complex sound in the human brain. *NeuroReport, 4*, 503–506.

Nashida, T., Yabe, H., Sato, Y., Hiruma, T., Sutoh, T., Shinozaki, N., & Kaneko, S. (2000). Automatic auditory information processing in sleep. *Sleep, 23* (6), 821–828.

Novak, G., Ritter, W., & Vaughan, H. G., Jr. (1992a). Mismatch detection and the latency of temporal judgements. *Psychophysiology, 29*, 398–411.

Novak, G., Ritter, W., & Vaughan, H. G., Jr. (1992b). The chronometry of attention-modulated processing and automatic mismatch detection. *Psychophysiology, 29*, 412–430.

Novak, G. P., Ritter, W., Vaughan, H. G., & Wiznitzer, M. L. (1990). Differentiation of negative event-related potentials in an auditory discrimination task. *Electroencephalography & Clinical Neurophysiology, 75*, 255–275.

Paavilainen, P., Jiang, D., Lavikainen, J., & Näätänen, R. (1993). Stimulus duration and the sensory memory trace: An event-related potential study. *Biological Psychology, 35*, 139–152.

Paavilainen, P., Tiitinen, H., Alho, K., & Näätänen, R. (1993). Mismatch negativity to slight pitch changes outside strong attentional focus. *Biological Psychology, 37*, 32–41.

Pantev, C., & Lütkenhöner, B. (2000). Magnetoencephalographic studies of functional organization and plasticity of the human auditory cortex. *Journal of Clinical Neurophysiology, 17*, 130–142.

Pekkonen, E., Jousmäki, V., Kononen, M., Reinikainen, K., & Partanen, J. (1994). Auditory sensory memory impairment in Alzheimer's disease: An event-related potential study. *NeuroReport, 5*, 2537–2540.

Pekkonen, E., Jousmäki, V., Partanen, J., & Karhu, J. (1993). Mismatch negativity area and age-related auditory memory. *Electroencephalography & Clinical Neurophysiology, 87*, 321–325.

Rinne, T., Antila, S., & Winkler, I. (2001). Mismatch negativity is unaffected by top-down predictive information. *NeuroReport, 12*, 2209–2213.

Ritter, W., Simson, R., Vaughan, H. G., & Friedman, D. (1979). A brain event related to the making of a sensory discrimination. *Science, 203*, 1358–1361.

Ritter, W., Sussman, E., Deacon, D., Cowan, N., & Vaughan, H. G., Jr. (1999). Two cognitive systems simultaneously prepared for opposite events. *Psychophysiology, 36*, 835–838.

Sallinen, M., Kaartinen, J., & Lyytinen, H. (1994). Is the appearance of mismatch negativity during stage 2 sleep related to the elicitation of K-complex? *Electroencephalography & Clinical Neurophysiology, 91* (2), 140–148.

Schröger, E. (1996). A neural mechanism for involuntary attention shifts to changes in auditory stimulation. *Journal of Cognitive Neuroscience, 8*, 527–539.

Schröger, E. (1997). On the detection of auditory deviations: A pre-attentive activation model. *Psychophysiology, 34*, 245–257.

Shiffrin, R. M., & Schneider, W. (1977). Controlled and automatic human information processing: II. Perceptual learning, automatic attending and a general theory. *Psychological Review, 84*, 127–190.

Shutara, Y., Koga, Y., Fujita, K., Takeuchi, H., Mochida, M., & Takemasa, K. (1996). An event-related potential study on the impairment of automatic processing of auditory input in schizophrenia. *Brain Topography, 8* (3), 285–289.

Stevens, J. C., & Hall, J. W. (1966). Brightness and loudness as functions of stimulus duration. *Perception & Psychophysics, 1*, 319–327.

Sussman, E., Ritter, W., & Vaughan, H. G., Jr. (1998a). Attention affects the organization of auditory input associated with the mismatch negativity system. *Brain Research, 789*, 130–138.

Sussman, E., Ritter, W., & Vaughan, H. G., Jr. (1998b). Predictability of stimulus deviance and the mismatch negativity. *NeuroReport, 9* (18), 4167–4170.

Sussman, E., Winkler, I., & Schröger, E. (in press). Top-down control over involuntary attention switching in the auditory modality. *Psychonomic Bulletin & Review*.

Szymanski, M. D., Yund, E. W., & Woods, D. L. (1999). Phonemes, intensity and attention: Differential effects on the mismatch negativity (MMN). *Journal of the Acoustical Society of America, 106* (6), 3492–3505.

Tervaniemi, M., Rytkönen, M., Schröger, E., Ilmoniemi, R. J., & Näätänen, R. (2001). Superior formation of cortical memory traces for melodic patterns in musicians. *Learning & Memory, 8*, 295–300.

Tiitinen, H., May, P., Reinikainen, K., & Näätänen, R. (1994). Attentive novelty detection in humans is governed by pre-attentive sensory memory. *Nature, 372*, 90–92.

Trejo, L. J., Ryan-Jones, D. L., & Kramer, A. F. (1995). Attentional modulation of the mismatch negativity elicited by frequency differences between binaurally presented tone bursts. *Psychophysiology, 32* (4), 319–328.

Winkler, I., Karmos, G., & Näätänen, R. (1996). Adaptive modeling of the unattended acoustic environment reflected in the mismatch negativity event-related potential. *Brain Research, 742*, 239–252.

Winkler, I., Kujala, T., Tiitinen, H., Sivonen, P., Alku, P., Lehtokoski, A., Czigler, I., Csepe, V., Ilmoniemi, R. J., & Näätänen, R. (1999). Brain responses reveal the learning of foreign language phonemes. *Psychophysiology, 36*, 638–642.

Winkler, I., Lehtokoski, A., Alku, P., Vainio, M., Czigler, I., Csepe, V., Aaltonen, O., Raimo, I., Alho, K., Lang, H., Iivonen, A., & Näätänen R. (1999). Pre-attentive detection of vowel contrasts utilizes both phonetic and auditory memory representations. *Cognitive Brain Research, 7*, 357–369.

Winkler, I., Reinikainen, K., & Näätänen, R. (1993). Event-related brain potentials reflect traces of echoic memory in humans. *Perception & Psychophysics, 53*, 443–449.

Winkler, I., Schröger, E., & Cowan, N. (2001). The role of large-scale perceptual organization in the mismatch negativity event-related brain potential. *Journal of Cognitive Neuroscience, 13*, 59–71.

Woldorff, M. G., Hackley, S. A., & Hillyard, S. A. (1991). The effects of channel-selective attention on the mismatch negativity wave elicited by deviant tones. *Psychophysiology, 28*, 30–42.

Woldorff, M. G., & Hillyard, S. A. (1991). Modulation of early auditory processing during selective listening to rapidly presented tones. *Electroencehalography & Clinical Neurophysiology, 79*, 170–191.

Woldorff, M. G., Hillyard, S. A., Gallen, C. C., Hampson, S. R., & Bloom, F. E. (1998). Magnetoencephalographic recordings demonstrate attentional modulation of mismatch-related neural activity in human auditory cortex. *Psychophysiology, 35* (3), 283–292.

IV

Neural and
Representational Models

Guest Editorial

Ad Aertsen

Albert-Ludwigs Universität, Freiburg, Germany

A model is an attempt to capture the essence of things. Hence, as a rule, a model strives to be as simple as possible, admitting complexity only as necessary. This is a very sensible rule, in fact. Approaches that disregard it tend to produce a muddle rather than a model—an insight I owe to Valentino Braitenberg. Thus, we generally use models as simplified versions of reality. They summarize our knowledge from previous experiments, allow us to make predictions to be tested in new experiments, and, above all, they enable us to make a conceptual interpretation of our results and insights.

The brain is an enormously complex system. The total number of possible states in a network comprising some 10^{11} neurons is exceedingly large. In fact, only a vanishing fraction of them will actually occur during a lifetime. This complexity has important strategic implications, both for experimental and theoretical approaches to brain function. In such a system, we cannot expect that the underlying principles will simply pop out from merely observing the neuronal activity during an experiment. A formal theory is needed to work out testable predictions regarding the functioning of the system. These predictions, in turn, lead to the design of new experiments that can critically test the theory. At the same time, a theory of such complex and only partially observable system must incorporate the relevant biological constraints. Otherwise, it runs the danger of degenerating into a sterile formal game. Thus a close interaction of experiment and theory provides the optimal research strategy to make substantial progress in brain research.

Ideas on possible principles of brain function may well be formulated on the basis of common sense. At the level of neuronal activity, however, this approach is often misleading, or even incorrect. A serious discourse on brain function could develop only several decades ago, after researchers attempted to abstractly define and actually mimic "intelligent behavior" in terms of models and simulated these on electronic computers. This started a new process of scientific inquiry in areas such as artificial intelligence, cognitive science, and computational neuroscience that, in turn, served as a rich source of inspiration for brain theoreticians. At the same time, insights and findings from brain research provided useful ideas for the understanding of complex artificial systems as studied in engineering and computer science. Thus, in our experience, the conceptual connections among modern brain science and physics, mathematics, and computer science are the most exciting and fruitful ones.

The new field of computational neuroscience presents a good case in point. A recent special issue of the journal *Nature Neuroscience* states that "Perhaps the most exciting and difficult challenge currently facing biological scientists is to understand how complex biological systems work. These systems exist at all levels of organization, from the genetic determinants of protein structure to the complex interplay of individual neurons in orchestrating behavior." In response to this challenge, computational neuroscience was developed "to provide a solid theoretical foundation and a set of technological approaches, aimed to enhance our understanding of nervous system function by providing modeling tools that describe and transcend these many different levels of organization" (National Institute of Health, 2000, p. 1161).

The issue we are dealing with here—understanding human brain function—is quite formidable, indeed. The brain enables us to actively interact with our environment. Speed, fault tolerance, adaptivity, and creativity characterize normal brain operation and ultimately guarantee that we successfully master our daily lives. The combination of these various properties is unprecedented among current technical systems. The neural networks of the brain have to integrate a steady stream of sensory inputs with previously stored experiences. Likewise, they must produce a continuous flow of output commands to control behavior that, in turn, influences sensory perception. Many of the associated brain processes run in parallel and are distributed over multiple brain areas, giving rise to fast and well-coordinated transients of neural activity. Thus, the brain represents a complex and high-dimensional dynamical system, the function of which can be fully understood only in its behavioral context.

Ever since the times of Sherrington (1941) and Hebb (1949), neurobiologists have pursued the notion that neurons do not act in isolation, but rather that they organize into assemblies for the various computational tasks involved in organizing meaningful behavior (see also James, 1890, for an early formulation of this concept). Over the years, different definitions of "neural assembly" have been proposed, each implying different functions and properties. Some of these were phrased in terms of anatomy, others in terms of shared function or shared stimulus response (see Gerstein, Bedenbaugh, & Aertsen, 1989, for a review, with many references to the original literature). One operational definition for the cell assembly has been particularly influential: near-simultaneity or some other specific timing relation in the firing of the participating neurons. As, for instance, elaborated in the concept of the "synfire chain" (Abeles, 1991), the synaptic influence of multiple neurons converging onto others in the cortical network is much stronger if they fire in (near-)coincidence (Diesmann, Gewaltig, & Aertsen, 1999). Thus, temporal coherence or synchronous firing, postulated as a mechanism for perceptual integration (Hebb, 1949), is in fact directly available to the brain as a potential neural code (Johannesma, Aertsen, van den Boogaard, Eggermont, & Epping, 1986; Perkel & Bullock, 1968).

The notion that the functional organization of the cortex is based on interactions within and among groups of cells in large neural networks is supported by the anatomical structure and, in particular, by the massive connectivity of this part of the brain (Braitenberg & Schüz, 1991). Until recently, however, few physiological data have directly addressed the cell assembly hypothesis. Neither the study of global activity in large populations of neurons, nor the recording of single-neuron activity allows for a critical test of this concept. Rather, one seeks to observe the activities of many separate neurons simultaneously, preferably in awake, behaving animals, and to analyze these multiple single-neuron activities for possible signs of (dynamic) interactions between them. Results of such analyses are then used to draw inference regarding the processes taking place within and between hypothetical cell assemblies. Thus, in recent years, it has become possible to study directly various phenomena associated with neuronal assemblies. The salient result of these direct assembly observations has been that the neuronal interaction structure and, hence, the membership and internal organization of the observed assemblies depend on stimulus—and behavioral context, exhibiting systematic dynamic changes on several different time scales, with time constants down to the millisecond range (see Aertsen, Erb, & Palm, 1994, for a review and discussion on possible mechanisms involved).

These modulations of functional inter-neuron coupling form an interesting and novel feature of cortical network organization. In particular, they are the signature of an ongoing process of dynamical and activity-related "linking" and "unlinking" of neurons into modifyible, coherent groups. This process may have interesting functional implications at different levels of observation. At the single-neuron level, it may explain how even little specificity in anatomical connections could be dynamically sorted out to yield the complex functional properties that have been observed for cortical neurons. Thus, it might provide a natural mechanism for the physiologically measured context-dependence and intrinsic dynamics of receptive fields in central sensory neurons. At the multiple-neuron level, dynamic coupling may account for coherence variations in a spatially distributed neural code. Several phenomena in neocortical activity point at possible candidates for such distributed codes. One example is the observation of stimulus-specific oscillatory events in the visual cortex, with coherence properties that may extend over wide ranges of cortex (reviewed in Singer, 1999). A second is the relative exuberance of highly accurate and behavior-related spatio—temporal spike patterns in cortical activity, pointing at the presence of "synfire reverberations" (Prut et al., 1998). Finally, at the level of the organization of perception and action, modulation of functional coupling in interconnected neural networks may provide a mechanism for the selection and successive ignition of neural assemblies within and across such networks. Spatio-temporal variation of input activity, carried onto target networks by divergent-convergent projections, could effectively modulate the activity levels in these networks (Kuhn, Rotter, & Aertsen, 2003) and, hence, provide the means to select and dynamically switch from activation of one cell assembly to the next. Such "threshold control'-like (Braitenberg, 1978; Palm, 1982) mechanisms, possibly in combination with learning by means of spike-time-dependent synaptic plasticity (Bi & Poo, 2001) have, in fact, been proposed to implement the flexible generation of Hebbian "phase sequences" (Hebb, 1949) of cell assemblies and the dynamic flow of neural information associated with them (Aertsen et al., 1994; Salinas & Sejnowski, 2001).

In summary, the highly dynamic interplay of activity and connectivity in the cortical network gives rise to an ongoing process of rapid functional reorganization. Everchanging groups of neurons, each one recruited for brief periods of time, become co-activated and again de-activated, following each other in rapid succession. It is our conjecture that this dynamic reorganization provides the neural substrate to implement the computations involved in "higher brain function," including our capacity to perceive, to behave, and to learn.

The various contributions to this section on neural and representational models are firmly rooted in these recent developments in neuroscience. This holds, in particular, for Grossberg's perspective of "the complementary brain" and its relation to neural dynamics (chap. 19, this volume). Here, the author presents a readable account of his ambitious proposal for a neural-dynamics-based implementation of the classical view that the external world is paralleled by an appropriate internal representation in the brain (e.g., Craik, 1943; McCulloch, 1965). Unlike the classical view of computer-inspired collections of independent black boxes, however, his approach makes effective use of the emerging properties of a complex dynamical system of interacting feedforward and feedback processing streams. Much in the same vein, Kompass (chap. 20, this volume) addresses the temporal structure of human perception and cognition in terms of neural network dynamics. His contribution makes a case for a discrete mental time frame with an atomic unit of approximately 4.5 ms, and relates this temporal organization with the synchronization dynamics in Abelesian synfire chain networks. Leeuwenberg, finally, takes a more abstract view in his exploration of "structual information theory" as a formal vehicle to represent the perception of visual form (chap. 21, this volume). Here, the relation to a possible neuronal implementation scheme is neither sought, nor is it obvious from the mathematical formalism. Thus, the intrigued reader with a background in biology is provided with the interesting challenge of working out a biologically feasible realization of this mathematical elegance.

With these contributions in a book on *psychophysics beyond sensation* we have truly come a long way from the view that "psychophysics is the scientific discipline that studies phenomena which cease to be interesting once you clearly perceive them" (a view prevalent at the time I started out as a student in neuroscience). At the same time, the chapters you are about to read underline another important development, that of *"models beyond boxology"*. Biological and mathematical sophistication have matured to the extent that we can truly hope that a moderately realistic model of brain function is within reach. Whether that model (or—more likely—a collection of models) is ultimately correct is less important than that it is inspiring and capable of organizing our theoretical and experimental endeavors. Certainly, one criterion should be firmly kept in mind: The models we develop should preferably outqualify Salman Rushdie's M2C2Ds for P2C2E (*"machines too complicated to describe"* to control *"processes too complicated to explain"*) (Rushdie, 1991). The proof of the present pudding is left as an exercise to the reader.

REFERENCES

Abeles, M. (1991). *Corticonics. Neural circuits in the cerebral cortex.* Cambridge, England: Cambridge University Press.

Aertsen, A., Erb, M., & Palm, G. (1994). Dynamics of functional coupling in the cerebral cortex: an attempt at a model-based interpretation. *Physica D, 75,* 103–128.

Bi, G., & Poo, M. (2001). Synaptic modification by correlated activity: Hebb's postulate revisited. *Annual Review of Neurosciences, 24,* 139–166.

Braitenberg, V. (1978). Cell assemblies in the cerebral cortex. In R. Heim & G. Palm (Eds.), *Theoretical approaches to complex systems: Vol. 21. Lecture Notes in Biomathematics* (pp. 171–188). Berlin: Springer.

Braitenberg, V., & Schüz, A. (1991). *Anatomy of the cortex. Statistics and geometry.* Berlin: Springer.

Craik, K. (1943). *The nature of explanation.* Cambridge, England: Cambridge University Press.

Diesmann, M., Gewaltig, M.-O., & Aertsen, A. (1999). Stable propagation of synchronous spiking in cortical neural networks. *Nature (London), 402,* 529–533.

Gerstein, G. L., Bedenbaugh, P., & Aertsen, A. M. H. J. (1989). Neuronal assemblies. *IEEE Transactions on Biomedical Engineering, 36,* 4–14.

Hebb, D. (1949). *The organization of behavior. A neuropsychological theory.* New York: Wiley.

James, W. (1890). *Psychology: Briefer course.* New York: Holt.

Johannesma, P., Aertsen, A., van den Boogaard, H. Eggermont, J., & Epping, W. (1986). From synchrony to harmony: Ideas on the function of neural assemblies and on the interpretation of neural synchrony. In G. Palm & A. Aertsen (Eds.), *Brain theory* (pp. 25–47). Berlin: Springer.

Kuhn, A., Rotter, S., & Aertsen, A. (2003). Higher-order statistics of input ensembles and the response of simple model neurons. *Neural Computation, 15,* 67–101.

McCulloch, W. S. (1965). *Embodiments of mind*. Cambridge, MA: MIT Press.

National Institutes of Health (2000). Sponsors' foreword: Computational neuroscience at the NIH. *Nature Neuroscience Supplements, 3*, 1161–1164.

Palm, G. (1982). *Neural assemblies. An alternative approach to artificial intelligence*. Berlin: Springer.

Perkel, D. H., & Bullock, T. H. (1968). Neural coding. *Neuroscience Research Program Bulletin, 6*, 221–344.

Prut, Y., Vaadia, E., Bergman, H., Haalman, I., Slovin, H., & Abeles, M. (1998). Spatiotemporal structure of cortical activity: properties and behavioral relevance. *Journal of Neurophysiology, 79*, 2857–2874.

Rushdie, S. (1991). *Haroun and the sea of stories*. London: Granta Books (Penguin).

Salinas, E., & Sejnowski, T. J. (2001). Correlated neuronal activity and the flow of neural information. *Nature Reviews Neuroscience, 2*, 539–550.

Sherrington, C. (1941). *Man on his nature. The Gifford lectures, Edinburgh 1937–38*. Cambridge, UK: Cambridge University Press.

Singer, W. (1999). Neuronal synchrony: A versatile code for the definition of relations? *Neuron, 24*, 49–65.

19

The Complementary Brain: From Brain Dynamics to Conscious Experiences

Stephen Grossberg
Boston University

Many computer scientists have suggested that intelligent systems, our brains included, are organized into independent modules, as in a digital computer, and we see by processing perceptual qualities, such as form, color, and motion, by using these independent modules. The brain's organization into processing streams (DeYoe & van Essen, 1988) supports the idea that brain processing is specialized, but it does not in itself imply that these streams contain independent modules. Independent modules should be able to compute fully their particular processes on their own. Much perceptual data argue against the existence of independent modules, however, because strong interactions are known to occur between perceptual qualities (Egusa, 1983; Faubert & von Grunau, 1995; Kanizsa, 1974; Pessoa, Beck, & Mingolla, 1996; Smallman & McKee, 1995). For example, changes in perceived form or color can cause changes in perceived motion, and conversely; and changes in perceived brightness can cause changes in perceived depth, and conversely. How and why do these qualities interact? An answer to this question is needed to determine the functional and computational units that govern behavior as we know it.

This chapter reviews evidence, along the lines of Grossberg (2000a), that the brain's processing streams compute *complementary* properties. Each stream's properties are related to those of a complementary stream, much as a lock fits its

TABLE 19.1

Some Complementary Pairs of Brain Processes

Boundary completion	Surface filling-in
Boundary orientation	Motion direction
"What" learning and matching	"Where" learning and matching
Attentive learning	Orienting search
Object tracking	Optic flow navigation
Color	Luminance
Vergence	Spherical angle
Motor expectation	Volitional speed
Sensory cortical representation	Learned motivational feedback
Working memory order	Working memory rate

key or two pieces of a puzzle fit together. It is also suggested how the mechanisms that enable each stream to compute one set of properties prevent it from computing a complementary set of properties. As a result, each of these streams exhibits complementary strengths and weaknesses. How then are these complementary properties synthesized into a consistent behavioral experience? It is proposed that *interactions* between these processing streams overcome their complementary deficiencies and generate behavioral properties that realize the unity of conscious experiences. In this sense, *pairs* of complementary streams are the functional units because it is only through their interactions that key behavioral properties can be competently computed. This conclusion suggests that pairs of complementary streams may comprise the structural units that the brain uses to derive complete information about the environment and that emergent properties that are due to interactions between these streams are the functional units that govern behavior. As subsequently illustrated, these interactions may be used to explain many of the ways in which perceptual qualities are known to influence each other. Table 19.1 is a summary of some pairs of complementary processes that will be described herein.

Why does the brain often need several processing stages to form each processing stream? Accumulating evidence suggests that these stages realize a process of *hierarchical resolution of uncertainty*. 'Uncertainty' here means that computing one set of properties at a given stage can suppress information about a different set of properties at that stage. As I illustrate in the next section, these uncertainties are proposed to be overcome by use of more than one processing stage to form a stream. Overcoming informational uncertainty utilizes both hierarchical interactions within the stream and the parallel interactions between streams that overcome their complementary deficiencies. This observation illustrates from yet another perspective that the computational unit is not a single processing stage; it is, rather, proposed to be an ensemble of processing stages that interact within and between complementary processing streams.

According to this view, the organization of the brain obeys principles of uncertainty and complementarity, just as does the physical world with which brains interact and of which they form a part. I propose that these principles reflect each brain's role as a self-organizing measuring device *in* the world and *of* the world. Experimental and theoretical evidence for complementary processes and processing streams will be described in subsequent sections.

In most of these cases, evidence for the existence of processing streams and their role in behavior has been developed by many investigators. The fact that pairs of these streams exhibit complementary computational properties and that successive processing stages realize a hierarchical resolution of uncertainty has only gradually become clear through neural modeling, primarily from our group and colleagues. Through a large number of such modeling studies, it gradually became clear that different pairs of streams realize different combinations of complementary properties, as illustrated in the next sections. As of this writing, so many streams seem to follow this pattern that I now suggest that complementarity may be a general principle of brain design.

COMPLEMENTARY BOUNDARIES AND SURFACES IN VISUAL FORM PERCEPTION

Visual processing, from the retina through the inferotemporal and parietal cortices, provides excellent examples of parallel processing streams (Fig. 19.1). What evidence is there to suggest that these streams compute complementary properties, and how is this done? A neural theory, called FACADE (Form-And-Color-And-DEpth) theory, proposes that perceptual *boundaries* are formed in the LGN–interblob–interstripe–V4 (LGN stands for lateral geniculate nucleus) stream, whereas perceptual *surfaces* are formed in the LGN–blob–thin stripe–V4 stream (Grossberg, 1994). Many experiments have supported this prediction (e.g., Elder & Zucker, 1998; Lamme, Rodriguez-Rodriguez, & Spekreijse, 1999; Rogers-Ramachandran & Ramachandran, 1998).

FACADE theory suggests how and why perceptual boundaries and perceptual surfaces compute complementary properties. Figure 19.2(a) illustrates three pairs of complementary properties that are clarified by using the illusory contour percept of a Kanizsa square (Kanizsa, 1974). In response to both images of this figure, boundaries form *inwardly* between cooperating pairs of incomplete disk (or pac man) inducers to form the sides of the square. These boundaries are *oriented* to form in a collinear fashion between like-oriented inducers. The square boundary in Fig. 19.2(a) can be both seen and recognized because of the enhanced illusory brightness of the Kanizsa square. In contrast, the square boundary in Fig. 19.2(b) can be recognized even though it is not visible; that is, there is no brightness or color difference on either side of the boundary. Figure 19.2(b) shows that *some* boundaries can be recognized even though they are invisible. FACADE theory predicts

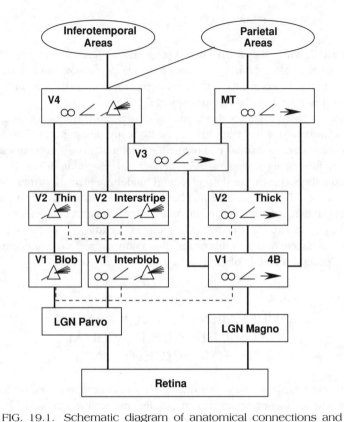

FIG. 19.1. Schematic diagram of anatomical connections and neuronal selectivities of early visual areas in the macaque monkey. LGN, lateral geniculate nucleus (parvocellular [parvo] and magnocellular [magno] divisions). Divisions of visual areas V1 and V2: blob, cytochrome oxidase blob regions; interblob, cytochrome oxidase-poor regions surrounding the blobs; 4B, lamina 4B; thin, thin (narrow) cytochrome oxidase stripes; interstripe, cytochrome oxidase-poor regions between the thin and thick stripes; thick, thick (wide) cytochrome oxidase stripes; V3, visual area 3; V4, visual area(s) 4; and MT, middle temporal area. Areas V2, V3, V4, and MT have connections to other areas not explicitly represented here. Area V3 may also receive projections from V2 interstripes or thin stripes. Heavy lines indicate robust primary connections, and thin lines indicate weaker, more variable connections. Dashed lines represent observed connections that require additional verification. Icons: rainbow = tuned, opponent, or both, wavelength selectivity (incidence at least 40%), angle symbol = orientation selectivity (incidence at least 20%), spectacles = binocular disparity selectivity, strong binocular interactions, or both (V2; incidence at least 20%), and right-pointing arrow = direction of motion selectivity (incidence at least 20%). [Adapted by E. A. DeYoe and D. C. van Essen, 1988, "Concurrent Processing Streams in Monkey Visual Cortex," Trends in Neurosciences, 11, pp. 219–226. Copyright 1988 by Elsevier Science. Adapted with permission.]

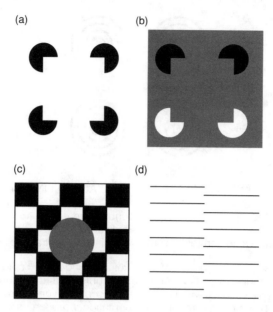

FIG. 19.2. (a) Kanizsa square, (b) a reverse-contrast Kanizsa square. The emergent Kanizsa square can be seen and recognized because of the enhanced illusory brightness within the illusory square. The reverse-contrast Kanizsa square can be recognized but not seen. (c) The boundary of the gray disk can form around its entire circumference even though the relative contrast between the disk and the white and black background squares reverses periodically along the circumference. (d) The vertical illusory contour that forms at the ends of the horizontal lines can be consciously recognized even though it cannot be seen by virtue of any contrast difference between it and the background.

that *all* boundaries are invisible within the boundary stream, which is proposed to occur in the interblob cortical processing stream (Fig. 19.1). This prediction has not yet been directly tested through a neurophysiological experiment, although several studies have shown that the distinctness of a perceptual grouping, such as an illusory contour, can be dissociated from the visible stimulus contrast that is associated with it (Hess, Dakin, & Field, 1998; Petry & Meyer, 1987).

The invisible boundary in Fig. 19.2(b) can be traced to the fact that its vertical boundaries form between black and white inducers that possess opposite contrast polarity with respect to the gray background. The same is true of the boundary around the gray disk in Fig. 19.2(c). In this figure, the gray disk lies in front of a textured background whose contrasts with respect to the disk reverse across space. To build a boundary around the entire disk, despite these contrast reversals, the boundary system pools signals from opposite contrast polarities at each position.

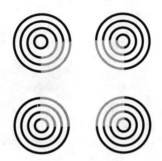

BOUNDARY COMPLETION   SURFACE FILLING-IN

oriented   unoriented
inward   outward
insensitive to contrast polarity   sensitive to contrast polarity

FIG. 19.3.   In this example of neon color spreading, the color in the gray contours spreads in all directions until it fills the square illusory contour. An explanation of this percept is given in Grossberg (1994). Three complementary computational properties of visual boundaries and surfaces are also described. Boundaries are predicted to be completed within a boundary contour system that passes through the interblobs of cortical area V1, whereas surfaces are filled in within a feature contour system that passes through the blobs of cortical area V1 (see Fig. 19.1).

This pooling process renders the boundary system output *insensitive* to contrast polarity. The boundary system hereby loses its ability to represent visible colors or brightnesses, as its output cannot signal the difference between dark and light. It is in this sense that *all boundaries are invisible*. These properties of boundary completion are summarized in Fig. 19.3. Figure 19.2 illustrates another invisible boundary that can be consciously recognized.

If boundaries are invisible, then how do we see anything? FACADE theory predicts that visible properties of a scene are represented by the surface processing stream, which is predicted to occur within the blob cortical stream (Fig. 19.1). A key step in representing a visible surface is called *filling-in*. Why does a surface filling-in process occur? An early stage of surface processing compensates for variable illumination or "discounts the illuminant" (Helmholtz, 1910/1925; Land, 1977) to prevent illuminant variations from distorting all percepts. Discounting the illuminant attenuates color and brightness signals except near regions of sufficiently rapid surface change, such as edges or texture gradients, which are relatively uncontaminated by illuminant variations. Later stages of surface formation fill in the attenuated regions with these relatively uncontaminated color and brightness signals and do so at the correct relative depths from the observer through a process called *surface capture*. This multistage process is an example of hierarchical resolution of uncertainty, because the later filling-in stage overcomes uncertainties about brightness and color that were caused by discounting the illuminant at an earlier processing stage.

How do the illuminant-discounted signals fill in an entire region? Filling-in behaves like a diffusion of brightness across space (Arrington, 1994; Grossberg & Todorović, 1988; Paradiso & Nakayama, 1991). In response to the display in Fig. 19.3, filling-in spreads *outwardly* from the individual gray inducers in all directions. Its spread is thus *unoriented*. How is this spread of activation contained? FACADE theory predicts that signals from the boundary stream to the surface stream define the regions within which filling-in is restricted. This prediction has not yet been neurophysiologically tested. Without these boundary signals, filling-in would dissipate across space, and no surface percept could form. Invisible boundaries hereby indirectly ensure their own visibility through their interactions with the surface stream.

For example, in Fig. 19.2(a), the square boundary is induced by four black pac man disks that are all less luminant than the white background. In the surface stream, discounting the illuminant causes these pac men to induce local brightness contrasts within the boundary of the square. At a subsequent processing stage, these brightness contrasts trigger surface filling-in within the square boundary. The filled-in square is visible as a brightness difference because the filled-in activity level within the square differs from the filled-in activity of the surrounding region. Filling-in can lead to visible percepts because it is *sensitive* to contrast polarity. These three properties of surface filling-in are summarized in Fig. 19.3. They are clearly complementary to the corresponding properties of boundary completion.

In Fig. 19.2(b), the opposite polarities of the two pairs of pac men with respect to the gray background lead to approximately equal filled-in activities inside and outside the square, so the boundary can be recognized but not seen. In Fig. 19.2(d), the white background can fill in uniformly on both sides of the vertical boundary, so no visible contrast difference is seen.

These remarks just begin the analysis of filling-in. Even in the Kanizsa square, one often perceives a square hovering in front of four partially occluded circular disks, which seem to be completed behind the square. FACADE theory predicts how surface filling-in is organized to help such figure–ground percepts to occur in response to both two-dimensional pictures and three-dimensional scenes (Grossberg, 1994, 1997; Grossberg & McLoughlin, 1997).

In summary, boundary and surface formation illustrate two key principles of brain organization: hierarchical resolution of uncertainty and complementary interstream interactions. Figure 19.3 summarizes three pairs of complementary properties of the boundary and surface streams. Hierarchical resolution of uncertainty is illustrated by surface filling-in: Discounting the illuminant creates uncertainty by suppressing surface color and brightness signals except near surface discontinuities. Higher stages of filling-in complete the surface representation by use of properties that are complementary to those whereby boundaries are formed, guided by signals from these boundaries.

COMPLEMENTARY FORM AND MOTION INTERACTIONS

In the visual cortex, a third parallel processing stream, passing through LGN–4B–thick stripe–MT (MT indicates the middle temporal area), processes motion information (Fig. 19.1) (Albright, Desimone, & Gross, 1984; Maunsell & van Essen, 1983; Newsome, Gizzi, & Movshon, 1983). Why does a separate motion stream exist, given that individual cells in cortical area V1 are already sensitive to aspects of both form and motion? In what sense are form and motion computations complementary? What do interactions between form and motion accomplish from a functional point of view? Modeling work suggests how these streams and their mutual interactions compensate for complementary deficiencies of each stream toward generating percepts of moving-form-in-depth (Baloch & Grossberg, 1997; Francis & Grossberg, 1996). Such motion percepts are called *formotion* percepts because they arise from a form–motion interaction.

The form system uses *orientationally* tuned computations whereas the motion system uses *directionally* tuned computations. In the formotion model, the processing of form by the boundary stream uses orientationally tuned cells (Hubel & Wiesel, 1977) to generate emergent object representations, such as the Kanizsa square (Fig. 19.2). Such emergent boundary and surface representations, rather than just the energy impinging on our retinas, define the form percepts of which we are consciously aware. Precise orientationally tuned comparisons of left-eye and right-eye inputs are also used to compute sharp estimates of the relative depth of an object from its observer (Ohzawa, DeAngelis, & Freeman, 1990; von der Heydt, Hanny, & Dursteler, 1981) and thereby to form three-dimensional boundary and surface representations of objects separated from their backgrounds (Grossberg, 1994; Grossberg & McLoughlin, 1997; McLoughlin & Grossberg, 1998).

How is this orientation information used by the motion stream? An object can contain contours of many different orientations that all move in the same direction as part of the object's motion. Both psychophysical and neurophysiological experiments have shown that the motion stream pools information from many orientations that are moving in the same direction to generate precise estimates of a moving object's direction and speed (Albright et al., 1984; Ben-Av & Shiffrar, 1995; Maunsell & van Essen, 1983; Newsome et al., 1983; Watanabe, 1997; Wuerger, Shapley, & Rubin, 1996). Lesions of the form system also show that, on its own, the motion system can make only coarse depth estimates (Logothetis, Schiller, Charles, & Hurlbert, 1990; Schiller, Logothetis, & Charles, 1990). Thus it seems reasonable that the orientationally tuned form system generates emergent representations of forms with precise depth estimates, whereas the directionally tuned motion system—on its own—can generate only coarse depth estimates. In this conception, orientation and direction are complementary properties, whereby orientation is computed parallel to a contour, whereas, at least in the absence of contextual constraints, direction is computed perpendicular to it (Wallach, 1976).

How does the motion stream pool information across space from many oriented contours to generate precise estimates of an object's direction and speed? How do the emergent object boundaries that are computed with precise depth estimates in the form stream get injected into the motion stream and thereby enable the motion stream to track emergent object representations in depth? These are large questions with complex answers on which many investigators are working. Classical computational models of motion detection involving Reichardt-like or motion–energy mechanisms have focused on the recovery of local motion directions (Adelson & Bergen, 1985; van Santen & Sperling, 1984; Watson & Ahumada, 1985). Cells in motion-processing areas such as MT, however, are sensitive to both the direction and the speed of moving patterns (Allman, Miezin, & McGuinness, 1985; Maunsell & van Essen, 1983), and both direction and speed estimates are needed to track moving objects. More recent models have proposed how motion signals can be differentiated and pooled over multiple orientations and spatial locations to form global estimates of both object direction and speed (Chey, Grossberg, & Mingolla, 1997, 1998).

The present discussion of motion perception focuses on how the complementary uncertainties of the form and motion streams may be overcome by their interaction. There is evidence for an interstream interaction from area V2 of the form stream to area MT of the motion stream (Fig. 19.1). This interaction could enable depthful form representations that are computed in area V2 to be tracked by the motion stream at their correct depths as they move through time. A model of this formotion interaction has successfully simulated many perceptual and brain data about motion perception (Baloch & Grossberg, 1997; Chey et al., 1997; Francis & Grossberg, 1996; Grossberg & Rudd, 1992). This model also predicts an important functional role for percepts of long-range apparent motion, whereby observers perceive continuous motion between properly timed but spatially stationary flashes of color or brightness. These continuous motion interpolations can be used to track targets, such as prey and predators, that intermittently disappear as they move at variable rates behind occluding cover, such as bushes and trees in a forest. The "flashes" are the intermittent appearances of the prey or predator. This prediction has not yet been tested neurophysiologically.

Figure 19.4 illustrates an experimental display that vividly illustrates such a formotion interaction. In frame 1 (in the upper half of the figure), the pac men at the left-hand side of the figure define a Kanizsa square by means of the boundary completion process that takes place within the form stream. In frame 2 (in the lower half of the figure), the pac men are replaced with closed disks, and a square region is cleared in the line array to the right. As a result, an illusory square forms adjacent to the line ends. The pac men and the line arrays were designed

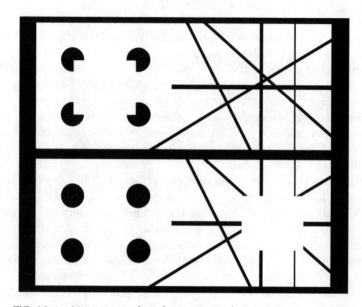

FIG. 19.4. Images used to demonstrate that apparent motion of illusory figures arises through interactions of the static illusory figures, but not from the inducing elements themselves. Frame 1 (the upper left-hand corner) is followed by frame 2 (the lower left-hand corner) in the same spatial locations. With correctly chosen image sizes, distances, and temporal displacements, an illusory square is seen to move continuously from the inducers in the left-hand picture of frame 1 to the inducers in the right-hand picture of frame 2. [From "Apparent Motion of Subjective Surfaces," by V. S. Ramachandran, 1985, *Perception*, pp. 127–134. Copyright 1985 by Pion. Reprinted with permission.]

so that none of their features could be matched. Only the emergent squares have matching features. When frame 2 is turned on right after frame 1 is turned off, the square appears to move continuously from the pac man array to the line array. This percept is an example of apparent motion because nothing in the images actually moves. The percept is a "double illusion" because both the emergent forms and their motions are visual illusions. The theory suggests that the illusory square boundaries are generated in the form stream before being injected into the motion stream, where they are the successive "flashes" that generate a wave of apparent motion.

It seems plausible that some of the quantized temporal effects that Geissler, Elliott, and their colleagues have reported during apparent motion experiments (see this volume) may be at least partially explained by how these model mechanisms respond to a repetitive sequence of flashes, particularly the way in which habituative transmitter gates (or depressing synapses) within the transient channels of the models are periodically inactivated and recover in response to such repetitive sequences.

COMPLEMENTARY WHAT AND WHERE PROCESSING: EXPECTATION LEARNING AND MATCHING

Complementary form and motion processing are proposed to be part of a larger design for complementary processing whereby objects in the world are cognitively recognized, spatially localized, and acted on. The form stream inputs to the inferotemporal cortex, whereas the motion stream inputs to the parietal cortex (Fig. 19.1). Many cognitive neuroscience experiments have supported the hypotheses of Mishkin, Ungerleider, and Macko. (Mishkin, Ungerleider, & Macko, 1983; Ungerleider & Mishkin, 1982) and of Goodale and Milner (1992) that the inferotemporal cortex and its cortical projections learn to categorize and recognize *what* objects are in the world, whereas the parietal cortex and its cortical projections learn to determine *where* they are and *how* to deal with them by locating them in space, tracking them through time, and directing actions towards them. This design thus separates sensory and cognitive processing from spatial and motor processing.

These hypotheses have not, however, noted that sensory and cognitive learning processes are complementary to spatial and motor learning processes on a mechanistic level. Neural modeling has clarified how sensory and cognitive processes solve a key problem, called the *stability–plasticity dilemma* (Carpenter & Grossberg, 1991; Grossberg, 1999b; Grossberg & Merrill, 1996), and can thus rapidly and stably learn about the world throughout life without catastrophically forgetting our previous experiences. In other words, our brains remain *plastic* and open to new experiences without risking the *stability* of previously learned memories. This type of fast stable learning enables us to become experts at dealing with changing environmental conditions: Old knowledge representations can be refined by changing contingencies, and new ones built up, without destroying the old ones due to catastrophic forgetting.

On the other hand, catastrophic forgetting is a *good* property for spatial and motor learning. We have no need to remember all the spatial and motor representations (notably motor maps and gains) that we used when we were children. In fact, the parameters that controlled our small childhood limbs would cause major problems if they continued to control our larger and stronger adult limbs. This forgetting property of the motor system should not be confused with the more stable sensory and cognitive representations with which they interact that, for example, help us to ride a bike after years of disuse.

These distinct What and Where memory properties are proposed to follow from complementary mechanisms whereby these systems *learn* expectations about the world and *match* these expectations against world data. To see how we use a sensory or cognitive expectation, suppose you were asked to "find the yellow ball within one-half second, and you will win a $10,000 prize." Activating an expectation of "yellow balls" enables more rapid detection of a yellow ball, and with a more energetic neural response, than if you were not looking for it. Neural correlates of such excitatory priming and gain control have been reported by several laboratories (Hupé et al., 1998; Kapadia, Ito, Gilbert, & Westheimer, 1995; Luck, Chelazzi, Hillyard, & Desimone, 1997; Motter, 1993; Reynolds, Nicholas, Chelazzi, & Desimone, 1999; Roelfsema, Lamme, & Spekreijse, 1998; Watanabe, Sasaki, Nielsen, Takino, & Miyakawa, 1998). Sensory and cognitive top-down expectations hereby lead to *excitatory matching* with confirmatory bottom-up data. On the other hand, mismatch between top-down expectations and bottom-up data can suppress the mismatched part of the bottom-up data and thereby start to focus attention on the matched, or expected, part of the bottom-up data. This sort of excitatory matching and attentional focusing of bottom-up data with top-down expectations is proposed to generate resonant brain states that support conscious experiences (Carpenter & Grossberg, 1991; Grossberg, 1999b; Grossberg & Merrill, 1996). I proposed in the mid-1970s that "all conscious states are resonant states," and I believe that subsequent data are still compatible with this hypothesis. Paradoxical data about conscious perceptual experiences from several modalities have been explained as emergent properties of such resonant states, including properties of synchronous binding (Grossberg, 1999b; Grossberg & Somers, 1991).

In contrast, a motor expectation represents where we *want* to move, such as to the position where our hand can grasp a desired object. Such a motor expectation is matched against where the hand *is*. After the hand moves to the desired position, no further movement is required, and movement stops. Motor expectations hereby control *inhibitory matching*. Inhibitory matching does not lead to brain resonance, so motor processing is not conscious. In summary, in the present theory, sensory and cognitive matching are excitatory, whereas spatial and motor matching are inhibitory. These are complementary properties.

Recent modeling work predicts some of the cells and circuits that are proposed to carry out these complementary types of matching. For example, recent modeling has suggested how top-down sensory matching is controlled in visual cortex, notably from cortical area V2 to V1 and, by extension, in other sensory and cognitive neocortical circuits (Grossberg, 1999a; Grossberg & Raizada, 2000). This top-down circuit is part of a larger model of how bottom-up, top-down, and horizontal interactions are organized within the laminar circuits of visual cortex; see Fig. 19.5. The circuit generates top-down outputs from cortical layer 6 of V2 that activate, by means of a possibly polysynaptic pathway, layer 6 of V1. Cells in layer 6 of V1, in turn, activate an on-center off-surround circuit to layer 4 of V1. The on-center is predicted to have a modulatory effect on layer 4, because of the balancing of excitatory and inhibitory inputs to layer 4 within the on-center. The inhibitory signals in the off-surround can suppress unattended visual features. This top-down circuit realizes a type of *folded feedback*, whereby feedback inputs from

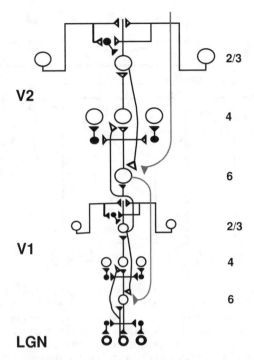

FIG. 19.5. The LAMINART model synthesis of bottom-up, top-down, and horizontal interactions in LGN, V1, and V2. Cells and connections with open symbols denote preattentive excitatory mechanisms that are involved in perceptual grouping. Solid black symbols denote inhibitory mechanisms. Dashed symbols denote top-down attentional mechanisms. (From "How Does the Cerebral Cortex Work? Learning, Attention, and Grouping by Laminar Circuits of Visual Cortex," by S. Grossberg, 1999, *Spatial Vision, 12*, pp. 163–187. *Copyright 1999 by VSP. Adapted with permission*)

V2 are folded back into the feedforward flow of information from layer 6 to layer 4 of V1. The modulatory nature of the layer 6-to-4 connections helps explain a curious fact about bottom-up cortical design: Despite the fact that the LGN activates layer 4 of V1 indirectly by means of inputs to layer 6, a separate, direct excitatory pathway exists from LGN to layer 4 of V1. It is predicted that this direct pathway is needed to enable the LGN to drive layer 4 cells to suprathreshold activity levels, because the indirect LGN–6–4 pathway is modulatory. The modeling articles summarize neurophysiological, anatomical, and psychophysical experiments that are consistent with these predictions.

Recent modeling work also predicts some of the cells and circuits that are proposed to carry out top-down motor matching, notably in cortical areas 4 and 5 (Bullock, Cisek, & Grossberg, 1998; Cisek, Bullock, & Grossberg, 1998). Inhibitory matching is predicted to occur between a Target Position Vector (TPV),

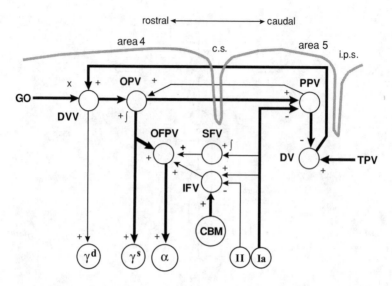

FIG. 19.6. The VITE circuit model. Thick connections represent
the kinematic feedback control aspect of the model, with thin
connections representing additional compensatory circuitry. GO,
scaleable gating signal; DVV, desired velocity vector; OPV, outflow
position vector; OFPV, outflow force + position vector; SFV, static
force vector; IFV, inertial force vector; CBM, assumed cerebello-
cortical input to the IFV stage; PPV, perceived position vector; DV,
difference vector; TPV, target position vector; γ^d, dynamic gamma
motoneuron; γ^s, static gamma motoneuron; α, alpha motoneuron; Ia, type Ia afferent fiber; II, type II afferent fiber (position error feedback); c.s., central sulcus; i.p.s., intraparietal sulcus. The
symbol + represents excitation, – represents inhibition, × represents multiplicative gating, and $+\int$ represents integration. [From
"Cortical Networks for Control of Voluntary Arm Movements Under
Various Force Conditions," D. Bullock, P. Cisek, and S. Grossberg,
1998, *Cerebral Cortex, 8*, pp. 48–62. Copyright 1998 by Oxford
University Press. Reprinted with permission.]

which represents where we want to move our arm, and a Present Position Vector (PPV) which computes an outflow representation of where the arm is now
(Fig. 19.6). This comparison is proposed to occur in cortical area 5 at Difference
Vector (DV) cells, which compute how far, and in what direction, the arm is com-
manded to move. This Difference Vector is, in turn, predicted to be transmitted
to cortical area 4, where is multiplicatively gated by a GO signal (a scalable gating signal) that is under volitional control. Turning on the GO signal determines
whether the limb will move, and its amplitude scales the speed of movement. The
product of DV and GO hereby determines a Desired Velocity Vector (DVV). Such
a DV is predicted to be computed at area 5 phasic cells and its corresponding DDV
at area 4 phasic MT cells. The modeling articles summarize neurophysiological,

anatomical, and psychophysical experiments that are consistent with these predictions. It should also be noted that various other cell types within cortical areas 4 and 5 do *not* do inhibitory matching, and may even support resonant states.

The learning processes that accompany these complementary types of matching are also proposed to exhibit complementary properties. Learning within the sensory and cognitive domain is often *match learning*. Match learning occurs only if a good enough match occurs between active top-down expectations and bottom-up information. When such an approximate match occurs, previously stored knowledge can be refined. If novel information cannot form a good enough match with the expectations that are read out by previously learned recognition categories, then a memory search is triggered that leads to selection and learning of a new recognition category, rather than to catastrophic forgetting of an old one (Carpenter & Grossberg, 1991; Grossberg, 1999b; Grossberg & Merrill, 1996). In contrast, learning within spatial and motor processes is proposed to be *mismatch learning* that continuously updates sensory–motor maps (Guenther, Bullock, Greve, & Grossberg, 1994) or the gains of sensory–motor commands (Fiala, Grossberg, & Bullock, 1996; Ito, 1984). Thus both learning and matching within the What and Where streams may have complementary properties. As a result, we can stably learn what is happening in a changing world, thereby solving the stability–plasticity dilemma while adaptively updating our representations of where objects are and how to act on them by using bodies whose parameters change continuously through time.

COMPLEMENTARY ATTENTIVE LEARNING AND ORIENTING SEARCH

Match learning has the great advantage that it leads to stable memories in response to changing environmental conditions. However, it also has a potentially disastrous disadvantage: If you can learn only when there is a good enough match between bottom-up data and learned top-down expectations, then how do you ever learn anything that you do not already know? Some popular learning models, such as back propagation, try to escape this problem by assuming that the brain does only "supervised learning." During supervised learning, an explicit correct answer, or teaching signal, is provided in response to every input. This teaching signal forces learning to track the correct answer. Such a model cannot learn if an explicit answer is not provided. It appears, however, that much human and animal learning, especially during the crucial early years of life, takes place in a relatively unsupervised fashion.

Other models do allow "unsupervised learning" to occur. Here, the key problem to be solved is: if a teacher is not available to force the selection and learning of a representation that can map onto a correct answer, then the internal dynamics of the model must do so on their own. To escape the problem of not being able to learn something that one does not already know, some of these models assume that we *do* already know (or, more exactly, have internal representations for) everything

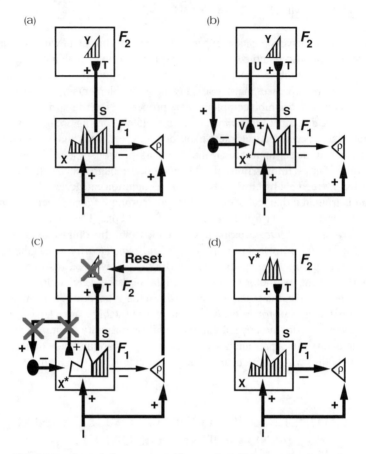

FIG. 19.7. Search for a recognition code within an adaptive resonance theory learning circuit: (a) Input pattern **I** is instated across
the feature detectors at level F_1 as a short-term memory (STM)
activity pattern **X**. Input **I** also nonspecifically activates the orienting subsystem ρ. STM pattern **X** is represented by the hatched
pattern across F_1. Pattern **X** both inhibits ρ and generates the output pattern **S**. Pattern **S** is multiplied by long-term memory (LTM)
traces, or learned adaptive weights. These LTM-gated signals are
added at F_2 nodes to form the input pattern **T**, which activates the
STM pattern **Y** across the recognition categories coded at level
F_2. (b) Pattern **Y** generates the top-down output pattern **U**, which
is multiplied by top-down LTM traces and added at F_1 nodes to
form the prototype pattern **V** that encodes the learned expectation of the active F_2 nodes. If **V** mismatches **I** at F_1, then a new
STM activity pattern **X*** is generated at F_1. **X*** is represented by the
hatched pattern. It includes the features of **I** that are confirmed by
V. Mismatched features are inhibited. The inactivated nodes corresponding to unconfirmed features of **X** are not hatched. The reduction in total STM activity that occurs when **X** is transformed
into **X*** causes a decrease in the total inhibition from F_1 to ρ.

432

that we may ever wish to know, and that experience just selects and amplifies these representations (Edelman, 1987). These models depend on the bottom-up filtering of inputs, and a very large number of internal representations that respond to these filtered inputs, to provide enough memory to represent whatever may happen. Having such a large number of representations leads to a combinatorial explosion, with an implausibly large memory. Thus, although using a very large number of representations can help with the problem of catastrophic forgetting, it creates other, equally serious, problems instead. Other unsupervised learning models shut down learning as time goes on to avoid catastrophic forgetting (Kohonen, 1984).

I propose that these problems are averted in the brain through use of another complementary interaction. This complementary interaction helps to balance between processing the familiar and the unfamiliar, the expected and the unexpected. It does so by using complementary processes of resonance and reset, which are predicted to subserve properties of attention/consciousness and memory search, respectively. This interaction enables the brain to discover and stably learn new representations for novel events in an efficient way without assuming that representations already exist for as yet unexperienced events. It hereby solves the combinatorial explosion while also solving the stability–plasticity dilemma.

One of these complementary subsystems is just the What stream that already was described, with its top-down expectations that are matched against bottom-up inputs. When a recognition category activates a top-down expectation that achieves a good enough match with bottom-up data, this match process focuses attention on those feature clusters in the bottom-up input that are expected (Fig. 19.7). Experimental evidence for such matching and attentional processes has been found in neurophysiological data about perception and recognition (Bullier, Hupé, James, & Girard, 1996; Hupé et al., 1998; Motter, 1994a, 1994b; Reynolds et al., 1999; Roelfsema et al., 1998; Sillito, Jones, Gerstein, & West, 1994). Many behavioral and neural data have been explained by assuming that such

←_____

(Continued) (c) If inhibition decreases sufficiently, ρ releases a non-specific arousal wave to F_2, which resets the STM pattern $\mathbf{Y}$ at F_2. (d) After $\mathbf{Y}$ is inhibited, its top-down prototype signal is eliminated, and $\mathbf{X}$ can be reinstated at F_1. Enduring traces of the prior reset lead $\mathbf{X}$ to activate a different STM pattern $\mathbf{Y}$ at F_2. If the top-down prototype that is due to $\mathbf{Y}$ also mismatches $\mathbf{I}$ at F_1, then the search for an appropriate F_2 code continues until a more appropriate F_2 representation is selected. Then an attentive resonance develops, and learning of the attended data is initiated. [From *Carpenter & Grossberg*, "A Massively Parallel Architecture for a Self-Organizing Neural Pattern Recognition Machine," by G. A. Carpenter and S. Grossberg, 1987, *Computer Vision, Graphics, and Image Processing, 37*, pp. 54–115. Copyright 1987 by Harcourt. Adapted with permission.]

top-down feedback processes can lead to resonant brain states that play a key role in dynamically stabilizing both developmental and learning processes (Carpenter & Grossberg, 1991; Grossberg, 1982, 1987, 1999a, 1999b; Grossberg, Boardman, & Cohen, 1997; Grossberg & Merrill, 1996; Grossberg & Myers, 2000).

How does a sufficiently bad mismatch between an active top-down expectation and a bottom-up input drive a memory search, say because the input represents an unfamiliar type of experience? This mismatch within the attentional system is proposed to activate a complementary *orienting system*, which is sensitive to unexpected and unfamiliar events. Output signals from the orienting system rapidly reset the recognition category that has been reading out the poorly matching top-down expectation [Figs. 19.7(b) and 19.7(c)]. The cause of the mismatch is hereby removed, thereby freeing the system to activate a different recognition category [Fig. 19.7(d)]. The reset event hereby triggers memory search, or hypothesis testing, which automatically leads to the selection of a recognition category that can better match the input. If no such recognition category exists, say because the bottom-up input represents a truly novel experience, then the search process can automatically activate an as yet uncommitted population of cells with which to learn about the novel information. This learning process works well under both unsupervised and supervised conditions. Supervision can force a search for new categories that may be culturally determined and are not based on feature similarity alone. For example, separating the letters E and F into separate recognition categories is culturally determined; they are quite similar based on visual similarity alone. Taken together, the interacting processes of attentive-learning and orienting-search realize a type of error correction through hypothesis testing that can build an ever-growing, self-refining internal model of a changing world.

The complementary attentive-learning and orienting-search subsystems and how they interact have been progressively developed since the 1970s within Adaptive Resonance Theory (ART) (Carpenter & Grossberg, 1991; Grossberg, 1999b; Grossberg & Merrill, 1996). Neurobiological data have elsewhere been reviewed in support of the ART hypothesis that the attentive-learning system includes such What processing regions as inferotemporal cortex and its projections in prefrontal cortex, whereas the orienting-search system includes circuits of the hippocampal system (Grossberg & Merrill, 1996). Data about mismatch cells in the hippocampal system are particularly relevant to this hypothesis (Otto & Eichenbaum, 1992). ART predicts that these interactions between inferotemporal cortex and the hippocampal system during a mismatch event offset the inability of the What processing stream to search for and learn appropriate new recognition codes on its own. This deficiency of the What stream has been used to predict how hippocampal lesions can lead to symptoms of amnesic memory (Grossberg & Merrill, 1996). Because of their ability to learn stably in real time about large amounts of information in a rapidly changing world, ART models have also been used in pattern recognition applications in technology (Carpenter & Grossberg, 1996).

COMPLEMENTARY
ADDITIVE AND SUBTRACTIVE
INTRASTREAM PROCESSING

The two types of matching across the What and Where processing streams use different combinations of excitatory and inhibitory neural signals. Complementary processes that use excitatory and inhibitory interactions can also arise *within* a processing stream. Thus each processing stream may be broken into complementary substreams. Several examples are now mentioned wherein parallel combinations of additive and subtractive neural signals can be computed within a single processing stream. A classical example in the What processing stream combines outputs from long-wavelength (L) and medium-wavelength (M) retinal photoreceptors into parallel luminance (L + M) and color (L − M) channels (Mollon & Sharpe, 1983). The color channels compute reflectances, or ratios, by discounting the illuminant, whereas the luminance channel computes luminant energy. When both channels are used, the illuminant can be discounted without information about luminant energy being thrown away.

Intrastream complementarity also seems to occur within the Where stream. Here, cortical area MT activates area Medial Superior Temporal Area (MST) (not shown in Fig. 19.1) on the way to parietal cortex. In macaque monkeys, the ventral part of MST helps to track moving visual objects, whereas dorsal MST helps to navigate in the world using global properties of optic flow (Duffy & Wurtz, 1995; Tanaka, Sugita, Moriya, & Saito, 1993). These tasks are behaviorally complementary: The former tracks an object moving in the world with respect to an observer, whereas the latter navigates a moving observer with respect to the world. The tasks are also neurophysiologically complementary: Neurons in ventral MST compute the relative motion of an object with respect to its background by *subtracting* background motion from object motion, whereas neurons in dorsal MST compute motions of a wide textured field by *adding* motion signals over a large visual domain (Tanaka et al., 1993). Corresponding to MST's breakdown into additive and subtractive subregions, area MT of owl monkeys possesses distinct *bands* and *interbands* (Born & Tootell, 1992). Band cells have additive receptive fields for visual navigation, whereas interband cells have subtractive receptive fields for computing object–relative motion. Modeling studies have shown how these complementary properties can be used, on the one hand, for visual navigation based on optical flow information and, on the other hand, for predictive tracking of moving targets with pursuit eye movements (Grossberg, Mingolla, & Pack, 1999; Pack, Grossberg, & Mingolla, 2001). These studies make a number of neurophysiological predictions, including how the log polar mapping that is defined by the cortical magnification factor helps to achieve good navigational properties. A remarkable prediction is that the biologically observed spiral tuning curves that were found by Graziano, Andersen, and Snowden (1994) in cortical area MST maximize the amount of position invariance of which the positionally-variant log polar map is capable.

Intrastream complementarity is also predicted to occur during sensory–motor control, or How processing. To see this, suppose that both eyes fixate an object that can be reached by the arms. Psychophysical (Foley, 1980) and neurophysiological data (Grobstein, 1991; Sakata, Shibutani, & Kawano, 1980) suggest that the vergence of the two eyes, as they fixate the object, is used to estimate the object's radial distance, while the spherical angles that the eyes make relative to the observer's head estimate the object's angular position. Distance and angle are mathematically independent properties of an object's position with respect to an observer. How does the brain compute the distance and angle to an object that the eyes are fixating? A neural model proposes how addition and subtraction can again realize the necessary computations by exploiting the bilateral symmetry of the body (Guenther et al., 1994). In particular, eye movement control pathways give rise to parallel branches, called corollary discharges, that inform other brain systems of the present position of the eyes (Helmholtz, 1910/1925). These outflow movement control pathways have an opponent organization to control the body's agonist and antagonist muscles. Neural modeling has mathematically proved that, when both eyes fixate an object, accurate spherical angle and vergence estimates of object position may be derived by the addition and the subtraction, respectively, of the ocular corollary discharges that control the two eyes while their opponent relationships are preserved, at separate populations of angle and vergence cells (Guenther et al., 1994).

These examples illustrate how complementary behavioral capabilities can be derived by "brain arithmetic," whereby outputs of a processing stage are segregated into additive and subtractive parallel computations at a subsequent processing stage. Such additive and subtractive combinations can occur both between processing streams and within a single processing stream. These simple computations generate very different behavioral properties when applied to different sensory inputs or different stages of a processing stream. The next sections illustrate several ways in which complementary multiplication and division operations may enter the brain's arithmetic repertoire.

FACTORIZATION OF
PATTERN AND ENERGY:
RATIO PROCESSING AND SYNCHRONY

Multiplication and division occur during processes that illustrate the general theme of how the brain achieves *factorization of pattern and energy* (Grossberg, 1982). Here, "pattern" refers to the hypothesis that the brain's functional units of short-term representation of information, and of long-term learning about this information, are distributed patterns of activation and of synaptic weight, respectively, across a neuronal network. "Energy" refers to the mechanisms whereby pattern processing is turned on and off by activity-dependent modulatory processes.

Why do pattern and energy need to be processed separately? Why cannot a single process do both? One reason is that cell activities can fluctuate within only a narrow dynamic range. Often input amplitudes can vary over a much wider dynamic range. For example, if a large number of input pathways converge on a cell, then the number of active input pathways can vary greatly through time, and with it, the total size of the cell input. Owing to the small dynamic range of the cell, its activity could easily become saturated when a large number of inputs is active. If all the cells became saturated, then their activities could not sensitively represent the relative size, and thus importance, of their respective inputs. One way to prevent this would be to require that each individual input be chosen very small so that the sum of all inputs would not saturate cell activity. However, such small individual inputs could easily be lost in cellular noise. The cell's small dynamic range could hereby make it insensitive to both small and large inputs as a result of noise and saturation, respectively, at the lower and upper extremes of the cell's dynamic range. This *noise-saturation dilemma* faces all biological cells, not merely nerve cells. Interactions across a network of cells are needed to compute the *relative* sizes of inputs to cells in the network and thereby to overcome noise and saturation. This kind of pattern processing sacrifices information about the absolute amplitude of inputs in order to enable the cells to respond sensitively to their relative size over a wide dynamic range. Because the pattern-processing network discards information about absolute input size, a separate channel is needed to track information about the *total* amplitude, or "energy," of the inputs.

Retaining sensitivity to the relative size of inputs can be accomplished by on-center off-surround interactions between cells that obey the membrane equations of neurophysiology (Douglas, Koch, Mahowald, Martin, & Suarez, 1995; Grossberg, 1982; Heeger, 1993). In a feedforward on-center off-surround network, feedforward inputs excite their target cells while inhibiting a broader spatial range of cells. To store inputs temporarily in short-term (or working) memory, excitatory feedback between nearby cells and inhibitory feedback between a broader spatial range of cells can solve the noise-saturation dilemma. Stated in another way, these networks define mass–action interactions among short-range cooperative and longer-range competitive inputs or activities. The mass–action terms of membrane equations introduce multiplication into brain arithmetic by multiplying cell inputs with cell voltages, or activities. Membrane equations respond to on-center off-surround interactions by dividing each cell's activity by a weighted sum of all the cell inputs (in a feedforward interaction) or activities (in a feedback interaction) with which it interacts. This operation keeps cell activities away from the saturation range by *normalizing* them while preserving their sensitivity to input ratios.

The ubiquitous nature of the noise-saturation dilemma in all cellular tissues clarifies why such on-center off-surround anatomies are found throughout the brain. For example, when ratio processing and normalization occur during visual perception, they help to control brightness constancy and contrast (Arrington, 1994; Grossberg & Todorović, 1988) as well as perceptual grouping and attention (Gove, Grossberg, & Mingolla, 1995; Grossberg, 1999a; Grossberg, Mingolla, & Ross, 1997; Grossberg & Raizada, 2000). At higher levels of cognitive processing, these mechanisms can provide a neural explanation of the "limited capacity" of cognitive short-term memory (Grossberg, 1987).

The cooperative–competitive interactions that preserve cell sensitivity to relative input size also bind these cell activities into functional units. Indeed, *relative* activities need to be computed *synchronously*, and early theorems about short-term and long-term memory processing (Grossberg, 1982) predicted an important role for synchronous processing between the interacting cells. Subsequent neurophysiological experiments have emphasized the functional importance of synchronous brain states (Eckhorn et al., 1988; Gray & Singer, 1989). More recent neural modeling has shown how such synchronized activity patterns can, for example, quantitatively explain psychophysical data about temporal order judgments during perceptual grouping within the visual cortex (Grossberg & Grunewald, 1997). The synchronous states that arise in ART networks are another example of the synchronizing property of suitably defined cooperative–competitive networks.

FACTORIZATION OF MOTOR
EXPECTATION AND VOLITION

Factorization of pattern and energy shows itself in many guises. For example, it helps to explain how motor expectations (pattern) interact with volitional speed signals (energy) to generate goal-directed arm movements (Bullock, Grossberg, & Mannes, 1993; Georgopolous, Schwartz, & Kettner, 1986; Horak & Anderson, 1984), as during the computation of the DVV in the cortical area 4 circuit of Fig. 19.6. As noted in the discussion of Where and How processing, a motor expectation represents where we want to move, such as to the position where our hand can grasp a desired object. Such a motor representation, or TPV, can *prime* a movement, or get us ready to make a movement, but by itself, it cannot release the movement (Bullock et al., 1998; Georgopolous et al., 1986). First the TPV needs to be converted into a DV, which triggers an overt action only when a volitional signal (Horak & Anderson, 1984) that multiplicatively gates action is read out. The volitional signal for controlling movement speed is called a GO signal, as in Fig. 19.6. The signal for controlling size is called a GRO signal. Neural models have predicted how such GO and GRO signals may, for example, alter the size and the speed of handwritten script without altering its form (Bullock et al., 1993; Grossberg & Paine, 2000). As noted in Fig. 19.6, some motor expectations seem to be computed in the parietal and motor cortex. Volitional signals seem to be computed within the basal ganglia (Brown, Bullock, & Grossberg, 2000; Horak & Anderson, 1984).

The vector integration to end point, or VITE, neural model, summarized in Fig. 19.6, of how these arm-controlling pattern and energy factors combine within cortical areas 4 and 5 has been used to predict the functional roles of six identified cortical cell types and to simulate quantitatively their temporal responses during a wide range of behavioral tasks (Bullock et al., 1998; Cisek et al., 1998). These results support model hypotheses about how variable-speed and variable-force arm movements can be carried out in the presence of obstacles. The model hereby provides a detailed example of how task-sensitive volitional control of action realizes an overall separation into pattern and energy variables.

FACTORIZATION OF ATTENTIVE COGNITIVE–EMOTIONAL INTERACTIONS

Cognitive–emotional learning enables sensory and cognitive events to acquire emotional and motivational significance. Both classical and instrumental conditioning can be used for this purpose (Kamin, 1969; Pavlov, 1927; Skinner, 1938; Staddon, 1983). For example, during classical conditioning, an irrelevant sensory cue, or conditioned stimulus (CS), is paired with a reinforcing event, or unconditioned stimulus (US). The CS hereby acquires some of the reinforcing properties of the US; it becomes a "conditioned reinforcer" with its own motivational properties. The manner in which the thalamocortical representation of a conditioned reinforcer CS is influenced by motivational signals represents, I suggest, another example of factorization of pattern and energy. Here, the activities across the thalamocortical representations of recently presented sensory events, including the CS, constitute the "pattern." This pattern is normalized by the feedback on-center off-surround interactions that are used to store the activities in short-term memory without saturation. If one or more of these sensory events is a conditioned reinforcer, then it can amplify its own activity by means of learned motivational feedback signals, which play the role of energy in this example (Grossberg, 1982; Grossberg & Merrill, 1996). These amplified representations can, in turn, attentionally block (Kamin, 1969), or inhibit, the representations of irrelevant sensory events by means of the off-surround of the feedback network. Attentional blocking is one of the key mechanisms whereby animals learn which consequences are causally predicted by their antecedent sensory cues and actions, and which consequences are merely accidental. A more detailed summary of how blocking is proposed to happen is now given.

During cognitive–emotional learning, at least three types of internal representations interact: Sensory and cognitive representations (S), drive representations

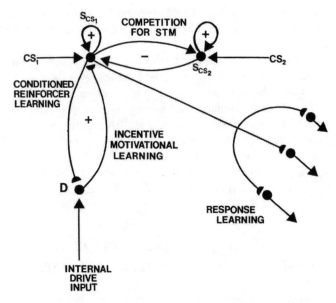

Fig. 19.8   Schematic conditioning circuit: Conditioned stimuli (CS_i) activate sensory categories (S_{CS_i}), which compete among themselves for limited-capacity short-term memory (STM) activation and storage. The activated S_{CS_i} representations, where $i = 1, 2$, elicit trainable signals to drive representations D and motor-command representations M. Learning from a sensory representation S_{CS_i} to a drive representation D is called conditioned reinforcer learning. Learning from D to a S_{CS_i} is called incentive motivational learning. Signals from D to S_{CS_i} are elicited when the combination of conditioned sensory plus internal drive inputs is sufficiently large. Sensory representations that win the competition in response to the balance of external inputs and internal motivational signals can activate motor-command pathways.

(D), and motor representations (M) (Grossberg, 1982; Grossberg & Merrill, 1996), as shown in Fig. 19.8. The sensory representations S are thalamocortical representations of external events, like the ones previously described within the What processing stream. They include representations of CSs. D representations include the hypothalamic and amygdala circuits at which homeostatic and reinforcing cues converge to generate emotional reactions and motivational decisions (Aggleton, 1993; Davis, 1994; LeDoux, 1993). M representations include cortical and cerebellar circuits for controlling discrete adaptive responses (Ito, 1984; Thompson, 1988). As noted, the S representations represent the pattern information in this example. They interact with one another by means of an on-center off-surround feedback network that stores their activities in short-term memory, while also solving the noise-saturation dilemma. The D representations supply modulatory energy owing to the action of the following types of learning processes:

1. *"Conditioned reinforcer learning"* occurs in the S → D pathways and enables a sensory event, such as a conditioned stimulus CS, to become a conditioned reinforcer that can activate a drive representation D. This may be accomplished by pairing the CS with an unconditioned stimulus US. The CS activates its sensory representation S. The US activates its own sensory representation, which in turn activates D. Adaptive weights in the S → D pathway can grow in response to this correlated activity. Future presentations of the CS can hereby lead to the activation of D, which controls various emotional and motivational responses.

2. Because of this pairing of CS and US, "incentive motivational learning" can also occur in the adaptive weights within the D → S pathway. This type of learning allows an activated drive representation D to prime, or modulate, the sensory representations S of all sensory events that have consistently been activated with it in the past. Speaking intuitively, these sensory events are motivationally compatible with D.

3. S → M *"habit learning,"* or motor learning, trains the sensorimotor maps and gains that control appropriate and accurately calibrated responses to the CS. These processes include circuits such as those summarized in Fig. 19.6.

Conditioned reinforcer learning and incentive motivational learning combine to control attentional blocking in the following way. As already noted, sensory representations S are the pattern variables that store sensory and cognitive representations in short-term memory by using on-center off-surround feedback networks. Because of the self-normalizing properties of these networks, the *total* activity that can be stored in short-term memory across the entire network is limited. This is thus, once again, an example of the noise-saturation dilemma. Because of activity normalization, sufficiently great activation of one sensory representation implies that other sensory representations cannot be stored in short-term memory. In the present example, conditioning of a CS to an US strengthens both its S → D conditioned reinforcer and D → S incentive motivational pathways. Thus when a conditioned reinforcer CS activates its sensory representation S, learned S → D → S positive feedback quickly amplifies the activity of S. This S → D → S feedback pathway supplies the motivational energy that focuses attention on salient conditioned reinforcers. These amplified sensory representations inhibit the storage of other sensory cues in short-term memory by means of the lateral inhibition that exists among the sensory representations S. Blocking is hereby explained by use of the incentive motivational "energy" to amplify conditioned reinforcer CS representations within the self-normalized sensory "pattern" that is stored in short-term memory. This S → D → S feedback causes a cognitive–emotional resonance to occur. The model prediction of how drive representations D, such as those in the amgydala, influence blocking by delivering incentive motivational feedback to thalamocortical sensory representations has not yet been tested.

It was proposed in Grossberg (2000b) how such a cognitive–emotional model, which is called a CogEM model, can explain many data about the negative symptoms of schizophrenia when its drive representations D become depressed. It was also shown how all the circuit elements of the recent Damasio (1999) model of "core consciousness" can be naturally mapped onto those of the CogEM model. In particular, activation of the S ↔ D feedback loop causes a cognitive–emotional resonance that is predicted to support conscious states. This linkage predicts how depression of D can influence core consciousness in schizophrenics.

FACTORIZATION OF RATE-INVARIANT SPEECH AND RHYTHM

Factorization of pattern and energy also seems to play an important role in temporally organized cognitive processes such as speech and language. Here sequences of events are transformed into temporally evolving spatial patterns of activation that are stored within working memories (Baddeley, 1986). The 'pattern' information that is stored in working memory represents both the event itself—its so-called *item* information—and the temporal *order* in which the events occurred. The 'energy' information encodes both the temporal *rate* and *rhythm* with which the events occur (Grossberg, 1987). Factorization of information about item and order from information about rate and rhythm helps us to understand speech that is spoken at variable rates: A *rate-invariant* representation of speech and language in working memory avoids the need to define multiple representations of the same speech and language utterance at every conceivable rate. This representation can, in turn, be used to learn speech and language codes, or categories, that are themselves not too sensitive to speech rate. Because rate and rhythm information are substantially eliminated from the rate-invariant working-memory representation, rate and rhythm need to be computed by a separate process. This is a problem of *factorization*, rather than of independent representation, because the speech rate and rhythm that are perceived depend on the categorical language units, such as syllables and words, that are familiar to the listener. What these language units are, in turn, depends on how the listener has learned to group together and categorize the temporally distributed speech and language features that have previously been stored in the rate-invariant working memory.

Rate-invariant working memories can be designed from specialized versions of the on-center off-surround feedback networks that are used to solve the noise-saturation dilemma (Bradski, Carpenter, & Grossberg, 1994; Grossberg, 1982, 1987). In other words, the networks that are used to store *spatially* distributed feature patterns, without a loss of sensitivity to their identity and relative size, can be specialized to store *temporally* distributed events, without a loss of sensitivity to their identity and temporal order. The normalization of these stored activities is the basis for their rate-invariant properties. Thus this model predicts that a process such as discounting the illuminant, in the spatial domain, uses a variant of the same mechanisms that are used to process rate-invariant speech, in the temporal domain. A key problem concerns how the rate-invariant working memory can maintain the same representation as the speech rate speeds up. The model predicts that the energy information that is computed from the speech rate and rhythm can be used to automatically gain-control the processing rate of the working memory to maintain its rate-invariant speech properties (Boardman, Grossberg, Myers, & Cohen, 1999). In particular, the rate at which the working memory stores individual events needs to keep up with the overall rate at which successive speech sounds are presented. A neural model of this process has been progressively developed to quantitatively simulate psychophysical data concerning the categorization of variable-rate speech by human subjects (Boardman et al., 1999; Grossberg, Boardman et al., 1997; Grossberg & Myers, 2000) and to functionally interpret neurophysiological data that are consistent with model properties (Grossberg & Myers, 2000). In this model, the working memory interacts with a categorization network by means of bottom-up and top-down pathways, and conscious speech is a resonant wave that emerges through these interactions.

UNIFYING VIEW OF HOW THE BRAIN IS FUNCTIONALLY ORGANIZED IN THE LARGE

Much experimental evidence has supported the idea that the brain is organized into processing streams, but how these streams are determined and how they interact to generate behavior is still a topic of active research. This chapter summarized some of the rapidly growing empirical and theoretical evidence that our brains compute *complementary* operations within *parallel pairs* of processing streams. Table 19.1 summarizes some of the processes for which evidence of complementarity has been collected from behavioral and neural data and models. The variety of these behavioral processes provides some indication of the generality of this organizational principle in the brain. Interstream interactions are proposed to overcome complementary processing deficiencies within each stream. Hierarchical interactions between the several levels of each processing stream are proposed to overcome informational uncertainties that occur at individual processing stages within that stream. Hierarchical intrastream interactions and parallel interstream interactions work together to generate behavioral properties that are free from these uncertainties and complementary insufficiencies. Such complementary processing may occur on multiple scales of brain organization.

Many experimentalists have described properties of functional specialization and integration in their neural data. Some neural modelers have attempted to characterize such properties by using concepts about how the brain may work to achieve information maximization. Information, as a technical concept, is well defined for stationary information channels or channels whose statistical properties tend to persist through time. In contrast, brains self-organize on a relatively fast time scale through development and lifelong learning and do so in response to nonstationary, or rapidly changing, statistical properties of their environments. I propose that hierarchical intrastream interactions and parallel interstream interactions between complementary systems are a manifestation of this capacity for self-controlled and stable self-organization. This observation leads to my final remarks.

How do complementary sets of properties arise, rather than some other combination of properties? How is the organization of smaller-scale complementary properties organized within larger-scale complementary properties? The simplest hypothesis, for which little direct experimental evidence is yet available, is that each pair of complementary processes represents two sides of a larger brain system. Complementarity could arise if, during brain development, precursors of the larger system bifurcated into complementary streams through a process of symmetry breaking that operates on multiple scales of organization. In this view, complementary systems are an integral part of the self-organization process that enables the brain to adapt to a rapidly changing world. This view of brain development is not in conflict with prevailing views of specific developmental mechanisms (Obermayer, Ritter, & Schulten, 1990). Rather, it points to a global organizational principle that may be capable of coordinating them.

Thus, just as in the organization of the physical world with which it interacts, it is proposed that the brain is organized to obey principles of complementarity, uncertainty, and symmetry breaking. In fact, it can be argued that known complementary properties exist because of the need to process complementary types of information in the environment. The processes that form perceptual boundaries and surfaces provide a particularly clear example of this hypothesis. The 'complementary brain' may thus perhaps best be understood through analyses of the cycles of perception, cognition, emotion, and action whereby the brain is intimately linked to its physical environment through a continuously operating feedback cycle. One useful goal of future research may be to study more directly how complementary aspects of the physical world are translated into complementary brain designs for coping with this world.

ACKNOWLEDGMENTS

This work was supported in part by grants from the Defense Advanced Research Projects Agency and the Office of Naval Research (ONR N00014-95-1-0409), the National Science Foundation (NSF ITI-97-20333), and the Office of Naval Research (ONR N00014-95-1-0657). The author thanks Robin Amos and Diana Meyers for their valuable assistance in the preparation of the manuscript.

REFERENCES

Adelson, E. H., & Bergen, J. R. (1985). Spatiotemporal energy models for the perception of motion. *Journal of the Optical Society of America, 2*, 284–299.

Aggleton, J. P. (1993). The contribution of the amygdala to normal and abnormal emotional states. *Trends in Neurosciences, 16*, 328–333.

Albright, T. D., Desimone, R., & Gross, C. G. (1984). Columnar organization of directionally sensitive cells in visual area MT of the macaque. *Journal of Neurophysiology, 51*, 16–31.

Allman, J., Miezin, F., & McGuinness, E. (1985). Direction- and velocity-specific responses from beyond the classical receptive field in the middle temporal visual area (MT). *Perception, 14*, 105–126.

Arrington, K. F. (1994). The temporal dynamics of brightness filling-in. *Vision Research, 34*, 3371–3387.

Baddeley, A. D. (1986). *Working memory*. Oxford, England: Clarendon.

Baloch, A. A., & Grossberg, S. (1997). A neural model of high-level motion processing: Line motion and formotion dynamics. *Vision Research, 37*, 3037–3059.

Ben-Av, M. B., & Shiffrar, M. (1995). Disambiguating velocity estimates across image space. *Vision Research, 35*, 2889–2895.

Boardman, I., Grossberg, S., Myers, C., & Cohen, M.A. (1999). Neural dynamics of perceptual order and context effects for variable-rate speech syllables. *Perception and Psychophysics, 61*, 1477–1500.

Born, R. T., & Tootell, R. B. H. (1992). Segregation of global and local motion processing in primate middle temporal visual area. *Nature (London), 357*, 497–499.

Bradski, G., Carpenter, G. A., & Grossberg, S. (1994). STORE working memory networks for storage and recall of arbitrary sequences. *Biological Cybernetics, 71*, 469–480.

Brown, J. W., Bullock, D., & Grossberg, S. (2000). How laminar frontal cortex and basal ganglia circuits interact to control planned and reactive saccades. Manuscript submitted for publication.

Bullier, J., Hupé, J. M., James, A., & Girard, P. (1996). Functional interactions between areas V1 and V2 in the monkey. *Journal of Physiology (Paris), 90*, 217–220.

Bullock, D., Cisek, P., & Grossberg, S. (1998). Cortical networks for control of voluntary arm movements under variable force conditions. *Cerebral Cortex, 8*, 48–62.

Bullock, D., Grossberg, S., & Mannes, C. (1993). A neural network model for cursive script production. *Biological Cybernetics, 70*, 15–28.

Carpenter, G. A., & Grossberg, S. (1987). A massively parallel architecture for a selforganizing neural pattern recognition machine. *Computer Vision, Graphics, and Image Processing, 37*, 54–115.

Carpenter, G. A., & Grossberg, S. (Eds.). (1991). *Pattern recognition by self-organizing neural networks*, Cambridge, MA: MIT Press.

Carpenter, G. A., & Grossberg, S. (1996). Adaptive resonance theory. In J. D. Irwin (Ed.), *The industrial electronics handbook* (pp. 1286–1298). Boca Raton, FL: CRC.

Chey, J., Grossberg, S., & Mingolla, E. (1997). Neural dynamics of motion grouping: From aperture ambiguity to object speed and direction. *Journal of the Optical Society of America A, 14*, 2570–2594.

Chey, J., Grossberg, S., & Mingolla, E. (1998). Neural dynamics of motion processing and speed discrimination. *Vision Research, 38*, 2769–2786.

Cisek, P., Bullock, D., & Grossberg, S. (1998). A cortico-spinal model of reaching and proprioception under multiple task constraints. *Journal of Cognitive Neuroscience, 10*, 425–444.

Damasio, A. (1999). *The Feeling of What Happens*. New York: Harcourt Brace.

Davis, M. (1994). The role of the amygdala in emotional learning. *International Review of Neurobiology, 36*, 225–265.

DeYoe, E. A., & van Essen, D. C. (1988). Concurrent processing streams in monkey visual cortex. *Trends in Neuroscience, 11*, 219–226.

Douglas, R. J., Koch, C., Mahowald, M., Martin, K. A. C., & Suarez, H. H. (1995). Recurrent excitation in neocortical circuits. *Science, 269*, 981–985.

Duffy, C. J., & Wurtz, R. H. (1995). Medial superior temporal area neurons respond to speed patterns in optic flow. *Journal of Neuroscience, 17*, 2839–2851.

Eckhorn, R., Bauer, R., Jordan, W., Brosch, M., Kruse, W., Munk, M., & Reitböck, H. J. (1988). Coherent oscillations: A mechanism of feature linking in the visual cortex? *Biological Cybernetics, 60*, 121–130.

Edelman, G. M. (1987). *Neural Darwinism: The theory of neuronal group selection*. New York: Basic Books.

Egusa, H. (1983). Effects of brightness, hue, and saturation on perceived depth between adjacent regions in the visual field. *Perception, 12*, 167–175.

Elder, J. H., & Zucker, S. W. (1998). Evidence for boundary-specific grouping. *Vision Research, 38*, 143–152.

Faubert, J., & von Grunau, M. (1995). The influence of two spatially distinct primers and attribute priming on motion induction. *Vision Research, 35*, 3119–3130.

Fiala, J. C., Grossberg, S., & Bullock, D. (1996). Metabotropic glutamate receptor activation in cerebellar Purkinje cells as substrate for adaptive timing of the classically conditioned eye-blink response. *Journal of Neuroscience, 16*, 3760–3774.

Foley, J. M. (1980). Binocular distance perception. *Psychological Review, 87*, 411–434.

Francis, G., & Grossberg, S. (1996). Cortical dynamics of form and motion integration: Persistence, apparent motion, and illusory contours. *Vision Research, 36*, 149–173.

Georgopolous, A. P., Schwartz, A. B., & Kettner, R. E. (1986). Neuronal population coding of movement direction. *Science, 233*, 11416–1419.

Goodale, M. A., & Milner, D. (1992). Separate visual pathways for perception and action. *Trends in Neuroscience, 15*, 10–25.

Gove, A., Grossberg, S., & Mingolla, E. (1995). Brightness, perception, illusory contours, and cortico-geniculate feedback. *Visual Neuroscience, 12*, 1027–1052.

Gray, C. M., & Singer, W. (1989). Stimulus-specific neuronal oscillations in orientation columns of cat visual cortex. *Proceedings of the National Academy of Sciences, USA, 86*, 1698–1702.

Graziano, M. S. A., Andersen, R. A., & Snowden, R. (1994). Tuning of MST neurons to spiral motions. *Journal of Neuroscience, 14*, 54–67.

Grobstein, P. (1991). Directed movement in the frog: A closer look at a central representation of spatial location. In M. A. Arbib & J.-P. Ewert (Eds.), *Visual structure and integrated functions* (pp. 125–138). Berlin: Springer.

Grossberg, S. (1982). *Studies of mind and brain*. Norwell, MA: Kluwer Academic.

Grossberg, S. (1987). *The adaptive brain: Vol. II. Vision, speech, language, and motor control*. Amsterdam: Elsevier/North-Holland.

Grossberg, S. (1994). 3-D vision and figure-ground separation by visual cortex. *Perception and Psychophysics, 55*, 48–120.

Grossberg, S. (1997). Cortical dynamics of three-dimensional figure–ground perception of two-dimensional pictures. *Psychological Review, 104*, 618–658.

Grossberg, S. (1999a). How does the cerebral cortex work? Learning, attention, and grouping by the laminar circuits of visual cortex. *Spatial Vision, 12*, 163–187.

Grossberg, S. (1999b). The link between brain learning, attention, and consciousness. *Consciousness and Cognition, 8*, 1–44.

Grossberg, S. (2000a). The complementary brain: Unifying brain dynamics and modularity. *Trends in Cognitive Sciences, 4*, 233–246.

Grossberg, S. (2000b). The imbalanced brain: From normal behavior to schizophrenia. *Biological Psychiatry, 48*, 81–98.

Grossberg, S., Boardman, I., & Cohen, M. A. (1997). Neural dynamics of variable-rate speech categorization. *Journal of Experimental Psychology: Human Perception and Performance, 23*, 481–503.

Grossberg, S., & Grunewald, A. (1997). Cortical synchronization and perceptual framing. *Journal of Cognitive Neuroscience, 9*, 117–132.

Grossberg, S., & McLoughlin, N. (1997). Cortical dynamics of three-dimensional surface perception: Binocular and half-occluded scenic images. *Neural Networks, 10*, 1583–1605.

Grossberg, S., & Merrill, J. W. L. (1996). The hippocampus and cerebellum in adaptively timed learning, recognition, and movement. *Journal of Cognitive Neuroscience, 8*, 257—277.

Grossberg, S., Mingolla, E., & Pack, C. (1999). A neural model of motion processing and visual navigation by cortical area MST. *Cerebral Cortex, 9*, 878–895.

Grossberg, S., Mingolla, E., & Ross, W. D. (1997). Visual brain and visual perception: How does the cortex do perceptual grouping? *Trends in Neuroscience, 20*, 106–111.

Grossberg, S., & Myers, C. (2000). The resonant dynamics of conscious speech: Interword integration and duration-dependent backward effects. *Psychological Review, 107*, 735–767.

Grossberg, S., & Paine, R. W. (2000). A neural model of corticocerebellar interactions during attentive imitation and predictive learning of sequential handwriting movements. *Neural Networks, 13*, 999–1046.

Grossberg, S., & Raizada, R. (2000). Contrast-sensitive perceptual grouping and object-based attention in the laminar circuits of primary visual cortex. *Vision Research, 40*, 1413–1432.

Grossberg, S., & Rudd, M. (1992). Cortical dynamics of visual motion perception: Short-range and long-range apparent motion. *Psychological Review, 99*, 78–121.

Grossberg, S., & Somers, D. (1991). Synchronized oscillations during cooperative feature linking in a cortical model of visual perception. *Neural Networks, 4*, 453–466.

Grossberg, S., & Todorović, D. (1988). Neural dynamics of 1-D and 2-D brightness perception: A unified model of classical and recent phenomena. *Perception and Psychophysics, 43*, 723–742.

Guenther, F. H., Bullock, D., Greve, D., & Grossberg, S. (1994). Neural representations for sensory-motor control, III: Learning a body-centered representation of 3-D target position. *Journal of Cognitive Neuroscience, 6*, 341–358.

Heeger, D. J. (1993). Modeling simple-cell direction selectivity with normalized, half-squared linear operators. *Journal of Neurophysiology, 70*, 1885–1898.

Helmholtz, H. L. F. von (1925). *Treatise on physiological optics*. (J. P. Southall, Trans.). New York: Dover. (Original work published 1910)

Hess, R. F., Dakin, S. C., & Field, D. J. (1998). The role of "contrast enhancement" in the detection and appearance of visual contours. *Vision Research, 38*, 783–787.

Horak, F. B., & Anderson, M. E. (1984). Influence of globus pallidus on arm movements in monkeys. I. Effects of kainic acid-induced lesions. *Journal of Neurophysiology, 52*, 290–322.

Hubel, D. H., & Wiesel, T. N. (1977). Functional architecture of macaque monkey visual cortex. *Proceedings of the Royal Society London, Series B, 198*, 1–59.

Hupé, J. M., James, A. C., Payne, B. R., Lomber, S. G., Girard, P., & Bullier, J. (1998). Cortical feedback improves discrimination between figure and background by V1, V2 and V3 neurons. *Nature (London), 394*, 784–787.

Ito, M. (1984). *The cerebellum and neural control*. New York: Raven.

Kapadia, M. K., Ito, M., Gilbert, C. D., & Westheimer, G. (1995). Improvement in visual sensitivity by changes in local context: Parallel studies in human observers and in V1 of alert monkeys. *Neuron, 15*, 843–856.

Kamin, L. J. (1969). Predictability, surprise, attention, and conditioning. In B. A. Campbell & R. M. Church (Eds.), *Punishment and aversive behavior* (pp. 279–298). New York: Appleton-Century-Crofts.

Kanizsa, G. (1974). Contours without gradients or cognitive contours. *Italian Journal of Psychology, 1*, 93–113.

Kohonen, T. (1984). *Self-organization and associative memory*. Berlin: Springer.

Lamme, V. A. F., Rodriguez-Rodriguez, V., & Spekreijse, H. (1999). Separate processing dynamics for texture elements, boundaries and surfaces in primary visual cortex of the macaque monkey. *Cerebral Cortex, 9*, 406–413.

Land, E. H. (1977). The retinex theory of color vision. *Scientific America*, *237*, 108–128.

LeDoux, J. E. (1993). Emotional memory systems in the brain. *Behavioral Brain Research*, *58*, 69–79.

Logothetis, N. K., Schiller, P. H., Charles, E. R., & Hurlbert, A.C. (1990). Perceptual deficits and the activity of the color-opponent and broad-band pathways at isoluminance. *Science*, *247*, 214–217.

Luck, S. J., Chelazzi, L., Hillyard, S. A., & Desimone, R. (1997). Neural mechanisms of spatial selective attention in areas V1, V2, and V4 of macaque visual cortex. *Journal of Neurophysiology*, *77*, 24–42.

Maunsell, J. H. R., & van Essen, D. C. (1983). Response properties of single units in middle temporal visual area of the macaque monkey. I. Selectivity for stimulus duration, speed, and orientation. *Journal of Neurophysiology*, *49*, 1127–1147.

McLoughlin, N., & Grossberg, S. (1998). Cortical computation of stereo disparity. *Vision Research*, *38*, 91–99.

Mishkin, M., Ungerleider, L. G., & Macko, K.A. (1983). Object vision and spatial vision: Two cortical pathways. *Trends in Neuroscience*, *6*, 414–417.

Mollon, J. D., & Sharpe, L. T. (1983). *Colour vision*. New York: Academic Press.

Motter, B. C. (1993). Focal attention produces spatially selective processing in visual cortical areas V1, V2, and V4 in the presence of competing stimuli. *Journal of Neurophysiology*, *70*, 909–919.

Motter, B. C. (1994a). Neural correlates of attentive selective memory and pop-out in extrastriate area V4. *Journal of Neuroscience*, *14*, 2178—2189.

Motter, B. C. (1994b). Neural correlates of attentive selective memory and pop-out in extrastriate area V4. *Journal of Neuroscience*, *14*, 2190—2199.

Newsome, W. T., Gizzi, M. S., & Movshon, J. A. (1983). Spatial and temporal properties of neurons in macaque MT. *Investigative Ophthalmology and Visual Science*, *24*, 106.

Obermayer, K., Ritter, H., & Schulten, K. (1990). A principle for the formation of the spatial structure of retinotopic maps, orientation and ocular dominance columns. *Proceedings of the National Academy of Sciences, USA*, *87*, 8345–8349.

Ohzawa, I., DeAngelis, G. C., & Freeman, R. D. (1990). Stereoscopic depth discrimination by the visual cortex: Neurons ideally suited as disparity detectors. *Science*, *249*, 1037–1041.

Otto, T., & Eichenbaum, H. (1992). Neuronal activity in the hippocampus during delayed non-match to sample performance in rats: Evidence for hippocampal processing in recognition memory. *Hippocampus*, *2*, 323–334.

Pack C., Grossberg, S., & Mingolla, E. (2001) A neural model of smooth pursuit control and motion perception by cortical area MST. *Journal of Cognitive Neuroscience*, *13*, 102–120.

Paradiso, M. A., & Nakayama, K. (1991). Brightness perception and filling-in. *Vision Research*, *31*, 1221–1236.

Pavlov, I. P. (1927). *Conditioned reflexes*. London: Oxford University Press.

Pessoa, L., Beck, J., & Mingolla, E. (1996). Perceived texture segregation in chromatic element-arrangement patterns: High intensity interference. *Vision Research*, *36*, 1745–1760.

Petry, S., & Meyer, G. (Eds.). (1987). *The perception of illusory contours*. Berlin: Springer.

Ramachandran, V. S. (1985). Apparent motion of subjective surfaces. *Perception*, *14*, 127–134.

Reynolds, J. H., Nicholas, J. Chelazzi, L., & Desimone, R. (1999). Competitive mechanisms subserve attention in macaque areas V2 and V4. *Journal of Neuroscience*, *19*, 1736–1753.

Roelfsema, P. R., Lamme, V. A. F., & Spekreijse, H. (1998). Object-based attention in the primary visual cortex of the macaque monkey. *Nature (London)*, *395*, 376–381.

Rogers-Ramachandran, D. C., & Ramachandran, V. S. (1998). Psychophysical evidence for boundary and surface systems in human vision. *Vision Research*, *38*, 71–77.

Sakata, H., Shibutani, H., & Kawano, K. (1980). Spatial properties of visual fixation neurons in posterior parietal association cortex of the monkey. *Journal of Neurophysiology*, *43*, 1654–1672.

Schiller, P. H., Logothetis, N. K., & Charles, E. R. (1990). Role of the color-opponent and broad-band channels in vision. *Visual Neuroscience*, *5*, 321–326.

Sillito, A. M., Jones, H. E., Gerstein, G. L., & West, D. C. (1994). Feature-linked synchronization of thalamic relay cell firing induced by feedback from the visual cortex. *Nature (London)*, *369*, 479–482.

Skinner, B. F. (1938). *The behavior of organisms*. New York: Appleton-Century-Crofts.

Smallman, H. S., & McKee, S. P. (1995). A contrast ratio constraint on stereo matching. *Proceedings of the Royal Society London, Series B, 260*, 265–271.

Staddon, J. E. R. (1983). *Adaptive behavior and learning*. New York: Cambridge University Press.

Tanaka, K., Sugita, Y., Moriya, M., & Saito, H. A. (1993). Analysis of object motion in the ventral part of the medial superior temporal area of the macaque visual cortex. *Journal of Neurophysiology, 69*, 128–142.

Thompson, R. F. (1988). The neural basis of basic associative learning of discrete behavioral responses. *Trends in Neurosciences, 11*, 152–155.

Ungerleider, L. G., & Mishkin, M. (1982). Two cortical visual systems: Separation of appearance and location of objects. In D. L. Ingle, M. A. Goodale, & R. J. W. Mansfield (Eds.), *Analysis of visual behavior* (pp. 549–586). Cambridge, MA: MIT Press.

van Santen, J. P. H., & Sperling, G. (1984). Temporal covariance model of human motion perception. *Journal of the Optical Society of America, 1*, 451–473.

von der Heydt, R., Hanny, P., & Dursteler, M. R. (1981). The role of orientation disparity in stereoscopic perception and the development of binocular correspondence. In E. Grastyan & P. Molnar (Eds.), *Sensory functions: Vol. 16. Advances in Physiological science*. Oxford, England: Pergamon.

Wallach, H. (1976). *On perception*. New York: Quadrangle.

Watanabe, T. (1997). Velocity decomposition and surface decomposition–Reciprocal interactions between motion and form processing. *Vision Research, 37*, 2879–2889.

Watanabe, T., Sasaki, Y., Nielsen, M., Takino, R., & Miyakawa, S. (1998). Attention-regulated activity in human primary visual cortex. *Journal of Neurophysiology, 79*, 2218–2221.

Watson, B., & Ahumada, A. E. J. (1985). Model of human visual-motion sensing. *Journal of the Optical Society of America, 2*, 322–342.

Wuerger, S., Shapley, R., & Rubin, N. (1996). "On the visually perceived direction of motion" by Hans Wallach: 60 years later. *Perception, 25*, 1317–1367.

20

Universal Temporal Structures in Human Information Processing: A Neural Principle and Psychophysical Evidence

Raul Kompass
University of Leipzig, Germany

In this chapter a very old problem is reexamined: Is human cortical information processing continuous or temporally discretely structured? Many early contributions to this problem argued in favor of the second possibility: Fechner (1860) related consciousness to a superimposition of fast and slow rhythms. In 1864, von Baer (von Baer, 1864) suggested that temporal resolution of our perception is limited by a smallest unit called *moment*. This led to the view that we perceive the outside world as a stream of short static impressions (Uexkuell, 1928). The discovery of the electroencephalogram (EEG) (Berger, 1938) and its band structure and later the interpretation of cortical processes by computer analogies motivated attempts to prove that a temporal structure exists in form of a cortical central clock, which, however, did not succeed (Allport, 1968; Harter & White, 1968; Stroud, 1955; Vroon, 1974). Many of the current approaches to psychophysical modeling rest on the assumption that the information flow in the perceptual system is continuous or that its discreteness can be neglected (Luce & Green, 1972; McGill, 1963; Townsend & Ashby, 1983; Wickens, 1982). If perceptual decisions on a macroscopic scale are modeled by stochastic processes, as in random-walk models, on the microscopic scale this usually corresponds to an assumed random mode of operation of single information processing units that accumulate their contributions independently of each other.

In neurophysiology, this rationale is paralleled by the interpretation of neurons as independent units that integrate noisy spike-rate-coded information on the basis of differing synaptic weights yielding again a rate-coded output within an ensemble of some 100–1000 neurons. However, advanced neurophysiological methods that allow for in vivo monitoring of the activity of several neurons in parallel at different brain sites led to observations that question this interpretation. Neurons do not act independently of each other and are highly sensitive to coincidences in their input firing patterns (e.g., Softky & Koch, 1993). The understanding of neurons as coincidence detectors is part of a new concept, called synfire chain. In a synfire chain, volleys of simultaneous activity of groups of neurons traverse the brain in a chain, or "braid," possibly involving loops. Abeles and colleagues (Abeles et al., 1993) presented neurophysiological evidence that the firing of neurons within such a chain can be temporally very precise. The observed variation of up to ± 1 ms within delays as large as 450 ms exceeds perceptual performance by an order of magnitude. Combining such high temporal precision of neural delays with the assumption of recurrence of cortical information flow allows the derivation of a neurophysiological processing schema, here referred to as the delay oscillation interaction schema (DOIS), in which periods of oscillatory representation in neural feature maps and neural delays have integer or simple fractional ratios.

The main purpose of this chapter is to relate this physiologically predicted property to selected psychophysical evidence that is at variance with the assumption of temporally continuous brain operation. The presented results show that cortical information processing is highly noncontinuous and may exhibit precise discrete temporal values that can be related to each other by integer or simple rational size relations. This structural similarity between psychophysics and neurophysiology can be further explored by the inspection of correspondences of specific temporal intervals.

In what follows, evidence in favor of highly precise neural firing patterns and the concept of synfire chains are presented. In the second step, arguments suggesting that neural information processing is essentially recurrent are outlined. Thereafter both properties are combined in the prediction that, to yield optimal interaction of different kinds of neural representations, total neural delays and oscillation periods are related by near-integer or simple fractional ratios. Such rational size relations can exist in the neural substrate between periods that by themselves are variable in time, or they may be implemented in relation to a fixed absolute reference period (or a reference oscillation). The latter possibility is stated as part of Geissler's (1985, 1987, 1992; Geissler, Schebera, & Kompass, 1999) taxonomic time quantum model (TQM). This model postulates a smallest reference interval of ~ 4.5 ms, called quantum. Some physiological results that are compatible with the existence of such a quantum are presented.

An outline of psychophysical evidence in favor of discrete mental timing constitutes the second part of this chapter. Besides historical findings, such as the one by von Békésy (1936), several new results are presented. Among these are the preferred temporal values that occur during perceptual switches from perceived motion to flicker found with apparent motion (AM) of both the beta and the gamma type. The novel set of discrete intervals, although obtained in a different perceptual modality, is surprisingly similar to the system of values found by von Békésy (1936).

In the final section of this chapter, the presented psychophysical findings are discussed, put in the context of Geissler's taxonomic model, the TQM, and consequences resulting from the link between physiology and psychophysics enabled on the basis of the discrete temporal structuring are briefly considered.

A NEURAL PRINCIPLE FOR STRUCTURED MENTAL TIMING

The Synfire Chain Concept

A change in the understanding of the principles of cortical function began within the past decade. The traditional assumption that neural processing essentially relies on integration of stochastic excitatory and inhibitory input, thereby contributing to a rate-coded output signal within an ensemble of some 100 neurons, was questioned by a number of neurophysiological observations. Temporal precision of neural activity in reaction to arriving stimuli was found to be much greater than expected on the assumption of rate coding (Berry, Warland, & Meister, 1997). At the same time, the firing of cortical neurons (without external stimulation) was found to be too irregular to be compatible with integration of stochastically arriving input spikes (Softky & Koch, 1993).

As a new principle of neural operation, coincidence detection of input activity was suggested (Abeles, 1982; Softky & Koch, 1993; see also Shadlen & Newsome, 1994). Coincidence detection is suitable for the detection of synchronous firing patterns that in the visual cortex are functionally linked to the binding of several stimulus aspects to a common percept (see, e.g., Engel, König, Kreiter, Schillen, & Singer, 1992). However, the occurrence of synchronous firing patterns is not limited to peripheral representations, instead it seems to be ubiquitous throughout the neocortex. Abeles and colleagues (Abeles et al., 1993) found repeatable patterns of precisely timed spike discharges in the frontal cortex of monkeys. Interspike intervals as large as 450 ms had a temporal precision of ±1 ms. This precision of relative timing exceeds human performance in duration discrimination by an order of magnitude. The very high precision of timing is restricted to internal firing patterns though. Time locking to external stimuli was found to be much looser, having a precision of ±50 ms (Abeles & Prut, 1996). To explain these findings, Abeles et al. suggested a new coding scheme called synfire chain. The principal idea of a synfire chain is sketched in Fig. 20.1. Synchronous volleys of spikes traversing through a feedforward neural network constitute a transient form

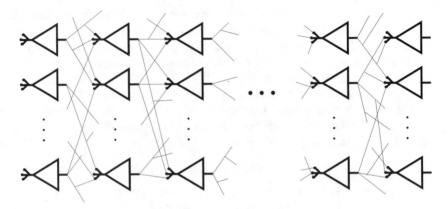

FIG. 20.1. Schematic representation of a synfire chain (after Abeles et al., 1993).

of neural information representation. Such representations yield a very efficient coding scheme as the same neurons can participate in several different chains. Many different synfire chains can run concurrently with few interactions because one chain with some 100 neurons per link requires only a very small percentage of the brain to be active at a time.

According to Bienenstock (1995), some additional advantages of synfire chains over other candidate coding schemes, such as fixed-point attractors (Amit, 1989; Hopfield, 1982) and cardinal cells (Barlow, 1972), are their consistency with a selection principle of brain operation and their ability to provide a more plausible framework for compositionality than other solutions, such as phase locking of neural oscillators.

Synfire chains can occur only if the number of neurons participating in a volley as well as their phase differences remain stable during propagation of activity along the chain. In model simulations, Diesmann, Gewaltig, and Aertsen (1999) could show that these requirements are met by simple leaky integrate-and-fire neurons. In their study, the temporal jitter within a volley in the chain has a stable fix point at ~0.5 ms standard deviation of firing for volley sizes above 90 neurons. The activity of the neurons in the volleys (once the volleys are established) also remains stable. For volleys of size 100, ~95 neurons fire in each volley. Extrapolation of these results may explain the fine absolute precision of timing despite the high overall synfire chain delay.

Recurrence as a Principle of Neural Information Processing

When we remember a past experience or imagine what would happen if we acted in a certain way in a hypothetical situation, we somehow generate mental represen-tations that are at an abstract level equivalent to those induced by real experiences.

It was suggested (Neisser, 1967) that the generation of mental representations is not limited to only imaginary contents of mind but is rather a property of conscious perception in general. Within a larger theoretical framework, the adaptive resonance theory, Grossberg (1999) formulated the hypothesis that all conscious states are resonant states. He proposes that conscious information processing is characterized by permanent resonance of bottom-up (concept activation) and top-down (concept evaluation) processes. In Grossberg's view, recurrence has a much more fundamental functional role than simple regulation of bottom-up processing, as was assumed in early attention models (Broadbent, 1952; Treisman, 1960). This role is best understood within the framework of Bayesian information processing.

Bayes' rule (Jaynes, 1995) allows us to determine the probability of a hypothesis by calculating its ability to model empirical data. In perception this rule allows the processing system to select the most appropriate (probable) mental concept (hypothesis) out of a number of alternatives by evaluating their ability to top-down model the sensory activity (the data). The highly complicated task of deriving an abstract representation from a many-dimensional sensory description can thus be replaced with several simpler constructive tasks. The idea of modeling is central in Bayesian information processing, which led to substantial progress in automatic pattern recognition, artificial intelligence, and machine learning. Two developments in this direction are the minimum-description-length (Rissanen, 1978) method and the Helmholtz machine (Hinton, Dayan, Frey, & Neal, 1994). The power of Bayes' rule, which inherently involves a preference for simple hypotheses, a sort of Occam's Razor (Berger, 1985), suggests that our nervous system operates in a Bayesian manner. Its operation must then be recurrent because the outlined models have to interact with the sensory acitvity they try to emulate. Neurophysiological investigations revealed that recurrent connections are present between many processing areas in the cortex (see Fellemann & Van Essen, 1991).

Recurrence of simple artificial neural networks may contribute to superior generalization performance. Recently it was shown that an unsupervised network that learns to predict its own input through a sequence of nontrivial low-complexity mappings may perform sparse or factorial coding, depending on the statistics of the data, and may outperform special learning rules such as principal-component analysis or independent-component analysis (Hochreiter & Schmidhuber, 1999). Synfire chains are compositional (Bienenstock, 1995), which makes them perfectly suited for processing complicated compositional and hierarchical models. Recurrent synfire chains are therefore likely to be an architecture the brain uses for information processing.

Apart from these information-theoretic and neurophysiological arguments, there is much psychophysical evidence available for a fundamental role of recurrent processing. For one example, partial report experiments with color cueing of the letters to be reported (Sperling, 1960; Tsal & Lavie, 1988) revealed that errors still occurred on the basis of spatial information. This, among other evidence, led van der Heijden (1993) to suggest a model of visual processing wherein spatial information is fed back to a sensory coding level to enhance the readout of semantic features at the cued positions. Extending van der Heijden's model by further recurrent feedback of semantic information might explain other results like that of Graves (1976), who found that the number of letters that could be identified (given the letter to be identified after display offset) was twice as large (approximately eight) as the number that could be reported in full report (approximately four) (Graves, 1976; Sperling, 1960). Preliminary information that is already present in semantic representations apparently has to be fed back to the sensory level to stabilize, resonate, and enter conscious memory. It may be speculated that the magical number of four items that occurs in many attentional and memory paradigms (Cowan, 2001) represents an upper bound on the ability of the perceptual system to feed back information and resonate and stabilize several percepts in parallel.

The Interaction of Recurrent Synfire Chains With Oscillatory Representations

Neural feature maps, for instance those discovered by Hubel and Wiesel (1977), enable representation of information in highly specialized codes that often preserve the topology of the stimuli. The activity in such maps was found to be oscillatory. Synchrony between different units coding compatible features at different positions thereby reflects global stimulus properties such as connectedness or colinearity (see, e.g., Engel et al., 1992). The functional role of synchrony, however, is still not clear. Synchrony might contribute to the detection of such global properties and the "binding" of special information of different sources to coherent object representations or reflect the action of other binding mechanisms that, by means of top-down recurrent activation, lead to synchrony of their inputs. The latter possibility is supported by models of Grossberg and Somers (1991) and Grossberg and Grunewald (1997) within the form-and-color-and-depth theory of the visual system.

The assumption that oscillatory activity in neural feature maps and dynamic activity in synfire chains as two principally different types of neural representation have to interact leads to the DOIS. In this schema, the central assumption that Hebb's (1949) principle holds is made. This principle says that interaction occurs when the dendritic activity that drives a neuron is approximately simultaneous to the firing output of the neuron. Recently it was neurophysiologically supported by the findings of Markram, Lübke, Frotscher, & Sakman (1997) and Zhang, Tao, Holt, Harris, & Poo (1998). Zhang et al. found that the weights of synapses that were active shortly (5–20 ms) before the postsynaptic neuron fired were subsequently strengthened and the weights of those that were active shortly after postsynaptic activity were weakened. Hebb's principle is also realized by synaptic plasticity, depending on the differential firing of neurons as a result of coincidence in their input. Gerstner, Kempter, Hemmen, and Wagner (1996) described such a mechanism that allowed for spiking accuracy and recognition of input coincidence with a precision far below 1 ms.

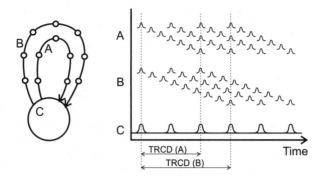

FIG. 20.2. Left, matching activity in the DOIS; right, total recurrent chain delays (TRCDs) of synfire chains A and B are integer multiples of the oscillation period of activity in the feature map C.

Optimal interaction of oscillatory representations and recurrent synfire chain activity constrains the delays of the chain to approximately integer multiples of the oscillation period (Fig. 20.2). For different recurrent synfire chains acting on the same feature maps, this leads to the constraint that their total recurrent chain delays (TRCDs) are related by simple rational ratios. Such ratios are known from psychological data on discrete timing (see the next subsection). Therefore the hypothesis is made that distinguished temporal intervals associated with discrete timing in psychological experiments have their neurophysiological equivalent in total delays of recurrent synfire chains. The relations between synfire chain delays and oscillation periods could be dynamically established during evolution of perceptual representation by adjustment of delays and periods. The models by Grossberg and collaborators (Grossberg & Grunewald, 1997; Grossberg & Somers, 1991) can be interpreted as examples of such adjustment in which the synfire chains, consisting of just of one element, determine the oscillation periods.

It would be beneficial, however, if integer relations were supported from the beginning by suitable permanent adjustment of TRCDs. Permanent adjustment of TRCDs implies that discrete temporal intervals are invariant in absolute size. Psychophysical findings exhibit such an invariance.

Geissler's Quantum

Invariance of discrete temporal intervals that have rational relations to each other allows the specification of all these intervals as integer multiples of a fixed small unit. On the basis of perceptual data, Geissler suggested that this unit has the same value of 4.5–4.6 ms, called time quantum Q_0, in different modalities and cognitive demands. Specification of this value is part of the taxonomic system TQM (Geissler, 1985, 1987, 1992; Geissler et al., 1999), which is subsequently discussed. The hypotheses forming the TQM were motivated exclusively by psychophysical observations. When psychophysical discrete timing has its counterpart in neural delays, however, as claimed in this chapter, there might also exist neural delays that correspond to Q_0. Neurophysiological data seem to support such a correspondence:

Psychophysical measurements of interhemispheric transmission time with the Poffenberger paradigm (1912) give an estimate of this delay of 3–5 ms (Brysbaert, 1994), which is about the same size as Geissler's time quantum Q_0.

Another fundamental delay, brainstem transmission time (BTT), assessed by means of early evoked electrical responses to auditory clicks, could be shown to remain quite constant with variations of stimulus intensity (Fabiani, Sohmer, Tait, Gafni, & Kinarti, 1979). During early development (0–7 years of age), BTT decreases from ~6 ms to 4.5 ± 0.2 ms, a value equivalent to the Geissler constant Q_0. The reduction is thought to result from increased myelination of axons.

Signal transmission delays in general should have an impact on fast oscillations as they may prevent global synchronization without phase lags. This for some time gave rise to a puzzle: It was known that neural oscillations in the gamma range (~30–70 Hz, which corresponds to periods of ~14–33 ms) are synchronous throughout the whole cortex (Basar & Demiralp, 1995; Llinas & Ribary, 1993), although the conduction delays globally may exceed 10 ms. Recently a mechanism for the alignment of gamma phases in the hippocampus, despite such large delays, was proposed by Traub, Whittington, Stanford, and Jefferys (1996). Excitatory neurons firing in phase with the inhibitory cells of the same neural column give delayed excitation to inhibitory cells of neighboring columns. This external excitation is able to evoke a second spiking of the inhibitory neurons, which results in the generation of spike doublets. The adjustment of the doublet width can compensate for the phase difference between the distant columns. In physiological measurements of rat hippocampal slices, a doublet width of 4–5 ms was found. This interval also agrees with Geissler's time quantum Q_0.

Cortical layer 5 pyramidal neurons are able to bind inputs of different cortical layers by a new cellular mechanism discovered by Larkum, Zhu, and Sakman (1999). Sensitivity to concurrent synaptic inputs in lower and upper layers is optimal when there is a slight asynchrony of ~5 ms between these inputs.

In the rat hippocampus very fast collective oscillations ("ripples") were found that have a frequency of 200–250 Hz (Buzsaki, Horvath, Urioste, Hetke, & Wise, 1992). Such ripples might, if present in humans at the same frequency range, be linked to discrete timing. They are thought to be involved in long-term-memory (LTM) formation because, as they occur during periods of rest, they replay temporal patterns that entered the hippocampus before, during periods of activity, in temporally compressed (~5:1) form, thereby activating cortical structures that are associated with memory function (Chrobak & Buzsáki, 1998; Skaggs & McNaughton, 1996). These ripples, which have periods of 4–5 ms, might not only update LTM but also adjust synfire chain delays. In the DOIS, oscillatory representations may be interpreted as working memory and synfire chains connecting them as LTM. Updating of LTM and adjustment of TRCDs thus would be results of the same process.

Alternative Approaches to Neural Timing

The DOIS should be understood as only a rough first approximation to the description of discrete regularities of neural temporal activity. There is another principle schema, termed *temporal coding* by Stevens and Zador (1995), which makes use of relative timing as coding dimension. Hopfield (1995) showed that with simple integrate-and-fire neurons a fire-rate intensity code can easily be converted to a temporal code, representing analog signal strength by the phase difference of action potentials to a central clock and pointed out the advantages of this code for further processing. There are neurophysiological findings regarded as evidence in favor of temporal coding: O'Keefe and Recce (1993) found that the activity of hippocampal place cells in rats, which code location, is phase shifted systematically relative to the theta rhythm during passage through a labyrinth. Richmond and Optican (1990) found that stimulus-onset spike latencies of neurons in the inferior temporal cortex of monkeys are related to the encoding of visual forms. However, the interpretation of these findings is not unambiguous because slight asynchronies of firing activity may represent not analog phase coding but sequential activity within cyclic activation of different units. Wehr and Laurent (1996), for example, found that olfactory neurons in the locust were cyclically active in different order, depending on the odor presented. Temporal coding in Stevens' and Zador's sense and the DOIS therefore do not contradict each other and may reflect different aspects of a more complicated neural temporal coding regime.

PSYCHOPHYSICAL EVIDENCE FOR THE EXISTENCE OF DISCRETE MENTAL TIMING MECHANISMS

Perceptual and Fusion Thresholds of Oscillatory Stimuli

The empirical results subsequently presented deviate from the mainstream of mental chronometry, in which functional questions are the focus of research, by a different role of variation of temporal intervals. In the paradigm of Sternberg (1966), for example, the experimenter varies the set size to observe a change of reaction time. Then an argument for the serial character of the memory scanning process is derived from the functional dependence of both. In many of the experiments presented in this chapter, systematic variation of experimental parameters is important only as a source of variability in the temporal variable. The interesting result is an universal structure within this variation, for example discrete temporal values and their size relations or commonly preferred intervals across different mental tasks. The first, to my knowledge, empirical contribution to this line of research was given by Lalanne (1876), who pointed out that the frequency of stimulus fusion in the tactile, auditory, and visual modality equals 18 Hz. Lalanne conjectured a common, yet unknown, mechanism behind this.

Measuring tactile stimulus fusion, Brecher (1932) found that the critical frequency did not depend on intensity of stimulation or the cutaneous receptor density: Stimulation of the tips of tongue and fingers gave approximately the same critical frequency value as stimulation of the back or the feet. Variability between participants was very small: Individual averages of 14 participants yielded an overall mean period of 55.3 ms (18.1 Hz) and a standard deviation of 1.2 ms between participants. This seemed surprising because it was known that other well-determinable psychological constants such as Weber fractions differ much more among participants.

Almost at the same time von Békésy (1936) (later Nobel laureate) made an important discovery during measurement of absolute thresholds of the perception of low-frequency sinusoidal sounds. He found that the dependence of the threshold frequency on sound-pressure amplitude, globally a hyperbolic function, at a number of points exhibited local invariance. The left-hand side of Fig. 20.3 shows the result of his measurement.

At 18 Hz (corresponding to a period of 55 ms), where this invariance extended over the largest range, it comprised at least seven successive adjustments of amplitude between trials. At this well-known frequency the sound became tonal in character. Besides this particular frequency value, 10 other locally invariant frequencies were found. Von Békésy attributed this result to the quantal character of the nervous processes without explicitly mentioning many nearly exact integer relations between the distinguished frequencies. These relations are presented on the right-hand side of Fig. 20.3.

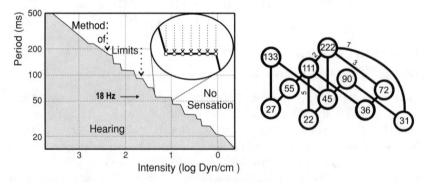

FIG. 20.3. Left, absolute intensity threshold in the perception of low-frequency sound as a function of frequency exhibits intervals of local invariance. Arrows denote the trajectories of adjustment. Results for 18 Hz after von Békésy (1936). Right, locally invariant periods and near-integer relations. The same integer ratios 2:1, 3:1, and 5:1, are represented by connections with the same orientations.

Reaction Time Studies

The evaluation of reaction times (RTs) in different experiments revealed signs of discrete mental-timing processes. The first studies reported, however, lacked thorough statistical analysis and were possibly flawed: Temporal autocorrelation functions (ACFs) of simple RT data exhibited periodicities of ~25 ms (e.g. Harter & White, 1968). The modulation of the ACFs, however, optimal with ~50 data points, disappeared when a larger number of RTs were analyzed. Drifting of the periods could have been a cause for this. However, it could be shown (Vroon, 1974) that random data, evaluated in a similar way, also exhibited strong modulations with similar periods.

That RTs still may contain periodicities was demonstrated by Latour (1967) with a study of the optokinetic nystagmus, elicited by continuously moving dots: the analysis of eye-pursuit simple RT, the analysis of the detection rate of a small flash as function of the time to the next saccade, and the analysis of detection rates for one flash conditional on the perception of a previously presented spatially displaced flash. Latour found three periods in these RTs that he set into relation to three EEG periods: 110 ms (dominant EEG α before experiment) $\approx 3/2 \times 72$ ms (dominant EEG α during experiment), 72 ms $\approx 5 \times 14.5$ ms (period in ocular left $\rightarrow$ right reaction, also period in optokinetic nystagmus), 14.5 ms $\times 2 \approx 29.7$ ms (dominant EEG γ during experiment), 29.7 ms $\approx 3 \times 9.7$ ms (period in ocular right $\rightarrow$ left reaction).

After collecting a large number of simple manual choice reaction times from different subjects, Dehaene (1993) made spectral analyses of the RT distributions and found 14 statistically significant dominant periods having one of the following values: 12.2, 13.5, 15, 18.3, 19.7, 21.3, 28.4, and 36.6 ms. Among these values the periods 13.5, 28.4, and 36.6 were repeatedly significant with more than one participant; they are nearly multiples 3, 6, and 8 of 4.5 msec.

Saccadic RTs in several cases were found to exhibit multimodal distributions (see Fischer & Weber, 1993). Gezeck, Fischer, and Timmer (1997) found with a very large data set comprising more than 90,000 saccadic RTs that individual RT distributions exhibited stable modes that were altered only in size, not in position, by training or variation of the gap, a break between fixation stimulus offset, and target flash onset. Superposition of all saccadic RTs of a gap condition across individuals yielded both with trained and naive participants three RT modes at similar positions: 107 ± 14 ms, 148 ± 18 ms, and 203 ± 11 ms for trained and 106 ± 11 ms, 148 ± 21 ms, and 209 ± 19 ms for naive participants.

Memory Scanning

Mental memory scanning periods are exquisite candidates for discrete timing because they are characteristics of a highly automated task and they can be determined with very high accuracy and great robustness. The 37-ms scanning period of digits

(Sternberg, 1966) can be viewed as a discrete temporal value. Recently it was demonstrated that this value is subject to slight variation by external rhythmic stimulation (Burle & Bonnet, 2000; see also subsequent discussion).

In a recent study Petzold and Edeler (1995) found clusters of processing time in a more complex memory task. Participants had to decide whether a presented behavioral act or a personality attribute matched a memorized description. The clustering of participants allowed considerable reduction of overall RT variability and enabled detailed analyses of different processing strategies. This involved calculation of mental operation times that clustered at 163, 216, and 267 ms. These numbers are very close to the multiples 3, 4, and 5 of 54 ms.

The Investigation of Time Perception

Other evidence for a discrete structure of mental time was found in studies of time perception. Kristofferson (1967) in an asynchrony detection task found a psycho-metric function in agreement with the assumption of periodic sampling of sensory information. The 48-ms sampling period, called quantum, was significantly cor-related with half the period of the participants' dominant EEG alpha spindles.

In 1980 Kristofferson reported an experiment in which he had examined, after extensive training, his ability to discriminate two-click intervals in a procedure without standard stimuli (feedback after each trial allowed for the formation of a purely mental standard). Discriminability, as a function of base duration, deviated from the linear characteristic expected on the basis of Weber's law to form a stair-caselike function (Kristofferson, 1980). Figure 20.4 illustrates this result. Allan and Kristofferson had, in former experiments (Allan, 1971), shown that the psy-chometric function for this type of discrimination task could be well characterized as an integral of a triangular probability function and argued that this reflected the action of discrete temporal processes such as periodic sampling. Discriminability therefore was given in terms of a quantum equaling half the base length of the triangle. The staircase characteristic given in Fig. 20.4 may be interpreted as an adjustment of the quantum to various base durations through subsequent doubling.

In another experiment (Kristofferson, 1990) investigation of the discriminability of the asynchrony of the last click in a train of four clicks led to the observation that the quantum that characterizes discrimination performance takes at least the value of 8.6 ms (10.3 ms for another participant). Reducing the period of clicks below 250–300 ms did not improve discrimination beyond this.

Influencing Internal Pacemakers—The Treisman Paradigm

Another fundamentally different approach to demonstrate the discrete nature of the mechanisms for time perception was taken by Treisman, Faulkner, Naish, and Brogan (1990), who investigated the influence of a continuously presented external

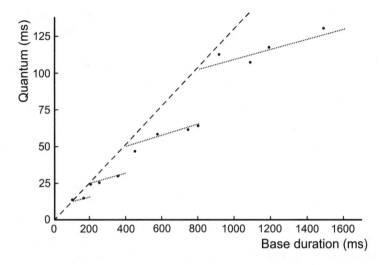

FIG. 20.4. Duration discriminability in a single-stimulus method after prolonged training and regression given by Kristofferson (1980). Discrimination errors (expressed as quantal values) and corresponding intervals exhibit doubling relations. The discrimination error (JND) relates to the quantum q as JND = 0.27 q.

click rhythm on the estimation of temporal intervals ranging from 0.5 to 0.8 s. Characteristic changes of estimated duration were found with minima at the click-rhythm frequencies 3.5, 4.5, 5.5, 9, 11.5, 13.5, 16, 18, and 24 Hz (with periods of approximately 42, 55, 62, 74, 87, 111, 182, 222, and 286 ms). Near-integer relations of these periods were 55 ms × 2 ≈ 111 ms, 111 ms × 2 = 222 ms, 222 ms ≈ 3 × 74 ms, 182 ms ≈ 3 × 62 ms, and 42 ms × 2 ≈ 87 ms. Treisman previously (1963) had proposed the existence of internal pacemakers consisting of a variable-frequency oscillator and an additional output multiplier. The pacemakers could cover a wide frequency range and might serve to represent stimulus intensities or to time motor actions. The influence of the external click rhythm on the time estimate was explained by the rhythmic driving of the pacemaker that represented time. With the assumption that driving requires simple frequency ratios of clicks and internal pacemaker, the pacemaker frequency was assessed, yielding either 24.75 or 49.5 Hz in one and 37.3 Hz in another experiment. In another study (Treisman, Faulkner, & Naish, 1992), the analysis yielded frequencies from 49.6 to 50 Hz that were rationally related to the driving rhythm. The closeness of these values to the 50-Hz frequency of both the power lines and the CRT used in the experiment was discussed by Treisman et al. (1992), who presented arguments against a synchronization of the internal rhythms to such weak external stimulation.

The paradigm of driving internal clocks by task-independent periodic stimulation has proved to be fruitful in further studies. Visual instead of auditory stimulation led to similar results in time estimation (Treisman & Brogan 1992). The performance in machine typing could be shown to vary with click rate (Treisman et al., 1992). In a neurophysiological study it was shown that the frequency of EEG activity shifted slightly in reaction to the inducing stimuli. The frequency shifts occurred at frequencies that were multiples of 12.8 Hz ($\cong$78 ms) (Treisman, Cook, Naish, & MacCrone, 1994).

Burle and Bonnet (1999) in a "Simon"-type choice reaction task (Simon & Small, 1969) restricted the frequencies of accompanying auditory clicks to a small range and found, for both congruent and incongruent stimulus-response arrangements, the same characteristic deviations of reaction time. Their results are shown on the left-hand side of Fig. 20.5. A similar investigation (Burle & Bonnet, 2000) showed that, in a short-term-memory search (Sternberg, 1969), residual slope and intercept in RT list length regression varied equally depending on the click rhythm. This is shown on the right-hand side of Fig. 20.5. The residuals allow for the extraction of driving frequencies that, despite locking, do not change the internal regimen. In Figure 20.5, right-hand side, these are 19.7 Hz ($\cong$50.8 ms) and 21.8 Hz ($\cong$45.9) ms. Their periods differ by 4.9 ms, which is approximately Geissler's constant.

Two Experiments on Apparent Motion

Recently at our department at Leipzig University two experiments on AM were conducted (Geissler et al., 1999; Kompass, 2001; Kompass, Geissler, & Schebera, 2003) that yielded a set of discrete time values as large as those of von Békésy. In both experiments a paradigm that resembles the one used by von Békésy (1936) was applied: A temporal variable was determined in a method of limits while an additional parameter influencing the measure in a reproducible way was varied between trials. Long-range AMs of both the beta and the gamma type were used in the experiments. In long-range AM, timing is the most important factor that influences the resulting percept (Holt-Hansen, 1974; Neuhaus, 1930).

The stimulus sequences presented to induce the AM are shown in the insets of the top graphs of Fig. 20.6. There were 46 participants in the beta-motion experiment and 33 in the gamma-motion experiment. Timing was parameterized in terms of exposure duration (ED) of a flash or a bar and interstimulus interval (ISI). In the case of gamma motion the small square present during the ISI served as only a point of fixation. If ED and ISI were large, participants perceived an alteration of two flashes or periodic appearance and disappearance of the vertical bar. As ED and ISI became smaller, participants saw a forward and backward movement of *one* flash or extension and contraction of the bar, possibly with a break between. When ED and ISI were decreased flicker was perceived: Both spots or the bar, respectively, flickered in place or even seemed periodically to pop out of the background in depth. The ISI of transition from AM to flicker was determined with a gradual decrease of ISI in a method of limits. ED was varied between trials in

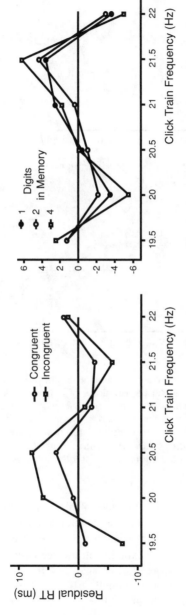

FIG. 20.5. Rhythmic click driving causes systematic deviations of RTs: left, Residual RT as a function of driving frequency in a Simon-type choice reaction task exhibits the same characteristic pattern for incongruent and congruent trials; right, Residual RT as a function of driving frequency in Sternberg's memory search.

465

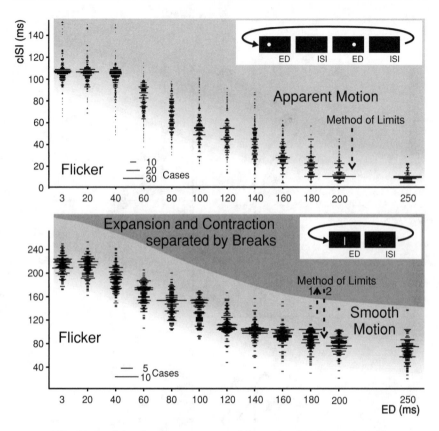

FIG. 20.6. Stimulus sequences and interstimulus intervals critical for transition to flicker as functions of exposure duration (ED)
in (top) beta motion and (bottom) gamma motion. The critical interstimulus intervals are collapsed across subjects and angular separations. There are preferred critical interstimulus interval values
that are constant across EDs, although the central tendencies of
the critical interstimulus intervals are strictly decreasing functions
of the ED.

12 discrete steps: 3, 20, 40, . . . , 180, 200, and 250 ms. In the gamma experiment, ISI
reduction started after an increase of this parameter until the participants reported
breaks between contraction and expansion, which served to equalize starting conditions (see Fig. 20.6). In the beta experiment, the decrease in ISI had to stop at
zero. Only positive ISI values were further analyzed. In principle, however, beta
motion can be seen with overlapping stimuli.

The main results (combined data for different angular distance/size of stimuli,
which have a minor influence on the percept) are presented in Fig. 20.6. The
ISIs critical for transition to flicker (cISIs) are decreasing functions of ED with

similar slope for both types of AM. In both experiments there were preferred values for perceptual switching. To evaluate these preferences statistically, all cISI were combined in common distributions that exhibited a number of modal values. Significance of the modes was then assessed with density-estimation methods. A significance bound for the maximum of the estimated density was computed with a Monte Carlo approach, and, independently, the local variation of the density was evaluated in different scales of resolution with a method that determines significant zero crossings of the derivative of the density (Chaudhuri & Marron, 1999). The sets of significant modal values for both experiments were, for beta motion {4–5, 9–10, 22–23, 27, 37, 44, 54, 107, and 142–147 ms} and for gamma motion {77, 104, 154, and 210 ms}.

These discrete intervals are compatible to the structure of invariant periods found by von Békésy (1936) in the auditory dimension. The 103-ms mode in gamma motion and 107 ms in beta motion, both being highly significant, are likely to correspond to the 110-ms value found by von Békésy. Near-integer relations among the modal values of either experiment are sketched on the left-hand side of Fig. 20.7.

In search of a microperiod underlying the manifestation of discrete timing, differences of cISI were analyzed. With the beta-motion data, absolute cISI differences of trials that were identical except for the ED parameters, which were neighbors in the sense that $|ED_1 - ED_2| = 20$ ms (analogously for ED = 3 or 250 ms) and that had cISI values no larger than ~40 ms, exhibited a multimodality in their distribution, which had a period of ~4.4 – 4.7 msec. The right-hand side of Fig. 20.7 shows the histogram of differences and the results of fitting with varying modulations. Such an approach did not work with gamma motion. An analysis of a larger set of 16 modal values, including many modes that were not significant

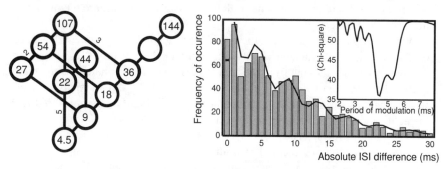

FIG. 20.7. Left, Significant cISI in the beta-motion experiment and integer relations; right, small cISI values (<40 ms) in the beta-motion experiment exhibit a microperiod of 4.2–4.6 ms. Absolute values of differences of cISIs of trials with neighboring EDs (e.g., 180 and 200 ms) are given in the histogram. Inset, approximation with modulated mixture of normal distributions gives the best fit for a modulation period of 4.56 ms (small graph).

as single values, however, seemed to support existence of a 9-ms microperiod in gamma motion, twice the value of the microperiod in beta motion.

Other Research and General Difficulties in the Investigation of Discrete Timing

Another experimental result that suggests temporal discreteness of mental activity is presented by Elliott and Müller in this book. Although the many findings for discrete timing seem convincing when presented together, they represent only a small segment of current psychophysical research. Apart from the fact that many researchers seem to be unaware of discrete timing, a major reason for this situation seems to be the special difficulties that arise in researching it. In contrast to the investigation of other psychophysical quantities, with discrete times the property of discreteness has to be proved at some step of the analysis. This may be achieved by a demonstration of the invariance of discrete temporal values as a function of other perceptually important parameters or by a demonstration of the increased probability of their occurrence, as compared with other values. Accordingly, experiments that are planned to yield discrete values often require a larger number of measurements, or very precise measurements. For example, many results from the investigation of perceptual dynamics indicate that qualitative changes may occur when temporal parameters of ~100 or ~200 ms are exceeded (see Breitmeyer, 1984, for examples in visual masking). Mostly, however, the resulting data seem not to be invariant and precise enough to put them in the context of discrete timing. A case for which this seems possible is the investigation of the double-flash effect (Springer, Deutsch, & Stanley, 1975), which exhibited an interval of 105 ± 5 ms. In general, subtleties of the experimental procedure often are critical for the occurrence of discreteness. In what follows some critical points are mentioned to illustrate the problem.

Von Békésy (1936) noted that the local invariance in his experiment depended on the direction of parameter adjustment in the method of limits. He increased the frequency, thus moving from the area in parameter space where no perception occurred to the area where perception occurred (see Fig. 20.3). Measurements with adjustment in the opposite direction led to a gliding of the threshold and to highly increased inaccuracy of measurement, which von Békésy associated with frequency locking. The observation of discrete timing therefore required not only the application of a method of limits, which no longer is the first choice in psychophysics as it was in Fechner's and Wundt's days (Wundt, 1874), but also its use in a fashion that deviates from the one that is found in standard textbooks (e.g., Gescheider, 1976). It is obvious that the method of constant stimuli that leads to interpolated, not directly perceptually observed, thresholds is not suited to yield discreteness in the measured variable.

Application of the method of limits also in the experiments on AM (Geissler et al., 1999; Kompass et al., 2003) raised new critical issues. The reduction of the

ISI had to proceed at the right pace. A reduction that was too fast resulted in a coarse-grained ISI because only after a new exposure duration could another ISI be applied, which might differ too much from the previously presented value to allow precise measurement. If the reduction was too slow (below 2-ms ISI per second of experiment), the perceptual switch changed its character and a situation of ambiguous perception arose with apparently random switching from motion to flicker and back again. This seemed to be accompanied by a change in the regimen of internal rhythms, which was indicated by the tendency of appearance of a 6.7-ms microperiod in cISI differences (Kompass 2001).

Latour (1967) mentioned that the periodicities he observed occurred only with almost complete adaptation to darkness. The participants consequently reacted to stimuli that were not very different in intensity from the absolute threshold. Likewise the proper illumination was needed for the appearance of the double-flash effect (Springer et al., 1975). In Kristofferson's (1980) experiment the application of a method without standards may have been critical (there were essentially two stimulus intensities that were judged, and subsequent feedback was given). This again is an infrequently used experimental method.

DISCUSSION

Combination of Discrete Intervals

The first step toward a unified analysis of empirically observed discrete intervals may be made by their combination into a common system. Many such intervals fit in a "periodic system" that emerges when the data of von Békésy (1936) and Geissler et al. (1999) are combined (Fig. 20.8). This applies to the following temporal intervals: 55 ms, found by Lalanne (1876) and Brecher (1932), 72 and 110 ms by Latour (1967), 107 and 203–209 ms by Gezeck et al. (1997), 105 ms by Springer et al. (1975), 13.5, 28, and 37 ms by Dehaene (1993), 37 ms by Sternberg

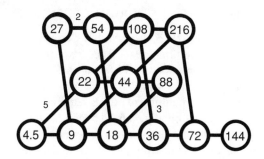

FIG. 20.8.   System of periods composed of discrete intervals from several sources. Connections indicate approximate integer relations. The same ratios correspond to the same orientations.

(1969), 216 ms by Petzold & Edeler (1995), 9 ms by Kristofferson (1990), 55, 111, 222, 74, 42, and 87 ms by et al. Treisman and colleagues (Treisman, 1990; Treisman & Brogan, 1992; Treisman et al., 1992), and 104 and 210 ms by Kompass et al. (2003). In the system, distinguished values may be represented as near-integer multiples (1, 2, 4, 8, 16, 32, 3, 6, 12, 24, 48, 5, 10, 20) of Geissler's quantum Q_0 of 4.5 ms. Such a representation is therefore an indirect argument for the existence of the quantum Q_0.

As in musical scales, contradictions appear when near-integer relations in this periodic system are interpreted as exact values. The two routes (4.5, 9, 18, 36, and 110 ms and 4.5, 22, and 110 ms) in Fig. 20.8 show that 110 ms is interpreted in the graph both as 24 times and 25 times the quantum. Near-integer ratios thus reflect the limited precision of the system, which is $\sim 1/24$. For the preceding selected discrete intervals, assignment to multiples of the quantum within Fig. 20.8 is mostly unambiguous. It seems ambiguous for some other values because of the limited precision. For example, in gamma motion (Kompass et al., 2003) the 77- and 154-ms cISI modes are assigned to the multiples 18 and 36 of Q_0. They are quite close to the multiples 16 and 32, however, and their interpretation essentially depends on the "context" of other discrete values. In such a situation, size relations within one data set have to be considered as more important than those to other data sets or to an abstract system, such as the one given in Fig. 20.8.

Consideration of simple size relations within the same data sets also helps to avoid the general problem of overfitting: Availability of a sufficiently fine grid of ideal values allows the fitting of arbitrary data, which makes the fact that such a fit is possible meaningless. With the present data, a high precision of discrete values from the same source and the simplicity of the integer relations make their occurrence by chance unlikely and are therefore good indicators of discrete timing. For future research more powerful statistical tools are needed to assess the likelihood that a set of apparently related intervals have integer or near-rational size relations.

The Taxonomic Model of Quantal Timing

In Geissler's TQM (Geissler, 1985, 1987, 1992; Geissler et al., 1999), another unified description of discrete timing data, integer size relations are exact and a limitation of precision is incorporated in a different way. The result of Kristofferson (1980) indicated that quantization and Weber law are compatible if the representation of mental intervals t as multiples of quanta requires bigger quanta for larger intervals. In the TQM, this is formally realized by limitations placed on the multiplicity in representations of time intervals to a *coherence bound M*. M is estimated to be ~ 30, in accordance with human duration discrimination performance. In contrast to the previous periodic system, 24 and 25 times the quantum are regarded as different values. However, the representation of 220 ms, for example, is possible only as 24 times a quantum of 9 ms because of the coherence bound. In a simplified form the TQM can be presented by the following hypotheses:

1. Mental timing is quantal. Quantum values are multiples of an *elementary quantum* $Q_0 \approx 4.5$ ms.
2. Concatenation of quanta leads to mental representation of larger intervals. The length of trains is bound to a multiplicity of M quanta (coherence bound). M is assumed to be ~ 30.
3. Representations of intervals form *hierarchies*. Short trains can thus serve as quanta at a higher level of the hierarchy.

In addition, to account for the observation that only selected multiples of the quantum occur, the following assumption is made:

4. There is a *preference* for simple compound multiples such as 24 (= 2*2* 2*3).

The formation of hierarchies, which is illustrated on the left-hand side of Fig. 20.9, can be used to derive preferences of the multiples of a quantum. On the right-hand side of Fig. 20.9, a system of preferences is presented that was obtained by a count of all possible hierarchies that do not exceed M and contain the multiple on an intermediate level.

The TQM was the theoretical basis and motivation for a number of recent research activities, including the two AM studies. The fundamental role of Q_0 in mental timing is now, as was shown, supported by several neurophysiological and psychophysical results. There is some evidence, however, that under certain conditions there may occur another smallest unit of quantization, 6.7 ms, which is not an integer multiple of Q_0 but equals $3/2 * Q_0$ (Kompass, 2001).

The observation that the higher discrete intervals also have higher distances, and hence larger greatest common divisors, supports Hypotheses 2 and 3 of the

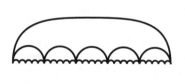 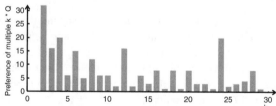

FIG. 20.9. Illustration of two hypotheses of the taxonomic model of quantal timing: left, hierarchy formation. Short queues of periodic activity can serve as quantal units of larger queues. Right, preference system of multiples of the absolute quantum Q_0. Simple multiples such as 12 or 24 are more likely to occur in a mental task than others.

TQM. Direct experimental testing of Hypothesis 2, the *limited coherence*, and experimental determination of M are difficult, however. This is mainly because of the character of the taxonomic system used as a predictive system, which describes observable intervals by a finer, less observable structure. The predicted discrete intervals with highest preference have distances from each other that are mostly larger than the underlying quantum (see the right-hand graph of Fig. 20.9). Consequently testing of Hypothesis 2 and determination of M require extraction of the finer structure, that is, inference of the less preferred intervals from the experimental data or direct determination of the underlying quantum. In the experiment on beta motion (Geissler et al., 1999; Kompass, 2001) a signature of ~ 4.5 ms, indicating involvement of Q_0, could be extracted from cISI values up to ~ 40 ms (right-hand graph of Fig. 20.7). This allows us to conclude that $M \geq 9$. In the experiment on gamma motion (Kompass et al., 2003), the regular spacing of the modes that were not significant as single values indicated that a fine structure with a 9-ms microperiod underlays quantal timing at least up to 105-ms, which suggests a new constraint of $M \geq 12$. To a lesser extent, the regular spacing is even apparent up to represented intervals of 210 ms, suggesting that $M \geq 24$. A possible upper bound for M results from the assumption that cISIs in beta motion are limited by the coherence bound. This leads to values from $M = 24$ up to $M = 32$ for different subjects.

The Precision of Discrete Timing

For many of the problems related to discrete timing, including understanding the role of the coherence bound M in the TQM, the issue of temporal precision and resolution seems central. Obviously different levels of precision and resolution that are involved in discrete timing have to be distinguished. If it is assumed that the DOIS explanation properly reflects the underlying physiological mechanisms, the following levels should be considered:

1. Precision of firing in a synfire chain. Relative precision according to Abeles et al. (1993) can be as high as 1/200 and better.

2. Resolution of oscillation periods of oscillating neural maps that are connected with recurrent synfire chains. This resolution is limited by the intervolley interval of the synfire chains. Selected neurophysiological data by Abeles et al. (1993) (see the right-hand side of Fig. 20.5) indicate an intervolley interval of ~ 10 ms. In the simulations of Diesmann et al. (1999) intervolley intervals equaled 6–7 ms after the synaptic delays were arbitrarily set to 5 ms.

3. Counting of oscillation periods leads to another, more coarse, measure of elapsed time. The resolution of this measure is the oscillation period itself. Fast oscillations in neural feature maps in the high gamma range may have frequencies of up to 90 Hz (Eckhorn, 1999), which corresponds to a resolution of down to

~10 ms. Often the resolution is worse, however, because typical frequencies are in the 40-Hz range or below.

4. Embedding of fast oscillations in slower ones, as in the short-term-memory model of Lisman and Idiart (1995), leads to a further coarse notion of resolution by relating the high and low oscillation periods involved. From physiological investigations it may be concluded that theta and gamma oscillations are involved in common neural representations that give relative resolutions of up to 1:12 (Skaggs & McNaughton, 1996).

There is evidence for different levels of precision also in psychophysical observations:

In the AM experiments (Geissler et al., 1999; Kompass et al., 2003), the precision of repeated cISI measures increased at preferred cISI. Computation of Weber fractions from these differences at selected ISIs in gamma motion led to fractions as small as 1/60, which obviously are too precise to conform to Weber's law as known from duration discrimination experiments (Kompass, 2001). Relating this observation to the preceding hierarchy of precisions and resolutions indicates that synfire chain precision should be involved in measurement here.

Ordinary Weber law precision in psychophysics motivated the estimate $M = 30$ in the TQM. It might be linked to the second considered level of physiological precision, the resolution of oscillation periods. Such an interpretation would be compatible with Geissler's TQM, if intervolley intervals might be as small as 4.5 ms and if they were preferredly integer multiples of this value. The representation of discrete intervals as multiples of a quantum then would correspond to the number of links in the recurrent synfire chain representing the interval.

The most frequently observed discrete temporal intervals have a coarser resolution, which is evident from the scheme in Fig. 20.8, the system of discrete periods. Such a resolution may correspond to the spacing of periods of related neural feature map oscillations, thus reflecting the preceding levels 3 and 4.

There is another fundamental question related to the precision of timing: How constant is discrete timing across individuals and perceptual phenomena? The investigation by Brecher (1932) showed that the average individual periods of nearly 55 ms varied with only ~3% standard deviation across individuals. In the AM experiments several observers contributed to narrow peaks of cISI density, which is possible only with, at most, a similarly low variability of discrete timing. A relative variation of ~3% thus can be regarded as a crude upper bound for variability across individuals who exhibit the same general pattern. The precision of timing across different modalities and perceptual tasks should be at least almost comparably high; this is suggested by the relation of the discrete temporal values that are combined to the periodic system in Fig. 20.8. The variability considered here includes several kinds of systematic and random experimental errors. For example, RT in the method of limits leads to systematically smaller cISIs in the AM experiments (Kompass et al., 2003). Discrete timing under ideal conditions may therefore be much more precise than the estimate of 3%. It is possible, however, to systematically influence discrete temporal values. In the Treisman paradigm such a systematic variation is exploited, and the results by Treisman et al. (1992) and Burle and Bonnet (2000) proved its existence. The relative variation of the search rate in the Sternberg task by Burle and Bonnet (2000) is as large as $\pm 2.5\%$. How can discrete intervals and thus the quantum be so constant? If the constancy is the result of developmental adjustment of physiological delays, as suggested by Fabiani et al. (1979) for the BTT, are there external influences that allow the quantum to adjust to the same value for different individuals? We can only speculate here. A very precise permanent external rhythm is the day–night cycle. Possibly a multitude of intermediate physiological rhythms would allow for adjustment of the time quantum relative to such a huge period.

The Link Between Physiology and Psychophysics

Relating two different research fields can be very beneficial for both sides, because well-known laws in one field may be translated to the other and studied and tested there. For this and also for philosophical reasons there was always a strong interest in relating psychological findings to neurophysiology (Wundt, 1874). Neurophysiology, on the other side, needs psychology to motivate investigations and to interpret otherwise meaningless data. Attempts to link both fields were, and still are, successful in explaining sensory performance with the physiology of the senses (e.g., Laming, 1986). Little success, however, was achieved in extending these connections to inner psychophysics (Uttal, 1996). The importance of discrete timing research partially results from the fact that it can provide a basis for such a link. In what follows, three possible directions in which such a link may contribute to future research are shortly discussed.

Neurophysiological investigation of spike latencies and oscillation periods may benefit from the psychologically derived taxonomy in Fig. 20.8 and from the TQM. Spike timing often exhibits a high temporal variability that may conceal possible regularities behind it. If a superimposition of temporal coding (Stevens & Zador, 1995) with highly precise average timing is assumed, inspection of some single-neuron simultaneous activity may seem to have little temporal precision at all. I hypothesize that central measures of spike latencies and oscillation periods may exhibit more regularity than currently expected.

Relating the several findings on discrete timing may contribute to the development of physiologically plausible neural network models. Such models may incorporate recurrent information flow, the DOIS, or both, and still use temporal coding. The different levels of temporal resolution discussed in this chapter make even nested levels of temporal coding possible: Synfire chain precision allows for different latencies of links relative to the typical intervolley interval and different link orders in a chain may, on a higher level, serve for temporal information coding. The short-term-memory model of Lisman and Idiart (1995) is an example of the latter.

In psychology better understanding of quantal timing may help to disentangle the contributions of discretely and continuously structured processes to mental operation. Consequently it may help to discover the functional algorithmic patterns and to resolve individually different processing strategies. The investigation of Petzold and Edeler (1995) is a nice example of this: Individually different characteristic periods in memory search were found to be differing multiples of the same period. There is a similar earlier finding of Sternberg, who observed that the search time per digit in memory search was the same in students and two kinds of participants with mental impairments, despite high absolute RT differences.

REFERENCES

Abeles, M. (1982). Role of cortical neuron: Integrator or coincidence detector? *Israel Journal of Medical Sciences, 18*, 83–92.

Abeles, M., & Prut, Y. (1996). *Precise firing times in the frontal cortex.* Paper presented at the workshop on Neural Information and Coding at Jackson Folge, Wyoming (Abstract). Retrieved on-line January 5, 2001, from http://www.sloan.salk.edu/~zador/JHabstracts2/node1.html

Abeles, M., Vaadia, E., Bergman, H., Prut, Y., Haalman, I., & Slovin, H. (1993). Dynamics of neuronal interactions in the frontal cortex of behaving monkeys. *Concepts in Neuroscience, 4* (2), 131–158.

Allan, L. G. (1971). Duration discrimination of brief light flashes. *Perception & Psychophysics, 9*, 327–334.

Allport, D. A. (1968). Phenomenal simultaneity and the perceptual moment hypothesis. *British Journal of Psychology, 59*, 395–406.

Amit, D. J. (1989). *Modeling brain function: The world of attractor neural networks.* Cambridge, England: Cambridge University Press.

Barlow, H. B. (1972). Single units and sensation: a neuron doctrine for perceptual psychology? *Perception, 1*, 371–394.

Basar, E., & Demiralp, T. (1995). Fast rhythms in the hippocampus are a part of the diffuse gamma-response system. *Hippocampus, 5*, 240–241.

Berger, H. (1938). *Das Elektroenkephalogramm des Menschen* [The human electroencephalogram]. Reprinted in Acta Nova Leopoldina. Neue Folge, 6, 173. Halle (Saale), Germany.

Berger, J. (1985). *Statistical decision theory and Bayesian analysis.* New York: Springer.

Berry, M. J., Warland, D. K, & Meister, M. (1997). The structure and precision of retinal spike trains. *Proceedings of the National Academy of Sciences, USA, 94*(10), 5411–5416.

Bienenstock, E. (1995). Model of neocortex. *Computation in Neural Systems, 6*, 179–224.

Brecher, G. A. (1932). Die Entstehung und biologische Bedeutung der subjektiven Zeiteinheit— des Moments [The emergence and biological significance of the subjective time unit perceptual moment]. *Zeitschrift für vergleichende Physiologie, 18*, 204–243.

Breitmeyer, B. G. (1984) *Visual masking: An integrative approach.* England: Oxford: Clarendon.

Broadbent, D. E. (1952). Speaking and listening simultaneously. *Journal of Experimental Psychology, 43*, 267–273.

Brysbaert, M. (1994). Behavioral estimates of interhemispheric transmission time and the signal detection method: A reappraisal. *Perception & Psychophysics, 56*, 479–490.

Burle, B., & Bonnet, M. (1999). What's an internal clock for? From temporal information processing to temporal processing of information. *Behavioural Processes, 45*, 59–72.

Burle, B., & Bonnet, M. (2000). High-speed memory scanning: A behavioral argument for a serial oscillatory model. *Cognitive Brain Research, 9*, 327–337.

Buzsáki, G., Horvath, Z., Urioste, R., Hetke, J., & Wise, K. (1992). High frequency network oscillation in the hippocampus. *Science, 256*, 1025–1027.

Chaudhuri, P., & Marron, J. S. (1999). SiZer for exploration of structures in curves. *Journal of the American Statistical Association, 94*, 807–823.

Chrobak J. J., & Buzsáki G. (1998). Gamma oscillations in the entorhinal cortex of the freely moving rat. *Journal of Neuroscience, 18*, 388–398.

Cowan, N. (2001). The magical number 4 in short-term memory: A reconsideration of mental storage capacity. *Behavioral and Brain Sciences, 24*, 87–114.

Dehaene, S. (1993). Temporal oscillations in human perception. *Psychological Science, 4*, 264–269.

Diesmann, M., Gewaltig, M. O., & Aertsen, A. (1999). Stable propagation of synchronous spiking in cortical neural networks. *Nature (London), 402*, 529–533.

Eckhorn, R. (1999). Neural mechanisms of visual feature binding investigated with microelectrodes and models. *Visual Cognition, 6*, 231–265.

Engel, A., König, P., Kreiter, A., Schillen, T., & Singer, W. (1992). Temporal coding in the visual cortex: New vistas on integration in the nervous system. *Trends in Neuroscience, 15*, 216–226.

Fabiani, M., Sohmer, H., Tait, C., Gafni, M., & Kinarti, R. (1979). A functional measure of brain activity: Brain stem transmission time. *Electroencephalography and Clinical Neurophysiology, 47*, 483–491.

Fechner, G. T. (1860). *Elemente der Psychophysik* [Elements of Psychophysics] (2nd edition). Leipzig: Breitkopf und Haertel.

Fellemann, D. J., & Van Essen, D. C. (1991). Distributed hierarchical processing in the primate cerebral cortex. *Cerebral Cortex, 1*, 1–47.

Fischer, B., & Weber, H. (1993). Vision and visual attention. *Behavioral and Brain Sciences, 16*, 553–610.

Geissler, H.-G. (1985). Sources of seeming redundancy in temporally quantized information processing. In G. d'Ydewalle (Ed.), *Cognition, information processing, and motivation* (pp. 233–241). Amsterdam: North-Holland.

Geissler, H.-G. (1987). The temporal structure of central information processing: Evidence for a tentative time-quantum model. *Psychological Research, 49*, 99–106.

Geissler, H.-G. (1992). New magic numbers in mental activity? On a taxonomic system for critical time periods. In H.-G. Geissler, S. W. Link, & J. T. Townsend (Eds.), *Cognition, information processing and psychophysics* (pp. 293–322). Hillsdale, NJ: Lawrence Erlbaum Associates.

Geissler, H.-G., Schebera, F.-U., & Kompass, R. (1999). Ultra-precise quantal timing: Evidence from simultaneity thresholds in long-range apparent movement. *Perception & Psychophysics, 61*, 707–726.

Gerstner, W., Kempter, R., van Hemmen, J. L., & Wagner, H. (1996). A neuronal learning rule for sub-millisecond temporal coding. *Nature (London), 383*, 76–78.

Gescheider, G. (1976). *Psychophysics: Method and theory*. Hillsdale, NJ: Lawrence Erlbaum Associates.

Gezeck, S., Fischer, B., & Timmer, J. (1997). Saccadic reaction times: A statistical analysis of multimodal distributions. *Vision Research, 37*, 2119–2131.

Graves, R. E. (1976). Are more items identified than can be reported? *Journal of Experimental Psychology: Human Learning and Memory, 2*, 208–214.

Grossberg, S. (1999). The link between brain learning, attention, and consciousness. *Consciousness and Cognition, 8*, 1–44.

Grossberg, S., & Grunewald, A. (1997). Cortical synchronization and perceptual framing. *Journal of Cognitive Neuroscience, 9*, 117–132.

Grossberg, S., & Somers, D. (1991). Synchronized oscillations during cooperative feature linking in a cortical model of visual perception. *Neural Networks, 4*, 453–466.

Harter, M. R., & White, C. T. (1968). Periodicity within reaction time distributions and electromyograms. *The Quarterly Journal of Experimental Psychology, 20*, 157–166.

Hebb, D. O. (1949). *The organization of behaviour.* New York: Wiley.

Hinton G. E., Dayan, P., Frey, B., & Neal, R. M. (1994). The wake–sleep algorithm for unsupervised neural networks. *Science, 268*, 1158–1161.

Hochreiter, S. & Schmidhuber, J. (1999). Feature extraction through LOCOCODE. *Neural Computation, 11*, 679–714,

Holt-Hansen, K. (1974). Duration of experienced lenghtening and shortening of straight lines. *Perceptual and Motor Skills, 39*, 987–996.

Hopfield, J. (1982). Neural networks and physical systems with emergent collective computational abilities. *Proceedings of the National Academy of Sciences, USA, 79*, 2554–2588.

Hopfield, J. J. (1995). Pattern recognition computation using action potential timing for stimulus representation. *Nature (London), 376*, 33–36.

Hubel, D. H., & Wiesel, T. N. (1977). Functional architecture of macaque monkey visual cortex (Ferrier lecture). *Proceedings of the Royal Society of London, Series B, 198*, 1–59.

Jaynes, E. T. (1995). *Probability theory: The logic of science* (fragmentary edition). Retrieved on-line February 10, 2001 from http://bayes.wustl.edu/etj/ prob.html

Kompass, R. (2001). *Analyse diskreter zeitlicher Strukturen perzeptiver Prozesse* [Analysis of discrete temporal structures in perceptual processes]. Lengerich, Germany: Pabst Science Publishers.

Kompass, R., Geissler, H.-G., & Schebera, F. (2003). Quantal timing in gamma movement. Manuscript submitted for publication.

Kristofferson, A. B. (1967). Successiveness discrimination as a two-state, quantal process. *Science, 158*, 1337–1339.

Kristofferson, A. B. (1980). A quantal step function in duration discrimination. *Perception & Psychophysics, 27*, 300–306.

Kristofferson, A. B. (1990). Timing mechanisms and the threshold for duration. In H.-G. Geissler (Ed.), in collaboration with M. H. Müller and W. Prinz, *Psychophysical explorations of mental structures* (pp. 269–277). Toronto: Hogrefe & Huber.

Lalanne, L. (1876). Sur la durée de la sensation tactile [On the duration of tactile sensations]. *Note Comptes Rendus de l'Acadenue des Sciences Paris, 1314–1316.

Laming, D. (1986). *Sensory analysis.* London: Academic Press.

Larkum, M. E., Zhu, J. J., & Sakman, B. (1999). A new cellular mechanism for coupling inputs arriving at different cortical layers. *Nature (London), 398*, 338–341.

Latour, P. L. (1967). Evidence of internal clocks in the human operator. *Acta Psychologica, 27*, 93–100, 341–348.

Lisman, J. E., & Idiart, M. A. P. (1995). Storage of 7 ± 2 short-term memories in oscillatory subcycles. *Science, 267*, 1512–1515.

Llinas, R., & Ribary, U. (1993). Coherent 40-Hz oscillation characterizes dream state in humans. *Proceedings of the National Academy of Sciences, USA, 90*, 2078–2081.

Luce, R. D., & Green, D. M. (1972). A neural timing theory for response times and the psychophysics of intensity. *Psychological Review, 79*, 14–57.

Markram, H., Lübke, J., Frotscher, M., & Sakman, B. (1997). Regulation of synaptic efficacy by coincidence of postsynaptic APs and EPSPs. *Science, 275*, 213–215.

McGill, W. J. (1963). Stochastic latency mechanisms. In R. Luce, R. R. Bush, & E. Galanter (Eds.), *Handbook of mathematical psychology* (Vol. 1, pp. 311–360). New York: Wiley.

Neisser, U. (1967). *Cognitive psychology.* New York: Appleton-Century-Crofts.

Neuhaus, W. (1930). Experimentelle Untersuchungen der Scheinbewegung. [Experimental investigation of apparent movement]. *Archiv für die gesamte Psychologie, 75*, 315–458.

O'Keefe, J., & Recce, M. L. (1993). Phase relationship between hippocampal place units and the EEG theta rhythm. *Hippocampus, 3*, 317–330.

Petzold, P., & Edeler (1995). Organization of person memory and retrieval processes in recognition. *European Journal of Social Psychology, 25*, 249–267.

Poffenberger, A. (1912). Reaction time to retinal stimulation with special reference to the time lost in conduction through nervous centres. *Archiv der Psychologie, 23*, 1–73.

Richmond, B. J., & Optican, L. M. (1990). Temporal encoding of two-dimensional patterns by single units in the primate visual cortex. II. Information transmission. *Journal of Neurophysiology, 64*, 370–380.

Rissanen, J. (1978). Modeling by shortest data description. *Automatica, 14*, 465–471.

Shadlen, M. N., & Newsome, W. T. (1994). Noise, neural codes and cortical organisation. *Current Opinion in Neurobiology, 4*, 569–579.

Simon, J. R., & Small, A. M., Jr. (1969). Processing auditory irrelevant information: Interference from an irrelevant cue. *Journal of Applied Psychology, 53*, 433–435.

Skaggs, W. E., & McNaughton, B. L. (1996). Replay of neuronal firing sequences in rat hippocampus during sleep following spatial experience. *Science, 271*, 1870–1873.

Softky, W. R., & Koch, C. (1993). The highly irregular firing of cortical cells is inconsistent with temporal integration of random EPSPs. *Journal of Neuroscience, 13*, 334–350.

Sperling, G. (1960). The information available in brief visual presentations. *Psychological Monographs, 74*, 1–29.

Springer, R. M., Deutsch, J. A., & Stanley, G. (1975). Double flashes from single pulses of light. *Perception & Psychophysics, 18*, 398–400.

Sternberg, S. (1966). High-speed scanning in human memory. *Science, 153*, 652–654.

Sternberg, S. (1969). Memory-scanning: Mental processes revealed by reaction-time experiments. *American Scientist, 57*, 421–457.

Stevens, C. F., & Zador, A. (1995). Neural coding: The enigma of the brain. *Current Biology, 5*, 1370–1371.

Stroud, J. M. (1955). The fine structure of psychological time. In H. Quastler, (Ed.), *Information theory in psychology* (pp. 140–207). Glencoe, IL: Free Press.

Townsend, J. T., & Ashby, F. G. (1983). *The stochastic modeling of elementary psychological processes*. Cambridge, England: Cambridge University Press.

Traub, R. D., Whittington, M. A., Stanford, I. M., & Jefferys, J. G. R. (1996). A mechanism for generation of long-range synchronous fast oscillations in the cortex. *Nature (London), 383*, 621–624.

Treisman, A. (1960). Contextual cues in selective listening. *Quarterly Journal of Experimental Psychology, 12*, 242–248.

Treisman, M. (1963). Temporal discrimination and the indifference interval: Implications for a model of the internal clock. *Psychological Monographs, 77*(Whole No. 576), 1–31.

Treisman, M., & Brogan, D. (1992). Time perception and the internal clock: Effects of visual flicker on the temporal oscillator. *European Journal of Cognitive Psychology, 4*, 41–70.

Treisman, M., Cook, N., Naish, P. L. N., & MacCrone, J. K. (1994). The internal clock: Electroencephalographic evidence for oscillatory processes underlying time perception. *The Quarterly Journal of Experimental Psychology, 47A* (2), 241–289.

Treisman, M., Faulkner, A., & Naish, P. L. N. (1992). On the relation between time perception and the timing of motor action: Evidence for a temporal oscillator controlling the timing of movement. *The Quarterly Journal of Experimental Psychology, 45A* (2), 235–263.

Treisman, M., Faulkner, A., Naish, P. L. N., & Brogan, D. (1990). The internal clock: Evidence for a temporal oscillator underlying time perception with some estimates of its characteristic frequency. *Perception, 19*, 705–743.

Tsal, Y., & Lavie, N. (1988). Attending to color and shape: The special role of location in selective visual processing. *Perception & Psychophysics, 44*, 15–21.

Uexkuell, J. von (1928). *Theoretische Biologie* [Theoretical biology] (2nd ed.). Berlin: Springer.

Uttal, W. R. (1996). Do bridges exist between psychophysics and neurophysiology? In S. Masin (Ed.), *Proceedings of the 12th Annual Meeting of the International Society for Psychophysics* (pp. 1–22). Padua, Italy: The International Society for Psychophysics.

Van der Heijden, A. H. C. (1992). *Selective attention in vision.* London, New York: Routledge.

Von Baer, K. V. (1864). Welche Auffassung der lebendigen Natur ist die richtige? Und wie ist diese Auffassung auf die Entomologie anzuwenden? [Which view of the living nature is the right one? And how is it to be applied to entomology?]. In H. Schmitzdorf (Ed.), *Reden, gehalten in wissenschaftlichen Versammlungen, und kleine Aufsätze vermischten Inhalts,* (pp. 237–283). St. Petersburg: Verlag der Kaiserlichen Hofbuchhandlung.

Von Békésy, G. (1936). Über die Hörschwelle und Fühlgrenze langsamer sinusförmiger Luftdruckschwankungen [Low-frequency thresholds for hearing and feeling]. *Annalen der Physik, 26* (5), 554–556.

Vroon, P. A. (1974). Is there a time quantum in duration experience? *American Journal of Psychology, 87,* 237–245.

Wehr, M., & Laurent, G. (1996). Odour encoding by temporal sequences of firing in oscillation neural assemblies. *Nature (London), 384,* 162–166.

Wickens, T. D. (1982). *Models for behavior: Stochastic processes in psychology.* San Francisco: Freeman.

Wundt, W. (1874). *Grundzüge der physiologischen Psychologie* [Basics of physiological psychology]. Leipzig: Verlag von W. Engelmann.

Zhang, L. I., ,Tao, H. W., Holt, C. E., Harris, W. A., & Poo, M. (1998) A critical window for cooperation and competition among developing retinotectal synapses. *Nature (London), 395,* 37–44.

21

Structural Information Theory and Visual Form

Emanuel Leeuwenberg
University of Nijmegen, The Netherlands

This chapter deals with a specific approach to visual form—the *structural information theory* or, briefly, SIT. In fact, this theory is on pattern structure, irrespective of whether this structure is visual. However, historically, SIT was developed in connection with visual perception research at the Nijmegen Institute for Cognition and Information (NICI). It was initialized by Leeuwenberg (1969) and elaborated on by various other researchers. Some attended to experimental evidence (Boselie & Leeuwenberg, 1986; Geissler, Klix, & Scheidereiter, 1978; Mens & Leeuwenberg, 1988; Restle, 1982; van Leeuwen, Buffart, & van der Vegt, 1988; van Lier, Leeuwenberg, & van der Helm, 1997; van Tuyl & Leeuwenberg, 1979), while others focused on theoretical issues (Buffart, Leeuwenberg, & Restle, 1983; Collard & Buffart, 1983; van der Helm & Leeuwenberg, 1991; van Lier, van der Helm, & Leeuwenberg, 1994).

The focus is on three characteristics of SIT in relation to visual form perception. As an introduction, a few general features of the approach are sketched, namely, assumptions on visual form perception, cornerstones of SIT, and SIT applications to visual form.

ASSUMPTIONS ON VISUAL FORM
PERCEPTION

Irrespective of whether perception deals with structured patterns or not, its research has a specific tricky character. All sciences, including perception research, are based on observations. Hence, in all sciences, perception is used as a mediating mental instrument of study. However, in perception research, perception is also the studied object; thus it is both topic and instrument of all investigations in this field.

This characteristic of perception research easily leads to confusion on these two functions and gives rise to the wrong conclusion that objects are the input stimuli of perception. As any research makes use of observations and aims at establishing properties of given objects, the assumption seems plausible that perception itself also establishes properties of given objects. However, rather the opposite is true: Perception establishes objects on the basis of stimulus properties. The stimulus, being its input, just consists of patches of light on various independent parts of the retina, and the role of perception is to assess which patches of light belong together and constitute objects. Thus these objects belong to the output of perception and not to the input. Indeed, an observer looks at a stimulus but does not see the stimulus.

An extra source of confusion is the fact that perception is rapid, without effort and beyond any conscious control. This suggests that perception is a trivial process of copying stimuli. In fact, this concept agrees with the aforementioned naive idea that objects belong to the visual input, implying that perception just turns objects into objects.

In my view, the mentioned misunderstanding explains why perception is hardly acknowledged by laypeople as a research topic and why perception is a topic of a young science. This science was not initialized until around 1900, primarily by Gestalt psychologists. Besides, perception is still approached by innumerable independent and loose theories, being plausible in some respects and untenable in other respects. In line with this fate and for similar arguments Aristotle made the following prediction: "In a shorter time more will be known about the most remote objects, namely the stars, than about the most close topic, namely perception".

The confusion of the visual output and input has a slightly different implication in the case in which perception deals with structured patterns. If knowledge about object categories is supposed to be the product of perception, perception is a trivial process if this knowledge is also a visual input. Indeed, memory traces of percepts of immediate context may affect the perception but merely that of visual ambiguous patterns (Rock, 1983). Beyond these restricted conditions, we assume that a separable autonomous process of form perception is not affected by acquired knowledge. This assumption is in line with the microgenetic experiments of Bachmann and Allik (1976) and of Mens and Leeuwenberg (1988) that show context effects of unambiguous patterns as the result of response biases. In my view, these observations at least justify a definition of visual form perception as a modular process that is not affected by acquired knowledge.

To a great extent the autonomy of perception is propagated by the Gestalt psychologists. They discovered the so-called Gestalt cues, which are properties of the retinal stimulus pattern that indicate which pattern elements are visually grouped together. The grouped pattern elements are supposed to reflect the perceived objects. However, the relative visual strengths of these cues are not specified. Therefore the Gestalt approach does not make clear to what extent these cues contribute to grouping pattern elements and how these cues are related within a pattern representation. My approach aims at solving this topic and integrating Gestalt cues.

Another basic assumption of my approach is that visual pattern representation is determined not by criteria dealing with the process but by criteria dealing with the final product of this process. This product is the visual stimulus representation. It is assumed to reflect the visual interpretation, including the segmentation and classification of a pattern. Thus the assumption is that perception aims at a pattern representation that satisfies certain criteria whereas the process aims at reaching this representation in one way or another. Without a doubt, the process from input to output is of great importance. Nevertheless, I perceive it as an issue of secondary relevance. Besides, information about the visual process is hardly accessible and is very ambiguous. The brain process reveals itself still piecemeal and incompletely. Therefore it is taken as a black box. After all, various kinds of processes can be hypothesized that lead to the same representation.

The Gestalt psychologists attempted to integrate their Gestalt cues by assuming a governing visual principle that is supposed to select the visually preferred representation from various hypothetical representations of the stimulus. Their principle is called the *law of pragnanz*. It means that the most "balanced," "harmonious," "plausible," and "concise" pattern representation is visually preferred. However, such attributes are not clearly defined. My approach deals with a related selection criterion, namely the *simplicity principle*. It states that the simplest representation is selected from innumerable possible representations of a pattern. In my approach this principle is well defined and allows quantitative predictions about the preferred pattern representation.

An alternative selection criterion is the *likelihood principle*. It states that the most likely representation is selected from innumerable possible representations of a pattern. Although this principle is appealing, as it guarantees veridical predictions, I refute this principle, again in the case of the perception of structured patterns, as the likelihood principle presumes the role of knowledge in form perception.

A distinction can be made between ontogenetic and phylogenetic knowledge. The first is acquired during a human's life span and the second during evolution. Indeed, the likelihood principle applies to cognition at the level at which knowledge is used, that is, in conscious reasoning that is of use, for instance, in scientific research. After all, the goal of scientific research is opposed to that of perception. As has been said, scientific research aims at establishing properties of objects whereas perception rather aims at establishing objects on the basis of stimulus properties. Its output is the input of scientific research.

CORNERSTONES OF SIT

SIT supplies a theoretical framework for representing structures. Whether these structures refer to visual patterns, auditory tone series, or DNA chains is irrelevant. It deals with ordered symbols irrespective of their semantic meaning. The theory is actually elaborated for series of ordered symbols. The goal is to account for the regular structure of the symbols, such as a symmetrical or a repetitive structure.

In my view, an essential feature of SIT can best be clarified for the actual symbol series **AAAAAA**. As it is given, this series is called a *primitive code*. The reason is illustrated as follows. Suppose **A** refers to an apple. Thus the series represents "apple, apple, apple, apple, apple, apple." Without doubt, this description is conceived of as unintelligent, because it takes no account of the insight that its components are identical. Another representation is "four apples plus two apples," or, in terms of symbols, $4 * (A) 2 * (A)$. It is better indeed but still not optimal, because it does not completely reflect all identities of the apples. For this reason "six apples," or, in terms of symbols, $6 * (A)$ is the best representation. The latter code optimally reflects the internal identity structure. Note that all three codes still represent the primitive code equally well.

A coincident property of the optimal code, $6 * (A)$, is its compactness. It comprises the least amount of the identifiable **A** symbols. This amount is called the *structural information load* (I). For **AAAAAA** the load is $I = 6$, whereas it is $I = 1$ for $6 *(A)$. Thus the choice of the best code is determined by the simplicity principle mentioned in the preceding section. It implies that the more a code is simple the more it describes regularity in a series. For having a simplicity principle that is operational and tenable, various questions have to be answered. In fact, all these questions are answered, some with formal proofs, by van der Helm and collaborators (van der Helm, 2000; van der Helm & Leeuwenberg, 1991, 1996; van der Helm, van Lier, & Leeuwenberg, 1992).

1.   What are regularities? As an answer, van der Helm proposed his so-called accessibility criterion (van der Helm & Leeuwenberg, 1991). His analysis of all possible structures reveals that just three kinds of regularity are of use. Two of them are repetition and bilateral symmetry.

2.   How is information load defined? In the past, various load measures were proposed, for instance, by Buffart and Leeuwenberg (1983), but the most recent and justifiable measure was proposed by van der Helm et al. (1992). It states that the load equals the number of elements on all "hierarchical" levels of a code. The

lowest-level elements are symbols, and the higher-level elements are chunks in the representation.

3. Is the simplicity principle justifiable, that is, veridical? The answer is positive for viewpoint-dependent aspects of objects. For aspects of objects independent of the viewpoint, the answer stems from algorithmic information theory and is tentatively positive (van der Helm, 2000).

4. Can the simplest code be established without an excessive search of all possible codes of a series? Indeed, part of an answer is offered by van der Helm's PISA algorithm (van der Helm & Leeuwenberg, 1986). It definitely establishes the simplest code of a given primitive series of symbols without an excessive search. In practice, the program needs a few seconds for finding the simplest code of a series of ~1,000 symbols.

SIT APPLICATIONS TO VISUAL FORM

The application of SIT to perception requires establishing which pattern elements are to be represented by symbols. Commonly we use line lengths and turns along the contour as elements of a simple surface, but any other heuristic for "semantic mapping" may be just as good. Desirable restrictions are that the pattern elements are visually relevant and that the stimulus can be reconstructed from the pattern elements. For a three-dimensional (3D) object we commonly make use of its two-dimensional (2D) surface components. Often the description reflects an hierarchical structure of these surface components.

From the illustration in the preceding section it is clear that the simplest code, 6 * (A), describes both the initial primitive code, AAAAAA, and the optimal identity structure. In the application to perception in which these symbols refer to pattern elements, the simplest code describes both the visual input and the output, depending on how the symbols are conceived.

If the symbols specify the quantities of pattern elements, the code describes the stimulus. The mental reconstruction of the stimulus from the simplest code leads to an image that is of use for deriving pattern properties that are not represented by the simplest code.

If the code disregards the preceding metrical aspects, the code describes the abstract structure of the pattern. This is of use for visual pattern classification. The *abstract code* describes all patterns with the regularities represented by the code. For instance, the simplest code of a parallelogram describes all parallelograms. These patterns differ only with respect to metrical aspects of their dimensions.

The preferred abstract pattern representation describes the class of patterns with the same structure, but also the pattern interpretation as revealed in experiments on serial pattern segmentation and surface completion. Related to surface completion are topics such as figure–ground, transparency, subjective contours, neon–illusion, assimilation and contrast.

Beside the simplest codes, there are three properties of the simplest codes that refer to visual salience effects. Two of them deal with quantitative measures:

1. *Pattern goodness* is determined by the amount of identical pattern elements as established by the simplest code and the total amount of elements of a pattern. This property is characteristic for a pattern and may affect the detection of symmetry and repeat structures.

2. *Preference strength* is determined by the information load of the simplest code and that of a rival code. It is characteristic for the visual interpretation of a pattern and may affect the detection of embedded figures and similarity judgments.

Another property of the simplest code, called *hierarchical dominance*, refers to a qualitative salience effect, but merely applies to shapes whose simplest code has a hierarchical structure. The assumption is that the highest hierarchical level refers to a more salient shape component than lower hierarchical levels do. This hierarchical dominance can be tested by prime experiments and has effects on temporal order, mental rotation, and unity and variety judgments.

PROCESS VERSUS REPRESENTATION CRITERIA FOR PATTERN CLASSIFICATION

From now on, we attend to three basic characteristics of the SIT approach that are the subjects of discussion. Although these characteristics are described in various publications within their own context, here they are presented within each other's context. To show their plausibility, they are each compared to emerge alternative models of perception.

The first topic deals with *process criteria versus representation criteria*. Process criteria merely apply to the choice of process stages whereas representation criteria merely apply to properties of the preferred pattern representation, being the product of perceptual processes. Here, we select just one process criterion and one representation criterion. Both deal with hierarchical structures.

A Process Criterion: Global Precedence

A simple process criterion is expressed by the *global-precedence* hypothesis of Navon (1977). His hypothesis remains appealing to students of perception. It states that the visual process starts with the global shape and ends with details. The global shape is the low-spatial-frequency structure. It misses differentiation of details and agrees with the pattern seen by squinting eyes. The details appear at increasing spatial-frequency levels. The relation between these levels is formally

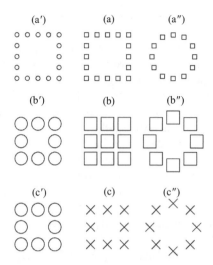

FIG. 21.1. Patterns designed for testing the global-precedence hypothesis.

well described by the scale–space model proposed by Koenderink & van Doorn (1976).

The global-precedence hypothesis is supposed to characterize the processing of 2D patterns, especially of configurations of separate equal subpatterns. At least, the classification experiments of Hoffman (1975) and Navon (1977) with these configurations have given rise to this hypothesis. An illustration is presented in Fig. 21.1.

Figures 21.1(a) and 21.1(a′) share global shapes, whereas Figs. 21.1(a) and 21.1(a″) share the detailed subpattern shapes. The first two figures are judged to be more related than the second two figures, and this classification supports the global-precedence hypothesis. However, this hypothesis has been criticized by various perception researchers.

Kinchla (1977) found that the hypothesis roughly holds if the stimuli do not exceed a visual angle of 7°. If they exceed this angle the details may be decisive for classification.

Martin (1979) demonstrated that the classification of compound patterns is not based on a categorical but on a gradual visual effect of the global shape. If the size of subpatterns increases and its amount decreases, the global effect decreases. This is illustrated by Figs. 21.1(b), 21.1(b′), and 21.1(b″). The judged similarity of the first two figures is approximately the same as the judged similarity of the latter two figures.

Furthermore, Kimchi and Palmer (1982) have shown that the structures of the subpatterns codetermine the pattern classification. An illustration is given for closed and open subpatterns in Figures 21.1(c), 21.1(c′), and 21.1(c″). The judged similarity of the first two figures is even less than the judged similarity of the latter two figures.

Finally, a restriction of the global-precedence hypothesis is concerned with color. A conflicting case of colors overrules almost any shape organization. For instance, if Fig. 21.1(a′) is blue and Figs. 21.1(a) and 21.1(a″) are red, the latter two parts are probably grouped together (Beck, 1982; de Weert, 1999).

The following comment is more general. If the global-precedence hypothesis is restricted to special compound texture-alike configurations, a preliminary stage has to be supposed that precedes the processing of the global shape. This preliminary stage should identify stimuli as compound texture-alike configurations. It should occur on the basis of their characteristics, which are the global structures and the subpatterns. However, these characteristics are precisely the pattern aspects that are classified in the stages dictated by the global-precedence hypothesis itself. It implies that stimulus classification should precede stages for establishing stimulus classification.

The global-precedence hypothesis applies to the perceptual domain of art production indeed. Usually, painters and composers of music begin with a global sketch and end with the elaboration of details. This order is efficient, as the global shape can be drawn without subpatterns, whereas subpatterns cannot be drawn without their positions being determined by the global shape. Internally correct subpatterns, which are at wrong positions, have to be redrawn. However, art is opposed to perception: Art deals with the process from code to pattern, whereas perception deals with the process from pattern to code.

A Representation Criterion: Descriptive Hierarchy

Another assumption is that the quality of the process product, being the representation, determines the interpretation of a pattern and its salience. We first focus on configurations whose global shapes specify only the positions of the subpatterns. These configurations give rise to metrical hierarchy. Later we consider configurations whose global shapes specify both the positions and the orientations of the subpatterns. Such configurations give rise to structural hierarchy.

Metrical Hierarchy. We consider again the kinds of configurations used by Navon (1977). These are shown in Fig. 21.2. Their subpatterns are in parallel, that is, they have the same orientation. This implies that the global shape specifies the positions of the subpatterns and not their orientations. Care is taken that the amount of subpatterns is equal to the amount of points in each subpattern. The reason will subsequently become clear. The assumption is that the code of each pattern describes two components, namely an S structure and an ellipsoidal structure. Our concern is with the relations between these components.

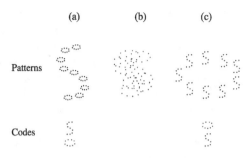

FIG. 21.2. Patterns characterized by metrical hierarchy. The difference between the patterns is merely due to the size of its components.

Figure 21.2(a) is conceived of as an S structure of ellipsoidal subpatterns, whereas Fig. 21.2(c) is conceived of as an ellipse of S-shaped subpatterns. These concepts are reflected by the visualized and informal codes presented below the figures. In each code, the upper part refers to the global shape and the lower part to the subpattern. In this way, these codes reflect hierarchical structures. Our concern is the character of this hierarchy.

The relations between the three patterns in Fig. 21.2 reveal this character. From Fig. 21.2(a) to Fig. 21.2(c), the size of the global S structure gradually decreases and the size of ellipsoidal substructure gradually increases. Figure 21.2(b) is an intermediate step. As a result, the hierarchy of Fig. 21.2(c) seems to be opposed to the hierarchy of Fig. 21.2(a). However, this is not true. Each pattern of Fig. 21.2 can be represented by two hierarchical codes. One reflects an S structure of ellipsoidal subpatterns, and the other reflects an ellipse of S-shaped subpatterns.

This conclusion can also be derived from their codes, if these are perceived as recipes for pattern reconstruction. In that case, each code should be accomplished with information about the orientation of the subpatterns with respect to the global structure. Then each code describes three reconstruction stages. These stages are illustrated first for the reconstruction of Fig. 21.2(a), from its most plausible code presented below this figure: First, construct an S shape of points. Second, attach an orientation at each point. Third, attach an ellipse at each orientation. Note that the ellipses do not overlap each other. In other words, the ellipses are "spatially contiguous." Another reconstruction is possible from the code with a reverse hierarchy. The three stages are as follows: First, construct a small ellipse of points. Second, attach an orientation at each point. Third, attach a large S shape at each orientation. This reconstruction of Fig. 21.2(a) is correct although contraintuitive. After all, the various S-shaped subordinate structures overlap each other, that is, they are not spatially contiguous. According to van der Helm and Leeuwenberg (1996), pattern codes are subdue to *spatial contiguity*. It means that code components should refer to well-separated pattern components.

The spatial-contiguity constraint favors the salience of the global shape, and its extension is merely a quantitative or "metrical" pattern aspect. This idea is in line with MacKay's view (1969) that the extension of a structure contributes to its "weight of evidence." However, according to this analysis, the processing of the global structure does not precede the processing of the subpatterns, as advocated by Navon (1977). The global structure is just dominant over details merely because of its extension. Eventually global precedence can be taken as a suggestive side effect of global dominance. Thus, for configurations of parallel-oriented subpatterns, there is no structural argument but just a metrical argument for the visual dominance of the global structure.

Structural Hierarchy.   Now codes are considered that are hierarchical both with respect to the positions and to the local orientations of substructures. In Figs. 21.3(a) and 21.3(b), patterns are shown with such hierarchical codes. Their substructures are not in parallel, but are constant with respect to the local orientations of the global shape.

For Fig. 21.3(a), two codes can be considered. According to one code, the pattern is described as an S structure of points that specify both the positions and the orientations of ellipses. These orientations are orthogonal to the local orientations of the S structure. This code is visualized in Fig. 21.3(a′) by an S at the top and an ellipse at the bottom. The orientation that relates the S and the ellipse, is not indicated in this visualized code. The code describes the following three stages for reconstructing the pattern: Construct an S shape of points, specify a 90° angle at each point, and attach an ellipse to each angle.

According to another code, shown in Fig. 21.3(a″), the pattern is described as an ellipse of points that specify both the positions and the orientations of S shapes. However, all these S shapes are slightly different. Besides, almost all local orientations of these S shapes are slightly different. Thus this code is very complex and therefore implausible. The hierarchy of the latter code is appropriate for the simple code of Fig. 21.3(b), shown in Fig. 21.3(b′). Its complex and implausible

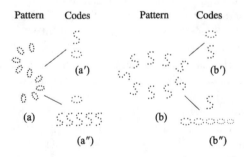

FIG. 21.3.   The two patterns, (a) and (b), are characterized by structural hierarchy: Their upper codes are more simple than their bottom codes.

Shape   Codes   Shape   Codes

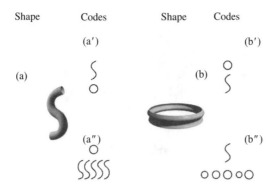

FIG. 21.4. The two objects, (a) and (b) are characterized by structural hierarchy: Their upper codes are more simple than their bottom codes.

code is illustrated by Fig. 21.3(b″). It describes an S structure of ellipses. All these ellipses have different sizes: In the center of Fig. 21.3(b), the ellipses are small, and outside the center they are large.

Similar to the 2D configurations in Fig. 21.3, the 3D objects in Fig. 21.4 can be represented each by a simple and a complex code. Again the substructures are arranged orthogonal to the global structure. Their subpattern orientations are not 2D but 3D. In the simple code of Fig. 21.4(a), the S-shape is the highest code component, and in the simple code of Fig. 21.4(b), the circle is the highest code component. Their alternative codes, having reversed hierarchies, are very complex.

The difference between the aforementioned metrical hierarchy and the more complete hierarchy under discussion is the following. In case of a pure metrical hierarchy, codes with opposed hierarchies are equally complex. This is actually because the parallel orientations of the subpatterns are not determined by the global structure. For the more complete hierarchy under discussion this is not the case: The codes with opposing hierarchies are not equally complex. Therefore the latter, more complete, hierarchy is called a structural hierarchy, and we call the highest level of this structural hierarchy, not a global structure, but a *superstructure*, and the lowest level not a substructure, but a *subordinate structure*.

For all shapes in Figs. 21.3 and 21.4, the global structures coincide with the superstructures. Indeed, this is valid for codes of 2D configurations, but not necessarily for codes of 3D objects. In Fig. 21.5 an illustration is given in which this coincidence is absent. It presents a vase object with its simplest structural code. Like the simplest code of Fig. 21.4(b), this code consists of a circular superstructure and an S-shaped subordinate structure. Because the circle is small and the S shape extended, we can conceive of neither the circle as the global structure nor the S shape as the substructure.

Shape   Code

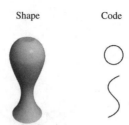

FIG. 21.5.   The superstructure does not coincide with the global structure.

In line with the previous global-dominance assumption for codes with metrical hierarchy, the hypothesis is made that the superstructure is dominant because of its high-level position in codes with structural hierarchy (Leeuwenberg & van der Helm, 1991). To ensure that the dominance of the superstructure cannot be attributed to global dominance, appropriate experiments deal with 3D objects.

Here a brief sketch is given of an experiment by van Lier that is designed to test the superstructure-dominance hypothesis and, in general, the visual relevance of structural hierarchy of shape representation (van Lier et al., 1997). He makes use of the prime-matching paradigm (Sekuler & Palmer, 1992). In each trial, he presented a test pair of object drawings, preceded by a prime. This prime agreed either with the superstructure or with the subordinate structure of the test objects. The object matching was found to be facilitated more by priming superstructures than by priming subordinate structures. Care is taken that the superstructures of shapes in the experiment do not coincide with their global structures. Therefore the global-precedence hypothesis does not explain the results.

Summary

Navon explains the perceptual classification of compound configurations, characterized by a global shape and many separate equal subpatterns, on the basis of a process criterion. According to his global-precedence hypothesis, the processing of the global shape precedes the processing of the subpatterns. However, various factors, such as the number, the size, the shape, and the color of the subpatterns, undermine this hypothesis. An alternative explanation of SIT assumes a representation criterion. In the case in which the global shape merely determines the positions of the subpatterns, the global shape is not precedent, but rather is dominant because of its size. Such configurations are characterized by metrical hierarchy. In the case in which a shape determines both the positions and the orientations of the subpatterns, the configurations are characterized by a structural hierarchy of superstructures and subordinate structures. It means that one code is more simple than the other code with a reverse hierarchy. The superstructure does not necessarily coincide with the global shape. Prime-matching experiments support the superstructure-dominance assumption.

CODES FROM COMPONENTS VERSUS COMPONENTS FROM CODES

From now on, our discussion is restricted to representation models, and again, we chose just one approach as opponent: the "recognition-by-components" (RBC) model, proposed by Biederman (1987). This model provides an appealing account of object perception but differs in many respects from SIT.

Codes from Components: RBC

The basic idea of RBC is that visual scenes are composed of components in the same way that words are composed of letters. For words, less than ~26 letters are sufficient. For describing complex objects, Biederman (1987) discerns 24 simple geometric components, such as cones, wedges, blocks and cylinders, which he refers to as "geons." Some are shown in Fig. 21.6.

Any complex object can be seen as a composition of geons, and the border between two geons is supposed to be inferred from local concavities. The geons themselves are each supposed to be identified or recognized from the retinal properties of their projections.

Here, we consider neither the actual geon identification process, as elaborated by Biederman, nor his experiments, which show how well geons are visually identified from projections of complex and degraded objects. We merely consider how simple objects are classified as geons on the basis of variable aspects of their retinal properties. In Fig. 21.6, this geon classification is illustrated. Four aspects of a given geon determine its code. Three aspects apply to the cross section and one aspect deals with the axis of a geon. The cross section is assumed to be orthogonal

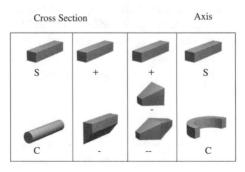

FIG. 21.6. An illustration of Biederman's (1987) geon representation (RBC).

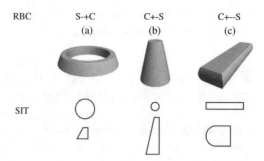

FIG. 21.7. According to RBC, the objects (b) and (c) are similar. According to SIT, the objects (a) and (b) are similar.

to the axis. Commonly, the axis is the longest component of a geon object. If there is no longest component, the axis is the one for which the cross section is constant or symmetric. The four aspects are as follows:

1. *Edge cross section*: The contour of the cross-section consists of either straight-line segments (**S**) or includes one or more curves (**C**).
2. *Symmetry cross section*: The cross section is either bilaterally symmetrical (+) or not bilaterally symmetrical (−).
3. *Course cross section*: Going along the axis, the cross section is constant (+), expanding (−), or both expanding and contracting (−−).
4. *Shape axis*: The axis is either straight (**S**) or curved (**C**).

The four variables, with their two or three subcategories each, give rise to 2 * 2 * 3 * 2 = 24 geons and specify each geon code. In Fig. 21.7, some geon codes are illustrated. They are given above each shape.

The geon code of Fig. 21.7(a) is **S** − + **C**. The longest component of the object is a circle, and the cross section a trapezoid. The **S** stems from the straight edges of the cross section, the − is due to the asymmetry of the cross section, the + refers to the constant crosssection, and the **C** refers to the circular axis.

For the object in Fig. 21.7(b), the geon code is **C** + − **S**. The longest component is a straight vertical axis. The cross section is a gradually increasing circle.

The geon code of Fig. 21.7(c) is **C** + − − **S**. The longest component is a straight line. The cross section is an increasing and decreasing rectangle with a circular component.

Components from Codes: SIT

According to RBC, the cross section and axis components of a geon are prespecified by stimulus properties. The reverse applies to SIT. According to SIT, the simplest code of an object is primary and the object components are derived from the simplest code. This is subsequently demonstrated.

As an introduction to object components, we first focus on the classification of objects. As was argued in the previous section, the simplest SIT code of Fig. 21.7(a) consists of a circle as superstructure and a trapezoid as subordinate structure. This code, shown at the bottom of this figure, is in agreement with the RBC code, or, more specifically, the superstructure agrees with the axis of the RBC code. However, the arguments for this common structure are different. The choice of the circular axis of the RBC code is based on its length, that is, a metrical and not a structural aspect of the object, whereas the choice of the circular superstructure of the SIT code is based on the simplicity of this code. A SIT code of Fig. 21.7(a) with a reversed hierarchy, that is, with a trapezoid as superstructure and circles as subordinate structures, is very complex.

For this same reason, the SIT code of Fig. 21.7(b), shown at the bottom of this figure, consists of a circle as superstructure and a trapezoid as subordinate structure. However, for this figure, this superstructure does not agree with the axis but with the cross section of its RBC code. Thus sometimes the superstructure agrees with the axis and sometimes with the cross section of the RBC code.

RBC and SIT components may also differ with respect to their shapes. Axes in RBC codes either are straight lines or (semi)circles, whereas superstructures in SIT codes may have any shape. For instance, the superstructure in the simplest SIT code of Fig. 21.7(c) is a rectangle.

In fact, the SIT code of Fig. 21.7(c), shown at the bottom of this figure, describes the way in which a carpenter would construct this object. Probably a carpenter would take a rectangular plank and manufacture its sides with a U-shaped saw. In this sense, a SIT code is taken as a procedural description, being a formula for the construction of the represented object.

Note that the RBC codes of Figs. 21.7(a) and 21.7(b) are completely different and those of Figs. 21.7(b) and 21.7(c) are almost equal, whereas the SIT codes of Figs. 21.7(a) and 21.7(b) are equal and those of Figs. 21.7(b) and 21.7(c) are completely different. The latter code relations agree with the visual relations established by a judged similarity experiment (Leeuwenberg, van der Helm, and van Lier, 1994).

Code components have an impact on relations not only between objects but also on relations within objects. According to SIT, a complex object is taken as a whole. If its simplest code consists of separate components, the visual object is assumed to reveal segments, and inversely, if its simplest code does not consist of separate components, the object should not reveal visual segments. This is illustrated in the next paragraph.

Figure 21.8(a) is commonly perceived as a dual shape and Figs. 21.8(b) and 21.8(c) as unitary shapes. RBC does not make this differentiation. Each object consists of just two geons. This is not true for SIT. Only the code of Fig. 21.8(a) has two superstructures: The superstructure of the upper part is a semicircle and the superstructure of the bottom part is a complete circle. The other two shapes are

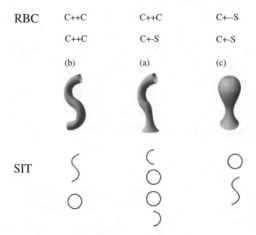

FIG. 21.8. According to SIT, (b) and (c) are integrated objects, whereas (a) is a "dual" object. According to RBC, all three objects are equally dual.

each described by a single superstructure. The superstructure of Fig. 21.8(b) is an S shape, and the superstructure of Fig. 21.8(c) is a circle. Because superstructures are the most decisive components of codes, these codes explain why Fig. 21.8(a) is commonly perceived as a dual shape and Figs. 21.8(b) and 21.8(c) as unitary shapes. This is shown by van Bakel (1989).

Summary

The differences between RBC and SIT are as follows: (a) According to RBC, a complex object is taken as a composition of elementary object components, called geons. Each geon is characterized by prespecified properties of its cross section and axis. According to SIT, there are no prespecified object components. The simplest code of a whole complex object is primary, and the object components are derived from the simplest code. (b) In as far as RBC coding deals with hierarchy, the hierarchy is primarily determined by metrical aspects of shapes. After all, the axis of a geon is the longest object component. Besides, the axis is either straight or circular. A SIT code deals primarily with structural hierarchy determined by the simplicity of the representation. There is no restriction on the shape of its superstructure and of its subordinate structure. The superstructure coincides with either the cross section or with the axis of a geon. As a consequence, the RBC and the SIT classifications of objects are different.

THE LIKELIHOOD VERSUS THE
SIMPLICITY PRINCIPLE OF PERCEPTION

Commonly, one interpretation of the countless possible interpretations of a pattern is visually preferred. According to the likelihood principle, this preferred stimulus interpretation agrees with the most probable actual structure in reality. Thus this interpretation has an external origin. Of course, this external structure has to be known. According to the simplicity principle, the preferred interpretation reflects the simplest representation of the pattern. This interpretation has an internal origin.

In the discussion of the likelihood principle, two factors of the Bayes rule are relevant. One factor is the prior or unconditional probability. It accounts for the frequencies of structures that are present in the real world. These structures, taken irrespectively of their viewpoint, are supposed to be stored in memory during evolution by our ancestors. This factor is called *world-based likelihood*. The other factor deals with the conditional probability that a hypothetical structure produces the actual retinal stimulus. In the case in which this structure is a 3D object, its conditional likelihood is determined by the projective invariance under varying viewpoints. For this reason this factor is called *view-based likelihood*. In fact, the unconditional and the conditional factors are also relevant for the simplicity principle.

The Likelihood Principle: Regularity
Derived From Sets

View-Invariant Properties. The RBC of Biederman (1987) makes use of nonaccidental properties (NAPs), and the validity of these NAPs is supposed to be based on the likelihood principle. Here NAPs and their use are briefly explained.

NAPs are properties of retinal projections that are assumed to hold for 3D objects. For instance, the linearity or straightness of a line is a NAP, because a straight line probably is the projection of a straight edge in three dimensions from a general point of view. The argument is that the projection of a straight edge, under any orientation or viewpoint, is steadily a straight line, whereas the projection of, say, a hook shape, given the restricted visual resolution of vision, rarely is a straight line. The specific length of a line is not a NAP, as a short line may be the projection of a short but also of a long edge under a certain slant. Therefore quantitative aspects are not considered to be NAPs.

Not only linearity, but also symmetry and parallellity are NAPs. However, the latter two properties are less-invariant NAPs. Under some orientations, symmetrical and parallel structures in 3D space do not generate symmetrical and parallel projections. Indeed, asymmetrical and nonparallel structures rarely generate symmetrical and parallel projections.

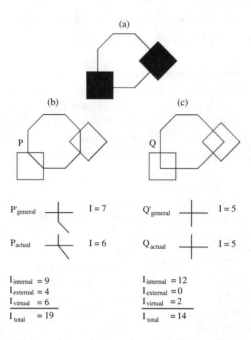

FIG. 21.9. Objects (b) and (c) are interpretations of (a). According to Kanisza (Kanizsa & Gerbino, 1982), the simplicity principle favors (b), whereas (c) is visually preferred. According to van Lier's coding analysis (van Lier, van der Helm, & Leeuwenberg, 1994), the simplicity principle still favors (c).

Invariant Compositions.   We have referred to the general-viewpoint assumption for explaining the view-based likelihood interpretation of stimulus properties. This assumption is that each stimulus usually presents itself such that it does not bring forward coincidental features that might be due to a specific accidental point of view. A milder version of this general-viewpoint assumption is Rock's "avoidance of coincidence principle." Rock (1983) applies this principle not only to views of objects but also to positions and orientations of 2D pattern components. His principle is illustrated by visual interpretations of an occlusion pattern.

Figure 21.9(a), designed by Kanizsa and Gerbino (1982), can be interpreted in two ways. The interpretation of Fig. 21.9(b) as two black squares occluding a regular polygon is not preferred, whereas the other interpretation of Fig. 21.9(c) as two black squares occluding an irregular polygon is commonly preferred.

The explanation of Rock (1983) is as follows. In Fig. 21.9(b), the position of the squares and the position of the regular polygon are very coincidental and therefore improbable. At each junction between the square and the polygon, the contour of this polygon makes a turn. A small displacement of the polygon would dramatically change the stimulus pattern toward a more general-view image of the hypothetical surfaces (Buffart et al., 1983). Therefore this interpretation should be avoided. As this coincidence is absent in Fig. 21.9(c), this interpretation is preferred.

The Simplicity Principle: Sets Derived From Regularity

Any model of perception should explain and not assume visual classification. Thus any model of perception should merely assume nonvisual "template" categories for each stimulus. However, the two previously presented approaches, based on the likelihood principle, namely invariant-view properties and invariant compositions, do not satisfy this requirement. Before the simplicity principle is discussed, their negative implications for line interpretations are illustrated by reference to the Bayes rule.

Comment on View-Invariant Properties. Here we discuss the linearity NAP. According to this NAP, a retinal straight line probably is the projection of a straight edge and not the projection of an edge that is not straight. Thus with respect to the view-based likelihood of the Bayes rule, the linearity NAP is justifiable. However, with respect to the world-based likelihood of the Bayes rule, the linearity NAP is hardly justifiable. Straight edges and nonstraight edges are not two equally probable options. There are, in principle, a few straight edges, whereas there are, in principle, countless template categories of nonstraight line edges with varying numbers of angles whose projections may still give rise to straight lines, given the restricted visual resolution. Besides, a set of possible complex edges of each category is larger than a set of possible simple edges.

Indeed, what counts are the actual numbers of straight and nonstraight template categories, and, without doubt, these actual numbers deviate from the numbers of possible different versions of edges. If the actual numbers would agree with the possible numbers, the world would be completely chaotic. This world would allow neither perception nor life. However, as researchers, we do not have any access to information about the actual frequencies of view-independent structures. Hence, it is implausible that the world-based likelihood of the Bayes rule can be specified, and the question cannot be answered whether the preceding indicated view-based likelihood of linearity overrules the world-based likelihood. A solution is to assume that perception is a priori sensitive to regularity and selects the simplest stimulus representation that describes a maximum of regularity.

Comment on Invariant Compositions. Here Rock's (1983) avoidance of coincidence principle is discussed through use of the illustration in Fig. 21.10. Figure 21.10(a) can be interpreted as a single cross object [Fig. 21.10(a′)] or as two sticks, one overlapping the other [Fig. 21.10(a″)]. Figure 21.10(b) can be interpreted as a single long stick [Fig. 21.10(b′)] or as two small sticks, one in line with the other [Fig. 21.10(b″)]. According to Rock's avoidance of coincidence principle,

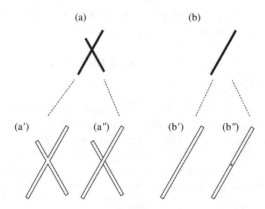

FIG. 21.10. Pattern (a) is rather interpreted as a composition of two objects, i.e., as (a″) instead of (a′). In contrast, pattern (b) is rather interpreted as one single object, i.e., as (b′) instead of (b″). According to Rock (1983), the likelihood principle provides an explanation whereas, according to SIT, this explanation is invalid.

Fig. 21.10(a) is seen rather as a composition of two small sticks and Fig. 21.10(b) as one single long stick. The reasoning is that the probability of throwing two matchsticks with the result of an arbitrary composition [Fig. 21.10(a″)] is larger than that with the result of a good continuing composition [Fig. 21.10(b″)].

My comment is as follows. The probability of throwing two matchsticks with the result of the actual composition of Fig. 21.10(a″) is approximately equal to the probability of throwing two matchsticks with the result of the actual composition of Fig. 21.10(b″).

Indeed, the probabilities are different if each composition is conceived of as representing a class of sticks with the same regular structure. Only under this condition is the class size of collinear sticks smaller than the class size of "randomly" positioned matches. However, the difference between these class sizes is determined by the regularity of these configurations itself. Hence, beforehand, perception should be sensitive to regularity. In other words, visual categorization is needed on the basis of regularity detection, that is, on the basis of the simplicity principle. This means that the avoidance of coincidence principle presupposes that regularity should be inferred from different class sizes whereas these different class sizes actually stem from different regularities themselves.

So far, the circularity of this likelihood explanation applies to the conditional view component of the Bayes rule. Without this circularity, the outcome of this view component is actually indifferent. For Fig. 21.10(b), there is even a reason to doubt about the preference for the single long stick interpretation of Fig. 21.10(b′). This reason stems from the unconditional world likelihood. The argument is as follows: There are more short lines than long lines because long lines consist of many short lines whereas short lines do not consist of long lines. Thus, as only template pattern categories are allowed, the conclusion is that the world-based likelihood of the Bayes rule favors short lines. This implies that the whole Bayes account of the likelihood principle even may favor the interpretation of Fig. 21.10(b″).

As has been said, researchers do not have any access to information about the actual template categories of structures and about their frequencies. It is even a question as to whether the visual system itself has access to the actual frequency distribution of objects in the world. If so, we have to assume that the visual system of our ancestors, over the time span of evolution, stored all perceived objects and all their frequencies and that this information is hereditary. The main bottleneck is that our ancestors dealt with retinal images, but the useful information deals with frequencies of viewpoint independent objects. Thus our ancestors also coped with the object interpretation of retinal images (Rock, 1983). In other words, the unconditional likelihood principle is equally circular as the conditional likelihood principle: The presupposition is that perception explains perception (Hoffman, 1996).

Simplest Compositions. Figure 21.9(a) was actually designed by Kanizsa and Gerbino (1982) to demonstrate that perception not always tends to "global simplicity" but sometimes tends to "local simplicity." As said, the irregular polygon interpretation, shown in Fig. 21.9(c), is preferred above the regular polygon interpretation, shown in Fig. 21.9(b). It is only at the local level that Fig. 21.9(c) is simpler than Fig. 21.9(b). However, according to Kanizsa and Gerbino, the actual simplicity principle should apply to the whole pattern.

van Lier was not convinced by Kanizsa's argument. He developed a model that integrated global and local simplicity (van Lier et al., 1994). For each interpretation of a pattern, he discerned three structures. One is the *internal structure*. This structure refers to the viewpoint-independent surface components that are assumed by the stimulus interpretation under consideration (in fact, this structure corresponds to the unconditional factor of the Bayes rule). The other two structures refer to viewpoint-dependent aspects of the pattern (they correspond to the conditional factor of the Bayes rule). The latter two structures deal with the way the actual stimulus reveals the hypothetical surfaces that constitute the internal structure.

One viewpoint-dependent pattern aspect is the *external structure*. This structure reflects the positions and orientations of the hypothetical surfaces in the way these appear from the perceiver's point of view. The more these positions and orientations are arbitrary and in line with the general viewpoint, the more the assumed surfaces of the internal structure are independent and the more the hypothesized interpretation is supported. If these positions and orientations are coincidental and regular, they give rise to misleading visual associations between the hypothetical surfaces. Thus coincidental positions and orientations undermine the hypothetical interpretation.

The other viewpoint-dependent pattern aspect is the *virtual structure*. This structure consists of the occluded part that is being imagined by the perceiver. The more invisible the stimulus elements, the less the support for the interpretation. van Lier has shown that the three structures can be varied independently of each other (van Lier et al., 1994). Of greatest importance is that he expressed these structures in terms of information load and not in terms of probabilities. The load of each structure contributes to the total load of an interpretation.

Here his approach is illustrated for the two interpretations of Fig. 21.9(a). The internal structure of the interpretation, shown in Fig. 21.9(b), consists of two squares and the regular polygon. The load of the two squares is $I = 3 + 3$, and the load of the regular polygon is $I = 3$. In contrast, the internal structure of the alternative interpretation [Fig. 21.9(c)] consists of two squares and the irregular polygon. Their loads, respectively, are $I = 3 + 3$ and $I = 6$. Thus if the interpretation selection were to be determined merely by the internal structure, Kanizsa's conclusion would be correct: The simplest interpretation is not preferred.

However, there is more. The more the positions and orientations of surfaces are coincidental and deviate from the general-viewpoint structure, the more the load of the external structure should be. This load is assessed for each local junction between the two hypothetical surfaces. The quantification of this load is illustrated for the top junction P in Fig. 21.9(b). This load is equal to the load of P ($I = 7$) of the junction in a general-viewpoint version minus the load of P ($I = 6$) of the actual more regular junction. Thus the load of this junction is $I = 1$. It reflects one coincidence. There are four such junctions; thus the load of the external structure is $I = 4$. In the same way, the load of the external structure of Fig. 21.9(c) is specified for Q junctions. This load is $I = 0$, because their actual junctions agree with the general-viewpoint structures. These actual junctions do not reveal any coincidence.

The load of the virtual structure is specified by the amount of angles and lines between these angles in the invisible part. For the option in Fig. 21.9(b), the load of the virtual structure is $I = 3 + 3$ (behind each square: two angles and one line). For the option in Fig. 21.9(c), the load of the virtual structure is $I = 1 + 1$ (behind each square: one angle). As a result, the total load of Fig. 21.9(c), $I = 14$, is less than the total load of Fig. 21.9(b), $I = 19$. This predicts the visual preference of Fig. 21.9(c).

According to this formula, van Lier has analyzed 144 figures, and for 96% of these figures his predictions appeared to agree with the visual interpretations (van Lier et al., 1994).

Summary

The distinction between viewpoint-dependent and viewpoint-independent aspects of pattern interpretations is relevant for comparing the likelihood and the simplicity principles. With respect to the viewpoint-dependent pattern aspects, the predictions on completion phenomena stemming from the likelihood principle coincide with those of the simplicity principle indeed. However, the likelihood principle predicts pattern classification by presuming pattern classification. With respect to the viewpoint-independent pattern aspects the likelihood explanation is equally circular, although its predictions may differ from those of the simplicity principle (van der Helm, 2000).

The simplicity principle seems to favor global completion of occlusion patterns whereas, in some cases, local completion is visually preferred (Kanizsa & Gerbino, 1982). Thus this principle seems to be falsified. However, van Lier has shown that this is not true if viewpoint-dependent aspects of the patterns are taken into account (van Lier et al., 1994). Simplicity, which applies to both the hypothesized surfaces and to their positions, explains visual occlusion phenomena rather well.

DISCUSSION

SIT's merits for explaining visual pattern classification were emphasized. However, the fact that SIT merely deals with a representation criterion for selecting structure implies an obvious gap. Beforehand, it does not supply an algorithm of the process from stimulus to representation. A subproblem concerns the character of the primitive code of a visual stimulus. However, note that this is not an issue of SIT, being a syntactic theory on structure representation, but of the semantics of visual form within the domain of SIT application. My comment on this topic is as follows.

In perception, the process order is supposed to start with the stimulus and to end with the representation. However, according to the SIT approach, only the reverse order is accessible:

$$\text{stimulus} \leftarrow \text{primitive code} \leftarrow \text{reduced code.}$$

The reason is that a reduced code describes just one primitive code, and a primitive code describes just one stimulus, whereas a stimulus can be described by many different correct primitive codes, and a primitive code can be described by many different reduced codes. The descriptive simplicity principle implies that all possible reduced codes of a stimulus should be tested to select the simplest code. However, this gives rise to the question of whether the simplicity principle is a tenable and realistic principle.

Indeed, in part an answer is offered by van der Helm's PISA algorithm (van der Helm & Leeuwenberg, 1986), which makes use of the shortest route solution. As was stated in the introduction, it definitely establishes the simplest code of a given primitive series of symbols without an explosive search of all possible codes. However, van der Helm does not claim to offer a model of perception.

There is, so far, no solution for the processing of stimuli that are supposed to stand for projections of 3D objects. Their coding gives rise to an extra problem: Within the constraint of projective geometry, a single proximal stimulus may be the projection of countless distal objects, each described by a different primitive code. Thus, in practice, the coding of these stimuli requires the intervention of human intuition. Even a simple 2D proximal pattern gives rise to many options for primitive representations within the constraint that a code should represent the stimulus. In other words, the semantic mapping of visual patterns is still a topic of study.

REFERENCES

Bachmann, T. & Allik, J. (1976). Integration and interruption in the masking of form by form. *Perception, 5*, 79–97.

Beck, J. (1982). Textural segmentation. In J. Beck (Ed.), *Organization and representation in perception* (pp. 285–318). Hillsdale, NJ: Lawrence Erlbaum Associates.

Biederman, I. (1987). Recognition by components: A theory of human image understanding. *Psychological Review, 94*, 115–147.

Boselie, F., & Leeuwenberg, E. (1986). A test of the minimum principle requires a perceptual coding system. *Perception, 15*, 331–354.

Buffart, H., & Leeuwenberg, E. (1983). Structural information theory. In H. Geissler, H. Buffart, E. Leeuwenberg, & V. Sarris (Eds.), *Modern issues in perception* (pp. 48–72). Berlin: VEB Deutscher Verlag der Wissenschaften.

Buffart, H., Leeuwenberg, E., & Restle, F. (1983). Analysis in visual pattern completion. *Journal of Experimental Psychology: Human Perception and Performance, 9*, 980–1000.

Collard, R. F., & Buffart, H. F. (1983). Minimization of structural information: A set-theoretical approach. *Pattern Recognition, 16*, 231–242.

de Weert, Ch. (1999). The role of colour in pattern perception. *ASCI '99. Proceedings of the 5th annual conference of the advanced school for computing and imaging* (pp. 10–15). Heijen, The Netherlands, June 15–17.

Geissler, H., Klix, F., & Scheidereiter, U. (1978). Visual recognition of visual structure: Evidence of a two-stage scanning model. In E. Leeuwenberg & H. Buffart (Eds.), *Formal theories of visual perception* (pp. 299–314). Chichester, England: Wiley.

Hoffman, D. D. (1996). What do we mean by "the structure of the world"? In D. Knill & W. Richards (Eds.), *Perception as Bayesian inference* (pp. 219–221). Cambridge, England: Cambridge University Press.

Hoffman, J. (1975). Hierarchical stages in the processing of visual information. *Perception & Psychophysics, 18*, 348–354.

Kanizsa, G., & Gerbino, W. (1982). Amodal completion: Seeing or thinking? In J. Beck (Ed.), *Organization and representation in perception* (pp. 167–190). Hillsdale, NJ: Lawrence Erlbaum Associates.

Kimchi, R., & Palmer, S. (1982). Form and texture in hierarchically constructed patterns. *Journal of Experimental Psychology: Human Perception and Performance, 8*, 521–535.

Kinchla, R. (1977). The role of structural redundancy in the perception of visual targets. *Perception & Psychophysics, 22*, 19–30.

Koenderink, J., & van Doorn, A. (1976). The singularities of the visual mapping. *Biological Cybernetics, 24*, 51–59.

Leeuwenberg, E. (1969). Quantitative specification of information in sequential patterns. *Psychological Review, 76*, 216–220.

Leeuwenberg, E., & van der Helm, P. (1991). Unity and variety in visual form. *Perception, 20*, 595–622.

Leeuwenberg, E., van der Helm, P. & van Lier, R. (1994). From geons to structure. A note on object representation. *Perception, 23*, 505–515.

MacKay, D. (1969). *Information, mechanism and meaning.* Cambridge, MA: MIT Press.

Martin, M. (1979). The role of sparsity. *Memory and Cognition, 7*, 476–484.

Mens, L., & Leeuwenberg, E. (1988). Hidden figures are ever present. *Journal of Experimental Psychology: Human Perception and Performance, 14*, 561–571.

Navon, D. (1977). Forest before trees: The precedence of global features in visual perception. *Cognitive Psychology, 9*, 353–383.

Restle, F. (1982). Coding theory as an integration of Gestalt psychology and information processing. In J. Beck (Ed.), *Organization and representation in perception* (pp. 31–56). Hillsdale, NJ: Lawrence Erlbaum Associates.

Rock, I. (1983). *The logic of perception.* Cambridge, MA: Bradford.

Sekuler, A., & Palmer, S. (1992). Perception of partly occluded objects: A microgenetic analysis. *Journal of Experimental Psychology: General, 121*, 95–111.

van Bakel, A. (1989). *Perceived unity and duality as determined by superstructure components of pattern codes.* Unpublished master's thesis, NICI, University of Nijmegen, The Netherlands.

van der Helm, P. (2000). Simplicity versus likelihood in visual perception: From surprisals to precisals. *Psychological Bulletin, 126*, 770–800.

van der Helm, P., & Leeuwenberg, E. (1986). Avoiding explosive search in automatic selection of simplest pattern codes. *Pattern Recognition, 19*, 181–191.

van der Helm, P., & Leeuwenberg, E. (1991). Accessibility: A criterion for regularity and hierarchy in visual pattern codes. *Journal of Mathematical Psychology, 35*, 151–213.

van der Helm, P., & Leeuwenberg, E. (1996). Goodness of visual regularities: A nontransformational approach. *Psychological Review, 103*, 429–456.

van der Helm, P., van Lier, R., & Leeuwenberg, E. (1992). Serial pattern complexity: Irregularity and hierarchy. *Perception, 21*, 517–544.

van Leeuwen, C., Buffart, H., & J., van der Vegt. (1988). Sequence influence on the organization of meaningless serial stimuli: Economy after all. *Journal of Experimental Psychology: Human Perception and Performance, 14*, 481–502.

van Lier, R., van der, Helm, P., & Leeuwenberg, E. (1994). Integrating global and local aspects of visual occlusion. *Perception, 23*, 883–903.

van Lier, R., Leeuwenberg, E., & van der Helm, P. (1997). In support of structural hierarchy in visual shape. *Psychological Research, 60*, 134–143.

van Tuyl, H., & Leeuwenberg, E. (1979). Neon color spreading and structural information measures. *Perception & psychophysics, 25*, 269–284.

Author Index

Subject Index

40 Hz, *see* Oscillation

A

Accumulation function, 119–121, 125, 126, 129, 131
Adaptive resonance theory (ART), 432F, 434, 438, 455
Anchoring, 71
Apparent motion, 425, 426, 464–468
Articulation
  rate, 350, 356, 361, 365
  suppression of, 320, 321, 324–327
  time, 351, 360, 361, 362T, 363T, 364T, 365–368
Assimilation, *see* Context effects
Attention
  -al blink, 301
  automatic capture of, 290, 293, 295, 302, 303
  focal, focus of, 224, 225, 228, 371, 372, 374, 383, 384
  recapturing, 297, 298
  and sensory memory, 344
  visual, 221–223
    dimension-based, 237, 239–243
    object-based, 221, 222, 239–241
Auditory sensory memory, 331–346, 390–403
  in animals, 334
  attention effects, 344, 395–397
  automaticity, 394–397
  bottom-up and top-down effects, 390, 394–403
  capacity, 337–341
  duration, *see* lifetime
  functions, 391, 397–399
  interference, 341–343
  lifetime, 334–337, 395–397
  phases, 332, 391
  as compared to sensory registers, 344
  training effects, 334, 335, 399–403
Automatic processing, 394–397

B

Bayes rule, 455, 497, 499–501
Behavioral properties, 4
Bias, 71, 275, 283, 290
  decision, 247
  response, 251, 278, 482
  selection, 326
Binding by synchronization, 138, 151, 456
Boundary completion, 419–425
Brightness, 28, 29, 31, 32, 35, 422, 423, 438

C

Capacity, *see* Auditory sensory memory
Categorical memory, *see* Short-term memory
Cell assembly, *see* Neural assembly
Code
  abstract, 485
  category, 168–171, 176, 180, 191, 192F
  constituents, 158, 191–193
  contraction, 170, 174
  generation time, 121
  primitive, 483, 485, 503, 504
  processing, 168–177, 193
Color differences
  spherical model of, 27–33, 35, 39–41
Color-opponent channels, 29, 30, 32
Common coding, 133, 190, 263
Configural effects
  and category of stimuli, 62–64
  interaction of range and stimulus position, 55–62
Consciousness, 344, 428, 433, 442
Context effects, 4, 6, 71–75
  assimilation, 45–48
  contrast, 45–48, 73, 75, 76
  shift, 71, 79–81
Contrast, *see* Context effects

521